CW01424708

ONE TO ONE

Bilingual Dictionary

English-Nepali
Nepali-English
Dictionary

Compiled by
Anil Mandal

ibs BOOKS (UK)

© Publishers

All rights reserved with the Publishers. No part of this publication may be reproduced or transmitted in any form or by any means, electronic, mechanical, photocopying, recording or otherwise, without the prior written permission of the Publishers.

First Edition: 2011
Second Edition: 2012

Published by

STAR PUBLICATIONS PVT. LTD.
4/5 B, Asaf Ali Road, New Delhi-110 002
E-mail- starpub@satyam.net.in

Printed in India at
Star Print-O-Bind, New Delhi-110020

About this Dictionary

Developments in science and technology today have narrowed down distances between countries, and have made the world a small place. A person living thousands of miles away can learn and understand the culture and lifestyle of another country with ease and without travelling to that country. Languages play an important role as facilitators of communication in this respect.

To promote such an understanding, **ibs BOOKS (UK)** has planned to bring out a series of bilingual dictionaries in which important English words have been translated into other languages, with Roman transliteration in case of languages that have different scripts. This is a humble attempt to bring people of the world closer through the medium of language, thus making communication easy and convenient.

These dictionaries have been compiled and edited by teachers and scholars of relative languages.

ONE TO ONE

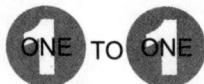

Bilingual Dictionaries in this Series

English-Afrikaans / Afrikaans-English	Abraham Venter
English-Amharic / Amharic-English	Girun Asanke
English-Arabic / Arabic-English	Rania-al-Qass
English-Bengali / Bengali-English	Amit Majumdar
English-Bosnian / Bosnian-English	Boris Kazanegra
English-Bulgarian / Bulgarian-English	Vladka Kocheshkova
English-Cantonese / Cantonese-English	Nisa Yang
English-Chinese (Mandarin) / Chinese (Mandarin)-Eng	Y. Shang & R. Yao
English-Croatian / Croatain-English	Vesna Kazanegra
English-Czech / Czech-English	Jindriska Poulova
English-Dari / Dari-English	Amir Khan
English-Estonian / Estonian-English	Lana Haleta
English-Farsi / Farsi-English	Maryam Zaman Khani
English-Greek / Greek-English	Lina Stergiou
English-Gujarati / Gujarati-English	Sujata Basaria
English-Hindi / Hindi-English	Sudhakar Chaturvedi
English-Hungarian / Hungarian-English	Lucy Mallows
English-Latvian / Latvian-English	Julija Baranovska
English-Lithuanian / Lithuanian-English	Regina Kazakeviciute
English-Marathi / Marathi-English	Sahard Thackerey
English-Nepali / Nepali-English	Anil Mandal
English-Pashto / Pashto-English	Amir Khan
English-Polish / Polish-English	Magdalena Herok
English-Punjabi / Punjabi-English	Teja Singh Chatwal
English-Romanian / Romanian-English	Georgeta Laura Dutulescu
English-Russian / Russian-English	Katerina Volobuyeva
English-Serbian / Serbian-English	Vesna Kazanegra
English-Slovak / Slovak-English	Zozana Horvathova
English-Somali / Somali-English	Ali Mohamud Omer
English-Tagalog / Tagalog-English	Jefferson Bantayan
English-Tamil / Tamil-English	Sandhya Mahadevan
English-Thai / Thai-English	Suwan Kaewkongpan
English-Turkish / Turkish-English	Nagme Yazgin
English-Ukrainian / Ukrainian-English	Katerina Volobuyeva
English-Urdu / Urdu-English	S. A. Rahman
English-Vietnamese / Vietnamese-English	Hoa Hoang

More languages in print

ibs BOOKS (UK)
London W1T 5NW (UK)

ENGLISH-NEPALI

A

A *a* एक ek

a back अनिवार्य कुरा aniwarya kura

abacus *n.* अंकगणक ankganak

abandon *v* छोड्नु chhodnu

abashed *adj.* लज्जित lajjit

abate *v.* कम गर्नु kam garnu

abbey *n.* साधुहरूको आश्रम sadhuharuko ashram

abbreviate *v.* छोटो पार्नु chhoto parnu

abdicate *v.* त्यागनु tayaganu

abdomen *n.* पेट pett

abduct *v.* अपहरण गर्नु apharan garnu

abhor *v.* घृणा गर्नु ghrina garnu

abide *v.* सहनु sahnu

ability *n* योग्यता yogyata

abject *adj.* फेंकनु pheknu

able *adj.* योग्य yogya

ablutions *n.* स्नान sanan

abnormal *adj.* असामान्य asamanya

aboard *adv.prep.* जहाज वा रेलमा jahaj va railma

abode *n.* बासस्थान bassthan

abolish *adj.* समाप्त गर्नु smapat garnu

abominable *adj.* साह्रै नराम्रो sahai naramro

aborigines *n.* आदिवासी adivasi

abort *v.* गर्भपात हुनु garbhapath hunu

abound *v.* प्रशस्त हुनु prashasta hunu

about *prep.* लगभग lagbhag

above *adv* माथि maathi

abrasive *n.* रगड्ने वस्तु ragharne vastu

abreast *adv.prep.* सँगै-सँगै sange-sange

abridge *v.* छोटो पार्नु chhoto parnu

abroad *adv.* परदेश pardesh

abrupt *adj.* अकस्मात् akasmaat

absatin *v.* अलग रहनु alag rahanu

abscess *n.* पिप peep

abscond *v.* सुटुक्क भाग्नु suttuk bhagnu

absence *n.* अनुपस्थिति anupasthiti

absolute *adj.* पूर्ण purn

absorb *v.* सोस्नु sosnu

abstemious *adj.* खान-पानमा संयमी khan-panma sanyami

abstrat *n.* अमूर्त amurt

absurd *adv.* वाहियात wahiyat

abundance *n.* प्रचुरता prachurta

abundant *adj.* प्रशस्त prashasta

abuse *n.* गाली दिनु gaali denu

acacia *n.* गम पाइने रूख gam paene rukh

academic *adj.* शिक्षा वा शिक्षण संबंधी shiksha va shikshan sambandhi

accde *v.* स्वीकार गर्नु swikar garnu

accelerate *v.* गति वा चाल बढ़ाउनु gati va chal badhanu

accent *n.* उच्चारण uccharan

accentuate *v.* जोर दिनु jordinu

accept *v.* स्वीकार/मन्जुर गर्नु swikar/manjur garnu

access *n.* पहुँच pahunch

accessible *adj.* पुग्न सकिने pugna sakine

accessory *n.* अतिरिक्त वस्तु atirikt vastu

accident *n* दुर्घटना durgha Tana

acclaim *v.* जयजयकार गर्नु jaijaikar garnu

acclimatize *v.* नयाँ जलवायुमा बानी पार्नु naya jalbayuma bani parnu

accolade *n.* प्रशंसा prashansa

accommodate *v.* मिलाउनु milaunu

accommodation *n.* बास बस्ने ठाउँ bas basne thaun

accompany *v.* साथ दिनु sath dinu

accomplice *n.* अपराध काममा सघाउने साथी apradh kamma saghaune sathi

accomplish *v.* पूरा गर्नु pura garnu

accord *v.* सित मेल खानु sith mail khanu

according to *adv.* अनुसार anusar

accordion *n.* बाजा baja

account *n.* हिसाब-किताब hisabkitab

accountant *n.* लेखापाल lekha pal

accrue *v.* थपिनु thapinu

accumulate *v.* थुपार्नु thurpanu

accurate *adj.* ठीक thik

accurately *v.* ठीकसँग thik sanga

accusation *v.* दोष dosh

accuse *v.* दोष लगाउनु dosh lagannu

accustom *v.* बानी बसाल्नु bani basalnu

ace *n.* एक्का ekka

acetic *adj.* अमिलो amelo

ache *n.* दुख्नु dukhnu

achieve *v.* प्राप्त गर्नु prapt garnu

achievement *n.* उपलब्धि uplabdhi

acid *n.* तेजाब tejab

acidity *n.* अमलपित्त amal pitta

acknowledge *v.* आभार मान्नु abhar

acknowledgement *n.* स्वीकृति swlkriti

acne *n.* नाकको स्वचाको खटिरो nakko twaghako kathira

acorn *n.* कटुस katus

acoustic *adj.* ध्वनि वा श्रवण सम्बन्धी dhwani va shravan sambandhi

acquaint *v.* परिचय गराउनु parichaya garaunu

acquaintance *n.* चिनजान chinjan

acquire *v.* प्राप्त गर्नु prapat garnu

acquit *v.* छुटकारा chhutkara

acquit *v.* निर्दोष घोषित गर्नु nirdosh ghoshit garnu

acqwuisition *n.* प्राप्ति prapti

acrid *n.* कड़ा kada

acrobat *n.* कसरत देखाउने व्यक्ति kasrat dekhaune vyakti

across *prep.* वारपार warpar

act *n.* ऐन yain

action *n.* कारबाई karbai

activate *v.* क्रियाशील बनाउनु kriyasheel banaunu

active *adj.* जाँगरिली jangarilo

activity *n.* संक्रियता sankriyata

actor *n.* अभिनेता abhineta

actress *n.* अभिनेत्री abhinetrl

actual *adj.* वास्तविक wastawik

acute *adj.* तीक्ष्ण teekshan

adage *n.* उखान ukhaan

adamant *adj.* एक कडा बस्तु ek kada bastu

adapt *v.* अनुकूल बनाउनु anukool banaunu

add *v.* जोड्नु jodnu

addict *v.* लत लाग्नु lat lagnu

addition *n.* जोड़ jodh

additional *adj.* अतिरिक्त atirikta

address *n.* ठेगाना thegana

adept *adj.* सिपालु sipalu

adequate *adj.* पर्याप्त, योग्य paryapt

adhere *v.* टाँसिनु tansinu

adhesive *adj.* टाँस्ने वस्तु taasne vastu

adjacent नजीकमा रहेको najeekma raheko

adjective *n.* विशेषण visheshan

adjourn *v.* स्थगित गर्नु staggit garnu

adjust *v.* मिलाउनु milaunu

administer *v.* शासन गर्नु shashan garnu

administrator *n.* प्रशासक prashasak

admire *v.* प्रशंसा गर्नु prashansagarnu

admission *n.* प्रवेश prawesh

admit *v.* भर्ती गर्नु bharti garnu

adolescence *n.* किशोरावस्था kishoravastha

adorable *adj.* पूजनीय pujniya

adore *v.* पूजा गर्नु puja garnu

adorn *v.* सिंगार्नु, सज्नु singarnu

adrift *adv.* बग्दै गरेको bagdae gareko

adroit *adj.* दक्ष daksh

adult *n.* युवा व्यक्ति yuva vyakti

adulterate *v.* मिलावट गर्नु milavat garnu

adultery *n.* परगमन pargaman

advance *n.* पेस्की peski

advantage *n.* फाइदा phaida

advent *n.* आगमन aagman

adventure *n.* साहसिक काम sahasik kam

adventurous *adj.* साहसिलो sahasilo

adverb *n.* क्रियाविशेषण kriyavisheshan

adverse *adj.* प्रतिकूल pratikool

adversity *n.* दुर्भाग्य durbhagya

advertisement *n.* विज्ञापन advertisement

advice *n.* सल्लाह sallah

advisor *n.* सल्लाहकार sallah kar

advocate *n.* वकील vakeel

aerial *n.* रेडियो radio

aerodrome *n.* हवाईअड्डा hawaiaddha

aeronautics *n.* उड्डानको विज्ञान udhanko vigyan

aeroplane *n.* विमान wiman

aesthetic *adj.* सौन्दर्य सम्बन्धी saundarya sambandhi

affable *adj.* मिलनसार milansaar

affair *n.* कार्य karya

affect *v.* प्रभाव पार्नु prabhaw parnu

affectation *n.* झूटो प्रेम jhuto prem

affection *n.* माया maya

affestionate *adj.* मायालु mayalu

affidavit *n.* शपथ पत्र shapath patra

affinity *n.* गहिरो सम्बन्ध gahior sambandh

affirm *v.* निश्चयसँग भन्नु nishchaya sanga bhannu

afflict *v.* कष्ट दिनु kasht dinu

affluent *adj.* धनी dhani

afford *v.* खर्च गर्न सक्नु Kharcha garna saknu

afforestation *n.* वनरोपण vanropan

aflame *adj.* जल्दे गरेको jaldae gareko

afloat *adj.* पानीमा उत्रेको, बगी रहेको pani ma utreko, bagi raheko

afoot *adv.* पैदल paidal

aforesaid *adj.* उपर्युक्त upruyukt

afraid *adj.* डराएको daraeko

afresh *adv.* नया ढँगले naya dhangle

after *prep.* पछि pachhi

afternoon *n.* अपरान्ह apranha

afterwards *adv.* पछि बाट pachhi bata

again *adv.* फेरि pheri

against *prep.* विरुद्ध wiruddha

age *n.* उमेर umer

agency *n.* एजेन्टको काम agentko kaam

agenda *n.* सभाको कार्यसूची sabhako karyasuchi

agent *n.* कर्त्ता karta

age-old *adj.* बूढो budho

aggrandize *v.* बढ़ाउनु badhaunu

aggravate *v.* गंभीर बनाउनु gambhir banaunu

aggregate *n.* कुलयोग kulyog

aggression *n.* आक्रमण akarman

aghast *adj.* आतंकित aatankit

agile *adj.* फुर्तिलो phurtilo

agitate *v.* उत्तेजित गर्नु uttejit garnu

aglow *adj.* चहकिलो chehkilo

agnostic *adj.* भगवान छकि छैन भन्ने व्यक्ति bhagwan chaki chaain bhanne vyakti

ago *adv.* अघि aghi

agony *n.* पीड़ा peerha

agrarian *adj.* भूमिको सम्बन्धी bhoomisambandhi

agree *v.* स्वीकार गर्नु swikar garnu

agreement *n.* मन्जूरी नामा manjuri nama

agriculture *n.* कृषि krishi

ahead *adv.* अघि aghi

aid *n.* सहायता/मद्दत गर्नु sahayata/ maddat garnu

aids *n.* योन रोग yaun rog

aim *n.* लक्ष्य laksha

air *n.* हावा hawa

airhostess *n.* विमान परिचारिका wiman paricharika

airline *n.* विमानसेवा wiman sewa

airport *n.* विमानस्थल wiman sthal

airy *adj.* प्रशस्त हावा लाग्न prashast hava lagne

aisle *n.* गिर्जाघरको खण्ड girjaghar ko khand

alacrity *v.* तत्परता tatparta

alarm *n.* खतराको संकेत khatarako sanket

alas *inter.* शोकसूचक शब्द sokhsuchak sabdha

albatross *n.* सामुद्रिक चरो samudrik charo

albino *n.* सेतो setho

album *n.* तस्वीर राख्ने किताब taswir rakhne kitab

albumen *n.* फुलको सेतो भाग phulko seto bhag

alchemy *n.* मध्ययुगको रासायनिक शास्त्र madhyayugko rasayanik shashtra

alcohol *n.* रक्सी raksi

alcove *n.* कोठाको छुट्टिएको भाग kothako chutiyeko bhag

ale *n.* बियर beer

alert *adj.* होशियार hoseyar

algebra *n.* बीजगणित beejganit

alias *n.* उपनाम upnaam

alienate *v.* अलग पार्नु alag parnu

alight *adj.* जल्दे गरेको jaldae gareko

align *v.* सोझो राख्नु sojho rakhnu

alike *adj.* एकैनासको ekai nas ko

alimentary *adj.* आहारको aaharko

aline *n.* परदेशी pardeshi

alive *adj.* जिउँदो jiundo

alkali *n.* क्षारीय kshariya

all *adj.* सबै sabai

allege *v.* आरोप aarop

allegiance *n.* निष्ठा nishta

alleviate *v.* कम गर्नु kam garnu

alley *n.* गल्ली galli

alliance *n.* सन्धि sandhi

alliteration *n.* अनुप्रास anupras

allocate *v.* निर्धारित गर्नु nirdharit garnu

allot *v.* व्यक्ति को हिस्सा तोक्नु vyaktiko hissa toknu

allow *v.* अनुमति दिनु anumati dinu

allowance *n.* भत्ता bhattha

alloy *n.* मिश्र धातु mishra dhatu

allude *v.* संकेत गर्नु sanket garnu

ally *v.* जोडिनु jodinu

almanac *n.* पात्रे patro

almighty *n.* सर्वशक्तिमान् sarwa shakti man

almond *n.* बदाम badam

almost *adv.* प्रायः prayah

alms *n.* भिक्षा bhiksha

alone *adj.* एक्लो eklo

along *prep.* साथमा sathma

aloof *adj.* टाडा tadha

aloud *adv.* ठूलो स्वरमा thulo swarma

alphabet *adv.* वर्णमाला warn mala

already *adv.* अघि नै aghi nai

alright *adj.* ठीक thik

also *adv.* पनि pani

altar *n.* वेदी vedi

alter *v.* बदल्नु badalnu

alteration *n.* अदलबदल adal badal

alternate *adj.* पालैपालो palai palo

alternately *adv.* पालैपालोसँग palai palo sanga

alternative *adj.* वैकल्पिक waikalpik

although *conj.* यद्यपि yadyapi

altitude *n.* उचाइ uchai

altogether *adv.* जम्मै jammai

alum *n.* फिटकिरि phitkiri

aluminium *n.* सेतो धातु seto dhatu

always *adv.* सधैँ sadhain

amalgam *n.* मिश्रण mishran

amateur *n.* सोखिन sokhin

amazing *adj.* अचम्मको achamma ko

ambassador *n.* राजदूत rajdut

ambience *n.* परिवेश pariwesh

ambiguous *adj.* अर्थ स्पष्ट नभएको arth spasht nabheyko

ambition *n.* आकांक्षा akansha

ambulance *n.* एम्बुलेन्स embulens

ameliorate *v.* अझ राम्रो पार्नु ajh ramro parnu

amen *int.* तथास्तु tathastu

amenity *n.* सुविधा suwidha

amiable *adj.* मिलनसार milansaar

amid, amidst *prep.* बीचमा beechma

ammonia *n.* अमोनिया amoniea

ammunition *n.* गोला बारूद gola-barood

amnesia *n.* स्मृति लोप smriti-lop

amoeba *n.* एक कोषीय प्राणी ek koshiya prani

among *prep.* बीच bich

amorous *adj.* प्रेम गरिहाल्ने prem garihaalne

amount *n.* रकम rakam

ample *adj.* प्रचुर prachur

amplify *v.* विस्तार गर्नु vishthar garnu

amputate *v.* काट्नु katnu

amulet *v.* जन्तर janter

amuse *n.* रमाउनु ramaunu

amusement *n.* मनोरंजन manoranjan

anaemia *n.* रक्तक्षीनताले पीडित raktshintale pidhit

anaesthetic *n.* बेहोशीकी अवस्था behoshi ki avashta

analyse *v.* विश्लेषण गर्नु vishleshan garnu

anarchy *n.* अराजकता arajakta

anatomy *n.* शरीर रचना को विज्ञान sharir-rachnako vigyan

ancestor *n.* पुर्खा purkha

anchor *n.* लंगर खसाल्नु langar khasalnu

ancient *adj.* प्राचीन prachin

and *conj.* र ra

anecdote *n.* छोटो किस्सा chhoto kissa

angel *n.* देवदुत dewdut

angle *n.* कोण kon

angry *adj.* रिसाएको risaeko

anguish *n.* वेदना vedna

animal *n.* जानवर janwer

animate *v.* प्राण हाल्नु pran halnu

animosity *n.* घृणा ghrina garnu

aniseed *n.* सौंफ saunf

anklet *n.* पाउजेब paujeb

anniversary *n.* वार्षिकी warshiki

announce *v.* घोषणा गर्नु ghoshana garnu

announcement *n.* घोषणा ghoshnana

annoy *v.* दिक्क लाउनु dikka launu

annual *adj.* वार्षिक warshik

annuity *n.* सालाना भत्ता salana battha

annul *v.* रद्द गर्नु radh garnu

anonymous *adj.* गुमनाम gumnaam

another *adj.* अर्को arko

answer *n.* जवाफ jawaph

ant *n.* कमिला kamila

antarctic *adj.* दक्षिण ध्रुव प्रदेश dakshin dhruv pradesh

antelope *n.* हरिण harin

antenna *n.* रेडियो आदि को एरियल radio adiko ariel

anthem *n.* प्रार्थनागान prarthnagaan

anthracite *n.* कड़ा कोइला kada koila

anthropology *n.* मानव विज्ञान manav vigyan

antibiotic *n. adj.* जीवाणु मार्ने औषधि jeevanu marne aushadhi

antibody *n* रोग रोक्ने तत्व rog rokne tattva

antifreeze *n.* हिमनिरोधी himnirodhi

antisocial *adj.* समाजविरोधी samajvirodhi

antler *n.* जरायोकोसीङ jaraekoseengh

antonym *n.* उल्टो अर्थको शब्द ulto artha ko shabda

anus *n.* मलद्वार maldwar

anxiety *n.* चिन्ता chinta

anxious *adj.* चिन्तित chintit

any *adj.* कुनै kunai

anyhow *adv.* जसरी पनि jasari pani

anyone *pron.* कुनै व्यक्ति kunai wyakti

anyway *adv.* जे होस् je hos

anywere *adv.* कहीं पनि kahin pani

apart *adv.* अलग alag

apartment *n.* कोठा kotha

ape *n.* पुच्छर नभएको बाँदर pucchar nabhayko bandar

aperture *n.* छिद्र chiddra

apex *n.* शिखर shikhar

apology *n.* क्षमायाचना ksham yachna

apparel *n.* वस्त्र धारण गर्नु wastra dharan garnu

apparent *adj.* स्पष्ट spastha

appartus *n.* उपकरण upkaran

appeal *n.* बिन्ती गर्नु ujur/bintigarnu

appear *v.* देखा पर्नु dekha parnu

appearance *n.* अनुहार anuhar

appeased *v.* सन्तुष्ट गर्नु santush garnu

appetite *n.* भोक bhok

apple *n.* स्याउ syau

appliance *n.* उपकरण वा यन्त्र upkaran va yantra

application *n.* प्रार्थना पत्र prarthna patra

appluad *v.* तारिफ/प्रशंसा गर्नु tariph

apply *v.* प्रयोगमा ल्याउनु paryog ma lyaunu

appoint *v.* नियुक्त गर्नु niyukta garnu

appreciate *v.* गुन मान्नु gun mannu

apprentice *n.* काम सिक्ने व्यक्ति kam sikne vyakti

approach *v.* नजीक आउनु najeek aaunu

appropriate *adj.* सुहाउँदो suhaoudho

approval *n.* मन्जुरी manjuri

approve *v.* मन्जुरी manjuri

approximately *adv* अन्दाजी andaji

apricot *n.* खुर्पानी फल khurpani phal

apt *adj.* झुकाउ भएको jukao bhaeko

aptitude *n.* क्षमता kschamta

aquarius *n.* कुम्भराशि kumbhrashi

arable *adj.* कृषि-योग्य krishi yogya

arachind *n.* माकुरा makura

arc *n.* चाप chap

arch *n.* मुख्य mukhya

archaeology *n.* पुरातत्व puratattva

archipelago *n.* द्वीपसमूह dweepsmuh

architect *n.* वास्तुकार wastukar

architecture *n.* भवन निर्माण कला bhawan nirman kala

arctic *adj.* अति ठण्डा ati thanda

ardent *adj.* प्रबल prabal

arduous *adj.* कठिन kathin

area *n.* क्षेत्रफल kshetra phal

arehaic *adj.* अहिले प्रयोग नहुने ahile prayog nahune

arena *n.* रंगभूमि rangbhoomi

argue *v.* बहस गर्नु bahas garnu

argument *n.* तर्क tark

arid *adj.* सुक्खा sikkha

aries *n.* मेष राशि mesh rashi

arise *v.* उठ्नु uthnu

aristrocracy *n.* अभिजाततंत्र abhijattantra

arithmetic *n.* अंकगणित ank ganit

arm *n.* पाखुरा paakhura

armour *n.* जंगी जहाज jangi jahaj

arms *n.* हातहतियार hathatiyar

army *n.* सेना shyna

aroma *n.* सुगन्धित sugandhit

around *adv.* चारैतिरि charaitira

arouse *v.* उत्तेजित गराउनु uttejit garaunu

arrangement *n.* बन्दोबस्त bandobast

arrest *v.* गिरफ्तार गर्नु giraphtar garnu

arrival *n.* आगमन agaman

arrive *v.* आइपुग्नु aipignu

arrogant *adj.* अहंकारी ahankari

arrow *v.* तीर tir

arson *n.* घर जलाउने दोष ghar jalouney dosh

art *n.* कला kala

artery *n.* धमनी dhamni

arthritis *n.* गठियावात gathiawat

article *n.* लेख lekh

artifact *n.* कला निर्मित बस्तु kala nirmith bastu

artificial *adj.* बनावटी banawati

artisan *n.* शिल्पी shilpi

artist *n.* कलाकार kalakar

as *adv.* जस्तो jasto

ascend *v.* उक्लनु uklanu

ascent *n.* चढ़ाइ chadhai

ascertain *v.* पत्ता लाउनु patta launu

ascetic *n.* सन्यांसी sanyasi

ashamed *adj.* लाज लागेको laj lageko

ashes *n.* खरानी kharani

ashore *adv.* किनारमा kinarma

aside *adv.* एकापट्टि ekapatti

ask *v.* सोध्नु sodhnu

ask for *v.* माग्नु magnu

asleep *v.* निदाएको nidaeko

aspect *n.* रूप rup

asphalt *n.* अलकत्रा alkatra

asphyxiate *v.* निसासिने पार्नु nisasine parnu

aspire *v.* आकांक्षा गर्नु akanksha garnu

aspirin *n.* पीड़ानाशक peerhanashak

ass *n.* गधा gadha

assassin *n.* हत्यारा hatyara

assassination *n.* हत्या hatya

assault *n.* कुटपिट kutpit

assemble *v.* जम्मा हुनु jamma hunu

assembly *n.* सभा sabha

assent *v,* सहमत हुनु sahmat hunu

assess *v.* मूल्याकन गर्नु mulyankan garnu

assessment *n.* महसूल mahasul

asset *n.* सम्पत्ति sampati

assiduous *adj.* परिश्रमी parishrami

assign *v.* निर्दिष्ट गर्नु nirdishta garnu

assignment *n.* सुम्पिएको काम sumpieko kam

assisant *n.* सहायक sahayak

assist *v.* सहायता गर्नु sahayata garnu

assocation *n.* संगठन sangathan

associate *v.* मिलाउनु millaunu

assorted *adj.* मिश्रित mishrit

assume *n.* मालिलिनु manilinu

assurance *n.* भरोसा bharosa

asthma *n.* दमको रोग dam ka rog

astonishment *n.* आश्चर्य ashcharya

astrologer *n.* जयोतिषी jyotishi

astrology *n.* ज्योतिष शास्त्र jyotish shastra

astronaut *n.* अन्तरिक्ष यात्री antariksha yatri

astronomy *n.* खगोल विज्ञान सम्बन्धी khagol vigyansambandhi

asylum *n.* पागलखाना pagalkhana

at *prep.* माथि mathi

atheist *n.* नास्तिक nastik

athlete *n.* मल्लयोद्धा maalyodha

atlas *n.* मानचित्रवली maanchirawali

atmosphere *n.* वायुमण्डल wayumandal

atoll *n.* प्रवाल द्वीप prawal dweep

atom *n.* परमाणु parmanu

atrocious *adj.* अति नराम्रो ati naramro

attach *v.* गाँस्नु gansnu

attachment *n.* लगाव lagaw

attack *v.* हमला गर्नु hamla garnu

attain *v.* प्राप्त गर्नु prapat garnu

attampt *v.* प्रयत्न गर्न prayatna garnu

attend *v.* हाजिर हुनु hajir hunu

attendance *n.* हाजिरी hajiri

attention *n.* ध्यान dhyan

attire *vc.* लुगा लगाउनु luga lagaunu

attitude *n.* ढाँचा dhancha

attract *v.* आकर्षित गर्नु akarshit garnu

attraction *n.* आकर्षण akarshan

auction *n.* लिलाम lilam

audacious *adj.* साहस sahas

audible *adj.* सुन्न सकिने sunna sakine

audience *n.* श्रोतागण shrota gan

audit *v.* लेखा जाँच्नु lekha janchnu

auditor *n.* लेखा परीक्षक lekha parikshak

auditorium *n.* सभाकक्षा sabha kakasha

augment *v.* वृद्धि गर्नु vridhi garnu

august *n.* अगस्त महीना august mahina

aunt *n.* काकी kaki

auspices *n.* तत्त्वाधान tattwawdhan

auspicious *adj.* शुभ shubha

auster *adj.* अति सरल ati saral

authentic *adj.* विश्वसनीय wishwasnlya

author *n.* लेखक lekhak

authority *n.* अधिकार adhikar

autobiography *n.* आत्मकथा atamkatha

autocrat *n.* तानाशाही tanashahi

autograph *adj.* हस्ताक्षर hastakshar

automatic *adj.* आफै चल्ने aphai chalne

automobile *n.* मोटरगाड़ी motargadi

autumn *n.* ारद ऋतु sharad ritu

available *adj.* उपलब्ध uplabdha

avalanche *n.* हिउँको पहिरो hiunko pahiro

avenge *v.* बदला लिनु badla linu

avenue *n.* मार्ग marg

average *n.* औसत ausat

avert *v.* कुरा तर्नु kura tarnu

aviary *n.* चराचुरूंगी राख्ने ठाउँ chrachurungi rakhne thaun

avid *adj.* उत्सुक utsuk

avoid *v.* टार्नु tarnu

await *v.* प्रतीक्षा गर्नु prateeksha garnu

awake *adj.* जगाउनु jagaaunu

award *n.* पुरस्कार puraskar

aware *adj.* सतर्कता satarkta

away *adv.* टाढ़ा tadha

awe *n.* श्रद्धा र डर shradha r dar

awful *adj.* भयानक bhayanak

awhile *adv.* एक छिन ek chiine

awkward *adj.* भद्दा bhadda

axe *n.* बन्चारो bancharo

axis *n.* धुरी dhuri

azure *n.* आसमानी रंग asmani rang

B

babe *n.* नानी nani

baboon *n.* लंगूर langoor

baby *n.* बच्चा bachcha

bachelor *n.* विवाह नभएको मानिस wiwah na bhaeko manis

backbone *n.* ढाड dhad

backwards *adv.* पछिल्तिर pacchil tira

backwoods *n.* पछौटे ठाउँ pachhote thaun

bacteria *n.* जीवाणु jeevanu

bad *adj.* खराब kharab

badge *n.* बिल्ला billa

bag *n.* झोला jhola

baggage *n.* मालमत्ता mal matta

baggy *adj.* धोक्रे dhokre

bagpipes *n.* मसक बाजा masakbaja

bail *n.* जमानी jamani

bailiff *n.* चपरासी charparsasi

bait *n.* चारा chara

bake *v.* सेक्नु seknu

bakery *n.* पाउरोटी बनाउने पसल pauroti banaune pasal

balance *n.* तराजु (scales) taraju

balcony *n.* बार्दली bardali

bald *adj.* तालुखुइले talu khuile

baleful *adj.* खराब kharab

ball *n.* भकुण्डो bhakundo

ballast *n.* रोड़ा rorha

ballet *n.* नृत्य nritya

balloon *n.* गुब्बारा belun

ballot *n.* गुप्तमतदान guptmatdan

balm *n.* मलम malam

bamboo *n.* बाँस bans

ban *n.* निषेध nishedh

banana *n.* केरा kera

band *n.* घेरा ghera

bandage *n.* पट्टी patti

bandit *n.* डाँकु danku

bandy *v.* भनाभन गर्नु bhanban garnu

bang *n.* जोरको आवाज jorko awaaz

bangle *n.* चुरा chura

bangle *n.* चुरा chura

banish *v.* देशभाट निकाल्नु deshbat niklanu

bank *n.* बैंक baink

bankrupt *adj.* दिवालिया बनाउनु diwaliya banaunu

banner *n.* ध्वजपताका dhwaja pataka

banquet *n.* भोज bhoj

banyan *n.* बरको रुख bar ko rukh

bar *n.* डण्डा danda

barber *n.* हजाम hajam

bard *n.* गाइने gyane

bare *adj.* नांगो nango

barely *adv.* मुस्किलले muskil le

bargain *n.* मोलमोलाइ mol molai

barium *n.* बेरिअम berium

bark *n.* रूखको बोक्रा rukh ko bokra

barley *n.* जौ jau

barometer *n.* वायुचापमापक vayuchapmapak

barracks *n.* छाउनी chauni

barrel *n.* बन्दूकको नाल bandukko naal

barrier *n.* हद hadh

barrister *n.* उच्च अदालत का वकील ucch adalatka vakil

barter *n.* साटफेर satpher

basalt *n.* कालो रंग का चट्टान kalo rangko chattan

base *n.* पीण्ड pindh

basin *n.* भाँडा bhanda

basis *n.* आधारभूत adhar bhut

basket *n.* टोकरी tokari

bassoon *n.* मुखले बजाउने बाजा mukhle bajaune baaja

bat *n.* चमेरा chamero

batch *n.* बथन bathan

bath *n.* स्नान snan

battalion *n.* स्थल वाहिनी sthal wahini

batter *v.* लगातार हान्नु lagatar hannu

battery *n.* ब्याट्री byatri

battle *n.* लडाइँ ladin

bawdy *adj.* फोहोर fohor

bayonet *n.* संगीन sangeen

be *v.* हुनु hunu

beach *n.* किनारा kinarar

bead *n.* पोतेको गेडा pote ko geda

beagle *n.* शिकारी कुकुर shikari kukkur

beak *n.* चुच्चो chuchcho

beam *n.* किरण kiran

bean *n.* सिमी simi

bear *n.* भालु bhalu

beard *n.* दाही darhi

bearing *n.* आचरण aachran

beat *n.* ढुकढुकी dhukdhuki

beatific *adj.* आनन्द प्रदर्शित गर्ने anand pradarshit garne

beautiful *adj.* सुन्दर sundar

because *conj.* किनकि kinaki

become *v.* हुनु hunu

becoming *adj.* सुहाउँदो suhaundo

bed *n.* बिछ्यौना bichhyauna

bedbug *n.* उडुस udus

bedeeked *adj.* सिँगारिएको singareako

bedlam *n.* पागलखाना pagakhana

bee *n.* माहुरी mahuri

beef *n.* गाईको मासु gaiko masu

beehive *n.* माहुरीको चाका mahuri ko chaka

beekon *v.* हात इशाराले बोलाउनु haatko isharale bolaunu

beer *n.* बियर biyar

beet *n.* चुकन्दर chukandar

beetle *n.* गोब्रे कीरा gobre kira

befall *v.* घट्नु ghatnu

before *prep.* अगाडि agadi

beforehand *adv.* पहिले नै pahile nai

beg *v.* माग्नु magnu

beggar *n.* माग्ने magne

begin *v.* थाल्नु thalnu

beginning *n.* शुरुवात shuruwat

begrudge *v.* ईर्ष्या गर्नु irshya garnu

behalf *n.* को पक्षमा ko pakshma

behave *v.* व्यवहार गर्नु wyawahar garunu

behavio(u)r *n.* व्यवहार wyawahar garunu

behind *adv.* पछाडि pachhadi

behold *v.* हेर्नु hernu

beholden *adj.* आभारी abahari

being *n.* अस्तित्व astitva

belch *v.* डकार्नु dakarnu

belief *n.* विश्वास wishwas

believe *v.* विश्वास गर्नु wishwas garnu

bell *n.* घण्टी ghanti

belladonna *n.* धतरो dhaturo

belle *n.* सुन्दरी नारी sundari naari

belly *n.* पेट pet

belong *v.* कसैको हुनु kasai to hunu

below *adv.* मुन्तिर muntira

belt *n.* पटुका patuka

bench *n.* बेंच bench

bend *n.* मोड mod

beneficent *adj.* उपकार गर्ने upkaar garne

beneficial *adj.* लाभदायक labh dayak

benevolent *adj.* दयालु dayalu

benign *v.* नम्र र दयालु namra dayalu

bereavement *n.* वियोग wiyog

berry *n.* गेडा फल geda phal

berth *n.* बस्ने र सुल्ने ठाउँ basne ra sutne thaun

besides *prep.* बाहेक bahek

besmirch *v.* मैला पार्नु mailla parnu

best *adj.* सवभन्दा असल sab bhanda asal

bestow *v.* दिनु dinu

bet *n.* बाजी baji

betel *n.* पान pan

betel nut *n.* सुपारी supari

betray *v.* धोखा दिनु dhokha dinu

better *adj.* भन्दा राम्रो bhanda ramro

between *adv./prep.* बीच bichhyauna

beverage *n.* पिउने वस्तु piune wastu

beware *v.* सावधान हुनु sawdhan hunu

bewilder *v.* हडबडाउनु hadbadaunu

beyond *adv.* पर para

bias *n.* पक्षपात paksha pat

bickskin *n.* मृग को छाला mrigko chhal

bicscuit *n.* biskut

bicycle *n.* साइकल saikal

bid *v.* दाम लगाउनु dam lagaunu

big *adj.* ठूलो thulo

bigamy *n.* दुई विवाह गर्ने व्यक्ति dui vivah garne vyakti

bike *n.* साइकल saikal

bile *n.* पित्त pitta

bilingual *n.* दोभाषे dobhase

bill *n.* बिल billa

billet *n.* सिपाहीहरुको डेरा sipahiharuko dera

billion *n.* दश खरब dash kharab

billy-goat *n.* बोका boka

bin *n.* भकारी bhakari

bind *v.* बाँध्नु bandhnu

bingo *n.* ताशको खेल taashko khel

binoculars *n.* दुर्बिन durbin

biped *n.* दुईखुट्टे dul khutte

birch *n.* सउर saur

bird *n.* चरा chara

birth *n.* जन्म janma

birthday *n.* जन्मदिन janmadin

bishop *n.* बिशप bishop

bit *n.* टुक्रा tukra

bitch *n.* कुकुर्नी kukurni

bite *n.* टोक्नु toknu

bizarre *adj.* अनौठो anutho

black *adj.* कालो kalo

blackguard *n.* बदमाश badmaash

blacksmith *n.* कामी kami

bladder *n.* मूत्राश्य mutrashaya

blade *n.* छुरी chhuri

blame *n.* दोष dosh

blank *n.* रिक्तता riktata

blanket *n.* कम्बल kambal

blatant *adj.* स्पष्ट spasht

blaze *n.* ज्वाला jwala

bleak *adj.* उजाड ujjadh

bleary *adj.* धमिलो आँखा भएको dhamilo ankha bhaeko

bleed *v.* रगत बग्नु ragat bagnu

bleep *n.* तीखो आवाज teekho awaaz

blemish *n.* दाग daag

bless *v.* आशीर्वाद/आसिक दिनु ashirwad/asik dinu

blind *adj.* अन्धो andho

blink *v.* आँखा झिमझिम गर्नु ankha jhimjhim garnu

bliss *n.* आनन्द anand

blister *n.* पानी फोका pank phoka

blithe *adj.* प्रसन्न prasann

blitz *n.* हमला hamla

blizzard *n.* हिउँको आँधी hiunko aandhi

block *n.* काठको मुढो kathko mudho

blockade *v.* नाकाबन्दी गर्नु nakkabandi garnu

blockage *n.* अवरोध awrodh

bloke *n.* मान्छे manchhe

blood *n.* रगत ragat

bloodshed *n.* रक्तचाप rakta pat

bloom *v.* फुल्नु phulnu

blouse *n.* चोलो cholo

blow *n.* ठक्कर thakkar

blowzy *adj.* फोहोरी fohori

blue *adj.* नीलो nilo

blueprint *n.* रूपरेखा rooprekha

bluff *n.* ठाड्रो भीर tharho bheer

blunder *n.* ठूलो भूल गर्नु thulo bhul garnu

blunder *n.* भूलचूक bhoolchook

blunt *adj.* नभएको dhar na bhaeko

blurt *v.* नसोची भन्नु nasochi bhannu

blush *n.* सरम sharam

boa *n.* अर्जीगर arjigar

boar *n.* बँदेल bandel

board *n.* पाटी pati

boast *v.* धाक लाउनु dhak launu

boat *n.* डुंगा dunga

boater *n.* परालको टोपी paraalko topi

bobbin *n.* कोया koya

bobby *n.* पुलीस को सिपाही police ko sipahi

bodice *n.* चोलो cholo

body *n.* शरीर sharir

boffin *n.* वैज्ञानिक vaigayanik

bog *n.* दलदल dal dal

bogus *adj.* झठो jhutho

boil *n.* फोका phoka

bold *adj.* शूरो shuro

bolt *n.* छेस्किनी chheskini

bomb *n.* बम गोला bam gola

bombard *v.* बमबारी गर्नु bambari garnu

bonafide *adj.* असली asli

bonanza *n.* धनको खानी dhan ko khani

bond *n.* बन्धन bandhan

bone *n.* हड्डी haddi

bon-homie *n.* मिलनसारी milansaari

bonus *n.* बोनस bonus

book *n.* किताब kitab

booklet *n.* पुस्तिका pustika

boon *n.* वरदान wardan

boor *n.* असभ्य व्यक्ति asabhya vyakti

boot *n.* जूता jutta

booth *n.* मतदान सील matdan sthal

booty *n.* लूटको माल lutko mal

borax *n.* सोहाग sohaag

border *n.* सिमाना smiana

bore *n.* उच्चाट लाग्नु uchchat lagnu

boredom *n.* पट्टाई pattai

born *adj.* जन्मेको janmeko

borrow *v.* सापट लिनु sapat linu

bosom *n.* छाती chhati

boss *n.* हाकिम hakim

botch *v.* कच्चा काम गरेर बिगार्नु kachha kaam garer bigarnu

both *adj.* दुवै duwai

bother *v.* कष्ट दिनु kasht dinu

bottle *n.* सिसी sisi

bottom *n.* पींध pindh

boudoir *n.* स्त्रीको निजी कोठा striko niji kotha

bough *n.* हाँगा hangan

boulder *n.* ठूलो ढुंगा thulo dhunga

boulevard *n.* फराकिलो बाटो frakilo baato

bounce *v.* उफ्रनु uphranu

boundary *n.* सिमाना simana

boundless *adj.* अपार apaar

bountiful *adj.* दानशील daanshil

bounty *n.* उदारता uddarta

bouquet *n.* फुलको गुच्छा phulko guchchha

bourgeosis *adj.* मध्यम वर्गको madhyamvargko

bovine *adj.* गोरू जस्तो goru jasto

bow *n.* धनुष dhanush

bowel *n.* आँद्रा, आँत andra, aant

bow-legged *adj.* बाङखट्टे baangkhatte

bowler *n.* बल फयाँक्ने मानिस bowl phyankne manis

box *n.* बाकस bakas

boxer *n.* मुक्केबाज mukke baj

boxing day *n.* क्रिस्मसको पछिको दिन chritsmasko pachiko din

boy *n.* केटा keta

boycott *v.* बहिष्कार गर्नु bahishkar garnu

bra *n.* ढाक्ने चोली dhakne choli

brace *n.* कस्ने चीज kasne cheej

bracelet *n.* बाला bala

bracing *adj.* स्फूर्ति दिने sphurti dine

brackish *adj.* अलि नुनिलो ali nunilo

brain *n.* दिमाग dimag

brake *n.* गतिरोधक gati rodhak

bramble *n.* कांढादार झाड़ी kaarhadaar jhari

bran *n.* चोकर chokar

branch *n.* हाँगा hanga

brand *n.* डामेको चिन्ह dameko chinha

brandish *v.* हल्लाउनु hallaunu

brandy *n.* ब्राण्डी brandy
brash *adj.* ढीठ dheeth
brass *n.* पित्तल pittal
brat *n.* बालक balak
bravado *n.* साहस देखाउने काम sahas dekhune kaam
brave *adj.* बहादुर bahadur
bravo *int.* स्याबास syabaas
brawl *n.* झगड़ा गर्नु jhagrha garnu
brazier *n.* अँगेठी angethi
breach *n.* भंग bhang
bread *n.* पाउरोटी pauroti
breadth *n.* चौडाइ chaudai
break *v.* टुटाउनु tutaunu
breakfast *n.* नास्ता nasta
breast *n.* छाती chhati
breath *n.* श्वास sawas
breed *v.* पाल्नु palnu
breeze *n.* अंगार angaar
brethren *n.* दाजु daazu
breviary *n.* प्रार्थनाको पुस्तक prarthanako pustak
bribe *n.* घूस ghus
brick *n.* ईंटा inta
bridal *adj.* विवाहको vivahko
bride *n.* बेहुली behuli
bridegroom *n.* बेहुलो behulo
bridge *n.* पुल pul
bridle *n.* लगाम lagam
brief *adj.* छोटकरी chhotkari
brigade *n.* सेनाको एक विभाग senako ek vibhaag

bright *adj.* चम्किलो chamkilo
brilliant *adj.* अति चतुर ati chatur
brimstone *n.* गन्धक gandhak
bring *v.* ल्याउनु lyaunu
bring down *v.* झार्नु jharnu
bring out *v.* निकाल्नु nikalnu
bring up *v.* हुर्काउनु hurkaunu
brink *n.* किनारा kinara
brisk *adj.* फुर्तिलो phurtilo
brisket *n.* हयाकुलो hayakulo
brittle *adj.* नाजुक najuk
broad *adj.* चौडाई chaudai
broke *adj.* भाँच्नु vachnu
broker *n.* दलाल dalal
brolly *n.* छाता chaata
bromide *n.* ब्रोमाइड bromide
bronze *n.* काँस kans
brook *n.* सहनु sahanu
broom *n.* कुचो kucho
brothel *n.* रन्डीघर randi ghar
brother *n.* दाजु daju
brother-in-law *n.* जेठाजु jethaju
brougham *n.* बन्दगाड़ी bandh garhi
brow *n.* आँखीभौं ankhibhaun
brown *adj.* खैरो khairo
bruise *n.* चोट लगाउनु वा लाग्नु chot lagaunu va lagnu
brunette *n.* कालो कपाल भएकी आइमाई kalo kapal bhaeki aimai
brunt *n.* धक्का dhakka
brush *n.* कुचो kucho

brusque *adj.* अशिष्ट ashisht

brutal *adj.* निर्दयी nirdayi

brute *n.* पशुतुल्य pashutulya

bubble *n.* पानी फोका panil phoka

buccaneer *n.* समुद्री डाकू samudari daaku

buck *n.* उफ्रनु uphranu

bucket *n.* बाल्टी balti

buckle *n.* खींप लाउनु khip launu

buckwheat *n.* फापर phapar

bud *n.* कोपिला kopila

buddy *n.* साथी saathi

budge *v.* सर्नु sarnu

budget *n.* आय-व्ययक aya-wyayak

buff *n.* राँगाको मासु ranga ko masu

buffalo *n.* भोंसी bhainsi

buffer *n.* ने वस्तु dhakka thamne wastu

buffoon *n.* विदूषक vidushak

bug *n.* उड्स udus

bugle *n.* बिगुल bigul

bugle *n.* बिगुल bigul

build *n.* निर्माण गर्नु nirman garnu

builder *n.* बनाउने banaune

building *n.* भवन bhawan

bulb *n.* चिम chim

bulge *n.* फुल्नु phulnu

bulk *n.* थोक thok

bull *n.* साँढे sandhe

bulldog *n.* बुलडग कुक्कुर bulldug kukkur

bullet *n.* गोली goli

bullock *n.* गोरू goru

bulrush *n.* नरकट narkat

bum *n.* सापट लिनु sapat linu

bump *v.* ठक्कर खानु thakkar khanu

bumptious *adj.* अहंकारी ahankari

bun *n.* मीठो केक वा रोटी meetho cake va roti

bunch *n.* झुप्पा jhuppa

bundle *n.* पोको poko

bunkum *n.* फजुल कुरा fazool kura

bunsen burner *n.* ग्यास बर्नर gas burner

burden *n.* भारी bhari

bureau *n.* विभाग wibhag

bureaucracy *n.* कर्मचारी तन्त्र karmchari tantra

burgeon *v.* कोपिला हाल्नु kopila halnu

burial *n.* चिहानमा गाड्ने काम chihan ma gadne kam

burly *adj.* हट्टा कट्टा hattakatta

burn *n.* पोल्नु polnu

burst *n.* फुट्नु phutnu

bury *v.* गाड्नु gadnu

bus *n.* बस bas

bush *n.* झाड़ी jhadi

bushel *n.* अन्नको नाप annako naap

businesslike *adj.* व्यवस्थित wyawasthit

businessman *n.* व्यापारी wyapari

bust *n.* शरीरको माथिल्लो आधा भाग sharir ko mathillo adha bhag

bustle *n.* हलचल halchal

busy *adj.* व्यस्त wyasta

but *conj.* तर tara

butcher *n.* बगरे bagare

butt *v.* बन्दूकको कुन्दा bandukko kunda

butter *n.* नौनी nauni

butter *n.* मक्खन, नौनी makhan, nauni

butterfly *n.* पुतली putali

buttocks *n.* चाक chak

button *n.* टाँक tank

buy *n.* किन्नु kinnu

buzz *v.* हतार hattar

buzzard *n.* मासु खाने चरा masu khane chara

by *prep.* सँग sanga

bye *n.* विदाई bidai

bye-bye *int.* बिदाई bidai

bygone *adj.* विगत wigat

by-law *n.* उपनियम upniyam

by-pass *n.* उपमार्ग लिनु upmarg linu

byre *n.* पाठशाला pathshala

by-road *n.* गोरेटो goreto

by-word *n.* उक्ति ukati

C

cab *n.* ट्याक्सी tayksi

cabbage *n.* बन्दाकोभी banda kobhi

cabin *n.* कोठा koyha

cabinet *n.* दराज daraj

cable *n.* डोरी dori

cacao *n.* कोकोको बीज वा रूख cococo beej va rukh

cackle *n.* जोरले हाँस्नु jorle hansnu

cactus *n.* सिउँडी sinudi

cadaver *n.* लाश lash

cadre *n.* तालीम प्राप्त दल taleem prapt dal

caftan *n.* अनुसंधान anusandhan

cage *n.* पिँजड़ा pinjada

cahier *n.* खजान्ची khajanchi

cairn *n.* ढुंगा को स्मारक dhungako smarak

cajole *v.* मीठा कुराले फुस्ल्याउनु meetha kurale fuslayanu

cake *n.* केक kek

calamity *n.* आपत्ति appati

calculate *n.* हिसाब गर्नु hisab garnu

calendar *n.* पात्रो patro

calf *n.* बाच्छो bachchho

calico *n.* सूती लुगा suti luga

call *n.* बोलावट bolawat

call girl *n.* वेश्या weshya

callous *adj.* निर्दय nirday

callow *adj.* अनुभवहीन anubhavheen

calm *n.* शान्ति shanti

calumny *n.* निन्दा ninda

camel *n.* ऊँट ute

camera *n.* क्यामेरा kyamera

camouflage *n.* भेष बदलने काम bhesh badalne kam

camp *n.* क्याम्प kyamp

camphor *n.* कपूर kapur

campus *n.* क्याम्पस kyampas

can *n.* सक्नु saknu

canal *n.* नहर nahar

can-can *n.* नाच naach

cancel *v.* रद्द/बदर गर्नु radda/ badar garnu

cancer *n.* कर्कट रोग karkat rog

candid *adj.* सरल saral

candidate *n.* उम्मेदवार ummed war

candle *n.* मैनबत्ती main batti

candour *n.* स्पष्टवादिता sapashtwadita

candy *n.* मिस्त्री misri

cane *n.* बेत bet

canister *n.* डिब्बा dibba

canteen *n.* चमेनाघर chamena ghar

canto *n.* सर्ग sarg

canvas *n.* मोटो कपडा moto kapada

canyon *n.* नदी बग्ने घाटी nadi bagne ghatti

cap *n.* टोपी topi

capable *adj.* योग्य yogya

capacity *n.* हैसियत haisiyat

cape *n.* अन्तरीप antreep

capital *n.* राजधानी raj dhani

capitalism *n.* पूंजीवाद punjiwad

capricorn *n.* मकर makar

capsule *n.* चक्की chakki

captain *n.* कप्तान kaptan

caption *n.* शीर्षक sheershak

captivate *v.* मोहित पार्नु mohit pamu

captivate *n.* मोहित गर्नु mohit garnu

capture *n.* पक्राउ pakrau

car *n.* मोटर गाड़ी motar gadi

carafe *n.* पानी वा मदिराको बोतल paani va madirako bottle

caravan *n.* यात्री समूह yatri samuh

caraway *n.* जीरा jeera

carburettor *n.* काबुरेटर carburettor

carcass *n.* जनावर को लाश janawarko laash

card *n.* तास tas

cardamom *n.* अलैंची alainchi

cardboard *n.* गत्त gatta

cardigan *n.* स्वेटर sweater

care *n.* हेरचाह herchah

career *n.* जीवनचर्या jiwan charya

careful *adj.* होशियार hoshiyar

careless *adj.* बेपरवाह beparwah

caress *v.* माया गर्नु mayagarnu

cargo *n.* जहा/गाडीमा लगिने मलमत्ता jahaj/gadima lagine mal matta

caries *n.* हड्डी वा दाँतको क्षय haddi va danthko kshay

carmine *n.* गाढ़ा रातो रंग garrha ratto rang

carnivorous *adj.* मांसाहारी mansahari

carp *n.* माछा विशेष machha vishesh

carpenter *n.* सिकर्मी sikarmi

carpet *n.* गलैंचा galaincha

carriage *n.* वाहन शुल्क wahan sulk

carrier *n.* कुल्ली kulli

carrion *n.* सड़ेको मासु sadeko masu

carrot *n.* गाजर gajar

carry *v.* बोक्नु boknu

cart *n.* बैलगाडी bail gadi

cartel *n.* उत्पादक संघ uttpadak-sangh

cartoon *n.* व्यंग्य चित्र wyanga chitra

carve *v.* काटमा नाक्शा खन्नु kath ma naksha khanu

cascade *n.* छागो chhango

case *n.* मुद्दा mudda

casein *n.* छेना chhena

cash *n.* नगद nagad

cashew nut *n.* काजु kaju

cashier *v.* बर्खास्त गर्नु barkhast garnu

casino *n.* जूवा घर juwa ghar

cassette *n.* क्यासेट kyaset

cassock *n.* लामो पोशाक lamo poshak

caste *n.* जात jate

castle *n.* महल mahal

castor-oil *n.* अँडिरको तेल aandirko tel

casualty *n.* हताहत hatahat

cat *n.* बिरालो biralo

cataclysm *n.* भयानक विपत्ति bhyanak vipati

catacombs *n.* क्रबहरूको तहखाना krubharuko tehkhana

catalogue *n.* सूचीपत्र suchipatra

cataract *n.* आँखाको फुलो aankhako phulo

catch *n.* समाल्नु samathnu

catchword *n.* सूचक-शब्द suchak-shabad

category *n.* श्रेणी shreni

caterpillar *n.* लोभी मानिस lovi manis

catharsis *n.* विरेचन virechan

cathedral *n.* मुख्य गिरजाघर mukhya girijaghar

cattle *n.* गाईवस्तु gaivastu

cauliflower *n.* फुलकोभी phulkobhi

cause *n.* कारण karan

caustic *adj.* कटु kattu

caution *adj.* होशियार hoshiyar

cavalier *n.* घोड़चढ़ी godh chadhi

cave *n.* गुफा gupha

cavort *v.* उत्तेजिक भएर उफ्रनु utaigik bhayara uffranu

cease *v.* बन्द गर्नु band garnu

ceaseless *adj.* लगातार lagatar

cedar *v.* देवदार devdar

celebrate *v.* उत्सव मनाउनु utsaw manaaunu

celestial *adj.* आकाशीय akashlya

celibacy *n.* अविवाहित जीवन awiwahit jiwan

cell *n.* जीवकोष्ठ jiwkosth

celling *n.* छाना chhana

cello *n.* भाइलिन जस्तै बाजा violion jasto baja

cement *n.* सिमण्टी simanti

cemetery *n.* कब्रिस्तान kabristan

censor *n.* जाच janch

census *n.* जनगणना jan ganan

cent *n.* प्रतिशत pratisath

centenary *n.* शतवार्षिकी shat warshiki

centennial *adj.* शतवर्षीय satabarsiya

centimetre *adj.* सैन्टीमीटर centimetre

central *adj.* केन्द्रीय kendriya

centre (ter) *n.* केन्द्र kendra

century *n.* शताब्दी shatabdi

cerebral *adj.* मगजको magajako

ceremony *n.* समारोह samaroh

ceritifcate *n.* प्रमाणपत्र praman patra

certain *adj.* निश्चित nischith

certify *n.* प्रमाणित गुर्न pramanit granu

cessation *n.* समाप्ति samapati

chaff *n.* भुस vush

chain *n.* जंजीर janjir

chair *n.* कुर्सी kursi

chairman *n.* अध्यक्ष adhyaksha

chaise *n.* रिक्सा rikshaw

chalet काठको घर kathko ghar

chalk *n.* खरी khari

challenge *n.* चुनौती chunauti

chamber *n.* कोठा kotha

chameleon *n.* छेपारो cheparo

champagne *n.* फ्रेन्च मदिरा french madera

champion *n.* विजेता wijeta

chance *n.* मौका mauka

chancellor *n.* कुलपति kulpati

chancery *n.* राजदूतावासको कार्यालय rajdutawas ko karyalaya

chancy *adj.* अनिश्चित anischit

change *n.* अदलबदल adal badal

chant *v.* गाउनु gauaunu

chaos *n.* अस्त-व्यस्त ast wyasta

chap *n.* फुट्नु phutnu

chapel *n.* सानो गिर्जाघर samp gorkagjar

chapter *n.* अध्याय adhyaya

character *n.* चरित्र charitra

characteristc *n.* विशिष्ट गुण wishisht gun

charade *n.* प्रहेलिका praheiika

charcoal *n.* आरोप aarop

charge *n.* जिम्मा jimma

chariot *n.* रथ rath

charisma *n.* ईश्वरीय दान ishwariya dan

charity *n.* दान dan

charming *adj.* मोहक mohak

chart *n.* नक्सा naksa

chase *n.* लखेटाइ lakhetai

chat *v.* बात मार्नु bat marnu

chateau *n.* महल mahal

chattle *n.* घरको चल वस्तु gharko chal bastu

chauffeur *n.* मोटरचालक motarchalak

cheap *adj.* सस्तो sasto

cheat *n.* ठग thag

check *n.* रोक rok

cheek *n.* गाला gala

cheerful *adj.* प्रसन्न prasanna

cheese *n.* खुवा khuwa

cheetah *n.* चिता cheta

chef *n.* होटलको मुख्य भान्से hotel ko mukhiya vansay

chemical *adj.* रासायनिक rasayanik

cheque/check *n.* चेक chek

cheroot चुरोट churote

cherry *n.* सानो रातो फल sano rato phal

chess *n.* बुद्धिचाल buddhichal

chest *n.* छाती chhati

chestnut *n.* कटुस katus

chew *v.* चपाउनु chapaunu

chick *n.* चल्ला challa

chicken *n.* कुखुरा kukhura

chicken pox *n.* ठेउला theula

chicory *n.* एक प्रकारको पौधा ek prakar ko podha

chide *v.* हप्काउनु hapkaunu

chief *n.* प्रधान pradhan

children *n.* बच्चाहरू bachcha haru

chilli/chili *n.* खोर्सानी khorsani

chimera *n.* असत्य asathya

chimney *n.* चिउडो dhuwankas

chin *n.* चिउँडो chiundo

china *n.* चिनियाँ माटोका भाडा chiniyan mtoka bhanda

chip *n.* टुका tukra

chisel *n.* छिनु chinu

chit *n.* सानो बच्चा sano baccha

chitchat *n.* कुराकानी kurakani

chlorine *n.* क्लोरीन chlorine

chocolate *n.* चकलेट chaklet

choice *n.* छनोट chhanot

choir *n.* गायकहरूको दल gayak haru ko dal

cholera *n.* हैजा haija

chop *n.* टुका पार्नु tukra parnu

choral *adj.* गायक-दलको gayak dalko

chord *n.* तार taar

chorus *n.* गायकहरूको दल gayak haru ko dal

christian *n.* इसाई isai

christmas *n.* क्रिस्मस चाड krismas chad

chrome *n.* क्रोम crome

chronicle *n.* घटनाहरूको क्रमिक विवरण ghatnaharu ko kramik vitran

chronometer *n.* ठीक समय बताउने घड़ी theek samay bataune ghari

chrysanthemum *n.* गोदावरी फूल godawari phul

chuckle *v.* दबेको हाँसो dabeko haanso

chum *n.* घनिष्ठ साथी ghanisht saathi

church *n.* गिर्जाघर girja ghar

churn *n.* मदानी madani

chute *n.* चिप्लेटी cheplete

chutney *n.* चटनी chutney

cigar *n.* सिगार cigar

cigarette *n.* चुरोट churot

cinema *n.* चलचित्र chal chitra

cinnamon *n.* दालचिनी dalchini

circuit *n.* बिजुली-पथ bijuli-path

circular *adj.* गोलो golo

circulation *n.* प्रचार prachar

circumference *n.* परिधि paridhi

circumspect *adj.* सावधान sabddhan

circumstance *n.* स्थिति sthiti

circus *n.* सर्कस sarkas

cirrhosis *n.* कलेजोको रोग kalegeo ko rog

citizen *n.* नागरिक nagrik

citron *n.* बिमिरा bimiro

citrus *n.* सुन्तला suntala

city *n.* शहर shahar

civil *adj.* निजामती nijamati

civilization *n.* सभ्यता sabhyata

clad *adj.* लगाएको lagaeko

claim *n.* दाबा dabha

clam *n.* ठूलो सीपी thulo sipi

clamp *n.* च्याप्ने पुर्जा chyapne purja

clan *n.* कुल वंश kul bansh

clap *n.* थपड़ी thapadi

claret *n.* रातो फ्रेन्च मदिरा rato french madira

clarify *v.* स्पष्ट गर्नु spasht garnu

clarion *adj.* आह्वान aahawan

clash *n.* भिडन्त bhidanta

class *n.* दर्जा darja

classify *v.* श्रेणीबद्ध shreni baddha

clay *n.* चिप्लो माटो chiplo mato

clean *adj.* सफा sapha

clear *adj.* स्पष्ट spasht

cleft *n.* धाँजा dhanja

clergy *n.* गिर्जाघरका पादरीहरू girjagharka padariharu

clerk *n.* पादरी padhari

clever *adj.* सिपालु sipalu

cliff *n.* चट्टान chattan

climate *n.* हावापानी hawapani

climax *n.* पराकाष्ठा parakasta

climb *v.* चढ्नु chadhnu

cling *v.* टाँसियनु tansinu

clinic *n.* उपचार गृह upchar grih

clip *n.* किलिप kilip

clique *n.* गुट gute

cloak *n.* बहाना bahana

clock *n.* घडी ghadi

cloister *n.* मठ math

close *n.* अन्त ant

closet *n.* दराज daraj

cloth *n.* कपडा kapada

clothes *n.* लुगाफाटो luga phato

cloud *n.* बादल badal

cloudy *adj.* बदली लागेको badali lageko

clove *n.* ल्वांग lwan

clown *n.* पाखे pakhe

clumsy *adj.* बंढंगो bedhang ko

coach *nb.* प्रशिक्षक prashikshak

coal *n.* कोइला koila

coarse *adj.* खस्रो khasro

coast *n.* किनारा kinara

coat *n.* कोट kotha

cobalt *n.* कोबाल्ट cobalt

cobbler *n.* सार्की sarki

cobra *n.* गोमन goman

cobweb *n.* माकुराको जालो makura ko jali

cock *n.* भाले कुखुरा bhale kukhura

cock-eyed *adj.* टेढ़ो thedo

cockroach *n.* साहीनउंदग्ला sanglo

cocksure *adj.* सुनिश्चित sunenischit

coconut *n.* नरिवल nariwal

cocoon *n.* रेशमको कोया resham ko koya

cod *n.* समुद्री माछा samundari maccha

co-education *n.* सहशिक्षा saha shiksha

coerce *v.* बाध्य गर्नु badhiya garnu

co-exist *v.* सँगै रहनु sangai rahanu

co-existence *n.* सहअस्तित्व saha astitwa

coffee *n.* कफी kaphi

coffin *n.* लाश राख्ने वाकस iash rakhne bakas

cognac *n.* फ्रेन्च ब्रान्डी french brandi

cognition *n.* ज्ञान gyan

cohabit *v.* अविवाहित पुरूष-स्त्री avivahit purush&stri

cohort प्राचीन रोमन फौजको कम्पनी prachin roman phhojko company

coin *n.* सिक्का sikka

coincide *v.* सन्जोग पर्नु sanjog parnu

coir *n.* नरिवल को जटा nariwal ko jata

coke *n.* कोक kok

cold *adj.* चिसो chiso

colic *n.* सूल sul

collapse *v.* ढल्नु dhalnu

collar *n.* कठालो kathalo

collate *v.* दाँज्नु dajnu

colleague *n.* मित्र mitra

collect *v.* जम्मा गर्नु jamma garnu

collection *n.* सङ्कलन sankalan

college *n.* क्याम्पस kyampas

collide *v.* ठक्कर खानु thakkar khanu

collision *n.* धक्का dhakka

colloquial *adj.* बोलचालको bol chal ko

collusion *n.* साठगाँठ santhganth

collyrium *n.* गाजल gajal

colo(u)r *n.* रंग rang

colonel *n.* मकगजरमाथिको अफिसर makgajarmathiko officer

colonialism *n.* उपनिवेशवाद upniwesh wad

colony *n.* बस्ती basti

colt *n.* घोडा को बच्चा ghoda ko bachcha

column *n.* खम्बा khamba

coma *n.* गहिरो निन्द्रा gahiro nindra

comb *n.* काहीनउंदगियो kangiyo

combat *n.* लड़ाई ladai

combine *v.* जोर्नु jornu

combustible *adj.* सजिलै जल्ने sajellai jalnai

come *v.* आउनु aunu

comedian *n.* हास्य-अभिनेता hasya abhineta

comedy *n.* संयोगान्त नाटक samyogant natak

comely *adj.* सुन्दर sundar

comet *n.* धूमकेतु dhumketu

comfort *n.* आराम aram

comfortable *adj.* आरामदायी aram dayi

comma *n.* अर्धविराम ardh wiram

command *n.* आज्ञा agya

commemorate *v.* स्मरण गर्नु smaran garnu

commence *v.* थाल्नु thalnu

commend *v.* तारिफ गर्नु tariph garnu

comment *n.* टिका-टिप्पणी tika-tippani

commerce *n.* वाणिज्य wanijya

commercial *adj.* व्यावारिक wyaparik

commision *n.* कमिसन kamisan

commit *v.* वचनबद्ध हुनु wachan baddh hunu

committee *n.* समिति samiti

commodious *adj.* फराकिलो pharakilo

commodity *n.* बेपारी सामग्री bepari samagri

commodore *n.* नाविक आफिसर nabik officer

common *adj.* साझा sajha

common sense *n.* सामान्य ज्ञान samanya gyan

commotion *n.* होहल्ला hohalla

communicate *v.* सन्देश दिनु sandesh dinu

communication *n.* संचार sanchar

communion *n.* सहभागिता sahabhagita

communique *n.* विज्ञप्ति bigapith

communism *n.* साम्यवाद samyawad

communist *n.* साम्यवादी samyawadi

community *n.* समुदाय samudaya

compact *adj.* सघन saghan

companion *n.* साथी sathi

company *n.* संस्था samstha

comparable *adj.* तुलना गर्न सकिने tulna garn sakne

compare *v.* दाँज्नु danjnu

compartment *n.* रेलको डब्बा rail ko dabba

compass *n.* कम्पास kampas

compassion *n.* दया daya

compel *v.* कर लाउनु kar launu

compensation *n.* भर्ना bharna

compere *n.* सूत्रधार sutradhar

compete *v.* प्रतियोगिता गर्नु pratiyogita garnu

competence *n.* योग्यता, क्षमता yogayta

competent *adj.* लायक layak

competition *n.* प्रतिस्पर्धा pratispardha

complacent *adj.* आत्मसन्तुष्ट aatma santust

complain *v.* सिकायत गर्नु sikayat garnu

complete *adj.* पूरा pura

completion *n.* सम्पन्न sampanna

complex *n.* कठिन kathin

complexion *n.* अनुहार anuhar

compliance *n.* पालन palan

complication *n.* अलझो alijho

complicity *n.* सहभागिता saha bhagita

compliment *n.* तारिफ गर्नु tariph

compose *v.* रच्नु rachnu

composer *n.* रचयिता rachayita

composition *n.* रचना rachna

composure *n.* शान्ति shanti

compound *n.* मिश्रण mishran

comprehend *v.* बुभ्नु bujhnu

compress *v.* खाँदनु khadnu

compromise *n.* समझौता samjhauta

compulsion *n.* कर लाउनु kar launu

compulsory *adj.* गर्नै पर्ने garnai parne

computer *n.* शुशंक्य sushankya

comrade *n.* साथी sathi

conceal *v.* लुकाउनु lukaunu

conceit *n.* घमण्ड ghamand

concentration *n.* एकाग्रता ekagrata

concept *n.* विचार wichar garnu

concern *n.* चासो chaso

concerning *prep/* बारेमा barema

concert *n.* संगीत कार्यक्रम sdangit karyakram

conch *n.* शंख sankh

conciliation *n.* मेल मिलाप mel milap

concise *adj.* छोटकरी chhotkari

conclave *n.* गुप्त सभा gupt sabha

conclude *v.* निष्कर्ष निकाल्नु nishkarsh nikalnu

conclusion *n.* निचोड़ nichod

concordance *n.* सामंजस्य samanjasya

concrete *adj.* रोडा roda

concur *v.* स्वीकार गर्नु swikar garnu

condemn *v.* दोषी ठहऱ्याउनु doshi thaharyaunu

condescend *v.* तल झर्नु tal jharnu

condition *n.* हालत halat

condolence *n.* श्रद्धांजलि shraddhanjali

condom *n.* गर्भनिरोधक garbh nirodhak

condone *v.* माफ गर्नु maaf garnu

conduct *n.* चरित्र charitra

conduit *n.* पानी जाने नल paani jane nal

confectionery *n.* मिठाई mithai

confederacy *n.* राज्यहरूको संघ rajyaharu sangh

confer *v.* परामर्श गर्नु paramarsh garnu

conference *n.* सभा sabha

confess *v.* स्वीकार गर्नु swikar garnu

confession *n.* कायलनामा kayalnama

confidence *n.* भरोसा bharosa

confine *v.* सीमित राख्नु simit rakhnu

confirm *v.* पुष्टि गर्नु pushti garnu

confiscate *v.* जफत japhat

conflict *n.* विरोध wirodh

confluence *n.* दोभान dobhan

confluence *n.* संगम sangam

confront *v.* सम्मुख पर्नु sammukh parnu

confused *adj.* भ्रमित bhramit

confusion *n.* गोलमाल golmal

confute *v.* खण्डन गर्नु khandan garnu

congeal *v.* जम्नु jamnu

congenital *adj.* जन्मैदेखिको जन्मगत janmedekhiko janamgat

congested *adj.* भीड़भाड़ भएको bhirhbhar bhaeko

congratulate *v.* बधाई दिनु badhai dinu

congratulation *n.* बधाई दिनु badhai dinu

congress *n.* सभा sabha

congruous *adj.* संगत sangat

conifer *n.* शंकुधारी sakundhari

conjugal *adj.* वैवाहिक baibayhik

conjugate *v.* क्रियारूप बनाउनु kriyarup banananu

conk *v.* बिग्रनु bigarnu

connect *v.* जोड्नु jodnu

connive *v.* नदेखेको जस्तो गर्नु najekhaiko jasto garnu

conquer *v.* जिल्नु jitnu

conquest *n.* विजय wijaya

conscious *adj.* होसमा भएको hosma bnhaeko

consecrate *v.* पवित्र पार्नु pavitra parnu

consensus *n.* सर्वसम्मति sarvsammati

consent *v.* मान्नु mannu

consequence *n.* फल phal

conservation *n.* संरक्षण samrakshan

conservative *adj.* परिवर्तन नचाहने parivartan nachahane

conserve *v.* संरक्षण sanrakshan

consider *v.* विचार गर्नु wichar garnu

consistent *adj.* अनुरूप anurup

consmos *n.* विश्व vishav

consolation *n.* तसल्ली tasalli

consonant *n.* व्यंजन wyanjan

conspiracy *n.* षड्यंत्र shadyantra

constant *adj.* स्थिर sthir

constellation *n.* तारागण taragan

consternation *n.* विस्मय visamay

constipation *n.* कब्जियत kabjiyat

constituion *n.* संविधान samwidhan

constitutency *n.* चुनाउ क्षेत्र chunau khestra

constrain *v.* बाध्य गर्नु badhya garnu

construct *v.* बनाउनु banaunu

construction *n.* निर्माण nirman

consul *n.* महावाणिज्यदूत maha wanijyadut

consume *v.* खपत/उपभोग गर्नु khapat/upbhog garnu

consummate *adj.* पक्का pakka

consumptive *n.* क्षयरोग kshaya rog

contact *n.* सम्पर्क sampark

contagious *adj.* सर्ने sarne

contain *v.* भित्र हुनु bhitar hunu

contained *adj.* रहेको raheko

container *n.* भाँडो bhando

contaminate *v.* फोहोर/दूषित पार्नु phohor/dushit parnu

contamination *n.* दूषण dushan

contemporary *adj.* समकालीन samkaleen

contempt *n.* घृणा ghrina

contend *v.* विवाद गर्नु wiwad garnu

contention *n.* विवाद, कलह wiwad, kalah

contest *n.* विवाद wiwad

context *n.* संदर्भ sandarbh

continent *n.* महाद्वीप mahadwip

continuation *n.* क्रम kram

continue *v.* लागिरहनु lagi rahanu

continuously *adv.* लगातार lagatar

contort *v.* बटारिनु batarinu

contour *n.* रूपरेखा rooprekha

contraband *n.* अवैध माल awaidhmal

contraception *n.* गर्भनिरोध garbhnirodhak

contract *n.* ठेक्का thekka

contractor *n.* ठेकेदार thekedar

contradict *v.* खण्डन गर्नु khandan garnu

contraption *n.* अनौठो यन्त्र anutho yantra

contrariety *n.* प्रतिकूलता pratikulta

contrary *adj.* विपरीत wiparit

contrast *n.* भेद bhed

contravene *v.* उल्लंघन ullanghan

contribute *v.* मदत/पैसा दिनु madat/paisa dinu

control *n.* नियन्त्रण niyantran

controversy *n.* विवादास्पद wiwadaspad

conuslt *v.* सल्लाह लिनु sallah linu

convection *n.* संवहन sawahan

convenient *adj.* पायक payak

convent *n.* भिक्षुनीहरूको मठ bhikshuniharuko math

conversant *adj.* परिचित parichit

conversation *n.* कुराकानी kurakani

converse *v.* बात गर्नु baatgarnu

convert *n.* दल्ले व्यक्ति dharm badalne wyakti

convex *adj.* बाहिरतिर उठेको bahirtir utheko

convey *v.* सन्देश पुऱ्याउनु/सुनाइदिनु sandesh pury aunu/sunaidinu

convict *n.* अभियुक्त abhiyukta

convince *v.* विश्वास गराउनु wiswas garaunu

convivial *adj.* मिलनसार milansar

convocation *n.* आह्वान ahawaan

convoy *n.* सँगै जाने जहाजी बेडा sangai jane jahaji beda

cook *n.* भान्छे bhanchhe

cool *adj.* चिसो chiso

coop *n.* खोर khor

cooperate *v.* सहयोग गर्नु sahyog garnu

coordinate *v.* समन्वय गर्नु samanwaya garnu

cop *v.* पुलीस police

cope *v.* सामना गर्नु samna garnu

copious *adj.* प्रचुर prachur

copper *n.* तामा tama

copulate *v.* सम्भोग/मैथुन गर्नु sambhog/maithun garnu

copy *n.* प्रतिलिपि pratilipi

coral *n.* मूंगा munga

cord *n.* डोरी dorie

cordial *adj.* हार्दिक hardik

corduroy *n.* मोटो सूती लुगा moto suti luga

coriander *n.* धनिया dhaniya

corn *n.* अनाज anaj

cornerstone *n.* आधारशिला adharshila

cornet *n.* बाजा baaja

cornice *n.* कार्निस karnis

corollary *n.* स्वाभाविक परिणाम swabhavik parinam

coronation *n.* राज्याभिषेक rajyabhishek

corporal *adj.* शारीरिक shareerik

corporation *n.* निगम nigam

corpse *n.* मुर्दा murda

corpulent *adj.* मोटो moto

corpuscle *n.* कणिका kanika

corral *n.* पशु राख्ने घेरा pashu rakhne ghera

correct *thik* ठीक shuddha

correspondence *n.* लेखापढी lekha padhi

corridor *n.* मटान matan

corrigendum *n.* शुद्धिपत्र shudhipatra

corroborate *v.* पुष्टि गर्नु pushti garnu

corrugated *v.* लहरदार lehardar

corruption *n.* भ्रष्टाचार bhrashachar

cortege *n.* ताँती tanti

cosmic *adj.* ब्रह्माण्ड को bramhand ko

cosmos *n.* सम्पूर्ण ब्रह्मण्ड sampurn bhrahmand

cost *n.* मूल्य mulya

costly *adj.* महँगो mahango

costume *n.* पोशाक poshak

cot *n.* सानो खाट sano khaat

cote *n.* गोठ goth

coterie *n.* मण्डली mandali

cottage *n.* कुटी kuti

cottage industry *n.* घरेलु उद्योग gharelu

cotton *n.* कपास kapas

couch *v.* व्यक्त गर्नु vyakat garnu

cough *v.* खोक्नु khoknu

council *n.* परिषद् parishad

counsel *n.* सल्लाह sallah

counsellor *n.* सल्लाहकार sallahkar

count *n.* गन्ती ganti

countenance *n.* अनुहार anuhar

counterfeit *adj.* नकली, जाली nakali, jaali

counterfoil *n.* रसीद rasid

counterpart *n.* प्रतिरूप pratirup

countersigh *v.* थप सही गर्नु thap sahi garnu

country *n.* देश desh

countryside *n.* गाउँघर gaun ghar

county *n.* प्रान्त prant

coup d'etat *n.* विद्रोह widroh

couple *n.* जोडा joda

coupon *n.* कुपन kupan

courage *n.* साहस sahas

courageous *adj.* साहसी sahasi

course *n.* पाठ्यक्रम pathya kram

court *n.* अदलात adalat

courteous *adj.* सुशील sushil

courtesy *n.* आद adar

courtier *n.* दरबारिया darbaria

courtship *n.* प्रणय-याचना pranay-yachna

courtyard *n.* चोक chok

cove *n.* सानो खाड़ी sano khari

cover *n.* बिर्को birko

covert *adj.* गुप्त gupt

cow *n.* गाई gai

coward *adj.* कातर kathar

cower *v.* डरले लुरूक्क पर्नु darle luruk parnu

cowl *n.* चिम्नीको ढकनी chimniko dhakni

cowshed *n.* गाईगोठ gai goth

crab *n.* गँगटो gangato

crack *n.* चेर्केको धर्का charkeko dharka

crackpot *n.* सनकी व्यक्ति sanki vyakti

craft *n.* सीप sip

crag *n.* ठाड़ो पहाड़ वा चट्टान tharo pahad wa chattan

cramp *n.* बाउँडिने रोग baundine rog

crane *n.* सारस saras

cranium *n.* खोपड़ी khopari

crank *n.* सनकी व्यक्ति sanki vyakti

cranny *n.* चिरा chira

crap *n.* बेकवाद bekwad

crash *n.* धड़ाका dhadaka

crass *adj.* अति ठूलो ati thulo

craven *adj.* कातर kattar

crawl *v.* घस्रनु ghasranu

crayon *n.* रंगीन पेन्सिल rangin pencil

craze *n.* धुन dhun

crazy *adj.* बौलाहा baulaha

cream *n.* मलम malam

crease *n.* दोब्याएको dobryaeko doro/rekha

create *v.* सृजना/रचना गर्नु srijana/ rachna garnu

creator *n.* सृष्टिकर्ता srishti karta

creature *n.* प्राणी prani

credible *adj.* पत्यारिलो patyarilo

credit *n.* इज्जत ijjat

creditable *adj.* प्रशंसनीय prashansniya

credo *n.* मत mat

creed *n.* मत mat

cremation *n.* दाहसंस्कार dah sanskar

crescent *adj.* अर्द्धचन्द्र ardhchandra

cress *n.* चंसूर chansur

crest *n.* जुरो juro

crestfallesn *adj.* निराश nirasha

cretain *n.* लठुवा lathuwa

crevasse *n.* हिम-दरार him-darar

cricket *n.* क्रिकेट kriket

crime *n.* अपराध apradh

criminal *n.* अपराधी apradhi

crimp *v.* घुँगुरो बनाउनु ghungro banaunu

crimson *n.* गाढ़ा रातो रंग garha rato rang

crinkle *v.* मुजा पर्नु वा पार्नु muja parnu wa paarnu

cripple *n.* लङ्गडो langado

crisis *n.* संकट sankat

critic *n.* आलोचक alochak

critical *adj.* नाजुक najuk

criticize *v.* आलोचना गर्नु alochana garnu

crochet *n.* काँटाको बुनाइ kantako bunai

crockery *n.* माटाका भाँड़ा वा त्यसको खपटा mataka bhanda wa tyasko khapta

crocodile *n.* गोही gohi

croft *n.* सानो खेत sano khet

crone *n.* जराजीर्ण बुढ़िया jarajirn budhiya

croon *n.* गुनगुनाउनु gungunaunu

crop *n.* बाली bali

crore *n.* करोड़ crore

cross *n.* सूली suli

cross-examination *n.* बन्द सवाल band sawal

crossroads *n.* चौबाटो chaubato

crossword *n.* शब्द पहेली shabd paheli

crotchet *n.* पादस्वर padswar

crow *n.* काग kag

crowd *n.* भीड bhid

crowded *adj.* भीडभाडपूर्ण bhidbhadpurn

crown *n.* श्रीपेच shripech

crucial *adj.* ठूलो महत्त्व को thulo mahtav ko

crucible *n.* धातु पगाल्ले भाँडो dhatu pagale bharo

cruel *adj.* निर्दयी nirdayi

cruel *adj.* निर्दय nirday

cruiser *n.* वेगवानू जंगी जहाज begwan jango jahaj

crumple *v.* खुम्चिनु khrimchinu

crunch *v.* आवाज निकाल्दै चपाउनु awaz nikarldae chapaunu

crush *v.* किच्नु kichnu

crusty *adj.* पाप्रा जस्तो papra jasto

crutch *n.* बैसाखी baisakhi

cry *v.* रुनु runu

crypt *n.* गिर्जामुनिको कोठा girjamuniko kotha

crystal *n.* काँच kanch

cub *n.* छाउरो chhauro

cube *n.* घन ghan

cubicide *n.* सानो छुट्टै कोठा sano chutai kotha

cubit *n.* हातको नाम hatko nam

cuckoo *n.* कोयली koyali

cucumber *n.* काँक्रो kankro

cud *n.* पागुर pagur

cuddle *v.* प्यारो गरेर अँगाल्नु piaro garer angalnu

cuff *n.* नाड़ीको छेउ nariko cheu

cuisine *n.* पकाउने तरीका pakaune tarika

culpable *adj.* दोषी ठहरिन योग्य doshi thehrin yogya

cultivation *n.* खेती गर्नु kheti garnu

cultural *adj.* सांस्कृतिक sanskritik

culvert *n.* बाटामुनिबाट पानी जाने batamunibat pani jane

cumbersome *adj.* भारी bhari

cunning *n.* धूर्त duhurt

cup *n.* कचौरा kachaura

cupboard *n.* दराज daraj

cupid *n.* कामदेव kamdev

cupidity *n.* धनको लोभ dhanko lobh

cupola *n.* गुम्बज gumbaj

cur *n.* भुस्याहा कुकुर bhusyaha kukur

curable *adj.* निको हुनसक्ने niko huna sakne

curate *n.* पुरोहित purohit

curative *adj.* रोग नाश गर्ने rog nash garne

curb *n.* प्रतिबन्ध गर्नु pratibandh garnu

curcumscribe *v.* रेखाले घेर्नु rekhale ghernu

curd *n.* दही dahi

cure *v.* निको तुल्याउनु niko tulyaunu

curfew *n.* कर्फ्यू karphyu

curious *adj.* उत्सुक utsuk

currency *n.* मुद्रा mudra

current *n.* हालसालको halsalko

curse *n.* सराप sarap

curtail *v.* छोटो र रूखो choto r rukho

curtain *n.* पर्दा parda

cushion *n.* गद्दा gadda

custard apple *n.* सरिफा saripha

custgoms *n.* भन्सार अड्डा bhansaradda

custody *n.* हिरासत hirasat

custom *n.* रीतिथिति ritithiti

customer *n.* गाहक gahak

cut *n.* कटान katan

cuticle *n.* कड़ा त्वचा को बाहिरी तह kara twacha ko bahiri the

cutlass *n.* सानो तरवार sano tarwar

cutlet *n.* कटलेट cutlet

cut-throat *n.* हत्यारा hatyara

cyanide *n.* विष vish

cycle *n.* चक्र chakra

cyclone *n.* आँधी andhi

cymbals *n.* झयाली jhyali

D

dacoit *n.* डाँकू danku

daddy *n.* बाबु babu

dafame *v.* निन्दा गर्नु ninda garnu

daft *adj.* मूर्ख murkh

dagger *n.* कटारी katari

dagger *n.* कटार kattar

dahlia *n.* लाहुरे फूल lahure phul

daily *adv.* दिनदिनै din dinai

dairy *n.* दूध पाइने ठाउँ dudh paine Thaun

dais *n.* मंच manch

daisy *n.* फूल phul

dale *n.* उपत्यका upatyaka

dam *n.* बाँध bandh

damage *n.* हानि hani

dame *n.* उच्च पद की महिला ucch pad ki mahila

damsel *n.* ठिटी thiti

dance *n.* नृत्य nritya

dandruff *n.* चाया chaya

danger *n.* खतरा khatra

danger *n.* खतरा khatra

dangerous *adj.* खतरनाक khatarnak

dangle *v.* लटकिनु latkinu

dare *v.* साहसे/हिम्मत गर्नु sahas/ himmat garnu

daring *adj.* सूरो suro

dark *adj.* अँध्यारो andhyaro

darling *n./adj.* प्रिये priye

darn *v.* रफ्फू भर्नु raphphu bharnu

dash *v.* हुत्तिनु huttinu

dashing *adj.* फुर्तिलो phurtilo

dastardly *adj.* कातर kattar

data *n.* तथ्यांक tathanyak

date *n.* मिति miti

dating *n.* मिल्ने/भेट्ने काम milne/ bhetne kam

daughter *n.* छोरी chhori

daughter-in-law *n.* बुहारी buhari

daunt *v.* तर्साउनु tarsaunu

dawn *n.* बिहान सबेरै bihana saberai

day *n.* दिनदिनै din dinai

day after tomorrow *n.* पर्सि parsi

day before yesterday *n.* अस्ति asti

daybreak *n.* झिसमिसे बिहान jhismise bihana

daydream *n.* दिवास्वप्न diwaswapna

daylight *n.* दिनको उज्यालो din ko ujyalo

daylong *n.* दिनभरि din bhari

daytime *n.* दिउँसो diunso

daze *v.* रन्थनिनु ranthninu

dazzle *v.* आँखा तिर्मिराउनु ankha tirmir aunu

dead *adj.* मरेको mareko

deadline *n.* समयसीमा samaya sima

deaf *adj.* बहिरा bahiro

deal *v.* दिनु dinu

dealing *n.* व्यवहार wyawahar

dear *adj.* प्यारो pyaro

dearness *n.* महँगाइ mahangai

dearth *n.* अभाव abhav

death *n.* मृत्यु mrityu

death penality *n.* मृत्युदण्ड mrityu dand

debacle *n.* पतन patan

debar *v.* रोक्नु roknu

debate *n.* वादविवाद wadwiwad

debenture *n.* ऋणपत्र rinpatra

debilitate *v.* कमजोर बनाउनु kamjor banaunu

debonair *adj.* मिलनसार milansar

debt *n.* ऋण rin

debunk *v.* असली रूप देखाउने asli roop dekhaune

decade *n.* दस वर्षको समय das warsh ko samaya

decapitate *v.* टाउको काट्नु tauko katnu

decay *n.* क्षय kshaya

deceased *adj.* मृत mrit

deceit *n.* छल-कपट chal-kapat

deceitful *n.* कपटी kapati

deceive *v.* ठग्नु thagnu

decent *v.* उचित uchit

decide *v.* फेसला phaisala

deciduous *adj.* पतनशीलता pathansilta

decimal *n.* दसमलब dasamalab

decipher अर्थ निकाल्नु arth nikalnu

decision *n.* फैसला phaisala

declaim *v.* प्रभाव पार्ने गरी बोल्नु prabhav parne gari bolnu

declare *v.* घोषित गर्नु ghoshit garnu

declension *n.* शब्द रूप shabd rup

decline *v.* नमान्नु namanun

decor *n.* कोठा को सजावट kothako sajawat

decorate *v.* स्रिगार्नु singarnu

decorum *n.* शिष्टाचार shishtachar

decrease *n.* कमी kami

dedicate *v.* समर्पित गर्नु samarpit garnu

dedication *n.* अर्पण arpan

deduce *v.* परिणाम निकाल्नु parinam nikalnu

deduct *v.* काट्नु katnu

deed *n.* काम kam

deep *adj.* गहिरो gahiro

defeated *v.* हारेको hareko

defecate *n.* हग्नु hagnu

defective *n.* दोष भएको dosh bhaeko

defence/defense *v.* रक्षा raksha

defensive *n.* रक्षा आत्मक raksh atmak

defiante *n.* अवज्ञा awagya

deficiency *adj.* कमी kami

deficient *n.* कमी/अभाव भएको kami/abhaw bhaeko

deficit *adj.* घाटा ghata

defiled *v.* जुठो jutho

definition *n.* परिभाषा paribhasha

deflection *adj.* मार्ग विचलन marg wichalan

deft *v.* चतुर chatur

deft *adj.* दक्ष daksh

defy *v.* विरोध गर्नु wirodh garnu

degrade *v.* हच्याउनु hochyunu

degree *n.* दर्जा darja

dehydrate *v.* निर्जल गर्नु nirjal garnu

dehydration *n.* पानीको कमी pani ko kami

deity *n.* देवी dewi

delay *n.* ढिलाई dhilai

delegate *n.* प्रतिनिधि pratinidhi

delegation *n.* खटाउने/सुम्पने काम khataune/sumpane kam

delete *v.* मेट्नु metnu

deliberate *adv.* जानेर गरिएको janera garieko

delicacy *n.* स्वादिलो खाना swadilo khana

delicate *adj.* कोमल komal

delicious *adj.* मीठो mitho

delight *n.* खुसी khusi

delighted *adj.* खुसी khusi

delirious *adj.* अचेत अवस्थामा बर्बराउने achet awastha ma barbaraune

deliver *v.* छोड्नु chhodunu

delude *v.* छल्नु chalnu

deluxe *adj.* उच्चकोटिको ucchkotiko

demand *n.* माग mag

demerit *n.* बैगुन baigun

demi-god *n.* अर्धदेव ardhdev

demise *n.* मृत्यु mrityu

democracy *n.* प्रजातन्त्र prajatantra

demolish *v.* भत्काउनु bhatkaunu

demon *n.* दैत्य daitya

demonstrate *v.* प्रदर्शन गर्नु pradarshan garnu

demoralize *v.* निरुत्साहित गर्नु nirutsashit garnu

demotion *n.* पद अवनति pad awanati

demure *adj.* शान्त shant

den *n.* गुफा gupha

denial *n.* खण्डन khandan

denomination *n.* मूल्यवर्ग mulyawarg

denote *v.* बताउनु bataunu

denounce *v.* निन्दा गर्नु ninda garnu

dense *adj.* घना ghana

dent *n.* खोपिल्टो khopilto

dental *adj.* दाँत सम्बन्धी dant sambandhi

dentist *n.* दाँतको डाक्टर dant ko daktar

denture *n.* नकली दाँत nakali dant

deny *v.* इन्कार गर्नु inkar garnu

depart *v.* प्रस्थान गर्नु prasthan

department *n.* फाँट phant

departure *n.* रमाना ramana hunu

depend *v.* निर्भर हुनु nirbhar hunu

dependable *adj.* भरपर्दो bhar pardo

deplete *v.* कम गर्नु वा खाली गर्नु kam garnu wa khali garnu

deplorable *adj.* शोचनीय shochniya

deplore *v.* अफसोस गर्नु aphsos garnu

deploy *v.* तैनाथ गर्नु tainath garnu

deployment *n.* तैनाथी tainathi

depopulate *v.* जनसंख्या घटाउनु jansankhya ghataunu

deporatation *n.* देशनिकाला desh nikala garnu

deport *v.* देश निकाला गर्नु desh nikala garnu

deposit *n.* जम्मा jamma

depot *n.* भण्डार bhandar

depressed *adj.* झोक्रिएको jhokrieko

depth *n.* गहिराइ gahirai

deputation *n.* प्रतिनिधि-मण्डल pratinidhi mandal

depute *v.* प्रतिनिधि नियुक्त गर्नु pratinidhi niyukat garnu

deputy *n* नायब nayab

deranged *adj.* बौलाहा bolaha

derive *v.* बाट उत्पत्ति हुनु bata utpatti hunu

derogatory *adj.* अपमानजनक apmanjanak

derrick *n.* भारी उठाउने यंत्र bhari uthaune yantra

descend *v.* ओर्लनु orlanu

descent *n.* उतार uttar

description *n.* वर्णन/बयान गर्नु warnan/bayan garnu

descry *v.* देख्नु dekhnu

desert *n.* मरुभूमि maru bhumi

deserts *n.* आफूले पाउनुपर्ने फल aphule paunuparne phal

deserve *v.* योग्य/उचित हुनु yogya/uchit hunu

desiccated *adj.* सुकाएको sukaeko

design *n.* जुक्ति jukti

desire *n.* इच्छा ichchha

desk *n.* छेस्क desk

desolate *adj.* न्य shunya

despair *n.* निराशा nirasha

despatch हेर्नु hernu

desperate *adj.* निराशा nirasha

desperate *adj.* निराशाजनक nirashajanak

despite *n.* दुराचार durachar

despoil *v.* लुट्नु lutnu

despot *n.* प्रजापीडक शासक prajapidak shasak

despot *n.* भोजनपछि खाने मिष्टान्न bhojanpachi khane mishthan

destination *n.* जाने ठाउँ jane thaun

destination *n.* गन्तव्य स्थान gantavya sthan

destiny *n.* भाग्य bhagya

destiny *n.* भाग्य bhagya

destroy *v.* नाश/नष्ट गर्नु nash/ nasht garnu

destroy *v.* नष्ट गर्नु nasht garnu

destruction *n.* नाश nash

detach *v.* बाट अलग गर्नु baat alag garnu

detail *n.* तपसिल tapsil

detain *v.* रोक्नु roknu

detect *v.* पत्ता लाउनु patta launu

detect *v.* पत्ता लाउनु patta launu

detective *n.* जासूस jasus

détente *n.* तनाउको कमी tanau ko kami

detention *n.* रोक्नु roknu

detention *n.* थुना thuna

deter *v.* रोक्नु roknu

deteriorate *v.* बिग्रनु bigranu

determination *n.* दृढता dridhta

determine *v.* आँट्नु antnu

deterrent *n.* रोक्ने कुरा rokne kura

detest *v.* घृणा गर्नु ghrina garnu

detract *v.* कम गर्नु वा खाली गर्नु kam garnu wa khali garnu

detriment *n.* हानि hani

develop *v.* विकास गर्नु wikas garnu

development *n.* विकास wikas

deviate *v.* ठीक बाटोबाट हट्नु thik batobat hatnu

device *n.* तारिका tarika

devil *n.* सैतान saitan

devil *n.* शैतान shaitaan

devise *v.* उपाय/जुक्ति गर्नु upaya/ jukti garnu

devitalize *v.* शक्तिहीन पार्नु shaktiheen parnu

devote *v.* दत्तचित्त हुनु datta chitta hunu

devotee *n.* भक्त bhakta

devotion *n.* भक्ति bhakti

devour *v.* हसुर्नु hasurnu

devout *adj.* धार्मिक dharmik

dew *n.* ओस os

dew *n.* शीत sheet

dexterity *n.* दक्षता dakshta

diabetes *n.* मधुमेह madhumeh

diabolic, diablical *adj.* अति दुष्ट ati dusht

diadem *n.* मुकुट किरीट mukut kirit

diagnose *v.* रोग पत्ता लाउनु rog patta launu

diagonal *n.adj.* विकर्ण vikaran

diagram *n.* रेखा चित्र rekha chitra

dial *v.* सुर्य घडी surya ghadi

dialect *n.* भाषा bhasha

dialect *n.* उपभाषा upbhasha

dialectic *adj.* द्वन्द्वात्मक dwandatamak

dialogue *n.* कुराकानी kurakani

diameter *n.* व्यास vyas

diamond *n.* हीरा hira

diarrh(o)ea *n.* पखाला pakhala

diary *n.* दैनिक विवरण dainik wiwaran

dice *n.* पासा pasa

dichotomy *n.* दुई विभाजन dui vibhajan

dicky *adj.* कमजोर बनाउनु kamjor banaunu

dictate *v.* आदेश दिनु adesh dinu

dictator *n.* तानाशाह tana shah

diction *n.* शब्द-योजना shabd yojna

dictionary *n.* शब्द कोश shabd kosh

didactic *adj.* शिक्षा दिने shiksha dine

die *v.* मर्नु marnu

diesel *n.* डिजेल dijel

diet *n.* आहार ahar

different *adj.* फरक pharak

difficult *adj.* गाह्यो gahyo

diffident *adj.* संकोच sankoch

diffuse *v.* धेरै शब्द प्रयाग गर्ने dherai shabd prayag garne

dig *v.* खन्नु khannu

digestion *n.* पाचनक्रिया pachan kriya

dignify *v.* सम्मान दिनु samman dinu

dignitary *n.* उच्च पदका अधिकारी ucch padka adhikari

dignity *n.* मान maan

dike, dyke *n.* बाँध baandh

dilatory *adj.* विलम्ब गर्ने vilamb garne

dilemma *n.* दोधार dodhar

diligent *adj.* उद्योगी udyogi

dim *adj.* धमिलो dhamilo

dimenstion *n.* आयाम ayam

diminish *v.* घटाउनु ghataunu

dimple *n.* हाँस्दा गालामा पर्ने खाडल hansda galama parne khadal

din *n.* हल्ला halla

din *n.* कोलाहल kolahal

dine *v.* भोजन गर्नु bhojan garnu

dinghy *n.* सानो डुङ्गा sano dunga

dingy *adj.* मेला mela

dinner *n.* रातको खाना rat ko khana

dinosaur *n.* एक किसिमको घस्रने जन्तु ek kisimko ghasrne jantu

dint *n.* सानो खोपिल्टी sano khopilti

dip *v.* डुबाउनु dubaunu

diploma *n.* उपाधि upadhi

diplomacy *n.* कूटनीति kutniti

diplomatic *adj.* कूटनैतिक kutnaitik

diptheria *n.* घाँटीको रोग ghaantiko rog

dire *adj.* भयानक bhayanak

direct *v.* निर्देश दिनु nirdesh dinu

direction *n.* दिशा disha

director *n.* निर्देशक nirdeshak

dirge *n.* शोक-गीत shok-geet

dirty *adj.* फोहोरी phohori

disable *v.* नसक्ने बनाउनु naskane banaunu

disabled *adj.* अपाङ्ग apang

disadvantage *n.* हानि hani

disagnose *v.* रोग खुट्ट्याउनु rog khuttaunu

disagree *v.* नामुजूर/अस्वीकार गर्नु namanjur/aswikar garnu

disallow *v.* अनुमति नदिनु anumati nadinu

disappear *v.* अल्पनु alpanu

disappoint *v.* निराश गर्नु nirash garnu

disapprove *v.* नमान्नु namannu

disarrange *v.* अस्तव्यस्त गर्नु astvyast garnu

disaster *n.* आपत् apat

disavow *v.* अस्वीकार गर्नु aswikar garnu

disc, disk *n.* गोलो वस्तु golo vastu

discard *v.* त्याग्नु tyagnu

discharge *n.* छुट्कारा chhutkara

disciple *n.* चेला chela

discipline *n.* अनुशासन anushasan

disclose *v.* प्रकट गर्नु prakat garnu

discomfort *n.* असुविधा asuvidha

disconsolate *adj.* दुःखी dukhi

discontent *n.* असन्तोष asantosh

discontinue *v.* रोक्नु roknu

discord फूट phoot

discount *n.* छूट chhut

discourage *v.* निरुत्साहित गर्नु nirutsahit garnu

discover *v.* पत्ता लाउनु patta launu

discredit *n.* बदनामी badnami

discriminate *v.* भेदभाव गर्नु bhed bhaw garnu

discuss *v.* छलफल गर्नु chhal phal garnu

discussion *n.* छलफल chhal phal

disease *n.* रोग rog

disembark *v.* उत्रनु utranu

disembodied *adj.* शरीरबाट अलग भएको sharirbaat alag bhaeko

disfavour *n.* अरूचि aroochi

disfigure *v.* रूप बिगार्नु roop bigarnu

disgrace *n.* अपमानजनक apmanjanak

disguise *n.* भेष बदल्नु bhesh badalnu

dish *n.* थाल thal

dishevelled *adj.* नकोरेको nakoreko

dishonest *adj.* बेइमान beiman

disillusion *v.* भ्रम हटाउनु bhram hataunu

disjointed *adj.* असम्बद्ध asambadh

dislike *n.* घिन ghine

dislodge *v.* हटाउनु hataunu

dismal *adj.* उदास udaas

dismantle *v.* भत्काउनु bhatkaunu

dismay *n.* डर र निराशाको भावना dar r nirashako bhawna

dismiss *v.* खोस्नु khosnu

disobey *v.* नटेर्नु na ternu

disoblige सहायता गर्न इन्कार गर्नु sahayta garn inkar garnu

disorder *n.* होहल्ला hohalla

disown *v.* आफ्नो होइन भन्नु apno hoin bhanu

disparage *v.* तुच्छ सम्झनु tuch samjhanu

dispatch *n.* सन्देश sandesh

dispensary *n.* औषधालय aushdhalaya

dispirited *adj.* हतोत्साह hatoutsaw

displace *v.* हटाउनु hataunu

display *n.* प्रदर्शन pradarshan garnu

displeasure *n.* नाराजी naraji

dispossess *v.* कब्जा हरण गर्नु kabja haran garnu

disprove *v.* असत्य प्रमाणित गर्नु asatya pramanit garnu

dispute *n.* झगडा jhagada

disquiet *v.* पीर पार्नु peer parnu

disquisition *n.* लामो भाषण lamo bhashan

disregard *n.* अनादर anadar

disrepair जीर्णोवस्था jeernovastha

disrepute *n.* बदनामी badnami

disrespect *n.* अनादर anadar

disseminate *v.* प्रचार गर्नु prachar garnu

dissent *v.* असम्मत हुनु asammat hunu

dissimilar *adj.* असमान asamaan

dissolute *adj.* अनैतिक anaitik

dissolution विघटन vighatan

dissonance *n.* बेसुरापन besurapan

distance *n.* दूरी duri

distaste *n.* अरूचि aroochi

distend *v.* फुलाउनु फुल्नु phulaunu phulnu

distiguish *v.* भेद bhed

distillery *n.* भट्टी bhatti

distinct *adj.* छुट्टै chhuttai

distinguish *v.* छुट्ट्याउनु chhuttyaunu

distinguished *adj.* विशिष्ट wishisht

distract *v.* अर्कोतिर खिँच्नु arkotir khichnu

distress *n.* कष्ट kasht

distribute *v.* बाँछ्नु bandnu

district *n.* जिल्ला jilla

distrust *n.* अविश्वास awishwas

disturb *v.* बाधा दिनु badha dinu

disturbance *n.* बाधा दिनु badha

ditch *n.* खाल्डो khaldo

ditto *n.* उही uhi

ditty *n.* साधारण गीत sadharan geet

diurnal *adj.* दिनको dinko

dive *n.* गोता gota

diverse *adj.* विविध vividh

diversion *n.* मोड़ modh

divert *v.* बहलाउनु bahalaunu

divest *v.* वंचित गर्नु vanchit garnu

divide भाग गर्नु bhag garnu

divination *n.* भविष्यकथन bhavishya kathan

divisible *adj.* भाग लगाउन सकिने bhag lagaun sakine

divorce *n.* पारपाचुके parpachuke

dizzy *adj.* रिंगटा ringata lageko

do *v.* गर्नु garnu

doctor *n.* डाक्टर daktar

doctrine *n.* सिद्धान्त siddhant

document *n.* कागजपत्र kagaj patra

dodder *v.* काम्नु kamnu

dodge *n.* छलने/छक्याउने काम chhalne/chhakyaune kam

doe *n.* मृगी mrigi

doer *n.* कर्ता karta

dog *n.* कुकुर kukur

dogged *adj.* दृढ dridh

doggerel *n.* कुकविता kukavita

doggy *n.* कुकुर kukur

dole *v.* वितरण गर्नु vitran garnu

doll *n.* पुतली putali

dollar *n.* संयुक्त राज्य अमेरिका sanyukt rajya america

dolly *n.* पुतली putli

dolphin *n.* समुद्री जन्तु samudari jantu

dome *n.* गुम्बज gumbaj

domestic *adj.* घरेलु gharelu

domicile *n.* प्रवास prabas

domicole *n.* निवास-स्थान niwas-sthan

dominant *adj.* मुख्य mukhya

dominate *v.* दबाउनु dabaunu

domination *n.* प्रभुत्व prabhutwa

don *v.* लाउनु launu

donate *v.* दान/चन्दा दिनु dan/chanda dinu

donkey *n.* गधा gadha

donor *n.* दाता data

door *n.* दैलो dailo

doorkeeper *n.* पाले pale

dormant *adj.* सुप्त supt

dormitory *n.* ठूलो सुत्ने कोठा thulo sutne kotha

dorsal *adj.* पिठ्यूँको pithuyuko

dosage *n.* औषधिको खुराक aushadhiko khurak

dose *n.* मात्रा matra

dot *n.* थोप्लो thoplo

dote *v.* पुल्पुल्याउनु pulpulaunu

double *adj.* दोब्बर dobbar

doubt *n.* शंका shanka

doubtful *adj.* शंकाजनक shanka janak

doubtless *adj.* निस्सन्देह nissandeh

dour *adj.* कड़ा kardha

douse पानी खन्याउनु pani khanyanu

dove *n.* ढुकुर dhukur

dowdy *adj.* भद्दा bhadda

down *n.* तल tala

downcast *adj.* झोक्राएको jhokraeko

downfall *n.* पतन patan

downhill *n.* ओरालो orali

downpour *n.* मुसलधार पानी musaldhar pani

downstairs *adv.* तलतिर tala tira

dowry *n.* दाइजो daijo

doyen *n.* वरिष्ठ सदस्य varisht sadasya

doze *v.* उँघ्नु unghnu

dozen *n.* दर्जन darjan

drab *adj.* नीरस neeras

drag *v.* तान्नु tannu

dragon *n.* प्वाँखे सर्प pwankhe sarpa

drain *n.* नाल nal

drake *n.* भाले हाँस bhale haans

dram *n.* तरल पदार्थको तौल taral padarthko tol

drama *n.* नाटक natak

dramatic *adj.* नाटकीय natkiya

drastic *adj.* कठोर kathor

draught *n.* कोठामा हावाको झोंक्का kothama hawako jhokka

draw *n.* खिंचातानी khichatani

drawback *n.* दोष dosh

drawer *n.* घर्रा gharra

drawing *n.* रेखाचित्र rekha chitra

drawing room *n.* बैठक baithak

drawl *v.* लेग्रो legro

dread *n.* डर dar

dreadful *adj.* भयानक bhayanak

dream *n.* सपना sapna

dreary *adj.* नीरस neeras

dregs *n.* थेग्रो thegro

drench *v.* भिज्नु bhijnu

dress *n.* लुगा luga

driblet *n.* तप्कने थोपा tapkane thopa

drift *v.* बग्नु bagnu

drill *n.* बर्मा barma

drink *n.* पेय peya

drip *v.* तप्किनु tapikanu

drive *n.* हँकाइ hankai

drivel *v.* बकम्फूस bakamphoos

driver *n.* चालक chalak

drizzle *n.* सिमसिम पानी simsim pani

droll *adj.* विचित्र vichitar

drool *v.* राल चुहाउनु ral chuhaunu

droop *v.* लत्रनु latranu

drop *n.* थोपा thopa

dross *n.* धातु को मैला dhatuko maila

drought *n.* सुक्खा sukkha

drove *n.* खेदिएको गाई-वस्तुको हूल khediyeko gaivastuko hool

drown *v.* डुब्नु dubnu

drub *v.* लगातार पिट्नु lagatar pitnu

drug *n.* औषधि aushadhi

drugstore *n.* औषधि पसल
aushadhi pasal

drum *n.* ढोल dhol

drunk *adj.* मातेको mateko

drunkard *n.* रक्सी खाने dherai
raksi khane

dry *adj.* सुकेको sukeko

dual *adj.* दुईजनाको duijanako

dubiety *n.* सन्दिग्धता sandigdhta

duck *n.* हाँस hans

duct *n.* नली nali

dud *n.* काम नलाग्ने चीज kam
nalagne cheej

due *adj.* उचित uchit

duel *n.* दुई जनाको भिडन्त dui jana
ko bhidant

dues *n.* ऋण rin

duet *n.* युगलगान yugal gan

duffer *n.* निकम्मा व्यक्ति nikamma
vyakti

dug *n.* थुन thun

dulcet *adj.* मीठो meetho

dull *adj.* मन्द mand

dullard *n.* लठुवा lathuwa

duly *adv.* ठीकसँग thiksang

dump *v.* फ्याँक्नु phayankanu

dumpy *adj.* पुड्कोर मोटो punkur
moto

dunderhead *n.* मूर्ख व्यक्ति murkh
vyakti

dune *n.* बालुवाको ढिस्को baluwako
dhisko

dungeon *n.* कालकोठरी kalkothari

dunk *v.* बिस्कुट वा रोटी चोपल्नु
biscuit va roti chopalnu

dupe *v.* धोखा दिनु dhoka dinu

duplicate *adj.* दोहोरो dohoro

durable *adj.* टिकाउ tikau

duration *n.* अवधि awadhi

duress *n.* धम्की dhamki

during *prep.* मात्रा ma

during *prep.* को समयमा ko
samyama

dusk *n.* गोधूलि godhuli

dusky *adj.* कालो रंगको kaloranko

dust *n.* धूलो dhulo

dutiful *adj.* आज्ञापालक agya palak

duty *n.* काम kam

dwarf *n.* बाउन्ने baunne

dwelling *n.* निवास niwas

dye *n.* रंगाउनु rang aunu

dynamite *n.* विस्फोटक visphotak

dynamo *n.* विद्युत् निकाल्ने एक यंत्र
vidhyut nikalne ek yantra

dynasty *n.* वंश wamsha

dysentery *n.* आउँ aun

dyspepsia अपच apach

E

each *adj.* हरेक harek

eager *adj.* उत्सुक utsuk

eagle *n.* चील chil

ear *n.* कान kan

earl *n.* अंग्रेजी कुलीन पुरूष angrezi kuleen purush

early *adj.* सबेरै saberai

earmark *v.* खास कामको लागि कोष छुट्टयाउनु khas kam ko lago kosh chhuttyaunu

earn *v.* कमाउनु kamaunu

earnest *adj.* गंभीर gambhir

earning *n.* कमाइ kamai

earshot *n.* आवाज सुन्न सकिने दूरी awaz sun sakine duri

earth *n.* पृथ्वी prithwi

earthquake *n.* भुइँचालो bhuinchalo

ease *n.* आराम aram

easel *n.* चित्र अङ्ग्याउने काठको ढाँचा chitra adaune kathko dhancha

easily *adv.* सजिलोसँग sajilo sanga

east *n.* पूर्व purwa

eastern *adj.* पूर्वी purwi

easy *adj.* सजिलोसँग sajilo sanga

eat *v.* खानु khanu

eatables *n.* खानूकुरा khane kura

ebony *n.* कड़ा कालो काठ karha kalo kath

ebullient *adj.* उल्लसित ullasit

eccelesiastic *n.* पादरी padri

eccentric *n.* झक्की jhakki

echo *n.* प्रतिध्वनि pratidhwani

éclair *n.* केक cake

eclipse *n.* सुर्य ग्रहण surya grahan

eclipse *n.* ग्रहण grahan

ecology *n.* पर्यावरण paryawaran

economic *adj.* आर्थिक arthi

economical *adj.* कम खर्चिलो kam kharchilo

economize *v.* कम खर्च/किफायत गर्नु kam kharch kiphayat garnu

economy *n.* अर्थतन्त्र arth tantra

eczema *n.* दाद dad

eddy *n.* भुँवरी bhuwanri

edge *n.* छेउ chheu

edgy *adj.* झोकी jhoki

edible *adj.* खान हुने khana hune

edifice *n.* भवन bhawan

edit *v.* सम्पादन गर्नु sampadan garnu

educate *v.* शिक्षा दिनु shiksha dinu

education *n.* शिक्षा shiksha

eel *n.* बाम माछा bammachha

effect *n.* असर asar

effective *adj.* राम्रो असर पार्ने ramroasar parne

effete *adj.* दुर्बल durbal

efficiency *n.* दक्षता dakshata

efficient *adj.* दक्ष daksh

effigy *n.* पुतला putala

effort *n.* मिहिनेत mihinet

effrontery *n.* धृष्टता dhrishtata

effulgent *adj.* उज्जवल ujjawal

egalitarian *n.* समतावादी samata wadi

egg *n.* फुल phul

eggplant *n.* भण्टा bhanta

ego *n.* अहम aham

egress *n.* बाहिर जाने काम bahir jane kam

eight *n.* आठ aath

eighteen *n.* अठार athara

eighth *adj.* आठौं athaun

eighty *adj.* अस्सी assi

ejaculate *v.* सिर्का छोड्नु sirka chhodnu

ejaculation *n.* स्खलन skhalan

eject *v.* निकाल्नु nikalnu

eke out कुनै कुरामा थपथाप kunai kurama thapthaap

elaborate *adj.* विस्तृत wistrit

elan *n.* फुर्ति phurti

elapse *v.* बित्नु bitnu

elastic *adj.* तन्कने tankane

elated *adj.* खुस khus

elbow *n.* कुहिना kuhina

elder *adj.* जेठो jetho

elderly *adj.* प्रौढ praudh

elect *v.* चुन्नु chunnu

election *n.* चुनाउ chunau

electric shock *n.* बिजुलीको करेण्टको धक्का bijuli ko karent ko dhakka

electricity *n.* बिजुली bijuli

electrocute *v.* बिजुलीको करेण्ट लागेर मर्नु bijuli ko karent lagera marnu

elegant *adj.* सुन्दर sundar

element *n.* तत्त्व tattwa

elephant *n.* हात्ती hatti

elevate *v.* उचाल्नु uchalnu

elevation *n.* ऊँचाइ unchai

elevator *n.* लिफ्ट lipht

eleven *n.* एघार eghara

elicit *v.* निकाल्नु nikalnu

eligible *adj.* छान्नयोग्य chhanna yogya

eliminate *v.* लोप गराउनु lop garaunu

elixir *n.* अमृत amrit

elk *n.* एक जातको हरिण ek jaatko harin

elm *n.* रूख विशेष rukh vishesh

elocution *n.* बोल्ने कला bolne kala

elongate *n.* लामो पार्नु lamo parnu

elope *v.* चम्पत हुनु champat hunu

elopquent *adj.* राम्रो बोल्ने ramro bolne

else *pron.* अर्को arko

elsewhere *adj.* अन्तै antai

elucidate *v.* स्पष्ट गर्नु sapasht garnu

emaciated *adj.* दुब्लो भएको dublo bhaeko

emancipate *v.* मुक्त गर्नु mukt garnu

emancipation *n.* मुक्ति mukti

embankment *n.* बाँध bandh

embargo *n.* रोक्का rokka

embark *v.* जहाज चढ्नु jahaj chadhnu

embarkation *n.* आरोहण arohan

embarrass *v.* अप्ठ्यारोमा पार्नु apthyaro ma parnu

embarrassment *n.* अप्ठ्यारोमा पार्नु apthyaro ma parnu

embassy *n.* दूतावास dutawas

embed *v.* जड्नू jadnu

embers *n.* आगोको झरिलो रहल agoko jharilo rahal

emblazon *v.* अलंकृत गर्नु alankrit garnu

emblem *n.* चिनो chino

embolden *v.* हिम्मत बढ़ाउनु himmat badhaunu

emboss *v.* कुँदेर बेलबुट्टा भर्नु kunder belbutta bharnu

embrace *v.* अँगालो हाल्नु angalo halnu

embroidery *n.* कार्चोप karchop

embryo *n.* भ्रूण bhurun

emerald *n.* पन्ना panna

emerge *v.* निक्लनु niklanu

emergency *n.* संकट sankat

emergent *adj.* नवोदित nawodit

emery *n.* पालिस गर्ने धातु palis garne dhatu

emigrant *n.* प्रवासी prawasi

émigré *n.* प्रवासी prawasi

eminent *adj.* नामी nami

emissary *n.* दूतावास dutawas

emit *v.* छोड्नु chodnu

emotion *n.* भाव bhawan

empathy *n.* समानुभूति samanubhuti

emperor *n.* सम्राट samrat

emphasis *n.* जोर jor

empire *n.* साम्राज्य samrajya

employ *v.* काम दिनु kam dinu

employee *n.* काम गर्ने kam garnue

employment *n.* काम kam

empower *v.* अधिकार दिनु adhikar dinu

empress *n.* सम्राज्ञी samragi

empty *adj.* रित्तो ritto

en masse *adv.* सामूहिक रूपले samuhik ruple

en route *adv.* बाटोमा batoma

enable *v.* योग्य∕लायकबनाउनपु yogya/layak banaunu

enable *v.* समर्थ वा योग्य बनाउनु samrath va yogya banaunu

enact *v.* अभिनय गर्नु abhinay garnu

enamel *n.* एनामेल enamel

encase *v.* डिब्बामा बन्द गर्नु dibbama band garnu

encephalitis *n.* मस्तिष्क ज्वर mastishka jwar

enchant *v.* टुना∕मोहित गर्नु tuna/mohit garnu

enchant *v.* मोहित गर्नु mohit garnu

enchantment *n.* मोह moh

enclose *v.* घेर्नु ghernu

enclosure *n.* घेरा ghera

encounter *v.* लड्नू ladnu

encounter *v.* सित भेट्नु sit bhetnu

encourage *v.* उक्साउनु uksaunu

encouragement *n.* हौसला hausala

encumber *v.* भार हाल्नु bhaar halnu

encyclop(a)edia *n.* विश्वकोश wishwa kosh

end *n.* आखिर akhir

end *n.* अन्त anth

endanger *v.* खतरामा हाल्नु khatrama halnu

endear *v.* प्यारो बनाउनु piaro banaunu

endeavo(u)r *n.* प्रयल prayatna

endless *adj.* अनन्त anant

endorse *v.* लेखेर स्वीकार/दरपीठ गर्नु lekhera swikar/darpith garnu

endorse *v.* समर्थन samrathan

endow *v.* दिनु dinu

endurance *n.* सहनशीलता sahan shilta

endure *v.* सहनु sahanu

endure *v.* सहनु sahnu

enema *n.* डूस doos

enemy *n.* त्रु shatru

energy *n.* बल bal

energy *n.* ऊर्जा oorja

enervate *v.* दुर्बल बनाउनु durbal banaunu

enfold *v.* लपेट्नु lapetanu

enforce *v.* कर लगाउनु kar lagaunu

enforcement *n.* लागू गर्ने काम lagu garne kam

engage *v.* काममा लाग्नु kam ma lagnu

engaged *adj.* काममा लागेको/व्यस्त kam ma lageko/wyasta

engagement *n.* काम kam

engender *v.* उत्पन्न गर्नु uttpan garnu

engine *n.* कल kal

engineer *n.* इन्जिनियर injiniyar

england *n.* बेलायत belayat

english *n.* अँग्रेज angrej

engrave *v.* खोप्नु khopnu

engulf *v.* ग्रास गर्नु gras garnu

enhance *v.* बढ्नु badhnu

enigma *v.* पहेली paheli

enjoin *v.* आदेश दिनु aadesh dinu

enjoy *v.* रमाउनु ramaunu

enjoyable *adj.* आनन्द दिने anand dine

enjoyment *n.* मजा maja

enlarge *v.* ठूलो गर्नु thulo garnu

enlighten *v.* प्रकाश पार्नु prakash parnu

enlightenment *n.* ज्ञान gyan

enmesh *v.* फसाउनु phasaunu

enmity *n.* शत्रुता shatruta

enough *adv.* यथेष्ट yathesht

enquire *v.* सोधपुछ गर्नु sodh puchh garnu

enquual *adj.* असमान asaman

enrage *v.* क्रुद्ध पार्नु krudh parnu

ensconce *v.* आरामसित बसाउनु aramsit basaunu

ensign *n.* झण्डा jhanda

enslave *v.* दास बनाउनु das banaunu

entangle *v.* फस्नु phasnu

entanglement *n.* अल्झाइ aljhai

entente *n.* सन्धि sandhi

entente *n.* सन्धि sandhi

enter *v.* पस्नु pasnu

enterprise *n.* उद्यम udyam

enterprising *adj.* उद्यमी udyami

entertain *v.* मन बहलाउनु man bahalaunu

entertainment *n.* मनोरंजन manoranjan

enthral *v.* मोहित गर्नु mohit garnu

enthrone *v.* राजगद्दीमा राख्नु rajgaddima rakhnu

enthuse *v.* उत्साह देखाउनु utsaw dekhaunu

enthusiasm *n.* जोश josh

entice *v.* फकाउनु phakaunu

entirely *adv.* पूर्ण रूपले purn ruple

entitle *v.* अधिकार दिनु adhikar dinu

entourage *n.* दलबल dalbal

entrails *n.* आन्द्रा aandra

entrance *n.* प्रवेश prawesh

entrap *v.* फसाउनु phasaunu

entreat *v.* बिन्ती/अनुरोध गर्नु binti/anurodh garnu

entrepreneur *n.* उद्यमी udyami

entrust *v.* सुम्पनु sumpanu

entry *n.* प्रवेश prawesh

entwine *v.* बेरिनु berinu

envelop *v.* घेर्नु ghernu

envelope *n.* खाम kham

envelope *n.* खाम kham

enventual *adj.* अन्तिम antim

enviable *adj.* ईर्ष्या गर्न योग्य irshya garn yogya

environment *n.* वातावरण watawaran

envy *n.* डाहा daha

enzyme *n.* इन्जाइम enzyme

epic *n.* महाकाव्य maha kawya

epidemic *n.* महामारी mahamari

epilepsy *n.* छारेरोग chhare rog

epilogue *n.* उपसंहार upsanhar

episode *n.* प्रसंग prasang

epistle *n.* चिठी chithi

equal *adj.* बराबर barabar

equanimity *n.* मनको स्थिरता manko sthirta

equator *n.* भूमध्य रेखा bhumadhya rekha

equestrian *n.* घोड्चढी ghod chadhi

equiality *n.* बराबरी barabari

equinox *n.* दिन र रात समान हुने समय din r rat saman hune samay

equip *v.* सजाउनु sajaunu

equipment *n.* उपकरण upkaran

equivalent *adj.* बराबर barabar

era *n.* युग yug

eradicate *v.* निर्मूल/उन्मूलन गर्नु nirmul/unmulan garnu

erase *v.* मेट्नु metnu

eraser *n.* मेट्ने रबर metne rabar

ere *adv.* अघि aghi

erect *v.* बनाउनु banaunu

erode *v.* ख्याउनु khyaunu

erosion *n.* कटान katan

erotic *adj.* कामुक kamuk

err *v.* गल्ती गर्नु galti garnu

errand *n.* बाहिर गई गरिने काम bahir gal garine kam

erroneous *adj.* अशुद्ध ashudh

error *n.* गल्ती galti

escalate *v.* बढाउनु batdhaunu

escalator *n.* आफै चल्ने भरेङ्ग aphai chalne bhareng

escapade *n.* जोखिमपूर्ण काम jokhimpurn kam

escape *v.* फुल्कनु phutkanu

escarpment *n.* करालो परेको ठाउँ karalo pareko thaun

especial *adj.* विशेष vishesh

especially *adv.* विशेषगरी wishesh gari

espionage *n.* जासूसी jasusi

espouse *v.* बिहे गर्नु bihe garnu

espy *v.* देख्नु dheknu

essay *n.* निबन्ध nibandh

essence *n.* सार sar

essential *adj.* जरूरी jaruri

establish *v.* सीपना/खडा गर्नु sthapana/khada garnu

establishment *n.* सीपना sthapana

esteem *n.* आदर adar

estimate *adv.* लागत lagat

estrange *v.* विमुख गराउनु vimukh garaunu

estuary *n.* नदीमुख nadimukh

eternal *adj.* अनन्त anant

ethereal *adj.* सुकुमार sukumar

ethical *n.* नैतिक naitik

ethics *n.* नीतिशास्त्र niti shastra

ethos *n.* जातीय गुण jatiya gun

etiquette *n.* काइदा kaida

eunuch *n.* खसी परेको व्यक्ति khasi pareko vyakti

euphoria *n.* सुख वा उल्लास को स्थिति sukh va ullas ko sthiti

euquilibrium *n.* सन्तुलन santulan

euquitable *adj.* न्यायसंगत nayaysangat

evacuate *v.* खाली गर्नु khali garnu

evade *v.* बाट बाच्नु baat bachnu

evaluate *v.* मूल्यांकन mulyankan

evaporate *v.* बाफ बन्नु baph bannu

eve *n.* उत्सवको अघिल्लो साँझ utsavko aghilo saanjh

eveing *n.* बेलुका beluka

even *adv.* पनि pani

event *n.* घटना ghatna

eventual *adj.* अन्तिम antim

ever *adv.* सधैं sadhain

evergreen *adj.* सदाबहार sadabahar

everlasting *adj.* सधैं रहने sadhain rahane

every *adj.* हरेक harek

everybody *n.* हर व्यक्ति har wyakti

everything *n.* हर चीज har chij

everywhere *adv.* जहाँसुकै jahan sukai

evict *v.* निकाल्नु nikalnu

evidence *n.* साक्षी sakshi

57

evident *adj.* प्रत्यक्ष pratyaksha

evil *n.* दुष्टता dushtata

evince *v.* देखाउनु dekhaunu

evoke *v.* उत्पन्न गर्नु uttapan garnu

evolution *n.* विकास wikas

evolve *v.* विकसित हुनु वा गर्नु wiksit hunu wa garnu

ewer *n.* घड़ा gharha

exacerbate *v.* तीव्र बनाउनु tivra banaunu

exact *adj.* ठीक thik

exactly *adv.* ठीकसँग thik sanga

exaggeration *n.* बढाई चढाई गरेको कुरा badhai chadhai gareko kura

examination *n.* जाँच janch

examine *v.* जाँच्नु janchnu

example *n.* ददाहरण udaharan

exasperate *v.* रीस उठाउनु rees uthaunu

excavate *v.* खनेर निकाल्नु khanera nikalnu

exceed *v.* बढ्नु badhnu

excel *v.* जिल्नु jitnu

excellency *n.* महामहिम maha mahim

excellent *adj.* उत्तम uttam

except *prep.* सिवाय siwaya

exception *n.* नियमबाहिरको कुरा niyam bahira ko kura

excess *n.* ज्यादा jyada

excessive *adj.* अत्यधिक atyadhik

exchange *n.* साटासाट satasat

exchequer *n.* राजकोष rajkosh

excite *v.* उत्तेजित गर्नु uttejit garnu

excitement *n.* उत्तेजना uttejana

exclaim *v.* कराउनु karaunu

exclude *v.* भाग लिन नदिनु bhag lin nadinu

excrement *n.* दिसा disha

excrescence *n.* अपवृद्धि apvridhi

excursion *n.* सफर saphar

excuse *n.* क्षमा kshama

execrable *adj.* अति नराम्रो ati naramro

execute *v.* गर्नु garnu

executive *n./adj.* कार्यकारिणी karya karini

exempt *v.* छूट दिनु chhut dinu

exemption *n.* छूट दिनु chhut dinu

exercise *n.* अभ्यास abhyas

exert *v.* काममा ल्याउनु kamma lyaunu

exhale *v.* सास छोड्नु saas chodnu

exhaust *v.* सिद्धिनु siddhinu

exhausted *adj.* थाकेको thakeko

exhibition *n.* प्रदर्शनी pradarshani

exhort *v.* उपदेश दिनु updesh dinu

exile *n.* निष्कासन nishkasan

exist *v.* बाँच्नु banchnu

existence *n.* अस्तित्व astitwa

exit *n.* निस्कने बाटो niskane bato

exobitant *adj.* ज्यादै बढी jyadai badhi

exodus *n.* प्रस्थान prasthan

exorbitant *adj.* अत्यधिक atyadhik

exorcise *v.* भूत धपाउनु bhut dhapaunu

exotic *adj.* नौलो naulo

expand *v.* बढ्नु badhnu

expansion *n.* विस्तार wistar

expect *v.* आशा asha

expectant *adj.* आशा गर्ने asha garne

expectorant *v.* कफनासक coughnasak

expectorate *v.* कफ निकाल्नु coughnikalnu

expedite *v.* चाँडो/ताकिता गर्नु chando/takita garnu

expedition *n.* यात्रा yatra

expel *v.* निकाल्नु nikalnu

expenditure *n.* खर्च kharch

expensive *adj.* महंगो mahango

experience *n.* अनुभव anubhav

experienced *adj.* अनुभवी anubhavi

experiment *n.* प्रयोग prayog

expert *adj.* सिपालु sipalu

expertise *n.* विशेष सीप vishesh seep

expiate *v.* प्रायश्चित गर्नु prayashchit garnu

expionage *n.* जासूसी jasoosi

expire *v.* मर्नु marnu

explain *v.* बताउनु bataunu

explanation *n.* व्याख्या wyakhya

explode *v.* पड्कनु padkanu

explore *v.* खोज/अन्वेषण गर्नु khoj/anweshan garnu

explosion *n.* विष्फोटन wishphotan

export *n.* निर्यात निकासी गर्नु niryat nikasi garnu

express *v.* बोल्नु bolnu

expression *n.* अभिव्यक्ति abhiwyakti

expropriate *v.* हरण गर्नु haran garnu

exquisite *adj.* उत्तम uttam

ex-serviceman *n.* भूतपूर्व सैनिक bhutpurv sainik

extempore *adj.* बिना तयारी bina tayari

extend *v.* फेलाउनु phailaunu

extension *n.* जोडिएको भाग jodiyeko bhaag

extepore *adv. adj.* बिना तयारी bine tyari

exterior *adj.* बाहिरी bahiri

exterminate *v.* खतम गर्नु khatam garnu

external *adj.* बाहिरी bahiri

external *adj.* बाहिरको bahirko

extinct *adj.* बिलाउको bilaeko

extinguish *v.* निभाउनु nibhaunu

extirpate *v.* उन्मूलन गर्नु unmulan garnu

extra *adj.* अतिरिक्त atirikta

extract *v.* झिक्नु jhiknu

extradite *v.* सुम्पनु sumpanu

extradition *n.* सुपुर्दगी supurdagi

extraneous *adj.* असम्बद्ध asambadh

extraordinary *adj.* असाधारण asadharan

extravagant *adj.* खर्चिलो kharchilo

extreme *adj.* उग्र ugra

extricate *v.* मुक्त गर्नु mukt garnu

exude *v.* देखाउनु dekhaunu

eye *n.* आँखा ankha

eyeball *n.* आँखीगेडी ankhi gedi

eyebrow *n.* आँखीभौं ankhi bhaun

eyeglasses *n.* चस्मा chasma

eyelash *n.* परेला parela

eyesight *n.* दृष्टि drishti

eyewitness *n.* प्रत्यक्षदर्शी pratyakshadarshi

F

f(a)eces *n.* दिसा disa

fable *n.* कथा katha

fabric *n.* कपड़ा kapada

fabricate *v.* बनाउनु banaunu

fabulous *adj.* ऋख्यात prakhat

façade *n.* भवनको सामुन्ने भाग bhavanko samune bhag

face *n.* मुख mukh

facial *adj.* अनुहारको anuharko

facile *adj.* सहज sahaj

facility *n.* सुविधा suwidha

facsimile *n.* अनुलिपी anulipi

fact *n.* कुरा kura

faction *n.* गुट gut

factitious *adj.* कृत्रिम kritrim

factor *n.* तत्त्व tattwa

factory *n.* कारखाना karkhana

faculty *n.* सङ्काय sankaya

fad *n.* धुन dhun

fade *v.* खुइलनु khuilanu

faeces *n.* विष्ठा vishtha

faggot *n.* दाउराको बिटा daurako bita

fahrenheit *adj.* फारेनहाइट fahrenheit

fail *v.* निष्फल हुनु nishphal hunu

failure *n.* असफलता asaphalta

faint *adj.* मूर्छित murchhit

fair *n.* मेला mela

fairy *n.* परी pari

faithful *adj.* इमानदार imandar

fake *n.* नक्कली वस्तु nakkali wastu

falcon *n.* बाज baj

fall *v.* खस्नु khasnu

fallible *adj.* गलती गर्न सक्ने galti garn sakne

falls *n.* झरना jharna

falsetto *n.* पुरूषमा हुने purushma hune

fame *n.* कीर्ति kirti

familiar *adj.* चिनेजानेको chine janeko

family *n.* परिवार pariwar

famine *n.* अनिकाल anikal

famous *adj.* प्रसिद्ध prasiddha

fan *n.* पंखा pankha

fanatic *n./adj.* धर्मान्ध dharmandh

fanfare *n.* धूमधाम dhumdham

fang *n.* दाह्रा Darha

fantastic *adj.* विलक्षण wilakshan

far *adj.* टाढा tadha

fard-headed *adj.* व्यावहारिक wyawharik

farewell *n.* विदाइ bidai

far-fetched *adj.* अस्वाभाविक aswabhawik

farm *n.* खेत khet

farmer *n.* किसान kisan

farrier *n.* घोड़ा को टापमा नाल ठोक्ने मानिस ghorako tapma nal thokne manis

farrow *v.* सुँगरले बच्चा जन्माउनु sungurle bacha janmaunu

fart *v.* पादनु padnu

fascinate *v.* 13 mohit/akarshit garnu

fashion *n.* चलन chalan

fast *adj.* छिटो chhito

fasten *v.* बाँध्नु bandhnu

fat *n.* चिल्लो chillo

fatal *adj.* ज्यान जाने jyanjane

fatal *adj.* घातक ghatak

fate *n.* भाग्य bhagya

father *n.* बाबु babu

father-in-law *n.* ससुरा sasura

fathom *n.* पानीको गहिराइको नाप paniko gahiraiko nap

fatigue *n.* थकाइ thakai

faucet *n.* टुटी tuti

fault *n.* गलती galti

fauna *n.* प्राणीहरू prani haru

faux pas *n.* गलती galti

favo(u)r *n.* कृपा kripa

favo(u)rite *n.* प्यारो pyaro

fear *n.* डर Darha

fearful *adj.* डरलाग्दो dar lagdo

fearless *adj.* निडर nidar

feasible *adj.* सम्भव sambhaw

feast *n.* भोज bhoj

feat *n.* कठिन काम kathin kaam

feather *n.* प्वाँख pwankh

feckless *adj.* लापरवाह laparwah

fecund *adj.* धेरै उब्जनी हुने dherai ubjani hune

fed विरक्त वा वाक्क भएको virakt wa wak bhaeko

fee *n.* शुल्क shulka

feeble *adj.* कमजोर kamjor

feed *v.* ख्वाउनु khwaunu

feel *v.* महसुस गर्नु mahsus garnu

feeling *n.* भाव bhaw

feet *n.* पाउ खट्टाहरू pau/khutta haru

feint *n.* बहाना bahana

felicitate *v.* बधाई दिनु badhai dinu

felicitation *n.* बधाई दिनु badhai dinu

feline *adj.* बिरालोको biraloko

fell *v.* रूख काट्नु rukh katnu

fellow *n.* साथी sathi

felon *n.* घोर अपराधी ghor apradhi

female *n.* स्त्री stri

feminine *adj.* स्त्रीलिंग striling

femur *n.* तिघ्राको हड्डी tighrako haddi

fen *n.* धाप dhap

fence *n.* बार bar

fend *v.* आफ्नो बचाउ गर्नु apno bachau garnu

fennel *n.* सोंप soanp

fenugreek *n.* मेथी methi

ferment *v.* उत्तेजित गर्नु वा हुनु uttejit garnu wa hunu

fern *n.* उन्यू unyu

ferocious *adj.* डरलाग्दो dar lagdo

ferry *n.* डुंगा dunga

fertile *adj.* उब्जाउ ubjau

fertilizer *n.* मल mal

fervent *adj.* व्यग्र wyagra

fervo(u)r *n.* जोश josh

fester *v.* पाक्नु paknu

festival *n.* चाड chad

festive *adj.* रमाइलो ramailo

fetch *v.* लिएर आउनु liera aunu

feud *n.* झगडा jhagada

fever *n.* जरो jaro

feverish *adj.* ज्वरग्रस्त jwar grast

few *adj.* अलिकति ali kati

fiction *n.* काल्ललिक बयान kalpanik bayan

fictitious *adj.* काल्पनिक kalpanik

fiddle *n.* सारंगी sarangi

field *n.* खेत khet

fierce *adj.* डरलाग्दो dar lagdo

fifteen *n.* पन्ध्र pandhra

fifth *adj.* पाँचौ panchaun

fig *n.* अन्जीर anjir

fight *n.* लडन्त ladant

fighting *n.* लडाइँ ladain

figure *n.* अंक ank

file *n.* रेती reti

fill *v.* भर्नु bharnu

film *n.* चलचित्र chal chitra

filter *n.* फिल्टर philtar

filthy *adj.* फोहोरी phohori

fin *n.* माछाको पखेटा machhako pakheta

final *adj.* अन्तिम antim

finally *adv.* अन्तमा nantma

find *v.* फेला पार्नु phela parnu

fine *adj.* असल asal

finery *n.* सुन्दर वस्त्र र गहनापात sundar vastra r gehnapat

finger *n.* औंला aunla

fingernail *n.* नङ् nantma

fingerprint *n.* ल्याप्चे lyapche

finish *v.* सिध्याउनु siddhyaunu

finite *adj.* सीमित simit

fir *n.* सल्ला, देवदारू salla, devdaru

fire *n.* आगो ago

fire brigade *n.* दमकल damkal

fire engine *n.* दमकल damkarl

firefly *n.* जूनकीरी junkiri

fireman *n.* आगो निभाउने मानिस ago nibhaune manis

fireplace *n.* अगेनु agenu

firewood *n.* दाउरा daura

fireworks *n.* आतशबाजी atash baji

firmament *n.* आकाश akash

firms *n.* कम्पनी kampani

first *adj.* पहिलो pahilo

firth *n.* मुहान muhan

fiscal year *n.* आर्थिक वर्ष Arthik warsh

fish *n.* माछा machhako pakheta

fisherman *n.* मल्लाह mallah

fist *n.* मुट्ठी muthi

fit *adj.* लायक layak

fitness *n.* योग्यता yogyata

five *n.* पाँच panchaun

fix *n.* दोधार dodhar

fizz *v.* यस्तो आवाज yasto awaz

fizzle *v.* विफल हुनु viphal hunu

flabbergasted *adj.* जिल्ल परेको jill pareko

flag *n.* झंडा jhanda

flagellate *v.* कोर्रा लाउनु korara launu

flagrant *adj.* स्पष्ट spasht

flail *n.* मुसल musal

flair *n.* योग्यता yogayta

flame *n.* आगो को लप्का ago ko lapka

flank *n.* छेउ chheu

flannel *n.* फलालिन phalatin

flannel *n.* फलालिन phalatin

flap *n.* फड्फडाहट phadphadahat

flare *n.* ज्वाला jwala

flash *n.* झिल्को jhilko

flashback *n.* पूर्व-दृश्य purv-drishya

flashlight *n.* टर्चलाइट tarch lait

flat *adj.* सम्म samma

flatly *adv.* स्पष्टसँग spasht sanga

flatter *v.* बढाइ गर्नु badhai garnu

flatulence *n.* वायु उत्पन्न गर्ने vayu uttapan garne

flaunt *v.* देखाउनु dekhaunu

flavo(u)r *n.* स्वाद swad

flaw *n.* खोट khot

flawless *adj.* निर्दोष nirdosh

flea *n.* उपियाँ upiyan

fleck *n.* दाग, धब्बा daag, dhabha

flee *v.* भाग्नु bhagnu

fleece *n.* ऊन कत्रनु oon katranu

flesh *n.* मासु masu

flexible *adj.* लच्किने lachkine

flick *v.* हल्का चालले हान्नु वा छुनु halka challe hanu wa chunu

flicker *vg.* धिपधिप गर्नु dhipdhip garnu

flight *n.* उडान udan

flinch *v.* पछि हट्नु pachi hatnu

flint *n.* चकमक chakmak

flirt *n.* नाठी nathi

float *n.* पानीमा उत्रने वस्तु pani ma utrane wastu

flock *n.* बथान bathan

flog *v.* कोर्रा हान्नु korra hannu

flood *n.* बाढी badhi

flooded *adj.* बाढी आएको badhi aeko

floor *n.* कोठाको kotha ko bhuin

flop *v.* भ्यात्त खस्नु bhayat khasnu

flora *n.* वनस्पति wanaspati

floriculture *n.* फूलको कृषि phoolko krishi

florist *n.* माली mali

florist *n.* फूल बेच्ने व्यक्ति phool bechne vyakti

flortilla *n.* बेड़ा bedha

flour *n.* पीठो pitho

flourish *v.* मौलाउनु maulaunu

flow *n.* प्रवाह prawah

flower *n.* फूल phul

flowerpot *n.* गमला gamla

flu *n.* रूघा, खोकी, ज्वरो आदि rugha, khoki, jwaro adi

fluent *adj.* फर्र बोल्ने pharra bolne

fluid *n.* तरल वस्तु taral wastu

fluke *n.* संयोगको सफलता sanyogko safalta

flunkey *n.* वर्दी लाउने नोकर vardi laune nokar

flurry *n.* हावा वा हावाको झोक्का hawa wa hawako jhoka

flush *n.* मुख को लाली mukh ko lali

flustered *adj.* हडबडाएको hadbadaeko

flute *n.* बाँसुरी bansuri

fly *n.* झिंगा jhinga

foam *n.* फींज phinj

fodder *n.* गाईवस्तुको दाना gaivastuko dana

foe *n.* शत्रु shatru

foetus *n.* पेटको बच्चा pethko bachha

fog *n.* कुइरो kuiro

foggy *adj.* कुहिरो लागेको kuhiro lageko

foible *n.* चरित्रको दोष charitarko dosh

fold *n.* खोर khor

foliage *n.* पातहरू patharu

folk *n.* साथी sathi

folk music *n.* लोकसंगीत lok sangit

folk song *n.* लोकगीत lokgit

folklore *n.* जनश्रुति jan shruti

follow *v.* पछिलाग्नु pachhi lagnu

follower *n.* समर्थक samarthak

foment *v.* सेक्नु seknu

fond *adj.* माया गर्ने maya garne

fondle *v.* सुमसुम्याउनु sum sumyaunu

food *n.* खानेकुरा khane kura

fool *n./adj.* मूर्ख murkh

foot *n.* पाउ pau

football *n.* भकुण्डा bhakundo

footpath *n.* पेटी peti

footprint *n.* पाइला paila

footstep *n.* कदम kadam

footwear *n.* जुत्ता jutta

for *prep.* लाई lai

foray *n.* हमला hamla

forbear *n.* पूर्खा poorkha

forbid *v.* रोक्नु roknu

forbidden *adj.* मनाही गरिएको manahi garieko

force *n.* बल bal

forearm *n.* पाखुरा pakhura

forecast *n.* भविष्यवाणी bhawishyawani

forefather *n.* पुर्खा purkha

forefinger *n.* चोरऔँला chor aunla

forehead *n.* निधार nidhar

foreign country *n.* विदेश widesh

foreigner *n.* विदेशी wideshi

foremost *adj.* सबभन्दा पहिलो sab bhanda phailo

forensic *adj.* अदालत को adalatko

forest *n.* बन ban

foretaste *n.* पूर्वानुभव purvanubhav

foretell *v.* पहिले नै धन्नु pahile ne dhanu

forethought *n.* पूर्वविचार purvvichar

forever *adv.* हमेशाको लागि hamesha ko lagi

forewarn *v.* पहिले नै चेतावनी दिनु pahile ne chetauni dinu

forfeit *v.* गुमाउनु gumaunu

forgather *v.* भेला हुनु bhela hunu

forgery *n.* बनावटी banawati

forget *v.* बिर्सनु birsanu

forgetful *adj.* बिर्सने birsane

forgive *v.* माफ/क्षमा गर्नु maph/ kshama garnu

fork *n.* काँटा kanta

form *n.* आकार akar

formal *adj.* नियमानुसार niyam anusar

formality *n.* औपचारिकता aupcharikta

format *n.* पुस्तकको आकार pustakko akaar

former *adj.* अधिको aghi ko

formerly *adv.* उहिले uhile

formidable *adj.* भंयकर bhayankar

formula *n.* सूत्र sutra

formulate *v.* स्पष्ट रूपले व्यक्त गर्नु sapasht roople vyakt garnu

fornication *n.* व्यभिचार vyabhichar

forntier *n.* सिमाना simana

fort *n.* किल्ला killa

forthcoming *adj.* आगामी agami

fortitude *n.* धैर्य dhairya

fortnight *n.* चौध दिन chaudha din

fortress *n.* किल्ला killa

fortunate *adj.* भाग्यमानी bhagya mani

fortune teller *n.* ज्योतिषी jyotishi

forty *n.* चालीस chalis

forum *n.* मंच manch

forward *adj.* अगाडिको agadi ko

foster *v.* पाल्नु palnu

foul *adj.* दुर्गन्थी durgandhi

found *v.* पायो payo

foundation *n.* जग jag

founder *n.* संस्थापक sansthapak

foundry *n.* ज्यासल jyasal

fount *n.* स्रोत sarot

fountain *n.* झर्ना jharna

four *n.* चार char

four-footed *adj.* चारखुट्टे char khutte

fourth *adj.* चाथो chautho

fowl *n.* कुखुरा kukhura

fox *n.* फ्याउरो phyauro

fraction *n.* अंश amsh

fractious *adj.* कचिङ्गल गर्ने kanchil garne

fracture *n.* भंग bhang

fragment *n.* टुक्रा tukra

fragmentation *n.* विखंडन wikhandan

fragrant *adj.* सुगन्धि sugandhit

frame *n.* घेरा ghera

frank *adj.* फरासिलो pharasilo

frankly *adj.* खुलस्तसँग khulast sanga

fraternity *n.* भाइचारा bhai chara ko

fraud *n.* धोका dhoka

freak *n.* लहड lahad

free *adj.* स्वतंत्र swantantra

free of cost *adj.* सित्तै sittai

freely *adv.* स्वतंत्र रूपले swatantra ruple

freeze *v.* जम्नु jamnu

freight *n.* मालढुबानी भाडा maldhuwani bhada

freight train *n.* मालगाडी malgadi

frequent *adj.* बराबर/बारम्बार भइ आएको barabar/barambar bhai aeko

frequently *adv.* घरीघरी gharighari

fresh *adj.* ताजा taja

fret *v.* पिरल्नु piralnu

friable *adj.* झुरिने jhurine

friar *n.* भिक्षु bhikshu

friction *n.* रगड ragad

Friday *n.* शुक्रवार shukra war

friend *n.* साथी sathi

friendly *adj.* मिलनसार milansar

friendship *n.* मित्रता mitrata

frighten *v.* तर्साउनु tarsaunu

fritter *v.* नष्ट गर्नु nasht garnu

frog *n.* भ्यागुतो bhyaguto

from *prep.* बाट bata

frond *n.* पातहरू patharu

front *advj.* अगाडिको agadiko

frost *n.* तुसारो tusaro

frostbite *n.* हिउँले खाएको घाउ hiun le khaeko ghau

froth *n.* फींज feerj

frowzy *adj.* फोहोरे fohare

frugal *adj.* किफायती kiphayati

fruit *n.* फल phal

fruitful *adj.* फलदायक phaldayak

fruition *n.* चिताएको कुरा पुग्ने काम chitaeko kura pugne kam

frustrate *v.* निराश/हतोत्साह गराउनु nirash/hatotsah garaunu

fry *v.* भुट्नु bhutnu

fuck *v.* संभोग गर्नु sambhog garnu

fuel *n.* इन्धन indhan

fug *n.* गुम्सेको वातावरण gusseko vatavaran

fugitive *n.* भगुवा bhaguwa

fulcrum *n.* आलम्ब aalamb

fulfil *v.* पूरा गर्नु pura garnu

full *adj.* भरिएको bharieko

fumble *v.* छामछाम-छुमछुम गर्नु chamacham chumchum garnu

66

fume *n.* धुँवा लाएर कीटाणुहरू मार्नु dhua laer kitanuharu marnu

fun *n.* तमासा tamasa

function *n.* काम kam

fund *n.* कोष kosh

fundamental *adj.* आधारभूत adhar bhut

funeral *n.* मलामी malami

funnel *n.* सोली soli

funny *adj.* रमाइलो ramailo

fur *n.* भुवा bhuwa

furbish *v.* टलकाउनु talkaunu

furious *adj.* रिसले चूर ris le chur

furl *v.* बूर्नु boornu

furlong *n.* 201 मीटर 201 metre

furniture *n.* टेबुल, कुर्ची आदि tebul, kurchi, adi

furrier *n.* भुत्लाको व्यापारी bhulako vyopari

furry *adj.* भुवा जस्तो bhuwa jasto

further *adv.* पर para

fury *n.* रिसले चूर ris

fuse *n.* फ्युज phyuj

fusillade *n.* गोलाबारी golabari

fuss *n.* खलबल khalbal

fussy *adj.* नाटीकुटी गर्ने natikuti garne

futile *adj.* व्यर्थ wyartha

future *n.* भविष्यमानी bhawishyawani

G

ga(u)ge *n.* नाप्ने डन्डी napne dandi

gab *n.* बकबक bakbak

gadfly *n.* डाँस dance

gadget *n.* साना-कल sana-kal

gag *n.* बुजो bujo

gagina *n.* पुति putti

gain *n.* फाइदा phaida

gainsay *v.* विरोध गर्नु wirodh garnu

gait *n.* चाल chal

gaiter *n.* खुट्टा ढाक्ने पट्टी khuta dhakne patti

gal *n.* ठिटी thitti

gala *n.* उत्सव utsaw

galaxy *n.* आकाशगंगा akash ganga

gale *n.* आँधी andhi

gall *n.* पित्त pitta

gallant *adj.* बीर bir

galleon *n.* स्पेनको जहाज spainko jahaj

gallery *n.* बरन्डा baranda

gallon *n.* ग्यालन gyalan

gallop *n.* पैयाँ paiyan

gallows *n.* फाँसीको तखता phansiko takhta

galore *adj.* प्रचुर prachur

gamble *v.* जूवा खेल्नु juwa khelnu

gambler *n.* जुवाडी juwadi

gambling *n.* जूवा juwa

game *n.* खेल khel

gamine *n.* दुब्ली र आकर्षक केटी dubli ra akarshak keti

gamut *n.* सबै sabai

gander *n.* भाले हाँस bhale haans

gang *n.* दल dal

gannet *n.* समुद्री चरा samudari chara

gaol *n.* जेल jail

gap *n.* छिद्र chhidra

gape *v.* मुख बाएर हेर्नु mukh baer hernu

garage *n.* मोटर कारखाना motar karkhana

garb *n.* लुगा luga

garbage *n.* फोहरमैला phohar maila

garden *n.* बगैंचा bagaincha

garden *n.* बगैंचा bagaincha

gardener *n.* माली mali

gargantuan *adj.* विशाल wishal

gargle *v.* कुल्ला गर्नु kulla garnu

garland *n.* माला mala

garlic *n.* लसुन lasun

garment *n.* लुगा luga

garner *v.* एकत्र गर्नु ekktar garnu

garnet *n.* दामी पत्थर dami pathar

garnish *v.* सिँगार्नु singarnu

gas *n.* वायु wayu

gasbag *n.* गफी gaphi

gash *n.* गहिरो घाउ gahiro ghau

gasoline *n.* पेट्रोल petrol

gasp *v.* हाँफ्नु hanphnu

gastric *adj.* पेटको petko

gastronomy *n.* राम्रो भोजन तयार गर्ने कला ramro bhojan tyar garne kala

gate *n.* ढोका dhoke

gatecrasher *n.* निम्ताबिनाको पाहुना nimtabinako pahuna

gatekeeper *n.* ढोके dhoke

gather *v.* जम्मा गर्नु jamma garnu

gathering *n.* जमघट jamghat

gaudy *adj.* भड्किलो bhadkilo

gauge *v.* नाप्नु napnu

gaunt *adj.* दुब्लो-पातलो dublo-patlo

gawky *adj.* भद्दा bhadda

gay *adj.* रमाइलो ramailo

gaze *n.* एकटकको हेराइ ek tak ko herai

gazelle *n.* सानो सुन्दर हरिण sano sundar harin

gazette *n.* राजपत्र raj patru

gear *n.* सज्जा sajja

gecko *n.* माउसुली mausuli

geese *n.* राजहाँसहरू raj hans haru

gelatine *n.* सरेस sares

gelding *n.* खसी पारेको घोड़ा khasi pareko ghora

gem *n.* रत्न ratna

gemini *n.* मिथुन राशि mithun rashi

gender *n.* लिंग ling

gene *n.* जीन gene

genealogy *n.* वंशावली vanshawali

general *n.* जर्नेल jarnel

general knowledge *n.* सामान्य ज्ञान samanya gyan

general post office *n.* गोस्वारा हुलाक goswara hulak

generation *n.* पुस्ता pusta

generosity *n.* उदारता udarta

genie *n.* हुरी huri

genius *n.* प्रतिभाशाली व्यक्ति pratibhashali wyakti

genocide *n.* जातिसंहार jatisanhar

genre *n.* शैली shaili

gentleman *n.* भलादमी bhaladmi

gently *adv.* हलुका ढंगले haluka dhangle

gentry *n.* ठूलाबाड़ा thulabadha

genuine *adj.* सक्कली sakkali

genus *n.* वर्ग warg

geodesy *n.* भूगणित bhuganit

geography *n.* भूगोल bhugo

geology *n.* भूगर्भशास्त्र bhugarbh shastra

geometry *n.* रेखागणित rekha ganit

georgette *n.* पातलो रेसमी कपडा patalo resami kapada

germ *n.* कीटाणु kitanu

germinate *v.* उम्रनु umranu

gestation *n.* गर्भधारण garbh dharan

gesticulate *v.* हावभाव गर्नु hawbhaw garnu

gesture *n.* इशारा ishara

get *v.* पाउनु paunu

get away *v.* भाग्नु bhagnu

get out of *v.* हट्नु hatnu

get ready *v.* तयार हुनु tayar hunu

get up *v.* उठ्नु uthnu

get-together *n.* सामाजिक जमघट samajik jamghat

ghetto *n.* गरिब बस्ती garib basti

ghost *n.* भूत bhut

ghoul *n.* मुर्दा खाने पिशाच murda khane pishach

giant *n.* दानव danaw

gibbet *n.* फाँसीको तखता phansiko takhta

giddiness *n.* रिंगटा ringata

gift *n.* कोसेली koseli

gig *n.* टमटम tumtum

gigantic *adj.* ज्यादै ठूलो jyadai thulo

ginger *n.* अदुवा aduwa

gingham *n.* धर्के सूती लुगा dharke suti luga

gipsy *n.* फिरन्ता जातिको सदस्य phiranta jatiko sadasya

giraffe *n.* जिराफ giraffe

gird *v.* बाँध्नु bhandnu

girdle *n.* पेटी peti

girl *n.* केटी keti

girlfriend *n.* प्रेमिका premika

gist *n.* मुख्य विषय mukhya vishya

give *v.* दिनु dinu

give and take *n.* आदानप्रदान adan pradan

give away *v.* दिनु dinu

give in *v.* आत्मसमर्पण गर्नु atma samarpan garnu

give out *v.* सिद्धिनु siddhinu

give up *v.* छोड्नु chhodnu

give way *v.* दबाबमा हार मान्नु dabab mahar mannu

glacier *n.* हिमनदी him nadi

glad *adj.* खुश गर्नु khush garnu

glade *n.* बनको खुला ठाउँ banko khula thaun

glance *n.* झलक jhalak

gland *n.* तिर्खा girkha

glare *n.* तेज tej

glass *n.* काँच kanch

glaucoma *n.* दृष्टि कम हुने रोग drishti kam hune rog

glaze *n.* चिल्लो हुनु chilo hunu

glazier *n.* इयालमा शीशा हाल्ने व्यक्ति ialama sheesha halne vyakti

gleam *n.* चमक chamak

glen *n.* उपत्यका upatyaka

glide *v.* चिप्लनु chiplanu

glimpse *n.* झलक jhalak

glint *v.* टलकनु talkanu

glitter *v.* चम्कनु chamkanu

globe *n.* पृथ्वी prithwi

globule *n.* थोपा thopa

gloom *n.* अन्धकार andhkar

gloomy *adj.* मलिन malin

glorify *v.* गुणगान गर्नु gungan garnu

glorious *adj.* तेजस्वी tejaswi

glove *n.* पंजा panja

glow *n.* झलक jhalak

glow-worm *n.* जूनकीरी junkiri

glue *n.* गुँद gund

glutton *n.* धेरै खाने dherai khane

glycerine *n.* ग्लिसरीन glycerine

gnash *v.* दाँतपिस्नु dantpisnu

gnat *n.* भुसुना bhusuna

gnu *n.* हुरी huri

go *v.* जानु janu

go down *v.* ओर्लनु orlanu

go off *v.* पड्कनु padkanu

go under *v.* निष्फल/पराजित हुनु nishphal/parajit hunu

goad *n.* प्रेरित गर्नु prerit garnu

goal *n.* उद्देश्य uddeshya

goat *n.* बोको boko

gobble *v.* खपाखप खानु khapakhap khanu

go-between *n.* बीचको मान्छे bich ko manchhe

goblet *n.* पिउने भाँड़ो piune bharho

goblin *n.* पिशाच pishach

god *n.* ईश्वर Ishwar

goddess *n.* देवी dewi

godown *n.* गोदाम godam

go-getter *n.* साहसी व्यक्ति sahasi wyakti

goggle *v.* आँखा फारेर हेर्नु ankhan pharer hernu

goggles *n.* घाममा लाउने कालो चस्मा gham ma laune kalo chasma

goitre *n.* गाँड gand

gold *n.* सुन sun

golden *adj.* सुनौलो sunaulo

goldsmith *n.* सुनार sunar

golf *n.* गल्फको खेल galafko khel

gong *n.* घण्टी ghanti

gonorrh(o)ea *n.* सुजाक sujak

good *adj.* असल asal

goodbye *n.* नमस्ते namaste

goods *n.* माल mal

goodwill *n.* मित्रभाव mitrabhav

goose *n.* राजहाँस rajhans

gooseberry *n.* फल विशेष phal vishesh

gorge *n.* खोंच khonch

gorgeous *adj.* भव्य bhawya

gorse *n.* झाड़ी jhari

gory *adj.* रक्तरंजित raktranjit

gospel *n.* यिशु का उपदेशहरू yishu ka updeshharu

gossamer *n.* माकुराको जालो makurako jalo

gossip *n.* गफ gaphi

goulash *n.* उसिनेको मासु र सब्जी usineko masu r sabji

gourd *n.* लौका lauka

gout *n.* बाथ bath

govern *v.* शासन चलाउनु shasan chalaunu

government *n.* सरकार sarkar

governor *n.* राज्यपाल rajyapal

gown *n.* फरिया phariya

grab *v.* खोस्नु khosnu

grace *n.* कृपा kripa

graceful *adj.* राम्रो ramro

gracious *adj.* दयालु dayalu

grade *n.* दर्जा darja

gradient *n.* बाटेको ढल्काइ batteko dhalkai

gradually *adv.* अलि अलि गरी ali ali gari

graduate *n.* स्नातक snatak

graft *n.* घूस ghus

grain *n.* अन्न anna

grain *n.* कण kan

graminivorous *adj.* धाँस खाने जन्तु ghans khane jantu

grammar *n.* व्याकरण wyakaran

gramophone *n.* ग्रामोफोन gramophone

granary *n.* भकारी bhakari

grand *adj.* भव्य bhawya

granddaughter *n.* नातिनी natini

grandeur *n.* रौनक raunak

grandfather *n.* बाजे baje

grandmother *n.* बजै bajai

grandson *n.* नातिनी natini

granite *n.* ग्रेनाइट granite

granny *n.* बज्यै bajyai

grant *n.* अनुदान anudan

granular *adj.* दानादार danadar

granule *n.* दाना danaw

grape *n.* अंगुर angur

grapevine *n.* अंगुर को लहरा angur ko lahar

grasp *n.* मुठी muthi

grass *n.* घाँस ghans khane jantu

grasshopper *n.* फटेङ्ग्रो phatengro

grateful *adj.* आभारी abhari

gratify *v.* खुसी पार्नु khusi parnu

grating *n.* जाली jaali

gratis *adv.* सित्तै sittai dieko

gratitude *n.* आभारी abhari

gratuitous *adj.* बिनामूल्य गरिएको वा दिइएको binamulya gariyeko wa diyeko

grave *adj.* गम्भीर gambhir

gravel *n.* रोड़ा rorha

gravitate *v.* खिँचिनु khichnu

gravity *n.* गुरुत्वाकर्षण gurutwakarshan

gravy *n.* लेदो ledo

graze *v.* चर्नु charnu

grease *n.* चिल्लो chillo

greasy *adj.* चिल्लो chillo

great *adj.* ठूलो thulo

great granddaughter *n.* पनातिनी panatini

great grandfather *n.* जिजु बाजे jiju baje

great grandmother *n.* जिजु बाजै jiju bajai

great grandson *n.* पनाति panatini

greatly *adv.* बेसरी besari

greatness *n.* महानता mahanta

greed *n.* लोभ lobh

greedy *adj.* लोभी lobhi

green *adj.* हरियो hariyo

greenery *n.* हरियोपरियो hariyo pariyo

greenhouse *n.* बिरुवाघर biruwa ghar

greet *v.* अभिनन्दन/सलाम गर्नु abhinandan/salam garnu

greetings *n.* बन्दना bandan

grenade *n.* हातगोला hatgola

grey *adj.* खरानी रंगको kharani ranga ko

griddle *n.* तावा tawa

grief *n.* दुःख duhkh

grievance *n.* उजूर ujur

grieve *v.* दुःख दिनु dukh dinu

grim *adj.* भयानक bhayanak

grimace *n.* मुख-विकृति mukh vikrati

grind *v.* पिँध्नु pindhnu

grip *n.* पकड padkad

gripses *n.* पेटको पीड़ा pet ko peerha

grisly *adj.* डरलाग्दो darlagdo

grist *n.* पिस्ने अन्न pisne anna

gristle *n.* मासुमा कड़ा रबर जस्तो वस्तु masuma karha rubber jasto vastu

groan *v.* दुख दिनु dhukh denu

grocer *n.* बनिया baniya

grog *n.* रक्सी raksi

groom *n.* बेहुला behula

groove *n.* खाल्डो khaldo

gross *n.* ठोस toss

grotesque *adj.* अनौठो anutho

grotto *n.* सानो गुफा sano gupha

grotty *adj.* फोहोर-मैला phohor maila

groundless *adj.* निराधार niradhar

groundnut *n.* बादाम badam

groundwork *n.* आधार adhar

group *n.* समूह samuh

grow *v.* उम्रनु umranu

growl *v.* झर्कनु jharkanu

growth *n.* वृद्धि vridhi

grudge *n.* ईख ikh

gruel *n.* खोले khole

gruelling *adj.* थकाउने thakaune

gruesome *adj.* भयानक bhayanak

grumble *v.* असन्तोष देखाउनु asantosh dekh aunu

guano *n.* समुद्री चराको सुली samudri charako suli

guarantee *n.* ग्यारण्टी gyaranti

guard *n.* पहरेदार paharedar

guardian *n.* अभिभावक abhibhawak

guava *n.* अम्बा amba

guess *n.* अन्दाज andan

guest *n.* पाहुना pahuna

guide *n.* मार्ग दर्शक marg darshak

guile *n.* छलकपट chalkapat

guillotine *n.* टाउको कोट्ने मेशिन tauko kotne machine

guilt *n.* दोष dosh

guilty *adj.* दोषी doshi

guinea *n.* गिन्नी ginni

guinea pig *n.* चौगडा chaugada

guip *n.* गाँस gans

guise *n.* वेश vesh

guitar *n.* गितार gitar

gully *n.* पानीले काटेको कुलो panile kateko kulo

gum *n.* गिजा gija

gun *n.* बन्दुक banduk

gunny *n.* टाट tatt

gunpowder *n.* बारूद barud

guru *n.* गुरु gurutwakarshan

gust *n.* हावा को झोक्का hawa ko jhokka

gut *n.* आन्द्राभुँडी andra bhundi

gutter *n.* कुलो kulo

guy *n.* डोरी dori

gym, gymnasium को छोटो रूप ko choto roop

gymnasiu *n.* व्यायामशाला wyayamshala

gymnast *n.* व्यायामी wyayami

gymnastics *n.* कसरत kasrat

gyn(a)ecologist *n.* स्त्रीरोग विशेषज्ञ stri rog wisheshgya

gynaecology *n.* स्त्रीरोग विज्ञान strirog vigyan

gypsum *n.* जिप्सम jipsum

gypsy फिरन्ता जातिको सदस्य phiranta jatiko sadasya

gyrate *v.* चक्कर खानु chakkar khanu

H

ha *int.* हर्ष आश्चर्च आदि जाहेर गर्ने शब्द harsh ashchurch adi jaher garne shabd

habit *n.* बानी bani

habitable *adj.* बस्न/बासयोग्य basna/basyogya

habitation *n.* वास vaas

habitual *adj.* बानी परेको bani paereko

habituated *adj.* बानी परेको bani paereko

hacksaw *n.* फलाम काट्ने आरी phalam katne aari

haemorrhoids *n.* हर्सा harsa

haft *n.* बंचरो आदिको बीड़ँ bancharo adiko beerh

haggle *v.* झगडा गर्नु jhagada garnu

hair *n.* कपाल raun

haircut *n.* कपाल कटाइ kapal latai

hairdo *n.* कश सज्जा kesh sajja

hairpin *n.* कपालको काँटा kapal ko kanta

hair'sbreadth *n.* धेरै निकट dherainiket

hairy *adj.* धेरै रौँ भएको dherai raun bhaeko

hale *adj.* स्वस्थ swasth

half *n.* आधार adha

half-brothher *n.* सौतिनी दाजु sautinidaju

half-hearted *adj.* कम आँटिलो kam antilo

half-mast *adj.* आधा झुकेको adha jhukeko

half-moon *n.* अर्धचन्द्र adha chandra

half-past *n.* साढे sadhe

half-time *n.* मध्यान्तर madhyantar

hall *n.* बैठक baithak

hallmark *n.* नम्बरी सुन चाँदी nambari sun chandi

hallow पवित्र पार्नु pavitar parnu

halo *n.* तेजमण्डल tejmandeal

halt *n.* अवरोध abharod

halve *v.* आधा आधा गर्नु adha-adha garnu

ham *n.* जाँघ jangh

hamlet *n.* सानो गाउँ sano gaun

hammer *n.* धन ghan

hammock *n.* झोलुङ्गे jholungo

hamper *v.* बाधा पार्नु badha parnu

hand *n.* हातगोला hat

hand in hand *adv.* हातेमालो hatemalo

handbag *n.* हाते ब्याग hate byag

handbill *n.* पर्चा parcha

handbook *n.* निर्देशिका nirdeshika

handcuffs *n.* हतकडी hatkadi

handel *n.* बीण्ड bind

handful *n.* मुट्ठीभर को परिमाण muthibhar ko pariman

handicap *n.* असुविधा asuwidha

handicapped *adj.* अपाङ्ग apang

handicraft *n.* हस्तकला hast kala

handkerchief *n.* रुमाल rumal

handmaid *n.* नोकर्नी nokrani

handover *v.* सुम्पनु sumpanu

hand-picked *adj.* राम्ररी छानिएको ramrai chhanieko

handsome *adj.* राम्रो ramro

handwriting *n.* हस्ताक्षर hastakshar

handy *adj.* सजिलो sajilo

handyman *v.* विभिन्न काम गर्नमा सिपालु व्यक्ति vibhin kam garnma sipalu vyakti

hang *v.* झुण्ड्याउनु jhundyaunu

hang up *v.* कुरा सकेपछि टेलिफोन राख्नु kura sake teliphon rakun

hangaround *v.* धेरै टाढा नजानु dherai tadha najanu

hanger *n.* लुगा आदि झुण्ड्याउने हयाङ्गर luga adi jhundyaune hyanger

hank ऊन, धागो आदिको लच्छा वा गुच्छा oon, dhago adiko lacha wa gucha

hanky *n.* पकेट रुमाल paket rumal

hanky-panky *n.* गोलमाल gol-mal

hansom *n.* दुई चक्के घोड़ा गाड़ी dui chakke ghora gadi

haphazar *adj.* जथाभाबी jatha bhabi

hapless *adj.* अभागी abhagi

happen *v.* हुनु hannu

happily *adv.* खुशीले khushile

happiness *n.* खुशी khushi

happy *adj.* खुश khush

harass *v.* सताउनु sataunu

harbinger *n.* अगुवा aguwa

harbo(u)r *n.* बन्दरगाह bandar gah

hard *adj.* साह्रो sarho

hard and fast *adj.* कडा र सख्त kada ra sakht

hard cash *n.* नगद nagad

hardliner *n.* कट्टर kattar

hardship *n.* कष्ट kasht

hardware *n.* घरमा चलाउने फलाम का सामान gharma chalaune phalam ka saman

hardy *adj.* बलियो baliya

hare *n.* खरायो kharayo

harem *n.* जनानाघर janana ghar

hark *v.* सुन्नु sunnu

harlot *n.* वेश्या weshhah

harm *n.* हानि hani

harm *n.* हानि hani

harmful *adj.* हानिकारक hanikarak

harmless *adj.* हानिरहित hani rahit

harmonica *n.* मुख-बाजा mukh baja

harmonious *adj.* मिल्दो mildo

harmony *n.* मेल mel

harpsichord *n.* पियानो जस्तो बाजा piano jasto baja

harsh *adj.* कडा kada

harvest *n.* बाली baliya

hashish *n.* चरेस chares

hasp *n.* अन्तराप antraap

haste *n.* हतार hatar

hasten *v.* हतार गर्नु hatar garnu

hasty *adj.* हतपते hatpate

hat *n.* टोप top

hatch *n.* जहाज को ढोका jahaj ko dhoka

hatchet *n.* सानो बन्चरो sano bancharo

hate *n.* घृणा ghrina

hatred *n.* घृणा ghrina

haughty *adj.* घमण्डी ghamandi

haughty *adj.* घमण्डी ghamandi

haul *v.* तनाव tannab

haunch *n.* पुट्ठा puttha

haunt *v.* बराबर दिमागमा आउनु barabar dimag ma aunu

have *v./aux.* सँग हुनु sanga hunu

haven *n.* आश्रय ashraya

haversack *n.* पिठ्यूँमा बोक्ने झोला pithuma bokne jhola

havoc *n.* विनाश winash

hawk *n.* बाज baj

hawker *n.* फेरीवाला pheri wala

hay *n.* परालु parai

haystack *n.* परालको कुन्यू paral ko kunyu

haywire *adj.* अव्यवस्थित awyawasthit+C3512

hazard *n.* संकट sankat

hazardous *n.* खतरनाक khatarnak

haze *adj.* तुवाँलो tuwanlo

hazel *n.* बिरूवाको किसिम biruwako kisim

h-bomb *n.* हाइड्रोजन बम hydrogen bum

he *pron.* ऊन oon

head *n.* टाउको, शिर tauko shir

headache *n.* शिरदर्द shir dard

headdress *n.* शिरपोश shir posh

headlight *n.* अगाडिको बत्ती agadi ko batti

headline *n.* शीर्षक shirshak

headlong *n.* टाउको ठोकिने गरी Tauko thokine gari

headmaster *adv.* प्रधानाध्यापक pradhan adhyapak

headquarters *n.* मुख्य कार्यालय mukhya karyalaya

headstrong *adj.* हठी hathi

headway *n.* प्रगति pragati

heady *adj.* मात लाग्ने mat lagne

heal *n.* निको हुनु niko hunu

heap *adj.* थुप्रो thupro

hear *n.* सुन्नु sunnu

hearing *v.* सुनवाइ sunwai

hearken *v.* सुन्नु sunu

hearsay *n.* सुनेको कुरा suneko kura

hearse *n.* मुर्दा लैजाने गाड़ी murda lejane gadi

heart *n.* मुटु mutu

heart attack *n.* हृदयघात hridaya ghat

heartbeat *n.* मुटुको ढुकढुकी mutuko dhukdhuki

heartbreaking *adj.* चित्त दुखाउने chitta dukhaune

heartburn *n.* छाती पोल्ने रोग chhati polne rog

heartfelt *adj.* दिली delhi

heart-rending *adj.* हृदयविदारक hridaya widarak

hearts *n.* मुटु mutu

heart-throb *n.* मायालु mayalu

heart-to-heart *adj.* खुलस्त khulast

hearty *adj.* हार्दिक hardik

heat *n.* गर्मी garmi

heat rash *n.* घमौरा ghamaura

heatwave *n.* ताप लहर tap lahar

heaven *n.* स्वर्ग swarg

heavenly *adj.* स्वर्गीय swargiya

heavy *adj.* गहौं gahraun

heavy industry *n.* भारी उद्योग bhari udyog

heavy-duty *adj.* कडा प्रयोगको लागि बनाइएको kada prayog ko lagi banaieko

hectare *n.* क्षेत्र को नाप kshetrako nap

hedgehog *n.* पोथ्रे दुम्सी pothre dumsi

heed *v.* ध्यान दिनु dhyan dinu

heel *n.* कुर्कुच्चा kurkuchcha

hegemony *n.* नेतृत्व netritava

heifer *n.* कोरली गाई korali gai

height *n.* उचाइ uchai

heinous *adj.* घोर ghor

heir *n.* हकदार hakdar

heir apparent *n.* युवराज yuwaraj

heiress *n.* युवराज्ञी yuwaragyi

helicopter *n.* हेलिकाप्टर helicopter

helium *n.* हिलियम helium

hell *n.* नरक narak

hello *n./excl.* हेलो helo

helmet *n.* फलामे टोप phalame top

help *n.* मदत madat

helpful *adj.* उपकारी upkari

helpless *adj.* असहाय asahaya

helter-skelter *adv.* हडबडमा hadbadma

hemisphere *n.* गोलार्ध golardh

hemlock *n.* विषालु वनस्पति vishalu vanaspati

hemp *n.* पटुवा patua

hemp *n.* सन sun

hen *n.* कुखुरी kukhuri

hen *n.* कुखुरी kukhuri

hence *adv.* अतः atach

henceforth *adv.* अबदेखि aba dekhi

henna *n.* मेंहदी mehendi

henpecked *adj.* स्वास्नीको वशमा रहने swasni ko wash ma rahane

hepatitis *n.* कलेजोको रोग kalejoko rog

heptagon *n.* सप्तभुज saptbhuj

her *pron.* उनको un ko

herald *n.* दूत dut

herb *n.* जडीबुटी jadibuti

herd *n.* बगाल bagai

herdsman *n.* गोठालो gothalo

here *adv.* यहाँ yahan

hereby *adv.* यसले yas le

heredity *n.* बाबुबाजेको गुण babu baje ko gun

heresy *n.* विधर्म widharm

heritage *n.* स्रोत sarawoth

hermit *n.* साधु sadhu

hernia *n.* हर्निया hernia

heroic *adj.* वीरतापूर्ण veertapurn

heroin *n.* लागू पदार्थ lagu padarth

heroine *n.* वीरांगना veerangna

heron *n.* बकुल्लो bakullo

herpes *n.* लुतो luto
herring *n.* हिलसा hilsa
herself *pron.* उनी आफै uni aphai
hesitant *adj.* हिचकिचाउने hichkichaune
hesitate *v.* हिचकिचाउनु hichkichaunu
hesitation *n.* हिचकिचाहट hichkichahat
hew *v.* बन्चरोले काट्नु bancharo le katnu
hexagon *n.* षड्भुज shadbhuj
hey *int.* जय-जय jai-jai
heyday *n.* सफलता का दिन saphalta ka din
hi *n./excl.* नमस्ते namaste
hidden *adj.* अदृश्य adrishya
hide *v.* लुक्नु luknu
hide and seek *n.* लुकामारी lukamari
hideous *adj.* घिनलाग्दो ghin lagdo
hideout *n.* लुक्ने ठाउँ lukne thaun
hiding *n.* पिटाइ pitai
high *adj.* अग्लो aglo
high court *n.* उच्च न्यायालय uchcha nyayalaya
high-handed *adj.* स्वेच्छाचारी swechchhachari
high-level *adj.* उच्चस्तरीय uchchastariya
high-rise *adj.* धेरै तला भएको dherai tala bhaeko
highway *n.* राजमार्ग raj marg

hijack *v.* विमान अपहरण गर्नु wiman apharan garnu
hike *n.* पैदल यात्रा गर्नु paidal yatra garnu
hilarious *adj.* रमाइलो ramailo
hill *n.* पहाड pahad
hill *n.* पहाड़, पर्वत pahad, parwat
hilly *adj.* पहाडी pahadi
him *pron.* उसलाई uslai
himself *pron.* ऊ आफै u aphai
hindrance *n.* बाधा पार्नु badha parnu
hinge *n.* चुकुल chukul
hint *n.* संकेत sanket
hip *n.* पुट्ठा puttha
hire *n.* किराया kiraya
his *pron.* उसको us ko
his Majesty's Government *n.* श्री पाँचको सरकार shri panch ko sarkar
historian *n.* इतिहासकार itihas kar
historical *adj.* ऐतिहासिक aitihasik
histroinic *adj.* नाटक वा अभिनयसम्बन्धी natak wa abhinaysambandhi
hit *n.* सफलता saphalta
hitch *n.* धक्का dhakka
hitherto *adv.* अहिलेसम्म ahile samma
hoard *n.* थुप्रो thupro
hoarding *n.* विज्ञापन टाँस्ने फल्याक vigypan tasne phalyak
hoarse *adj.* धोक्रो dhokro

hoary *adj.* उमेरले सेतो भएको umerle seto bhaeko

hoax *v.* छकाउनु chakaunu

hobby *n.* सोख sokh

hobgoblin *n.* प्रेत pret

hobo *n.* घुमिहिँड्ने बेकार व्यक्ति ghumhindne bekar vyakti

hoe *n.* कोदालो kodalo

hogwash *n.* काम नलाग्ने वस्तु kamna lagne wastu

hoi polloi *n.* जनसाधारण jansadharan

hoist *v.* उचाल्नु uchalnu

hoity-toity *adj.* घमण्डी ghamandi

hold *n.* पंकड pakad

hold out *v.* प्रतिरोध कायम गर्नु pratirodh kayam garnu

holdall *n.* गुन्टा कस्ने ब्याग gunta kasne byag

holder *n.* बीण्ड bind

hold-up *n.* लूट lut

hole *n.* दुलो dulo

holiday *n.* बिदा bida

holler *v.* चिच्च्याउनु chichaunu

hollow *adj.* खोक्रो khokro

holster *n.* पिस्तोल वा रिभल्भरको खोल pistol wa revolverko khol

holy *adj.* पवित्र pawitra

homage *n.* श्रद्धांजलि shraddhanjali

home *n.* घर ghar

homeless *adj.* घर नभएको ghar na bhaeko

homesich *adj.* घर सम्झिरहने ghar samjhi rahane

homework *n.* गृह कार्य grih karya

homicide *n.* नरहत्या nar hatya

homily *n.* उपदेश updesh

homosexual *adj.* समलिंगी sam lingi

hone *n.* सानढुङ्गा sandhunga

honest *adj.* इमानदार imandar

honey *n.* मह maha

hono(u)rable *adj.* माननीय manniya

hoodlum *n.* गुंडा gunda

hoodoo *n.* लोदर lodar

hoodwink *v.* आँखामा धुलो हाल्नु ankhama dhulo halnu

hoof *n.* खुर khur

hook *n.* अंकुश ankush

hookah *n.* हुक्का hukka

hookworm *n.* अङ्क्से-जुका ankse juka

hooligan *n.* बदमास badmas

hoop *n.* चक्र chakra

hooping cough *n.* लहरे खोकी lehare khoki

hoot *v.* बजाउनु bajaunu

hop *v.* एक खुट्टामा उफ्रनु ekkhuttama uphranu

hope *n.* आशा asha

hopeful *adj.* आशाजनक asha janak

hopeless *adj.* निराश nirash

horde *n.* भीड़ bheer

horizon *n.* क्षितिज kshitij

horizontal *adj.* तेर्सो terso

hormone *n.* अन्त anth

horn *n.* सिङ्ग singh

hornbill *n.* चरा dharnesh chara

hornet *n.* अरिङ्गाल aringal

horoscope *n.* जन्मपत्रिका janma patrika

horrible *adj.* भयानक bhayanak

horror *n.* डर dar

horse *n.* घोडा ghoda

horse laugh *n.* चर्को भद्दा हाँसो charko bhadda hanso

horsepower *n.* काम गर्नू दरको युनिट kam garne darko yunit

horseshoe *n.* नाल nal

horticulture *n.* बागवानी bagwani

hospice *n.* यात्रीहरू बस्ने ठाउँ yatrihare basnu thaun

hospitable *adj.* सत्कारशील satkarshil

hospital *n.* अस्पताल aspatal

hospitality *n.* सत्कार satkar

host *n.* आतिथेय aththeya

hostage *n.* बन्धक bandhak

hostel *n.* छात्रावास chhatrawas

hostess *n.* महिला मेजमान mahila majman

hostile *adj.* विपक्षी wipakshi

hot *adj.* तातो tato

hotchpotch/hodgepodge *n.* लठिबज lathibajra

hotel *n.* होटेल hotel

hot-headed *adj.* गरम मिजासको garam mijas ko

hound *n.* शिकारी कुकुर shikari kurkur

hour *n.* घण्टा ghanta

house *n.* घर ghar

house arrest *n.* नजरबन्दी najar bandi

household *n.* घरपरिवार ghar pariwar

housemaid *n.* नोकर्नी nokarni

house-warming *n.* गृहप्रवेश समारोह grih prawesh samaroh

housewife *n.* गृहिणी grihini

housing *n.* आवास निर्माण asas nirman

hovel *n.* झोपड़ी jhopari

hover *v.* एकै ठाउँमा उडिरहनु ekai thaun ma udi rahanu

how *adv.* कसरी kasari

however *adv.* त्यसो भए तापनि tyaso bhae ta pani

howl *v.* गर्जनु garjanu

hub *n.* चक्काको केन्द्र chakka ko kendra

hubble-bubble *n.* हुक्का hukka

hubbub *n.* गोलमाल golmal

hubbub *n.* हल्ला halla

hubby *n.* लोग्ने logne

huckster *n.* फेरीवाल pheriwal

hug *n.* अङ्गालो हाल्नु angali halnu

huge *adj.* विशाल wishal

hum *v.* गुनगुनाउनु gun gunaunu

human *adj.* मानवीय manawiya

human (being) *n.* मानवीय manawiya

human interest *n.* जन अभिरूचि jan abhiruchi

human nature *n.* मानव स्वभाव manaw swabhaw

human rights *n.* मानव अधिकार manaw adhikar

humane *adj.* दयालु dayalu

humanity *n.* मानवता manawta

humble *adj.* नम्र namra

humbug *n.* छल chhal

humdrum *adj.* नीरस neeras

humid *adj.* ओसिएको osieko

humidity *n.* आर्द्रता ardrata

humiliate *v.* अपमान/खिसी गर्नु apman/khisi garnu

humiliation *n.* अपमान/खिसी गर्नु apman/khisi garnu

hummock *n.* ढिस्को dhisko

humorous *adj.* लहडी lahadi

hunchback *n.* कूँजो kunjo

hundred *n.* सय saya

hundred percent *n.* सय प्रतिशत saya prati shat

hundred thousand *n.* एक लाख ekh lakh

hungry *adj.* भोकाएको bhokaeko

hunt *v.* शिकार खेल्नु shikar khelnu

hunter *n.* शिकारी shikari

hurdle *n.* बाधा पार्नु badha parnu

hurl *v.* हुल्याउनु hutyaunu

hurricane *n.* आँधी andhi

hurry *n.* हतार hatar

hurt *v.* चोट लाग्नु chot lagnu

husband *n.* लोग्ने logne

husbandry *n.* खेती kheti

hush *n.* मौन manu

hush money *n.* पाले नखोल्न दिइने घूस pol na kholna diine ghus

husk *n.* चोकर chokar

hut *n.* झुपडी jhupadi

hutch *n.* खरायो राख्ने खोर kharayo rakhne khor

hybrid *n. adj.* वर्णसंकर varansankar

hydroelectricity *n.* जल विद्युत jal widyut

hydrophobia *n.* पानीदेखि डर pani dekhi Dar

hygiene *n.* स्वास्थ्य विज्ञान swasthya wigyan

hymn *n.* भजन bhajan

hyphen *n.* योजक चिन्ह yojak chinha

hypocrisy *n.* पाखण्ड pakhand

I

Ice *n.* बरफ baraph

ice cream *n.* आइस्क्रीम ais krim

icon *n.* मूर्ति murti

idea *n.* विचार wichar

ideal *adj.* काल्पनिक kalpanik

identical *adj.* उस्तै ustai

identification *n.* पहिचान pahichan

identity (ID) card *n.* परिचयपत्र parichaya patra

ideology *n.* विचारधारा wichar dhara

ideosyncrasy *n.* सनक sanakhat

idiocy *n.* मूर्खता murkhta

idiom *n.* वाकृपद्धति wakpadyati

idiot *n.* पटमूर्ख patmurkh

idle *adj.* अल्छी alchhi

idol *n.* मूर्ति murti

idyll *n.* सुखद sukhad

if. *conj.* यदि yadi

ignoble *adj.* नीच neech

ignoramus *n.* अज्ञानी व्यक्ति agyani vyakti

ignorance *n.* अज्ञानता agyanta

ignorant *adj.* अज्ञानी agyani

ignore *v.* उपेक्षा गर्नु upeksha garnu

ill *adj.* बिरामी birami

ill-advised *adj.* नराम्रो सल्लाह पाएको na ramro sallah paeko

ill-bred *adj.* असभ्य asabhya

illegal *adj.* गैरकानूनी gair kanuni

illegible *adj.* पढ्न नसकिने padhna na sakine

illegitimate *adj.* ऐनले नदिएको ainle na dieko

ill-favoured *adj.* कुरूप kurup

ill-gotten *adj.* अन्यायपूर्वक प्राप्त गरेको anyaya purwak prapt gareko

illicit *adj.* गैरकानूनी gair kanuni

illimitable *adj.* असीम aseem

illiterate *adj.* निरक्षर nirakshar

illness *n.* बिमारी bimari

illogical *adj.* तर्कविरूद्ध tarkvirudh

ill-temerped *adj.* रिसाहा risaha

ill-treatment *n.* दुर्व्यवहार durwyawahar

illuminate *v.* झिलिमिली पार्न jhilimili parnu

illusion *n.* भ्रम bhram

illustrate *v.* व्याख्या गर्नु wyakhya garnu

illustration *n.* उदाहरण udaharan

illustrious *adj.* प्रसिद्ध prasidh

image *n.* चित्र chitra

imaginary *adj.* मनचिन्ते manchinte

imagination *n.* कल्पना kalpana

imam *n.* मुस्लिमको धर्मगुरू muslimko dharamguru

imbalance *n.* असन्तुलन asantulan

imbecile *adj.* मूर्ख murkh

imbroglio *n.* जटिल अवस्था jatir awastha

imbue *v.* मनमा भर्नु manma bharnu

imitate *v.* देखासिकी गर्नु dekha siki garnu

imitation *n.* नक्कल nakkal

immature *adj.* काँचो kancho

immediate *adj.* तुरून्त हुने turnta hune

immediately *adv.* तूरुन्तै turuntai

immense *adj.* ज्यादै ठूलो jyadai thulo

immerse *v.* डुब्नु dubnu

immigrant *n.* आप्रवासी aprawasi

imminent *adj.* हुन आँटेको huna anteko

immobile *adj.* चल्न नसक्ने chalan naskane

immoderate *adj.* अति ati

immodest *adj.* निर्लज्ज nirlajj

immoral *adj.* पापी papi

immortal *adj.* अमर amar

immovable *adj.* अचल achal

immune *adj.* सुरक्षित surakshit

immunity *n.* रोग प्रतिरोध क्षमता rog pratirodh kshamata

imp. *n.* बदमाश बालक badmash balak

impact *n.* प्रभाव prabhaw

impale *v.* रोप्नु ropnu

imparitiality *n.* निष्पक्षता nishpakshata

impart *v.* प्रदान गर्नु pradan garnu

impasse *n.* गतिरोध gati rodh

impassioned *adj.* भावपूर्ण bhavpurn

impassive *adj.* शान्त shant

impatient *adj.* अधीर adheer

impede *v.* छेक्नु cheknu

impediment *n.* बाधा badha

imperative *adj.* आवश्यक awashyak

imperfect *adj.* अपूर्ण apurn

imperialism *n.* साम्राज्यवाद samraija wad

imperialist *n.* साम्राज्यवादी samrajyawadi

imperious *adj.* हुकुम चलाउने hukum chalaune

imperishable *adj.* नाश नहुने nash nahune

impertinent *adj.* अटेरी ateri

impetus *n.* प्रेरणा prerana

impiety *n.* अश्रद्धा ashradha

impinge *v.* असर पर्नु asar parnu

impious *adj.* अधर्मी adharmi

impish *adj.* बदमासी गर्ने badmasi garne

implacable *adj.* सन्तुष्ट पार्न नसकिने santusht parn naskine

implement *v.* कार्यमा परिणत गर्नु karyama parinat garnu

implicate *v.* सरिक गराउनु sarik garaunu

implore *v.* प्रार्थना गर्नु prarthana garnu

imply *v.* मतलब बुझाउनु matlab bujhaunu

import *v.* आयात/पैठारी गर्नु ayat/ paithari garnu

important *adj.* महत्वपूर्ण mahattwa purn

impose *v.* लादनु ladnu

impossible *adj.* असम्भव asambhaw

impotent *adj.* नामर्द namard

impractical *adj.* असाध्य asadhya

imprecation *n.* सराप sarap

impregnable *adj.* दुर्जेय durjay

impregnate *n.* गर्भधारण गराउनु garbhdharan garaunu

impress *v.* प्रभाव पार्नु prabhaw parnu

impressive *adj.* प्रभावशाली prabhaw shali

imprison *v.* जेल हाल्नु jelhalnu

imprisonment *n.* थुना thuna

improbable *adj.* असम्भव asambhaw

impromptu *adj.* तात्कालिक tatkalik

improper *adj.* अनुचित anuchit

improve *v.* सुधार्नु sudharnu

imprudent *adj.* अविवेकी aviveki

impugn *v.* सन्देह प्रकट गर्नु sandeh prakat garnu

impulse *n.* संवेग samweg

impure *adj.* अपवित्र apawitra

in *prep.* भित्र bhitra

inability *n.* असामर्थ्य asamarthya

inaccessible *adj.* दुर्गम durgam

inaccurate *adj.* बेठीक bethik

inadequate *adj.* नपुग napug

inalienable *adj.* हरण गर्न नमिल्ने haran garna nam milne

inane *adj.* निरर्थक nirarthak

inanimate *adj.* निर्जीव nirjeev

inappropriate *adj.* अनुचित anuchit

inasmuch *adv.* किनभने kina bhane

inasmuch as *adv.* किनभने kinbhane

inattentive *adj.* असावधान asawdhan

inaudible *adj.* सुन्न नसकिने sunna na sakine

inaugural *adj.* उद्घाटनको udghatan ko

inaugurate *v.* उद्घाटन गर्नु udghatan garnu

inauguration *n.* उद्घाटन udghatan garnu

inauspicious *adj.* अशुभ ashubh

incantation *n.* मन्त्र mantra

incapable *adj.* अयोग्य ayogya

incapacitate *v.* अयोग्य बनाउनु ayogya banaunu

incarnation *n.* अवतार awtar juni

incense *n.* अगरबत्ती agarbatti

incentive *n.* प्रोत्साहन protsahan

inception *n.* प्रारम्भ prarambh

incessant *adj.* लगातारको lagatarko

incest *n.* हाडनाता करणी hadnata karani

inch *n.* इन्ची inchi

incident *n.* घटना ghatana

incidental *adj.* आकस्मिक akasmik

incivility *n.* अशिष्टता ashishtata

inclement *adj.* खराब kharab

inclination *n.* झुकाव jhukaw

inclined *adj.* झुकेको jhukeko

include *v.* गाभ्नु gabhnu

including *prep.* लगायत lagayat

incognito *adv./adj.* छद्म भेषमा chhadma bhesh ma

income *n.* आम्दानी amdani

income *n.* आमदनी amdani

income tax *n.* आयकर ayakar

incommensurate *adj.* तुलना नहुने tulna nahune

incommode *v.* असुविधा गराउनु asuvidha garaunu

incommunicable *adj.* भन्न नसकिने bhanna na sakine

incomparable *adj.* अतुलनीय atulniya

incompeten *adj.* अयोग्य ayogya

incomplete *adj.* अपूरो apuro

incomprehensible *adj.* नबुझिने nabujhine

inconclusive *adj.* टुङ्गोमा नपुग्ने tungoma napungame

inconsequential *adj.* महत्वहीन mahattwahin

inconstant *adj.* अस्थिर asthir

incontinent *adj.* दिसा-पिसाब रोक्न नसक्ने disa-pisab rokan naskane

inconvenient *adj.* असुविधाजनक asuwidhajanak

incorrect *adj.* अशु; ashuddha

increase *v.* बढ्नु badhnu

incredible *adj.* अविश्वसनीय awishwasniya

increment *n.* वृद्धि wriddhi

incubate *v.* ओथारो बस्नु otharo basnu

inculcate *v.* आग्रह गर्नु agraha garnu

incumbent *adj.* बहालवाला bahai wala

incurable *adj.* निको नहुने niko na hune

incursion *n.* धावा dhawa

indebted *adj.* ऋणी rini

indedent *adj.* अनुचित anuchit

indeed *adv.* वास्तवमा wastaw ma

indelible *adj.* मेटाउन नसकिने metaunu naskine

indemnify *v.* क्षति पूरा गर्नु kshati pura garnu

indenture *n.* अनुबन्ध पत्र anbandh patra

independence *n.* स्वतन्त्रता swatantrata

indescribable *adj.* वर्णन गर्न नसकिने varnan garn naskine

indestructible *adj.* नाश हुन नसक्ने nash huna na sakne

index *n.* सूची suchi

index finger *n.* चोरऔँला chor aunla

indicate *v.* देखाउनु dekhaunu

indication *n.* संकेत sanket

indifference *n.* लापर्वाही laparbahi

indigent *adj.* गरीब garib

indigestion *n.* अपच apach

indigestion *n.* अपच apach

indignant *adj.* रिसाएको risaeko

indignation *n.* क्रोध krodh

indirect *adj.* परोक्ष paroksha

indiscreet *adj.* असावधान asawdhan

indiscriminate *adj.* अन्धाधुन्ध andhadhund

indispensable *adj.* नभै नहुने na bhai na hune

indisputable *adj.* निर्विवाद nirvivad

indissoluble *adj.* नटुट्ने nattune

individual *n.* व्यक्तित्व wyaktitwa

indivisible *adj.* भाग गर्न/लाउन नसकिने bhag garna/launa na sakine

indolent *adj.* आलस्य alasya

indomitable *adj.* हिम्मत नहार्ने himmat na harne

indoors *adv.* घरभित्र ghar bhitra

induce *v.* फकाउनु phakaunu

indulge *v.* आशक्त हुनु ashakta hunu

industrious *adj.* परिश्रमी parishrami

industry *n.* उद्योग udyog

industry *n.* उद्योग-धंधा udyog dhanda

inebriated *adj.* मातेको mateko

inedible *adj.* खान नहुने khan nahune

ineffable *adj.* वर्णन गर्न नसकिने varnan garn naskine

ineffective *adj.* असर नपर्ने asar na parne

ineffectual *adj.* निष्फल nishphal

inefficient *adj.* अयोग्य ayogya

inelegant *adj.* असुन्दर asundar

ineligible *adj.* अयोग्य ayogya

ineluctable *adj.* बाट उम्कन नसिकने baat umkan naskine

inept *adj.* अयोग्य ayogya

inequality *n.* असमानता asamanta

inevitable *adj.* अनिवार्य aniwarya

inexorable *adj.* अटल atal

inexpensive *adj.* सस्तो sasto

inexperienced *adj.* अनुभव नभएको anubhaw na bhaeko

inexplicable *adj.* व्याख्या गर्न नसकिने vyakhaya garn naskine

infamous *adj.* बदनाम badnam

infancy *n.* शैशव काल shaishaw kal

infant *n.* शिशु shishu

infantry *n.* पैदल सेना paidalsena

infatuated *adj.* मोहित mohit

infection *n.* सरुवा रोग saruwa rog

infectious *adj.* सरुवा रोग saruwa rog

inferior *adj.* तल्लो tallo

inferiority *n.* हीनता hinta

infernal *adj.* नरकको narakko

infertile *adj.* बाँझो banjho

infidel *n.* नास्तिक nastik

infidelity *n.* विश्वासघात wishwasghat

infiltrate *v.* पस्नु pasnu

infiltration *n.* घुसपैठ ghus paith

infinity *n.* अनन्त anant

inflammation *n.* सुज suj

inflation *n.* मुद्रास्फीति mudra sphiti

inflict *v.* कष्ट दिनु kasht dinu

influence *n.* प्रभाव prabhaw

influential *adj.* प्रभावशाली prabhawshali

influenza *n.* कड़ा kardha

influx *n.* अन्तर आगमन antar agaman

inform *v.* थाहा दिनु thaha dinu

information *n.* सूचना suchana

infrastructure *n.* पूर्वाधार purwadhar

ingenious *adj.* दक्ष daksha

ingfratitude *n.* कृतघनता kritghanta

ingienook *n.* अगेनुको कुना agenuko kuna

inglorious *adj.* लज्जाजनक lajjajanak

ingredient *n.* अवयव awayaw

inhabit *v.* बास गर्नु bas garnu

inhabitable *adj.* बास गर्न योग्य bas garna yogya

inhabitant *n.* बासिन्दा basinda

inhale *v.* सास लिनु sas linu

inherit *v.* पुर्खा आदिबाट पाउनु purkha adi bata paunu

Inheritance *n.* अंश ansh

inhuman *adj.* निर्दयी nirdayi

inimitable *adj.* अद्वितीय adwitiya

initial *n.* नामको पहिलो अक्षर nam ko pahilo akshar

initiative *n.* पहल phala

inject *v.* सूई लाउनु sui launu

injection *n.* सुई sui

injure *v.* चोट लगाउनु chot lagaunu

injurious *adj.* हानिकारक hani karak

injury *n.* चोट लगाउनु chot lagaunu

injustice *n.* अन्यायपूर्वक प्राप्त गरेको anyaya purwak prapt gareko

ink *n.* मसी masi

inkling *n.* संकेत sanket

ink-pot *n.* मसीदानी masi dani

inlaid *adj.* बुट्टा जडिएको butta jadieko

inlet *n.* उपखाड़ी upkhari

inmate *n.* बासिन्दा basinda

inmost *adj.* अन्तरतम antartam

inn *n.* पाटी pati

inner *adj.* भित्री bhitri

innocent *adj.* निर्दोष nirdosh

innovate *v.* नयाँ कुरा ल्याउनु nayan kura liaunu

innovation *n.* नवीन प्रवर्तन nawin prawartan

innuendo *n.* छेड chhed

innumerable *adj.* अनगिन्ती anginti

inoculate *v.* सुई दिनु suidinu

inoculation *n.* खोप khop

inoperable *adj.* चिरफार chirphar

inordinate *adj.* अत्यधिक ataydhik

inquest *n.* अदालती जाँच adalat janch

inquiry *n.* सोधपुछ sodh puchh

inroad *n.* धाबा dhaba

insane *adj.* बौलाहा baulaha

inscription *n.* लेख lekh

insecticide *n.* कीटनाशक kitnashak

insects *n.* कीरा kira

insensate *adj.* बेहोश behosh

inseparable *adj.* अलग नहुने alag na hune

inside *prep.* भित्र bhitra

insight *n.* अन्तरदृष्टि antar drishti

insignificant *adj.* निरर्थक nirarthak

insipid *adj.* खल्लो khallo

insist *v.* जोड दिनु joddinu

insolent *adj.* बेअदब be adab

insomnia *n.* अनिद्रा anidra

inspection *n.* जाँच janchnu

inspector *n.* निरीक्षक nirikshak

inspiration *n.* प्रेरणा prerana

inspire *v.* प्रेरित गर्नु prerit garnu

instal(l)ment *n.* किस्ता kista

install *v.* स्थापित गर्नु sthapit garnu

instance *n.* उदाहरण udaharan

instant *n.* तात्कालिक क्षण tatkalik kshan

instantly *adv.* तुरुन्त turunt

instead of *adv.* बदलामा badla ma

instigate *v.* उक्साउनु uksaunu

institute *n.* संस्थान sansthan

instruct *v.* सिकाउनु skiaunu

instruction *n.* आदेश adesh

instructor *n.* गुरु guru

instrument *n.* औजार aujar

insufficent *adj.* कम kam

insulator *n.* बिजुलीको करेण्ट आदि छेक्ने बस्तु bijuli ko karent

insulin *n.* इन्सुलिन insulin

insult *n.* अपमान apman

insupportable *adj.* असह्य asahay

insurance *n.* बीमा bima

insure *v.* पक्का गर्नु pakka garnu

insurrction *n.* विद्रोह widroh

intact *adj.* पूर्ण purn

integral *adj.* अभिन्न abhinna

integrity *n.* पूर्णता purnta

intellect *n.* बुद्धि buddhi

intellectual *n.* बुद्धिजीवी buddhi jiwi

intelligence *n.* बुद्धिमान buddhiman

intend *v.* चिताउनु chitaunu

intense *adj.* तीव्र tiwra

intensity *n.* तीव्रता tiwrata

intention *n.* इच्छा ichchha

intentional *adj.* जानाजानी jana jani

intercept *v.* बीचैमा रोक्नु blchai ma roknu

intercourse *n.* सम्पर्क sampark

interesting *adj.* रहर/चाखलाग्दो rahar/chakh lagdo

interfere *v.* बाधा दिनु badha dinu

interference *n.* हस्तक्षेव hastakshep

interim *adj.* अन्तरिम antarim

interior *adj.* भित्री bhitri

interlace *v.* जोडिनु jodinu

interlink *v.* जोड्नु jodnu

intermarry *v.* अन्तःविवाह गर्नु anthavivah garnu

intermediate *adj.* बीचको bich ko

intermission *n.* मध्यान्तर madhyantar

intermittent *adj.* रोकिँदे हुने rokide hune

internal *adj.* भित्री bhitri

international *adj.* अन्तर्राष्ट्रिय antarashtriya

interplay *n.* पारस्परिक क्रिया parasparik kriya

interpol *n.* अन्तरराष्ट्रिय पुलिस antarrashtriya police

interpose *v.* बीचमा बोल्नु beechma bolnu

interpret *v.* अर्थ बताउनु arth bat aunu

interpreter *n.* दोभाषे do bhashe

interrogate *v.* प्रश्न गर्नु prashna garnu

interrogation *n.* प्रश्न गर्नु prashna garnu

interrupt *v.* बिथोल्नु bitholu

interruption *n.* अवरोध awrodh

intersection *n.* चौबाटो chaubato

interstellar *adj.* ताराहरूमध्यको taraharu madhyako

interstice *n.* चिरा chira

interval *n.* मध्यान्तर madhyantar

interview *n.* अन्तरवार्ता antar warta

intestate *adj.* वसयतनामा नलेखी vasiyatnama nalekhi

intestine *n.* आन्द्रो andro

intimate *adj.* घनिष्ठ ghanishth

intimation *n.* जनाउ janau

intimidate *v.* धम्क्याउनु dhamkyaunu

into *prep.* भित्र bhitra

intolerable *adj.* सहन नसकिने sahana na sakine

intoxicate *v.* लट्ठ पार्नु latthaparnu

intrepid *adj.* निडर nidar

intricate *adj.* जटिल jatil

intrigue *n.* गुप्त प्रेम गर्नु gupt prem garnu

introduce *v.* चिनजान/परिचय गराउनु chinjan/parichaya garaunu

introduction *n.* चिनजान chinjan

introvert *n.* अन्तर्मुखी व्यक्ति antarmukhi vyakti

intrusion *n.* जबर्जस्ती प्रवेश jabarjasti prawesh

inure *v.* अभ्यस्त गर्नु abhyast garnu

invade *v.* हमला/आक्रमण गर्नु hamla/akraman garnu

invalid *adj.* नाकाम nakam

invaluable *adj.* अनमोल anmol

invasion *n.* हमला/आक्रमण गर्नु hamla/akraman garnu

inveigle *v.* मीठो बोली वा चाल गरेर फुस्लाउनु mitho boli wa chal garer phuslaunu

invent *v.* आविष्कार गर्नु awishkar garnu

invention *n.* आविष्कार awishkar

invest *v.* लगानी गर्नु lagani garnu

investigate *v.* जाँचपड़ताल गर्नु janchpadtal garnu

investigation *n.* जाँचपडताल janchpadtal

invicible *adj.* अजेय ajeya

invitation *n.* निम्तो nimto

invite *v.* निम्तो दिनु nimto dinu

invoice *n.* बिल bil

involve *v.* सरिक/समावेश गर्नु sarik/ samawesh garnu

involvement *n.* संलग्नता samlagnata

inward *adj.* भित्रतिर bhitra tira

iron *n.* फलाम phalam

ironical *adj.* विडम्बनापूर्ण widambanapurn

ironmonger *n.* कामी kami

irony *n.* श्लेश salesh

irrational *adj.* तर्कहीन tark hin

irregular *adj.* अनियमित aniyamit

irrelevant *adj.* असम्बद्ध asambaddh

irremovable *adj.* हटाउन नसकिने hataun naskine

irreparable *adj.* मरम्मत गर्न नसकिने marammat garna na sakine

irrepressible *adj.* अदम्य adamay

irresistible *adj.* विरोध गर्न नसकिने wirodh garna na sakine

irretrievable *adj.* वापस पाउन नसकिने vapas paun naskine

irrgation *n.* सिँचाइ sinchai

irrigate *v.* पटाउनु pataunu

irritate *v.* रिस उठाउनु ris uthaunu

irritation *n.* रिस ris

is *v./aux.* छ chha

island *n.* टापु tapu

isle *n.* टापू tapu

isolate *v.* अलग्याउनु alagyaunu

isotope *n.* आइसोटोप isotope

issue *n.* सन्तान santan

it *pron.* यो yo

itch *n.* चिलाइ chilai

item *n.* विषय wishaya

itinerary *n.* यात्रा तालिका yatra talika

its *pron.* यसको yas ko

itself *pron.* यो आफै yo aphai

ivory *n.* हस्तिहाड hathihad

ivy *n.* चिरहरितलता chirharitalta

J

jab घोच्नु ghochnu

jack *n.* मोटर उचाल्ने औजार moter uhcalne aujar

jack in office *n.* रवाफिलो कर्मचारी rawaphilo karmchari

jack of all trades *n.* सबै विषय अलि अलि जान्ने sabai washaya ali ali janne

jackal *n.* स्याल syal

jackass *n.* भाले गधा bhale gadha

jacket *n.* ज्याकोट jyaket

jackfruit *n.* रूख कटहर rukh kathar

jackknife *n.* ठूलो चक्कु thulo chakku

jade *n.* थकेको घोडा thakeko ghoda

jail *n.* झयालखाना jyalkhana

jailor *n.* घ्यालखानाको हाकिम jhyal khana ko hakim

jalopy *n.* पुरानो थोत्रो गाड़ी purano thotro gadi

jam *n.* रुकावट rukawat

jamboree *n.* आनन्द anand

jar *n.* ठूलो सिसी thulo sisi

jargon *n.* विशिष्ट बोली wishist boli

jarsey *n.* गन्जी gangi

jasmine *n.* चमेली chameli

jasper *n.* सूर्यकान्त मणि surya kant mani

jaundice *n.* पाण्डु रोग pandu rog

jaunt *n.* सैर sair

javelin *n.* भाला bhala

jaw *n.* बङ्गारा bandara

jazz *n.* अमेरिकी हब्सी मूलको सङ्गीत amerika habsi mul ko sangit

jazzy *adj* चड्का chadak

jealous *adj* इखालु ikhalu

jean *n.* जीन कपडा jin kapada

jeep *n.* जीप (vehical) jip

jeer *v.* गिज्याउनपु gijyaunu

jeopardy *n.* शंका shanka

jeremiad *n.* बिलौना bilona

jerk *n.* झट्का jhatka

jester *n.* ठट्टा गर्ने thatta garne

jet *n.* चिक्का chhirka

jet endine *n.* सिर्काको जोडले चल्ने इन्जिन sira ko jodle chalne injin

jet plane *n.* जेटविमान jet wiman

jet-black *adj.* गाडा कालो gadha kalo

jew *n.* यहूदी tahudi

jewel *n.* रतन ratan

jeweller *n.* जुहारी juhari

jewellery *n.* गहना gahana

jibe *n.* खिसी, उपहास khisi, uphas

jiffy *n.* क्षण kshan

jiggered *adj.* थकित thakit

jihad *n.* मुस्लिमहरूको धार्मिक युद्ध muslimharuko dharmik yudh

jim crow *n.* हब्शी habshi

jingal *n.* साना धंटी को टनटन आवाज sana ghantuko tan tan awaj

jinx *n.* अलच्छिना व्यक्ति वा वस्तु alachchhin waykti wa wastu

job *n.* नौकरी nokri

jobless *adj.* ढाके dhakre

jockey *n.* घोडदौड को सबार ghod daud kosabar

jocular *adj.* ठट्यौलौ thatyaulo

jog *v.* घचघच्याउनु ghach ghachy aunu

join *v.* जोर्नु jornu

joint *adj.* संयुक्त samyukta

joist *n.* दलिन dalin

joke *n.* ठट्टा thatta

joker *n.* ठट्टा गर्ने व्यक्ति thata garne vyakti

jolly *adj.* खुश khush

jolt *n.* धक्का dhakka

jornalism *n.* पत्रकारिता patra karita

jot *n.* थोरै thorai

journal *n.* बहिखाता bahi khata

journalist *n.* पत्रकार patrakar

journey *n.* यात्र yatra

jovial *adj.* आनन्दी anandi

jowl *n.* गाला को निम्न भाग gala ko niman bhag

joy *n.* खुशी khushi

jubilant *adj.* प्रसन्न prashna

jubilation *n.* अन्यानन्द aanyanand

jubilee *n.* जयन्ती jayanti

judg(e)ment *n.* इन्साफ insaph

judge *n.* न्यायाधीश nuayadhish

judicial *adj.* अदालती adalati

judiciary *n.* न्यायपालिका nyayapalika

judicious *adj.* विवेकी wiweki

judo *n.* जापानी कुस्ती japani kusti

jug *n.* जग jag

juggler *n.* जादुगर jadugar

juice *n.* रस ras

juicy *adj.* रसिलो rasilo

jumble *n.* थुप्रो thupro

jumbo *adj.* बडेमान bademan

jumbo jet *n.* अति ठूलो जेटविमान ati thulo jet wiman

jump *n.* उफ्राइ uphrai

jump the gun *v.* बेला नभई सुरु गर्नु bela na bhal suru garnu

jumper *n.* ऊनी सुइटर uni suitar

junction *n.* जोर्नी jorni

juncture *n.* सङ्कट को स्थिति sankat ko sthiti

jungle *n.* वन wan

junior *n.* नायब nayab

juniper *n.* चेप्टे सल्ला chepte salla

junket *n.* दही को मिष्टान्न dahiko misthanan

junketing *n.* भोज bhoj

jupiter *n.* बृहस्पति ग्रह wrihaspati graha

just *adj.* न्यायी nyayi

just before *adv.* अलि अघि ali aghi

just now *adv.* भखरै bharkharai

justice *n.* न्याय nyayapalika

justify *v.* उचित देखाउनु uchit

jut *n.* चुच्चो chuchcho

jute *n.* सन san

juvenile *adj.* तरुण tarun

juvenile delinquency *n.* नाबालिग अपराध nabalig apradh

juxtapose *n.* सँगै-सँगै राख्नु sange-sange rakhnu

K

kale *n.* एक किसिमको बन्दकोपी ek kisimko bandkopi

kaleidoscope *n.* बराबर बदलिरहने दृश्य barabar badli rahane drishya

kaolin *n.* सेतो माटो seto mato

kapok *n.* तकिया आदिमा हाल्ने सिमलको रूई takia adima halne simalko rui

kaput *n.* बिग्रेको bigreko

karate *n.* जापानी कुश्ती japani kusti

kayak *n.* एस्किमो डुङ्गा eskimo dunga

keel *n.* नौतल nautal

keen *adj.* टाठो tatho

keenness *n.* तीव्रता tiwrata

keep *v.* राख्नु rakhnu

keepsake *n.* चिनु chinu

keg *n.* पीपा peepa

ken *n.* ज्ञानको सीमा gyanko seema

kennel *n.* कुकुर खोर kukur khor

kerchief *n.* मजेत्रो majetro

kernel *n.* गुदी gudi

kerosene *n.* मट्टीतेल mattitel

kestrel *n.* एक किसिमको सानो बाज ek kisimko sano baaj

ketch *n.* जहाज jahaj

kettle *n.* किटली kitli

key *n.* साँचो sancho

keyhole *n.* साँचो छिराउने प्वाल sancho chhiraune pwal

keynote *n.* प्रमुख विचार pramukh wichar

keyring *n.* साँचोहरु हाल्ने रिङ. sancho haru halne rin

khaki *n.* खाकी कपडा kihaki kapada

kick *n.* लात lat

kick out *n.* निकालिदिनु nikali dinu

kickback *n.* कमिसन kamisan

kick-off *n.* खेल आदि शुरू khel adi shuru

kid *n.* केटाकेटी keta keti

kidnap *v.* अपहरण गर्नु apaharan garnu

kidney *n.* मिर्गौला mirgaula

kill *v.* मार्नु marnu

killer *n.* हत्यारा hatyara

kiln *n.* अवाल awal

kin *n.* नातादार nata dar

kind *adj.* दयालु dayalu

kindergarten *n.* शिशु विद्यालय shishu widyalaya

kindle *v.* बाल्नु balnu

kindly *adv.* दया/कृपापूर्वक daya/ kripapurwak

kindness *n.* दया daya

king *n.* राजा raja

kingdom *n.* अधिराज्य adhirajya

kingpin *n.* आवश्यक व्यक्ति awashyak wyakti

kingship *n.* राजाको पद raja ko pad

kinsfolk *n.* पुरुष नातादार purush natadar

kip *n.* सुल्ने ठाउँ sutne thau

kirk *n.* गिर्जा girja

kismet *n.* किस्मत kismat

kiss *n.* चुम्बन chumban

kit *n.* सामान saman

kitchen *n.* भान्साकोठा bhansa kotha

kitchen garden *n.* करेसाबारी karesa bari

kite *n.* चङ्गा changa

kith *n.* आफन्तहरू afantharu

kitten *n.* बिरालोको बच्चा birailo ko bachcha

kleptomania *n.* चोरी गर्न लालायित हुने रोग chori garna lalayit hune rog

knack *n.* युक्ति sip

knave *n./adv.* धूर्त dhurt

knead *v.* पिठो/माटो मुछ्नु pitho/ matho muchhnu

knee *n.* घुँडा ghunda

kneecap *n.* घुँडाको चक्का ghunda ko chakka

knee-deep *adj.* घुँडासम्मको गहिरो ghunda samma ko gahiro

kneel *v.* घुँडा टेक्नु ghunda teknu

knife *n.* चक्कु chakku

knit *v.* बुन्नु bunnu

knob *n.* गट्टा gatta

knock *n.* दनक danak

knock down *v.* पछार्नु pachharnu

knoll *n.* ढिस्को dhisko

knot *n.* गाँठो gantho

knotty *adj.* गठिलो gathilo

knout *n.* कोर्रा kora

know *v.* चिन्नु chinnu

know-how *n.* जानकारी jankari

knowingly *adv.* जानीजानी janijani

knowledge *n.* ज्ञान gyan

known *adj.* थाहा भएको thaha bhaeko

knuckle *n.* औंलाको जोर्नी aulako jorni

knuckle down *v.* मन दिएर काममा लाग्नु man diyera kam ma lagnu

knuckle under *v.* हार मान्नु har mannu

knuckly *n.* औंलाको जार्नी aunla ko jorni

koala *n.* रूख चढ्ने जनावर rukh chadne jnawar

kologram(m)e *n.* हजार ग्राम hajar gram

koran *n.* मुस्लिमहरूको धर्मग्रन्थ muslimharuko dharamgranth

kudos *n.* इज्जत ijjat

L

Lab *n.* प्रयोगशाला prayogshala

label *n.* चिन्हपत्र chinha patra

labelled *n.* लेबल टाँस्लु label taslu

labial *adj.* ओठको authko

labo(u)r *n.* काम kam

labo(u)rer *n.* ज्यामी jyami

laboratory *n.* प्रयोगशाला prayog shala

laborious *adj.* परिश्रमी parishrami

labour *n.* परिश्रम parshram

lace *n.* फित्ता phitta

lack *n.* कमी kami

lackadaisical *adj.* शिथिल shithil

lackey *n.* नोकर nokar

lacklustre *adj.* निस्तेज nistej

laconic *adj.* बोल्दा थोरै शब्द प्रयोग गर्ने bolda therai shabd prayog garne

lacquer बार्निस barnis

lactic *adj.* दूध को dudh ko

lacuna *n.* रिक्त स्थान rikt sthan

lad *n.* ठिटो thito

ladder *n.* भर्याङ्ग bharyan

ladle *n.* डाडु dadu

lady *n.* महिला mahila

ladykiller *n.* स्त्रीहरूलाई मोहित नार्ने पुरुष strirulai mohit narne purush

lady's finger *n.* रामतोरियाँ ram toriyan

lag *v.* पछि पर्नु pachhi parnu

lager *n.* हल्का बियर halka bear

lair *n.* जंगली जनावर को गुफा junglee janwarko gufa

laird *n.* जमीनदार jamindar

lake *n.* ताल tal

lama *n.* लामा lama

lamb *n.* पाठो patho

lambent *adj.* कान्तिमय kantimai

lame *adj.* लङ्गडो langado

lame duck *n.* शक्तिहीन व्यक्ति shaktihin wyakti

lament *v.* विलाप गर्नु wilap garnu

lamp *n.* बत्ती batti

land *n.* जमीन jamin

landholder *n.* जग्गाधनी jagga dhani

landlady *n.* घरपटिनी ghar patini

landlocked *adj.* भूपरिवेष्टित bhupariweshtit

landlord *n.* घरपटी ghar patini

landmark *n.* सरहद sarahd

landowner *n.* जग्गाधनी jagga dhani

landscape *n.* भूदृश्य bhudrishya

landslide *n.* पहिरो pahiro

lane *n.* गल्ली galli

language *n.* भाषा bhasha

languid *adj.* शिथिल shitil

languish *v.* शिथिल/दुर्बल हुनु shithil/durbal hunu

lanky *adj.* अग्लो र दुब्लो aglo ra dublo

lantern *n.* लाल्टिन laltin

lap *n.* काख kakh

lapel *n.* कठालो kathalo

lapse *n.* भूलचूक bhuichuk

larceny *n.* चोरी chori

large *adj.* ठूलो thulo

largely *adv.* विशालताले bishalthalay

largesse *n.* मुक्तहस्तले दिएको दान mukthastale diaeko dan

larynx *n.* कण्ठ kanth

lascivious *adj.* भ्रष्टाचारी bharsthachari

lash *n.* कोर्रा ठोक्नु korra thoknu

last *adj.* अन्तिम antim

last night *n.* पछिल्लो रात pachhillo rat

last time *n.* पछिल्लो पटक pachhillo patak

last year *n.* पोहोर (साल) pohor (sal)

lasting *adj.* टिकाउ tikau

lastly *adv.* आखिरमा akhir ma

latch *n.* चुकुल chukul

late *n.* अबेला abela

lately *adv.* हालै halai

latent *adj.* प्रकट नभएको prakat nabhaeko

later *adj.* पछि pachhi

latex *n.* रबर आदि को दुधिलो रस rubber adiko dudhilo ras

lath *n.* काठको लामो पातलो टुक्रा kathko lamo patlo tukra

lather *n.* साबुनको फाँज sabun ko phinj

lathi *n.* लाठी lathi

latitude *n.* अक्षांश akshansh

latreral *adj.* छेउको cheuko

latrine *n.* चर्पी charpi

latter *adj.* पछिल्लो pachhillo

laugh *n.* हाँस्नु hansnu

laughing gas *n.* हँसाउने ग्याँस hansaune gyans

laughing stock *n.* मजाक व ठट्टाको पात्र majak wa thatta ko patra

laughter *v.* हाँसो hanso

launch *v.* छोड्नु chon

laundry *n.* को घर dhobi ko ghar

lava *n.* लावा lawa

lavatory *n.* चर्पी charpi

lavish *adj.* मन फुकाएर खर्च गर्नु man phukaera kharch garnu

law *n.* कानून kanun

lawful *adj.* कानूनी kanuni

lawless *adj.* मनपरी गर्ने man pari garne

lawn *n.* चोरी chaur

lawsuit *n.* मुद्दा mudda

lawyer *n.* वकील wakil

lax *adj.* खुकुलो, फितलो khukulo, phitlo

laxative *n.* जुलाफ julaf

lay *v.* बिछ्याउनु bichhaunu

lay aside *v.* अलग राख्नु alag rakhnu

lay down *v.* बुझाउनु bujhaunu

lay waste *v.* नाश गर्नु nash garnu

layer *n.* तह tah

layman *n.* आम/साधारण व्यक्ति am/ sadharan wyakti

lay-off *n.* अस्थायी खारेजीको अवधि asthayi khareji ko awadhi

layout *n.* सजावट sajawat

laziness *n.* आलस्य alasya

lazy *adj.* अल्दी alchhi

lea *n.* चउर chaur

lead सीसा sheesa

leader *n.* नेता neta

leading *adj.* पुमुख prakmukh

leaf *n.* पात patho

leaflet *n.* पर्चा parcha

leak *n.* चुहावट chuhyawat

leakage *n.* चुहावट chuhawat

leaky *adj.* चुहिने chuhine

lean *adj.* दुब्लो dublo

leap *n.* छालाङ्ग chhalang

learn *v.* सिक्नु siknu

learned *adj.* पढेलेखेको padhe lekheko

learning *n.* विद्यान widya

leash *n.* दाम्लो damlo

least *adj.* सबैभन्दा थोरै sabai bhanda thorai

leather *n.* चमडा chamada

leave *n.* बिदा bida

leave off *v.* छोड्नु chon

leaven *n.* खमीर khamir

lectern *n.* गिर्जामा बाइबल राख्ने डेस्क girjama bible rakhne desk

lecture *n.* भाषण bhashan

lecturer *n.* उपप्राध्यावक up pradhyapak

ledger *n.* बही खाता bahi khata

leech *n.* जुका juka

leek *n.* प्याज जस्तो सब्जी pyaj jasto sabzi

left *adj.* देब्रे debre

left wing *n.* वामपन्थी दल wam panthi dal

leftist *n.* वामपन्थी wam panthi

leftover *adj.* उब्रिएको ubrieko

lefty *adj.* देब्रे हात चल्ने debre hat chalne

leg *n.* गोडा goda

legacy *n.* बपौती bapauti

legal *adj.* कानूनी kanuni

legate *n.* पोपको दूत popko dut

legend *n.* दन्त्य/पौराणिक कथा dantya/pauranik katha

leggings *n.* खुट्टा छोप्ने आवरण khutta chopne awaran

leggy *adj.* लामा-लामा खुट्टा हुने lama-lama khutta hune

leghorn *n.* एक जातको कुखुरा ek jatko kukhura

legible *adj.* पढ्न सकिने padhna sakine

legion *n.* रोमको सेना rom ko sena

legislation *n.* ऐन ain

legislative *adj.* व्यवस्थापिका wyawasthapika

legislature *n.* विधानसभा widhan sabha

legitimate *adj.* वैध waidh

legume *n.* गेडागुडी geda gudi

leisure *n.* फुर्सत phursat

leisurely *adv.* फुर्सतमा phursatma

lemon *n.* कागती kagati

lemonade *n.* निम्बूको शरबत nimbuko sharbat

lend *v.* सापट/ऋण दिनु sapat/rin dinu

length *n.* लम्बाइ lambai

lenient *adj.* कडिकड़ाउ नगर्ने karikadau nagarne

lenity *n.* दयालुता dyaluta

lens *n.* लेन्स lens

lentil *n.* दाल dal

leopard *n.* चितुवा chituwa

leper *n.* कोरी kori

leprosy *n.* कुष्ठ रोग kushth rog

lesbian *n.* समलिङ्गी स्त्री samlingi stri

lesion *n.* घाउ ghau

less *adj.* कमी kam

lessee *n.* पट्टाधारी pattadhari

lesson *n.* पाठो patho

lessor *n.* पट्टादाता pattadata

lest *conj.* भन्ने डरले bhanne darle

let *v.* गर्न दिनु garna dinu

let alone *v.* छोडिदिनु chhodi dinu

let down *v.* धोका दिनु dhoka dinu

let go *v.* छोड्नु chodnu

let in *v.* प्रवेश गर्नु दिनु prawesh garna dinu

let in for *v.* संलग्न गराउनु samlagna garaunu

let loose *v.* रिहा गर्नु riha garnu

let on *v.* गोप्य/कुरा खोल्नु gopya/ kura kholnu

let up *v.* कम/शिथिल हुनु kam/shithil hunu

lethal *adj.* घातक ghatak

lethargy *n.* उदासीनता udasinta

letter *n.* चिठी chithi

letter box *n.* पत्रमंजूषा patra manjusha

lettuce *n.* जिरीको साग jiri ko sag

let-up *n.* विराम wiram

leucocyte *n.* वेताणु vetanu

levant *v.* भाग्नु bhagnu

levee *n.* बाँध bandh

level *n.* तह tah

lever *n.* उत्तोलक uttolak

lever up *v.* उक्काउनु ukkanunu

lewd *adj.* कामुक kamuk

ley *n.* घाँसको मैदान ghasko maidan

liability *n.* दायित्व dayitwa

liable *adj.* जवाफदेह jawaph deh

liaison *n.* सम्पर्क sampark

liaison officer *n.* सम्पर्क अधिकृत sampark adhikrit

liar *n.* झूटो बोल्ने jhuto bolne

liberal *adj.* उदार udar

liberate *v.* मुक्त गर्नु mukta garnu

liberation *n.* मुक्ति mukti

liberty *n.* स्वाधीनता swadhinta

libra *n.* तुला राशि tula rashi

librarian *n.* पुस्तकाध्यक्ष pustak adhyaksha

library *n.* पुस्तकालय pustakalaya

lice *n.* जुम्राहरू jumra haru

licence *n.* आज्ञा/अनुमति पत्र agya/ anumati patra

lichen *n.* झयाउ jhyau

licit *adj.* वैध vaidhya

lick *v.* चाट्नु chatnu

lid *n.* बिर्को birko

lie *n.* झूटो कुरा jhuto kura

lie down *v.* सुल्नु sutnu

lie flat *v.* पस्रिनु pasrinu

life *n.* जीवन jiwan

life cycle *n.* जीवनचक्र jiwan chakra

life expectancy *n.* आयुराशा ayurasha

life insurance *n.* जीवनबीमा jiwan bima

lifeblood *n.* जीवन धान्ने वस्तु jiwan dhanne wastu

lifeless *adj.* बेजान bejan

lifelong *adj.* आजीवन ajiwan

lifer *n.* जन्मकैदी janamkaidi

life-size(d) *adj.* पूर्णकद purn kad

lifetime *n.* जुनी juni

lift *n.* लिफ्ट lipht

ligament *n.* स्नायु snayu

light *n.* प्रकाश prakash

light bulb *n.* बिजुली को गुलुप bijuli ko gulup

light industry *n.* प्रसन्नचित sanu udyog

light-fingered *adj.* हात फेर्ने hatpherne

light-headed *adj.* चपल chapal

light-hearted *adj.* आनन्दी anandi

lightning *n.* सानु उद्योग chatyan

lightsome *adj.* प्रसन्नचित prasanchit

lignite *n.* नरम कोइला naram koila

like *adj.* कम महत्त्वको jasto

likeness *n.* समानता samanta

likewise *adv.* त्यसैगरी tyasai gari

liking *n.* रुचि ruchi

lilt *n.* लय lai

lily *n.* नलिनी nalini

limb *n.* अङ्ग ang

lime *n.* चून chun

limestone *n.* चूनढुङ्गा chun dhunga

limit *n.* सीमा sima

limitation *n.* सीमितता simitta

limited *adj.* सीमित simit

limitless *adj.* सीमा रहित sima rahit

limousine *n.* बन्द मोटरगाडी band motar gadi

limousine *n.* मोटरगाड़ी motorgadi

limp *adj.* लुलो lulo

line *n.* रेखा rekha

lineage *n.* कुल kul

linen *n.* सुती कपडा suti kapada

line-up *n.* पंक्ति pankti

linguist *n.* भाषविद् bhasha wid

liniment *n.* मालिस malis

lining *n.* लुगाको भित्री luga ko bhitri

link *n.* जोड jod

linkage *n.* सम्बद्धता sambaddhta

linseed *n.* आलस्य alas

lion *n.* सिंह simha

lioness *n.* सिंहिनी simhini

lip *n.* ओठ oth

lip-service *n.* चेपारे बोली chepare boli

lipstick *n.* लाली lali

liquid *n.* तरल taral

liquidate *v.* मार्नु marnu

liquor *n.* रक्सी raksi

liquorice *n.* जेठीमधु jethimadhu

lira *n.* इटालीको मुद्रा italyko mudra

list *n.* सूची suchi

listejn *v.* सुन्नु sunnu

listener *n.* सुन्ने व्यक्ति sunne wyakti

literacy *n.* साक्षरता saksharta

literary *adj.* साहित्यसम्बन्धी sahityasambandhi

literate *adj.* लेखपढ गर्न जान्ने lekh padh garna janne

literature *n.* साहित्य sahitya

lithe *adj.* लचिलो lachilo

lithography *n.* अश्ममुद्रण ashammudran

litre *n.* लीटर litre

litter *n.* फोहरमैला phohar maila

little *adj.* सानु sanu

live *adj.* जिउँदो jiundo

live *v.* जीउनु, बाँच्नु jiunu, bachnu

livelihood *n.* जीविका jiwika

lively *adj.* फुर्तिलो phurtilo

liver *n.* कलेजो kalejo

liver *n.* कलेजो kalejo

livestock *n.* गाईवस्तु gai wastu

livid *adj.* सीसा रंग को seesa rangko

living *adj.* जीविका jiwika

living goddess *n.* कुमारी kumari

living room *n.* बैठक baithak

lizard *n.* छेपारो chheparo

load *n.* भारी bhari

loaf *n.* पाउरोटी pauroti

loafer *n.* आवारा awara

loan *n.* ऋण rin

loan *n.* ऋण, सापट rin, sapat

lobe *n.* कानको लोती kanko loti

lobster *n.* ठूलो चिङ्गडी माछा thulo chingdi machha

lobster *n.* चिँगड़ी chingari

locale *n.* घटनास्थल ghatnasthal

location *n.* स्थानीय sthaniya

loch *n.* झील jheel

lock *n.* ताल्चा talcha

lock up *v.* थन्क्याउनु thankyaunu

lockout *n.* कारखानामा तालाबन्दी karkhanama talabandhi

locust *n.* सलह salah

locust *n.* सलह salah

lode *n.* धातु रेखा dhaturekha

lodestar *n.* ध्रुवतारा dhruvtara

lodge *n.* लज laj

lofty *adj.* अग्लो र दुब्लो aglo ra dublo

log *n.* काठको मुढा kath ko mudha

logarithm *n.* लघुगुणक laghuganak

logic *n.* तर्क tark

logic *n.* तर्कशास्त्र tarkshastra

logical *adj.* तर्कसंगत tarksangat

loin *n.* कम्मर kammar

loin *n.* कम्मर kammar

loincloth *n.* कछाड kachhad

loiter *v.* भौंतारिनु bhauntarinu

lollipop *n.* मिठाई mithai

lone *adj.* एक्लो eklo

lonelinees *n.* एक्लोपन eklo pan

lonely *adj.* एकान्त ekant

long *adj.* लामो lamo

long distance *adj.* लामो दुरीको lamo duri ko

long face *n.* अँध्यारो मुख andhyaro mukh

long jump *n.* लामो दूरीको उफ्राइ lamo duri ko uphrai

long life *n.* लामो आयु lamo ayu

long range *adj.* धेरै दूरीको dherai duri ko

long shot *n.* अन्दाज andaj

longago *adv.* धेरै अघि dherai aghi

longevity *n.* दीर्घायु dirghayu

longitude *n.* देशान्तर deshantar

loo *n.* पाइखाना paikhana

look *n.* हेराइ herai

look after *v.* हेरविचार/स्याहार गर्नु herwichar/syahar garnu

look for *v.* खोज्नु khojnu

look forward to *v.* अपेक्षा गर्नु apeksha garnu

look into *v.* खोजतलास/छानबिन गर्नु khoj talas/chhan bin garnu

look like *v.* जस्तो देखिनु jasto dekhinu

look out *n.* रखबारी गर्ने ठाउँ/मानिस rakhbari garne thaun/manis

look up *v.* हेर्नु hernu

loom *n.* लुगा बुन्ने तान luga bunne tan

loony *adj.* पागल pagal

loop *n.* सुर्केनी surkeni

loophole *n.* नियम भङ्ग गर्ने niyam bhang garne upaya

loose *adj.* लुलो lulo

loosen *v.* फुकाउनु phukaunu

loot *n.* लुटेको माल luteko mal

looting *n.* लूटलाट lutlat

lord *n.* मालिक malik

lose *v.* हार्नु harnu

loser *n.* हरूवा haruwa

loss *n.* नोक्सान noksan

loss of face *n.* मानहानि man hani

lost *adj.* हराएको haraeko

lot(s) of *adj.* धेरै dherai

lotion *n.* रस ras

lottery *n.* चिट्ठा chittha

lotus *n.* कमलको फूल kamal ko phul

loud *adj.* चर्को charko

loudly *adv.* ठूलो आवाजले thulo awaj le

loudspeaker *n.* आवाज ठूलो पार्ने यन्त्र awaj thulo parne yantra

louse *n.* जुम्रो jumro

lout *n.* गँवार ganwar

love *n.* प्रेम prem

love affair *n.* मायाप्रीती mayapriti

love marriage *n.* प्रेम विवाह prem wiwah

lovebirds *n.* चखेवाचखेवी chakhewa chakhewi

lovelorn *adj.* विरही wirahi

lovely *adj.* सुन्दर sundar

lover *n.* प्रेमी premi

lovesick *n.* विरही प्रेमी wirahi premi

loving *adj.* माया गर्ने maya garne

low *adj.* होचो hocho

lower *adj.* तल्लो tallo

lowland *n.* निम्नभूमि nimanbhumi

lowly *adj.* नम्र namra

loyal *adj.* बफादार baphadar

loyalty *n.* बफादारी baphadari

lozenge *n.* चुस्ने मिठाई chusne mithai

lubricate *v.* तेल लगाउनु tel lagaunu

luck *n.* भाग्य bhagya

luckily *adv.* भाग्यवश bhagya wash

lucky *adj.* भाग्यमानी bhagya mani

lucrative *adj.* लाभदायक labh dayak

ludicrous *adj.* हास्यपद hasyaprad

lug *v.* घिसार्नु ghirsanu

luggage *n.* माल mal

lugubrious *adj.* दुःखी dukhi

lukewarm *adj.* मनतातो man tato

lull *n.* शान्ति shanti

lullaby *n.* लोरी lori

lumbago *n.* कम्मरको पीड़ा kammarko peerha

lumbar *adj.* कम्मरको kammarko

luminous *adj.* प्रकाशयुक्त prakash yukta

lump *n.* ढिका dhika

lunar *adj.* चन्द्रमाको chandrama ko

lunatic *n.* पागल pagal

lunch *n.* दिउसोको खना diuso ko khana

luncheon *n.* दिवाभोज diwa bhoj

lung *n.* फोक्सो phokso

lure *v.* लोभ्याउनु lobhyaunu

luscious *adj.* मीठो mitho

lust *n.* वासना wasna

lustre *n.* चमक chamak

lustrous *adj.* झल्कने jhalkan

luxuriant *adj.* धेरै dherai

luxurious *adj.* सोख सयल गर्ने sokh sayal garne

lyceum *n.* भाषण दिने हल bhashan dine hal

lyric *n.* गीत git

M

machine *n.* कल kal

mackintosh *n.* बर्सादी barsadi

macrocosm *n.* ब्रह्माण्ड brahmand

mad *adj.* बौलाहा baulaha

madam *n.* महोदया mahodaya

madcap *adj.* लापर्बाह laparbah

madden *n.* पागल वा क्रुद्ध बनाउनु pagal wa krudh banaunu

mademoiselle *n.* कुमारी kumari

madonna *n.* कुमारी मेरी kumari meri

maestro *n.* संगीतज्ञ sangeetagya

magazine *n.* पत्रिका patrika

mager/meager *adj.* कमसल kamsal

magic *n.* जादु jadu

magician *n.* जादुगर jadugar

magnet *n.* चुम्बक chumbak

magnificent *adj.* भव्य bhavya

magnify *v.* बढाउनु badhaunu

magnitude *n.* मात्रा matra

magnolia *n.* थलकमलको फूल thal kamal ko phul

magnum *n.* बोतल bottle

mahjong *n.* चारजनाले खेल्ने charjanale khelne

maid *n.* नोकिर्नी nokarni

maiden *n.* कुमारी केटी kumari keti

maiden speech *n.* पहिलो भाषण pahilo bhashan

maidservant *n.* नोकर्नी nokarni

mail *n.* डाँक dank

mailbox *n.* पत्रमंजूषा patra manjusha

mailman *n.* हुलाकी hulaki

main *adj.* मुख्य mukhya

mainly *adv.* प्रायः prayah

mainstay *n.* मुख्य सहारा mukhya sahara

mainstream *n.* मूलप्रवाह mul prawah

maintain *v.* हेरचाह her chah

maisonette *n.* सानो घर sano ghar

maize *n.* मकै makai

majestic *adj.* प्रभावशाली prabhaw shali

majority *n.* बहुमत bahumat

make *v.* बनाउनु banaunu

make-up *n.* श्रृंगार shringar

malady *n.* बिमारी bimari

malaise *n.* अस्वस्थता aswastata

malaria *n.* हिमज्वर himjowar

male *n.* भाले bhale

malediction *n.* सराप sarap

malefactor *n.* अपराधी apradhi

malevolent *adj.* अरूको अहित गर्न चाहने aruko ahit garn chahne

malformation *n.* कुरचना kurchana

malice *n.* डाहा daha

malignant *adj.* हानिकारक hani karak

mallard *n.* जंगली हाँस junglee haas

mallet *n.* मुङ्ग्रो mungro

mallet *n.* मुङ्ग्रो mungro

malnutrition *n.* कुपोषण kuposhan

malodorous *adj.* दुर्गन्धपूर्ण durgandhpurn

malpractice *n.* दुर्व्यवहार durwyawahar

malt *n.* बीयर bear

maltreatment *n.* दुर्व्यवहार durwyawahar

mammal *n.* स्तनपायी जन्तु stanpayi jantu

mammon *n.* धन dhan5

man *n.* मान्छे manchhe

manacle *n.* हतकड़ी hatkadi

manage *v.* संचालन गर्नु sanchalan garnu

management *n.* व्यवस्थापन wyawashtapan

manager *n.* व्यवस्थापक wyawsthapak

mane *n.* घोडाको जगर ghoda ko jagar

manful *adj.* साहसी sahasi

mango *n.* आँप anp

manhandle *v.* हात हाल्नु hat halnu

manhood *n.* पुरुषत्व purushtav

manifesto *n.* घोषणा-पत्र ghoshna patra

manifold *adj.* अनेक र विविध anek r vividh

mankind *n.* मनुष्यजाति manushya jati

manly *adj.* बलियो baliyo

manner *n.* काइदा kaida

manoeuvres *n.* युद्धाभ्यास yudhabhyas

manor *n.* जिमीदारी jimidari

manpower *n.* कामदरहरूको ठूलो जमात kamdarharuko thulo jamat

mansion *n.* भवन bhawan

manslaughter *n.* नरहत्या narhatya

mantelpiece *n.* अगेनुको मास्तिर रहेको काठ agenuko mastir raheko kath

manual *n.* विवरणपुस्तिका wiwaran pustika

manufacture *n.* उत्पादन गर्नु utpadn garnu

manure *n.* मल mal

manuscript *n.* पाण्डुलिपि pandulipi

manuscript *n.* पाण्डुलिपि pandulipi

many *adj.* धेरै dherai

map *n.* नक्सा naksa

maple *n.* केपासी kepasi

mar *v.* बिगार्नु bigarnu

marathon *n.* अति लामो दौड ati lamo daud

marble *n.* सङ्गमरमर stone

march *n.* मार्च महीना march mahina

mare *n.* घोडी ghodi

margin *n.* छेउ chheu

marigold *n.* सयपत्री फूल sata patri phul

marine *adj.* सामुद्रिक samudrik

marionette *n.* कठपुतली kathputali

marital *n.* दाम्पत्य dampatya

mark *n.* चिनो chino

market *n.* बजार bajar

marketing *n.* बेचबिखन bech bikhan

marketplace *n.* चोकबजार chok bajar

marksman *n.* निशानाबाज nishnabaz

maroon *n.* खैरो रातो रंग khairo rato rang

marriage *n.* हिबहे biha

marriageable *adj.* विवाहयोग्य wiwah yogya

married *adj.* विवाहित wiwahit

marry *v.* बिहे/विवाह गर्नु bihe

mars *n.* मंगल ग्रह mangal graha

marsh *n.* धाप dhap

mart *n.* बजार bazar

martial law *n.* जङ्गी ऐन jangi ain

martin *n.* भीर गौंथली bheer gonthali

martyr *n.* शहीद shahid

marval (i)ous *adj.* विचित्र wicitra

marxism *n.* मार्क्सवाद markswad

masculine *n.* पुलिङ्ग puling

mask *n.* मकुण्डा makundo

mason *n.* डकर्मी dakarmi

mass *n.* राशि rashi

mass midia *n.* आमसंचारका साधन amsancharka sadhan

mass movement *n.* जनआन्दोलन jan andolan

mass production *n.* बहुउत्पादन bahu utpadan

massacre *n.* काटमार katmar

massage *n.* मालिस malis

masseus *n.* मालिस गर्ने पेशावर स्त्री malis garne peshawar sthri

massive *adj.* ठूलो thulo

mast *n.* मस्तूल mastul

master *n.* मालिक malik

master plan *n.* गुरुयोजना guru yojana

masterpiece *n.* उत्कृष्ट कृति utkrisht kirti

masticate *v.* चपाउनु chapaunu

masturbate *v.* हस्तमैथुन गर्नु hastmaithun garnu

masturbation *n.* हस्तमैथुन hast maithun

masuoleum *n.* समाधि samadhi

mat *n.* चटाई chatai

match *n.* सलाई salai

matchbox *n.* सलाईको बट्टा salai ko batta

matchless *adj.* बेजोड bejod

matchmaker *n.* लमी lami

matchstick *n.* सलाईको काँटी salai ko kanti

matdriarch *n.* परिवार वा कुलकी मुखेनी pariwar wa kulki mukeni

mate *n.* साथी sahti

material *n.* माल mal

maternal *adj.* आमापट्टिटको amapattico

maternal uncle *n.* मामा mama

maternity hospital *n.* प्रसूतिगृह prasuti griah

maternity leave *n.* सुत्केरी बिदा sutkeri bida

mathematical *n.* गणित ganit

mathematics *n.* गणित ganit

matins *n.* बिहानको प्रार्थना bihanko prarthana

matricide *n.* मातृहत्या matri hatya

matricide *n.* मातृहत्या matrihatya

matrimonial *adj.* वैवाहिक waiwahik

matrimony *n.* बिहे bihe

matron *n.* घरकी मालिक्नी ghar ki malikni

matron *n.* अस्पताल प्रधान नर्स asaptal pradhan nurse

matter *n.* वस्तु wastu

matter of fact *n.* वास्तविक कुरो wastawik kuro

matting *n.* चटाई chatai

mattock *n.* गैंती gainti

mattress *n.* डसना dasna

mattress *n.* डसना dasna

maturate *v.* पाक्नु paknu

mature *adj.* पाको pako

maturity *n.* परिपक्वता paripakwata

maudlin *adj.* ज्यादै भावुक jyadae bhavuk

mausoleum भव्य समाधि bhavya smadhi

mauve *n.* फीका बैजनी रङ्ग phika baijani rang

mauve *n.* बैजनी baijani

maw *n.* पेट peth
mawkish *adj.* रोगी rogi
maxim *n.* उक्ति ukti
maximum *adj.* अधिकतम adhiktam
may *mod.* सक्नु sakun
maybe *adv.* हुनसक्छ huna sakhha
maybe *adv.* शायद shayad
mayor *n.* नगरप्रमुख nagar pramukh
mayor *n.* नगरपाल, नगरपति nagarpal, nagarpati
me *pron.* मलाई malai
me *pron.* मलाई malai
mead *n.* महको रक्सी mehko raksi
meadow *n.* चौर chaur
meadow *n.* घाँसको मैदान ghasko maidan
meal *n.* खाना khana
mean *adj.* छुच्चो chhuchcho
meaning *n.* माने mane
meaning *n.* अर्थ arth
meaningless *adj.* अर्थहीन arthhin
means *n.* जुक्ति jukti
meantime *adv.* यसैबीचमा yasai bich ma
meanwhile *adv.* यसैबीचमा yasai bich ma
measles *n.* दादुरा dadura
measles *n.* दादुरा dadura
measly *adj.* तुच्छा tucha
measure *n.* नाप nap
measure *n.* मात्रा matra
measurement *n.* नाप nap

meat *n.* मासु masu
mechanic *n.* मिस्त्री mistri
mechanical *adj.* कलपुर्जासम्बन्धी kalpurja sambandhi
medal *n.* पदक padak
medi(a)eval *adj.* मध्ययुगी madhya yugi
mediate *v.* मध्यस्थ हुनु madhyasth hunu
mediator *n.* मिलाप गराउने milap garaune
medical *adj.* डाक्टरी daktari
medicine *n.* ओखती okhati
medieval *adj.* मध्ययुको madhyauko
mediocre *adj.* साधारण sadharan
meditate *v.* ध्यान/चिन्तन गर्नु dhyan/chintan garnu
meditation *n.* ध्यान dhyan
medium *n.* मध्यम madhyam
meek *adj.* नम्र namra
meet *n.* जमघट jamghat
meeting *n.* सभा बैठक sabha baithak
melancholic *adj.* विषादग्रस्त vishadgrast
melancholy *n./adj.* उदासीनता udasinta
melee *n.* भिडन्त bhidant
melliflous *adj.* सुमधुर sumdhur
melodious *adj.* मनोहर manohar
melody *n.* मधुर गीत/संगीत madhur git/sangit
melon *n.* तरबुजा tarbuja

melong *n.* खर्बुजा kharbuja

melt *v.* पग्लनु paglanu

member *n.* सदस्य sadasya

membrane *n.* झिल्ली jhilli

memento *n.* सम्झौटो samjhoto

memo(randum) *n.* लेखोट lekhot

memorable *adj.* सम्झन लायकको samjhana layak ko

memorial *n.* स्मारक smarak

memorize *v.* याद गर्नु yad garnu

memory *n.* सम्झना samjhana layak ko

men *n.* लोग्नेमान्छेहरू logne manchhe haru

menace *n.* धमकी dhamki

mend *v.* मर्मत गर्नु marmat garnu

mendacious *adj.* झूटो jhuto

mendicant *v.* भिखारी bhikhari

menfolk *n.* लोग्ने-मानिसहरू logne manis haru

menstruation *n.* रजस्वला rajaswala

mental *adj.* मानसिक mansik

mention *n.* उल्लेख ullekh

mentor *n.* परामर्शदाता pramarshdata

menu *n.* खानेकुराको सूची khane kura ko suchi

merchandise *n.* व्यापारका मालसामान wyapar ka mal saman

merchant *n.* व्यापारी wyapari

merciful *adj.* दयालु dayalu

merciless *adj.* निष्ठुर nishthur

merciry *n.* पारो paro

mercury *n.* बुध ग्रह budh graha

mere *n.* पोखरी pokhari

merely *adv.* मात्रा matra

merge *v.* गाभ्नु gabhnu

merger *n.* मिसिने काम misine kam

merit *n.* गुण gun

meritorious *adj.* योग्य yogya

mermaid *n.* मत्स्यकन्या matsyakanya

merriment *n.* खसीयाली khusiyali

merry *n.* हर्ष harsh

mess *n.* लठीबज्र lathi bajra

messaenger *n.* सन्देश पुऱ्याउने sandesh puraune

message *n.* सन्देश sandesh

messiah *n.* यिसुखिष्ट yisukhisht

metal *n.* धातु dhatu

metamorphosis *n.* रूप-परिवर्तन roop-parivartan

meteor *n.* उल्का ulka

method *n.* उपाय upaya

meticulous *adj.* अति सावधान ati sawdhan

metre/meter *n.* मिटर mitar

metropolis *n.* महानगर maha nagar

mew *n.* म्याउम्याउ myau myau

mica *n.* अभ्रक abhrak

mice *n.* मूसाहरू musa haru

microbe *n.* जीवाणु jiwanu

microcosm *n.* लघु ब्रह्माण्ड laghu brahmand

microphone *n.* माइक maik

microscope *n.* सूक्ष्मदर्शक sukshamdarshak

midday *n.* मध्यान्ह madhyanha

midden *n.* फोहोरको थुप्रो fohorko thupro

middle *adj.* माझ majh

middle age *n.* अधबैंसे उमेर adhbainse umer

middle class *n.* मध्यम वर्ग madhyam warg

middleweight *n.* केजीसम्मको तौल pachhattar keji samma ko taul

midnight *n.* आधारात adha rat

midsummer *n.* मध्यग्रीष्म madhyagrishm

midwife *n.* सुँडेनी sundeni

mien *n.* व्यक्तिको चालढाल vyaktiko chaldhal

might *n.* बलियो baliyo

migraine *n.* कपाल दुख्ने रोग kapal dhukne rog

migrant *n.* प्रवासी prawasi

migration *n.* बसाइ सर्ने काम basai sarne kam

mild *adj.* नरम naram

mildew *n.* ढुसी dhusi

mile *n.* माइल mail

milestone *n.* कोसेढुङ्गा kose dhunga

milieu *n.* वातावरण watawaran

military *n.* सेना sena

milk *n.* दूध dudh

milkman *n.* ग्वाला gwala

milky *adj.* दूध जस्तो dudh jasto

milky way *n.* आकाशगंगा akash ganga

mill *n.* कारखाना karkhana

millennium *n.* हजार वर्षको अवधि hajar warsh ko awadhi

millepede *n.* खजूरो khajuro

miller घट्टको मालिक ghat ko malik

millet *n.* कोदो kodo

million *n.* दस लाख das lakh

millionaire *n.* लखपति lakhpati

millstone *n.* जाँतो janto

mind *n.* मन man

mindful *adj.* विचारशील wicharshail

mine *pron.* मेरो mero

mineral *n.* खनिज पदार्थ khanij padarh

mingle *v.* मिसिनु misnu

mingle *v.* मिसिनु misnu

mingy *adj.* नीच neech

miniature *n.* सानु आकार को वस्तु sanu akar ko wastu

minimum *n.* सबभन्दा कम sab bhanda kam

mining *n.* खानी खन्ने काम khani khanne kam

minister *n.* मंत्री mantri

ministry *n.* मन्त्रालय mantralaya

mink *n.* एक जन्तु ek jantu

minority *n.* अल्पसंख्या alpsankhya

minstrel *n.* गाइने gaine

mint *n.* टकसार taksar

minus *n.* घटाउ ghatau

minutely *adv.* ठीक हिसाबले thik hisab le

minx *n.* अटेरी ateri

miracle *n.* चमत्कार chamatkar

miraculous *adj.* चमत्कारपूर्ण chamatkarpurn

mirage *n.* मृगतृष्णा mrigtrishna

mire *n.* हिलो hilo

mirror *n.* ऐना aina

mirth *n.* हाँसो-खुशी haso-khushi

misadventrue *n.* दुर्भाग्य durbhagya

miscalculate *v.* गलत अन्दाज गर्नु galat andaj garnu

miscariage *n.* तुहिने काम tuhine kam

miscellaneous *adj.* विविध wiwidh

mischance *n.* दुर्भाग्य durbhagya

mischief *n.* उपद्रो upadro

mischievous *adj.* उपद्रयाहा upadhryaha

misconception *n.* गलत धारणा galat dharna

misconduct *n.* दुराचार durachar

miscontrue *v.* गलत अर्थ लाउने galat arth laune

miscount *v.* अशुद्ध गणना गर्नु ashudh ganana garnu

miscreant *adj.* दुष्ट dushta

miscreant *n.* आदिवासी adiwasi

misdeed *n.* खराब काम kharab kam

misdeed *n.* दुष्कर्म dushkaram

miserable *adj.* दुखी duhkhi

misery *n.* दुःख duhkhi

misfortune *n.* आपत् apat

misgiving *n.* शंका shanka

misguide *v.* बहकाउनु bahkaunu

mishap *n.* दुर्घटना durghatna

misinform *v.* गलत सूचना दिनु galat suchana dinu

misinterpret *v.* गलत अर्थ लगाउनु galat arth lagaunu

mislead *v.* कुबाटो लैजानु kubato laijanu

mismanage *v.* खराब बन्दोबस्त गर्नु kharab bandobast garnu

mismanagement *n.* खराब इन्तजाम kharab intjam

misprint *v.* गलत छाप्नु galat chapnu

misquote *v.* गलत उद्धरण दिनु galat udwaran dinu

misrule *n.* कुशासन kushasan

miss *n.* कुमारी kumari keti

missile *n.* क्षेप्यास्त्र kshepyastra

mission *n.* खटाएको काम khataeko kam

misspent *adj.* व्यर्थै न्ष्ट भएको vyarthe nasht bhaeko

mist *n.* कुहिरो kuhiro

mistake *n.* भूल bhul

mistaken *adj.* भ्रममा परेको bhram ma pareko

mister/Mr. *n.* महाशय mahashaya

mistletoe *n.* हरचुर harchur

mistress *n.* मालिक्नी malikni

mistrust *n.* अविश्वास awishwas

misunderstand *v.* गलत सम्झनु galat samjhanu

misunderstanding *n.* गलतफहमी galat phahami

misuse *n.* दुरुपयोग durupyog

mix *v.* मिसाउनु misaunu

mixture *n.* मिश्रण mishran

moan *v.* विलाप गर्नु wilap garnu

mob *n.* हूल hul

mobile *adj.* हलचल गर्न सक्ने halchal garna sakne

mock *n.* नक्कल nakkal

mode *n.* काइदा kaida

model *n.* नमूना namuna

moderate *adj.* ठिकैको thikari ko

modern *adj.* आधुनिक adhunik

modernize *v.* आधुनिक बनाउनु adhunik banaunu

modest *adj.* सेखी नगर्ने sekhi na garne

modesty *n.* नम्रता namrata

modicum *n.* थोरै परिमाण thorae pariman

moist *adj.* भिजेको bhijeko

moisture *n.* ओस os

molar *n.* चपाउने दाँत chapaune dant

mole *n.* छुचुन्द्रो chhuchundro

molecule *n.* अणु anu

molest *v.* सताउनु sataunu

molten *adj.* पग्लेको pagleko

moment *n.* छिन chhin

momentous *adj.* गहकिलो gahkilo

momentum *n.* गति gati

monarch *n.* राजा raja

monarchy *n.* राजतंत्र raj tantra

monastery *n.* मठ math

monday *n.* सोमवार somwar

monetary *adj.* आर्थिक arthik

money *n.* पैसा paisa

moneylender *n.* रिन दिने साहु rin dine sahu

mongoose *n.* न्याउरी मूसो nyarui muso

mongrel *n.* मिसाहा कुकुर misaha kukur

monk *n.* योगी yogi

monkey *n.* बाँदर bandar

monopoly *n.* एकाधिकार ekadhikar

monotonous *adj.* न्यास्रो nyasro

monsoon *n.* बर्खा barkha

monster *n.* राक्षस rakshas

month *n.* महिना mahina

monthly *adj.* मासिक masik

monument *n.* स्मारक smarak

moo *v.* गाई कराउनु gai karaunu

mood *n.* मन को अवस्था man ko awastha

moody *adj.* उदास udasinta

moon *n.* चन्द्रमा chandrama

moonlight *n.* जून jun

mop *v.* पुछ्नु puchhnu

moral *n.* नीतिशिक्षा niti siksha

moral courage *n.* नैतिक साहस naitik sahas

moral force *n.* नैतिक बल naitik bal

morale *n.* हौसला hausala

morality *n.* नैतिकता naitikta

morally *adv.* नैतिक ढङ्गले naitik dhang le

mordant *adj.* कटु katu

more *adj.* बढी badhi

moreover *adv.* अझ ajha

mores *n.* रीति-थिति riti-thiti

morning *n.* बिहान bihana

morning star *n.* ुक्रतारा shukra tara

morrow *n.* भोलिको दिन bholiko din

morsel *n.* गाँस gans

mortal *adj.* मरणशील maran shil

mortgage *n.* बन्धकी bandhaki

mortuary *n.* लाश राख्ने घर lash rakhne ghar

mosque *n.* मस्जिद masjid

mosquito *n.* लाम्खुट्टे lam khutte

mosquito net *n.* झूल jhul

moss *n.* काई kaida

most *adj./adv.* सबभन्दा sab bhanda kam

mostly *adv.* धेरैजसो dherai jaso

mote *n.* धूलोको कण dhuloko kan

mother *n.* आमा ama

mother tongue *n.* मातृभाषा matribhasha

mother-in-law *n.* सासू sasu

motherly *adj.* आमाको गुण भएकी ama ko gun bhaeki

mother-of-pearl *n.* सिपी sipi

motion *n.* चाल chal

motion picture *n.* चलचित्र chalchitra

motionless *adj.* स्थिर sthir

motor *n.* मोटर motar

motor car *n.* मोटरकार motarkar

motorcade *n.* मोटर.गाडीहरूको लाम motargadi haru ko lam

motorcycle *n.* मोटरसाइकल motar saikal

mottled *adj.* टाटेपाटे tatte-phate

motto *n.* सिद्धान्त siddhant

motto *n.* आदर्श-वाक्य adarsh vakya

moujik *n.* रूसी किसान rusi kisan

mould *v.* ढाल्नु dhalnu

moulder *v.* मक्किएर धूलो हुनु makkiaer dhulo hunu

mound *n.* ढिस्को dhiksko

mount *v.* घोडा चढ्नु ghoda chadhnu

mountain *n.* पहाड pahad

mountaineer *n.* पर्वतारोही parwatarohi

mountainous *adj.* पहाडी pahadi

mourn *v.* शोक मनाउनु shok manaunu

mourning *n.* आशौच ashauch

mouse *n.* मूसाहरू musa haru

moustache *n.* जुँघा jungha

mouth *n.* मुख mukh

mouthful *n.* मुखभरि mukhbhari

movable *adj.* चल्ने chalne sarne

move *n.* चाल chal

movement *n.* चाल chal

movie *n.* चलचित्र chalchitra

moving *adj.* मन छुने man chune

mr *n.* श्री shri

mrs *n.* श्रीमती shrimati

much *adj.* धेरै dherai

mucus *n.* सिँगान singan

mud *n.* हिलो hilo

muffler *n.* गलबन्दी gal bandi

mug *n.* गिलास gilas

mulberry *n.* किम्बु kimbu

mulct *v.* जरिमाना गर्नु jarimana garnu

mule *n.* खच्चर khachchar

mullet *n.* समुद्री माछाको प्रकार samudari machhako prakar

multi-colo(u)red *adj.* बहुरङ्गी bahi rangi

multiple *adj.* बहुल bahul

multiplication *n.* गुणा guna

multiply *v.* गुन्नु gunnu

multi-purpose *adj.* बहुमुखी bahu mukhi

multi-storey *n.* धेरै तला भएको dherai tala bhaeko

multitude *n.* घुइँचो ghuincho

mum चूप choop

mumps *n.* हाँडे रोग hande rog

munch *v.* चपाउनु chapaunu

mundane *adj.* सांसारिक sansarik

municipal *adj.* नगरपालिका nagarpalika

municipality *n.* नगरपालिका nagar palika

munitions *n.* हातहतियार hathatiyar

murder *n.* हत्या hatya

murderer *n.* हत्यारा hatyara

murky *adj.* अँध्यारो andhyaro

murmur *v.* गुनगुनाउनु gun gunaunu

muscle *n.* सुम्लो sumlo

muscular *adj.* पुष्ट pusht

museum *n.* म्युजियम myujiyam

mushroom *n.* च्याउ chyau

music *n.* संगीत सम्बन्धी sangit sambandhi

musical instrument *n.* साजबाज sajbaj

musician *n.* संगीकार sangit kar

musk *n.* कस्तूरी kasturi

musk deer *n.* कस्तूरी मृग kasturi mriga

muslim *n.* मुस्लिम muslim

muslin *n.* मलमल malmal

muss *n.* खजमजाउनु khajmajaunu

must *mod.* पर्छ parchha

mustang *n.* अमेरिकामा पाइने जंगली घोड़ा americama paine junglee ghora

mustard *n.* रायो raio

mustard green *n.* तोरी tori

muster *v.* एकत्र गर्नु ektar garnu

mute *adj.* लाटो lato

mutiny *n.* सैनिक विद्रोह sainik widroh

mutter *v.* फतफताउनु phat phataunu

mutton *n.* खसी khasi

mutual *adj.* आपसको apas ko

mutually *adv.* आपसमा apas ma

muzzle *n.* थुतुनु thutunu

muzzy *adj.* निस्तेज nistej

my *pron.* मेरो mero

mycology *n.* च्याउको विज्ञान chiauko vigyan

myriad *n.* ठूलो संख्या thulo sankhya

myself *pron.* म आफैँ ma aphain

mysterious *adj.* रहस्यमय rahasya maya

mystery *n.* रहस्य rahasya

mystique *n.* रहस्यात्मकता rahasyatamkata

myth *n.* पौराणिक कथा pauranik katha

mythology *n.* पौराणिक कथामाला pauranik kathamala

N

nab *v.* समाल्नु samatnu

nadir *n.* अधोबिन्दु adhobindu

naiad *n.* जलदेवी jaldevi

nail *n.* किला kila

nainsook *n.* मिहीन सुती लुगा mihin suto luga

naive *adj.* सोझो sojho

naked *adj.* नाङ्गो nango

name *n.* नाम nam

nameless *adj.* नाम नभएको namna bhaeko

nankeen *n.* सूती लुगा suti luga

nanny-goat *n.* बाखी bakhi

nap *n.* एक छिनको निद्रा ek chinko nidra

nappy *n.* नानीको थाङ्ना naniko thana

narcissism *n.* आत्ममोह atammoh

narcotic *n.* वर्णन गर्नु madak/lagu padarth

narrate *v.* वर्णन गर्नु warnan garnu

narrow-minded *adj.* सङ्कीर्ण sankirn

nasal *adj.* नाके nake

nasty *adj.* फोहोर phohor

natal *adj.* जन्मको janamko

nation *n.* राष्ट्र rashtra

national *adj.* राष्ट्रीय rashtriya

nationalism *n.* राष्ट्रवाद rashtrawad

nationality *n.* राष्ट्रीय rashtriyata

native *n.* बासिन्दा basinda

nativity *n.* जन्मको janamko

natural *adj.* प्राकृतिक prakritik

naturalism *n.* प्रकृतिवाद prakritiwad

naturalize *v.* नागरिकता दिनु nagrikta dinu

naturally *adv.* स्वभावैले swabhawai le

nature *n.* प्रकृति prakritik

naught *n.* केही होइन kehi hoin

naughty *adj.* दृष्ट dusht

nausea *n.* अमन aman
naval *adj.* सागरीय sagriye
navel *n.* नाइटो naito
navigable *adj.* जहाज चलाउने योग्य jahaj chalaune yogya
neap *n.* लघु ज्वारभाटा laghu jawarbhata
near *adv.* नजिक najik
nearby *adj.* नजिकैको najikai ko
nearly *adv.* लगभग lagbhag
near-skghted *adj.* निकटदर्शी nikat darshi
neat *adj.* सफा sapha
neat and clean *adj.* सफा-सुघर sapha sugghar
neatly *adv.* सफासँग sampha sanga
nebula *n.* नीहारिका niharika
nebulous *adj.* धमिलो dhamilo
necessaries *n.* बाँच्ने सामग्री banchhne samagri
necessary *adj.* जरुरी jaruri
necessitous *adj.* दरिद्र daridar
necessity *n.* जरुरत jarurat
neck *n.* गर्दन gardan
necklace *n.* हार har
necktie *n.* नेकटाइ nektai
necropolis *n.* चिहान chihan
nectar *n.* अमृत amrit
need *n.* खाँचो khancho
needful *adj.* आवश्यक awashyak
needle *n.* सियो siyo
needless *adj.* अनावश्यक anawashyak

needlework *n.* सिलाइ silai
neglect *n.* बेवास्ता bewasta
negligence *n.* लापर्बाही laparbahi
negligent *adj.* असावधान asawdhan
negotiation *n.* वार्ता warta
negro *n.* हब्सी habsi
neigh *v.* घोड़ा हिनहिनाउनु ghora hinhinaunu
neighbo(u)r *n.* छिमेकी chhimeki
neighbo(u)rhood *n.* छिमेक chhimek
neighbo(u)ring *adj.* छिमेक/आसपासको chiimek/aspas ko
neither *adj./adv./conj.* पनि pani
neo *pref.* नयाँ nayan
neolithic *adj.* नव प्रस्तर nav prastar
neologism *n.* नयाँ शब्द nayan shabd
neon *n.* रंगहीन ग्यास rangheen gyas
nephew *n.* भतिजा bhatija
nephritis *n.* मिर्गौंला सुनिने रोग mirgalo sunine rog
nepotism *n.* नातावाद natawad
neptune *n.* वरुण ग्रह warnungraha
nerve *n.* स्नायु snayu
nervous *adj.* आत्तिएको attieko
nervous system *n.* स्नायु प्रणाली snayu pranali
nest *n.* गुँड gund
nestle *v.* आरामसित बस्नु aramsit basnu

net *n.* जाली jal

nettle *n.* सिस्नु sisnu

network *n.* जालो jalo

neuralgia *n.* स्नायुरोग snayurog

neuter *adj.* नपुंसक napunsak

never *adv.* कहिले पनि होइन kahile pani hoina

never mind *v.* केही छैन kehi chhaina

nevertheless *adv.* त्यसो भए तापनि tyaso bhae tapani

new *adj.* नयाँ nayan

new moon *n.* औंसी aunsi

new year *n.* नयाँ/नव वर्ष nayan/ nawa warsh

newcomer *n.* नवागन्तुक nawagantuk

newly *adj.* हालको halko

newly-wed *n./adj.* हाल बिहे भएको halbihe bhaeko

news *n.* खबर khabar

newspaper *n.* अखबार akhbar

news-stand *n.* अखबार पसल akhbarpasal

newsworthy *adj.* समाचारयोग्य samachar yogya

newt *n.* छेपारा जस्तो प्राणी chepara jasto prani

next *adj.* अर्को arko

nib *n.* kalamko tuppo

nice *adj.* राम्रो ramro

nick *n.* सानो कटाइ sano katai

nickel *n.* निकल nikal

nickname *n.* उपनाम upnam

niece *n.* भतिजी bhatiji

niggrdly *adj.* कंजूस kanjus

nigh *adv.* नजीक najeek

night *n.* रात rat

nightingale *n.* जुरेली रनतमसप

nightlife *n.* रातको मनोरंजन rat ko manoranjan

nightmare *n.* डरलाग्दो सपना dar lagdo sapana

nightshirt *n.* सुल्ले बेलामा लाउने कमिज sutne bela ma laune kamij

nightsoil *n.* रातको दिसापिसाब rat ko disa pisab

nihillism *n.* शून्यवाद shunyawad

nil *n.* शून्य shunya

nimble *adj.* छिटो chhito

nimbus *n.* प्रभावमंडल prabhavmandal

nincompoop *n.* मूर्ख murkh

nine *n.* नौ nau

nineteen *n.* उन्नाइस unnais

ninety *n.* नब्बे nabbe

ninth *n.* नवौँ nawaun

nippers *n.* चिम्टा chimta

nipple *n.* स्तनको मुख esthan ko mukh

nippy *adj.* चिसो chiso

nirvana *n.* निर्वाण nirwan

nit *n.* लिखा likha

nitrogen *n.* नाइट्रोजन nitrogen

nitwit *n.* मूर्ख व्यक्ति murkh vyakti

no *adv.* अहँ ahan

no doubt *n.* निस्सन्देह nissandeh

no one *pron./adv.* पासो kohi pani hoina

noble *adj.* श्रेष्ठ shreshtha

nobody *n.* कोही होइन kohi hoina

nod *v.* टाउ को हल्लाउनु tauko hallaunu

noel *n.* क्रिस्मस christmas

noise *n.* आवाज awaj

noisome *adj.* हानिकर hanikar

noisy *adj.* ठूलो आवाज हुने thulo awaj hune

nomenclature *n.* नामावली namawali

nominal *adj.* नाम मात्र को nammatra ko

nominate *v.* मनोनीत गर्नु manonit garnu

nomination *n.* नियुक्ति niyukti

nominative *n.* कर्त्ता कारक kartakarak

nominee *n.* मनोनीत व्यक्ति manonit vyakti

none *adv.* कोही पनि होइन kohi pani hoina

non-existent *adj* काल्पनिक kalpanik

non-payment *n.* नतिर्ने काम natirne kam

nonplussed *adj.* छक्क परेको chhak pareko

nonsense *n.* बेमतलबको कुरो be matlab ko kuro

non-smoker *n.* धूम्रपान नगर्ने dhumra pan na gaarne

non-stop *adj.* न रोकिने na rokine

nook *n.* एक कुना मा ek kuna ma

noon *n.* मध्यान्ह madhyana

noose *n.* सामान्य paso

norm *n.* मानदंड mandand

normal *adj.* सामान्यतवरले samanya

normally *adv.* सामान्यतवरले samanya tawarle

north *n.* उत्तर uttar

north pole *n.* उत्तरी ध्रुव uttari dhruwa

north star *n.* ध्रुव तारा dhruwa tara

northern *adj.* उत्तरी uttari

northward *adv.* उत्तर तीर uttar tira

nose *n.* नाक naak

nose ring *n.* नाक को प्वाल bulaki

nosegay *n.* फूलको गुच्छा phulko gucha

nostril *n.* नाकको प्वाल nak ko pwal

not *adv.* नाइँ nain

notable *adj.* सम्झन लायकको samjhana layak ko

notation *n.* संकेत चिन्ह sanket chinha

note *n.* टिप्पणी tipaani

notebook *n.* सानु कापी sanu kapi

noted *adj.* प्रख्यात prakhyat

nothing *adj.* केही होइन kehi hoina

notice *n.* सूचना suchana

notify *v.* सूचित गर्नु suchit garnu

notion *n.* विचार wichar

notorious *adj.* बदनाम badnam

notwithstanding *adv.* तापनि tapani

nourish *v.* पोस्नु posnu

nourishment *n.* पोषण poshan

novel *n.* उपन्यास upanyas

novelist *n.* उपन्यासकार upanyaskar

novice *n.* अनाडी anadi

now *adv.* अहिले ahile

nowadays *adv.* आजकल ajkal

nowhere *adv.* कहीँ कतै पनि होइन kahin katai pani hoina

noxious *adj.* अहितकारी ahitkari

nozzle *n.* टुटी tuti

nub *n.* सानो गाँठो sano gantho

nubile *adj.* विवाह-योग्य vivah yogya

nuclear *adj.* विज सम्बन्धी beej sambandhi

nuclear energy *n.* आणविक शक्ति anwik shakti

nuclear family *n.* एकल परिवार ekal pariwar

nuclear power *n.* आणविक शक्ति anwik shakti

nucleus *n.* केन्द्र kendra

nude *adj.* नाङ्गो nango

nuisance *n.* हानी कारक बस्तु hani karak bastu

numb *adj.* लाटिएको latieko

number *n.* गन्ती ganti

number one *adj.* आफू एक नम्बर को afoo ek nambar ko

numerable *adj.* गन्ती गर्न सकिने ganti garn sakine

numeral *n.* अंक ank

numerous *adj.* धेरै dherai

nun *n.* जोगिनी jogini

nuptial *n.* विवाह सम्बन्धी wiwah sambandhi

nurse *n.* धाई dhai

nursing home *n.* नसिङ् होम narsin hom

nursling *n.* दूधे बालक dudhe balak

nurture *v.* पाल्नु palnu

nut *n.* सुपारी supari

nutcracker *n.* सरौता sarauta

nutmeg *n.* जाइफल jaiphal

nutrition *n.* पोषण poshan

nutritious *adj.* पौष्टिक paushtik

nuzzle *v.* नाकले छुनु वा दल्नु nakle chunu wa dalnu

nylon *n.* नाइलन nailan

nymph *n.* अप्सरा apsara

nymphet *n.* रहरलाग्दी reharlagdi

O

o, oh *int.* हो ho

oak *n.* कटुसको रूख katusko rukh

oat *n.* जौ jao

oath *n.* किरिया kiriya

oats *n.* जई धान्य jai dhanya

obdurate *adj.* हठी hathi

obedience *n.* आज्ञापालन agya palan

obedient *adj.* आज्ञाकारी agya kari

obeisance *n.* प्रणाम pranam

obelisk *n.* शुलाकार स्तम्भ shulakar stambh

obese *adj.* साहै मोटो sahe moto

obesity *n.* मोटोपन motopan

obey *v.* आज्ञा पालन गर्नु agya palan garnu

object *n.* वस्तु wastu

objection *n.* विरोध wirodh

objective *n.* लक्ष laksha

oblation *n.* नैवेद्य naivaidhya

obligate *v.* बाध्य गर्नु badhya garnu

obligation *n.* कर्त्तव्य kartawya

obligatory *adj.* कर/बाध्य गराउने kar/badhya garaune

oblige *v.* उपकार गर्नु upkar garnu

oblique *adj.* तेर्सो terso

obliterate *v.* मेट्नु metnu

oblong *adj.* लाम्चो lamcho

obnoxious *adj.* घृणित ghrinit

obscene *adj.* अश्लील ashlil

obscure *adj.* धमिलो पर्नु dhamilo parnu

obsequies *n.* अन्त्येष्टि antyeshti

observation *n.* अवलोकन awlokan

observatory *n.* वेधशाला wedhshala

observe *v.* अवलोकन awlokan garnu

obsolete *adj.* बेचल्तीको be chalti ko

obstacle *n.* तगारा tagaro

obstinate *adj.* जिद्दीवाल jiddiwal

obstruct *v.* बाधा दिनु badha dinu

obstruction *n.* अल्झो aljho

obtain *v.* पाउनु paunu

obtainable *adj.* मिल्ने योग्य milne yog

obverse *n.* मुख चित्त mukh chit

obviate *v.* हटाउनु hataunu

obvious *adj.* स्पष्ट spasht

occasion *n.* औसर ausar

occasionally *adv.* कहिलेकाहीँ हुने kahile kahin

occident *n.* पश्चिम को दिशा paschim ko desha

occult *adj.* गुप्त gupt

occupation *n.* पेशा pesha

occupy *v.* ओगट्नु ugatanu

occur *v.* हुनु hunu

occurrence *n.* संयोग sangyog

ocean *n.* महासागर mahasagar

o'clock *n.* बजे baje

octane *n.* पेट्रोलको गुण बुझाउने वस्तु petrolko gun bujhaune vastu

octroi *n.* चुँगी chungi

odd *adj.* अनौठो anautho

oddment *n.* रहलपहल rahalpahal

odds *n.* फरक pharak

odds and ends *n.* छूटफूट chhutphut

odour *n.* गन्ध gandh

odyssey *n.* घटनापूर्ण भ्रमण ghatnapurjha bhraman

of *prep.* को ko

off *adv.* अलग alag

off and on *adv.* बेलाबेलामा bela bela ma

off chance *n.* कम सम्भावना kam sambhawan

off colo(u)r *adj.* अस्वस्थ aswasth

offbeat *adj.* असामान्य asamanya

offence *n.* कसुर kasur

offend *v.* सताउनु sathauanu

offender *n.* अपराधी apradhi

offensive *n.* आक्रामक akramak

offer *n.* प्रस्ताव prastaw

offering *n.* सौगात saugat

offhand *adj.* बिनातयारी bina tayari

office *n.* कार्यालय karyalaya

officer *n.* अधिकृत adhikrit

offset *v.* क्षति पूरा गर्नु kshatipura garnu

offshoot *n.* हाँगा hanga

offspring *n.* सन्तान santan

often *adv.* अक्सर aksar

ogle *v.* आँखा लड़ाउनु aankha ladaunu

ogre *n.* मान्छे खाने राक्षस manche khane rakshas

ohm *n.* विद्युत प्रतिरोधको एकांक vidhyut pratirodhko ekank

oil *n.* तेल tel

oil colo(u)r *n.* तेल रङ्ग tel rang

oil painting *n.* तैलचित्र tail chitra

oil well *n.* तेलको कूवा tel ko kuwa

oilcake *n.* तेल बस्तु tel bastu

oilfield *n.* तेल खानी telkhani

oily *adj.* चिल्लो chillo

ointment *n.* लेप lep

okay(ok) *n.* स्वीकृति swikriti

okra *n.* रामतोरियाँ ram toriyan

old *adj.* पुरानो purano

old age *n.* बुढेसकाल budheskal

old hand *n.* अनुभवी मानिस anubhawi manis

old hat *adj.* पुरानो ढर्राको purano dharra ko

oldest *adj.* सबभन्दा जेठो sab bhanda jetho

old-fashioned *adj.* पुरानो ढाँचाको purano dhancha ko

oligarchy *n.* अल्प-तंत्र alap-tantra

olive *n.* जैतून jaitun

olive branch *n.* शान्तिको प्रतीक shanti ko pratik

omelet(te) *n.* अम्लेट amlet

omen *n.* शकुन shakun

omen *n.* शकुन shakun

ominous *adj.* अपशकुन apsakun

ominous *adj.* अनिष्टसूचक anishthasuchak

omission *n.* छूट chut

omit *v.* छोड्नु chon

omnipresence *n.* सर्वविषय ज्ञान sarvvishay gyan

on *prep.* मोटोपन ma

once *adv.* एक चोटि ek choti

once upon a time *adv.* एक समयमा eka samayma

oncoming *adj.* आउँदो aundo

one *n.* एक ek

one by one *adv.* एकएक गरेर ek ek garera

one-eyed *adj.* कानो kano

onerous *adj.* मेहनत चाहिने mehnat chahine

one-sided *adj.* एकतर्फी ek tarphi

ongoing *adj.* चल्दै गरेको chaldai gareko

onion *n.* प्याज pyaj

onlooker *n.* तमासे tamase

only *adj.* केवल kewal

onrush *n.* प्रवाह prawah

onset *n.* हमला hamla

onslaught *n.* भीषण आक्रमण bheeshan akarman

onward *adv.* अघिअघि aghi aghi

onyx *n.* दामी पत्थर dami pathar

ooze *v.* चुहनु chuhnu

opacity *n.* अपारदर्शिता apardarshita

opaque *adj.* अपारदर्शी apardarshi

open *adj.* खुला khula

open-air *adj.* खुला khula

open-handed *adj.* उदार udar

opening *n.* उद्घाटन udghatan

openly *adv.* खुलस्त khulast

open-minded *adj.* खुला मनको khulamanko

opera *n.* गीती-नाटय giti-natay

operable *adj.* चिरफार गर्न हुने chirphar garn hune

operate *v.* चलाउनु chalaunu

operation *n.* चिर फार chir phar

operator *n.* संचालक sanchalak

ophthalmic *adj.* आँखा को ankhako

opiate *n.* निद्रा लगाउने औषधि nindra lagune aushdhi

opinion *n.* विचार wichar

opium *n.* अफीम aphim

opponent *n.* विपक्षी wipakshi

opportunism *n.* अवसरवाद avsarwad

opportunity *n.* अवसर awsar

oppose *v.* विरोध गर्नु wirodh garnu

opposite *adj.* उल्टो ulto

opposition *n.* विरोध wirodh

oppress *v.* अत्याचार गर्नु atyachar garnu

opt *v.* चुन्नु chunu

optician *n.* चस्मा बनाउने ब्यक्ति chasma banaune baykti

optimist *n.* आशावादी asha wadi

optimum *adj.* अनुकूलतम anukultam

option *n.* रोजी roji

optional *adj.* इच्छाधीन ichchha dhin

opus *n.* संगीत रचना sangit rachna

or *conj.* अथवा athawa

oral *adj.* मुखको mukh ko

orange *n.* सुन्तला suntala

orb *n.* गोला gola

orbit *n.* आखाको घर aakha ko ghar

orchard *n.* बगैँचा bagaincha

orchid *n.* सुनाखरी sunakhari

ordeal *n.* कठिन परीक्षा kathin pariksha

order *n.* हुकुम hukum

orderly *n.* काइदासित kaida sita

ordinance *n.* अध्यादेश adhyadesh

ordinary *adj.* साधारण sadharan

ordnance *n.* युद्धसमग्री yudhsmagri

ore *n.* धाउ dhau

organ *n.* अङ्ग ang

organism *n.* जीव jeev

organization *n.* संस्था sanstha

organize *v.* बन्दोबस्त गर्नु bandobast garnu

orgasm *n.* कामोत्तेजनाको चरमबिन्दु kamuttejanako charambindu

orient *n.* पूर्वका purwaka

oriental *adj.* पूर्वीय purwiya

orientate *v.* अनुकूलन anukulan

orifice *n.* छिद्र chidra

origin *n.* उत्पत्ति utpatti

original *adj.* सक्कली sakkali

originate *v.* पैदा गराउनु/हुनु paida garaunu/hunu

ornament *n.* गहना gahana

ornithology *n.* चराचुरुङ्गीको विज्ञान chrachurangiko vigyan

orphan *n.* टुहुरो tuhuro

orphanage *n.* अनाथालय anathalaya

orthodox *adj.* कट्टर kattar

orthography *n.* हिज्जे hijje

ostler *n.* सईस sais

other *adj.* अर्को arko

otherwise *conj.* नत्र natra

ouch *n.* ऐय्या eya

ounce *n.* औंस auns

ounce *n.* तौलको एकांक tolko ekank

our *pron.* हाम्रो hamro

oust *v.* निकाल्नु nikalnu

out *n./v.* बाहिर bahira

out of date *adj.* गुज्रेको gujreko

out of order *adj.* बिग्रेको bigreko

out-and-out *adv.* हरेक तबरले harek tabar le

outboard *adj.* जहाज वा नाउको बाहिर राखिएको jahaj wa nauko bahir rakhiyeko

outbreak *n.* दङ्गाफसाद danga phasad

outcaste *n.* घर वा साथीविहीन व्यक्ति ghar wa sathivihin vyakti

outclass उछिन्नु uchhinu

outcome *n.* नतिजा natija

outdoor *adj.* बाहिरी bahiri

outdoors *adv.* बाहिर bahira

outer *adj.* बाकिहरी bahiri

outface *n.* सामना गर्नु samna garnu

outfall *v.* ठाउँ जहाँ पानी खस्छ thau jahan pani khach

outfit *n.* सजावट sajawat

outflow *n.* बहाउ bahau

outgrowth *n.* विकास vikas

outing *n.* सफर saphar

outlandish *adj.* अनौठो anutho

outlaw *n.* निर्वासित nirwasit

outlay *n.* खर्च kharch

outlet *n.* निकास nikas

outline *n.* रूपरेखा rup rekha

outlive *v.* भन्दा बढ्ता बाँच्नु bhanda badhta banchnu

outlook *n.* दृष्टिकोण drishti kon

outlying *adj.* दूरस्थ durasth

outnumber *v.* सङ्ख्या बढी हुनु sankhya badhi hunu

out-patient *n.* अस्पतालमा देखाउन आउने रोगी asptalma dekhaun aune rogi

outpost *n.* चौकी chauki

outpouring *n.* उद्गार udgar

output *n.* उत्पादन utpadan

outright *adj./adv.* स्पष्ट spasht

outset *n.* शुरु shuru

outside *adv.* बाहिरपट्टि bahira patti

outsize *adj.* सामान्य आकार वा नापभन्दा ठूलो samanya akar wa napbhanda thulo

outskirts *n.* शहरको बाहिरी भाग shahar ko bahiri bhag

outsmart *v.* चलाकीले जित्नु chalakile jitnu

outspoken *adj.* खुलस्त कुरा गर्ने khulast kura garne

outspread *adj.* फिँजाएको phijaiko

outstreched *adj.* फेलाएको phelaiko

outvote *v.* धेरै मतले पराजित गर्नु dherai matle prajit garnu

outward *adv.* बाहिरतिरको bahira tira ko

outworn *adj.* पुरानो purano

ova *adj.* अण्डाकार andakar

oval *adj.* अण्डाकार andakar

oven *n.* चूलो chulo

over *prep.* माथि mathi

over and over *adv.* बारम्बार barambar

overall *adj.* समस्त samast

overat *v.* अति अभिनय गर्नु ati abhinay garnu

overbearing *adj.* अहङ्कारी ahankari

overcast *adj.* बादल badal

overcharge *v.* अधिक दाम लिनु वा माग्नु adhik dam linu wa magnu

overcoat *n.* ओभरकोट overcoat

overcome *v.* पराजित गर्नु prajeet garnu

overcrowded *adj.* खचाखच भरिएको khachakhach bhariyeko

overdose *n.* औषधिको अधिक मात्रा aushadhi adhik matra

overdue *adj.* म्याद नाघेको myad nagheko

overeat *v.* जरूरतभन्दा ज्यादा खानु jarooratbandh jyada khanu

overhear *v.* थाहा नदिकन सुन्नु thaha nadikana sunnu

overjoyed *adj.* ज्यादै हर्षित jyadai harshit

overland *adv.* स्थलमार्गबाट sthalmargbat

overlap *v.* खप्टिनु khap tinu

overleaf *adv.* पन्नाको अर्कोपट्टि pannako arkopatti

overload *n.* बढी भार badhi bhar

overlook *v.* देख्न नसक्नु dekhna na saknu

overnight *adv.* रातभरि rat bhari

overpower *v.* जित्नु jitnu

overreach *v.* चलाकीले जित्नु chalakile jitnu

overrule *v.* बदर/खारेज गर्नु badar/ kharej garnu

overseas *adj.* समुद्रपार samudra par

oversight *n.* भूल bhul

oversleep *v.* अबेरसम्म सुत्नु abresum sutnu

overspill *n.* पोखिएको कुरा pokhiyeko kura

overstate *v.* बढ़ाई-चढ़ाईकन भन्नु badhai-chadhaika bhanu

overstay *v.* अधिक बस्नु adhik vastu

overstep *v.* अतिक्रमण गर्नु atikraman garnu

overstrung *adj.* अति व्यग्र ati vyagra

overt *adj.* खुलस्त khulast

overtake *v.* उछिन्नु uchhinnu

overthrow *v.* उल्टाइदिनु ultai dinu

overtime *adj.* बढी समय को badhi samaya ko

overturn *v.* पल्टाउनु paltaunu

overwhelm *v.* ढाक्नु dhaknu

ovum *n.* अण्डाणु andanu

owe *v.* ऋणी हुनु rini hunu

owl *n.* लाटोकोसेरो lato kosero

own *adj.* उपभोग गर्नु aphnai

owner *n.* मालिक malik

ox *n.* गोरु goru

oxygen *n.* अक्सिजन oxygen

oyster *n.* सिपी sippi

P

pace *n.* कदम kadam

pack *n.* पोको poko

package *n.* पोको poko

pact *n.* सन्धि sandhi

pad *n.* गद्दा gadda

paddy *n.* धान dhan

padlock *n.* ताल्चा talcha

paediatrics *n.* बाल चिकित्सा bal chikitsa

page *n.* पाना pana

pageant *n.* तमाशा tamasha

pagoda *n.* नेपाली शैलीको मन्दिर nepali shaili ko mandir

pail *n.* बाल्टी balti

pain *n.* दुख dukh

painful *adj.* पीडादायी pida dayi

painless *adj.* पीडारहित pida rahit

paint *n.* रङ्ग rang

painter *n.* चित्रकार chitrakar

painting *n.* चित्रकारी chitrakari

pair *n.* जोडी jodi

pal *n.* साथी sathi

pale *adj.* फिक्का पहेलो phikkapahenlo

paling *n.* घोचाको बार ghochako bar

pallet *n.* गुन्द्री gundri

pallor *n.* फीकापन phikkapan

palm *n.* हरकेला harkela

palpitate *v.* धड्कनु dhadkanu

palpitation *n.* ढुकढुक dhuk dhuk

palsy *n.* पक्षाघात pakshaghat

pamper *v.* पुलपुल्याउनु pul pulyaunu

pamphlet *n.* पर्चा parcha

pan *n.* तावा tawa

panacea *n.* सर्वौषधि sarwaushadhi

pancake *n.* मालपुवा malpuwa

pancreas *n.* पछाउनी pachauni

panegyric *n.* गुणगान gungaan

pang *n.* वेदना wedana

panic *n.* भय bhaya

pannikin *n.* कप cup

panoply *n.* कवच kawach

panorama *n.* खुला दृश्य khula drishya

pant *v.* स्वाँ स्वाँ गर्नु swan swan garnu

pantaloons *n.* पतलून patloon

panther *n.* चितुवा chituwa

pantomime *n.* मूकाभिनय mukabhinay

papa *n.* बुबा buba

papaya *n.* मेवा mewa

paper *n.* कागज kagaj

paperback *n.* कागजको जिल्ला भएको किताब kagaj ko jilla bhaeko kitab

paperwork *n.* अफिसका लिखित कामहरू aphis ka likhit kam haru

papyrus *n.* जलबिरूवा jalbiruwa

par *n.* बराबरी barabari

parachute *n.* प्यारासुट pyarasut

parad *n.* जुलुस julus

paradise *n.* स्वर्ग swarg

paragraph *n.* अनुच्छेद anuchhed

paralysis *n.* पक्षाघात pakshaghat

paramount *adj.* सर्वोच्च sarwochcha

paramour *n.* जार jar

parapet *n.* प्रखाल prakhal

paraphrase *v.* अकैं शब्दमा व्याख्या गर्नु akkai shabdma vyakhaya garnu

parasite *n.* अरूको मुख ताक्ने aru ko mukh takne

parasol *n.* घाम छाता gham chhata

parboil *v.* उसिन्नु ussinu

parcel *n.* पोको poko

parchment *n.* चर्मपत्र charampatra

pardon *n.* क्षमा kshama

parents *n.* आमाबाबु ama babu

pariticpate *v.* भाग लिनु bhag linu

park *n.* उद्यान udyan

parlance *n.* बोलीको शैली boliko shaili

parliament *n.* संसद sansad

parlo(u)r *n.* बैठक baithak

parody *n.* खराब लकल kharab lakal

parrot *n.* सुगा suga

parse *v.* पद-परिचय दिनु padh-parichay dinu

part *n.* भाग bhag

part and parcel *n.* आवश्यक भाग awashyak

part with *v.* छोड्नु chhodnua

partial *adj.* आंशिक amshik

partiality *n.* पक्षपात pakshpat

participant *n.* सहभागी sah bhagi

particle *n.* कण kan

particularly *adv.* विशेषगरी wishesh gari

particulars *n.* विवरणहरू wiwaran haru

partidge *n.* तित्रा titra

parting *n.* बिदाइ bidai

partition *n.* विभाजन wibhajan

partiuclar *adj.* विशेष wishesh

partly *adv.* आंशिक रूपमा amshik rup ma

partner *n.* साथी sathi

partridge *n.* तित्रा titra

part-time *adj./adv.* आंशिक समयका लागि amshik samaya ka lagi

party *n.* जन समूह jan samuh

pass away *v.* मर्नु marnu

passenger *n.* यात्री yatri

passion *n.* अनुराग anurag

passionate *adj.* रिसाहा risaha

passive *adj.* निष्क्रिय nishkriya

passport *n.* राहदानी rah dani

past *n.* भूतकाल bhutkal

paste *n.* टाँस्नु tasnu

pastime *n.* मनोरंजन manoranjan

pastry *n.* केक cake

pasture *n.* खर्क khark

pat *n.* धाप dhap

patch *n.* जमीनको टुक्रा jamin ko tukra

patch pocket *n.* टालेको जस्तो खल्ती taleko jasto khalti

patch up *v.* मिलाउनु milaunu

patchwork *n.* टालटुल गर्ने काम taltul garne kam

pate *n.* टाउको tauko

paternal *adj.* बाबुको बाबुपट्टिको babu ko babi patti ko

path *n.* बाटो bato

pathetic *adj.* दया मायालाग्दो daya maya lagdo

pathetic *adj.* करूणाजनक karunajanak

pathology *n.* रोगरूको विज्ञान rogruko vigyan

pathos *n.* करूणरस karunras

patience *n.* धैर्य dhairya

patient *n.* बिरामी birami

patio *n.* आँगन aangan

patios *n.* स्थानीय बोली sthaniya boli

patrician *adj.* कुलीन kuleen

patrimony *n.* पैतृक सम्पत्ति paitrik sampati

patriot *n.* देशभक्त desh bhakta

patron *n.* संरक्षक samrakshak

patronize *v.* संरक्षण दिनु samrakshan dinu

pattern *n.* बुट्टा butta

pauper *n.* कङ्गाल kangal

pause *n.* विराम wiram

pave *v.* ढुङ्गा छाप्नु dhunga chhapnu

pavement *n.* सडकको पेटी sadak ko peti

paw *n.* पंजा panja

pawn *v.* बन्धक राख्नु bandhak rakhnu

pay *n.* तलब talab

pay off *v.* राम्रो नतिजा ल्याउनु ramro natija

payable *adj.* तिर्नु पर्ने tirnu parne

payload *n.* पैसा तिरेर राखिने भारी paisa tirera rakhine bhari

payment *n.* भुक्तानी bhuktani

pay-off *n.* घूस ghus

payroll *n.* तलबी सूची talabi suchi

pea *n.* मटर matar

peace *n.* शान्ति shanti

peaceful *adj.* शान्तिपूर्ण shantipurn

peaceful coexistence *n.* शान्तिपूर्ण सहअस्तित्व shantipurn sahastitwa

peach *n.* आरु को बोट aru ko boat

peacock *n.* मयूर mayur

peahen *n.* पोथी मुजुर pothi mujur

peak *n.* चुचुरो chuchuro

peal *n.* गडगडाहट gad gadahat

peanut *n.* बदाम badam

pear *n.* नास्पाती naspati

pearl *n.* मोती moti

pearl button *n.* सिपीको टाँक sipi ko tank

pearl onion *n.* छ्यापी chhyapi

peasant *n.* किसान kisan

peasantry *n.* किसानवर्ग kisan warg

pebble *n.* गोलो सानु ढुङ्ग golo sanu dhunga

peck *v.* ठुङ्नु thunnu

peculiar *adj.* अनौठो anautho

peddling *adj.* तुच्छ tuch

pedestrian *n.* बटुवा batuwa

pedicure *n.* खुट्टाको चिकित्सा khuttako chikitsa

peek *v.* चियाउनु chiaunu

peel *n.* बोक्रा bokra

peep *v.* च्याउनु chyaunu

peephole *n.* च्याउने प्वाल chyaune pwal

peerless *adj.* तुलना गर्न नसकिने tulna garna na sakine

peg *n.* किला kila

pell-mell *adv.* हतार गरेर hatar garer

pen *n.* कलम kalam

pen pal *n.* पत्रमित्र patra mitra

penalty *n.* दण्ड dand

penance *n.* प्रायश्चित praishchit

penchant *n.* अभिरूचि abhiruchi

pencil *n.* सिसाकलम sisa kalam

pendent *adj.* लट्केको latkeko

pending *adj.* टुङ्गो नलागेको tungo na lageko

penetrate *v.* पसाउनु pasaunu

penetration *n.* छिराइ chhirai

penfriend *n.* पत्रमित्र patra mitra

penicillin *n.* पेन्सिलिन pensilin

peninsula *n.* प्रायद्वीप praidweep

penis *n.* लिंग ling

penknife *n.* सानु चक्कु sanu chakku

pen-name *n.* उपनाम upnam

penniless *adj.* पैसाविहीन paisavihin

pension *n.* पेन्सन pensan

pentagon *n.* पंचभुज panchbhuj

pentameter *n.* पंचचरण panchcharan

peon *n.* पिउन piun

people *n.* जनता janta

per annu, *adj.* प्रतिवर्ष prati warsh

per capita *adj.* प्रतिव्यक्ति prati wyakti

percent *adj.* सयकडा sayakada

perception *n.* धारणा dharna

perchance *adv.* संयोगले sanyogle

peregrination *n.* यात्रा yatra

peremptory *adj.* हुकुम चलाउने hukum chalaunu

perfect *adj.* बिलकुल ठीक bilkul thik

perfectly *adv.* पूरातवरले pura tawar le

perforce *adv.* विवश भएर vivash bhaer

perform *v.* काम गर्नु kam garnu

performance *n.* काम गराइ kam garai

perfume *n.* मधुर सुबासमा madhur subashna

perhaps *adv.* सायद sayad

perimeter *n.* परिधि paridhi

period *n.* अवधि awadhi

periodical *adj.* समय समयमा हुने samaya samaya ma hune

peripatetic *adj.* भ्रमणशील bhrmansheel

perish *v.* नासिनु nasinu

perishable *adj.* बिग्रने bigrane

perliminary *adj.* सुरुको shuru ko

permanent *adj.* स्थायी sthayi

permission *n.* अनुमति anumati

permit *n.* अनुमति पत्र anumati patra

peroration *n.* भाषणको उपसंहार bhashanko upsanhar

perpendicular *n.* लम्ब lamb

perplexed *adj.* व्याकुल baykul

perquisite *n.* वेतनबाहेक दिइने सुविधा vetanbahek dine suvidha

persecute *v.* सताएनु satunu

persecution *n.* जुलुम julum

perseverance *n.* लगन lagan

persimmon *n.* हलुवाबेद haluwabed

persist *v.* जोड गर्नु jod garnu

person *n.* व्यक्ति wyakti

persona non grata *n.* स्वीकार नगरिएको व्यक्ति swikar na garieko wyakti

personal *adj.* निजी niji

personality *n.* व्यक्तित्व wyaktitwa

personally *adv.* आफै aphai

personnel *n.* कर्मचारी/कामदारहरू karm chari/kamdar haru

perspective *n.* परिप्रेक्ष paripreksha

perspex *n.* ऐना जस्तो देखिने प्लास्टिक पदार्थ ena jasto dekhine plastic padarth

perspiration *n.* पसिना pasina

perspire *v.* आउनु aaunu

persuade *v.* मनाउनु manauinu

persuasion *n.* बिन्तीभाउ binti bhau

pert *adj.* धृष्ट dhrisht

pertain *v.* को हुनु ko hunu

pertinacious *adj.* दृढ़ dridh

pertinent *adj.* सुहाउँदो suhaundo

peruse *v.* ध्यान दिएर पढ्नु dhyan deir padhnu

pessimism *n.* निराशावाद nirashawad

pest *n.* नाशकारी व्यक्ति nashkari wyakti

pester *v.* सताउनु sataunu

pestilence *n.* महामारी mahamari

pestle *n.* मुसल musal

pet *n.* प्यारो बस्तु pyaro wastu

petal *n.* फूलको पात phul ko pat

petitbourgeois *n.* निम्न मध्य वर्गको व्यक्ति niman madhya wargko vyakti

petiticoat *n.* फरिया fariya

petition *n.* बिन्तीपत्र binti patra

petrol *n.* पेट्रोल petrol

petroleum *n.* खनिज khanij

pettish *adj.* चाँडो रिसाउने chando risaune

petty *adj.* सामान्य samanya

pew *n.* गिर्जाघरको बेन्च वा आसन girjagharko bench wa asan

phantom *n.* भूत bhut

pharmacist *n.* औषधि तयार गर्ने व्यक्ति aushadhi tayar garne vyakti

pharmacy *n.* औषधि पसल aushadhi pasal

phase *n.* चरण charan

pheasant *n.* कालिज kalij

pheasant impeyan *n.* डाँफे danphe

phenol *n.* फिनेल phenyl

phew *interj.* छिः छयाः chi chya

phial *n.* सानु सिसी sanusisi

philanthropy *n.* लोकहित lokhit

philately *n.* डाक टिकट संग्रह dak ticket sangrah

philosopher *n.* दार्शनिक darshanik

philosophy *n.* दर्शनशास्त्र darshanshastra

phlegm *n.* खकार khakar

phone *n.* टेलिफोन teliphon

phony *adj.* नक्कली nakkali

photo *n.* फोटो photo

photocopy *n.* फोटोकापी photokapi

photograph *n.* तस्वीर taswir

phrase *n.* छोटो वाक्य chhoto wakya

phut *adv.* बिग्रनु bigarnu

physical *adj.* म्6176शारीरिक sharirik

physical exercise *n.* कसरत kasrat

physician *n.* डाक्टर daktar

physics *n.* भौतिकशास्त्र bhautik shastra

piano *n.* प्यानो pyano

piazza *n.* चोक chok

pick *v.* कोट्याउनु kotyaunu

pick up *v.* टिप्नु tipnu

pickaback *adv.* पिठ्यूँमा pithyuma

pickaxe खन्ती khanti

pickle *n.* अचार achar

pickpocket *n.* बगलीमारा baglimara

picnic *n.* पिकनिकब piknik

pictursque *adj.* आकर्षक akarshak

picutre *n.* तस्वीर taswir

piddle *v.* पिशाब गर्नु pishab garnu

pidgin *n.* मिश्रित भाषा mishrit bhasha

piece *n.* टुक्रा tukra

piecemeal *adv.* एक-एक गरेर eke ek garera

pierce *v.* छेड्नु chhednu

piety *n.* धर्म-निष्ठा dharam-nishta

pig *n.* सुँगुर sungur

pig *n.* सुँगुर sungur

pigeon *n.* परेवा parewa

pig-headed *adj.* जिद्दी jiddi

pigtail *n.* टुपी tupi

pike *n.* भाला bhala

pilaster *n.* भित्ता-स्तम्भ bhitta-satabh

pile *n.* थुप्रो thupro

piles *n.* अलकाई alkai

pilgrim *n.* यात्रु yatru

pill *n.* चक्की chakki

pillage *n.* नाश nash

pillar *n.* खम्बा khamba

pillow *n.* तकिया takiya

pilot *n.* विमानचालक wiman chalak

pimp *n.* दलाल dalal

pimple *n.* डन्डीफोर dandi phor

pin *n.* आलपिन alpin

pin down *v.* विवश गर्नु wiwash garnu

pincers *n.* चिम्टा chimtra

pinch *n.* चिम्टी chimti

pine *n.* सल्लो sallo

pine cone *n.* सिम्टा simta

pineapple *n.* भुइँकटहर bhuin kathar

pineers *n.* चिम्टा chimta

pingpong *n.* टेबुलटेनिस tebul tenis

pink *adj.* गुलाफी gulaphi

pinpoint *v.* किट्नु kitnu

pinprick *n.* घोचपोच ghoch pech

pint *n.* तरल वस्तुको नाप taral wastu ko nap

pioneer *n.* अगुवा aguwa

pious *adj.* धर्मात्मा dharmatma

pipe *n.* नली nali

pipedream *n.* असम्भव इच्छा asambaw

piping *n.* मुरलीवादन murliwadan

piping hot *adj.* अति तातो ati tato

pirate *n.* समुद्री डाँकू samudari daku

pisces *n.* मीन राशि min rashi

pisctachio *n.* पेस्ता pesta

piss *v.* मुलु mutnu

pistachio *n.* पेस्ता pesta

pistol *n.* पिस्तोल pistol

pit *n.* खाडल khadal

pit-a-pat *adv.* ट्याप-ट्याप गरेर tyap-tyap garer

pitch *n.* अलकत्रा alkatra

pitch-dark *adj.* चकमन्न अँध्यारो chak manna andhyaro

pitcher *n.* गाग्रो gagro

pitful *n.* कोमल komal

pitiable *adj.* दयनीय

pitiless *adj.* निर्दयी nirdayi

pittance *n.* थोरै पैसा

pity *n.* दया मया लाग्दो daya maya lagdo

placard *n.* प्लेकार्ड ple kard

place *n.* ठाउँ thaun

placenta *n.* सालनाल salnal

placid *adj.* शान्त shant

plagiarize *v.* अर्काको विचार वा लेखाई चोर्नु arkako vichar va lekhai chornu

plain *n.* समतल मैदान samtal maidan

plain sailing *n.* सरल कार्य saral karya

plainspoken *adj.* स्पष्टवक्ता spasht wakta

plaintiff *n.* वादी vadi

plan *n.* योजना yojana

plane *n.* हवाईजहाज hawai jahaj

planet *n.* ग्रह graha

plank *n.* फल्याक phalayk

planning *n.* योजना yojana

plant *n.* बिरुवा biruwa

plantain *n.* केरा kera

plantation *n.* बोट बिरुवा लगाएको जग्गा bot wiruwa lagaeko jagga

plasma *n.* प्लाविका plawika

plaster *n.* मसाला masala

plastic *n.* प्लास्टिक plastik

plate *n.* थाल thal

plateau *n.* पठार pathar

platform *n.* मंच manch

platitude *n.* सामान्य उक्ति samanya ukti

platoon *n.* सेनाको एक भाग senako ek bhaag

play *n.* खेल khel

play down *v.* महत्त्व कम गर्नु mahatthwa kam garnu

player *n.* खेलाडी kheladi

playground *n.* खेल मैदान khel maidan

playing card *n.* तास tas

playmate *n.* दाँतरी dauntari

play-off *n.* अतिरिक्त समयको खेल atirikta samaya ko khel

playwright *n.* नाटककार natak kar

plaza *n.* चोक chok

plea *n.* बिन्ती binti

plead *v.* बिन्ती गर्नु binti garnu

pleader *n.* वकील wakil

pleasant *adj.* रमाइलो ramailo

pleasantry *n.* ठट्टा thatta

please *v.* रिझाउनु rijhaunu

pleased *adj.* खुश khush

pleasing *adj.* रोचक rochak

pleasure *n.* आनन्द anand

pleat *n.* मुजा muja

pledge *n.* वाचा wacha

plenty *n.* प्रशस्त prashat

plethora *n.* धेरै मात्रा dherai matra

pliable *adj.* कमलो हुने kamlo hune

pliers *n.* पेन्चिस penchish

plight *n.* हालत halat

plot *n.* जग्गा jagga

plough *n.* हलो halo

ploy *n.* चतुर चाल chatur chal

pluck *v.* टिप्नु tipnu

plum *n.* आलुबखडा alu bakhda

plumage *n.* चराको प्वाँख charakho pawankh

plumber *n.* धारामिस्त्री dharamistri

plume *n.* प्वाँख pwankh

plunder *n.* लूटको माल lut ko mal

plunderer *n.* लुटेरा lutera

plunge *v.* डुब्नु dubnu

plural *n.* बहुवचन bahu wachan

plus *n.* थाप thap

plush *adj.* विलासमय vilasmaya

pluto *n.* यम ग्रह yam graha

ply *n.* पत्र patra mitra

plywood *n.* प्लाइउड plaiud

pneumonia *n.* फोक्सोको सुज phokso ko suj

pocket *n.* खल्ती khalti

pocketbook *n.* खल्तीमा राख्ने सानु किताब khalti ma rakhne sanu kitab'

pod *n.* कोसा kosa

podgy *adj.* छोटो र मोटो choto r moto

poem *n.* कविता kawita

poet *n.* कवि kawi

poetess *n.* महिला कवि mahilakawi

poetry *n.* कविता kawita

pogrom *n.* आयोजित हत्याकाण्ड ayojit hatyakand

poignant *adj.* मनलाई पीर पार्ने manlai peer parne

poinsettia *n.* लालुपाते lalupate

point *n.* चुच्चो chuchcho

point of view *n.* विचार wichar

point-blank *adj.* सोझै sojhai

pointed *adj.* तीखो tikho

poison *n.* विष wish

poisonous *adj.* विषालु wishalu

poke *v.* घोच्नु ghochnu

poke fun at *phr.* ठट्टा गर्नु thatta garnu

polar *adj.* ध्रुवीय dhrawiya

pole *n.* खम्बा khamba

pole star *n.* ध्रुवतारा dhruwa tara

police *n.* पुलिस pulis

police station *n.* थाना thana

policeman *n.* पुलिस pulis

policy *n.* नीति niti

polish *n.* पालिस palis

polite *adj.* नम्र naran

political *n.* राजनैतिक raj nitigya

politics *n.* राजनीतिज्ञ raj nitigya

polling booth *n.* मतदानस्थल matdan

pollution *n.* प्रदूषण pradushan

polygon *n.* बहुभुज bahubhuj

polythene *n.* प्लास्टिक plastic

pomade *n.* कोश्मा लाउने लेप koshma laune lep

pomegranate *n.* अनार anar

pommel *v.* हातले हिर्काउनु hatle hirkaunu

pomp *n.* रबाफ rabaph

pompous *adj.* भड्किलो bhadkilo

pond *n.* पोखरी pokhari

ponder *v.* सोच्नु sochnu

pony *n.* टट्टु tattu

pool *n.* पोखरी pokhari

poor *adj.* गरीब garib

poor man *inter.* बिचरा bichara

populace *n.* आमजनता amjanata

popular *adj.* प्रचलित prachlit

popularity *n.* लोकप्रियता lok priyata

population *n.* जनसंख्या jan sankhya

populous *adj.* घना आवादी भएको ghana awadi bhaeko

porcelain *n.* चिनीमाटाका वस्तु chini mata ka wastu

porch *n.* डयौढी dyaudhi

porcupine *n.* दुम्सी dumsi

pore *n.* मन लगाउनु man lagaunu

pork *n.* सुँगुरको मासु sungurko maas

porous *adj.* छिद्र भएको chhidra bhaeko

port *n.* बन्दरगाह bandargah

portable *adj.* सजिलोसँग लैजान सकिने sajilo sanga laij ana sakine

portend *v.* पूर्वसूचना दिनु purvsuchna dinu

porter *n.* भरिया bhariya

portfolio *n.* मन्त्रीको विभाग mantri ko wibhag

portico *n.* बाहिरी बरण्डा bahiri baranada

portion *n.* भाग bhag

portrait *n.* चित्र chitra

portray *v.* चित्र बनाउनु chitra banaunu

pose *n.* हाउभाउ haubhau

posh *adj.* उच्च दर्जाको ucch darjako

position *n.* ढाँचा dhancha

positive *adj.* सकारात्मक sakaratmak

possess *v.* राख्नु rakhnu

possession *n.* भोग bhog

possessions *n.* धन-सम्पत्ति dhan sampatti

possibility *n.* सम्भावना sambhawana

possible *adj.* सम्भव sambhaw

possibly *adv.* हुन सक्छ huna sakchha

post *n.* खम्बा khamba

post office *n.* हुलाकअड्डा hulak adda

postage *n.* हुलाकमहसुल hulak mahsul

postage stamp *n.* हुलाकटिकट hulak tikat

postbox *n.* पोस्टबक्स postbaks

postcard *n.* पोस्टकार्ड postkard

poster *n.* पर्चा parcha

poster *n.* पोस्टर poster

posterity *n.* भावी पीढ़ी bhawi peerhi

postern *n.* पछाड़िको ढोका pachhariko dhoka

postman *n.* हुलाकी hulaki

postmaster *n.* हुलाकअड्डाको हाकिम hulakadda ko hakim

post-mortem *n.* मरणोत्तर marnottar

post-natal *adj.* जन्मपछि हुने janampachhi hune

postpone *v.* पछि सार्नु pachhi sarnu

postulate *v.* मानिलिनु maanilinu

posture *n.* हाउभाउ hau bhau

pot *n.* भाँडा bhanda

pot (belly) *n.* भुँडी bhundi

potable *adj.* पिउन हुने piuna hune

potato *n.* आलु alu

pot-bellied *adj.* भुँडे bhunde

pothhole *n.* गहिरा प्वाल gahiro pwal

potter *n.* कुम्हाले kumhale

pottery *n.* माटाका भाँडाकुँडा mataka bhanda kunda

pouch *n.* थैलो thailo

pouffe *n.* गद्दी gaddhi

poultry *n.* हाँस, कुखुरा आदि hans kukhura adi

pound *n.* धूलो पिठो पर्नु dhulo pitho parnu

pour *v.* खन्याउनु khanyaunu

poverty *n.* गरीबी garibi

poverty-striken *adj.* गरीब garib

powder *n.* पाउडर paudar

power *n.* बल bal

powerful *adj.* बलियो baliyo

powerless *adj.* शक्तिहीन shaktihin

pow-wow *n.* सम्मेलन sammelan

pox *n.* बिफर biphar

practical *adj.* व्यावहारिक wyawharik

practice *v.* अभ्यास गर्नु abhyas garnu

pragmatic *adj.* व्यावहारिक wyawharik

praise *n.* प्रशंसा prashamsa

praiseworthy *adj.* तारिफयोग्य tariph yogya

prate *v.* बकबक गर्नु bakbak garnu

prattle *v.* फतर-फतर बोल्नु fatar-fatar bolnu

prawn *n.* चिंगड़ी chingarhi

pray *v.* प्रार्थना/बिन्ती गर्नु prarthana/binti garnu

prayer wheel *n.* माने mane

preacher *n.* धर्मप्रचारक dharm pracharak

preamble *n.* प्रस्तावना prastavana

precarious *adj.* अनिश्चित anishchit

precaution *n.* सावधानी sawdhani

preceless *adj.* अमूल्य amulya

precious *adj.* कीमती kimti

precipice *n.* पहरो paharo

precipice *n.* ठाड़ो चट्टान tharho chattan

precipitous *adj.* भिरालो bhiralo

precis *n.* सार sar

precise *adj.* ठीक theek

precisely *adv.* ठीकसँग thik sanga

preclude *v.* निवारण गर्नु niwaran garnu

predecease *v.* भन्दा पहिले मर्नु bhanda pahile marnu

predecessor *n.* पूर्वज purwaj

predicament *n.* खराब अवस्था kharab awastha

prediction *n.* भविष्यवाणी bhawishyawani

predominant *adj.* अधिक adhik

preen *v.* प्वाँख मिलाउनु pwankh milaunu

prefer *v.* बढी रुचाउनु badhi ruchaunu

preferable *adj.* बढी रुचिकर badhi ruchikar

pregnancy *n.* पेट बोके को अवस्था petbokeko awastha

pregnant *adj.* गर्भवती garbhwati

prejudice *n.* पूर्वाग्रह purwagraha

premarital *adj.* विवाह-पूर्व vivah-purv

premature *adj.* अपरिपक्व aparipakwa

premier *adj.* अब्बल abble

premises *n.* हाता hata

premium *n.* बीमा-किस्ता bima-kista

premonition *n.* छनक chanak

prenatal *adj.* जन्मअघि janamaghi

preparation *n.* तयारी tayari

prepare *v.* तयार गर्नु tayar garnu

prepossessing *adj.* आकर्षक akarshak

preposterous *adj.* असंगत asangat

prerogrative *n.* विशेष अधिकार vishesh adhikar

presage *v.* पूर्वसूचना दिनु purvsuchna dinu

prescribe *v.* तोक्नु toknu

prescription *n.* पूर्जी purji

presence *n.* हाजिरी hajiri

present *adj.* हाजिरी hajir

preservation *n.* संरक्षण दिनु samrakshan

preside *v.* सभापतित्व गर्नु sabhapatitwa garnu

president *n.* राष्ट्रपति rashtrapati

press *n.* छापाखाना chhapa khana

press agency *n.* समाचार समिति samachar samiti

press agent *n.* प्रेस संवाददाता pres samwaddata

press conference *n.* पत्रकार सम्मेलन patrakar sammelan

pressure *n.* दबाब dabab

pressure group *n.* दबाव समूह dabab samuh

prestige *n.* इज्जत ijjat

presume *v.* भनिठान्नु bhani thannu

pretend *v.* बहाना गर्नु bahana garnu

pretext *n.* बहाना bahana

pretty *adj.* राम्रो ramro

prevent *v.* रोक्नु roknu

prevention *n.* रोकथाम rok tham

previous *adj.* अधिको aghi ko

previously *adv.* उहिले uhile

prey *n.* शिकार shikar

price *n.* मूल्य mulya

price list *n.* मूल्य सूचि mulya suchi

prick *n.* काँडा kanda

pride *n.* गर्व garwa

priest *n.* पुजारी pujari

prig *n.* आत्मसन्तुष्ट atamsantusht

prima *adj.* प्रथम pratham

primal *adj.* आदिम admim

primary *adj.* प्राथमिक prathymik

prime *adj.* मुख्य mukhya

prime minister *n.* प्रधानमंत्री pradhan mantri

primeval *adj.* आदिम adim

primitive *adj.* प्राचीन prachin

prince *n.* युवराज yuwaraj

princess *n.* राजकुमारी raj kumari

principal *adj.* प्रधान pradhan

principle *n.* सिद्धान्त siddhant

print *n.* छापा chhapa

printing press *n.* छापा,ाना chhapa khana

prior *adj.* पहिलेको pahile kor

prior to *adv.* भन्दा अघि bhanda aghi

priority *n.* प्राथमिकता prathmikta

prise *v.* तोड्नु todnu

prison *n.* झयालखान jhyalkhan

prisoner *n.* कैदी kaidi

privacy *n.* गुप्ति gupti

private *adj.* निजी niji

private enterprise *n.* निजी उद्यम niji udyam

private eye *n.* निजी गुप्तचार niji gupt char

private parts *n.* गुप्त अङ्ग gupt ang

privately *adv.* गुप्त रूपमा gupt rup ma

privilege *n.* सुविधा suwidha

privy *adj.* गुप्त, व्यक्तिगत gupt, vyaktigat

prize *n.* इनाम inam

pro rata *adj.* अनुपतामा anupatama

probable *adj.* हुन सक्ने huna sakne

probably *adv.* होला hola

probe *n.* डाक्टरको शलाका daktar ko shalaka

probity *n.* ईमानदारी imaandari

problem *n.* समस्या samsya

procedure *n.* कार्यविधि karya widhi

proceed *v.* अघि बढ्नु aghi badhnu

proceeding *n.* काम kam

proceeds *n.* नाफा napha

process *n.* प्रक्रिया prakriya

procession *n.* जुलुस julus

proclaim *v.* घोषण गर्नु ghoshana garnu

proclamation *n.* घोषणा ghoshana

proclivity *n.* झुकाउ jhukau

procure *v.* हासिल गर्नु hasil garnu

producer *n.* उत्पादक utpadak

product *n.* फल phal

production *n.* उत्पादन uptpadan

productive *adj.* उब्जाउ ubjau

profession *n.* पेशा pesha

professional *adj.* पेसेवर pesewar

professor *n.* प्राध्यापक pradhyapak

proffer *n.* अर्पित गर्नु arpit garnu

proficiency *n.* प्रवीणता praweenta

proficient *adj.* निपुण nipun

profit *n.* फाइदा phaida

profitable *adj.* नाफा दिने napha dine

profound *adj.* गहिरो gahiro

profuse *adj.* दानबीर daanbir

progenitor *n.* पूर्वज purwaj

progeny *n.* सन्तान santan

prognosis *n.* रोगको पूर्वानुमान rogko purwanumaan

program(m)e *n.* कार्यक्रम karya kram

progress *n.* प्रगति pragati

progressive *adj.* प्रगतिशील pragatishil

prohibition , मनाही गर्नु manahi garnu

project *n.* आयोजना ayojana

projectile *n.* अस्त्र astra

projector *n.* सिनेमा cinema

prominent *adj.* विशिष्ट wishisht

promise *n.* प्रतिज्ञा pratigya

promontory *n.* अन्तरीप antreep

promote *v.* बढाउनु badhaunu

promotion *n.* बढौती badhauti

prompt *adj.* छिटो chhito

promptly *adv.* तुरुन्त turunt

prone *adj.* घोप्टो ghopto

pronoun *n.* सर्वनाम sarwa nam

pronounce *v.* उच्चारण गर्नु uchcharan garnu

proof *n.* प्रमाण praman

proofread *v.* सच्याउनु sachyaunu

prop *v.* टेको दिनु teko dinu

propaganda *n.* झूटो प्रचार jhuto prachar

propagate *v.* फेलाउनु phelaunu

propel *v.* धकेल्नु dhakelnu

propeller *n.* हवाईजहाजको पङ्खा hawai jahaj ko pankha

proper *adj.* उचित uchit

properly *adv.* उचित तरिकाले uchit tarika le

property *n.* धन-सम्पत्ति dhan sampatti

prophecy *n.* भविष्यवाणी bhawishyawani

propitious *adj.* अनुकूल anukool

proponent *n.* प्रस्तावक prastawak

proposal *n.* प्रस्ताव prastaw

propose *v.* प्रस्ताव राख्नु prastaw rakhnu

proprietor *n.* मालिक malik

proprietor *n.* मालिक malik

propulsion *n.* अघि धकेल्ने काम aghi dhakelne kaam

prose *n.* गद्य gadya

prosecute *v.* मुद्दा चलाउनु mudda chalaunu

prosody *n.* छनद शास्त्र chand shastra

prospect *n.* आशा ahsa

prosper *v.* सप्रिनु saprinu

prosperity *n.* उन्नति unnati

prosperous *adj.* सम्पन्न sampanna

prostitute *n.* वेश्या weshya

prostitution *n.* वेश्यावृत्ति weshyawritti

prosy *n.* नीरस neeras

protect *v.* बचाउनु bachaunu

protection *n.* रक्षा rasksha

protective *adj.* रक्षा गर्ने raksha garne

protein *n.* प्रोटीन protin

protest *n.* विरोध wirodh

protocol *n.* कूटनैतिक शिष्टाचार kutnaitik shishtachar

proton *n.* प्रोटोन proton

protoplasm *n.* जीवद्रव्य jeevdrawya

proud *adj.* घमण्डी ghamandi

prove *v.* प्रमाणित गर्नु pramanit garnu

proverb *n.* दखान ukhan

provide *v.* जुटाउनु jutaunu

providence *n.* ईश्वर ishwar

province *n.* प्रान्त prant

provision *n.* व्यवस्था wyawastha

provisions *n.* दानापानी dana pani

proviso *n.* शर्त sharat

provocation *n.* उत्तेजना uttejana

provoke *v.* रिस उठाउनु ris uthaunu

prow *n.* अग्रभाग agrabhaag

proximity *n.* निकटता nikatata

proxy *n.* प्रतिनिधि prati nidhi

prudent *adj.* विवेकी wiweki

prune *v.* छिमल्नु chhimalnu

pseudo *adj.* मिथ्या mithya

psychology *n.* मनोविज्ञान manowigyan

pub *n.* भट्टी bhatti

puberty *n.* यौवनारम्भु yauwanarambh

public prosecutor *n.* सरकारी वकील sarkari wakil

public relation *n.* जन सम्पर्क jan sampark

public transport *n.* यातायात का साधन रेलए बस yatayat ka sadhan rell, bus

publican *n.* भट्टीवाल bhattiwal

publication *n.* प्रकाशन prakashan

publicity *n.* प्रचार prachar

publish *v.* प्रकाशित गर्नु prakashit garnu

publisher *n.* प्रकाशक prakashak

pudding *n.* खानापाछि खाने मिष्टान्न khanapachhi khane mishthan

puff *n.* सासको झोक्का sasko jhokka

puff up *v.* फुलाउनु phulaunu

pugilist *n.* मुक्काबाज mukkabaaj

pugnacious *adj.* झगड़ालु jhagralu

puill back *v.* भाग्नु bhagnu

pull *n.* तनाइ tanai

pull down *v.* भत्काउनु bhatkaunu

pull in *v.* नजिक जानु najik janu

pull off *v.* चुँडाल्नु chundalnu

pull out *v.* हट्नु hatnu

pull up *v.* उखेल्नु ukhelnu

pullet *n.* बच्चा कुखुरा bachha kukhura

pulley *n.* घिर्नी ghirni

pullover *n.* स्वेटर sweater

pulmonary *adj.* फोक्सोको focusko

pulsate *v.* धड़कनु dharkanu

pulse *n.* दाल dal

pulverize *v.* चूर्ण बनाउनु churn banaunu

pummel *v.* मुक्काले पिट्नु mukkale pitnu

pumpkin *n.* फर्सी pharsi

punch *n.* प्वाल पार्ने यंत्र pwal parne yantra

punctual *adj.* समय को पालना गर्ने samaya ko palna garne

puncture *n.* प्वाल पार्ने यंत्र pwal parne yantra

pungent *adj.* पिरो piro

punish *v.* दण्ड/सजाय दिनु dand/sajaya dinu

punishment *n.* सजाय sajaya

punster लेषकार leshkar

puny *adj.* सानो र दुब्लो sano r dublo

pup *n.* कुकुरको छाउरो kukur ko chhauro

pupil *n.* चेला chela

puppet *n.* कठपुतली kathputali

puppy *n.* कुकुरको छाउरो kukur ko chhauro

purchase *n.* खरीद kharid

pure *adj.* शुद्ध shuddha

purgative *n.* जुलाब julab

purge *v.* हटाउनु hataunu

purify *v.* शुद्ध तुल्याउनु shuddha tulyaunu

purity *n.* शुद्धता shudhta

purple *adj.* प्याजी pyaji

purpose *n.* उद्देश्य uddeshya

purposeful *adj.* ऑटिलो antilo

purposely *adv.* जानाजानी janajani

purse *n.* थैलो thaila

pursue *v.* पछि लाग्नु pachhi lagnu

pursuit *n.* खेदो khedo

pus *n.* पीप pip

push *n.* धक्का dhakka

push down *v.* बसाउनु basaunu

push in *v.* हुल्नु hunu

push off *v.* जानु janu

push through *v.* घुसार्नु ghusarnu

pushcart *n.* ठेलागाडा thela gada

pushover *n.* सजिलै हुने काम sajilai hune kam

put *v.* राख्नु rakhnu

put across *v.* सफलता का साथ काम गर्नु saphalta ka sath kam garnu

put away *v.* थन्क्याउनु thankyaunu

put down *v.* दबाउनु dabaunu

put in *v.* समय बिताउनु samaya bitaunu

put off *v.* फुकाल्नु phukalnu

put on *v.* लगाउनु lagaunu

put out *v.* निभाउनु nibhauanu

put together *v.* मिलाउनु milaunu

put up *v.* बनाउनु banaunu

put up with *v.* सहनु sahanu

puzzle *n.* रहस्य rahasya

pygmy, pigmy *n.* बामपुड्के bampunke

pyjamas *n.* पायजामा pyjama

pyorrhoea *n.* पाइरिया pyorrhoea

pyramid *n.* पिरामिड piramid

pyre *n.* चिता chita

python *n.* अजिङ्गर ajingar

Q

quack *n.* हाँसको बोली hans ko boli

quadrangle *n.* चौकोस मैदान chaukos maidan

quadrangular *adj.* चारचुच्चे char chuchche

quadrilateral *n.* चतुर्भुज chaturbhuj

quadrille *n.* चार जोड़ी नाच्ने नाच char jodi nachne nach

quadruped *n.* चौपाया जन्तु chaupaya jantu

quadruple *adj.* चौगुना संख्या chauguna sankhya

quagmire *n.* धाप dhap

quail *n.* बटेर batir

quaint *adj.* पुरानो खालको purano khalko

quake *n.* कम्पन kampan

qualification *n.* योग्यता yogyata

qualify *v.* योग्य बन्नु yogya bannu

quality *n.* गुण gun

qualm *n.* आशांखा aasankha

quandary *n.* दुविधा duvidha

quantify *v.* परिमाण बताउनु parmaan bataunu

quantum *n.* दिइएको मात्रा diieko matra

quarantine *n.* संसर्ग निषेध samsarga nishedh

quarrel *n.* झगडा jhagada

quarrelsome *adj.* झगडालु jhagadalu

quarry *n.* ढुङ्गाखानी dhunga khani

quart *n.* तरल वस्तुको नाप taral vastuko naap

quarter *n.* चौथाइ chauthai

quarterly *adj.* त्रैमासिक traimasik

quarters *n.* क्वाटर kwatar

quartet *n.* चारजनाको समूह char jana ko samuha

quartz *n.* फटिक phatik

quash *v.* बदर गर्नु badar garnu

quatrain *n.* चार चरणको पद्य char charanko padhe

quaver *v.* काँप्नु kanpnu

quay *n.* घाट ghaat

queen *n.* रानी rani

queen mother *n.* मुमा बडामहारानी muma bada maharani

queer *adj.* अनौठो anautho

quell *v.* दबाउनु dabaunu

query *n.* प्रश्न prashna

quest *n.* खोज khoj

question *n.* प्रश्न गर्नु parashna garnu

question mark *n.* प्रश्नचिन्ह prashna chinha

questionable *adj.* ांकास्पद shankaspad

questionnaire *n.* prashnawali

queue *n.* लाइन lain

quick *adj.* छिटो chhito

quicken *v.* चाँडो गर्नु/गराउनु chando garnu/garaunu

quicksilver *n.* पारो paro

quid *n.* चपाउने सुर्ती को डल्लो chapaune surtiko dallo

quid pro quo *n.* क्षतिपूर्तिको रूपमा दिइएको वस्तु kshati purti ko rup ma diieko wastu

quiet *adj.* शान्त shant

quietly *adv.* शान्तिसँग shanti sanga

quietude *n.* शान्ति shanti

quietus *n.* छुटकारा chutkara

quiff *n.* अलक alak

quill *n.* प्वाँख pwankh

quilt *n.* सिरक sirak

quinine *n.* कुनैन kunain

quinsy *n.* घाँटी सुनिने रोग ghanti sunine rog

quintal *n.* 100 किलो saya kolo

quip *n.* व्यंग bayang

quire *n.* 24 ताउ कागत 24 tau kagat

quit *v.* त्यागनु tyagnu

quite *adv.* बिलकुल bilkul

quits *n.* फच्छे phachchhe

quiver *n.* थरथराउनु thartharaunu

quixotic *adj.* अनौठो anautho

quiz *n.* सामान्य ज्ञानको प्रश्न samanya gyan ko prashna

quorum *n.* कोरम koram

quota *n.* तोकिए को मात्रा tokieko matra

quotable *adj.* उद्धृत गर्न लायकको uddhrit garna layak ko

quotation *n.* उद्धरण वाक्य uddharan wakya

quote *v.* कसैको कुरा kasai ko kura

quoth *v.* भन्यो bhanyo

quotient *n.* भागफल bhagphal

quzzical *adj.* बेढङ्गको bedhag ko

R

rabbit *n.* खरायो kharayao

rabid *adj.* रिसाहा risaha

race *n.* तेज चाल tej chal

rach *n.* खुला दराज khula daraj

racial *adj.* जातीय jaatiya

racism *n.* जाति भेद jati bhed

racist *n.* जातिवादी jati wadi

raconteur *n.* कथावाचक kathawachak

radar *n.* रेडार redar

raddle *n.* गेरु रङ्ग geru rang

radiant *adj.* चम्किलो chamkilo

radiation *n.* विकिरण wikiran

radical *adj.* स्वाभाविक swabhavik

radio *n.* रेडियो rediyo

radioactive *adj.* रेडियोधर्मी rediyo dharmi

radish *n.* मूला mula

radium *n.* रेडियम radium

raffle *n.* चिट्ठा chittha

raft *n.* मुढाहरूको बेडा mudha haru ko beda

rafting *n.* जलयात्रा jal yatra

rag *n.* झुत्रो jhutro

rage *n.* झोक jhok

ragged *adj.* थाङ्ने thanne

raid *n.* धावा dhawa

rail *n.* फलामे बार phalame bar

raillery *n.* दिल्लगी dillagi

railroad *n.* रेलमार्ग rel marg

railway *n.* रेलमार्ग rel marg

railway carriage *n.* रेलको डिब्बा rel ko dibba

railway engine *n.* रेलको इन्जिन rel ko injin

railway train *n.* रेलगाडी rel gadi

raiment *n.* वस्त्र wastra

rain *n.* वर्षा warsha

rainbow *n.* इन्द्रेणी indreni

raincoat *n.* बर्सादी barsadi

rainfall *n.* वर्षा warsha

rainy *adj.* बर्खे barkhe

rainy days *n.* दुःख का दिन duhkh ka din

rainy season *n.* वर्षाऋतु/याम warsha ritu/yam

raise *v.* उठाउनु uthaunu

raise *v.* उठाउनु uthaunu

raisin *n.* किसमिस kismis

rally *n.* भेला bhela

ram *n.* भेडा bheda

ramble *v.* डुल्नु dulnu

rampage *n.* हिंसात्मक व्यवहार hinsatmak wyawahar

rampant *adj.* अनियन्त्रित aniyantrit

ramshackle *adj.* पुरानो purano

random *adj.* अनियमित aniyamit

randy *adj.* कामुक kamuk

range *n.* क्षेत्र kshetra

rank *n.* दर्जा darja

rank and file *n.* साधारण सिपाही sadharan sipahi

ransack *v.* खूब खोज्नु khub khojnu

ransom *n.* फिरौती रकम phirauti rakam

rant *v.* प्रलाप गर्नु pralap garnu

rap *n.* हलुका घुस्सा हान्नु haluka ghussa hannu

rapacious *adj.* लोभी lobhi

rape *n.* बलात्कार balatkar

rapid *adj.* छिटो chhito

rapidly *adv.* छिटै chhitain

rapids *n.* तल झर्ने बेगवान नदी tala jharne wegwan nadi

rapport *n.* सम्बन्ध sambandh

rapprochement *n.* मैत्रीपूर्ण सम्बन्ध को पुनः स्थापन maitripurn sambandhko punh sthapan

rapture *n.* हर्ष harsh

rare *adj.* दुर्लभ durlabh

rascal *n.* पाजी paji

rash *n.* बिमिरा bimira

raspberry *n.* ऍसेलु ainselu

rat *n.* मूसो muso

ratable, rateable *adj.* कर लाग्ने kar laagne

rat-a-tat-tat *m.* ढोका आदिमा ठोकेको आवाज dhoka adami thokeko awaaz

rate *n.* दर darja

rather *adv.* बरू baru

ratify *v.* मन्जुर गर्नु manjur garnu

ration *n.* रासन raasan

rational *adj.* विवेकी wiweki

rationale *n.* आधारभूत कारण adharbhut karan

rat-tat *n.* ढकढक गरेको आवाज dakdak gareko awaaz

rattle *n.* थर्केको आवाज tharkeko awaj

raucous *adj.* कर्कश karkash

ravage *v.* बर्बाद barbad

rave *v.* पागल कुरा गर्नु pagal kura garnu

ravel *v.* जेलिनु jelinu

ravening *adj.* भोको bhoko

rave-up *n.* बृहत्पार्टी vrihat parti

ravine *n.* खोल्सा kholsa

raw *adj.* काँचो kancho

raw deal *n.* अनुचित व्यवहार anuchit wyawahar

raw material *n.* कच्चा माल kachchamal

raw-boned *adj.* ज्यादै दुब्लो jyadai dublo

ray *n.* किरण kiran

razor *n.* छुरा chhura

razor blade *n.* दौडादौड dauda daud

reach *v.* पुग्नु pugnu

react *v.* प्रतिक्रिया जनाउनु prati kriya janaunu

reaction *n.* प्रतिक्रिया जनाउनु pratikriya

reactionary *n.* प्रतिक्रियावादी pratikriyawadi

reactivate *v.* फेरि सक्रिय बनाउनु pheri sankriya banaunu

reactor *n.* अणुशक्ति उत्पन्न गर्ने यंत्र anushakti uttapan garne yantra

read *v.* पढ्नु padhnu

readable *adj.* पढ्न लायकको padhna layak ko

readdress *v.* ठेगाना बदली गर्नु thegana badli garnu

reader *n.* पाठक pathak

readily *adv.* तुरन्त turunt

readiness *n.* तयारी tayari

reading *n.* पठनपाठन pathan pathan

ready *adj.* तयारी tarya

ready money *n.* नगद nagad

ready-made *n.* तयारी वस्तु tayari wastu

real *adj.* साँचो sancho

real estate *n.* घरजग्गा ghar jagga

realism *n.* यथार्थवाद yatharthwad

reality *n.* वास्तविकता wastawikta

realize *v.* महसुस गर्नु mahsus garnu

really *adv.* साँच्चै sanchchai

realm *n.* राज्य rajya

ream *n.* कागज को 500 ताउ kagaj ko panch saya tau

reap *v.* बाली काट्नु ball katnu

reappear *v.* फेरि देखा पर्नु pheri dekha parnu

reappoint *v.* फेरि बहाल गर्नु pheri bahal garnu

rear *adj.* पछाडिको भाग pachhadi ko bhag

rearrange *v.* फेरि मिलाउनु pheri milaunu

reason *n.* कारण karani

reasonable *adj.* मनासिब manasib

reasonable *adj.* उचित uchhit

reassemble *v.* फेरि भेला हुनु pheri bhela hunu

reassure *v.* फेरि स्थापित गर्नु pheri sthapit garnu

rebel *n.* विद्रोही widrohi

rebellion *n.* विद्रोह widroh

rebirth *n.* पुनर्जन्म punar janma

rebuild *v.* फेरि बनाउनु pheri banaunu

rebuke *n.* हप्की hapki

recall *v.* फिर्ता बोलाउनु phirta bolaunu

recapitulate *v.* सारांश प्रस्तुत गर्नु saraansh prastut garnu

recapture *v.* फेरि पक्रनु pheri pakranu

recast *v.* सुधार्नु sudharnu

receipt *n.* भर्पाई bharpai

receipt *n.* रसिद rasid

receive *v.* पाउनु paunu

receive *v.* पाउनु paunu

receiver *n.* प्राप्त गर्ने prapt garne

recent *adj.* हालसालको ताजा halsal ko taja

receptacle *n.* भाँड़ा bhara

reception *n.* स्वागत swagat

receptionist *n.* स्वागत गर्ने swagat garne

recess *n.* अवकाश awkash

recipient *n.* पाउने व्यक्ति paune wyaki

reciprocal *adj.* आपसी apasi

reciprocate *v.* लेनदेन गर्नु len den garnu

recital *n.* वाचन wachan

reckless *adj.* लापरबाह laparbah

reckon *v.* ठान्नु thannu

reckoning *n.* गणना ganana

recline *v.* पछि सहारा लिनु pachi sahara lenu

recluse *n.* एक्लै बस्ने व्यक्ति ekalei basne vyakti

recognition *n.* पहिचान pahichan

recognize *v.* चिन्नु chinnu

recoil *v.* पछिल्तिर धक्का हान्नु pachhil tira dhakka hannu

recollect *v.* सम्झनु samjhanu

recommend *v.* सिफारिश गर्नु sipharish garnu

recommendation *n.* सिफारिश गर्नु sipharish garnu

reconcile *v.* मेलमिलाप गर्नु melmilap garnu

reconcillation *n.* मेलमिलाप mel milap

recondite *adj.* दुरूह durooh

reconfirm *v.* दोहोरो पुष्टि गर्नु dohoro pushti garnu

reconnaissance *n.* सैनिक सर्वेक्षण sainik sarwekshan

record *n.* लिखत likhat

record *n.* लिखित विवरण likhit vivran

recorder *n.* रकेर्ड गर्ने यन्त्र rekard garne yantra

recording *n.* रेकर्ड गर्ने काम rekard garne kam

recount *v.* पुनर्गणना punar ganana

recover *v.* निको/आराम हुनु niko/aram hunu

recovery *n.* स्वास्थ्यलाभ swasthya labh

recreate *v.* ताजा पार्नु taja parnu

recreation *n.* मनोरंजन manoranajan

recruit *n.* नयाँ सिपाही nayan sipahi

rectangle *n.* आयत ayat

rectangular *adj.* आयताकार ayatakar

rectify *v.* सच्याउनु sachyaunu

rector *n.* शिक्षाध्यक्ष shikshadhyaksha

rectum *n.* मलाश्य malashaya

recuperate *v.* आराम हुँदै जानु aram hundai janu

recuperation *n.* स्वास्थ्य लाभ swasthya labh

recur *v.* फेरि हुनु pheri hunu

recurrence *n.* दोहरिने काम doharine kam

red *adj.* रातो rato

red cross *n.* रेडक्रस redkras

red light *n.* खतरा को बत्ती khatara ko batti

red tape *n.* अति औपचारिकता ati aupcharikta

reddish *adj.* अलि अलि रातो ali ali rato

redeem *v.* मुक्त गर्नु mukta garnu

red-handed *adv.* थलैमा thalai ma

red-hot *adj.* तातेर रातो भएको tatera rato bhaeko

red-letter day *n.* खुशी को स्मरणीय दिन khushi ko smarniya din

red-light area *n.* वेश्या मोहल्ला weshya mohalla

redolent *adj.* सुगन्धित sugandhit

redouble *v.* दोबर गर्नु वा हुनु dobar garnu wa hunu

redress *v.* ठीक गर्नु thik garnu

reduce *v.* कम गर्नु kam garnu

reduction *n.* कमी kami

reed *n.* निगालो nigalo

reef *n.* समुद्री चट्टान samudri chattan

re-elect *v.* फेरि छान्नु/चुन्नु pheri chhannu/chunnu

re-enter *v.* फेरि पस्नु pheri pasnu

refer *v.* सन्दर्भ sandarbh

referee *n.* रेफ्री rephri

reference *n.* सन्दर्भ देखाउनु sandarbh dekhaunu

reference library *n.* सन्दर्भ पुस्तकालय sandarbh pustakalya

referendum *n.* जनमत संग्रह jan mat sangraha

referendum *n.* जनमत-संग्रह jan mat sangraha

refill *v.* फेरि भर्नु pheri bharnu

refine *v.* शुद्ध गर्नु shuddha garnu

refinery *n.* तेल सफा गर्ने कारखाना tel sapha garne karkhana

reflect *v.* प्रतिविम्बित गर्नु prati wimbit garnu

reflection *n.* प्रतिबिम्ब prati wimba

reform *n.* सुधार्नु sudharnu

refract *n.* बङ्ग्याउनु bangyaunu

refrain *v.* रोक्नु roknu

refresh *v.* ताजा गराउनु taja garaunu

refreshment *n.* जलपान jalpan

refrigerator *n.* चिसो पार्ने मेसिन chisoparne mesin

refuge *n.* शरण sharan

refugee *n.* शरणार्थी sharnarthi

refulgent *adj.* चहकिलो chehkilo

refund *v.* पैसा फिर्ता दिनु paisa phirta dinu

refuse *v.* अस्वीकार गर्नु aswikar garnu

regal *adj.* शाही shahi

regard *v.* आदर गर्नु adar garnu

regarding *prep.* बारेमा bare ma

regardless *adj.* लापरबाह laparbah

regatta *n.* नौका-दोड़ nauka-daur

regency *n.* राज प्रतिनिधिको पद raj pratinidhi ko pad

regeneration *n.* पुनर्जन्म punar janma

regent *n.* राजप्रतिनिधि rajpratinedhi

regicide *n.* राजाको हत्या rajako hatya

regime *n.* शासनकाल shasan kal

regimen *n.* शासन व्यवस्था shasan wyawastha

regiment *n.* पलटन paltan

region *n.* क्षेत्र kshetra

regional *adj.* क्षेत्रीय kshetriya

register *v.* दर्ता गर्नु darta garnu

registered *adj.* दर्ता गरेको darta gareko

registrar *n.* पाँजिकाधिकारी panjikadhikari

registration *n.* दर्ता darta

regret *n.* अफसोस aphsos

regrettable *adj.* शोचनीय shochniya

regular *adj.* नियमित niyamat

regularly *adv.* नियमित रूपमा niyamit rup ma

regulate *v.* नियमित niyamit

regulation *n.* नियम विधि niyam widhi

rehabilitate *n.* पहिलेको पद pahileko pad

rehabilitation *n.* पुनर्वास punarwas

rehearsal *n.* पूर्वाभ्यास purwabhyas

rehouse *v.* नयाँ बस्ने ठाउँ दिनु naya basne thaun dinu

reign *n.* राज गर्नु raj garnu

rein *n.* लगाम lagam

reincarnation *n.* अवतार .awtar

reinforce *v.* अरू बलियो बनाउनु aru baliyo banaunu

reject *v.* इन्कार/अस्वीकार गर्नु inkar/ aswikar garnu

rejection *n.* इन्कार गर्नु inkar garnu

rejoice *v.* खुश हुनु khush hunu

rejoicing *n.* खुशी khushi

relapse *v.* पहिलेको अवस्थामा जानु pahileko awasthama jaanu

relate *v.* बखान गर्नु bakhan garnu

related *adj.* सम्बन्धित sambandhit

relation *n.* नाता nata

relationship *n.* सम्बन्ध sambandh

relative *n.* नातागोता nata gota

relative *n.* साइनो saino

relax *v.* आराम गर्नु aram garnu

relaxation *n.* आराम aram

relay *v.* सन्देश पुन्याउनु sandesh puryaunu

relay race *n.* रिले दोड rile daud

release *v.* छोड्नु chodnu

relent *v.* नरम हुनु naram hunu

relentless *adj.* निर्दयी nirdayi

reliable *adj.* भरपर्दो bhar pardo

reliance *n.* भरोसा bharosa

relic *n.* अवशेष awshesh

relief *n.* आराम aram

relief fund *n.* उद्धार कोष uddhar kosh

relieve *v.* छोडिदिनु chhodi dinu

relievign *adj.* पालो दिनु palo dine

religion *n.* धर्म dharm

religious *adj.* धार्मिक dharmik

relish *v.* मनपराउनु manpraunu

reluctant *adj.* विरूद्ध wirudh

rely *v.* भर गर्नु/पर्नु bhar garnu/ parnu

remain *v.* बस्नु basnu

remainder *n.* बाँकी भाग banki

remaining *adj.* बाँकी भाग banki

remake *v.* फेरि बनाउनु pheri banaunu

remark *n.* भनाइ bhanai

remarkable *adj.* विशिष्ट wishisht

remedy *n.* उपचार upchar

remember *v.* सम्झनु samjhanu

remembrance *n.* सम्झना samjhana

remind *v.* सम्झना गराउनु samjhana garanunu

reminder *n.* सम्झौटो samjhauto

remission *n.* क्षमा kshama

remonstrate *v.* विरोध गर्नु virodh garnu

remorse *n.* पछुतो pachhuto

remorseless *adj.* निर्दयी nirdayi

remote *adj.* टाढाको tadha ko

removable *adj.* हटाउन लायकको hatauna layak ko

removal *n.* अपसरण upsaran

remove *v.* हटाउनु hataunu

remuneration *n.* नारिश्रमिक parishramik

renal *adj.* मिर्गौलाको mirgaulako

rend *v.* च्यात्नु chyatanu

render *v.* अनुवाद गर्नु anuwad garnu

rendezvous *n.* भेला हुने ठाउँ bhela hune thaun

renegade *n.* पक्षत्यागी pakshya tyagi

renew *v.* नयाँ पार्नु nayan parnu

renewal *n.* नयाँ बनाउने काम nayan banaune kam

renounce *v.* परित्याग गर्नु parityag garnu

renovate *v.* नयाँ बनाउनु nayan banaunu

renowned *adj.* प्रसिद्ध prasiddha

rent *n.* भाडा bhada

rental *n.* भाडाबाट आउने रकम bhada bata aune rakam

renunciation *n.* त्याग tyag

repair *v.* मर्म्मत गर्नु marammat garnu

repartee *n.* ओठे जवाफ authe jawaf

repast *n.* खाना khana

repay *v.* चुकाउनु chukaunu

repeal *v.* बदर/रद्द गर्नु badar/ radda garnu

repeat *v.* दोहोन्यानु dohoryaunu

repel *v.* पछि हटाउनु pachhi hataunu

repent *v.* पछुताउनु pachhutaunu

repentance *n.* पछुतो pachhuto

repetition *n.* दोहोन्याउने काम dohoryaune kam

replace *v.* बदल्नु badalnu

replacement *n.* प्रतिस्थापन pratisthapan

replete *adj.* भरिएको bhariyeko

replica *n.* नक्कल प्रतिकृति nakkal

reply *v.* जवाफ दिनु jawaph dinu

report *n.* रिपोर्ट riport

reportedly *adv.* सुनेअनुसार sune anusar

reporter *n.* संवाददाता samwaddata

repository *n.* चीजहरू राख्ने ठाउँ cheejharu rakhne thaun

represent *v.* सट्टामा खडा हुनु sattama khadahunu

representation *n.* प्रतिनिधित्व prati nidhitwa

representative *n.* प्रतिनिधित्व prati nidhitwa

repress *v.* दबाउनु dabaunu

repression *n.* दमन daman

reprimand *n.* नसिहत nashiat

reprint *n.* नयाँ प्रकाशन nayan prakashan

reproduce *v.* फेरि पैदा गर्नु pheri paida garnu

reproduction *n.* पुनरुत्पादन punarutpadan

reproof *n.* गाली gaali

reprove *v.* हप्काउनु hapkaunu

reptile *n.* घस्रने जन्तु ghasrane jantu

republic *n.* गणतंत्र gan tantra

repulse *v.* लखाट्नु lakhatnu

repulsive *adj.* घिनलाग्दो ghin lagdo

reputable *adj.* सम्मानित sammanit

reputation *n.* इज्जत ijjat

reputed *adj.* प्रसिद्ध prasiddha

request *n.* अनुरोध anurodh

requiem *n.* मृत mrit

require *v.* आवश्यक हुनु awashyak hunu

requirement *n.* आवश्यकता awashyakta

requisite *n.* चाहिने सामान chahine sasman

requite *v.* बदलामा दिनु badlama dinu

re-run *n.* नाटक natak

rescind *v.* रद्द गर्नु radh garnu

rescue *n.* रक्षा raksha

research *n.* अनुसन्धान anusandhan

researcher *n.* अनुसन्धान गर्ने anusandhan garne

resemblance *n.* समरूपता samarupta

resemble *v.* उकनाश हुनु ek nash hunu

resent *v.* रिसाउनु risaunu

resentment *n.* रिस ris

reservation *n.* आरक्षण arakshan

reserve *v.* सुरक्षित गर्नु surakshit garnu

reserved *adj.* सुरक्षित गर्नु surakshit garnu

reservoir *n.* जलाशय jalashaya

reshuffle *n.* पुर्न गठन गर्नु purna gathan garnu

reside *v.* बस्नु basnu

residence *n.* घर ghar jagga

resident *n.* निवासी niwasi

residential *adj.* आवासीय awasiya

residual *adj.* बाँकी रहेको baanki rahenko

residue *n.* शेष shesh

resign *v.* जागिर छोड्नु jagir chodnu

resign *v.* छोड्नु chodnu

resignation *n.* राजीनामा दिनु rajinama

resist *v.* विरोध गर्नु wirodh garnu

resistance *n.* बाधा badha

resole *v.* नयाँ तलुवा हाल्नु nayan tulwa halnu

resolute *adj.* कृतसंकल्प kritsankalp

resolution *n.* प्रस्ताव prastaw

resolve *v.* समाधान गर्नु sanmadhan garnu

resonant *adj.* गुंजिने gunjine

resort *v.* शरण sharan

resource *n.* स्रोत srot

respect *n.* आदर adar

respectable *adj.* आदरणीय adarniya

respectful *adj.* सम्मानजनक samman janak

respectfully *adj.* सादर sadar

respective *adj.* आ-आफ्नु a aphnu

respectively *adv.* क्रमैले kramai le

respiration *n.* वासप्रश्वास shwas prashwas

respire *v.* सास फेर्नु saas phernu

respite *n.* विलम्ब वा स्थगन vilamb wa sthagan

resplendent *adj.* उज्जवल ujjawal

respond *v.* उत्तर दिनु uttar dinu

response *n.* जवाफ दिनु jawaph dinu

responsibility *n.* जिम्मेवारी jimewari

rest *n.* आराम aram

restaurant *n.* भोजनालय bhojnalaya

restful *adj.* आराम दिने aaram dine

restive *adj.* बेचैन bechain

restless *adj.* चंचल chanchal

restlessness *n.* छटपटी chhatpati

restoration *n.* पुनस्थार्पना punarsthapna

restore *v.* फिर्ता गर्नु phirta garnu

restrain *v.* रोक्नु roknu

restraint *n.* विरोध wirodh

restrict *v.* रोक्नु roknu

restriction *n.* रोक्का rokka

result *n.* परिणाम parninam

resultant *adj.* परिणाम दिने parinam dine

resume *n.* बायोडाटा bayodata

resumption *n.* नयाँ सुरुआत nayan suruat

resurgent *adj.* हार haar

resuscitate *v.* सास र होस फर्काउनु sas ra hos pharkaunu

retail *n.* खुद्रा बिक्री khudra bikri

retain *v.* कायम राख्नु kayam rakhnu

retaliate *v.* बदला लिनु badla linu

retaliation *n.* बदला लिनु badla linu

retch *v.* वाक्क गर्नु waak garnu

retention *n.* राख्ने काम rakhne kaam

rethink *v.* फेरि सोच्नु pheri sochnu

retialer *n.* खुद्रा पसले khudra pasale

reticent *adj.* धेरै नबोल्ने dherai nabolne

retina *n.* दृष्टिपटल drishtipatal

retinue *n.* अनुचर anuchar

retire *v.* अवकाशप्राप्त awkash linu

retirement *n.* अवकाश awkash

retort *n.* ओठे जवाफ दिनु authe jawaf dinu

retract *v.* वापस लिनु vapas linu

retreat *n.* पछि हट्ने काम pacchi hatne kam

retribution *n.* दण्ड dandh

retrogress *v.* पछिल्तिर जानु pachhilitir jaanu

return *n.* वापसी wapasi

return ticket *n.* फिर्ती टिकट phirti tikat

reunion *n.* पुनर्मिलन punar milan

reunite *v.* फेरि सङ्गठित हुनु pheri sangathit hunu

rev *v.* इंजनको घुमाइ engine ko ghumai

revalue *v.* फेरि मूल्य लगाउनु pheri mulya lagaunu

reveal *v.* खोल्नु kholnu

revel *v.* होहल्ला गरी रमाइलो गर्नु ho halla gari ramailo garnu

revelation *n.* चमत्कार chamatkar

revelry *n.* उत्सव utsav

revenge *n.* बदला badla linu

reverberate *v.* घन्कनु ghankanu

reverberation *n.* गुँजन gunjan

revere *v.* मान गर्नु man garnu

reverence *n.* आदर adar

reverie *n.* चिन्तन chintan

reverse *n.* विपरीत wiparit

review *n.* समीक्षा samiksha

revise *v.* दोहोर्याउनु dohoryaunu

revision *n.* संशोधन sanshodhan

revive *v.* पुनर्जीवित गर्नु punar jiwit garnu

revoke *v.* रद्द/खारेज गर्नु radda/kharej garnu

revolt *n.* विद्रोह गर्नु widorh garnu

revolution *n.* आन्दोलन andolan

revolutionary *n.* क्रान्तिकारी krantikari

revolve *v.* घुम्नु ghumnu

revolver *n.* पिस्तौल pistaul

reward *n.* इनाम inam

rewrite *v.* फेरि लेख्नु pheri lekhnu

rhematism *n.* बात/बाथरोग bat/ bath rog

rhetoric *n.* आलङ्कारिक भाषा alankarik bhasha

rheumatic *adj.* बातरोग लागेको batrog lageko

rhinoceros *n.* गैंडा gainda

rhododendron *n.* गुराँस gurans

rhubarb *n.* फापर जातको साग fapar jatko saag

rhythm *n.* ताल tal

rib *n.* करङ karan

ribbon *n.* रिबन riban

rice *n.* भात bhat

rich *adj.* धनी dhani

riches *n.* धन dhan

rickshaw *n.* रिक्सा riksa

rid *v.* हटाउनु hataunu

riddle *n.* गाउँखाने कथा gaun khane katha

ride *v.* मोटर चढ्नु motar chadhnu

rider *n.* सवार sawar

ridge *n.* डाँडा danda

ridicule *n.* हँसी hansi

ridiculous *adj.* हाँसो hanso

rift *n.* दरार darar

rigging *n.* धाँधली dhandhali

right *adj.* दायाँ dayan

righteous *adj.* न्यायी nyayi

rightful *adj.* हकदार hak dar

right-hand man *n.* मुख्य सहायक mukhya sahayak

right-minded *adj.* ठीक विचार भएको thik wichar bhaeko

rigid *adj.* नगल्ने na galne

rigo(u)r *n.* कठोरता kathorta

rile *v.* चिढ्याउनु chirhaunu

rill *n.* सानो नदी sano nadi

rim *n.* बिट bit

ring *n.* मुन्द्री mundri

ring finger *n.* साहिली आँला sahili aunla

ring road *n.* चक्रपथ chakrapath

ringleader *n.* नेता neta

ringlet *n.* औठी authi

rinse *v.* पखाल्नु pakhalnu

riot *n.* हूलदङ्गा huldanga

rioter *n.* हुल्याहा hulyaha

ripe *adj.* पाकेको pakeko

ripen *v.* पाक्नु paknu

rip-off *n.* चोरी chori

riposte *n.* ओठे जवाफ authe jawaf

ripple *n.* सानो लहर sano lahar

rise *v.* उदाउनु udaunu

rising *adj.* उदीयमान udlyaman

risk *n.* जोखिम jokhim

risky *adj.* जोखिमपूर्ण jokhimpurn

risotto *n.* पुलाउ pulao

rite *n.* धार्मिक रीति dharmik riti

ritual *n.* संस्कार विधि विधान sanskar widhi widhan

rival *n.* प्रतिद्वन्द्वी prati dwandwi

river *n.* नदी nadi

rivulet *n.* खोला kholai

road *n.* सडक sadak

road hog *n.* मनपरी मोटर हाँक्ने man pari motar hankne

road map *n.* मार्गचित्र marg chitra

roadster *n.* खुला मोटरकार khula motorcar

roam *v.* घुमफिर गर्नु ghun phir garnu

roar *n.* गर्जन garjan

roast *n.* सेकुवा sekuwa

rob *v.* चोर्नु chornu

robber *n.* डाकु daku

robbery *n.* डकैती dakaiti

robe *n.* पोशाक poshak

robot *n.* रोबोट robot

robust *adj.* बलियो balio

rock *n.* चट्टान chattan

rocket *n.* रकेट raket

rod *n.* छडी chhadi

rodent *n.* मूसो, छुचुन्द्रो आदि muso chhuchundro adi

rogue *n.* उपद्र्याक्ष upadryaha

role *n.* भूमिका bhumika

roll *n.* मुठा mutha

roll away *v.* पल्टिँदै जानु paltindai janu

roll-call *n.* हाजिर hajir

rolled gold *n.* सुनको जलप sun ko jalap

roller *n.* बाटो पेल्ने इन्जिन bato pelne injine

romance *n.* प्रेमालाप premalap

romantic *adj.* काल्पनिक kalpanik

romp *v.* कुद्दै kuddai

roof *n.* छाना chhana

rook *n.* काग kag

rookie *n.* अनुभवहीन रिकुटे anubhavheen rikute

room *n.* कोठा kotha

roomy *adj.* फराकिलो pharakilo

rooster *n.* भाले bhale

root *n.* जरा jara

root out *n.* उखेल्नु ukhelnu

rope *n.* डोरी dori

rope in *v.* भाग लिन कर गर्नु bhag lina kar garnu

rosary *n.* जपमाला japmala

rosary *n.* जपमाला japmala

rose *n.* गुलाफ gulaph

rose water *n.* गुलाफजल gulaph jal

rosebud *n.* राम्री स्त्री ramristri

roster *n.* नामावली namawali

rostrum *n.* मंच manch

rosy *adj.* गुलाफी gulaphi

rot *v.* कुहिनु kuhinu

rotary *n.* घुम्नु यंत्र ghumne yantra

rotation *n.* चक्कर chakkar

rotor *n.* इंजनको घुम्ने भाग engineko ghumne bhaag

rotten *adj.* सडेगलेको sade galeko

rotter *n.* निकम्मा nikkama

rotund *adj.* गोलो golo

rouble *n.* रुसको मुद्रा rusko mudra

rouge *n.* लाली lali

rough *adj.* खस्रो khasro

rough and tumble *n.* हातपात hatpat

rough house *n.* झगडा jhagada

rough-and-ready *adj.* असभ्य भए पनि कारगर asabhya bhae pani kargar

roughly *adv.* अन्दाजी andaji

roughneck *n.* हल्याहा hulyaha

rough-tongued *adj.* अभद्र बोल्ने abhadra bolne

round *adj.* गोल gol

round up *v.* समाल्नु samatnu

roundabout *adj.* अन्दाजी andaji

roundel *n.* सानो थाल sano thal

round-table conference *n.* गोलमेज सम्मेलन golmej sammelan

round-up *n.* सार-सङ्क्षेप sar sankshep

roundworm *n.* गोलकृमि golkrimi

rouse *v.* जगाउनु jagaunu

rout *n.* दंगा danga

route *n.* बाटो bato

routine *n.* नियमित कार्य niyamit karya

rove *v.* घुमफिर गर्नु ghum phir garnu

rover *n.* घुमक्कड ghumakkad

rovwdy *adj.* गुण्डा gunda

row *n.* लहर lahar

rowdy *adj.* हुल्लड़बाज hullarhbaaj

royal *adj.* राजकीय rajkiya

royal road *n.* सजिलो उपाय sajilo upaya

royalty *n.* भत्ता battha

rub *v.* मल्नु malnu

rub in *v.* मालिस गर्नु malis garnu

rub out *v.* मेट्नु metnu

rubber *n.* रबर rabar

rubber *n.* रबर rabar

rubber stamp *n.* रबडको छाप rabad ko chhap

rubber-stamp *v.* नबिचारी स्वीकृति दिनु nabichari swikriti dinu

rubbish *n.* कसिङ्गर kasingar

ruby *n.* माणिक manik

ruck *n.* मुजा muja

rucksack *n.* पीठमा बोक्ने झोला pith ma bokne jhola

rudder *n.* कर्ण karan

rude *adj.* पाखे pakhe

rudiment *n.* शुरु shuru

ruffian *n.* बदमाश badmash

rug *n.* गलीचा galicha

rugged *adj.* रूखो rukho

ruin *n.* विनाश winash

rule *n.* नियम niyam

rule out *v.* हटाउनु hataunu

rule the roost *v.* वर्चस्व हुनु warchaswa hunu

ruler *n.* शासक shasak

rules and regulations *n.* नियम कानून niyam kanun

rum *n.* रम ram

rumbustious *adj.* हल्ला र विनोद गर्ने halla r vinod garne

rumo(u)r *n.* हल्ला halla

rump *n.* पशुको चाक pashuko chak

run *v.* दगुर्नु dagurnu

run away *v.* भाग्नु bhagnu

run down *v.* कमजोर हुनु kam jor hunu

run low *v.* थोरै बाँकी रहनु thorai banki rahanu

run off *v.* भाग्नु bhagnu

run out *v.* समाप्त हुनु samapt hune

run out on *v.* छाछिदिनु chhadi dinu

run over *v.* पोखिनु pokhinu

run short *v.* कमी हुनु kami hunu

run up चाँडै बढ्नु chandai badhnu

run up against *v.* कठिनाइ झेल्नु kathinai jhelnu

run-down *adj.* उपेक्षित upekshit

rung *n.* भरेङको खुड्किला bharen ko khud kila

runnel *n.* नाला nala

runner *n.* दौडने मान्छे daudane manchhe

runner-up *n.* उपविजेता upwijeta

running water *n.* खोला वा धाराको पानी kholawa dhara ko pani

run-of-the-mill *adj.* साधारण sadharan

runway *n.* धावन मार्ग dhawan marg

rupee *n.* रुपैयाँ rupaiyan

rural *adj.* गाउँले gaunle

ruse *n.* छल chal

rush *n.* घुइँचो ghuincho

rust *n.* खिया khiya

rusticate *v.* निकाल्नु nikalnu

rustle *n.* स्यारस्यार आवाज निक्लनु syar syar awaj niklanu

rusty *adj.* खिया लागेको khiya lageko

ruthless *adj.* निठुर nithur

rxpulsion *n.* निकाला nikala

S

sabotage *n.* तोडफोड topphod

sacaffold *n.* मचान machan

sack *n.* बोरा bora

sacrifice *n.* बलिदान balidan

sad *adj.* दुःखी dukhi

saddle *n.* भंज्याङ bhanjyan

safari *n.* शिकार को अभियान shikar ko abhiyan

safe *adj.* कुशल kushal

safe conduct *n.* अभयपत्र abhaya patra

safeguard *n.* रक्षा raksha

safely *adv.* सुविबस्तासँग subista sanga

safety pin *n.* सेप्टिपिन septi pin

safety razor *n.* सुरक्षित छुरा surakshit chhura

saffron *n.* केशर keshar

sag *v.* झुल्नु jhulnu

saga *n.* आख्यान akhyan

sage *n.* ऋषि rishi

sagittarius *n.* धनुराशि dhanu rashi

sago *n.* साबुदानाप sabudana

sail *n.* जहाज हिँड्नु jahaj ko pal

sailent *adj.* प्रमुख pramukh

sailor *n.* जहाजी jahaji

saint *n.* सन्त sant

sake *n.* कारण karan

salad *n.* salad

salad days *n.* किशोरावस्था kishorawastha

salamander *n.* माउसुली mausuli

salami *n.* मसालादार ससेज masaladar sasej

salary *n.* तलव talab

sale *n.* बिक्री bikri

saleable *adj.* बेच्नलायक bechna layak

salesman *n.* विक्रेता wikreta

salient *adj.* मुख्य mukhya

saline *adj.* नुनिलो nunilo

saliva *n.* राल ral

salt *n.* नुन nun

salted *adj.* नुनिलो nunilo

saltless *adj.* अलिनो alino

salute *n.* सलामी salami

salvation *n.* मुक्ति mukti

salve *n.* मलम malam

salver *n.* धातुको थाल वा ट्रे dhatuko thaal wa tray

same *adj.* उही uhi

sample *n.* नमूना namuna

sanatorium *n.* आरोग्यशाला arogya shala

sanction *n.* मंजुरी manjuri

sanctity *n.* पवित्रता pawitrata

sanctuary *n.* आरक्ष araksha

sand *n.* बालुवा baluwa

sandal *n.* चप्पल chappal

sandalwood *n.* श्रीखण्ड shrikhand

sandpaper *n.* खक्सी khaksi

sandwich *n.* स्याण्डबीच syandwich

sandy *adj.* बलौटे balaute samudritat

sane *adj.* स्वस्थ swasth

sang-froid *n.* संकटमा शान्त रहने शक्ति sankatma shant rehne shakti

sanguinary *adj.* रक्तपातपूर्ण raktpaatpurn

sanitary *adj.* स्वास्थ्यकर swasthyakar

sanitation *n.* सरसफाइ sar saphai

sap *n.* चोप chop

sapient *adj.* ज्ञानी gyani

sapling *n.* सानुबोट sanubot

sapphire *n.* नीलमणि nilmani

sarcasm *n.* घोचपेच ghochpech

sarcastic *adj.* व्यङ्ग्यपूर्ण wyangyapurn

sari *n.* साडी sadi

sarong *n.* लुङ्गी lungi

sated *adj.* तृप्त tripat

satellite *n.* उपग्रह upgraha

satin *n.* साटन sattan

satisfaction *n.* सन्तोष santosh

satisfactory *adj.* सन्तोषजनक santosh janak

satisfied *adj.* सन्तुष्ट santusht

satisfy *v.* सन्तुष्ट पार्नु santusht parnu

Saturday *n.* शनिवार shaniwar

saturn *n.* शनिग्रह shanigraha

satyr *n.* वन को देवता van ko devta

sauce *n.* रसदार व्यंजन rasdar wyanjan

saucepan *n.* ताप्के tapke

saucer *n.* रिकाबी rikabi

sausage *n.* ससेज sasej

savage *adj.* जङ्गली jangali

savagery *n.* जङ्गलीपन jangalipan

save *v.* बचाउनु bachaunu

save one's face *v.* ईज्जत बचाउनु ijjat bachananu

savings *n.* बचत bachat

savio(u)r *n.* मुक्तिदाता muktidata

saw *n.* हेर्नु hernu

sawdust *n.* काठको धुलो kathko dhulo

sawmill *n.* काठ चिर्ने कारखाना kath chiirne kar khana

sawyer *n.* काठ चिर्ने मान्छे kathchirne manchhe

say *v.* भन्नु bhannu

saying *n.* उखान ukhan

scab *n.* घाउको पाप्रा ghau ko papra

scabbard *n.* दाप dap

scabies *n.* लुतो luto

scaffold *n.* फाँसी दिने मंच phansi dine manch

scaffolding *n.* खाट khat

scald *v.* तातो पानी वा बाफले पोल्नु tatopani wa baph le polnu

scale *n.* कत्ला katla

scallop *n.* सिपी sippi

scaly *adj.* कत्ला भएको katla bhaeko

scamp *n.* गुण्डा gunda

scan *v.* ध्यानसँग हेर्नु dhyan sanga hernu

scandal *n.* बदनाम badnam

scansion *n.* छनद-परीक्षण chand-parikshan

scant *adj.* थोरै thorai

scanty *adj.* थोरै thorai

scapegoat *n.* अर्काको दोष बोक्ने arka ko dosh bokne

scar *n.* खत khat

scarce *adj.* अपुग apug

scarcely *adv.* मुस्किलले muskil le

scarcity *n.* कमी kami

scare *v.* तर्साउनु tarsaunu

scarf *n.* गलबन्दी galbadi

scarlet *adj.* गाडा रातो रङ्ग gadha rato rang

scary *adj.* डरलाग्दो darlagdo

scathing *adj.* कठोर kathor

scatter *v.* छर्नु chharnu

scavenger *n.* सिनु खाने पशु/चरा sinu khane pashu/chara

scene *n.* दृश्य drishya

scenery *n.* प्राकृतिक दृश्य prakritik drishya

scenic *adj.* रमणीय ramniya

scent *n.* बास्ना basna

sceptre *n.* राजदंड rajdand

schedule *n.* समयतालिका samayatalika

scheduled *adj.* तोकिएको tokieko

scheme *n.* योजना yojana

scholar *n.* विद्वान् widwan

scholarship *n.* छात्रवृत्ति chhatra writti

scholastic *adj.* शैक्षिक shekshik

school *n.* पाठशाला pathshala

science *n.* विज्ञान wigyan

scientist *n.* वैज्ञानिक waigyanik

scintillate *v.* चम्कनु chamkanu

scissors *n.* कैँची kainchi

scold *v.* हप्काउनु hapkaunu

scone *n.* केक cake

scoop *n.* पनिउँ paniun

scooter *n.* स्कूटर skutar

scope *n.* कार्यक्षेत्र karyakshetra

scorch *v.* झुर्रिनु jhurrinu

score *n.* बीस थान bisthan

scorer *n.* हिसाब राख्ने hisab rakhne

scorn *v.* हेप्नु hepnu

scorpio *n.* वृश्चिक राशि wrishehik rashi

scorpion *n.* बिच्छी bichchhi

scot-free *adj.* बिनासजाय उम्केको bina sajaya umkeko

scoundrel *n.* बदमास badmas

scount *n.* गुप्तचर guptchar

scourge *n.* महामारी maha mari

scout *n.* बालचर balchar

scraecrow *n.* बुख्याचा bukhyacha

scramble *v.* मुस्किले उक्लनु muskil le uklanu

scrap *n.* टुक्रा tukra

scrape *v.* ताछ्नु tachhnu

scraps *n.* जुठो पुरा jutho pura

scratch *n.* प्रस्थान रेखा prasthan rekha

scrawny *adj.* दुब्लो-पातलो dublo-patlo

scream *n.* चिच्याहट chichyahat

scredness *n.* पवित्रता pawitrata

screech *v.* तीखो teekho

screen *n.* पर्दा parda

screw *n.* पेच कस्नु pechkasnu

screwdriver *n.* पेचकस pechkas

scrimmage *n.* भिड्न्त bhidant

scrimp *v.* फारो गरेर चलाउनु pharo garer chalaunu

script *n.* लिपि lipi

scripture *n.* धर्मग्रन्थ dharmgranth

scrub *n.* दलेर सफा गुर्नु dalera sapha garnu

scrutinize *v.* ध्यानसँग जाँच्नु dhyan sanga janchnu

scrutiny *n.* सूक्ष्म परीक्षण suksham parikshan

scud *v.* सुगम रीतीले बगेर जानु sugam ritile bager janu

scuff *v.* खुट्टा घिसारेर हिँड्नु khuta ghisarer hindnu

scuffle *n.* झगडा jhagada

scull *n.* नाउ ख्याउने डाँडी nau khiyaune dandi

scullery *n.* भाँडा माइने कोठा bhanrha maine kotha

sculptor *n.* मूर्तिकार murtikar

sculpture *n.* मूर्तिकला murtikala

scurf *n.* चाया chaya

scurf *n.* चाया chaya

scurvy *n.* घृणित ghrinit

scythe *n.* हँसिया hansiya

sea *n.* समुद्र samundra

sea beach *n.* समुद्रीतट samudritat

sea level *n.* समुद्री सतह samudri sataha

seafarer *n.* समुद्री यात्री samudri yatri

seafood *n.* समुद्री खाना samudri khana

seal *n.* छाप chhap

seal of love *n.* चुम्बन chumban

seal off *v.* बाटो बन्द गर्नु bato band garnu

sealing wax *n.* लाहा laha

seam *n.* कपडाको जोर्नी kapada ko jorni

seamster *n.* दर्जी darji

seamstress *n.* दर्जिनी darjini

seaport *n.* समुद्री घाट samudri ghat

search *n.* खोजतलाश khojtalash

search party *n.* खोजी दल khojidal

seashore *n.* समुद्री किनार samudri kinar

seasickness *n.* समुद्री बिमारी samudri bimari

season *n.* ऋतु ritu

season *n.* ऋतु ritu

seasonal *adj.* मौसमी mausami

seasoned *adj* छिप्पिएको chhippieko

seat *n.* बस्ने ठाउँ basne thaun

seaweed *n.* समुद्री झार samudri jhar

seclusion *n.* एकान्तबासव ekant bas

second *n.* दोस्रो मान्छे dosro manchhe

second best *adj.* दोस्रो सर्वोत्तम dosro sarwottam

second fiddle *n.* दोस्रो सीन dosrosthan

second thought *n.* नयाँ विचार nayan wichar

second-hand *adj.* पुरानो purano

secrecy *n.* गोपनीयता gopniyata

secret *n.* गुप्ति कुरा guptikura

secret police *n.* गुप्त पुलिस gupt pulis

secret service *n.* जासूसी काम jasusi kam

secretariat सचिवालय sachiwalaya

secretary *n.* सेक्रेटरी secretari

sect *n.* सम्प्रदाय sampradya

section *n.* शाखा shakha

sector *n.* क्षेत्र kshetra

secular *n.* धर्मनिरपेक्ष dharm nirapeksha

secure *vc.* सुरक्षित गराउनु surakshit garaunu

security *n.* सुरक्षा suraksha

sedate *adj.* धीर dheer

sediment *n.* कसर kasar

sedition *n.* राजद्रोह raj droh

seduce *v.* बहकाउनु bahakaunu

seduction *n.* बहकाउ bahakau

see *v.* हेर्नु hernu

see off *v.* पुन्याउन जानु puryauna janu

see red *v.* ज्यादै रिसाउनु jyadai risaunu

see to *v.* ध्यान राख्नु dhyan rakhnu

seed *n.* बीउ bue

seedling *n.* बेर्ना berna

seek *v.* खोज्नु khojnu

seem *v.* देखिनु dekhiunu

seemingly *adv.* देख्दा dekhda

seemly *adj.* सुशील sushil

seemly *adj.* उचित uchit

seep *v.* रसाउनु rasaunu

seesaw *n.* ढिकिच्याउँ खेल dhiki chyaunkhel

see-through *adj.* पारदर्शक par darshak

segment *n.* खण्ड khand

seize *v.* समाल्नु samatnu

seizure *n.* पकड pakad

seldom *adv.* कहिलेकाहीँ मात्रै kahile kahin matai

select *v.* छान्नु chhannu

selection *n.* छनोट chhanot

self *n.* आफु aphu

self-abuse *n.* हस्तमैथुन hast maithun

self-confident *adj.* आत्मविश्वासी atma wishwasi

self-conscious *adj.* सङ्कोखी sankochi

self-control *n.* आत्मनियन्त्रण atma niyantran

self-determination *n.* आत्मनिर्णय atma nirnaya

self-evident *adj.* स्वयंसिद्ध swayamsiddha

self-help *n.* स्वावलम्बन swawlamban

self-indulgent *adj.* विलासी wilasi

self-interest *n.* स्वार्थ swarth

selfish *adj.* स्वार्थी swarthi

selfishness *n.* स्वार्थ swarth

selfless *adj.* निस्सवार्थ nisswarth

self-made *adj.* आफै बनेको aphai baneko

self-possessed *adj.* धैर्यवान dhairyawan

self-reliant *adj.* स्वावलमी swawlambi

self-respect *n.* आत्सम्मान atma samman

self-sacrifice *n.* आत्म बलिदान atma balidan

self-sufficient *adj.* आत्मनिर्भर atma nirbhar

sell *v.* बेच्नु bechnu

sell out *v.* धोका दिनु dhokha dinu

seller *n.* विक्रेता wikreta

semblance *n.* वाह्य आकृति vahya aakriti

semen *n.* वीर्य wirya

semester *n.* सेमेस्टर semestar

semi अर्ध ardh

semicircle *n.* आधा वृत्त adha writta

seminal *adj.* मूल mool

seminar *n.* गोष्ठी goshthi

senate *n.* सिनेट sinet

senator *n.* सिनेटर sinetar

send *v.* पठाउनु pathaunu

send for *v.* बोलाउन पठाउनु bolauna pathaunu

send off *v.* बिदा गर्नु bida garnu

senior *adj.* जेठो jetho

sensation *n.* हलचल halchal

sensational *adj.* सनसनीपूर्ण sansanipurn

sense *n.* अक्कल akkal

senseless *adj.* मूर्ख murkh

sensible *adj.* समझदार samajhdar

sensitive *adj.* संवेदनशील samwedanshil

sensory *adj.* संवेदिक samwedik

sentence *n.* वाक्य wakya

sentiment *n.* भावना bhawana

sentimental *adj.* भावुक bhawuk

sentinel *n.* पाले pale

separate *adj.* अलग alag

separately *adv.* बेग्लाबेग्लै begla beglai

sepia *n. adj.* गाढा खैरो gharha khairo

septic *adj.* विषाक्त vishakt

sequel *n.* परिणाम parinaam

sequence *n.* क्रम kram

sequester *v.* अरु मानिसबाट अलग राख्नु aru manisbaat alag rakhnu

seraglio *n.* अन्तःपुर antahpur

seraph *n.* देवदूत devdoot

serene *adj.* शान्त shant

serf *n.* दास das

serial *n./adj.* धारावाहिक dharawahik

serious *adj.* गम्भीर gambhir

serpent *n.* सर्प sarpa

servant *n.* नोकर nokar

serve *v.* पस्कनु paskanu

service *n.* सेवा sewa

serviciang *n.* मरम्मत marmarmat

serviette *n.* नेपकिन napkin

sesame *n.* तिल til

set *n.* सेट set

set about *v.* शरु गर्नु shuru garnu

set an example *v.* उदाहरण देखाउनु udahara dekhaunu

set eyes on *v.* देख्नु dekhnu

set upon *v.* आक्रमण गर्नु akraman garnu

setback *n.* निराशा nirasha

settle *v.* बसोबास गर्नु basobas garnu

settlement *n.* बस्ती basti

settler *n.* नयाँ बस्तीमा बस्ने nayanbasti ma basne

set-up *n.* व्यवस्था wyawastha

seven *n.* सात sat

seventeen *n.* सत्र satra

seventeenth *n./adj.* सत्रौं satraun

seventh *n./adj.* सातौं sataun

seventy *n.* सत्तरी sattari

sever *v.* अलग/विच्छेद गर्नु alag/ wichchhed garnu

several *adj.* धेरै dherai

severe *adj.* कडा kada

sew *v.* सिउनु siunu

sewer *n.* ढल dhal

sewing machine *n.* सिउने कल siune kal

sex *n.* लिङ्ग ling

sex appeal *n.* यौनाकर्षण yaunakarshan

sexy *adj.* कामोत्तेजक kamottejak

shackle *n.* बन्धन bandhan

shade *n.* छाया chhaya

shady *adj.* छायादार chhayadar

shaft *n.* माँझको भाग maghko dhag

shake *v.* हल्लाउनु hallaunu

shake down *v.* झार्नु jharnu

shake hands *v.* हात मिलाउनु hat milaunu

shake off *v.* पिण्ड छुटाउनु pind chhutaunu

shake-out *n.* हलचल halchal

shake-up *n.* हलचल halchal

shaky *adj.* चंचल chanchal

shall *mod.* लाहा laha

shallow *adj.* कम गहिरो kam gahiro

sham *adj.* बनावटी banawati

shame *n.* लज्जा lajja

shamefaced *adj.* लज्जालु lajjalu

shameless *adj.* निर्लज्ज nirlajja

shampoo *n.* स्याम्पू syampu

shape *n.* आकार akar

shapely *adj.* रूपवती rupwati

share *n.* अंश ansh

shareholder *n.* साझेदार sajhedar

sharp *adj.* तीखो tikho

sharpen *v.* तिखार्नु tikharnu

sharply *adv.* तेजले tej le

shatter *v.* फुटाउनु phutaunu

shave *n.* खौराइ khaurai

shawl *n.* ओढ्ने odhne

she *pron.* उनी uni

sheath *n.* खोल khol

shed *n.* छाप्रो chhapro

sheen *n.* चम्कनु chamkanu

sheep *n.* भेडा bheda

sheepish *adj.* लज्जालु lajjalu

sheet *n.* तन्ना tanna

shelf *n.* तखता takhta

shelter *n.* शरण sharan

shepherd *n.* भेडागोठालो bheda gothalo

shield *n.* ढाल dhal

shift *n.* साटो sato

shin *n.* नलिहाड nalihad

shine *n.* चमक chamak

shining *adj.* चम्किलो chamkilo

ship *n.* जहाज jahaj

shipment *n.* जहाजमा चलान गरिएको माल jahaj ma chalan garieko mal shire *n.* मण्डल mandal

shirt *n.* कमिज kamij

shiver *n.* कम्पन kampan

shock *n.* धक्का dhakka

shocking *adj.* चोट पुन्याउने chot puryaune

shoddy *adj.* घटिया ghatiya

shoe *n.* जुत्ता jutta

shoehorn *n.* बगलिस baglis

shoelace *n.* जुत्ता को फित्ता jutta ko phitta

shoemaker *n.* सार्की sarki

shoestring *n.* जुत्ता को फित्ता jutta ko phitta

shoot *n.* टुसा tusa

shooting *n.* बन्दुक वा पिस्तोल हान्ने काम banduk wa pistol hanne kam

shooting star *n.* सानो उल्का sano ulka

shop *n.* पसल pasal

shopkeeper *n.* पसले pasale

shopping *n.* किनमेल kinmel

shore *n.* बगर bagar

short *adj.* छोटो chhoto

short of *prep.* सिवाय siwaya

shortage *n.* अभाव abhaw

shortcut *n.* छोटोबाटो chhoto bato

shorten *v.* छोटो पार्नु chhoto parnu

shortfall *n.* घाटा ghata

shorthand *n.* छिटो लेख्ने विधि chhiti lekhne widhi

short-lived *adj.* छोटो जीवन भएको chhoto jiwan bhaeko

shortly *adv.* चाँडै chandai

shorts *n.* कट्टु kattu

short-sighted *adj.* निकटदर्शी nikatdarshi

short-tempered *adj.* चाँडै रिसाउने chandai risaune

short-term *adj.* अल्पकालिक alpkalik

short-witted *adj.* अल्पबुद्धि alp buddhi

shot *n.* तोपगोला top gola

should *v./mod.* पर्छ parchha

shoulder *n.* काँध kandh

shout *v.* कराउनु karaunu

shove *v.* घचेट्नु ghachetnu

shovel *n.* साभेल sabhel

show *n.* तमाशा tamasha

show off *v.* रबाफ देखाउनु rabaph dekhaunu

shower *n.* वर्षा warsha

showy *adj.* देखावटी dekhawati

shred *n.* त्यान्द्रो tyandro

shrewd *adj.* चलाख chalakh

shriek *n.* चिच्याहट chichyahat

shrill *adj.* तीखो tikho

shrimp *n.* झिंगे माछा jhinge machha

shrine *n.* तीर्थ tirth

shrine *n.* पवित्र स्थल pavitra sthal

shrink *v.* खुम्चिनु khumchinu

shrink *v.* सानो हुनु sano hunu

shroud *n.* कात्रो katro

shrug *v.* काँध खुम्च्याउनु kandh khum chyaunu

shudder *v.* डरले काम्नु dar le kammu

shuffle *v.* खुट्टा घिसारेर हिँड्नु khutta ghisarera hindnu

shun *v.* टाढा रहनु tadha rahanu

shut *v.* बन्द गर्नु band garnu

shut down *v.* बन्द गर्नु band garnu

shut off *v.* प्रवाह बन्द गरिदिनु prawah band garidinu

shut up *v.* चुप लाग chuplag

shutter *n.* झिलमिल jhilmil

shy *adj.* लज्जालु lajjalu

sibling *n.* सहोदर भाइ वा बहिनी sahodar bhai wa bahini

sibyl *n.* भविष्य बताउने स्त्री bhavishya bataune stri

sick *adj.* बिरामी birami

sick *adj.* बिमार bimar

sickle *n.* हँसिया hansiya

sickle *n.* हाँसिया hansiya

side *n.* छेउ chheu

side *n.* किनार kinar

side by side *adv.* सँगसँगै sang sangai

sidewalk *n.* पेटी peti

sideways *adv.* बगलतिर bagaltir

sieve *n.* चल्नी chalni

sigh *n.* लामो साँस लिनु lamo sas lenu

sight *n.* हेराइ herai

sight *n.* दृष्टि drishti

sightless *adj.* अन्धो andho

sightseer *n.* र्प्यटक paryatak

sign *v.* लामो सास फेर्नु lamo saas phernu

signal *n.* सङ्केत sanket

signature *n.* सही sahi

signboard *n.* सूचनापाटी साइनबोर्ड suchanapati

significance *n.* महत्त्व mahattwa

significant *adj.* महत्त्वपूर्ण mahattwapurn

signify *v.* जनाउनु janaunu

silence *n.* चुपचाप chupchap

silent *adj.* चुप लागेको chup lageko

silently *adv.* चुप लागेर chup lagera

silica *n.* सिलिका silika

silk *n.* रेशम resham

silkworm *n.* रेशमकीरा resham kira

silky *adj.* नरम naram

silly *adj.* लठुवा lathuwa

silver *n.* चाँदी chandi

silvery *adj.* चाँदीजस्तो सेतो chandi jasto seto

similar *adj.* उस्तै ustai

similarly *adv.* त्यसैगरी tyasaigari

simmer *v.* विस्तारै उम्लनु wistarai umlanu

simmer down *v.* कम उत्तेजित हुनु kam uttejit hunu

simple *adj.* सजिलो sajilo

simpleton *n.* मूर्ख murkh

simply *adv.* खालि khali

simulate *v.* हो-जस्तो गर्नु ho-jasto garnu

simultaneously *adv.* एकैचोटि ekaichoti

sin *n.* पाप pap

since *adv.* त्यस बेलादेखि tyas bela dekhi

sincere *adj.* साँचो sancho

sincerely *adv.* शुद्ध मनले shuddha manle

sine die *adv.* अनिश्चित कालसम्म anishchit kal samma

sine qua non *n.* अनिवार्य शर्त aniwarya shart

sinecure *n.* आरामको नोकरी aaram ko nokari

sinew *n.* नसा nasa

sinewy *adj.* गठिलो gathilo

sinful *adj.* पापी papi

sing *v.* गाउनु gauinu

singe *v.* पोल्नु polnu

singer *n.* गायक gayak

single *adj.* एक्लो eklo

single-handed *adj./adv.* एक्लै ले eklai le

single-minded *adj.* एकनिष्ठ ek nishth

singlet *n.* गन्जी ganji

singleton *adj.* एउटै eutai

sinister *adj.* अनिष्ट anisht

sink डुब्नु dubnu

sinus infection *n.* पिनास pinas

sir *n.* साहेब saheb

sissy *n.* स्त्री जस्तो पुरुष stri jasto purush

sister *n.* दिदी didi

sister-in-law *n.* भाउजू bhauju

sit *v.* बस्नु basnu

sit tight *v.* अडान लिनु adan linu

site *n.* निर्माणस्थल nirmal sthal

situation *n.* स्थिति sthiti

six *n.* छ chha

sixteen *n.* सोरह sorha

sixth *n./adj.* छैटौं chhaitaun

sixty *n.* साठी sathi

size *n.* नाप nap

sizzle *v.* छड्कनु charkanu

skeleton *n.* कङ्काल kankal

sketch *n.* हातले बनाएको चित्र hat le banaeko chitra

skewer *n.* झीर jheer

skiff *n.* सानो नाउ sano nau

skill *n.* सीप sip

skim *v.* तर झिक्नु tar jhiknu

skimish *n.* भिडन्त लडाइँ bhidant ladain

skin *n.* छाला chhala

skinflint *n.* कंजूस kanjoos

skinny *adj.* दुब्लो-पातलो dublo-patlo

skip *v.* बुरुक्क उफ्रनु burukka uphranu

skirt *n.* स्कर्ट skart

skull *n.* खोपडी khopadi

skullduggery *n.* चालबाजी chaalbaji

sky *n.* आकाश akash

sky-blue *adj.* आकाशे नीलो akashe nilo

skyjack *v.* विमान अपहरण गर्नु wiman apharan garnu

skyline *n.* खितिज kshitij

skyscraper *n.* गगनचुम्बी भवन gagan chumbi bhawan

slab *n.* शिला shila

slack *adj.* फितलो phitalo

slag *n.* धातुको मैला dhatuko maila

slam *v.* बजार्नु bajarnu

slander *n.* आरोप arop

slang *n.* अपभाषा ap bhasha

slant *adj.* तेर्सो terso

slap *n.* थप्पड thappad

slash *v.* चिर्नु chirnu

slate *n.* सिलोट silot

slaughter *v.* काट्नु katnu

slave *n.* दास das

slaver *v.* राल चुहाउनु raal chuhaunu

slavery *n.* दासता dasta

slay *v.* मार्नु marnu

sleazy *adj.* फोहोर fohor

sledgehammer *n.* ठूलो घन thulo ghan

sleep *v.* सुत्नु sutnu

sleeping bag *n.* सिलपिङ ब्याग slipin byag

sleeping pill *n.* निद्रा लाग्ने चक्की nidra lagne chakki

sleepy *adj.* निद्रा लागेको nidra lageko

sleeve *n.* बाहुला bahula

sleeveless *adj.* बाहुला नभएको bahula na bhaeko

slege *n.* अवरोध abrodh

slender *adj.* झिनो jhino

sleuth *n.* जासूस jasus

slew *v.* नयाँ दिशामा घुम्नु nayan dishama ghumnu

slice *n.* चाना chana

slide *v.* चिप्लनु chiplanu

slight *adj.* हल्का halka

slim *adj.* छरितो दुब्लो पातलो chharito dublo patalo

slime *n.* चिप्लो र हिले माटो chiplo r hile mato

sling *n.* झटारो jhataro

slingshot *n.* गुलेली guleli

slip *n.* भूल bjil

slip-knot *n.* सुर्केनी गाँठो surkeni gantho

slipper *n.* चप्पल chappal

slippers *n.* चट्टी chatti

slippery *adj.* चिप्लो chiplo

slipshod *adj.* फोहोरी phohori

slit *n.* चिरा chira

slogan *n.* नारा nara

slope *n.* उकालो ukalo

sloppy *adj.* बेढङ्ग bedhang

slot *n.* चिरा chira

slough *n.* गहिरो हिलो gahiro hilo

slow *adj.* ढीलो dhilo

slowloy *adv.* ढीलोगरी dhilogari

slug *n.* चिप्लेकीरो chiple kiro

sluggard *n.* अल्छी लोसे व्यक्ति alchhi lose vyakti

slum *n.* गन्दा बस्ती gandabasti

slumber *n.* निद्रा nidra

slur *v.* कलंक kalank

sly *adj.* धूर्त dhurt

small *adj.* सानो sano

small arms *n.* साना हतियार sana hatiyar

small change *n.* खुद्रा khudra

small hours *n.* आधारात तपछिको समय adharat pachhi ko samaya

small talk *n.* सानातिना कुरा sana tina kura

smallpox *n.* बिफर biphar

smallpox *n.* माई maai

smart *adj.* तेज tej

smartly *adv.* फुर्तिसिँग phurti sanga

smash *v.* फोड्नु phodnu

smattering *n.* थोरै ज्ञान thorae gyan

smear *v.* घस्नु ghasnu

smell *n.* सुगन्ध sugandh

smelt *v.* पगाल्नु pagaalnu

smile *n.* मुस्कान muskan

smiling *adj.* हँसिलो hansilo

smite *v.* हान्नु haanu

smith *n.* लोहार lohar

smoke *n.* धुँवा dhuwan

smokeless *adj.* धेवा नभएको dhuwan na bhaeko

smoker *n.* चुरोट⁄तमाखु खाने churot/tamakhu khane

smoking *n.* धुम्रपान dhurmrapan

smoky *adj.* घ्वाँसे dhawanse

smoothly *adv.* राम्रोसँग tamro sanga

smooth-tongued *adj.* मीठो बौल्ले miltho bolne

smother *v.* सास रोकिदिनु sas roki dinu

smoulder *v.* ज्वालाबिना जल्नु jwalabina jalnu

smudge *n.* दाग daag

smug *adj.* आत्म-सन्तुष्ट atam-santusht

smuggle *v.* तस्करी गर्नु taskari garnu

smuggler *n.* तस्कर व्यापारी taskar wyapari

snack *n.* खाजा khaja

snack bar *n.* चमेनाघर chamena ghar

snaffle *v.* नसोधी लैजानु nsodhi lejanu

snag *n.* समस्या samasya

snail *n.* शङ्खे कीरो shankha kiro

snake *n.* सर्प sarpa

snake charmer *n.* सपेरो sapero

snake in the grass *n.* लुकेको शत्रु lukeko shatru

snakebite *n.* सर्पको टोकाइ sapa ko tokai

snake-gourd *n.* चिचिण्डो chichindo

snakes and ladders *n.* बैकुण्ठ खेल baikunth khel

snap *v.* न्याक्क टोक्नु nyakka toknu

snapshot *n.* तस्वीर taswir

snare *n.* पासो paso

snarl *v.* ङ्यारङ्कुर गर्नु nyar nyur garnu

snatch *v.* खोस्नु khosnu

sneak *v.* सुटुक्क/लुकेर जानु sutukka/lukera janu

sneaking *adj.* गुप्तचर guptchar

sneer *v.* गिल्ला गर्नु gilla garnu

sneeze *n.* छिँक्क chhink

sniff *v.* सुर्कनु surknu

snigger *n.* दबेको हाँसो dabeko haanso

snob *n.* घमण्डी मान्छे ghamandi manchhe

snood *n.* केश बाँध्ने फिता kesh bandhne fitta

snore *v.* घुर्नु ghurnu

snout *n.* थुतुनो thutuno

snow *n.* हिउँ हिउँ पर्नु hiun

snow leopard *n.* हिउँ चितुवा hiun chituwa

snowball *n.* हिउँको डल्लो hiun ko dallo

snow-capped *adj.* हिउँले ढाकेको hiun le dhakeko

snowfall *n.* हिमपात himpat

snowline *n.* हिमरेखा him rekha

snowman *n.* हिममानव him manaw

snowstorm *n.* बरफिलो तूफान barphilo

snow-white *adj.* शुद्ध सेतो shuddha seto

snuff *n.* काजल kajol

so *adv./conj.* त्यसकारण tyas karan

so long as *adv.* त्यसो भएमा tyaso bhae ma

so on *pron.* इत्यादि ityadi

so-and-so *pron.* फलानु phalanu

soap *n.* साबुन sabun

soar *v.* अकासिनु akasinu

sob *n.* रुवाइ ruwai

sober *adj.* शान्त shant

so-called *adj.* तथाकथित tatha kathit

soccer *n.* फुटबल phut bal

social *adj.* सामाजिक samajik

social science *n.* सामाजिक विज्ञान samajik wigyan

social security *n.* सामाजिक सुरक्षा samajik suraksha

social services *n.* सामाजिक सेवा samajik sewa

social worker *n.* समाजसेवी samaj sewi

socialism *n.* समाजवाद samajwad

sociology *n.* समाज-विज्ञान samaj-vigyan

sock *n.* मोजा moja

sod *n.* चुपरीको थुप्रो chupriko thupro

soda *n.* सोडा soda

soda water *n.* सोडा पानी soda pani

sofa *n.* सोफा sopha

soft *adj.* कमलो kamalo

soft drink *n.* हलुका पेय haluka peya

soft(ly) spoken *adj.* मिजासिलो mijasilo

soft-hearted *adj.* कमलो kamalo

software *n.* कम्प्युटर कार्यक्रम kampyutar karya kram

soggy *adj.* भिजेको bhijeko

soil *n.* माटो mato

soiree *n.* सान्ध्य गोष्ठी saandhya goshti

sojourn *n.* बास बस्नु bas basnu

solace *n.* सान्त्त्वना santwana

solar *adj.* सूर्यको surya ko

solar eclipse *n.* सूर्यग्रहण surya grahan

solar system *n.* सौरमण्डल saur mandal

solder *n.* राङ raang

soldier *n.* सिपाही sipahi

sole *n.* पैताला paitala

solely *adv.* खालि khali

solemn *adj.* गम्भीर gambhir

solicit *v.* बिन्तीभाउ गर्नु binti bhau garnu

solid *adj.* ठोस thos

solitary *adj.* निर्जन nirjan

solution *n.* समाधान samadhan

solve *v.* हल/समाधान गर्नु hal/ samadhan garnu

solvent *adj.* ऋण तिर्न सक्ने rin tirn sakne

sombre *adj.* अँध्यारो andhyaro

some *adj.* केही kehi

somebody *pron.* कोही kohi

somehow *adv.* कुनै किसिमले kumnai kisimle

someone *pron.* कोही kohi

something *pron.* केही वस्तु kehi wastu

sometimes *adv.* कहिलेकाहीं kahile kahin matai

somewhere *adv.* कहीं kahin

somnolent *adj.* निद्रालु nidralu

son *n.* छोरा chhora

song *n.* गीत git

soon *adv.* चाँडै chandai

sooner or later *adv.* ढिलो वा चाँडो dhilo wa chando

soot *n.* ध्वाँसो dhwanso

soothe *v.* शमन गर्नु shaman garnu

soothsayer *n.* ज्योतिषी jyotishi

sorcerer *n.* बोक्सो bokso

sore *n.* घाउ ghau

sorrow *n.* दुःख duhkha

sorrowful *adj.* दुखी dukhi

sort *n.* किसिम kisim

sort out *v.* छुट्याउनु chhutyaunu

so-so *adj./adv.* ठिक्कै thikkai

sot *n.* जँड्याहा jangyaha

soul *n.* आत्मा atma

sound *n.* आवाजा awaj

sound asleep *adv.* मस्त निदाएको mast nidaeko

sound off *v.* जोडले कुरा गर्नु jod le kura garnu

sound sleep *n.* मस्तनिद्रा mast nidra

soundproof(ed) *adj.* आवाज नछिर्ने awaj na chhirne

soup *n.* रस ras

sour *adj.* अमिलो amilo

source *n.* मूल mul

south *n.* दक्षिण dakshin

southern *adj.* दक्षिणी dakkhini

southward *adj.* दक्षिणी dakshini

souvenir *n.* चिर्नु chinu

sovereign *n.* राजा raja

sovereignty *n.* प्रभुसत्ता prabhu satta

sow *v.* छर्नु chharnu

soya bean *n.* भटमास bhatmas

soya bean/soybean *n.* भटमास bhatmas

space *n.* ठाउँ thaun

space age *n.* अन्तरिक्ष युग antariksha yug

space station *n.* अन्तरिक्ष स्अेसन antariksha stesan

spacecraft *n.* अन्तरिक्षयान antariksha yan

spaceman *n.* अन्तरिक्षयात्री antariksha yatri

spaceship *n.* अन्तरिक्षयान antariksha yan

spacesuit *n.* अन्तरिक्ष पोशाक antariksha poshak

spacious *adj.* फराकिलो pharakilo

spade *n.* कोदालो kodalo

spades *n.* सुरथ surath

spadework *n.* शुरुको काम shuru ko kam

span *n.* विस्तार wistar

spare *n.* जगेडा jageda

spare parts *n.* जगेडा पुर्जाहरू jageda purja haru

spare time *n.* फुर्सद को समय phursad ko samaya

sparing *adj.* मितव्ययी mitvyaye

spark *n.* झिल्को jhilko

sparkle *v.* चम्कनु chamkanuj

sparrow *n.* भँगेरा bhangera

sparse *adj.* पातलिएको patlieko

spasm *n.* आक्रमण aakraman

spate *n.* बाढी badhi

spatial *adj.* आकाशीय aakashiya

spatter *v.* छर्किनु chharkinu

speak *v.* बोल्नु bolnu

speaker *n.* वक्ता wakta

spear *n.* भाला bhala

special *adj.* विशेष wishesh

specialist *n.* विशेषज्ञ wisheshagya

specially *adv.* विशेष गरी wishesh gari

specie *n.* धातु को सिक्का dhatuko sikka

specific *adj.* तोकिएको tokieko

specified *adj.* तोकिए को tokieko

specify *v.* तोक्नु toknu

specimen *n.* नमूना namuna

speck *n.* सानो कण sanokan

spectacular *adj.* हेर्न लायक को herna layak ko

spectator *n.* दर्शक darshak

speculate *v.* अनुमान/तर्कना गर्नु anuman/tarkana garnu

speculation *n.* अनुमान/तर्कना गर्नु anuman

speech *n.* बोली boli

speechless *adj.* लाटो lato

speed *n.* गति gati

speed limit *n.* गति सीमा gati sima

speedboat *n.* वेगसँग चल्ने मोटर डुङ्गा beg sanga chalne motar dunga

speedy *adj.* तेजिलो tejilo

spell *v.* हिज्जे गर्नु hijje garnu

spend *n.* खर्च गर्नु kharch garnu

spendthrift *n./adj.* फजुलखर्ची phajul kharchi

sphere *n.* डल्लो dallo

sphere of influence *n.* प्रभाव क्षेत्र prabhaw kshetra

spherical *adj.* गोलो golo

spice(s) *n.* मसला masla

spicy *adj.* मसालेदार masale dar

spider *n.* माकुरो makuro

spider *n.* माकुरा makura

spider's web *n.* माकुरा को जालो makura ko jalo

spike *n.* सुरो suro

spill *v.* पोख्नु pokhnu

spill the beans *v.* कुरा खोल्नु kura kholnu

spin *v.* फनफनी घुम्नु phan phani ghumnu

spinach *n.* पालुङ्गो palungo

spinal *adj.* मेरुदण्डको merudandko

spine *n.* डँडाल्नो dandalno

spinning top *n.* लट्टु lattu

spinning wheel *n.* चर्खा charkha

spire *n.* मिनार minar

spirit *n.* आत्मा atma

spiritual *adj.* आध्यात्मिक adhyatmik

spit *n.* थुक thuk

spiteful *adj.* इखालु ikhalu

spittle *n.* थुक thuk

spittoon *n.* थुक्ने भाँड़ो thukne bhadho

splash *n.* छ्यापछ्याप chhyap chhyap

spleen *n.* फियो phiyo

splendid *adj.* गानदार shandar

splendo(u)r *n.* चहक chahak

splint *n.* चोइटो choito

split *n.* विभाजित wibhajit

split personality *n.* विभाजित व्यक्तित्व wibhajit wyaktitwa

split second *n.* ज्यादै छोटो समय jyadai chhoto samaya

splotch *n.* धब्बा dhabba

spoil *v.* बिगार्नु bigarnu

spoilspert *n.* खेल बिगार्ने मान्छे khel bigarne manchhe

spokesperson *n.* प्रवक्ता prawakta

sponge *n.* स्पोंज sponj

spongy *adj.* सोसिलो sosilo

sponsor *n.* प्रायोजक prayojak

spontaneous *adj.* आफै भएको aphai bhaeko

spoof *v.* छलनु chhalnu

spool *n.* धागो वा फिलिम बेर्ने रिल dhago wa philim berne ril

spoon *n.* चम्चा chamcha

spore *n.* बीजाणु beejanu

sport(s) *n.* खेलकूद khelkud

sportsperson *n.* खेलाडी kheladi

spot *n.* दाग dag

spotless *adj.* बेदाग bedag

spotted *adj.* छिबिरि chhirbire

spouse *n.* जहान jahan

spout *n.* धारो dharo

sprain *n.* मर्कनु markanu

sprain *v.* मर्कनु makarnu

sprained *adj.* मर्केको markeko

spray *n.* पिचकारी pichkari

spread *v.* फेलनु phailanu

sprig *n.* सानो हाँगा sano haanga

spring *n.* बसन्त basant

spring on *v.* झम्अनु jhamtanu

sprinkle *v.* छर्कनु chharkanu

sprite *n.* युत yut

sprout *n.* अँकुर ankur

spud *n.* एक किसमको कोदालो ek kisimko kodhalo

spur *n.* थुम्को thela

spy *n.* जासूस jasus

squad *n.* टोली toli

squalid *adj.* फोहोरी phohori

squander *v.* फजुल खर्च गर्नु phajul kharch garnu

square *n.* चारपाटे char pate

square deal *n.* निष्कपट सौदेबाजी nish kapat saudebaji

square meal *n.* पेटभर भोजन pet bhar bhojan

square root *n.* वर्गमूल warg mul

squash *n.* स्कवास खेल skwas khel

squat *v.* टुक्रुक्क बस्नु tukrukka basnu

squatter *n.* सुकुम्बासी sukum basi

squeak *v.* चीँचीँ गर्नु chin chin garnu

squeeze *v.* निचर्नु nicharnu

squiffy *adj.* अलि मातेको ali mateko

squiggle *n.* बाङ्गोटिङ्गो रेखा bangotingo rekha

squint *adj.* डेढो dedho

squirrel *n.* लोखर्के lokharke

squirrel *v.* लोखर्के lokheken

stab *n.* छुरा धस्नु chhura dhasnu

stab in the back *n.* पिठ्युँमा प्रहार pinhyun ma prahar

stable *adj.* अचल achar

stadium *n.* रङ्गशाला rangshala

staff *n.* कर्मचारी karm chari

stag *n.* भाले जरायो bhale jarayo

stag party *n.* लोग्नेमान्छेहरूको पार्टी logne manchhe haru ko parti

stage *n.* रङ्गमंच rang manch

stagger *v.* लर्खराउनु larkharaunu

staid *adj.* गंभीर gambhir

stain *n.* दाग dag

stainless *adj.* बेदाग bedag

stainless steel *n.* खिया नलाग्ने इस्पात khiya na lagne ispat

stairs *n.* भरेङ bharen

stake सूली suli

stale *adj.* थोत्रो thotro

stalemate *n.* चालबन्द chalband

stalk *n.* डाँठ danth

stall *n.* तबेला tabela

stallion *n.* आँडु घोडा andu ghoda

stalwart *adj.* हट्टाकट्टा hattakatta

stamen *n.* पुंकेशर punkeshwar

stamina *n.* अड्ने शक्ति adne shakti

stammer *v.* भकभकाउनु bhak bhakaunu

stammer *v.* भकभकाउनु bhak bhakaunu

stammerer *n.* भकभके bhak bhake

stamp *n.* छाप chhap

stance *n.* गोली हान्दा उभिने ढंग goli handa ubhine dhang

stanch, staunch *v.* रोक्नु roknu

stand *v.* उभिनु ubhinu

stand by *v.* समर्थन गर्नु samarthan garnu

stand for *v.* प्रतिनिधित्व गर्नु prati nidhitwa garnu

stand off *v.* हट्नु hatnu

standard *n.* स्तर star

standard of living *n.* जीवन स्तर jiwan star

standard-bearer *n.* ध्वजावाहक dhwajawahak

standby *n.* सहारा sahara

standing committee *n.* स्थायी समिति sthayi samiti

standing order *n.* स्थायी आदेश sthayi adesh

standpoint *n.* दृष्टिकोण drishtikon

standstill *n.* मुकाम kukam

star *n.* तारा tara

starch *n.* माड़ maadh

stare at one another *v.* हेराहर गर्नु here her garnu

stargazer *n.* ज्योतिषी jyotishi

stark *adj.* दरो daro

start *n.* शुरु shuru

startle *v.* झस्किनु jhaskinu

starvation *n.* भोकमरी bhokmari

starve *v.* भोकै हुनु bhokai hunu

state *n.* स्थिति sthiti

state of affairs *n.* परिस्थिति paristhiti

state of mind *n.* मनस्थिति manasthiti

statement *n.* वक्तव्य waktawya

static *adj.* स्थिर sthir

station *n.* मुकाम mukam

statistics *n.* तथ्याङ्क tathyank

statue *n.* सालिक salik

status *n.* औकात aukat

status quo *n.* यथास्थिति yatha sthiti

status symbol *n.* जेथा jetha

statusquo यथापूर्व स्थिति yathapurv sthiti

staunch *adj.* वफादार baphadar

stay *v.* रहनु rahanu

stay put *v.* जहाँको त्यहीँ रहनु jahan ko tyhin rahanu

staying power *n.* अड्ने शक्ति adne shakti

steady *adj.* स्थिर sthir

steal *v.* चोर्नु chornu

steam *n.* बाफ baphadar

steel *n.* इस्पात ispat

steep *adj.* ठाडो thado

steeple *n.* गिर्जाघरको गजुर girjagharko gajur

steer *v.* परिचालन गर्नु parichalan garnu

steer clear of *v.* बचेर रहनु bachera rahanu

steering committee *n.* संचालक समिति sanchalak samiti

steering wheel *n.* स्टेरिङ sterin

stellar *adj.* तारायुक्त tarayukt

stem *n.* डाँठ danth

stench *v.* गनाउनु ganaunu

stencil *n.* स्टेन्सिल stensil

stenographer *n.* संकेत लेखक sanket lekhak

step *n.* खुड्किला khudkila

step down *v.* राजीनामा दिनु raji nama dinu

step in *v.* भित्र पस्नु bhitra pasnu

step up *v.* बढाउनु badhaun

stepbrother *n.* सौतिनी भाइ/दाजु sautini bhai/daju

stepdaughter *n.* झट्केली छोरी jhatkeli chhori

stepfather *n.* झङ्केलो बाबु jhadkelo babu

stepladder *n.* आफै अड्ने भरेङ aphai adne bharen

stepmother *n.* सौतिनी आमा sautini ama

stepsister *n.* सौतिनी बहिनी/दिदी sautini bahini/didi

stepson *n.* झट्केलो छोरा jhatkelo chhora

stereotyped *adj.* एकैनासे ekai nase

sterile *adj.* बाँझो banjho

stew *n.* बफाएको परिकार baphaeko parikar

steward *n.* प्रबन्धक prabandhak

stick *n.* लट्ठी latthi

stick aroujnd *v.* नजिकै रहनु najikari rahanu

stick out *v.* बाहिर निक्लेको हुनु bahira nikleko hunu

stick-in-the-mud *n.* पुरानो ढर्राको मानिस purano dharra ko mani

stiff *adj.* दरो daro

stifle *v.* निसासिनु nisasino

still *adv.* अझै ajhai

still life *n.* निर्जीव वस्तुको चित्र nirjiw wastu ko chitra

stillborn *adj.* janmada mareko

stimulate *v.* उत्तेजित गर्नु uttejit garnu

stimulation *n.* उत्तेजन uttejan

sting *n.* चिल्ने खिल chilne khil

stingy *adj.* कन्जुस kanjus

stink *v.* गनाउनु ganaunu

stipend *n.* भत्ता bhatta

stipulation *n.* शर्त shart

stir *v.* चलाउनु chalaunu

stitch *n.* टाँका tanka

stock *n.* सामान saman

stocking *n.* लामो मोजा lamo moja

stockpile *n.* माल को सँगालो mal ko sangalo

stocky *adj.* खँदिलो khandilo

stodge *adj.* पचाउन कठिन pachaun kathin

stomach *n.* भुँडी bhundi

stomp *v.* खुट्टा बजारेर हिँड्नु khutta bajarer hindanu

stone *n.* ढुङ्गा dhunga

stone age *n.* पत्थरयुग patthar yug

stone's throw *n.* छोटो दूरी chhoto duri

stool *n.* त्रिपाइ tripai

stool pigeon *n.* फसाउने मानिस phasaune manis

stoop *v.* निहुरनु nihuranu

stop *v.* रोक्नु roknu

stop dead *v.* टक्क अड्नु takkaadnu

stop short *v.* अचानक अड्नु achanak adnu

storage *n.* संग्रह sangraha

storehouse *n.* भण्डार bhandar

storekeeper *n.* भण्डारे bhandare

storey *n.* तला tala

stork *n.* सारस saras

storm *n.* आँधी andhi

stormy *adj.* आँधी चलेको andhi chaleko

story *n.* कथा katha

stout *adj.* बलियो baliyo

straight *adj.* सीधा sidha

straight away *adv.* तुरुन्त turunt

straight face *adj.* गम्भीर मुद्रा gambhir mudra

straighten *v.* सीधा पार्नु sidha parnu

straightforward *adj.* खरो kharo

strain *n.* तनाउ tanau

strange *adj.* अनौठो anautho

stranger *n.* नौलो/पराइ मान्दे naulo/parai manchhe

strangle *v.* घाँटी थुन्नु ghanti thunnu

strap *n.* फित्ता phitta

strata *n.* स्तर star

stratagem *n.* चाल chaal

strategy *n.* रणनीति ranniti

stratum *n.* चट्टानको पत्र वा तह chattanko patra wa the

straw *n.* पराल paral

strawberry *n.* भुइँ ऐँसेलु bhuin ainselu

stray *v.* बाटो बिराउनु bato biraunu

stream *n.* खोला khola

streamline *v.* सजिलो र सफल बनाउनु sajilo ra saphal banaunu

street *n.* सडक sadak

streetwalker *n.* वेश्या weshya

strength *n.* तागत tagat

strengthen *v.* बलियो बनाउनु baliyo banaunu

stress *n.* चाप chap

stretch *n.* तन्काइ tankai

stretch out *v.* पसार्नु pasarunu

stretcher *n.* विस्तारक bishtharak

strict *adj.* सख्त sakht

stride *n.* कदम kadam

stride *n.* कदम kadam

strident *adj.* चर्को charko

strife *n.* झगडा jhagada

strike *v.* हड़ताल hadtaal

strike home *v.* मर्म पहार गर्नु marm prahar garnu

strike off *v.* काट्नु katnu

string *n.* डोरी dori

strip *v.* फुकाल्नु lugaphukalnu

stripe *n.* धर्का dharka

striped *adj.* धर्के dharke

strive *v.* कोसिस गर्नु kosis garnu

stroke *n.* प्रहार prahar

stroll *v.* डुल्नु dulnu

strong *adj.* बलियो baliyo

strong point *n.* विशिष्टता wishishtta

strong-arm *adj.* बल प्रयोग गरिने bal prayog garine

stronghold *n.* गढ gadh

strong-minded *adj.* दृढनिश्चयी dridh nishchayi

strop *n.* छूरा उध्याउने छाला chura udhayune chhala

stroppy *adj.* हठी र रिसाहा hathi r risaha

structure *n.* संरचना samprachna

struggle *n.* संघर्ष sangharsh

stubborn *adj.* हठी hathi

student *n.* विद्यार्थी widyarthi

studio *n.* स्टूडियो studio

studious *adj.* अध्ययनशील adhayansheel

study *n.* पढाइ padhai

stuff *n.* चीज chij

stumble *v.* ठेस लाग्नु thes lagnu

stump *n.* ठुटा thuta

stun *v.* अचेत achet

stunned *adj.* दुखी dukhi

stunt *n.* कमाल kamal

stupid *adj.* मूर्ख murkh

stupor *n.* तन्द्रा tandra

stutter *v.* भकभकाउनु bhakbhakaunu

sty *n.* सुङ्गुरको खोर sungurko khor

style *n.* शैली shaili

stylish *adj.* ढाँचावाल dhanchawal

stylus *n.* ग्रामोफोनको सुई gramophoneko sui

subaltern *n.* सैनिक अफिसर sainik officer

subconscious *adj.* अवचेतन aw chetan

subcontinent *n.* उपमहाद्वीप upmahadweep

subdue *v.* जित्नु jitnu

subject *n.* विषय wishaya

subjection *n.* अधीनता adhinta

subjugate *v.* जित्नु jitnu

submerge *v.* पानीले ढाक्नु/डुबाउनु pani le dhaknu/dubaunu

submission *n.* अधीनता adhinta

subnormal *adj.* अवसामान्य avsamanya

subscriber *n.* ग्राहक grahak

subscription *n.* चन्दा chanda

subsequent *adj.* पछि आउने pachi aaune

subservient चापलूस chaploos

subside *v.* घट्नु ghatnu

substance *n.* चीज chij

substantiate *v.* प्रमाणित/साबित गर्नु pramanit/sabit garnu

substitue *n.* साटो sato

substratum *n.* तल्लो तह tallo the

subtle *adj.* कुशाग्र kushagra

subtract *v.* घटाउनु ghataunu

subtraction *n.* घटाउ ghataunu

success *n.* सफलता saphalta

successful *adj.* सफल saphal

successor *n.* उत्तराधिकारी uttaradhikari

such *adj.* यस्तो yasto

such as *adj.* जस्तो कि jasto ki

such-and-such *pron.* फलानो phalano

suck *v.* चुस्नु chusnu

suckle *v.* दूध ख्वाउनु dudh khwaunu

sudden *adj.* अचानक achanak

suddenly *adj.* अकस्मात् akasmat

suede *n.* नरम छाला naram chhala

suet *n.* गोरु वा भेड़ाको चर्बी goru wa bhedako charbi

suffer *v.* सहनु sahanu

suffering *n.* कष्ट kasht

sufficient *adj.* काफी kaphi

suffocate *v.* निसासिनु nisassinu

sugar *n.* चिनी chini

sugar beet *n.* चुकन्दर chukandar

sugar cane *n.* उखु ukhu

suggest *v.* सुझाउ दिनु sujhau dinu

suicide *n.* आत्महत्या atmahatya

suit *n.* सूट sut

suitable *adj.* सुहाउँदो suhaundo

suitcase *n.* लुगा राख्ने बाकस luga rakhne bakas

suitor *n.* झगडिया jhagadiya

sulk *v.* टुसिसनु thussinu

sullen *adj.* टुस्स परेको thussa pareko

sully *v.* कलुषित पार्नु kalushit parnu

sulphur/sulfur *n.* गन्धक gandhak

sultry *adj.* गर्मी garmi

sum *n.* जम्मा jamma

sum up *v.* जोड्नु jodnu

summary *n.* सारांश saransh

summit *n.* चुली chuli

summon *v.* डाक्नु daknu

sumptuous *adj.* बहुमूल्य bahu mulya

sun *n.* सूर्य surya

sunbath *n.* सूर्य स्नान surya snan

sunburnt *adj.* घामले डढेको ghanm le dadheko

sunday *n.* आइतबार aitbar

sunder *v.* अलग गर्नु alag garnu

sundial *n.* धूप-घड़ी dhoopghari

sundown *n.* सूर्यास्त suryast

sunflower *n.* सूर्यमुखी फूल surya mukhi phul

sunglasses *n.* घाम चस्मा gham chasma

sunny *adj.* घाम लागेको gham lageko

sunrise *n.* सूर्योदय suryodaya

sunset *n.* सूर्यास्त suryast

sunshine *n.* घाम gham

sunstroke *n.* लू lu

super *adj.* अति राम्रो atiramro

superb *adj.* शान्दार shandar

superfine *adj.* अति उत्तम atiuttam

superhuman *adj.* अतिमानवीय atimanviya

superintendent *n.* संचालक sanchalak

superior *adj.* श्रेष्ठ shreshth

supermarket *n.* विशाल बजार wishal bajar

supernatural *adj.* अलौकिक alaukik

supersition *n.* अन्ध विश्वास andh wishwas

supersititious *adj.* अन्धविश्वासी andh wishwasi

supertax *n.* आयकरमाथि लाग्ने थप कर aaykarmathi laagne thapkar

supervise *v.* रेखदेख गर्नु rekh dekh garnu

supervisor *n.* सुपरभाइजर supar bhajjar

supper *n.* कोमल komal

supplicate *v.* बिन्ती गर्नु binti garnu

supplies *n.* सरसामान sar saman

supply *n.* आपूर्ति apurti

support *n.* आड adhinta

supporter *n.* समर्थक samarthak

suppose *v.* अनुमान गर्नु anuman garnu

suppress *v.* दमन गर्नु daman garnu

supreme *adj.* सर्वोच्च sarwochcha

surcharge *v.* थप भाड़ा वा शुल्क thap bhada wa shulak

sure *adj.* पक्का pakka

sure-fire *adj.* पक्का padkka

sure-footed *adj.* खुट्टा नकमाउने khutta na kamaune

surface *n.* बाहिरी हिस्सा bahiri hissa

surgeon *n.* चिरफार गर्ने डाक्टर chir phar garne daktar

surgery *n.* विरफार chirphar

surmise *n.* अनुमान anumaan

surname *n.* उपनाम upnam

surpass *v.* जित्नु jitnu

surplus *n.* बढीती बाग badhti bagh

surprise *n.* आश्चर्य ashcharya

surprised *adj.* चकित chakit

surprising *adj.* अचम्म लाग्दो achamma lagdo

surrender *v.* आत्मसमर्पण गर्नु atma samarpan garnu

surround *v.* घेर्नु ghernu

surrounding *n.* सेरोफेरो sero phero

surtax *n.* अतिरिक्त कर atirikt kar

surveillance *n.* कड़ा निरीक्षण kadha parikshan

survey *v.* चारैतिर हेर्नु charai tira hernu

survive *v.* बाँच्नु banchnu

suspect *v.* शंका लागेको मानिस shanka lageko manis

suspend *v.* निलम्बन गर्नु nilamban garnu

suspense *n.* दुविधा duwidha

suspension *n.* झोलुङ्गे jholunge

suspension bridge *n.* झोलुङ्गे पुल jholunge pul

suspicioun *n.* सन्देह sandeh

suspicious *adj.* शंका लाग्ने shanka lagne

sustain *v.* थेग्नु thegnu

suzerain *n.* राजा raja

svelte *adj.* छरितो chharito

swab *n.* भुइँ आदि पुछ्ने साधन bhuin aadi poochne sadhan

swag *n.* चोरीको माल choriko maal

swagger *v.* अकडेर हिँड्नु akadera hindnu

swain *n.* गाउँले युवक gaunle yuvak

swallow *n.* गौंथली gaunthali

swamp *n.* दलदल dal dal

swan *n.* राजहाँस rajhans

swarm *n.* थुप्रो thupro

sway *v.* हल्लनु hallanu

swear *v.* किरिया खानु kiriyakhanu

sweat *n.* पसिना pasina

sweater *n.* स्वेटर swetar

sweep *v.* कुचो लाउनु kucho launu

sweep the board *v.* पूरा बाजी मार्नु pura baji marnu

sweeper *n.* कुचो लाउने मान्छे kucho launemanchhe

sweet *adj.* गुलियो guliyo

sweet potato *n.* सखरखण्ड sakharkhand

sweetheart *n.* प्रेमिका premika

sweetheart *n.* प्रेमी premi

sweetpea *n.* केराउको फुल kerau ko phul

swell *v.* सुनिनु suninu

swerve *v.* एक्कासि मोड़िनु ekkassi modhinu

swift *adj.* छिटो chhito

swig *v.* पिउनु piunu

swim *v.* पौडी खेल्नु paudi khelnu

swimmer *n.* पौडीबाज paudi baj

swimming *n.* पौडी paudi

swimming costume *n.* पौडी खेल्दा लाउने पोशाक paudi khelda laune poshak

swimming pool *n.* पौडी पोखरी paudi pokhari

swine *n.* सुँगुर sungur

swing *v.* झुलना jhulana

switch *n.* स्वीच swich

switch off *v.* निभाउनु nibhaunu

swoon *n.* मूर्छा murchha

swoop *v.* झम्अनु jhamaunu

swop, swap *v.* साट्नु saatnu

sword *n.* तरबार tarbar

syllable *n.* अक्षर aksha

syllabus *n.* पाठ्यक्रम pathyakram

symbol *n.* चिन्ह chinha

sympathy *n.* सहानुभूति sahanu bhuti

symptom *n.* लक्षण lakshan

syncopate *v.* ताल बदल्नु taal badlanu

syncope *n.* मूर्छा murchha

syndicate *n.* व्यवसाय-संघ vyavsaye-sangh

synonym *n.* उही अर्थ बुझाउने शब्द uhiarth bijhaune shabd

syphilis *n.* भिरिङ्गी रोग bhiringi rog

syringe *n.* पच्का packka

syrup *n.* चासनी chasni

system *n.* व्यवस्था wyawastha

systematic *adj.* रीति/नियमपूर्वक riti/niyam purwak

T

T.B. *n.* टि.बी. tibi

table *n.* टेबुल tebul

tableau *n.* चित्र chitra

tablecloth *n.* टेबुलपोशाक tebul poshak

tablet *n.* गोली goli

taboo *n.* वर्जित काम warjit kam

tabular *adj.* तालिकाबद्ध talikabadh

tabulate *v.* तालिकामा talikama

tacit *adj.* नभनिएको nabhniyeko

taciturn *adj.* कम बोल्ने kam bolne

tact *n.* सीप sip

tactful *adj.* निपुण nipun

tactics *n.* दाउपेच daupech

tactile *adj.* स्पर्शको sparshko

tadpole *n.* चेपागाँड़ा chepagaanda

tag *n.* लेबुल lebul

tail *n.* पुच्छर puchchhar

tail away *v.* पछि पर्नु pachhi parnu

tailor *n.* दर्जी darji

tailor-made *adj.* खुप मिलेको khup mileko

tailpiece *n.* अन्तिम भाग antim bhag

taint *v.* बिगार्नु bigarnu

take *v.* पक्रनु pakranu

take away *v.* लानु lanu

take hold *v.* समाल्नु samatnu

take off *v.* फुकाल्नु phukalnu

take out *v.* झिक्नु jhiknu

take over *v.* सम्हाल्नु samhalnu

take place *v.* घटित हुनु ghatit hunu

take to *v.* शुरु गर्नु shuru garnu

take to pieces *v.* भत्काउनु bhatkaunu

take-home pay *n.* कर आदि कटाई दिएको तलब karadi katai diyeko talab

tale *n.* कथा katha

talent *n.* योग्यता yogyata

talented *adj.* दक्ष daksha

talk *n.* कुराकानी kurakani

talk over *v.* छलफल गर्नु chhalphal garnu

talk tall *v.* गुड्डी हाँक्नु guddi hanknu

talkative *adj.* गफी gaphi

tall *adj.* अग्लो aglo

tall order *n.* अनुचित माग anuchit mag

tally *n.* लेनदेन len den

talon *n.* नङ्ग्रा nangra

tamarind *n.* इमली imali

tambourine *n.* खैंजड़ी khaijandhi

tame *adj.* पाल्तु paltu

tamp *v.* कोचार्नु kocharnu

tamper *v.* बिगार्नु bigarnu

tan *n.* खैरो रंग khairo rang

tangible *adj.* छुन सकिने chun sakine

tank *n.* कूवा kuwa

tantrum *n.* रीसको झोंक reesko jhonk

tap *n.* धारा dhara

tape *n.* फित्ता phitta

tapeworm *n.* फित्तेजुका phitte juka

tar *n.* अलकत्रा alkatra

tar *n.* अलकत्रा alkatra

tarantula *n.* विषालु माकुरा vishalu makura

tarboosh *n.* किनारा नभएको टोपी kinara nabhayeko topi

tardy *adj.* ढीलो dheelo

target *n.* निशाना nishana

tariff *n.* भन्सार महसुल bhansar mahsul

tarn *n.* सानो पार्वतीय ताल sano paarwartiya taal

tarnish *n.* धब्बा dhabba

taro *n.* पिँडालु pindalu

tarpaulin *n.* तिरपाल tirpaal

tarry *adj.* अलकत्रा लागेको alkatra lageko

task *n.* काम kam

tassel *n.* फुर्का phurka

taste *n.* स्वाद swad

tasteful *adj.* स्वादिलो swadilo

tasty *adj.* स्वादिलो swadilo

ta-ta *interj.* बिदा bidha

tatting *n.* किनारो kinaro

tattoo *n.* गोदना godna

taunt *v.* ताना मार्नु tana marnu

tavern *n.* भट्टी bhatti

tawny *adj.* कैलो-पहेंलो रंगको kailo-pahelo rangko

tax *n.* कर आदि कटाई दिएको तलब karadi katai diyeko talab

taxi *n.* ट्याक्सी tyaksi

tea *n.* चिया chiya

tea break *n.* चिया खाने छुट्टी chiya khane chhutti

tea estate *n.* चियाबगान chiya bagan

teach *v.* पढाउनु padhaunu

teacher *n.* शिक्षक shikshak

teak *n.* सागवान काठ sagwan kath

team *n.* टोली toli

teamwork *n.* मिलेर गरिने काम milera garine kam

teapot *n.* चियादान chiyadan

tear *n.* आँसु ansu

tear to pieces *v.* लुछ्नु luchhnu

tear up *v.* च्यातचुत पार्नु chyat chut parnu

tease *v.* जिस्क्याउनु jiskyaunu

teaspoon *n.* सानो चम्चा sano chamcha

teat *n.* दूधको मुण्टो dudh ko munto

technical *adj.* प्राविधिक prawidhik

technician *n.* प्राविधिज्ञ prawidhigya

technique *n.* प्रविधि prawidhi

technology *n.* प्रविधि prawidhi

teddy *n.* बालकले खेल्ने भालू baalkale khelne bhaalu

tedious *adj.* उच्चाट लाग्ने uchchat lagne

teens *n.* किशोराअवस्था kishorawastha

teeny *adj.* साहै सानो sahe sano

teeter *v.* अस्थिर भएर चल्नु वा उभिनु asthir bhaer chalnu wa ubhinu

teeth *n.* दाँतहरू dantharu

telegram *n.* तार tar

telephone *n.* टेलिफोन teliphon

telescope *n.* दूरबीन durbin

television *n.* टेलिभिजन teli bhijan

tell *v.* भन्नु bhannu

teller *n.* नोट गन्ने जाँच्ने not ganne janchne

temerity *n.* दुःसाहस dusaahas

temper *n.* मिजास mijas

temperament *n.* स्वभाव swabhaw

temperamental *adj.* चिरचिरे chirchire

temperature *n.* तापक्रम tapkram

tempered *adj.* रिसाहा risaha

tempest *n.* आँधी andhi

temple *n.* मन्दिर mandir

tempo *n.* रफ्तार raphtar

temporary *adj.* अस्थायी asthayi

tempt *v.* फसाउनु phasaunu

temptation *n.* लालच lalach

tempting *adj.* लोभलाग्दो lobh lagdo

ten *n.* दस das

tenacious *adj.* दृढ dridh

tenant *n.* बहालवाला bahalwala

tend *v.* हेरविचार गर्नु herwichar garnu

tendency *n.* झुकाउ jhukau

tender *adj.* कलिलो kalilo

tenet *n.* सिद्धान्त siddhant

tenner *n.* दशको नोट dashko not

tennis *n.* टेनिस खेल teniskhel

tense *adj.* तन्किएको tankieko

tension *n.* तन्केको अवस्था tankeko awastha

tent *n.* तम्बू tambu

tenure *n.* स्वामित्व swamitwa

term *n.* अवधिक awadhi

termagant *n.* झगड़ालु आइमाई jhagdalu aeimai

terminate *v.* समाप्त गर्नु samapt garnu

termination *n.* समाप्ति samapti

termite *n.* धमिरो dhamiro

terms *n.* मिल्नु milnu

terms of reference *n.* विचारार्थ विषय wichararth wishaya

terra firma *n.* स्थल sthal

terrace *n.* गरा gara

terrible *adj.* डरलाग्दो dar lagdo

terrify *v.* अत्याउनु atyaunu

territorial *adj.* क्षेत्रीय kshetriya

territory *n.* क्षेत्र kshetra

terror *n.* डर dar

tertiary *adj.* तेस्रो tesro

terylene *n.* टेरीलिन tereleem

test *n.* जाँच janch

testate *adj.* वसीयतनामा गरेर मर्ने wasiyatnama garer marne

testicle *n.* गुला gula

testify *v.* साक्षी बक्नु sakshi baknu

testimonial *n.* प्रमाण पत्र praman patra

testimony *n.* गवाही gawahi

tetanus *n.* घनुष्टङ्कार dhanushtankar

tetchy *adj.* झोंकी jhonki

text *n.* मूलपाठ mulpath

textbook *n.* पाठ्यपुस्तक pathyapustak

textile *n.* कपडा kapada

than *prep.* भन्दा bhanda

thank *v.* धन्यवाद दिनु dhanya wad dinu

thankful *adj.* आभारी abhari

thanks *inter.* धन्यवाद dhanyawad

thankyou *inter.* धन्यवाद dhanyawad

that *pron.* त्यो tyo

that is *conj.* अर्थात् arthat

thatch *n.* फुसको छाना phus ko chhana

thaw *v.* पग्लनु paglanu

the *def. art.* त्यो tyo

theatre/theater *n.* रङ्गमंच rang manch

theft *n.* चौरी chori

their *pron.* तिनी/उनीहरूको tini/uni haru ko

them *pron.* तिनी/उनीहरूलाई tini/uni haru lai

theme *n.* विषय wishaya

then *adj.* त्यसबेलाको tyas bela ko

thence *adv.* त्यहाँबाट tyahan bata

thence *adj.* त्यहाँदिखि tyahandikhi

thenceforth *adv.* त्यसउप्रान्त tyas upranta

theocracy *n.* पुरोहितवर्गको शासन purohitwargko shasan

theodolite *n.* कोण नाप्ने यंत्र kon napne yantra

theory *n.* सिद्धान्त siddhant

theosophy *n.* ब्रह्मविद्या brahmvidya

therapy *n.* चिकित्सा chikitsa

there *adv.* त्यहाँबाट tyahan bata

thereafter *adv.* तयसपछि tyas pachhi

thereby *adv.* त्यस उसले tyas us le

therefore *adv.* त्यसकारण tyas karan

therein *adv.* त्यहाँबाट tyahan bata

thereupon *adv.* त्यसपछि tyas pachhi

thermometer *n.* ताप नाप्ने tap napne

thermos *n.* थर्मस tharmas

thesaurus *n.* पर्यायवाची कोश prayayewachi kosh

these *pron.* यी yi

they *pron.* तिनीहरू tini haru

thick *adj.* मोटो moto

thicket *n.* झाङ jhan

thickness *n.* मोटाइ motai

thief *n.* चोरी chori

thigh *n.* तिघ्रा tighra

thimble *n.* औंलामा लाउने खोल olaama laune khol

thin *adj.* पातलो patalo

thing *n.* चीज chij

think *v.* विचार गर्नु wichar garnu

thinker *n.* विचारक wicharak

third *adj.* तेस्रो tesro

third-rate *adj.* घटिया ghatiya

thirsty *adj.* तिर्खाएको tirkhaeko

thirteen *n.* तेह्र terha

thirty *n.* तीस tis

this *pron.* यो yo

this day *n.* आज aja

this morning *n./adv.* आज बिहान aja bihana

thong *n.* छालाको डोरी chhalako dori

thorax *n.* वक्ष vaksh

thorn *n.* काँडा kanda

thorny *adj.* काँडे kande

thorough *adj.* पक्का pakka

thoroughfare *n.* मूल बाटो mul bati

thoroughtly *adv.* एकदम ek dam

those *pron.* उनीहरू uni haru

though *conj.* तापनि ta pani

thought *n.* विचार wichar

thoughtful *adj.* विचारशील wicharshil

thoughtless *adj.* वास्ता नगर्ने wasta na garne

thousand *n.* हजार hajar

thousands *n.* हजारौं hajaraun

thread *n.* धागो dhago

threadbare *adj.* झयाङ्प्वाले jhyang pwale

threat *n.* धम्की dhamki

threaten *v.* धम्क्याउनु dhamkyaunu

three *n.* तीन tin

threshold *n.* संघार sanghar

thrifty *adj.* कम खर्च गर्ने kam kharch garne

thrill *n.* सनसनी sansani

thrilling *adj.* रोमांचकारी romanch kari

thrive *v.* सप्रनु sapranu

throat *n.* घाँटी ghanti

throb *v.* बल्कुन balkanu

thrombosis *n.* मुटु वा रक्तनली-मा खून जम्ने क्रिया mutu wa raktnali-ma khoon jamne kriya

throne *n.* राजगद्दी rajgaddi

throng *v.* भीड bheer

through *prep.* मार्फत marphat

throughout *adv./prep.* पूर्णतया purntaya

throw *v.* फ्याँक्नु phyanknu

throw a party *v.* पार्टी दिनु parti dinu

throw out *v.* निकाल्नु nikalnu

thumb *n.* बूढी औँलो budhi aunlo

thumbnail sketch *n.* लघुचित्र laghu chitra

thumbprint *n.* औँठाछाप auntha chhap

thunder *n.* गर्जनु garjanu

thunderbolt *n.* चट्याङ chatyan

thunderous *adj.* गर्जने garjane

Thursday *n.* कबहीबार bihibar

thus *adv.* यसरी yasari

thy *adj.* तिम्रो timro

thyme *n.* वनज्वानु vanjawanu

thyroid *n.* थाराइड ग्रन्थि thyroid granthi

tiara *n.* त्रिमुकुट trimukut

tic *n.* अनुहार का पेशी को संकुचन anuhar ka peshiko sankuchan

tick *n.* टिक टिक आवाज tik-tik awaj

ticket *n.* टिकट tikat

tickle *v.* काउकुती kaukuti

ticklish *adj.* चाँडो कुतकुती लाग्ने chando kutkuti lagne

tidal *adj.* ज्वारभाटाको jwarbhatako

tide *n.* ज्वारभाटा jwar bhata

tidings *n.* समाचार samachar

tidy *adj.* सफा sapa

tie *v.* बाँध्नु bandhnu

tier *n.* तलाउ talau

tiff *n.* सानो झगड़ा saano jhagda

tiffin *n.* खाजा khaja

tiger *n.* बाघ bagh

tight *adj.* कसिउको kasieko

tight-fisted *adj.* कन्जूस kanjus

tight-lipped *adj.* केही नबोल्ने kehi na bolne

tile *n.* खपडा khapada

till *prep.* जबसम्म jaba samma

tillage *n.* खनजोत khanjot

tiller *n.* जोताहा jotaha

tilt *n.* झुल्नु ghulnu

tilth *n.* जोतेको जमीन joteko jameen

timber *n.* काठपात kathpat

time *n.* समय samaya

time and again *adv.* बारम्बार barambar

time and tide *n.* खोला र बेला khola ra bela

time immemorial *n.* अति प्राचीन काल ati prachin kal

time lag *n.* समयको अन्तर samaya ko antar

time limit *n.* निश्चित अवधि nishchit awadhi

time-hono(u)red *adj.* चिरसम्मानित chir sammanit

timely *adj.* सामयिक samayik

timepiece *n.* घडी ghadi

times *n.* युग yug

timetable *n.* समयतालिका samaya talika

timid *adj.* काथर kathar

timorous *adj.* कातर kaatar

timpani *n.* केटल ड्रम kettle drum

tin *n.* टिन tin

tinny *adj.* टिन जङ्गते tin jagayte

tint *n.* रङ्ग rang

tiny *adj.* धेरै सानो dherai sano

tip *n.* टुप्पो tuppo

tip-top *adj.* अत्युत्तम atyuttam

tire *v.* थकाइ लाग्नु thakai lagnu

tired *adj.* थाकेको thakeko

tiring *adj.* थकाउने thakaune

tissue *n.* पातलो नरम कागत paatlo naram kaagat

title *n.* दर्जामान darja

title page *n.* मुखपृष्ठ mukh prishth

title role *n.* प्रमुख भूमिका pramukh bhumika

to *prep.* लाई lai

to and fro *adv.* यताउति yata uti

toad *n.* खस्रे भ्यागुतो khasre bhyaguto

tobacco *n.* सुर्ती surti

today *n./adv.* आज aja

toddy *n.* रक्सी र गुलियो तातो पानी raksi r gulio tato paani

to-do *n.* खलबल khalbal

toe the line/mark *v.* आदेश पालन गर्नु adesh ko palan garnu

toehold *n.* सानो आधार sano adhar

toenail *n.* खुट्टाको नङ khutta ko nan

toffee *n.* टफी taphi

together *adv.* सँगै sangai

toilet *n.* हातमुख धुने haatmukh dhune

tokay *n.* हंगेरीको रक्सी hangeriko raksi

tolerable *adj.* सह्य sahya

tolerance *n.* सहनशीलता sahan shilta

tolerate *v.* सहनु sahanu

tomato *n.* गोलभेँडा gol bhenda

tomb *n.* चिहान chihan

tome *n.* ग्रन्थ grantha

tomeat *n.* भाले बिरालो bhaale biralo

tomfool *n.* महामूर्ख व्यक्ति mahamurkh vyakti

tommy-gun *n.* बन्दूक banduk

tommyrot *n.* रद्दी कुरा raddhi kura

tomorrow *n./adv.* भोलि bholi

ton(ne) *n.* टन tan

tone *n.* आवाज awaj

tone down *v.* नम्र हुनु namra hunu

tone up *v.* तीव्र पार्नु tiwra parnu

tongs *n.* चिम्टा chimta

tongue *n.* जिब्रो jibro

tongue-tied *adj.* अवाक् awak

tonic *n.* तागतको औषधि tagat ko aushadi

tonight *n./adv.* आज राती aja rati

too *adv.* अति ज्यादा ati prachin kal

tool *n.* औजार aujar

tooth *n.* दाँत dantharu

toothache *n.* दाँत दुखाइ dant dukhai

toothpaste *n.* मंजन manjan

toothpick दोत कोटयाउने सिन्को dant ko tyaune sinko

top *n.* शिखर shikhar

top secret *adj.* अति गोप्य ati gopya

topaz *n.* पुष्पराज pushpa raj

topcoat *n.* ओभरकोट obhar kot

topic *n.* विषय wishaya

top-notch *adj.* पहिलो दर्जाको pahilo darja ko

tops *n.* सबभन्दा राम्रो व्यक्ति वा वस्तु sabbhanda ramro vyakti wa vastu

topsoil *n.* माटोको माथिल्लो पत्र mato ko mathilo patra

topsy-turvy *adj.* उल्टोपल्टो ulto palto

torch *n.* टर्चलाइट tarch light

toreador *n.* साँढिसँग जुध्ने व्यक्ति sadhisang judhne vaykati

torment *v.* दुःख/यातना दिनु duhkh/yatna/dinu

torrent *n.* मुस्लो muslo

torrential *adj.* मुसलधारे musal dhare

torsion *n.* बटारिने क्रिया batarine kriya

tort *n.* अन्याय anayae

tortoise *n.* कछुवा kachhuwa

torture *n.* यातना yatna

toss *v.* सिक्का को हुत्याइ sikka ko huttyai

toss up *v.* सिक्का हुत्याउनु sikka huttyaunu

total *n.* जम्मा हिसाब jamma hisab

totally *adv.* जम्मै jammai

tote *v.* बोक्नु boknu

touch *n.* स्पर्श sparsh

touch down *v.* उत्रनु utranu

touch-and-go *adj.* जोखिमपूर्ण jokhimpurn

touching *adj.* मन छुने man chhune

toupee *n.* नकली कपाल nakali kapaal

tour *n.* यात्रा yatra

tour de force *n.* चमत्कार chamatkar

tourism *n.* प्रर्यटन paratan

tournament *n.* खेल प्रतियोगिता khel pratiyogita

tousle *v.* खजमज पार्नु khajmajh parnu

tow *v.* घिसार्नु ghisarnu

towards *prep.* तिर tira

towel *n.* तौलिया tauliya

tower *n.* अग्लो बुर्जा aglo burja

town *n.* नगर nagar

town hall *n.* सभागृह sabha griha

town planning *n.* नगर योजना nagar yojana

toxic *adj.* बिखालु bikhalu

toxin *n.* विष wish

toy *n.* खेलौना khelauna

tqraduce *v.* निन्दा गर्नु ninda garnu

trace *n.* खोज khoj

trachea *n.* वासनली vaasnali

trachoma *n.* फुलो phulo

track *n.* बाटो bato

track down *v.* सुराक लाउनु surak launu

tractor *n.* ट्याक्टर tryaktar

trade *n.* बेपार bepar

trade off *v.* सम्झौतासरी साटफेर गर्नु samjhauta sari sat pher garnu

trade on *v.* फाइदा उठाउनु phaida uthaunu

trade union *n.* मजदुर संघ majdur sangh

trademark *n.* व्यापारिक चिन्ह wyaparik chinha

trader *n.* व्यापारी wyapari

tradition *n.* रीतिथिति riti thiti

traditional *adj.* परम्परागत paramparagat

traffic *n.* ट्राफिक traphik

trafficker *n.* अवैध व्यापारी awaidh wyapari

tragedy *n.* दुःखद घटना duhkhad ghatna

tragic *adj.* दुःखद duhkhad ghatna

train *n.* रेल rel

trained *adj.* तालीम पाएको talim paeko

trainee *n.* तालिमे talime

training *n.* तालीम talim

trait *n.* स्वभाव swabhaw

traitor *n.* देशद्रोही desh drohi

tramp *n.* घुमन्ते ghumante

trample *v.* कुल्चिनु kulchinu

trampoline *n.* लचकदार गद्दा lachakdar gadda

trance *n.* तन्द्रा tandra

tranquility *n.* शन्ति shanti

transfer *v.* सरुवा गर्नु saruwa

transform *v.* रूप बदल्नु rup badalnu

transit *n.* पारवाहन parwahan

transitory *adj.* थोरै समय मात्र रहने thorea samay matra rahne

translate *v.* अनुवाद गर्नु anuwad garnu

translator *n.* अनुवादक anuwadak

transparent *adj.* पारदर्शी pardarshi

transplant *v.* अर्को ठाउँमा रोप्नु arko thaun ma ropnu

transport *n.* यातायात yatayat

trap *n.* पासो paso

trap-door *n.* छाना वा फर्समा भएको दरवाजा chhana wa pharsma bhaeko darwaza

trash *n.* थोत्रा रद्दी माल thotraraddimal

travail प्रसव पीड़ा prasav peerha

travel *v.* यात्रा/सफर गर्नु yatra/ saphar garnu

travel agent *n.* ट्राभल एजेण्ट trabhal ejent

travel(l)er *n.* यात्री yatri

tray *n.* किस्ती kisti

treacherous *adj.* छली chhali

treachery *n.* धोखा dhokha

tread *v.* हिंड्नु hindnu

treason *n.* राजद्रोह rajdroh

treasure *n.* धन dhan

treasurer *n.* खजांची khajanchi

treasury *n.* राजकोष raj kosh

treat *v.* व्यवहार गर्नु wyawahar garnu

treatise *n.* शोध-प्रबन्ध shodh-prabandhan

treatment *n.* उपचार upchar

treaty *n.* सन्धि sandhi

treble *adj.* तेहरो tehro

tree *n.* रूख rukh

trek *v.* पैदल यात्रा गर्नु paidal yatra garnu

trekker *n.* पदयात्री pad yatri

trekking *n.* पदयात्रा pad yatra

tremble *v.* थरथराउनु thar thar aunu

tremendous *adj.* घोर ghor

tremor *n.* थरथरी thar thari

trench *n.* सुरुङ surun

trenchant *adj.* कटु kattu

trend *n.* प्रवृत्ति prawritti

trend of thought *n.* विचारधारा wichar dhara

trepidation *n.* आशंका ashanka

trews *n.* कसिलो सुरूवाल kasilo suruwal

triad *n.* तीनको समूह teenko samuh

trial *n.* प्रयोग prayog

triangle *n.* त्रिभुज tri bhuj

tribal *adj.* जातीय jatiya

tribe *n.* जनजाति jan jati

tribulation *n.* दुःख dukh

tributary *n.* सहायक नदी sahayak nadi

tribute *n.* उपहार uphar

trick *n.* छल chhal

trickster *n.* चालबाज गर्ने व्यक्ति chaalbaj garne vyakti

tricolour *n.* तीन रंग भएको झंडा teen rang bhaeko jhanda

tricycle *n.* तीनपाङ्ग्रे साइकल tin pangre saikal

trident *n.* त्रिशूल trishul

trigger *n.* बन्दुक को जिब्री banduk ko jibri

trigonometry *n.* त्रिकोणमिति trikonmiti

trilateral *adj.* तीन पक्षीय teen pakshiya

trill *n.* कम्पित स्वर kampit swar

trim *adj.* टाम टुमे tam tune

trim one's sails *v.* बदलिँदो स्थितिमा ढल्नु badlindo sthiti mad dhalnu

trimaran *n.* डुङ्गा dunga

trinity *n.* त्रिमूर्ति tri murti

trinket *n.* गहनगुरिया gahana guriya

trio *n.* तीनजना को समूह tin jana ko samuha

trip *n.* सैर sair

triple *adj.* तेब्बर tebbar

triplex *adj.* तीनगुना teenguna

tripod *n.* त्रिखुटी tri khuti

tripper *n.* पर्यटक praytak

trite *adj.* सहलिया sahaliya

triumph *n.* विजय wijaya

trivial *adj.* बिना महत्त्वको bina mahtavko

troglodyte *n.* गुफाबासी gufawasi

trollop *n.* वेश्या veshya

trolly *n.* ट्राली trali

troop *n.* टोली toli

troops *n.* सेना sena

trophy *n.* उपहार uphar

tropical *adj.* गर्मीसम्बन्धी garmi sambandhi

troubadour *n.* गाइने gyane

trouble *n.* दुःख duhkh

trousers *n.* प्याण्ट pyant

trousseau *n.* बेहुलीको पोशाक behuliko poshak

trout *n.* एक जातको माछा ek jaatko machha

trowel *n.* कर्नी karni

truant *n.* स्कूल भगुवा school bhagua

truce *n.* युद्धविराम yddha wiram

truck *n.* ट्रक trak

truing *adj.* गाह्रो garho

truism *n.* जानेकै कुरा janneke kura

truly *adv.* वास्तवमा wastaw ma

trump *n.* तुरुप turup

trump up *v.* बनाउनु banaunu

trumpery *adj.* सस्तो भड़किलो वस्तु sasto bhadkilo vastu

trumpet *n.* बिगुल bigul

trunk *n.* मूलजीउ muljiu

trunkcall *n.* टाढाबाट गरिने टेलिफोन tadha bata garine teli phon

trust *n.* विश्वास wishwas

trustworthy *adj.* भरपर्दो bhar pardo

truth *n.* सत्य satya

truthful *adj.* साँचो sancho

try *v.* कोशिश गर्नु koshish garnu

try on *v.* लगाएर हेर्नु lagaera hernu

try out *v.* परीक्षा लिनु pariksha linu

tub *n.* टब tab

tube *n.* नली nali

tuber *n.* कन्द kand

tuberculossis *n.* क्षयरोग kshaya rog

Tuesday *n.* मंगलबार mangal bar

tuft *n.* गुच्छा guchchha

tug *v.* जोडले तान्नु jod le tannu

tug of war *n.* डोरी तान्ने खेल dori tanne khel

tuition *n.* ट्युसन tyusan

tulip *n.* घण्टाकार पुष्प ghantakar pushp

tumble *v.* खुरमुरिनु khur murinu

tummy *n.* पेट pet

tumo(u)r *n.* गाँठो gantho

tumult *n.* खैलाबैला khaila baila

tuna *n.* ठूलो समुद्री माछा thulo samudari machha

tune *n.* लय laya

tunic *n.* लुगा luga

tunnel *n.* सुरुङ surun

turban *n.* फेटा pheta

turbid *adj.* धमिलो dhamilo

turbulent *adj.* उग्र ugra

turf *n.* घाँस चौर ghanse chaur

turmeric *n.* हलेदो haledo

turmoil *n.* उत्पात utpat

turn *n.* घुमाउ ghumau

turn against *v.* विरुद्ध हुनु wiruddha hunu

turn down *v.* अस्वीकार aswikar

turn of the century *n.* युगसन्धि yug sandhi

turn off *v.* बन्द गर्नु band garnu

turn on *v.* खोल्नु kholnu

turn out *v.* निकाल्नु nikalnu

turn over *v.* उल्टाउनु ultaunu

turn to *v.* लाग्नु lagnu

turn turtle *v.* घोप्टिनु ghop tinu

turn up *v.* एकत्र हुनु ekatra hunu

turncoat *n.* दल छोडाहा dal chhodaha

turning *n.* मोड mod

turning point *n.* मोड mod

turnip *n.* सलगम salgam

turnkey *n.* जेलर jelar

turnover *n.* आय aya

turnpike *n.* शुल्कद्वार shulk dwar

turpentine *n.* तारपिनको तेल tarpinko tel

turpitude *n.* दुष्टता dushtta

turquoise *n.* फिरोज ढुङ्गा phiroj dhunga

turret *n.* बुर्जा burja

tusk *n.* हात्ती को दाह्रो hatti ko darho

tussle *n.* झगडा jhagada

tutelage *n.* संरक्षण sanrakshan

tutor *n.* गुरु guru

twain *n.* दुई dui

tweak *n.* निमोठ्नु nimothnu

tweed *n.* टुवीडको लुगा tweedko luga

twelve *n.* बाह्र barha

twentieth *adj.* बीसौँ biasaun

twice *adv.* दुईपल्ट duipalta

twig *n.* झिँझा jhinjha

twilight *n.* गोधूलि go dhuli

twin *n.* जुम्ल्याहा jumlyaha

twinkle *v.* चम्कनु chamkanu

twist *v.* बटार्नु batarnu

two *n.* दुईपल्ट duipalta

two-dimensional *adj.* दुई आयामको dulayamko

two-edged *adj.* दुईधारे dul dhare

two-faced *adj.* कपटी kapati

two-way *adj.* दोहोरो dohoro

type *n.* किसिम kisim

typewriter *n.* टाइपराइटर taip raitar

typhoid *n.* टायफाइड typhoid

typhoon *n.* प्रचण्ड तूफान prachand toofan

typhus *n.* जरो आउने सरूवा रोग jaro aaune saruwa rog

typical *adj.* खास khas

typist *n.* टाइपिस्ट taipist

tyrannical *adj.* निरङ्कुश nirankush

tyranny *n.* अत्याचार atyachar

tyre *n.* टायर taayar

U

udder *n.* कल्चौँडो kal chaundo

ugly *adj.* नराम्रो na ramro

ukulele *n.* चार तारे गिटार char taare gitar

ulcer *n.* घाउ ghau

ulterior *adj.* अव्यक्त awaykat

ultimate *adj.* अन्तिम antim

ultimately *adv.* अन्तमा antma

ultimatum *n.* आखिरी शर्त akhiri shart

ultra *pref.* अत्यधिक atadhik

ultramarine *n.adj.* उज्ज्वल नीलो ujjawal neelo

umbrella *n.* छाता chhata

umpire *n.* निर्णायक nirnayak

umpteen *adj.* धेरै dherae

unabashed *adj.* अलिज्जित alijjit

unabated *adj.* नघटेको naghateko

unabbreviated *adj.* असंक्षिप्त asankshipt

unable *adj.* नसक्ने na sakne

unacknowledged *adj.* अस्वीकृत aswikrit

unacquainted *adj.* चिनापर्ची नभएको china parchi na bhaeko

unactable *adj.* अभिनय गर्न नसकिने abhinay garn naskine

unadorned *adj.* नसिँगारिएको nasingariyeko

unaffected *adj.* सीधासाधा sidha sadha

unafraid *adj.* निडर nidar

unaimed *adj.* लक्ष्यहीन lakshyaheen

unallied *adj.* असम्बद्ध asambadh

unalterable *adj.* अपरिवर्तनीय apartivartinya

unaltered *adj.* अपरिवर्तित aparivartit

unambiguous *adj.* सुस्पष्ट susapshat

unanimous *adj.* एकमत ek mat

unappealable *adj.* अपील हुन नसक्ने apeel hun naskane

unapt *adj.* अनुपयुक्त anupyukt

unarmed *adj.* निहत्था nihattha

unassailable *adj.* अकाट्य akataya

unattached *adj.* खुकुलो khukulo

unaware *adj.* अनजान anjan

unblessed *adj.* अपवित्र apavitar

unbolt *v.* खोल्नु kholnu

unbred *adj.* अशिक्षित ashikshit

uncalled for *adj.* नबोलाएको nabolaiko

uncaring *adj.* निश्चिन्त nishchint

uncertain *adj.* अनिश्चित anishchit

unchaste *adj.* चोखो नभएको chokho nabhayko

uncivillised *adj.* असभ्य asabhya

unclas *adj.* नाङ्गो naango

unclassified *adj.* अवर्गीकृत awargikrit

uncle *n.* ठूलो बा thulo ba

unclench *v.* खोल्नु kholnu

uncomfortable *adj.* असजिलो asajilo

unconformable *adj.* असंगत asangat

unconformity *n.* असंगतता asangatata

unconnected *adj.* असम्बद्ध asambadh

unconquerable *adj.* अविजेय avijay

unconscious *adj.* बेहोश behosh

uncooked *adj.* काँचो kancho

uncork *v.* काग खोल्नु kaag kholnu

uncouple *v.* अलग गर्नु alag garnu

uncouth *adj.* गँवार ganwar

uncover *v.* आवरण उघार्नु awaran udharnu

uncrushable *adj.* अदम्य adamya

uncultured *adj.* असभ्य asabhya

undecided *adj.* अनिश्चित anishchit

under *prep.* मुनि muni

under age *adj.* अवयस्क awayask

underbred *adj.* अशिष्ट ashisht

underbrush *n.* झाड़ी jhaddi

undercarriage *n.* हवाईजहाजको उत्रने चक्का hawaijahaj unneko chakka

underclothes *n.* भित्रपट्टि लाउने लुगा bhitrpatti laune luga

underdog *n.* हरुवा haruwa

underdone *adj.* अधकल्चो adhkalvo

underestimate *v.* कम सम्झनु kam samjhanu

undergraduate *n.* स्नातक उपाधि प्राप्त नगरेको व्यक्ति sanatak upadhi prapt nagreko vyakti

underground *adj.* भूमिगत bhumi gat

underneath *adv.* मुन्तिर muntira

underrate *v.* कम महलत्तव दिनु kam mahattwa dinu

undersized *adj.* सानु कदको sanu kad ko

understand *v.* बुझ्नु bijhnu

understanding *n.* समझदारी samajh dari

undertake *v.* कबुल गर्नु kabul garnu

undertaking *n.* काम kam mahattwa dinu

underwear *n.* भित्री लुगा bhitri luga

underworld *n.* पाताल patal

undesirable *adj.* अवांछनीय awanchhaniya

undeveloped *adj.* अविकसित aviksit

undies *n.* स्त्रीको भित्री लुगा striko bhitri luga

undignified *adj.* मर्यादाहीन maryadaheen

undo *v.* फुकाउनु phukaunu

undoubtedly *adv.* निस्सन्देह nissandeh

undressed *adj.* लुगा नलाएको luga na laeko

undue *adj.* अनुचित anuchit

unearth *v.* खनेर निकाल्नु khaner nikalnu

uneasy *adj.* असजिलो asajilo

uneconomical *adj.* खर्चिलो kharchilo

unemployed *adj.* बेकार bekar

unemployment *n.* बेरोजगारी berojgari

unenlightened *adj.* राम्रो जानकारी नभएको ramro jaankari nabhayko

unequalled *adj.* बेजोड़ bejodh

uneven *adj.* बिजोर bijor

unexampled *adj.* अतुलनीय atulniya

unfair *adj.* पक्षपाती paksh pati

unfasten *v.* खोल्नु kholnu

unfathered *adj.* बतासे bataase

unfavo(u)rable *adj.* प्रतिकूल prati kul

unfavourable *adj.* प्रतिकूल prati kul

unfeeling *adj.* निष्ठुर nishthur

unfettered *adj.* स्वच्छन्द swachand

unfit *adj.* अयोग्य ayogya

unfold *v.* खोल्नु kholnu

unformed *adj.* निश्चित आकार nischit akaar

unfortunate *adj.* अभागी abhagi

unfreeze *v.* रोकटोक हटाउनु roktok hataunu

unfurl *v.* खोलिनु kholinu

unfurnished *adj.* फर्निचर नभएको furniture nabhayko

ungainly *adj.* भद्दा बेढंगको bhadda bedhangko

unhand *adj.* भारी bhaari

unhorse *v.* घोड़ाबाट लड़ाउनु ghodabaat ladaunu

unicameral *adj.* एक सदनीय ek sadaniya

unicellular *adj.* एक कोषीय ek koshiya

unicolour *adj.* एक रंगको ek rangko

unidimensional *adj.* सतही satahi

unification *n.* एकीकरण ekikaran

uniform *n.* बर्दी bardi

uniformity *n.* एकरूपता ek rupta

unify *v.* एक गराउनु ek garaunu

unimportant *adj.* महत्त्वहीन mahattwahin

uninhabitable *adj.* बस्न लायकको नभएको basn layakko nabhayko

unintelligent *adj.* मूर्ख moorkh

union *n.* एकता ekata

unique *adj.* बेजोड bejod

unit *n.* एकाइ ekai

unitary *adj.* एकात्मक ekatamak

unite *v.* जोड्नु jodnu

united *adj.* संयुक्त samyukta

unity *n.* एकता ekata

universal *adj.* विश्वव्यापी wishwa wyapi

universe *n.* ब्रह्माण्ड brahmand

university *n.* विश्वविद्यालय wishwa widyalaya

unjust *adj.* अन्यायी anyayi

unkind *adj.* निर्दय nirday

unknowable *adj.* अज्ञेय agyae

unknown *adj.* अज्ञात agyat

unlade *v.* उतार्नु utaarnu

unlash *v.* खोल्नु kholnu

unlearned *adj.* अनपढ़ anpad

unleash *v.* खोल्नु kholnu

unlikelihood *n.* असम्भाव्यता asambhavyta

unlimber *v.* तयार गर्नु tyar garnu

unlime *adj.* असमान asaman

unlimited *adj.* असीमित asimit

unload *v.* माल उतार्नु mal utarnu

unlucky *adj.* अभागी abhagi

unman *v.* हिम्मत तोड्नु himmat todhnu

unmanly *adj.* कमजोर kamjor

unmarked *adj.* अचिन्हित achinhit

unmarried *adj.* विवाह नभएको wiwahna bhaeko

unmeaning *adj.* निर्थक nirarthak

unnamed *adj.* अनाम anaam

unnatural *adj.* अप्राकृतिक aprakritik

unnecessary *adj.* नचाहिँदो na chahindo

unnoticed *adj.* नदेखेको na dekheko

unobstructed *adj.* नछेकिएको na chhekieko

unorthodox *adj.* अपरम्परागत aprampragat

unpack *v.* खोल्नु kholnu

unpaid *adj.* नतिरिएको na tirieko

unpeople *v.* जनशून्य गर्नु janshunya garnu

unpick *adj.* सिलाई खोल्नु silai kholnu

unpleasant *adj.* नरमाइलो na ramailo

unpopular *adj.* अलोकप्रिय alokpriya

unprecedented *adj.* पहिले नभएको pahile na bhaeko

unprepared *adj.* तयार नभएको tayar na bhaeko

unproductive *adj.* अनुत्पादक anutpadak

unpublished *adj.* अप्रकाशित aprakashit

unqualified *adj.* अयोग्य ayogya

unquote *v.* उद्धरणाचिन्ह बन्द गर्नु udwaranchinha bandh garnu

unready *adj.* अप्रस्तुत aprastut

unreasonable *adj.* बेमनासिब bemanasib

unrefined *adj.* अपरिष्कृत aparishkrit

unreliable *adj.* भर पर्न नसकिने bhar parn naskine

unrest *n.* अशान्तिगडबड ashanti

unriddle *v.* हल गर्नु hal garnu

unripe *adj.* काँचो kancho

unroll लपेटको वस्तु खोल्नु lapetko vastu kholnu

unroot *v.* उखाल्नु ukhalnu

unruly *adj.* अटेरी ateri

unsatisfactory *adj.* असन्तोषजनक asantoshjanak

unseen *adj.* नदेखिएको na dekhieko

unsheathe *v.* दाप वा म्यानबाट झिक्नु daap wa myanbaat jhiknu

unskillful *adj.* अदक्ष adaksh

unsociable *adj.* अरूको संगत नरूचाउने arooko sangat naruchaune

unsophisticated *adj.* सोझो sojho

unspeakable *adj.* अवर्णनीय awarnaniya

unspeakable *adj.* अकथनीय akathniya

unspotted *adj.* निष्कलंक nishkalank

unstable *adj.* अस्थिर asthir

unsteady *adj.* अस्थिर asthir

unsubstantial *adj.* निराधार niradhar

unsuccessful *adj.* असफल asaphal

unsuitable *adj.* अफाप aphap

unsure *adj.* अनिश्चित anishchit

unsuspected *adj.* असंदिग्ध asandigdh

unsuspecting *adj.* शंका नगरिने shanka na garine

untie *v.* फुकाउनु phukaunu

until *conj.* जबसम्म......हुँदैन jaba samma hundaina

untimely *adj.* असामयिक asakayik

untiring *adj.* नथाकीकन काम गरिरहने nathakeekan kaam garirehne

untitled *adj.* शीर्षकहीन sheershakheen

untouchable *n.* अछूत achhut

untouched *adj.* नछोएको nachoyeko

untoward *adj.* अशुभ ashubh

untrue *adj.* असत्य asatya

unusual *adj.* अनौठो anautho

unveil *v.* अनावरण गर्नु anawaran garnu

unwashed *adj.* असिंचित asinchit

unwell *adj.* बिसंचो bisancho

unwilling *adj.* बिराजी biraji

unwonted *adj.* अनभ्यस्त anbhyast

unworthy *adj.* अयोग्य ayogya

unzip *v.* जिप खोल्नु zip kholnu

up *prep/* माथि mathi

up against *adv.* निकट nikat

up against it *adv.* ठूलो कठिनाइमा thulo kathinai ma

up and coming *adj.* प्रगति गर्दै pragati gardai

upbraid *v.* डाँट्नु daantnu

upbringing *n.* शिक्षादीक्षा siksha diksha

upgrade *v.* पदोन्नति गर्नु paddonti garnu

upheaval *n.* उथलपुथल uthal puthal

uphill *adj.* उकालो ukalo

uphold *v.* समर्थन गर्नु samarthan garnu

uplift *n.* उन्नति unnati

upon *prep.* मा ma

upper *adj.* माथिल्लो mathillo

upperhand *n.* माथिल्लो हात mathillo hat

uppermost *adj.* सबभन्दा माथिल्लो sab bhanda mathilo

upright *adj.* खडा khada

uprising *n.* आन्दोलन andolan

uproar *n.* होहल्ला ho halla

uproot *v.* उखेल्नु ukhelnu

ups and downs *n.* तल माथि tala mathi

upset *v.* उल्टिनु ultinu

upside down *adj./adv.* उभिण्डो ubhindo

upstairs *n.* माथिल्लो तला mathillo tala

upstream *adv.* प्रवाहविपरीत prawah wiparit

upto *prep.* सम्म samma

upward *adj.* मास्तिर जाने mastir jaane

upwards *adv.* माथितिर mathi tira

uranium *n.* यूरेनियम urenium

uranus *n.* यूरेनस ग्रह urenus grah

urban *adj.* हरी shahari

urge *v.* जोर/ताकिता गर्नु jor/takita garnu

urgency *n.* महत्त्वहीन mahattwahin

urgent *adj.* जरुरी jaruri

uric *adj.* मूत्रको mutrako

urinal *n.* शौचालय shauchalaya

urine *n.* पिसाब pisab

urnate *v.* पिसाब गर्नु pishab garnu

us *pron.* हामीलाई hami lai

usage *n.* प्रयोग prayog

use *v.* प्रयोग prayog

use up *v.* सिद्ध्याउनु siddhyaunu

used *adj.* पुरानो purano

useful *adj.* उपयोगी upyogi

useless *adj.* निकम्मा nikamma

usher *n.* बस्ने ठाउँ देखाउनु basne thaun dekhaune

usual *adj.* साधारण sadharan

usually *adv.* अक्सर aksar

utensils *n.* भाँडाकुँडा bhanda kunda

uterus *n.* पाठेघर patheghar

utility *n.* उपयोगिता upyogita

utilization *n.* उपयोग upyogi

utilize *v.* उपयोग गर्नु upyog garnu

utmost *adj.* परम param

utter *v.* भन्नु bhannu

uvula *n.* किलकिले kilkile

V

vacant *adj.* खाली khali

vacation *n.* लामो छुट्टी lamo chhutti

vaccinate *v.* खोपाउनु khopaunu

vaccination *n.* खोप khopaunu

vaccine *n.* खोप khopaunu

vacillate *v.* दोमन गर्नु doman garnu

vagabond *n.* फिरन्ता phiranta

vagina *n.* योनि yoni

vague *adj.* अस्पष्ट aspasht

vain *adj.* व्यर्थ wyarth

valence *n.* संयोजकता sanjogota

valiant *adj.* साहसी sahasi

valid *adj.* मनासिब manasib

validity *n.* मान्यता manyata

valley *n.* उपत्यका upatyaka

valour *n.* वीरता veerta

valuable *adj.* मूल्यवान mulya wan

valuation *n.* मूल्यनिर्धारण mulya nirdharan

value *n.* मूल्य mulya

valueless *adj.* बेकारको bekar ko

valve *n.* कपाट kapaat

vamoose *v.* चाँड़ो जाऊ chando jaun

van *n.* बन्द गाडी bandgadi

vanish *v.* अल्पिनु alpinu

vanity *n.* घमण्ड ghamand

vanquish *v.* हराउनु haraunu

vapo(u)r *n.* बाफ baph

variable *adj.* बदल्ने badalne

variation *n.* परिवर्तन pariwartan

varied *n.* विविध wiwidh

variety entertainment *n.* विविध मनोरंजन wiwidh manoranjan

various *adj.* विभिन्न wibhinna

varsity *n.* को छोटो रूप ko chhoto roop

vary *v.* बदलिनु badlinu

vascular *adj.* संवहिनी swahini

vase *n.* फुलदान phuldan

vasectomy *n.* नसच्छेदन nas chchhedan

vaseline *n.* भेसलिन beslin

vast *adj.* विशाल wishal

vat *n.* टंकी tanki

vault *n.* गुम्बजदार छाना gumbaj dar chhana

vegetable *n.* तरकारी tarkari

vegetation *n.* वनस्पति wanaspati

vehement *adj.* प्रचण्ड prachand

vehicle *n.* सवारी sawari

veil *n.* घुम्टो ghumto

vein *n.* नसा nasa

vellum *n.* चर्मपत्र charampatra

velocity *n.* गति gati

velour *n.* मखमल जस्तो वस्त्र makhmal jasto vastra

velvet *n.* मखमल makhmal

vendor *n.* विक्रेता wikreta

venerable *adj.* आदरणीय adarniya

vengeance *n.* बदला badla

venial *adj.* क्षम्य shamya

venison *n.* मृगको मासु mrigko masu

venom *n.* विष wishal

venomous *adj.* विषालु wishalu

venous *adj.* शिराको shirako

vent *n.* निकास nikas

ventilation *n.* वायु संचालन wayu sanchalan

venture *n.* साहसको काम sahas ko kam

venus *n.* शुक्रग्रह shukra graha

verb *n.* क्रियापद kriyapad

verbal *adj.* मौखिक maukhik

verdict *n.* फैसला phaisla

verdure *n.* हरियाली haryali

verification *n.* प्रमाणीकरण pramanikaran

verify *v.* रुजू/प्रमाणित गर्नु ruju/pramanit garnu

verisimilitude *n.* साँचो जस्तो देखिने गुण saancho jasto dekine gun

veritable *adj.* साँचो saancho

verity *v.* सत्यता satyata

vermilion *n.* सिन्दूर sindur

vermouth *n.* सुरविशेष survishesh

vernacular *n.* स्वदेशी भाषा swadeshi bhasha

vernal *adj.* वसन्तको wasantko

verse *n.* कविता kawita

version *n.* अनुवाद anuwad

versus *prep.* विरुद्ध wiruddha

vertex *n.* शीर्ष sheersh

vertical *adj.* ठाडो thado

vertigo *n.* रिंगटा ringta

verve *n.* उत्साह utsaw

very *adv.* धेरै dherai

vessel *n.* भाँडो bhando

vest *n.* गन्जी ganji

veteran *n.* अनुभवी anubhawi

veto *n.* निषेध nishedh

via *prep.* भएर bhaera

viable *adj.* बाँच्न सक्ने banchna sakne

via-media मध्यमार्ग madhyamarg

vibraphone *n.* बाजा baaja

vibrate *v.* थर्कनु tharkanu

vibration *n.* कम्पन kampan

vice *n.* पाप pap

vice chancellor *n.* उपकुलपति upkulpati

vice president *n.* उपराष्ट्रपति uprashtrapati

vice versa *adv.* विपरीत wiprit

vicious *adj.* दुष्ट dusht

vicissitude *n.* उलटफेर ultatpher

vicnity *n.* आसपास aspasht

victim *n.* शिकार shikar

victimize *v.* शिकार बनाउनु shikar banaunu

victor *n.* विजेता wijeta

victorious *adj.* विजयी wijayi

victory *n.* जीत jitnu

victual *v.* खाद्यसामग्रीले भर्नु khadyasamagri bharnu

videlicet *adv.* अर्थात् arthaat

video *n.* भिडियो bhidiyo

vie *v.* प्रतिस्पर्धा गर्नु pratispardha garnu

view *n.* विचार wichar

viewpoint *n.* दृष्टिकोण drishtikon

vigilant *adj.* चनाखो chanakho

vigo(u)r *n.* शक्ति shakti

vigorous *adj.* जोडदार jod dar

vigorously *adv.* जोडसँग job sanga

vile *adj.* नीच nich

villa *n.* देहाती निवास dehati niwas

village *n.* गाउँ gaun

villager *n.* देहाती dehati

villain *n.* खलनायक khalnayak

villein *n.* सामन्ती प्रथाको दास samanti prathako das

vim *n.* उत्साह utsaw

vine *n.* लहरा lahara

vinegar *n.* सिरका sirka

vintner *n.* मदिराको बेपारी madira ko bepari

violate *v.* उल्लंघन गर्नु ullanghan garnu

violation *n.* उल्लंघन ullanghan

violence *n.* हिंसा hinsa

violent *adj.* हिंसात्मक hinsatmak

violet *adj.* बैजनी baijani

violin *n.* बेला bela

violinist *n.* बेलावादक bela wadak

viper *n.* विषालु सर्प vishalu sarp

virago *n.* भयानक कर्कशा आइमाई bhyanak karksha aeimai

virgin *n.* कन्याकेटी kanya keti

virgo *n.* कन्या राशि kanyariashi

virtual *adj.* झण्डैझण्डै jhandai jhandai

virtue *n.* सद्गुण sadgun

virtuous *adj.* सदाचारी sadachari

virus *n.* भाइरस bhairas

visa *n.* भिसा bhisa

visage *n.* अनुहार anuhaar

visible *adj.* देखिने dekhine

vision *n.* दृष्टिकोण drishtikon

visit *v.* भेट bhet

visitor *n.* आगन्तुक agantuk

visitor's book *n.* आगन्तुक पुस्तिका agantuk pustika

vista *n.* दृश्य drishya

visual *n.* दृष्टिसम्बन्धी drishti sambandhi

vital *adj.* आवश्यक awashyak

vitality *n.* जीवनशक्ति jiwan shakti

vitamin *n.* भिटामिन bhitamin

vivacious *adj.* सजीव sajiw

vivavoce *n.* मौखिक परीक्षा mokhik pariksha

vivid *adj.* उज्यालो ujyalo

vocabulary *n.* शब्दावली shabdawali

vocal *adj.* वाचिक wachik

vocalist *n.* गायक gayak

vocation *n.* पेशा pesha

vodka *n.* रूसी रक्सी roosi raksi

vogue *n.* चल्ती chalti

voice *n.* स्वर swar

voile *n.* मिहिन वस्त्र mihin vastra

volatile *adj.* चाँडै उड्ने chandai udne

volcano *n.* ज्वालामुखी jwalamukhi

vole *n.* मूसा जस्तो जन्त musa jasto jant

volleyball *n.* भलिबल bhalibal

volt *n.* भोल्ट bholt

volte-face *n.* पूर्ण परिवर्तन purn parvartan

voluminous *adj.* मोटो moto

voluntary *adj.* आफुखुशी aphu khushi

volunteer *n.* स्वयंसेवक swayam sewak

voluptuous *adj.* विषयभागी wishayabogi

vomit *n.* उल्टी ulti

voracious *adj.* पेटु petu

vote *n.* मत mat

vote down *v.* बहुमतले अस्वीकार गर्नु bahu mat le aswikar garnu

vote of no confidence *n.* अविश्वास को प्रस्ताव awishwas ko prastaw

vote of thanks *n.* धन्यवाद-ज्ञापन dhanyawad gyapan

voter *n.* मतदाता mat data

vow *n.* प्रतिज्ञा pratigya

vox *n.* आवाज awaaz

vulgar *adj.* अश्लील ashlil

vulva *n.* भग bhag

vying *adj.* होड़ गर्ने hodh garne

W

wade *v.* नदी हेलेर तर्नु nadi helera tarnu

waffle *n.* सानो केक sano cake

wag *v.* हल्लाउनु hallaunu

wag(g)on *n.* चारपाङ्ग्रे गाडी char pangre gadi

wage *n.* तलब talab

wager *n.* बाजी baji

waggle *v.* हल्लाउनु hallaunu

waif *n.* घरविहीन व्यक्ति gharwihin vyakti

wail *v.* विलाप गर्नु vilap garnu

waistcoat *n.* इस्टकोट istkot

wait *v.* पर्खनु parkhanu

waiter *n.* बेयरा beyara

waiting list *n.* प्रतीक्षा सूचि pratiksha suchi

waiting room *n.* प्रतीक्षालय pratikshalaya

waitress *n.* बेयराकेटी beyaraketi

wake *v.* जाग्नु jagnu

wake up *v.* जगाउनु jagaunu

walk *v.* हिँड्नु hindnu

walk off with *v.* चोरेर लैजानु chorera laijanu

walker *n.* डुल्ने dulne

walkover *n.* सजिलो जीत sajilojit

wall *n.* भित्ता bhitta

wallet *n.* परस purse

wallop *n.* ओखर okhar

walnut *n.* ओखर okhar

wampum *n.* कौड़ीको माला kodhiko maal

wander *v.* घुम्नु ghumnu

wanderer *n.* डुलुवा duluwa

wanderlust *n.* घुम्ने इच्छा ghumne iccha

wane *v.* घट्नु ghatnu

want *v.* चाहनु cjajami

wanted *adj.* आवश्यक awashyak

wanton *adj.* अकारण akaaran

wantonly *adv.* बेमतलबसँग be matlab sanga

war *n.* लडाइँ ladai

war cry *n.* लडाइँको नारा ladain ko nara

ward *n.* आश्रित ashrit

ward off *v.* रोक्नुबचाउनु roknu bachanu

warder *n.* इयालखानको रक्षक eyalkhanko rakshak

wardrobe *n.* दराज daraj

warehouse *n.* गोदाम godam

warfare *n.* युद्ध yuddha

warlike *adj.* न्यानो nyano

warm *adj.* तातो tatto

warm up *v.* तताउनु tataunu

warm-hearted *adj.* दयालु dayalu

warmth *v.* सावधान गर्नु sawdhan garnu

warn *v.* चेताउनी दिनु chetauni dinu

warning *n.* चेतावनी chetawani

warp *v.* विकृत गर्नु वा हुनु vikrit garnu va hunu

warrant *n.* वारण्ट warant

warrior *n.* योद्धा yoddha

warrior *n.* सिपाही sipahi

wart *v./aux.* थियो thiyo

was *v.* थियो thiyo

wash *v.* धुनु dhunu

wash up *v.* माझ्नु majhnu

washabasin *n.* कोपरा kopara

washable *adj.* धुन हुनु dhuna hune

washed out *adj.* थाकेको thakeko

washer *n.* वासर wasar

washerman *n.* धोबी dhobi

washy *n.* बारुलो barulo

wasp *n.* बारूलो barulo

wastage *n.* खेर khera

waste paper *n.* रद्दी कागज raddi kagaj

waste(paper) basket *n.* रद्दी को टोकरी raddi ko tokari

wasted *adj.* खेर गएको khera gaeko

wasteland *n.* बन्जर जग्गा banjar jagga

wastrel *n.* बेकामे व्यक्ति bekaame vyakti

watch *n.* घडी ghadi

watch out *v.* सतर्क रहनु satark rahanu

watchful *adj.* सावधान sawdhan garnu

watchmaker *n.* घडीसाज ghadisaj

watchman *n.* पाले pale

watchword *n.* संकेत शब्द sanket shabd

water *n.* पानी pani

water down *v.* कम गरी दिनु kam gari dinu

water lily *n.* सेतो कमल seto kamal

waterfall *n.* झरना jharna

watermelon *n.* तरबुजा tarbuja

watermill *n.* पानीघट्ट pani ghatta

waterpipe *n.* पानीको पाइप pani ko paip

waterproof *adj.* पानीले नबिगार्ने pani le na bigarne

watershed *n.* जलाधार jaladhar

waterspout *n.* जलस्तम्भ jal stambha

watery *adj.* पन्यालो panyalo

wave *n.* लहर lahar

waver *v.* हिचकिचाउनु hichkichaunu

wavy *adj.* लहरदार lahardar

wax *n.* मैन main

way *n.* बाटो bato

way of life *n.* जीवनचर्या jiwan charya

way out *adv.* धेरै बाहिर dherai bahir

wayback *n.* बटुवा batuwa

wayfarer *n.* बटुवा batuwa

waylay *v.* ढुक्नु dhuknu

way-out *adj.* असाधारण asadharan

wayside *adj.* जिद्दी jiddi

wayward *adj.* हठी hathi

we *pron.* हामी hami

weak *adj.* कमजोर kamjor

weaken *v.* कमजोर तुल्याउनु kam jor tuly aunu

weak-minded *adj.* सुस्त sust

weakness *n.* कल्याण kalyan

weal *n.* कल्याण kalyan

weal and woe *n.* सुखदुःख sukh duhkh

wealth *n.* धन dhan

wealthy *adj.* धनी dhani

weapon *n.* हतियार hatiyar

wear *v.* लाउनु launu

wear and tear *n.* टुटफुट tytphut

wear away *v.* खिइनु khiinu

wear out *v.* फाट्नु phatnu

weariness *n.* थकाइ thakai

weary *adj.* थाकेको thakeko

weasel *n.* काठे न्याउरीमूसो kathe nyauri muso

weather *n.* मौसम mausam

weather forecast *n.* मौसम भविष्यवाणी mausam bhawishya wani

weather-beaten *adj.* घाम पानी खाएको gham pani khaeko

weave *v.* बुन्नु bunnu

weaving *n.* बुनाइ bunai

web *n.* जाली jali

wed *v.* बिहे गर्नु bihe garnu

wedding *n.* बिहे bihe

wedding ring *n.* बिहेको औंठी bihe ko aunthi

wedge *n.* विवाहबन्धन wiwah bandhan

wedlock *n.* विवाहित अवस्था vivahit awastha

Wednesday *n.* बुधवार budh bar

weed *n.* झारण jharna

week *n.* साता satark rahanu

weekend *n.* हप्ताको आखिरी दिन hapta ko akhiri din

weekly *n.* साप्ताहिक saptahik

weep *v.* जोख्नु jokhnu

weigh *v.* तौलनु tolnu

weight *n.* ढक dhak

weightless *adj.* भारहीन bharhin

weighty *adj.* भारी bhari

weir *n.* नदीको बाँध nadiko bandh

weird *adj.* भयानक bhayanak

welcome *n.* स्वागत swagat

welcome arch *n.* स्वागत द्वार swagat dwar

weld *v.* तताएर पिटेर जोड्नु tattair piter jodnu

welfare *n.* कल्याण kalyan

welfare state *n.* कल्याणकारी राज्य kalyankari rajya

well *adj.* निको niko

well advised *adj.* बुद्धिमान् buddhiman

well and good *adv.* बेस bes

well balanced *adj.* सन्तुलित santulit

well bred *adj.* सुशील sushil

well done *adj.* स्याबाश syabash

well informed *adj.* जानिफकार janiph kar

well intentioned *adj.* राम्रो नियतको ramro niyat ko

well judged *adj.* राम्ररी गरिएको ramrai garieko

well known *adj.* प्रसिद्ध prasiddha

well off *adj.* धनी dhani

well read *adj.* सुपठित supathit

well tried *adj.* राम्ररी कोशिश गरेको ramrari koshish gareko

well-being *n.* कल्याण kalyan

well-to-do *adj.* खुसहाल khushhal

well-wisher *n.* हितैषी hitaishi

welter *n.* छयासमिस chiasmis

wench *n.* ठिटी thiti

were *v./aux.* थए their

west *n.* पश्चिम pashchim

western *adj.* पश्चिमी pashchimi

westernise *v.* पश्चिमी रंगमा रंगिनु pashchimi ranga ma ranginu

westernmost *adj.* सुदूरपश्चिम sudur pashchim

westward *adv.* पश्चिमतिर pashchim tira

wet *adj.* भिजेको bhijeko

wet blanket *n.* रंगमा भंग गर्ने ranga ma bhang garne

wet nurse *n.* धाई dhai

wether खसी पारेको भेड़ा khasi pareko bheda

wett *v.* तानमा हालेर कपड़ा बनाउने बाना tanma haler kapda banaune wala

whale *n.* ह्वेल माछा hwel machha

what *int. pron.* के ke

what for *int. pron.* के को लागि ke ko lagi

what have you *pron.* त्यस्तै अरू कुरा tyastai aru kura

whatever *pron.* जेसुकै je sukai

whatsoever *pron.* जेसुकै je sukai

wheat *n.* गहुँगो gahun

wheat stalk *n.* छवाली chhwali

wheedle *v.* फुस्ल्याउनु phuslayunu

wheel *n.* चक्का chakka

wheelchair *n.* पांग्रे मेच pangremech

whelp *n.* चिप्लेकीरा chiplekira

when *int. pron.* कहिले kahile

where *int. pron.* काँह kahan

whereabouts *adv.* ठेगाना thegana

wherever *adv.* जहाँसुकै jahan sukai

wherewithal *n.* पैसा आदि paisaadi

whether *conj.* कि ki

whetstone *n.* सान लाउने पत्थर san laune patthar

which *int.pron.* कुन kun

whiff *n.* फुस्स निस्केको हावा phuss niskeko hawa

while *con.* जबकि jaba ki

whim *n.* लहड lahad

whimsical *adj.* लहडी lahadi

whinny *v.* हिनहिनाउनु hinhinaunu

whip *n.* कोर्रा korra

whirl *v.* फनका ख्वाउनु phanka khwaunu

whisker *n.* जुँगा junga

whisper *v.* साउती गर्नु sauti garnu

whistle *n.* सिट्ठी sitthi

white *adj.* सेतो seto

white *adj.* सेतो seto

white elephant *n.* खर्चिलो हात्ति kharchilo hathi

white flag *n.* मिलापत्र झंडा mila patra jhanda

white hope *n.* आशाको ज्याति asha ko jyoti

white lie *n.* निदोष झूट nirdosh jhut

white paper *n.* वेतपत्र shwet patra

whitewash *n.* चुनको पोताइ chun ko potai

whither *adv.* कहाँ kahan

whitlow *n.* नङछुरी nan chhuri

whitsum *n.* इस्टरपछिको सातौं रविबार isterpachiko saathon ravibar

whittle *v.* काट्नु kaatnu

who *int. pron.* कोर्रा korra

whole *adj./adv.* सम्पूर्ण sampurn

wholehearted *adj.* सच्चा sachcha

wholesale *n.* थोक thok

wholesome *adj.* पौष्टिक paushtik

whom *int. pron.* कसलाई kaslai

whoop *v.* कराउनु karaunu

whooping cough *n.* लहरे खोकी lahare khoki

whore *n.* वेश्या veshya

whose *int.pron.* कस्को kasko

why *int. pron.* किन kina

wick *n.* बत्ती batti

wick *adj.* बदमास badmas

wicked *adj.* दुष्ट dusht

wicker *n.* बटारेको बेत batare ko bet

wide *adj.* चौडा chauda

wide awake *adj.* पूरा ब्यूँझेको pura byunjheko

wide-eyed *adj.* छक्क परेको chhakka pareko

widespread *adj.* व्यापक wyapak

widow *n.* विधवा widhwa

width *n.* चौडाइ chaudai

wield *v.* मच्चाउनु machchaunu

wife *n.* स्वास्नी swasni

wig *n.* नक्कली कपाल nakkali kapal

wiggle *v.* हल्लिनु halinu

wildcat *n.* बनबिरालो ban biralo

wilderness *n.* बंजर भूमि banjar bhoomi

wildfire *n.* डढेलो dadhelo

wiles *n.* चाल chaal

wilful *adj.* जिद्दी jiddi

will power *n.* इच्छाशक्ति ichchha shakti

willing *adj.* राजी raji

will-o-the-wisp *n.* राँकेभूत rankebhut

willy-nilly *adv.* इच्छा गरी वा नगरीकन iccha gari va nagrikan

wilt *v.* ओडलाउनु oilaunu

win *n.* जीत jit

wind *n.* हावा hawa

wind up *v.* समाप्त गर्नु samapt garnu

windbag *n.* बोलक्कड bolakkad

windfall *n.* झरेको फल jhare ko phal

windmill *n.* हावाघट्ट hawa ghatt

window *n.* झ्याल jhyal

windswept *adj.* धेरै हावाको मार परेको dherai hawa ko mar pareko

wine *n.* रक्सी raksi

wing *n.* पखेटा pakheta

wink at *v.* आँखा झिम्क्याउनु ankha jhimkyaunu

winner *n.* जितुवा jituwa

winnow *v.* निफन्नु niphannu

winnowing tray *adj.* राम्रो ramro

winsome *adj.* आकर्षक akarshak

winter *n.* हिउँद hiund

winter sports *v.* पुछ्नु puchhnu

wipe पुछ्नु puchhnu

wipe out *v.* मेट्नु metnu

wiper *n.* पुछ्ने वस्तु puchhne wastu

wire *n.* तार tarbuja

wireless *n.* बेतार betar

wirepulling *n.* लुकेर गरिने काम lukera garine kan

wiring *n.* बिजुली को तार जडान bijuli ko tar jadan

wiry *adj.* तार जस्तो taar jasto

wisdom *n.* ज्ञान gyan

wisdom tooth *v.* बुद्धि बङ्गरो buddhi bangaro

wise *adj.* बुद्धिमान् buddhiman

wisecrack *n.* घ्चुड्किला chudkila

wisely *adv.* बुद्धिमानी साथ buddhimani sath

wish *v.* इच्छा/कामना गर्नु ichchha/kamna garnu

wishful *adj.* इच्छुक ichchhuk

wishful thinking *n.* त्यान्द्रो tyandro

wisp *n.* सानो मूठा sanomootha

wistful *n.* ज्ञान gyan

wit *v.* अर्थात् arthat

witch *n.* बोक्सी boksi

witch doctor *n.* धामी dhami

witchcraft *n.* बोक्सी विद्या boksi widya

with *prep.* सँग snaga

withdraw *v.* पछि हटनु pachhi hatnu

withdrawal *v.* ओइलाउनु oilaunu

wither *v.* ओइलाउनु oilaunu

withhold *v.* रोक्नु roknu

within *prep.* भित्र bhitra

without *prep.* बिना bina

withstand *adj.* बेकुफ bekuph

witless *n.* साक्षी sakshi

witticism *n.* चुट्किलो chutkilo

witty *adj.* विनोदपूर्ण vinodpurn

wizard *n.* बोक्सो bokshi

wizened *adj.* सूकेको sukeko

wobble *v.* हल्लनु hallanu

woe *n.* दुःख duhkha

wolf *n.* ब्वाँसो bwanso

woman *n.* महिला mahila

womantizer *n.* कोख kokh

womb *n.* गर्भ garam

women *n.* महिलाहरू mahila haru

wonder *n.* आश्चर्य उदेक ashcharya

wonderful *adj.* अचम्मको achamma ko

wonky *adj.* अस्थिर asthir

wont *n.* आदत aadat

woo *v.* प्रेम गर्नु premgarnu

wood *n.* काठ kath

woodcutter *n.* दाउरे daure

wooded *adj.* रूखहरू भएको rukh haru bhaeko

wooden *adj.* काठको kathko

woodpecker *n.* काठकोटेरो kathko tero

wool *n.* ऊन un

woollen *adj.* ऊनी uni

word *n.* शब्द shabd

word fof honour *n.* वचन wachan

word of mouth *n.* मौखिक maukhik

work *n.* काम kam

workable *adj.* कामचलाउ kam chalau

workaday *n.* कामदार kamdar

worker *n.* वेतनभोगी vetanbhogi

workforce *n.* प्राप्त मजदूर संख्या prapt majdur sankhya

working knowledge *n.* कामचलाउ ज्ञान kam chalau gyan

workload *n.* कामको भार kam ko bhar

workmanship *n.* कालिगढी kali gadhi

workout *v.* हिसाब गर्नु hisab garnu

workshop *n.* कार्यशाला karyashala

world *n.* संसार sansar

world-famous *adj.* विश्वप्रसिद्ध wishwa prasiddha

worldly *adj.* सांसारिक sansarik

worm *n.* गडेऍलो gadeunlo

worn out *adj.* झुत्रो jhutro

worried *n.* चिन्ता chinta

worry *v.* चिन्ता गर्नु chinta garnu

worse *adj.* अरू बढी खराब aru badhi kharab

worsen *v.* खराब हुनु kharab hunu

worship *n.* पूजा गर्नु puja garnu

worshipper *n.* भक्त bhakta

worst *adj.* सबभन्दा खराब sab bhanda kharab

worsted *adj.* लायक layak

worth *n.* मूल्य mulya

worthiness *n.* योग्यता yogyata

worthless *adj.* निकम्मा nikamma

worthwhile *adj.* उचित uchit

worthy *adj.* योग्य yogya

would *mod.* भयो bhayo

would-be *adj.* हुनेवाला hunewala

wound *n.* घाउ ghau

wounded *inter.* बाफरे बाफ babh re baph

wow *n.* ठूलो सफलता thulo safalta

wrangle *n.* गरम बहस garam bahas

wrap *n.* रिस ris

wrath *n.* क्रोध krodh

wreak *v.* भयानक क्षति पुर्याउनु bhyanak khasti puryanu

wreath *n.* माला mala

wreck *v.* नाश गर्नु nash garnu

wreckage *n.* रेन्चु renchu

wrench *v.* बटार्नु batarnu

wrest *v.* बलले खोस्नु bal le khosnu

wrestie *v.* कुस्ती खेल्नु kusti khelnu

wrestler *n.* पहलमान pahalman

wrestling *n.* कुस्ती kusti

wretched *adj.* दुःखी duhkhi

wriggle *v.* चलमलाउनु chalmalaunu

wring *n.* चाउरी chauri

wrinkle *n.* नाडी nadi

wrist *n.* नाड़ी naadi

wristwatch *n.* रिट rit

writ *n.* परमादेश parmadesh

write *v.* लेख्नु lekhnu

write off *v.* माफ गर्नु map garnu

write up *v.* वर्णन/प्रशंसा गर्नु warnan/prashamsa garnu

writer *n.* लेखक lekhak

write-up *v.* वर्णन लेख warnan lekh

writhe *v.* दुःखले छटपटाउनु dukkha le chhat pataunu

writing *n.* लेखाइ lekhai

written *adj.* लेखेको lekheko

wrong *adj.* गलत galat

wrong doing *n.* दुराचार durachar

wrong-headed *adj.* हठी hathi

wry *adj.* व्यंग्यपूर्ण vyangyapurn

X

xenophobia *n.* फोटोकापी photokapi

xerox *n.* फोटोकापी photocopy

xmas *n.* क्रिसमस krismas

x-ray *n.* एक्सरे eksre

Y

yacht *n.* पालवाला डुङ्गा palwala dunga

yahoo *n.* चौंरी गाई chaunri gai

yak *n.* तरुल tarul

yam *n.* तरूल tarul

yard *n.* सुट sut

yarn *n.* सूत soot

yaw *n.* हाई गर्नु hal garnu

yawn *v.* हाई गुर्न high garnu

yaws *n.* गरम ठाँउमा हुने छालाको रोग garam thaunma hune chalako rog

yea *adv.* हो ho

year *n.* वर्ष warsh

year in and year out *adv.* निरन्तर nirantar

yearly *adj.* वार्षिक warshik

yearn *v.* रहर गर्नु rahar garnu

yearning *n.* मार्च march

yeast *n.* खमीर khameer

yell *v.* तीखो स्वर thekho soar

yellow *adj.* पहेँलो pahenlo

yellow fever *n.* पीतज्वर pit jwar

yellow press *n.* पीत पत्रकारिता pit patra karita

yelp *v.* छोटो chhoto

yeoman *n.* भूमिधर bhumi dhar

yeoman service *n.* खाँचो पर्दा गरिने सेवा khancho parda garine sewa

yes *n.* हो ho

yesman *n.* जीहजुरिया ji hajuriya

yesterday *adv.* अझै ajhai

yet *conj.adv.* अइसम्म ahism

yeti *n.* सोक्पा sokpa

yield *n.* पैदावार paidawar

yoga *n.* योग yog

yogurt, yoghurt *n.* दही dahi

yokel *n.* गाउँले gaunle

yolk *n.* अण्डा को पहेँलो भाग anda ko pahenlo bhag

yonder *adj.adv.* त्यहाँ tyehan

yore *n.* प्राचीन समय prachin samaya

you *pron.* तिमी timi

young *adj.* तरुण tarun

younger *adj.* कान्छो kanchho

youngest *adj.* सबभन्दा कान्छो sab bhanda kanchho

youngsters *n.* बालबालिका bal balika

your *pron.* तिम्रो timro

yourself *pron.* तिमी आफै timi aphai

youth *n.* यौवन yauwan

youthful *adj.* तरूण tarun

yowl *v.* लामो ठूलो स्वरले कराउनु lamo thulo swarle karaunu

Z

zany *n.* मसखरा maskhara

zap *v.* हमला गर्नु hamla garnu

zeal *n.* कट्टरपन्थी kattarpanthi

zealot *n.* कट्टर समर्थक kattar samarthak

zealous *adj.* उत्साही utsahi

zebra *n.* जेब्रा घोडा jebra ghoda

zen *n.* बौद्ध धर्मको एक रूप bodh dharamko ek roop

zephyr *n.* पश्चिमी वायु paschimi vayu

zero *n.* उत्साही utsahi

zest *n.* ठूलो रूचि thulo ruchi

zigzag *adj.* बाङ्गोटिङ्गो bango tingo

zinc *n.* जस्ता jasta

zipper *n.* जिपर jiper

zodiac *n.* राशिचक्र rashi chakra

zombie *n.* बुद्धिहीन व्यक्ति budhiheen vyakti

zone *n.* अंचल anchal

zone of peace *n.* शान्तिक्षेत्र shanti kshetra

zoo *n.* चिडियाखाना chidiya khana

zoological garden *n.* चिडियाखाना chidiya khana

zoologist *n.* प्राणीशास्त्री prani shastri

zoology *n.* पशुविज्ञान pashu wigyan

NEPALI-ENGLISH

A

a aphnu आ-आफ्नु *adj.* respective

aachran आचरण *n.* bearing

aadat आदत *n.* wont

aadesh dinu आदेश दिनु *v.* enjoin

aagman आगमन *n.* advent

aaharko आहारको *adj.* alimentary

aahawan आह्वान *adj.* clarion

aakashiya आकाशीय *adj.* spatial

aakha ko ghar आखाको घर *n.* orbit

aakraman आक्रमण *n.* spasm

aalamb आलम्ब *n.* fulcrum

aandirko tel अँडिरको तेल *n.* castor-oil

aandra आन्द्रा *n.* entrails

aangan आँगन *n.* patio

aankha ladaunu आँखा लड़ाउनु *v.* ogle

aankhako phulo आँखाको फुलो *n.* cataract

aanyanand अन्यानन्द *n.* jubilation

aaram dine आराम दिने *adj.* restful

aaram ko nokari आरामको नोकरी *n.* sinecure

aarop आरोप *v.* allege

aarop आरोप *n.* charcoal

aasankha आशांखा *n.* qualm

aatankit आतंकित *adj.* aghast

aath आठ *n.* eight

aatma santust आत्मसन्तुष्ट *adj.* complacent

aaunu आउनु *v.* perspire

aaykarmathi laagne thapkar आयकरमाथि लाग्ने थप कर *n.* supertax

aba dekhi अबदेखि *adv.* henceforth

abahari आभारी *adj.* beholden

abble अब्बल *adj.* premier

abela अबेला *n.* late

abhadra bolne अभद्र बोल्ने *adj.* rough-tongued

abhagi अभागी *adj.* hapless

abhagi अभागी *adj.* unfortunate

abhagi अभागी *adj.* unlucky

abhar आभर मान्नु *v.* acknowledge

abhari आभारी *adj.* grateful

abhari आभारी *n.* gratitude

abhari आभारी *adj.* thankful

abharod अवरोध *n.* halt

abhav अभाव *n.* dearth

abhaw अभाव *n.* shortage

abhaya patra अभयपत्र *n.* safe conduct

abhibhawak अभिभावक *n.* guardian

abhijattantra अभिजातततंत्र *n.* aristrocracy

abhinandan/salam garnu अभिनन्दन/सलाम गर्नु *v.* greet

abhinay garn naskine अभिनय गर्न नसकिने *adj.* unactable

abhinay garnu अभिनय गर्नु *v.* enact

abhineta अभिनेता *n.* actor

abhinetrl अभिनेत्री *n.* actress

abhinna अभिन्न *adj.* integral

abhiruchi अभिरूचि *n.* penchant

abhiwyakti अभिव्यक्ति *n.* expression

abhiyukta अभियुक्त *n.* convict

abhrak अभ्रक *n.* mica

abhyas अभ्यास *n.* exercise

abhyas garnu अभ्यास गर्नु *v.* practice

abhyast garnu अभ्यस्त गर्नु *v.* inure

abresum sutnu अबेरसम्म सुत्नु *v.* oversleep

abrodh अवरोध *n.* slege

achal अचल *adj.* immovable

achamma ko अचम्मको *adj.* amazing

achamma ko अचम्मको *adj.* wonderful

achamma lagdo अचम्म लाग्दो *adj.* surprising

achanak अचानक *adj.* sudden

achanak adnu अचानक अड्नु *v.* stop short

achar अचार *n.* pickle

achar अचल *adj.* stable

achet अचेत *v.* stun

achet awastha ma barbaraune अचेत अवस्थामा बर्बराउने *adj.* delirious

achhut अछूत *n.* untouchable

achinhit अचिन्हित *adj.* unmarked

adaksh अदक्ष *adj.* unskillful

adal badal अदलबदल *n.* alteration

adal badal अदलबदल *n.* change

adalat अदलात *n.* court

adalat janch अदालती जाँच *n.* inquest

adalati अदालती *adj.* judicial

adalatko अदालत को *adj.* forensic

adamay अदम्य *adj.* irrepressible

adamya अदम्य *adj.* uncrushable

adan linu अडान लिनु *v.* sit tight

adan pradan आदानप्रदान *n.* give and take

adar आद *n.* courtesy

adar आदर *n.* esteem

adar आदर *n.* reverence

adar आदर *n.* respect

adar garnu आदर गर्नु *v.* regard

adarniya आदरणीय *adj.* respectable

adarniya आदरणीय *adj.* venerable

adarsh vakya आदर्श-वाक्य *n.* motto

adesh आदेश *n.* instruction

adesh dinu आदेश दिनु *v.* dictate

adesh ko palan garnu आदेश पालन गर्नु *v.* toe the line/mark

adha आधार *n.* half

adha chandra अर्धचन्द्र *n.* half-moon

adha jhukeko आधा झुकेको *adj.* half-mast

adha rat आधारात *n.* midnight

adha writta आधा वृत्त *n.* semicircle

adha-adha garnu आधा आधा गर्नु *v.* halve

adhar आधार *n.* groundwork

adhar bhut आधारभूत *n.* basis

adhar bhut आधारभूत *adj.* fundamental

adharat pachhi ko samaya आधारात तपछिको समय *n.* small hours

adharbhut karan आधारभूत कारण *n.* rationale

adharmi अधर्मी *adj.* impious

adharshila आधारशिला *n.* cornerstone

adhayansheel अध्ययनशील *adj.* studious

adhbainse umer अधबैंसे उमेर *n.* middle age

adheer अधीर *adj.* impatient

adhik अधिक *adj.* predominant

adhik dam linu wa magnu अधिक दाम लिनु वा माग्नु *v.* overcharge

adhik vastu अधिक बस्नु *v.* overstay

adhikar अधिकार *n.* authority

adhikar dinu अधिकार दिनु *v.* empower

adhikar dinu अधिकार दिनु *v.* entitle

adhikrit अधिकृत *n.* officer

adhiktam अधिकतम *adj.* maximum

adhinta अधीनता *n.* subjection

adhinta अधीनता *n.* submission

adhinta आड *n.* support

adhirajya अधिराज्य *n.* kingdom

adhkalvo अधकल्चो *adj.* underdone

adhobindu अधोबिन्दु *n.* nadir

adhunik आधुनिक *adj.* modern

adhunik banaunu आधुनिक बनाउनु *v.* modernize

adhyadesh अध्यादेश *n.* ordinance

adhyaksha अध्यक्ष *n.* chairman

adhyatmik आध्यात्मिक *adj.* spiritual

adhyaya अध्याय *n.* chapter

adim आदिम *adj.* primeval

adivasi आदिवासी *n.* aborigines

adiwasi आदिवासी *n.* miscreant

admim आदिम *adj.* primal

adne shakti अड्ने शक्ति *n.* stamina

adne shakti अड्ने शक्ति *n.* staying power

adrishya अदृश्य *adj.* hidden

aduwa अदुवा *n.* ginger

advertisement विज्ञापन *n.* advertisement

adwitiya अद्वितीय *adj.* inimitable

afantharu आफन्तहरू *n.* kith

agadi अगाडि *prep.* before

agadi ko अगाडिको *adj.* forward

agadi ko batti अगाडिको बत्ती *n.* headlight

agadiko अगाडिको *advj.* front

agaman आगमन *n.* arrival

agami आगामी *adj.* forthcoming

agantuk आगन्तुक *n.* visitor

agantuk pustika आगन्तुक पुस्तिका *n.* visitor's book

agarbatti अगरबत्ती *n.* incense

agentko kaam एजेन्टको काम *n.* agency

agenu अगेनु *n.* fireplace

agenuko kuna अगेनुको कुना *n.* inglenook

agenuko mastir raheko kath अगेनुको मास्तिर रहेको काठ *n.* mantelpiece

aghi अघि *adv.* ago

aghi अघि *adv.* ahead

aghi अघि *adv.* ere

aghi aghi अघिअघि *adv.* onward

aghi badhnu अघि बढ्नु *v.* proceed

aghi dhakelne kaam अघि धकेल्ने काम *n.* propulsion

aghi ko अधिको *adj.* former

aghi ko अधिको *adj.* previous

aghi nai अघि नै *adv.* already

aglo अग्लो *adj.* high

aglo अग्लो *adj.* tall

aglo burja अग्लो बुर्जा *n.* tower

aglo ra dublo अग्लो र दुब्लो *adj.* lanky

aglo ra dublo अग्लो र दुब्लो *adj.* lofty

ago आगो *n.* fire

ago ko lapka आगो को लप्का *n.* flame

ago nibhaune manis आगो निभाउने मानिस *n.* fireman

agoko jharilo rahal आगोको झरिलो रहल *n.* embers

agrabhaag अग्रभाग *n.* prow

agraha garnu आग्रह गर्नु *v.* inculcate

aguwa अगुवा *n.* harbinger

aguwa अगुवा *n.* pioneer

agya आज्ञा *n.* command

agya kari आज्ञाकारी *adj.* obedient

agya palak आज्ञापालक *adj.* dutiful

agya palan आज्ञापालन *n.* obedience

agya palan garnu आज्ञा पालन गर्नु *v.* obey

agya/anumati patra आज्ञा/अनुमति पत्र *n.* licence

agyae अज्ञेय *adj.* unknowable

agyani अज्ञानी *adj.* ignorant

agyani vyakti अज्ञानी व्यक्ति *n.* ignoramus

agyanta अज्ञानता *n.* ignorance

agyat अज्ञात *adj.* unknown

aham अहम *n.* ego

ahan अहँ *adv.* no

ahankari अहंकारी *adj.* arrogant

ahankari अहंकारी *adj.* bumptious

ahankari अहङ्कारी *adj.* overbearing

ahar आहार *n.* diet

ahawaan आह्वान *n.* convocation

ahile अहिले *adv.* now

ahile prayog nahune अहिले प्रयोग नहुने *adj.* arehaic

ahile samma अहिलेसम्म *adv.* hitherto

ahism अइसम्म *conj.adv.* yet

ahitkari अहितकारी *adj.* noxious

ahsa आशा *n.* prospect

ain ऐन *n.* legislation

aina ऐना *n.* mirror

ainle na dieko ऐनले नदिएको *adj.* illegitimate

ainselu ऐँसेलु *n.* raspberry

aipignu आइपुग्नु *v.* arrive

ais krim आइस्क्रीम *n.* ice cream

aitbar आइतबार *n.* sunday

aitihasik ऐतिहासिक *adj.* historical

aja आज *n.* this day

aja आज *n./adv.* today

aja bihana आज बिहान *n./adv.* this morning

aja rati आज राती *n./adv.* tonight

ajeya अजेय *adj.* invicible

ajh ramro parnu अझ राम्रो पार्नु *v.* ameliorate

ajha अझ *adv.* moreover

ajhai अझै *adv.* still

ajhai अझै *adv.* yesterday

ajingar अजिङ्गर *n.* python

ajiwan आजीवन *adj.* lifelong

ajkal आजकल *adv.* nowadays

akaaran अकारण *adj.* wanton

akadera hindnu अकडेर हिँड्नु *v.* swagger

akanksha garnu आकांक्षा गर्नु *v.* aspire

akansha आकांक्षा *n.* ambition

akar आकार *n.* form

akar आकार *n.* shape

akarman आक्रमण *n.* aggression

akarshak आकर्षक *adj.* pictursque

akarshak आकर्षक *adj.* prepossessing

akarshak आकर्षक *adj.* winsome

akarshan आकर्षण *n.* attraction

akarshit garnu आकर्षित गर्नु *v.* attract

akash आकाश *n.* firmament

akash आकाश *n.* sky

akash ganga आकाशगंगा *n.* galaxy

akash ganga आकाशगंगा *n.* milky way

akashe nilo आकाशे नीलो *adj.* sky-blue

akashlya आकाशीय *adj.* celestial

akasinu अकासिनु *v.* soar

akasmaat अकस्मात् *adj.* abrupt

akasmat अकस्मात् *adj.* suddenly

akasmik आकस्मिक *adj.* incidental

akataya अकाट्य *adj.* unassailable

akathniya अकथनीय *adj.* unspeakable

akhbar अखबार *n.* newspaper

akhbarpasal अखबार पसल *n.* news-stand

akhir आखिर *n.* end

akhir ma आखिरमा *adv.* lastly

akhiri shart आखिरी शर्त *n.* ultimatum

akhyan आख्यान *n.* saga

akkai shabdma vyakhaya garnu अकैं शब्दमा व्याख्या गर्नु *v.* paraphrase

akkal अक्कल *n.* sense

akramak आक्रामक *n.* offensive

akraman garnu आक्रमण गर्नु *v.* set upon

aksar अक्सर *adv.* often

aksar अक्सर *adv.* usually

aksha अक्षर *n.* syllable

akshansh अक्षांश *n.* latitude

alachchhin waykti wa wastu अलच्छिना व्यक्ति वा वस्तु *n.* jinx

alag अलग *adv.* apart

alag अलग *adv.* off

alag अलग *adj.* separate

216

alag garnu अलग गर्नु *v.* sunder

alag garnu अलग गर्नु *v.* uncouple

alag na hune अलग नहुने *adj.* inseparable

alag parnu अलग पार्नु *v.* alienate

alag rahanu अलग रहनु *v.* absatin

alag rakhnu अलग राख्नु *v.* lay aside

alag/wichchhed garnu अलग/विच्छेद गर्नु *v.* sever

alagyaunu अलग्याउनु *v.* isolate

alainchi अलैंची *n.* cardamom

alak अलक *n.* quiff

alankarik bhasha आलङ्कारिक भाषा *n.* rhetoric

alankrit garnu अलंकृत गर्नु *v.* emblazon

alap-tantra अल्प-तंत्र *n.* oligarchy

alas आलस्य *n.* linseed

alasya आलस्य *adj.* indolent

alasya आलस्य *n.* laziness

alaukik अलौकिक *adj.* supernatural

alchhi अल्छी *adj.* idle

alchhi अल्छी *adj.* lazy

alchhi lose vyakti अल्छी लोसे व्यक्ति *n.* sluggard

ali aghi अलि अघि *adv.* just before

ali ali gari अलि अलि गरी *adv.* gradually

ali ali rato अलि अलि रातो *adj.* reddish

ali kati अलिकति *adj.* few

ali mateko अलि मातेको *adj.* squiffy

ali nunilo अलि नुनिलो *adj.* brackish

alijho अलझो *n.* complication

alijjit अलिज्जित *adj.* unabashed

alino अलिनो *adj.* saltless

aljhai अल्झाइ *n.* entanglement

aljho अल्झो *n.* obstruction

alkai अलकाई *n.* piles

alkatra अलकत्रा *n.* asphalt

alkatra अलकत्रा *n.* pitch

alkatra अलकत्रा *n.* tar

alkatra अलकत्रा *n.* tar

alkatra lageko अलकत्रा लागेको *adj.* tarry

alochak आलोचक *n.* critic

alochana garnu आलोचना गर्नु *v.* criticize

alokpriya अलोकप्रिय *adj.* unpopular

alp buddhi अल्पबुद्धि *adj.* short-witted

alpanu अल्पनु *v.* disappear

alpin आलपिन *n.* pin

alpinu अल्पिनु *v.* vanish

alpkalik अल्पकालिक *adj.* short-term

alpsankhya अल्पसंख्या *n.* minority

alu आलु *n.* potato

alu bakhda आलुबखडा *n.* plum

am/sadharan wyakti आम/साधारण व्यक्ति *n.* layman

ama आमा *n.* mother

ama babu आमाबाबु *n.* parents

ama ko gun bhaeki आमाको गुण भएकी *adj.* motherly

amal pitta अमलपित्त *n.* acidity

aman अमन *n.* nausea

amapattico आमापट्टिको *adj.* maternal

amar अमर *adj.* immortal

amba अम्बा *n.* guava

amdani आम्दानी *n.* income

amdani आमदनी *n.* income

amelo अमिलो *adj.* acetic

americama paine junglee ghora अमेरिकामा पाइने जंगली घोड़ा *n.* mustang

amerika habsi mul ko sangit अमेरिकी हब्सी मूलको सङ्गीत *n.* jazz

amilo अमिलो *adj.* sour

amjanata आमजनता *n.* populace

amlet अम्लेट *n.* omelet(te)

amoniea अमोनिया *n.* ammonia

amrit अमृत *n.* elixir

amrit अमृत *n.* nectar

amsancharka sadhan आमसंचारका साधन *n.* mass midia

amsh अंश *n.* fraction

amshik आंशिक *adj.* partial

amshik rup ma आंशिक रूपमा *adv.* partly

amshik samaya ka lagi आंशिक समयका लागि *adj./adv.* part-time

amulya अमूल्य *adj.* preceless

amurt अमूर्त *n.* abstrat

anaam अनाम *adj.* unnamed

anadar अनादर *n.* disregard

anadar अनादर *n.* disrespect

anadi अनाडी *n.* novice

anaitik अनैतिक *adj.* dissolute

anaj अनाज *n.* corn

anand आनन्द *n.* bliss

anand आनन्द *n.* jamboree

anand आनन्द *n.* pleasure

anand dine आनन्द दिने *adj.* enjoyable

anand pradarshit garne आनन्द प्रदर्शित गर्ने *adj.* beatific

anandi आनन्दी *adj.* jovial

anandi आनन्दी *adj.* light-hearted

anant अनन्त *adj.* endless

anant अनन्त *adj.* eternal

anant अनन्त *n.* infinity

anar अनार *n.* pomegranate

anathalaya अनाथालय *n.* orphanage

anautho अनौठो *adj.* odd

anautho अनौठो *adj.* peculiar

anautho अनौठो *adj.* queer

anautho अनौठो *adj.* quixotic

anautho अनौठो *adj.* strange

anautho अनौठो *adj.* unusual

anawaran garnu अनावरण गर्नु *v.* unveil

anawashyak अनावश्यक *adj.* needless

anayae अन्याय *n.* tort

anbandh patra अनुबन्ध पत्र *n.* indenture

anbhyast अनभ्यस्त *adj.* unwonted

anchal अंचल *n.* zone

anda ko pahenlo bhag अण्डा को पहेँलो भाग *n.* yolk

andaj अन्दाज *n.* long shot

andaji अन्दाजी *adv* approximately

andaji अन्दाजी *adv.* roughly

andaji अन्दाजी *adj.* roundabout

andakar अण्डाकार *adj.* ova

andakar अण्डाकार *adj.* oval

andan अन्दाज *n.* guess

andanu अण्डाणु *n.* ovum

andh wishwas अन्ध विश्वास *n.* supersition

andh wishwasi अन्धविश्वासी *adj.* supersititious

andhadhund अन्धाधुन्ध *adj.* indiscriminate

andhi आँधी *n.* cyclone

andhi आँधी *n.* gale

andhi आँधी *n.* hurricane

andhi आँधी *n.* storm

andhi आँधी *n.* tempest

andhi chaleko आँधी चलेको *adj.* stormy

andhkar अन्धकार *n.* gloom

andho अन्धो *adj.* blind

andho अन्धो *adj.* sightless

andhyaro अँध्यारो *adj.* dark

andhyaro अँध्यारो *adj.* murky

andhyaro अँध्यारो *adj.* sombre

andhyaro mukh अँध्यारो मुख *n.* long face

andolan आन्दोलन *n.* revolution

andolan आन्दोलन *n.* uprising

andra bhundi आन्द्राभुँडी *n.* gut

andra, aant आँद्रा, आँत *n.* bowel

andro आन्द्रो *n.* intestine

andu ghoda आँडु घोडा *n.* stallion

anek r vividh अनेक र विविध *adj.* manifold

ang अङ्ग *n.* limb

ang अङ्ग *n.* organ

angaar अंगार *n.* breeze

angali halnu अङ्कालो हाल्नु *n.* hug

angalo halnu अँगालो हाल्नु *v.* embrace

angethi अँगेठी *n.* brazier

anginti अनगिन्ती *adj.* innumerable

angrej अँग्रेज *n.* english

angrezi kuleen purush अंग्रेजी कुलीन पुरूष *n.* earl

angur अंगुर *n.* grape

angur ko lahar अंगुर को लहरा *n.* grapevine

anidra अनिद्रा *n.* insomnia

anikal अनिकाल *n.* famine

anischit अनिश्चित *adj.* chancy

anishchit अनिश्चित *adj.* precarious

anishchit अनिश्चित *adj.* uncertain

anishchit अनिश्चित *adj.* undecided

anishchit अनिश्चित *adj.* unsure

anishchit kal samma अनिश्चित कालसम्म *adv.* sine die

anisht अनिष्ट *adj.* sinister

anishthasuchak अनिष्टासूचक *adj.* ominous

aniwarya अनिवार्य *adj.* inevitable

aniwarya kura अनिवार्य कुरा a must

aniwarya shart अनिवार्य शर्त *n.* sine qua non

aniyamit अनियमित *adj.* irregular

aniyamit अनियमित *adj.* random

aniyantrit अनियन्त्रित *adj.* rampant

anjan अनजान *adj.* unaware

anjir अन्जीर *n.* fig

ank अंक *n.* figure

ank अंक *n.* numeral

ank ganit अंकगणित *n.* arithmetic

ankganak अंकगणक *n.* abacus

ankha आँखा *n.* eye

ankha jhimjhim garnu आँखा झिमझिम गर्नु *v.* blink

ankha jhimkyaunu आँखा झिम्क्याउनु *v.* wink at

ankha tirmir aunu आँखा तिर्मिराउनु *v.* dazzle

ankhako आँखा को *adj.* ophthalmic

ankhama dhulo halnu आँखामा धुलो हाल्नु *v.* hoodwink

ankhan pharer hernu आँखा फारेर हेर्नु *v.* goggle

ankhi bhaun आँखीभौं *n.* eyebrow

ankhi gedi आँखीगेडी *n.* eyeball

ankhibhaun आँखीभौं *n.* brow

ankse juka अङ्क्से-जुका *n.* hookworm

ankur अँकुर *n.* sprout

ankush अंकुश *n.* hook

anmol अनमोल *adj.* invaluable

anna अनन्न *n.* grain

annako naap अन्नको नाप *n.* bushel

anp आँप *n.* mango

anpad अनपढ़ *adj.* unlearned

ansh अंश *n.* inheritance

ansh अंश *n.* share

ansu आँसु *n.* tear

ant अन्त *n.* close

antahpur अन्तःपुर *n.* seraglio

antai अन्तै *adj.* elsewhere

antar agaman अन्तर आगमन *n.* influx

antar drishti अन्तरदृष्टि *n.* insight

antar warta अन्तरवार्ता *n.* interview

antarashtriya अन्तर्राष्ट्रिय *adj.* international

antariksha poshak अन्तिरिक्ष पोशाक *n.* spacesuit

antariksha stesan अन्तरिक्ष स्वेसन *n.* space station

antariksha yan अन्तरिक्षयान *n.* spacecraft

antariksha yan अन्तरिक्षयान *n.* spaceship

antariksha yatri अन्तरिक्ष यात्री *n.* astronaut

antariksha yatri अन्तरिक्षयात्री *n.* spaceman

antariksha yug अन्तरिक्ष युग *n.* space age

antarim अन्तरिम *adj.* interim

antarmukhi vyakti अन्तर्मुखी व्यक्ति *n.* introvert

antarrashtriya police अन्तररराष्ट्रिय पुलिस *n.* interpol

antartam अन्तरतम *adj.* inmost

anth अन्त *n.* end

anth अन्त *n.* hormone

anthavivah garnu अन्तःविवाह गर्नु *v.* intermarry

antilo ऑंटिलो *adj.* purposeful

antim अन्तिम *adj.* enventual

antim अन्तिम *adj.* eventual

antim अन्तिम *adj.* final

antim अन्तिम *adj.* last

antim अन्तिम *adj.* ultimate

antim bhag अन्तिम भाग *n.* tailpiece

antma अन्तमा *adv.* ultimately

antnu ऑंट्नु *v.* determine

antraap अन्तराप *n.* hasp

antreep अन्तरीप *n.* cape

antreep अन्तरीप *n.* promontory

antyeshti अन्त्येष्टि *n.* obsequies

anu अणु *n.* molecule

anubhav अनुभव *n.* experience

anubhavheen अनुभवहीन *adj.* callow

anubhavheen rikute अनुभवहीन रिकुटे *n.* rookie

anubhavi अनुभवी *adj.* experienced

anubhaw na bhaeko अनुभव नभएको *adj.* inexperienced

anubhawi अनुभवी *n.* veteran

anubhawi manis अनुभवी मानिस *n.* old hand

anuchar अनुचर *n.* retinue

anuchchhed अनुच्छेद *n.* paragraph

anuchit अनुचित *adj.* improper

anuchit अनुचित *adj.* inappropriate

anuchit अनुचित *adj.* indedent

anuchit अनुचित *adj.* undue

anuchit mag अनुचित माग *n.* tall order

anuchit wyawahar अनुचित व्यवहार *n.* raw deal

anudan अनुदान *n.* grant

anuhaar अनुहार *n.* visage

anuhar अनुहार *n.* appearance

anuhar अनुहार *n.* complexion

anuhar अनुहार *n.* countenance

anuhar ka peshiko sankuchan अनुहार का पेशी को संकुचन *n.* tic

anuharko अनुहारको *adj.* facial

anukool अनुकूल *adj.* propitious

anukool banaunu अनुकूल बनाउनु *v.* adapt

anukulan अनुकूलन *v.* orientate

anukultam अनुकूलतम *adj.* optimum

anulipi अनुलिपी *n.* facsimile

anumaan अनुमान *n.* surmise

anuman अनुमान/तर्कना गर्नु *n.* speculation

anuman garnu अनुमान गर्नु *v.* suppose

anuman/tarkana garnu अनुमान/तर्कना गर्नु *v.* speculate

anumati अनुमति *n.* permission

anumati dinu अनुमति दिनु *v.* allow

anumati nadinu अनुमति नदिनु *v.* disallow

anumati patra अनुमति पत्र *n.* permit

anupasthiti अनुपस्थिति *n.* absence

anupatama अनुपतामा *adj.* pro rata

anupras अनुप्रास *n.* alliteration

anupyukt अनुपयुक्त *adj.* unapt

anurag अनुराग *n.* passion

anurodh अनुरोध *n.* request

anurup अनुरूप *adj.* consistent

anusandhan अनुसंधान *n.* caftan

anusandhan अनुसन्धान *n.* research

anusandhan garne अनुसन्धान गर्ने *n.* researcher

anusar अनुसार *adv.* according to

anushakti uttapan garne yantra अणुशक्ति उत्पन्न गर्ने यंत्र *n.* reactor

anushasan अनुशासन *n.* discipline

anutho अनौठो *adj.* bizarre

anutho अनौठो *adj.* grotesque

anutho अनौठो *adj.* outlandish

anutho yantra अनौठो यन्त्र *n.* contraption

anutpadak अनुत्पादक *adj.* unproductive

anuwad अनुवाद *n.* version

anuwad garnu अनुवाद गर्नु *v.* render

anuwad garnu अनुवाद गर्नु *v.* translate

anuwadak अनुवादक *n.* translator

anwik shakti आण्विक शक्ति *n.* nuclear energy

anwik shakti आण्विक शक्ति *n.* nuclear power

anyaya purwak prapt gareko अन्यायपूर्वक प्राप्त गरेको *adj.* ill-gotten

anyaya purwak prapt gareko अन्यायपूर्वक प्राप्त गरेको *n.* injustice

anyayi अन्यायी *adj.* unjust

ap bhasha अपभाषा *n.* slang

apaar अपार *adj.* boundless

apach अपच dyspepsia

apach अपच *n.* indigestion

apach अपच *n.* indigestion

apaharan garnu अपहरण गर्नु *v.* kidnap

apang अपाङ्ग *adj.* disabled

apang अपाङ्ग *adj.* handicapped

apardarshi अपारदर्शी *adj.* opaque

apardarshita अपारदर्शिता *n.* opacity

aparipakwa अपरिपक्व *adj.* premature

aparishkrit अपरिष्कृत *adj.* unrefined

aparivartit अपरिवर्तित *adj.* unaltered

apartivartinya अपरिवर्तनीय *adj.* unalterable

apas ko आपसको *adj.* mutual

apas ma आपसमा *adv.* mutually

apasi आपसी *adj.* reciprocal

apat आपत् *n.* disaster

apat आपत् *n.* misfortune

apavitar अपवित्र *adj.* unblessed

apawitra अपवित्र *adj.* impure

apeel hun naskane अपील हुन नसक्ने *adj.* unappealable

apeksha garnu अपेक्षा गर्नु *v.* look forward to

aphai आफै *adv.* personally

aphai adne bharen आफै अड्ने भरेङ *n.* stepladder

aphai baneko आफै बनेको *adj.* self-made

aphai bhaeko आफै भएको *adj.* spontaneous

aphai chalne आफै चल्ने *adj.* automatic

aphai chalne bhareng आफै चल्ने भरेङ्ग *n.* escalator

aphap अफाप *adj.* unsuitable

apharan garnu अपहरण गर्नु *v.* abduct

aphim अफीम *n.* opium

aphis ka likhit kam haru अफिसका लिखित कामहरू *n.* paperwork

aphnai उपभोग गर्नु *adj.* own

aphsos अफसोस *n.* regret

aphsos garnu अफसोस गर्नु *v.* deplore

aphu आफु *n.* self

aphu khushi आफुखुशी *adj.* voluntary

aphule paunuparne phal आफूले पाउनुपर्ने फल *n.* deserts

apman अपमान *n.* insult

apman/khisi garnu अपमान/खिसी गर्नु *v.* humiliate

apman/khisi garnu अपमान/खिसी गर्नु *n.* humiliation

apmanjanak अपमानजनक *adj.* derogatory

apmanjanak अपमानजनक *n.* disgrace

apno bachau garnu आपनो बचाउ गर्नु *v.* fend

apno hoin bhanu आपनो होइन भन्नु *v.* disown

appati आपत्ति *n.* calamity

apradh अपराध *n.* crime

apradh kamma saghaune sathi अपराध काममा सघाउने साथी *n.* accomplice

apradhi अपराधी *n.* criminal

apradhi अपराधी *n.* malefactor

apradhi अपराधी *n.* offender

aprakashit अप्रकाशित *adj.* unpublished

aprakritik अप्राकृतिक *adj.* unnatural

aprampragat अपरम्परागत *adj.* unorthodox

apranha अपरान्ह *n.* afternoon

aprastut अप्रस्तुत *adj.* unready

aprawasi आप्रवासी *n.* immigrant

apsakun अपशकुन *adj.* ominous

apsara अप्सरा *n.* nymph

apthyaro ma parnu अप्ठ्यारोमा पार्नु *v.* embarrass

apthyaro ma parnu अप्ठ्यारोमा पार्नु *n.* embarrassment

apug अपुग *adj.* scarce

apurn अपूर्ण *adj.* imperfect

apuro अपूरो *adj.* incomplete

apurti आपूर्ति *n.* supply

apvridhi अपवृद्धि *n.* excrescence

arajakta अराजकता *n.* anarchy

araksha आरक्ष *n.* sanctuary

arakshan आरक्षण *n.* reservation

aram आराम *n.* comfort

aram आराम *n.* ease

aram आराम *n.* relaxation

aram आराम *n.* relief

aram आराम *n.* rest

aram dayi आरामदायी *adj.* comfortable

aram garnu आराम गर्नु *v.* relax

aram hundai janu आराम हुँदै जानु *v.* recuperate

aramsit basaunu आरामसित बसाउनु *v.* ensconce

aramsit basnu आरामसित बस्नु *v.* nestle

ardh अर्ध semi

ardh wiram अर्धविराम *n.* comma

ardhchandra अर्द्धचन्द्र *adj.* crescent

ardhdev अर्धदेव *n.* demi-god

ardrata आर्द्रता *n.* humidity

aringal अरिङ्गाल *n.* hornet

arjigar अर्जीगर *n.* boa

arka ko dosh bokne अर्काको दोष बोक्ने *n.* scapegoat

arkako vichar va lekhai chornu अर्काको विचार वा लेखाई चोर्नु *v.* plagiarize

arko अर्को *adj.* another

arko अर्को *pron.* else

arko अर्को *adj.* next

arko अर्को *adj.* other

arko thaun ma ropnu अर्को ठाउँमा रोप्नु *v.* transplant

arkotir khichnu अर्कोतिर खिँच्नु *v.* distract

arogya shala आरोग्यशाला *n.* sanatorium

arohan आरोहण *n.* embarkation

aroochi अरूचि *n.* disfavour

aroochi अरूचि *n.* distaste

arooko sangat naruchaune अरूको संगत नरूचाउने *adj.* unsociable

arop आरोप *n.* slander

arpan अर्पण *n.* dedication

arpit garnu अर्पित गर्नु *n.* proffer

arth अर्थ *n.* meaning

arth bat aunu अर्थ बताउनु *v.* interpret

arth nikalnu अर्थ निकाल्नु decipher

arth spasht nabheyko अर्थ स्पष्ट नभएको *adj.* ambiguous

arth tantra अर्थतन्त्र *n.* economy

arthaat अर्थात् *adv.* videlicet

arthat अर्थात् *conj.* that is

arthat अर्थात् *v.* wit

arthhin अर्थहीन *adj.* meaningless

arthi आर्थिक *adj.* economic

arthik आर्थिक *adj.* monetary

Arthik warsh आर्थिक वर्ष *n.* fiscal year

aru badhi kharab अरू बढी खराब *adj.* worse

aru baliyo banaunu अरू बलियो बनाउनु *v.* reinforce

aru ko boat आरु को बोट *n.* peach

aru ko mukh takne अरूको मुख ताक्ने *n.* parasite

aru manisbaat alag rakhnu अरु मानिसबाट अलग राख्नु *v.* sequester

aruko ahit garn chahne अरूको अहित गर्न चाहने *adj.* malevolent

asabhya असभ्य *adj.* ill-bred

asabhya असभ्य *adj.* uncivillised

asabhya असभ्य *adj.* uncultured

asabhya bhae pani kargar असभ्य भए पनि कारगर *adj.* rough-and-ready

asabhya vyakti असभ्य व्यक्ति *n.* boor

asadharan असाधारण *adj.* extraordinary

asadharan असाधारण *adj.* way-out

asadhya असाध्य *adj.* impractical

asahay असह्य *adj.* insupportable

asahaya असहाय *adj.* helpless

asajilo असजिलो *adj.* uncomfortable

asajilo असजिलो *adj.* uneasy

asakayik असामयिक *adj.* untimely

asal असल *adj.* fine

asal असल *adj.* good

asamaan असमान *adj.* dissimilar

asaman असमान *adj.* enquual

asaman असमान *adj.* unlime

asamanta असमानता *n.* inequality

asamanya असामान्य *adj.* abnormal

asamanya असामान्य *adj.* offbeat

asamarthya असामर्थ्य *n.* inability

asambaddh असम्बद्ध *adj.* irrelevant

asambadh असम्बद्ध *adj.* disjointed

asambadh असम्बद्ध *adj.* extraneous

asambadh असम्बद्ध *adj.* unallied

asambadh असम्बद्ध *adj.* unconnected

asambaw असम्भव इच्छा *n.* pipedream

asambhavyta असम्भाव्यता *n.* unlikelihood

asambhaw असम्भव *adj.* impossible

asambhaw असम्भव *adj.* improbable

asammat hunu असम्मत हुनु *v.* dissent

asandigdh असंदिग्ध *adj.* unsuspected

asangat असंगत *adj.* preposterous

asangat असंगत *adj.* unconformable

asangatata असंगतता *n.* unconformity

asankshipt असंक्षिप्त *adj.* unabbreviated

asantosh असन्तोष *n.* discontent

asantosh dekh aunu असन्तोष देखाउनु *v.* grumble

asantoshjanak असन्तोषजनक *adj.* unsatisfactory

asantulan असन्तुलन *n.* imbalance

asaphal असफॅल *adj.* unsuccessful

asaphalta असफलता *n.* failure

asaptal pradhan nurse अस्पताल प्रधान नर्स *n.* matron

asar असर *n.* effect

asar na parne असर नपर्ने *adj.* ineffective

asar parnu असर पर्नु *v.* impinge

asas nirman आवास निर्माण *n.* housing

asathya असत्य *n.* chimera

asatya असत्य *adj.* untrue

asatya pramanit garnu असत्य प्रमाणित गर्नु *v.* disprove

asawdhan असावधान *adj.* inattentive

asawdhan असावधान *adj.* indiscreet

asawdhan असावधान *adj.* negligent

aseem असीम *adj.* illimitable

asha आशा *v.* expect

asha आशा *n.* hope

asha garne आशा गर्ने *adj.* expectant

asha janak आशाजनक *adj.* hopeful

asha ko jyoti आशाको ज्याति *n.* white hope

asha wadi आशावादी *n.* optimist

ashakta hunu आशक्त हुनु *v.* indulge

ashammudran अश्ममुद्रण *n.* lithography

ashanka आशंका *n.* trepidation

ashanti अशान्तिगडबड *n.* unrest

ashauch आशौच *n.* mourning

ashcharya आश्चर्य *n.* astonishment

ashcharya आश्चर्य *n.* surprise

ashcharya आश्चर्य उदेक *n.* wonder

ashikshit अशिक्षित *adj.* unbred

ashirwad/asik dinu आशीर्वाद/आसिक दिनु *v.* bless

ashisht अशिष्ट *adj.* brusque

ashisht अशिष्ट *adj.* underbred

ashishtata अशिष्टता *n.* incivility

ashlil अश्लील *adj.* obscene

ashlil अश्लील *adj.* vulgar

ashradha अश्रद्धा *n.* impiety

ashraya आश्रय *n.* haven

ashrit आश्रित *n.* ward

ashubh अशुभ *adj.* inauspicious

ashubh अशुभ *adj.* untoward

ashuddha अशु; *adj.* incorrect

ashudh अशुद्ध *adj.* erroneous

ashudh ganana garnu अशुद्ध गणना गर्नु *v.* miscount

asimit असीमित *adj.* unlimited

asinchit असिंचित *adj.* unwashed

asli असली *adj.* bonafide

asli roop dekhaune असली रूप देखाउने *v.* debunk

asmani rang आसमानी रंग *n.* azure

aspasht अस्पष्ट *adj.* vague

aspasht आसपास *n.* vicnity

aspatal अस्पताल *n.* hospital

asptalma dekhaun aune rogi अस्पतालमा देखाउन आउने रोगी *n.* out-patient

assi अस्सी *adj.* eighty

ast wyasta अस्त-व्यस्त *n.* chaos

asthayi अस्थायी *adj.* temporary

asthayi khareji ko awadhi अस्थायी खारेजीको अवधि *n.* lay-off

asthir अस्थिर *adj.* inconstant

asthir अस्थिर *adj.* unstable

asthir अस्थिर *adj.* unsteady

asthir अस्थिर *adj.* wonky

asthir bhaer chalnu wa ubhinu अस्थिर भएर चल्नु वा उभिनु *v.* teeter

asti अस्ति *n.* day before yesterday

astitva अस्तित्व *n.* being

astitwa अस्तित्व *n.* existence

astra अस्त्र *n.* projectile

astvyast garnu अस्तव्यस्त गर्नु *v.* disarrange

asundar असुन्दर *adj.* inelegant

asuvidha असुविधा *n.* discomfort

asuvidha garaunu असुविधा गराउनु *v.* incommode

asuwidha असुविधा *n.* handicap

asuwidhajanak असुविधाजनक *adj.* inconvenient

aswabhawik अस्वाभाविक *adj.* far-fetched

aswastata अस्वस्थता *n.* malaise

aswasth अस्वस्थ *adj.* off colo(u)r

aswikar अस्वीकार *v.* turn down

aswikar garnu अस्वीकार गर्नु *v.* disavow

aswikar garnu अस्वीकार गर्नु *v.* refuse

aswikrit अस्वीकृत *adj.* unacknowledged

atach अतः *adv.* hence

atadhik अत्यधिक *pref.* ultra

atal अटल *adj.* inexorable

atamkatha आत्मकथा *n.* autobiography

atammoh आत्ममोह *n.* narcissism

atamsantusht आत्मसन्तुष्ट *n.* prig

atam-santusht आत्म-सन्तुष्ट *adj.* smug

atash baji आतशबाजी *n.* fireworks

ataydhik अत्यधिक *adj.* inordinate

ateri अटेरी *adj.* impertinent

ateri अटेरी *n.* minx

ateri अटेरी *adj.* unruly

athara अठार *n.* eighteen

athaun आठौं *adj.* eighth

athawa अथवा *conj.* or

aththeya आतिथेय *n.* host

ati अति *adj.* immoderate

ati abhinay garnu अति अभिनय गर्नु *v.* overat

ati aupcharikta अति औपचारिकता *n.* red tape

ati chatur अति चतुर *adj.* brilliant

ati dusht अति दुष्ट *adj.* diabolic, diablical

ati gopya अति गोप्य *adj.* top secret

ati lamo daud अति लामो दौड *n.* marathon

ati naramro अति नराम्रो *adj.* atrocious

ati naramro अति नराम्रो *adj.* execrable

ati prachin kal अति प्राचीन काल *n.* time immemorial

ati prachin kal अति ज्यादा *adv.* too

ati saral अति सरल *adj.* auster

ati sawdhan अति सावधान *adj.* meticulous

ati tato अति तातो *adj.* piping hot

ati thanda अति ठण्डा *adj.* arctic

ati thulo अति ठूलो *adj.* crass

ati thulo jet wiman अति ठूलो जेटविमान *n.* jumbo jet

ati vyagra अति व्यग्र *adj.*

overstrung

atikraman garnu अतिक्रमण गर्नु *v.* overstep

atimanviya अतिमानवीय *adj.* superhuman

atiramro अति राम्रो *adj.* super

atirikt kar अतिरिक्त कर *n.* surtax

atirikt vastu अतिरिक्त वस्तु *n.* accessory

atirikta अतिरिक्त *adj.* additional

atirikta अतिरिक्त *adj.* extra

atirikta samaya ko khel अतिरिक्त समयको खेल *n.* play-off

atiuttam अति उत्तम *adj.* superfine

atma आत्मा *n.* soul

atma आत्मा *n.* spirit

atma balidan आत्म बलिदान *n.* self-sacrifice

atma nirbhar आत्मनिर्भर *adj.* self-sufficient

atma nirnaya आत्मनिर्णय *n.* self-determination

atma niyantran आत्मनियन्त्रण *n.* self-control

atma samarpan garnu आत्मसमर्पण गर्नु *v.* give in

atma samarpan garnu आत्मसमर्पण गर्नु *v.* surrender

atma samman आत्सम्मान *n.* self-respect

atma wishwasi आत्मविश्वासी *adj.* self-confident

atmahatya आत्महत्या *n.* suicide

attieko आत्तिएको *adj.* nervous

atulniya अतुलनीय *adj.* incomparable

atulniya अतुलनीय *adj.* unexampled

atyachar अत्याचार *n.* tyranny

atyachar garnu अत्याचार गर्नु *v.* oppress

atyadhik अत्यधिक *adj.* excessive

atyadhik अत्यधिक *adj.* exorbitant

atyaunu अत्याउनु *v.* terrify

atyuttam अत्युत्तम *adj.* tip-top

august mahina अगस्त महीना *n.* august

aujar औजार *n.* instrument

aujar औजार *n.* tool

aukat औकात *n.* status

aulako jorni औंलाको जोर्नी *n.* knuckle

aun आउँ *n.* dysentery

aundo आउँदो *adj.* oncoming

aunla औंला *n.* finger

aunla ko jorni औंलाको जार्नी *n.* knuckly

auns औंस *n.* ounce

aunsi औंसी *n.* new moon

auntha chhap औंठाछाप *n.* thumbprint

aunu आउनु *v.* come

aupcharikta औपचारिकता *n.* formality

ausar औसर *n.* occasion

ausat औसत *n.* average

aushadhi औषधि *n.* drug

aushadhi adhik matra औषधिको
अधिक मात्रा *n.* overdose
aushadhi pasal औषधि पसल *n.*
drugstore
aushadhi pasal औषधि पसल *n.*
pharmacy
aushadhi tayar garne vyakti
औषधि तयार गर्ने व्यक्ति *n.*
pharmacist
aushadhiko khurak औषधिको
खुराक *n.* dosage
aushdhalaya औषधालय *n.*
dispensary
authe jawaf ओठे जवाफ *n.*
repartee
authe jawaf ओठे जवाफ *n.* riposte
authe jawaf dinu ओठे जवाफ दिनु
n. retort
authi औठी *n.* ringlet
authko ओठको *adj.* labial
avijay अविजेय *adj.* unconquerable
aviksit अविकसित *adj.*
undeveloped
avivahit purush&stri अविवाहित
पुरूष-स्त्री *v.* cohabit
aviveki अविवेकी *adj.* imprudent
avsamanya अवसामान्य *adj.*
subnormal
avsarwad अवसरवाद *n.*
opportunism
aw chetan अवचेतन *adj.*
subconscious
awaaz आवाज *n.* vox
awadhi अवधि *n.* duration

awadhi अवधि *n.* period
awadhi अवधिक *n.* term
awagya अवज्ञा *n.* defiante
awaidh wyapari अवैध व्यापारी *n.*
trafficker
awaidhmal अवैध माल *n.*
contraband
awaj आवाज *n.* noise
awaj आवाजा *n.* sound
awaj आवाज *n.* tone
awaj na chhirne आवाज नछिर्ने *adj.*
soundproof(ed)
awaj thulo parne yantra आवाज
ठूलो पार्ने यंत्र *n.* loudspeaker
awak अवाक् *adj.* tongue-tied
awal अवाल *n.* kiln
awanchhaniya अवांछनीय *adj.*
undesirable
awara आवारा *n.* loafer
awaran udharnu आवरण उघार्नु *v.*
uncover
awargikrit अवर्गीकृत *adj.*
unclassified
awarnaniya अवर्णनीय *adj.*
unspeakable
awashyak आवश्यक *adj.*
imperative
awashyak आवश्यक *adj.* needful
awashyak आवश्यक भाग *n.* part
and parcel
awashyak आवश्यक *adj.* vital
awashyak आवश्यक *adj.* wanted
awashyak hunu आवश्यक हुनु *v.*
require

awashyak wyakti आवश्यक व्यक्ति *n.* kingpin

awashyakta आवश्यकता *n.* requirement

awasiya आवासीय *adj.* residential

awayask अवयस्क *adj.* under age

awayaw अवयव *n.* ingredient

awaykat अव्यक्त *adj.* ulterior

awaz nikarldae chapaunu आवाज निकाल्दै चपाउनु *v.* crunch

awaz sun sakine duri आवाज सुन्न सकिने दूरी *n.* earshot

awishkar आविष्कार *n.* invention

awishkar garnu आविष्कार गर्नु *v.* invent

awishwas अविश्वास *n.* distrust

awishwas अविश्वास *n.* mistrust

awishwas ko prastaw अविश्वास को प्रस्ताव *n.* vote of no confidence

awishwasniya अविश्वसनीय *adj.* incredible

awiwahit jiwan अविवाहित जीवन *n.* celibacy

awkash अवकाश *n.* recess

awkash अवकाश *n.* retirement

awkash linu अवकाशप्राप्त *v.* retire

awlokan अवलोकन *n.* observation

awlokan garnu अवलोकन *v.* observe

awrodh अवरोध *n.* blockage

awrodh अवरोध *n.* interruption

awsar अवसर *n.* opportunity

awshesh अवशेष *n.* relic

awtar अवतार *n.* incarnation

awyawasthit+C3512 अव्यवस्थित *adj.* haywire

aya आय *n.* turnover

ayakar आयकर *n.* income tax

ayam आयाम *n.* dimenstion

ayat आयत *n.* rectangle

ayat/paithari garnu आयात/पैठारी गर्नु *v.* import

ayatakar आयताकार *adj.* rectangular

aya-wyayak आय-व्ययक *n.* budget

ayogya अयोग्य *adj.* incapable

ayogya अयोग्य *adj.* incompeten

ayogya अयोग्य *adj.* inefficient

ayogya अयोग्य *adj.* ineligible

ayogya अयोग्य *adj.* inept

ayogya अयोग्य *adj.* unfit

ayogya अयोग्य *adj.* unqualified

ayogya अयोग्य *adj.* unworthy

ayogya banaunu अयोग्य बनाउनु *v.* incapacitate

ayojana आयोजना *n.* project

ayojit hatyakand आयोजित हत्याकाण्ड *n.* pogrom

ayurasha आयुराशा *n.* life expectancy

B

baaja बाजा *n.* cornet

baaja बाजा *n.* vibraphone

baalkale khelne bhaalu बालकले खेल्ने भालू *n.* teddy

baandh बाँध *n.* dike, dyke

baangkhatte बाङखट्टे *adj.* bow-legged

baanki rahenko बाँकी रहेको *adj.* residual

baat alag garnu बाट अलग गर्नु *v.* detach

baat bachnu बाट बाच्नु *v.* evade

baat umkan naskine बाट उम्कन नसिकने *adj.* ineluctable

baatgarnu बात गर्नु *v.* converse

babh re baph बाफरे बाफ *inter.* wounded

babu बाबु *n.* daddy

babu बाबु *n.* father

babu baje ko gun बाबुबाजेको गुण *n.* heredity

babu ko babi patti ko बाबुको बाबुपट्टिटको *adj.* paternal

bachat बचत *n.* savings

bachaunu बचाउनु *v.* protect

bachaunu बचाउनु *v.* save

bachcha बच्चा *n.* baby

bachcha haru बच्चाहरू *n.* children

bachchho बाच्छो *n.* calf

bachera rahanu बचेर रहनु *v.* steer clear of

bachha kukhura बच्चा कुखुरा pullet

badal बादल *n.* cloud

badal बादल *adj.* overcast

badali lageko बदली लागेको *adj.* cloudy

badalne बदलने *adj.* variable

badalnu बदल्नु *v.* alter

badalnu बदल्नु *v.* replace

badam बदाम *n.* almond

badam बादाम *n.* groundnut

badam बदाम *n.* peanut

badar garnu बदर गर्नु *v.* quash

badar/kharej garnu बदर/खारेज गर्नु *v.* overrule

badar/radda garnu बदर/रद्द गर्नु *v.* repeal

bademan बडेमान *adj.* jumbo

badha बाधा दिनु *n.* disturbance

badha बाधा *n.* impediment

badha बाधा *n.* resistance

badha dinu बाधा दिनु *v.* disturb

badha dinu बाधा दिनु *v.* interfere

badha dinu बाधा दिनु *v.* obstruct

badha parnu बाधा पार्नु *v.* hamper

badha parnu बाधा पार्नु *n.* hindrance

badha parnu बाधा पार्नु *n.* hurdle

badhai chadhai gareko kura बढाई चढाई गरेको कुरा *n.* exaggeration

badhai dinu बधाई दिनु *v.* congratulate

badhai dinu बधाई दिनु *n.* congratulation

badhai dinu बधाई दिनु *v.* felicitate

badhai dinu बधाई दिनु *n.* felicitation

badhai garnu बढाइ गर्नु *v.* flatter

badhai-chadhaika bhanu बढ़ाई-चढ़ाईकन भन्नु *v.* overstate

badhaun बढाउनु *v.* step up

badhaunu बढ़ाउनु *v.* aggrandize

badhaunu बढाउनु *v.* magnify

badhaunu बढाउनु *v.* promote

badhauti बढौती *n.* promotion

badhi बाढी *n.* flood

badhi बढी *adj.* more

badhi बाढी *n.* spate

badhi aeko बाढी आएको *adj.* flooded

badhi bhar बढी भार *n.* overload

badhi ruchaunu बढी रुचाउनु *v.* prefer

badhi ruchikar बढी रुचिकर *adj.* preferable

badhi samaya ko बढी समय को *adj.* overtime

badhiya garnu बाध्य गर्नु *v.* coerce

badhnu बढ्नु *v.* enhance

badhnu बढ्नु *v.* exceed

badhnu बढ्नु *v.* expand

badhnu बढ्नु *v.* increase

badhti bagh बढीती बाग *n.* surplus

badhya garnu बाध्य गर्नु *v.* constrain

badhya garnu बाध्य गर्नु *v.* obligate

badla बदला *n.* vengeance

badla linu बदला लिनु *v.* avenge

badla linu बदला लिनु *v.* retaliate

badla linu बदला लिनु *n.* retaliation

badla linu बदला *n.* revenge

badla ma बदलामा *adv.* instead of

badlama dinu बदलामा दिनु *v.* requite

badlindo sthiti mad dhalnu बदलिँदो स्थितिमा ढल्नु *v.* trim one's sails

badlinu बदलिनु *v.* vary

badmaash बदमाश *n.* blackguard

badmas बदमास *n.* hooligan

badmas बदमास *n.* scoundrel

badmas बदमास *adj.* wick

badmash बदमाश *n.* ruffian

badmash balak बदमाश बालक *n.* imp.

badmasi garne बदमासी गर्ने *adj.* impish

badnam बदनाम *adj.* infamous

badnam बदनाम *adj.* notorious

badnam बदनाम *n.* scandal

badnami बदनामी *n.* discredit

badnami बदनामी *n.* disrepute

bagai बगाल *n.* herd

bagaincha बगैचा *n.* garden

bagaincha बगैंचा *n.* garden

bagaincha बगैंचा *n.* orchard

bagaltir बगलतिर *adv.* sideways

bagar बगर *n.* shore

bagare बगरे *n.* butcher

bagdae gareko बग्दै गरेको *adv.* adrift

bagh बाघ *n.* tiger

baglimara बगलीमारा *n.* pickpocket

baglis बगलिस *n.* shoehorn

bagnu बग्नु *v.* drift

bagwani बागवानी *n.* horticulture

bahadur बहादुर *adj.* brave

bahai wala बहालवाला *adj.* incumbent

bahakau बहकाउ *n.* seduction

bahakaunu बहकाउनु *v.* seduce

bahalaunu बहलाउनु *v.* divert

bahalwala बहालवाला *n.* tenant

bahana बहाना *n.* cloak

bahana बहाना *n.* feint

bahana बहाना *n.* pretext

bahana garnu बहाना गर्नु *v.* pretend

bahas garnu बहस गर्नु *v.* argue

bahau बहाउ *n.* outflow

bahek बाहेक *prep.* besides

bahi khata बहिखाता *n.* journal

bahi khata बही खाता *n.* ledger

bahi rangi बहुरङ्गी *adj.* multi-colo(u)red

bahir gal garine kam बाहिर गई गरिने काम *n.* errand

bahir jane kam बाहिर जाने काम *n.* egress

bahira बाहिर *n./v.* out

bahira बाहिर *adv.* outdoors

bahira nikleko hunu बाहिर निक्लेको हुनु *v.* stick out

bahira patti बाहिरपट्टि *adv.* outside

bahira tira ko बाहिरतिरको *adv.* outward

bahiri बाहिरी *adj.* exterior

bahiri बाहिरी *adj.* external

bahiri बाहिरी *adj.* outdoor

bahiri बाकिहरी *adj.* outer

bahiri baranada बाहिरी बरण्डा *n.* portico

bahiri hissa बाहिरी हिस्सा *n.* surface

bahirko बाहिरको *adj.* external

bahiro बहिरा *adj.* deaf

bahirtir utheko बाहिरतिर उठेको *adj.* convex

bahishkar garnu बहिष्कार गर्नु *v.* boycott

bahkaunu बहकाउनु *v.* misguide

bahu mat le aswikar garnu बहुमतले अस्वीकार गर्नुग *v.* vote down

bahu mukhi बहुमुखी *adj.* multi-purpose

bahu mulya बहुमूल्य *adj.* sumptuous

bahu utpadan बहुउत्पादन *n.* mass production

bahu wachan बहुवचन *n.* plural

bahubhuj बहुभुज *n.* polygon

bahul बहुल *adj.* multiple

bahula बाहुला *n.* sleeve

bahula na bhaeko बाहुला नभएको *adj.* sleeveless

bahumat बहुमत *n.* majority

baibayhik वैवाहिक *adj.* conjugal

baigun बैगुन *n.* demerit

baijani बैजनी *n.* mauve

baijani बैजनी *adj.* violet

baikunth khel बैकुण्ठ खेल *n.* snakes and ladders

bail gadi बैलगाडी *n.* cart

baink बैंक *n.* bank

baisakhi बैसाखी *n.* crutch

baithak बैठक *n.* drawing room

baithak बैठक *n.* hall

baithak बैठक *n.* living room

baithak बैठक *n.* parlo(u)r

baj बाज *n.* falcon

baj बाज *n.* hawk

baja बाजा *n.* accordion

bajai बजै *n.* grandmother

bajar बजार *n.* market

bajarnu बजार्नु *v.* slam

bajaunu बजाउनु *v.* hoot

baje बाजे *n.* grandfather

baje बजे *n.* o'clock

baji बाजी *n.* bet

baji बाजी *n.* wager

bajyai बज्यै *n.* granny

bakamphoos बकम्फूस *v.* drivel

bakas बाकस *n.* box

bakbak बकबक *n.* gab

bakbak garnu बकबक गर्नु *v.* prate

bakhan garnu बखान गर्नु *v.* relate

bakhi बाखी *n.* nanny-goat

bakullo बकुल्लो *n.* heron

bal बल *n.* energy

bal बल *n.* force

bal बल *n.* power

bal balika बालबालिका *n.* youngsters

bal chikitsa बाल चिकित्सा *n.* paediatrics

bal le khosnu बलले खोस्नु *v.* wrest

bal prayog garine बल प्रयोग गरिने *adj.* strong-arm

bala बाला *n.* bracelet

balak बालक *n.* brat

balatkar बलात्कार *n.* rape

balaute samudritat बलौटे *adj.* sandy

balchar बालचर *n.* scout

bali बाली *n.* crop

balidan बलिदान *n.* sacrifice

balio बलियो *adj.* robust

baliya बलियो *adj.* hardy

baliya बाली *n.* harvest

baliyo बलियो *adj.* manly

baliyo बलियो *n.* might

baliyo बलियो *adj.* powerful

baliyo बलियो *adj.* stout

baliyo बलियो *adj.* strong

baliyo banaunu बलियो बनाउनु *v.* strengthen

balkanu बल्कुन *v.* throb

ball katnu बाली काट्नु *v.* reap

balnu बाल्नु *v.* kindle

balti बाल्टी *n.* bucket

balti बाल्टी *n.* pail

baluwa बालुवा *n.* sand

baluwako dhisko बालुवाको ढिस्को *n.* dune

bam gola बम गोला *n.* bomb

bambari garnu बमबारी गर्नु *v.* bombard

bammachha बाम माछा *n.* eel

bampunke बामपुड्के *n.* pygmy, pigmy

ban बन *n.* forest

ban biralo बनबिरालो *n.* wildcat

banaune बनाउने *n.* builder

banaunu बनाउनु *v.* construct

banaunu बनाउनु *v.* erect

banaunu बनाउनु *v.* fabricate

banaunu बनाउनु *v.* make

banaunu बनाउनु *v.* put up

banaunu बनाउनु *v.* trump up

banawati बनावटी *adj.* artificial

banawati बनावटी *n.* forgery

banawati बनावटी *adj.* sham

bancharo बन्चारो *n.* axe

bancharo adiko beerh बंचरो आदिको बीड़ँ *n.* haft

bancharo le katnu बन्चरोले काट्नु *v.* hew

banchhne samagri बाँच्ने सामग्री *n.* necessaries

banchna sakne बाँच्न सक्ने *adj.* viable

banchnu बाँच्नु *v.* exist

banchnu बाँच्नु *v.* survive

band garnu बन्द गर्नु *v.* cease

band garnu बन्द गर्नु *v.* shut

band garnu बन्द गर्नु *v.* shut down

band garnu बन्द गर्नु *v.* turn off

band motar gadi बन्द मोटरगाडी *n.* limousine

band sawal बन्द सवाल *n.* cross-examination

banda kobhi बन्दाकोभी *n.* cabbage

bandan बन्दना *n.* greetings

bandar बाँदर *n.* monkey

bandar gah बन्दरगाह *n.* harbo(u)r

bandara बङ्गारा *n.* jaw

bandargah बन्दरगाह *n.* port

bandel बँदेल *n.* boar

bandgadi बन्द गाडी *n.* van

bandh बाँध *n.* dam

bandh बाँध *n.* embankment

bandh बाँध *n.* levee

bandh garhi बन्दगाड़ी *n.* brougham

bandhak बन्धक *n.* hostage

bandhak rakhnu बन्धक राख्नु *v.* pawn

bandhaki बन्धकी *n.* mortgage

bandhan बन्धन *n.* bond

bandhan बन्धन *n.* shackle

bandhnu बाँध्नु *v.* bind

bandhnu बाँध्नु *v.* fasten

bandhnu बाँध्नु *v.* tie

bandnu बाँछनु *v.* distribute

bandobast बन्दोबस्त *n.* arrangement

bandobast garnu बन्दोबस्त गर्नु *v.* organize

banduk बन्दुक *n.* gun

banduk बन्दूक *n.* tommy-gun

banduk ko jibri बन्दुक को जिब्री *n.* trigger

banduk wa pistol hanne kam बन्दुक वा पिस्तोल हान्ने काम *n.* shooting

bandukko kunda बन्दूकको कुन्दा *v.* butt

bandukko naal बन्दूकको नाल *n.* barrel

bango tingo बाङ्गोटिङ्गो *adj.* zigzag

bangotingo rekha बाङ्गोटिङ्गो रेखा *n.* squiggle

bangyaunu बङ्ग्याउनु *n.* refract

bani बानी *n.* habit

bani basalnu बानी बसाल्नु *v.* accustom

bani paereko बानी परेको *adj.* habitual

bani paereko बानी परेको *adj.* habituated

baniya बनिया *n.* grocer

banjar bhoomi बंजर भूमि *n.* wilderness

banjar jagga बन्जर जग्गा *n.* wasteland

banjho बाँझो *adj.* infertile

banjho बाँझो *adj.* sterile

banki बाँकी भाग *n.* remainder

banki बाँकी भाग *adj.* remaining

banko khula thaun बनको खुला ठाउँ *n.* glade

bans बाँस *n.* bamboo

bansuri बाँसुरी *n.* flute

bapauti बपौती *n.* legacy

baph बाफ *n.* vapo(u)r

baph bannu बाफ बन्नु *v.* evaporate

baphadar बफादार *adj.* loyal

baphadar वफादार *adj.* staunch

baphadar बाफ *n.* steam

baphadari बफादारी *n.* loyalty

baphaeko parikar बफाएको परिकार *n.* stew

bar बार *n.* fence

bar ko rukh बरको रुख *n.* banyan

barabar बराबर *adj.* equal

barabar बराबर *adj.* equivalent

barabar badli rahane drishya बराबर बदलिरहने दृश्य *n.* kaleidoscope

barabar dimag ma aunu बराबर दिमागमा आउनु *v.* haunt

barabar/barambar bhai aeko बराबर/बारम्बार भइ आएको *adj.* frequent

barabari बराबरी *n.* equiality

barabari बराबरी *n.* par

barambar बारम्बार *adv.* over and over

barambar बारम्बार *adv.* time and again

baranda बरन्डा *n.* gallery

baraph बरफ *n.* Ice

barbad बर्बाद *v.* ravage

bardali बार्दली *n.* balcony

bardi बर्दी *n.* uniform

bare ma बारेमा *prep.* regarding

barema बारेमा *prep/* concerning

barha बाह्र *n.* twelve

barkha बर्खा *n.* monsoon

barkhast garnu बर्खास्त गर्नु *v.* cashier

barkhe बर्खे *adj.* rainy

barma बर्मा *n.* drill

barnis बार्निस lacquer

barphilo बरफिलो तूफान *n.* snowstorm

barsadi बर्सादी *n.* mackintosh

barsadi बर्सादी *n.* raincoat

baru बरू *adv.* rather

barud बारूद *n.* gunpowder

barulo बारुलो *n.* washy

barulo बारूलो *n.* wasp

bas बस *n.* bus

bas basne thaun बास बस्ने ठाउँ *n.* accommodation

bas basnu बास बस्नु *n.* sojourn

bas garna yogya बास गर्न योग्य *adj.* inhabitable

bas garnu बास गर्नु *v.* inhabit

basai sarne kam बसाइ सर्ने काम *n.* migration

basant बसन्त *n.* spring

basaunu बसाउनु *v.* push down

basinda बासिन्दा *n.* inhabitant

basinda बासिन्दा *n.* inmate

basinda बासिन्दा *n.* native

basn layakko nabhayko बस्न लायकको नभएको *adj.* uninhabitable

basna बास्ना *n.* scent

basna/basyogya बस्न⁄बासयोग्य *adj.* habitable

basne ra sutne thaun बस्ने र सुत्ने ठाउँ *n.* berth

basne thaun बस्ने ठाउँ *n.* seat

basne thaun dekhaune बस्ने ठाउँ देखाउनु *n.* usher

basnu बस्रूपु *v.* remain

basnu बस्नु *v.* reside

basnu बस्नु *v.* sit

basobas garnu बसोबास गर्नु *v.* settle

bassthan बासस्थान *n.* abode

basti बस्ती *n.* colony

basti बस्ती *n.* settlement

bat marnu बात मार्नु *v.* chat

bat/bath rog बात⁄बाथरोग *n.* rhematism

bata बाट *prep.* from

bata utpatti hunu बाट उत्पत्ति हुनु *v.* derive

bataase बतासे *adj.* unfathered

batamunibat pani jane बाटामुनिबाट पानी जाने *n.* culvert

batare ko bet बटारेको बेत *n.* wicker

batarine kriya बटारिने क्रिया *n.* torsion

batarinu बटारिनु *v.* contort

batarnu बटार्नु *v.* twist

batarnu बटार्नु *v.* wrench

bataunu बातउनु *v.* denote

bataunu बताउनु *v.* explain

batdhaunu बढाउनु *v.* escalate

bath बाथ *n.* gout

bathan बथन *n.* batch

bathan बथान *n.* flock

batir बटेर *n.* quail

bato बाटो *n.* path

bato बाटो *n.* route

bato बाटो *n.* track

bato बाटो *n.* way

bato band garnu बाटो बन्द गर्नु *v.* seal off

bato biraunu बाटो बिराउनु *v.* stray

bato pelne injine बाटो पेल्ने इन्जिन *n.* roller

batoma बाटोमा *adv.* en route

batrog lageko बातरोग लागेको *adj.* rheumatic

batteko dhalkai बाटेको ढल्काइ *n.* gradient

battha भत्ता *n.* royalty

batti बत्ती *n.* lamp

batti बत्ती *n.* wick

batuwa बटुवा *n.* pedestrian

batuwa बटुवा *n.* wayback

batuwa बटुवा *n.* wayfarer

baulaha बौलाहा *adj.* crazy

baulaha बौलाहा *adj.* insane

baulaha बौलाहा *adj.* mad

baundine rog बाउँडिने रोग *n.* cramp

baunne बाउन्ने *n.* dwarf

bayang व्यंग *n.* quip

baykul व्याकुल *adj.* perplexed

bayodata बायोडाटा *n.* resume

bazar बजार *n.* mart

be adab बेअदब *adj.* insolent

be chalti ko बेचल्तीको *adj.* obsolete

be matlab ko kuro बेमतलबको कुरो *n.* nonsense

be matlab sanga बेमतलबसँग *adv.* wantonly

bear बीयर *n.* malt

bech bikhan बेचबिखन *n.* marketing

bechain बेचैन *adj.* restive

bechna layak बेच्नलायक *adj.* saleable

bechnu बेच्नु *v.* sell

bedag बेदाग *adj.* spotless

bedag बेदाग *adj.* stainless

bedha बेड़ा *n.* flortilla

bedhag ko बेढङ्गको *adj.* quzzical

bedhang बेढङ्ग *adj.* sloppy

bedhang ko बंढंगो *adj.* clumsy

beechma बीचमा *prep.* amid, amidst

beechma bolnu बीचमा बोल्नु *v.* interpose

beej sambandhi विज सम्बन्धी *adj.* nuclear

beejanu बीजाणु *n.* spore

beejganit बीजगणित *n.* algebra

beer बियर *n.* ale

beg sanga chalne motar dunga वेगसँग चल्ने मोटर डुङ्गा *n.* speedboat

begla beglai बेग्लाबेग्लै *adv.* separately

begwan jango jahaj वेगवान् जंगी जहाज *n.* cruiser

behosh बेहोश *adj.* insensate

behosh बेहोश *adj.* unconscious

behoshi ki avashta बेहोशीकी अवस्था *n.* anaesthetic

behula बेहुला *n.* groom

behuli बेहुली *n.* bride

behuliko poshak बेहुलीको पोशाक *n.* trousseau

behulo बेहुलो *n.* bridegroom

beiman बेइमान *adj.* dishonest

bejan बेजान *adj.* lifeless

bejod बेजोड *adj.* matchless

bejod बेजोड *adj.* unique

bejodh बेजोड़ *adj.* unequalled

bekaame vyakti बेकामे व्यक्ति *n.* wastrel

bekar बेकार *adj.* unemployed

bekar ko बेकारको *adj.* valueless

bekuph बेकुफ *adj.* withstand

bekwad बेकवाद *n.* crap

bela बेला *n.* violin

bela bela ma बेलाबेलामा *adv.* off and on

bela na bhal suru garnu बेला नभई सुरु गर्न *v.* jump the gun

bela wadak बेलावादक *n.* violinist

belayat बेलायत *n.* england

beluka बेलुका *n.* eveing

belun गुब्बारा *n.* balloon

bemanasib बेमनासिब *adj.* unreasonable

bench बेंच *n.* bench

bepar बेपार *n.* trade

bepari samagri बेपारी सामग्री *n.* commodity

beparwah बेपरवाह *adj.* careless

berinu बेरिनु *v.* entwine

berium बेरिअम *n.* barium

berna बेर्ना *n.* seedling

berojgari बेरोजगारी *n.* unemployment

bes बेस *adv.* well and good

besari बेसरी *adv.* greatly

beslin भेसलिन *n.* vaseline

besurapan बेसुरापन *n.* dissonance

bet बेत *n.* cane

betar बेतार *n.* wireless

bethik बेठीक *adj.* inaccurate

bewasta बेवास्ता *n.* neglect

beyara बेयरा *n.* waiter

beyaraketi बेयराकेटी *n.* waitress

bhaale biralo भाले बिरालो *n.* tomeat

bhaar halnu भार हाल्नु *v.* encumber

bhaari भारी *adj.* unhand

bhada भाडा *n.* rent

bhada bata aune rakam भाडाबाट आउने रकम *n.* rental

bhadda भद्दा *adj.* awkward

bhadda भद्दा *adj.* dowdy

bhadda भद्दा *adj.* gawky

bhadda bedhangko भद्दा बेढंगको *adj.* ungainly

bhadkilo भड्किलो *adj.* gaudy

bhadkilo भड्किलो *adj.* pompous

bhaera भएर *prep.* via

bhag भाग *n.* part

bhag भाग *n.* portion

bhag भग *n.* vulva

bhag garna/launa na sakine भाग गर्न/लाउन नसकिने *adj.* indivisible

bhag garnu भाग गर्नु divide

bhag lagaun sakine भाग लगाउन सकिने *adj.* divisible

bhag lin nadinu भाग लिन नदिनु *v.* exclude

bhag lina kar garnu भाग लिन कर गर्नु *v.* rope in

bhag linu भाग लिनु *v.* pariticpate

bhagnu भाग्नु *v.* flee

bhagnu भाग्नु *v.* get away

bhagnu भाग्नु *v.* levant

bhagnu भाग्नु *v.* puill back

bhagnu भाग्नु *v.* run away

bhagnu भाग्नु *v.* run off

bhagphal भागफल *n.* quotient

bhaguwa भगुवा *n.* fugitive

bhagwan chaki chaain bhanne vyakti भगवान छकि छेन भन्ने व्यक्ति *adj.* agnostic

bhagya भाग्य *n.* destiny

bhagya भाग्य *n.* destiny

bhagya भाग्य *n.* fate

bhagya भाग्य *n.* luck

bhagya mani भाग्यमानी *adj.* fortunate

bhagya mani भाग्यमानी *adj.* lucky

bhagya wash भाग्यवश *adv.* luckily

bhai chara ko भाइचारा *n.* fraternity

bhainsi भैंसी *n.* buffalo

bhairas भाइरस *n.* virus

bhajan भजन *n.* hymn

bhak bhakaunu भकभकाउनु *v.* stammer

bhak bhakaunu भकभकाउनु *v.* stammer

bhak bhake भकभके *n.* stammerer

bhakari भकारी *n.* bin

bhakari भकारी *n.* granary

bhakbhakaunu भकभकाउनु *v.* stutter

bhakta भक्त *n.* devotee

bhakta भक्त *n.* worshipper

bhakti भक्ति *n.* devotion

bhakundo भकुण्डो *n.* ball

bhakundo भकुण्डा *n.* football

bhala भाला *n.* javelin

bhala भाला *n.* pike

bhala भाला *n.* spear

bhaladmi भलादमी *n.* gentleman

bhale भाले *n.* male

bhale भाले *n.* rooster

bhale gadha भाले गधा *n.* jackass

bhale haans भाले हाँस *n.* drake

bhale haans भाले हाँस *n.* gander

bhale jarayo भाले जरायो *n.* stag

bhale kukhura भाले कुखुरा *n.* cock

bhalibal भलिबल *n.* volleyball

bhalu भालु *n.* bear

bhanai भनाइ *n.* remark

bhanban garnu भनाभन गर्नु *v.* bandy

bhanchhe भान्छे *n.* cook

bhanda भाँडा *n.* basin

bhanda भाँडा *n.* pot

bhanda भन्दा *prep.* than

bhanda aghi भन्दा अघि *adv.* prior to

bhanda badhta banchnu भन्दा बढ्ता बाँच्नु *v.* outlive

bhanda kunda भाडाँकुँडा *n.* utensils

bhanda pahile marnu भन्दा पहिले मर्नु *v.* predecease

bhanda ramro भन्दा राम्रो *adj.* better

bhandar भण्डार *n.* depot

bhandar भण्डार *n.* storehouse

bhandare भण्डारे *n.* storekeeper

bhandnu बाँध्नु *v.* gird

bhando भाँडो *n.* container

bhando भाँडो *n.* vessel

bhang भंग *n.* breach

bhang भंग *n.* fracture

bhangera भँगेरा *n.* sparrow

bhani thannu भनिठान्नु *v.* presume

bhanjyan भंज्याङ *n.* saddle

bhanna na sakine भन्न नसकिने *adj.* incommunicable

bhanne darle भन्ने डरले *conj.* lest

bhannu भन्नु *v.* say

bhannu भन्नु *v.* tell

bhannu भन्नु *v.* utter

bhanrha maine kotha भाँड़ा माइने कोठा *n.* scullery

bhansa kotha भान्साकोठा *n.* kitchen

bhansar mahsul भन्सार महसुल *n.* tariff

bhansaradda भन्सार अड्डा *n.* custgoms

bhanta भण्टा *n.* eggplant

bhanyo भन्यो *v.* quoth

bhar garnu/parnu भर गर्नु/पर्नु *v.* rely

bhar pardo भरपर्दो *adj.* dependable

bhar pardo भरपर्दो *adj.* reliable

bhar pardo भरपर्दो *adj.* trustworthy

bhar parn naskine भर पर्न नसकिने *adj.* unreliable

bhara भाँड़ा *n.* receptacle

bharen भरेङ *n.* stairs

bharen ko khud kila भरेङको खुड्किला *n.* rung

bharhin भारहीन *adj.* weightless

bhari भारी *n.* burden

bhari भारी *adj.* cumbersome

bhari भारी *n.* load

bhari भारी *adj.* weighty

bhari udyog भारी उद्योग *n.* heavy industry

bhari uthaune yantra भारी उठाउने यंत्र *n.* derrick

bharieko भरिएको *adj.* full

bhariya भरिया *n.* porter

bhariyeko भरिएको *adj.* replete

bharkharai भखैरै *adv.* just now

bharna भर्ना *n.* compensation

bharnu भर्नु *v.* fill

bharosa भरोसा *n.* assurance

bharosa भरोसा *n.* confidence

bharosa भरोसा *n.* reliance

bharpai भर्पाई *n.* receipt

bharsthachari भ्रष्टाचारी *adj.* lascivious

bharti garnu भर्ती गर्नु *v.* admit

bharyan भर्‍याङ्क *n.* ladder

bhasha भाषा *n.* dialect

bhasha भाषा *n.* language

bhasha wid भाषविद् *n.* linguist

bhashan भाषण *n.* lecture

bhashan dine hal भाषण दिने हल *n.* lyceum

bhashanko upsanhar भाषणको उपसंहार *n.* peroration

bhat भात *n.* rice

bhatija भतिजा *n.* nephew

bhatiji भतिजी *n.* niece

bhatkaunu भत्काउनु *v.* demolish

bhatkaunu भत्काउनु *v.* dismantle

bhatkaunu भत्काउनु *v.* pull down

bhatkaunu भत्काउनु *v.* take to pieces

bhatmas भटमास *n.* soya bean

bhatmas भटमास *n.* soya bean/ soybean

bhatta भत्ता *n.* stipend

bhattha भत्ता *n.* allowance

bhatti भट्टी *n.* distillery

bhatti भट्टी *n.* pub

bhatti भट्टी *n.* tavern

bhattiwal भट्टीवाल *n.* publican

bhauju भाउजू *n.* sister-in-law

bhauntarinu भाँतारिनु *v.* loiter

bhautik shastra भौतिकशास्त्र *n.* physics

bhavanko samune bhag भवनको सामुन्ने भाग *n.* façade

bhavishya bataune stri भविष्य बताउने स्त्री *n.* sibyl

bhavishya kathan भविष्यकथन *n.* divination

bhavpurn भावपूर्ण *adj.* impassioned

bhavya भव्य *adj.* magnificent

bhavya smadhi भव्य समाधि mausoleum

bhaw भाव *n.* feeling

bhawan भवन *n.* building

bhawan भवन *n.* edifice

bhawan भाव *n.* emotion

bhawan भवन *n.* mansion

bhawan nirman kala भवन निर्माण कला *n.* architecture

bhawana भावना *n.* sentiment

bhawi peerhi भावी पीढ़ी *n.* posterity

bhawishyawani भविष्यवाणी *n.* forecast

bhawishyawani भविष्यमानी *n.* future

bhawishyawani भविष्यवाणी *n.* prediction

bhawishyawani भविष्यवाणी *n.* prophecy

bhawuk भावुक *adj.* sentimental

bhawya भव्य *adj.* gorgeous

bhawya भव्य *adj.* grand

bhaya भय *n.* panic

bhayanak भयानक *adj.* awful

bhayanak भयानक *adj.* dire

bhayanak भयानक *adj.* dreadful

bhayanak भयानक *adj.* grim

bhayanak भयानक *adj.* gruesome

bhayanak भयानक *adj.* horrible

bhayanak भयानक *adj.* weird

bhayankar भंयकर *adj.* formidable

bhayat khasnu भ्यात्त खस्नु *v.* flop

bhayo भयो *mod.* would

bhed भेद *n.* contrast

bhed भेद *v.* distiguish

bhed bhaw garnu भेदभाव गर्नु *v.* discriminate

bheda भेडा *n.* ram

bheda भेडा *n.* sheep

bheda gothalo भेडागोठालो *n.* shepherd

bheer भीड़ *n.* horde

bheer भीड़ *v.* throng

bheer gonthali भीर गौंथली *n.* martin

bheeshan akarman भीषण आक्रमण *n.* onslaught

bhela भेला *n.* rally

bhela hune thaun भेला हुने ठाउँ *n.* rendezvous

bhela hunu भेला हुनु *v.* forgather

bhesh badalne kam भेष बदलने काम *n.* camouflage

bhesh badalnu भेष बदल्नु *n.* disguise

bhet भेट *v.* visit

bhid भीड *n.* crowd

bhidant भिडन्त *n.* melee

bhidant भिड़न्त *n.* scrimmage

bhidant ladain भिडन्त लडाइँ *n.* skimish

bhidanta भिडन्त *n.* clash

bhidbhadpurn भीडभाडपूर्ण *adj.* crowded

bhidiyo भिडियो *n.* video

bhijeko भिजेको *adj.* moist

bhijeko भिजेको *adj.* soggy

bhijeko भिजेको *adj.* wet

bhijnu भिज्नु *v.* drench

bhikhari भिखारी *v.* mendicant

bhiksha भिक्षा *n.* alms

bhikshu भिक्षु *n.* friar

bhikshuniharuko math भिक्षुनीहरूको मठ *n.* convent

bhiralo भिरालो *adj.* precipitous

bhirhbhar bhaeko भीड़भाड़ भएको *adj.* congested

bhiringi rog भिरिङ्गी रोग *n.* syphilis

bhisa भिसा *n.* visa

bhitamin भिटामिन *n.* vitamin

bhitar hunu भित्र हुनु *v.* contain

bhitra भित्र *prep.* in

bhitra भित्र *prep.* inside

bhitra भित्र *prep.* into

bhitra भित्र *prep.* within

bhitra pasnu भित्र पस्नु *v.* step in

bhitra tira भित्रतिर *adj.* inward

bhitri भित्री *adj.* inner

bhitri भित्री *adj.* interior

bhitri भित्री *adj.* internal

bhitri luga भित्री लुगा *n.* underwear

bhitrpatti laune luga भित्रपट्टि लाउने लुगा *n.* underclothes

bhitta भित्ता *n.* wall

bhitta-satabh भित्ता-स्तम्भ *n.* pilaster

bhog भोग *n.* possession

bhoj भोज *n.* banquet

bhoj भोज *n.* feast

bhoj भोज *n.* junketing

bhojan garnu भोजन गर्नु *v.* dine

bhojanpachi khane mishthan भोजनपछि खाने मिष्टान्न *n.* despot

bhojnalaya भोजनालय *n.* restaurant

bhok भोक *n.* appetite

bhokaeko भोकाएको *adj.* hungry

bhokai hunu भोकै हुनु *v.* starve

bhokmari भोकमरी *n.* starvation

bhoko भोको *adj.* ravening

bholi भोलि *n./adv.* tomorrow

bholiko din भोलिको दिन *n.* morrow

bholt भोल्ट *n.* volt

bhoolchook भूलचूक *n.* blunder

bhoomisambandhi भूमिको सम्बन्धी *adj.* agrarian

bhram भ्रम *n.* illusion

bhram hataunu भ्रम हटाउनु *v.* disillusion

bhram ma pareko भ्रममा परेको *adj.* mistaken

bhramit भ्रमित *adj.* confused

bhrashachar भ्रष्टाचार *n.* corruption

bhrmansheel भ्रमणशील *adj.* peripatetic

bhudrishya भूदृश्य *n.* landscape

bhuganit भूगणित *n.* geodesy

bhugarbh shastra भूगर्भशास्त्र *n.* geology

bhugo भूगोल *n.* geography

bhuichuk भूलचूक *n.* lapse

bhuin aadi poochne sadhan भुइँ आदि पुछ्ने साधन *n.* swab

bhuin ainselu भुइँ ऐंसेलु *n.*
strawberry

bhuin kathar भुइँकटहर *n.*
pineapple

bhuinchalo भुइँचालो *n.*
earthquake

bhuktani भुक्तानी *n.* payment

bhul भूल *n.* mistake

bhul भूल *n.* oversight

bhulako vyopari भुल्लाको व्यापारी
n. furrier

bhumadhya rekha भूमध्य रेखा *n.*
equator

bhumi dhar भूमिधर *n.* yeoman

bhumi gat भूमिगत *adj.*
underground

bhumika भूमिका *n.* role

bhunde भुँडे *adj.* pot-bellied

bhundi भुँडी *n.* pot (belly)

bhundi भुँडी *n.* stomach

bhupariweshtit भूपरिवेष्टित *adj.*
landlocked

bhurun भ्रूण *n.* embryo

bhusuna भुसुना *n.* gnat

bhusyaha kukur भुस्याहा कुकुर *n.*
cur

bhut भूत *n.* ghost

bhut भूत *n.* phantom

bhut dhapaunu भूत धपाउनु *v.*
exorcise

bhutkal भूतकाल *n.* past

bhutnu भुट्नु *v.* fry

bhutpurv sainik भूतपूर्व सैनिक *n.*
ex-serviceman

bhuwa भुवा *n.* fur

bhuwa jasto भुवा जस्तो *adj.* furry

bhuwanri भुँवरी *n.* eddy

bhyaguto भ्यागुतो *n.* frog

bhyanak karksha aeimai भयानक
कर्कशा आइमाई *n.* virago

bhyanak khasti puryanu भयानक
क्षति पुर्‍याउनु *v.* wreak

bhyanak vipati भयानक विपत्ति *n.*
cataclysm

biasaun बीसौं *adj.* twentieth

bich बीच *prep.* among

bich ko बीचको *adj.* intermediate

bich ko manchhe बीचको मान्छे *n.*
go-between

bichara बिचरा *inter.* poor man

bichchhi बिच्छी *n.* scorpion

bichhaunu बिछ्याउनु *v.* lay

bichhyauna बिछ्यौना *n.* bed

bichhyauna बीच *adv./prep.*
between

bida बिदा *n.* holiday

bida बिदा *n.* leave

bida garnu बिदा गर्नु *v.* send off

bidai विदाई *n.* bye

bidai बिदाई *int.* bye-bye

bidai विदाइ *n.* farewell

bidai बिदाइ *n.* parting

bidha बिदा *interj.* ta-ta

bigapith विज्ञप्ति *n.* communique

bigarnu बिग्रनु *v.* conk

bigarnu बिगार्नु *v.* mar

bigarnu बिग्रनु *adv.* phut

bigarnu बिगार्नु *v.* spoil

bigarnu बिगार्नु *v.* taint

bigarnu बिगार्नु *v.* tamper

bigrane बिग्रने *adj.* perishable

bigranu बिग्रनु *v.* deteriorate

bigreko बिग्रेको *n.* kaput

bigreko बिग्रेको *adj.* out of order

bigul बिगुल *n.* bugle

bigul बिगुल *n.* bugle

bigul बिगुल *n.* trumpet

biha हिबहे *n.* marriage

bihana बिहान *n.* morning

bihana saberai बिहान सबेरै *n.* dawn

bihanko prarthana बिहानको प्रार्थना *n.* matins

bihe बिहे/विवाह गर्नु *v.* marry

bihe बिहें *n.* matrimony

bihe बिहे *n.* wedding

bihe garnu बिहे गर्नु *v.* espouse

bihe garnu बिहे गर्नु *v.* wed

bihe ko aunthi बिहेको औँठी *n.* wedding ring

bihibar कबहीबार *n.* Thursday

bijhnu बुझनु *v.* understand

bijor बिजोर *adj.* uneven

bijuli बिजुली *n.* electricity

bijuli ko gulup बिजुली को गुलुप *n.* light bulb

bijuli ko karent बिजुलीको करेण्ट आदि छेक्ने बस्तु *n.* insulator

bijuli ko karent ko dhakka बिजुलीको करेण्टको धक्का *n.* electric shock

bijuli ko karent lagera marnu बिजुलीको करेण्ट लागेर मर्नु *v.* electrocute

bijuli ko tar jadan बिजुली को तार जडान *n.* wiring

bijuli-path बिजुली-पथ *n.* circuit

bikhalu बिखालु *adj.* toxic

bikri बिक्री *n.* sale

bil बिल *n.* invoice

bilaeko बिलाउको *adj.* extinct

bilkul बिलकुल *adv.* quite

bilkul thik बिलकुल ठीक *adj.* perfect

billa बिल्ला *n.* badge

billa बिल *n.* bill

bilona बिलौना *n.* jeremiad

bima बीमा *n.* insurance

bima-kista बीमा-किस्ता *n.* premium

bimar बिमार *adj.* sick

bimari बिमारी *n.* illness

bimari बिमारी *n.* malady

bimira बिमिरा *n.* rash

bimiro बिमिरा *n.* citron

bina बिना *prep.* without

bina mahtavko बिना महत्त्वको *adj.* trivial

bina sajaya umkeko बिनासजाय उम्केको *adj.* scot-free

bina tayari बिना तयारी *adj.* extempore

bina tayari बिनातयारी *adj.* offhand

binamulya gariyeko wa diyeko बिनामूल्य गरिएको वा दिइएको *adj.* gratuitous

bind बीण्ड *n.* handel

bind बीण्ड *n.* holder

bine tyari बिना तयारी *adv. adj.* extepore

binti बिन्ती *n.* plea

binti bhau बिन्तीभाउ *n.* persuasion

binti bhau garnu बिन्तीभाउ गर्नु *v.* solicit

binti garnu बिन्ती गर्नु *v.* plead

binti garnu बिन्ती गर्नु *v.* supplicate

binti patra बिन्तीपत्र *n.* petition

binti/anurodh garnu बिन्ती/अनुरोध गर्नु *v.* entreat

biphar बिफर *n.* pox

biphar ब्फिर *n.* smallpox

bir बीर *adj.* gallant

birailo ko bachcha बिरालोको बच्चा *n.* kitten

biraji बिराजी *adj.* unwilling

biralo बिरालो *n.* cat

biraloko बिरालोको *adj.* feline

birami बिरामी *adj.* ill

birami बिरामी *n.* patient

birami बिरामी *adj.* sick

birko बिर्को *n.* cover

birko बिर्को *n.* lid

birsane बिर्सने *adj.* forgetful

birsanu बिर्सनु *v.* forget

biruwa बिरुवा *n.* plant

biruwa ghar बिरुवाघर *n.* greenhouse

biruwako kisim बिरुवाको किसिम *n.* hazel

bisancho बिसंचो *adj.* unwell

biscuit va roti chopalnu बिस्कुट वा रोटी चोपल्नु *v.* dunk

bishalthalay विशालताले *adv.* largely

bishop बिशप *n.* bishop

bishtharak विस्तारक *n.* stretcher

biskut *n.* bicscuit

bisthan बीस थान *n.* score

bit बिट *n.* rim

bitholu बिथोल्नु *v.* interrupt

bitnu बित्लु *v.* elapse

biyar बियर *n.* beer

bjil भूल *n.* slip

blchai ma roknu बीचैमा रोक्नु *v.* intercept

bodh dharamko ek roop बौद्ध ६ र्मको एक रूप *n.* zen

boka बोका *n.* billy-goat

boknu बोक्नु *v.* carry

boknu बोक्नु *v.* tote

boko बोको *n.* goat

bokra बोक्रा *n.* peel

bokshi बोक्सो *n.* wizard

boksi बोक्सी *n.* witch

boksi widya बोक्सी विद्या *n.* witchcraft

bokso बोक्सो *n.* sorcerer

bol chal ko बोलचालको *adj.* colloquial

bolaha बौलाहा *adj.* deranged

bolakkad बोलककड *n.* windbag

bolauna pathaunu बोलाउन पठाउनु *v.* send for

bolawat बोलावट *n.* call

bolda therai shabd prayog garne बोल्दा थैरै शब्द प्रयोग गर्ने *adj.* laconic

boli बोली *n.* speech

boliko shaili बोलीको शैली *n.* parlance

bolne kala बोल्ने कला *n.* elocution

bolnu बोल्नु *v.* express

bolnu बोल्नु *v.* speak

bonus बोनस *n.* bonus

boornu बूर्नु *v.* furl

bora बोरा *n.* sack

bot wiruwa lagaeko jagga बोट बिरूवा लगाएको जग्गा *n.* plantation

bottle बोतल *n.* magnum

bowl phyankne manis बल फयाँक्ने मानिस *n.* bowler

brahmand ब्रह्माण्ड *n.* macrocosm

brahmand ब्रह्माण्ड *n.* universe

brahmvidya ब्रह्मविद्या *n.* theosophy

bramhand ko ब्रह्माण्ड को *adj.* cosmic

brandy ब्रान्डी *n.* brandy

bromide ब्रोमाइड *n.* bromide

buba बुबा *n.* papa

buddhi बुद्धि *n.* intellect

buddhi bangaro बुद्धि बङ्गारो *v.* wisdom tooth

buddhi jiwi बुद्धिजीवी *n.* intellectual

buddhichal बुद्धिचाल *n.* chess

buddhiman बुद्धिमान *n.* intelligence

buddhiman बुद्धिमान् *adj.* well advised

buddhiman बुद्धिमान् *adj.* wise

buddhimani sath बुद्धिमानी साथ *adv.* wisely

budh bar बुधवार *n.* Wednesday

budh graha बुध ग्रह *n.* mercury

budheskal बूढेसकाल *n.* old age

budhi aunlo बूढी औँलो *n.* thumb

budhiheen vyakti बुद्धिहीन व्यक्ति *n.* zombie

budho बूढो *adj.* age-old

bue बीउ *n.* seed

buhari बुहारी *n.* daughter-in-law

bujhaunu बुझाउनु *v.* lay down

bujhnu बुझ्नु *v.* comprehend

bujo बुजो *n.* gag

bukhyacha बुख्याचा *n.* scraecrow

bulaki नाक को प्वाल *n.* nose ring

bulldug kukkur बुलडग कुक्कुर *n.* bulldog

bunai बुनाइ *n.* weaving

bunnu बुन्नु *v.* knit

bunnu बुन्नु *v.* weave

burja बुर्जा *n.* turret

burukka uphranu बुरुक्क उफ्रनु *v.* skip

butta बुट्टा *n.* pattern

butta jadieko बुट्टा जडिएको *adj.* inlaid

bwanso ब्वाँसो *n.* wolf

byatri ब्याट्री *n.* battery

C

cake केक *n.* éclair

cake केक *n.* pastry

cake केक *n.* scone

carburettor काबुरेटर *n.* carburettor

centimetre सैन्टीमीटर *adj.* centimetre

chaal चाल *n.* stratagem

chaal चाल *n.* wiles

chaalbaj garne vyakti चालबाज गर्ने व्यक्ति *n.* trickster

chaalbaji चालबाजी *n.* skullduggery

chaata छाता *n.* brolly

chad चाड *n.* festival

chadak चड्का *adj* jazzy

chadhai चढ़ाइ *n.* ascent

chadhnu चढ्नु *v.* climb

chahak चहक *n.* splendo(u)r

chahine sasman चाहिने सामान *n.* requisite

chak चाक *n.* buttocks

chak manna andhyaro चकमन्न अँध्यारो *adj.* pitch-dark

chakaunu छकाउनु *v.* hoax

chakhewa chakhewi चखेवाचखेवी *n.* lovebirds

chakit चकित *adj.* surprised

chakka चक्का *n.* wheel

chakka ko kendra चक्काको केन्द्र *n.* hub

chakkar चक्कर *n.* rotation

chakkar khanu चक्कर खानु *v.* gyrate

chakki चक्की *n.* capsule

chakki चक्की *n.* pill

chakku चक्कु *n.* knife

chaklet चकलेट *n.* chocolate

chakmak चकमक *n.* flint

chakra चक्र *n.* cycle

chakra चक्र *n.* hoop

chakrapath चक्रपथ *n.* ring road

chal चाल *n.* gait

chal चाल *n.* motion

chal चाल *n.* move

chal चाल *n.* movement

chal छल *n.* ruse

chal chitra चलचित्र *n.* cinema

chal chitra चलचित्र *n.* film

chalak चालक *n.* driver

chalakh चालाख *adj.* shrewd

chalakile jitnu चलाकीले जित्नु *v.* outsmart

chalakile jitnu चलाकीले जित्नु *v.* overreach

chalan चलन *n.* fashion

chalan naskane चल्न नसक्ने *adj.* immobile

chalaunu चलाउनु *v.* operate

chalaunu चलाउनु *v.* stir

chalband चालबन्द *n.* stalemate

chalchitra चलचित्र *n.* motion picture

chalchitra चलचित्र *n.* movie

chaldai gareko चल्दै गरेको *adj.* ongoing

chalis चालीस *n.* forty

chalkapat छलकपट *n.* guile

chal-kapat छल-कपट *n.* deceit

challa चल्ला *n.* chick

chalmalaunu चलमलाउनु *v.* wriggle

chalne sarne चल्ने *adj.* movable

chalni चल्नी *n.* sieve

chalnu छलनु *v.* delude

chalti चल्ती *n.* vogue

chamacham chumchum garnu छामछाम-छुमछुम गर्नु *v.* fumble

chamada चमडा *n.* leather

chamak चमक *n.* gleam

chamak चमक *n.* lustre

chamak चमक *n.* shine

chamatkar चमत्कार *n.* miracle

chamatkar चमत्कार *n.* revelation

chamatkar चमत्कार *n.* tour de force

chamatkarpurn चमत्कारपूर्ण *adj.* miraculous

chamcha चम्चा *n.* spoon

chameli चमेली *n.* jasmine

chamena ghar चमेनाघर *n.* canteen

chamena ghar चमेनाघर *n.* snack bar

chamero चमेरा *n.* bat

chamkanu चम्कनु *v.* glitter

chamkanu चम्कनु *v.* scintillate

chamkanu चम्कनु *n.* sheen

chamkanu चम्कनु *v.* twinkle

chamkanuj चम्कनु *v.* sparkle

chamkilo चम्किलो *adj.* bright

chamkilo चम्किलो *adj.* radiant

chamkilo चम्किलो *adj.* shining

champat hunu चम्पत हुनु *v.* elope

chana चाना *n.* slice

chanak छनक *n.* premonition

chanakho चनाखो *adj.* vigilant

chanchal चंचल *adj.* restless

chanchal चंचल *adj.* shaky

chand shastra छनद शास्त्र *n.* prosody

chanda चन्दा *n.* subscription

chandai चाँडै *adv.* shortly

chandai चाँडै *adv.* soon

chandai badhnu चाँडै बढ्नु run up

chandai risaune चाँडै रिसाउने *adj.* short-tempered

chandai udne चाँडै उड्ने *adj.* volatile

chandi चाँदी *n.* silver

chandi jasto seto चाँदीजस्तो सेतो *adj.* silvery

chando garnu/garaunu चाँडो गर्नु/गराउनु *v.* quicken

chando jaun चाँडो जाऊ *v.* vamoose

chando kutkuti lagne चाँडो कुतकुती लाग्ने *adj.* ticklish

chando risaune चाँडो रिसाउने *adj.* pettish

chando/takita garnu चाँडो⁄ताकिता गर्नु *v.* expedite

chand-parikshan छनद-परीक्षण *n.* scansion

chandrama चन्द्रमा *n.* moon

chandrama ko चन्द्रमाको *adj.* lunar

changa चङ्गा *n.* kite

chansur चंसूर *n.* cress

chap चाप *n.* arc

chap चाप *n.* stress

chapal चपल *adj.* light-headed

chapaune dant चपाउने दाँत *n.* molar

chapaune surtiko dallo चपाउने सुर्ती को डल्लो *n.* quid

chapaunu चपाउनु *v.* chew

chapaunu चपाउनु *v.* masticate

chapaunu चपाउनु *v.* munch

chaploos चापलूस subservient

chappal चप्पल *n.* sandal

chappal चप्पल *n.* slipper

char चार *n.* four

char charanko padhe चार चरणको पद्य *n.* quatrain

char chuchche चारचुच्चे *adj.* quadrangular

char jana ko samuha चारजनाको समूह *n.* quartet

char jodi nachne nach चार जोडी नाच्ने नाच *n.* quadrille

char khutte चारखुट्टे *adj.* four-footed

char pangre gadi चारपाङ्ग्रे गाडी *n.* wag(g)on

char pate चारपाटे *n.* square

char taare gitar चार तारे गिटार *n.* ukulele

chara चारा *n.* bait

chara चरा *n.* bird

charai tira hernu चारैतिर हेर्नु *v.* survey

charaitira चारैतिरि *adv.* around

charakho pawankh चराको प्वाँख *n.* plumage

charampatra चर्मपत्र *n.* parchment

charampatra चर्मपत्र *n.* vellum

charan चरण *n.* phase

chares चरेस *n.* hashish

charitarko dosh चरित्रको दोष *n.* foible

charitra चरित्र *n.* character

charitra चरित्र *n.* conduct

charjanale khelne चारजनाले खेल्ने *n.* mahjong

charkanu छड्कनु *v.* sizzle

charkeko dharka चेर्केको धर्का *n.* crack

charkha चर्खा *n.* spinning wheel

charko चर्को *adj.* loud

charko चर्को *adj.* strident

charko bhadda hanso चर्को भद्दा हाँसो *n.* horse laugh

charnu चर्नु *v.* graze

charparsasi चपरासी *n.* bailiff

charpi चर्पी *n.* latrine

charpi चर्पी *n.* lavatory

chasma चस्मा *n.* eyeglasses

chasma banaune baykti चस्मा बनाउने ब्यक्ति *n.* optician

chasni चासनी *n.* syrup

chaso चासो *n.* concern

chatai चटाई *n.* mat

chatai चटाई *n.* matting

chatnu चाट्नु *v.* lick

chattan चट्टान *n.* cliff

chattan चट्टान *n.* rock

chattanko patra wa the चट्टानको पत्र वा तह *n.* stratum

chatti चट्टी *n.* slippers

chatur चतुर *v.* deft

chatur chal चतुर चाल *n.* ploy

chaturbhuj चतुर्भुज *n.* quadrilateral

chatyan सानु उद्योग *n.* lightning

chatyan चट्याङ *n.* thunderbolt

chaubato चौबाटो *n.* crossroads

chaubato चौबाटो *n.* intersection

chauda चौडा *adj.* wide

chaudai चौडाइ *n.* breadth

chaudai चौडाई *adj.* broad

chaudai चौडाइ *n.* width

chaudha din चौध दिन *n.* fortnight

chaugada चौगडा *n.* guinea pig

chauguna sankhya चौगुना संख्या *adj.* quadruple

chauki चौकी *n.* outpost

chaukos maidan चौकोस मैदान *n.* quadrangle

chauni छाउनी *n.* barracks

chaunri gai चाँरी गाई *n.* yahoo

chaupaya jantu चौपाया जन्तु *n.* quadruped

chaur चोरी *n.* lawn

chaur चउर *n.* lea

chaur चौर *n.* meadow

chauri चाउरी *n.* wring

chauthai चौथाइ *n.* quarter

chautho चाथो *adj.* fourth

chaya चाया *n.* dandruff

chaya चाया *n.* scurf

chaya चाया *n.* scurf

cheejharu rakhne thaun चीजहरू राख्ने ठाउँ *n.* repository

chehkilo चहकिलो *adj.* aglow

chehkilo चहकिलो *adj.* refulgent

chek चेक *n.* cheque/check

cheknu छेक्नु *v.* impede

chela चेला *n.* disciple

chela चेला *n.* pupil

chepagaanda चेपागाँड़ा *n.* tadpole

chepara jasto prani छेपारा जस्तो प्राणी *n.* newt

chepare boli चेपारे बोली *n.* lip-service

cheparo छेपारो *n.* chameleon

cheplete चिप्लेटी *n.* chute

chepte salla चेप्टे सल्ला *n.* juniper

cheta चिता *n.* cheetah

chetauni dinu चेताउनी दिनु *v.* warn

chetawani चेतावनी *n.* warning

cheuko छेउको *adj.* latreral

chha छ *v./aux.* is

chha छ *n.* six

chhadi छडी *n.* rod

chhadi dinu छाछिदिनु *v.* run out on

chhadma bhesh ma छद्म भेषमा *adv./adj.* incognito

chhaitaun छैटौं *n./adj.* sixth

chhak pareko छक्क परेको *adj.* nonplussed

chhakka pareko छक्क परेको *adj.* wide-eyed

chhal छल *n.* humbug

chhal छल *n.* trick

chhal phal छलफल *n.* discussion

chhal phal garnu छलफल गर्नु *v.* discuss

chhala छाला *n.* skin

chhalako dori छालाको डोरी *n.* thong

chhalang छालाङ्ग *n.* leap

chhali छली *adj.* treacherous

chhalne/chhakyaune kam छलने/छक्याउने काम *n.* dodge

chhalnu छलनु *v.* spoof

chhalphal garnu छलफल गर्नु *v.* talk over

chhana छाना *n.* celling

chhana छाना *n.* roof

chhana wa pharsma bhaeko darwaza छाना वा फर्समा भएको दरवाजा *n.* trap-door

chhango छागो *n.* cascade

chhanna yogya छान्नयोग्य *adj.* eligible

chhannu छान्नु *v.* select

chhanot छनोट *n.* choice

chhanot छनोट *n.* selection

chhap छाप *n.* seal

chhap छाप *n.* stamp

chhapa छापा *n.* print

chhapa khana छापाखाना *n.* press

chhapa khana छापा,गाना *n.* printing press

chhapro छाप्रो *n.* shed

chhare rog छारेरोग *n.* epilepsy

chharito छरितो *adj.* svelte

chharito dublo patalo छरितो दुब्लो पातलो *adj.* slim

chharkanu छर्कनु *v.* sprinkle

chharkinu छर्किनु *v.* spatter

chharnu छर्नु *v.* scatter

chharnu छर्नु *v.* sow

chhata छाता *n.* umbrella

chhati छाती *n.* bosom

chhati छाती *n.* breast

chhati छाती *n.* chest

chhati polne rog छाती पोल्ने रोग *n.* heartburn

chhatpati छटपटी *n.* restlessness

chhatra writti छात्रवृत्ति *n.* scholarship

chhatrawas छात्रावास *n.* hostel

chhauro छाउरो *n.* cub

chhaya छाया *n.* shade

chhayadar छायादार *adj.* shady

chhed छेड *n.* innuendo

chhednu छेड्नु *v.* pierce

chhena छेना *n.* casein

chheparo छेपारो *n.* lizard

chheskini छेस्किनी *n.* bolt

chheu छेउ *n.* edge

chheu छेउ *n.* flank

chheu छेउ *n.* margin

chheu छेउ *n.* side

chhidra छिद्र *n.* gap

chhidra bhaeko छिद्र भएको *adj.* porous

chhimalnu छिमल्नु *v.* prune

chhimek छिमेक *n.* neighbo(u)rhood

chhimeki छिमेकी *n.* neighbo(u)r

chhin छिन *n.* moment

chhink छिंक्क *n.* sneeze

chhippieko छिप्पिएको *adj* seasoned

chhirai छिराइ *n.* penetration

chhirbire छिबिरि *adj.* spotted

chhirka चिका *n.* jet

chhitain छिटै *adv.* rapidly

chhiti lekhne widhi छिटो लेख्ने विधि *n.* shorthand

chhito छिटो *adj.* fast

chhito छिटो *adj.* nimble

chhito छिटो *adj.* quick

chhito छिटो *adj.* rapid

chhito छिटो *adj.* swift

chhito छिटो *adj.* prompt

chhodi dinu छोडिदिनु *v.* let alone

chhodi dinu छोडिदिनु *v.* relieve

chhodnu छोड्नु *v* abandon

chhodnu छोड्नु *v.* give up

chhodnua छोड्नु *v.* part with

chhodunu छोड्नु *v.* deliver

chhora छोरा *n.* son

chhori छोरी *n.* daughter

chhotkari छोटकरी *adj.* brief

chhotkari छोटकरी *adj.* concise

chhoto छोटो *adj.* short

chhoto छोटो *v.* yelp

chhoto bato छोटोबाटो *n.* shortcut

chhoto duri छोटो दूरी *n.* stone's throw

chhoto jiwan bhaeko छोटो जीवन भएको *adj.* short-lived

chhoto kissa छोटो किस्सा *n.* anecdote

chhoto parnu छोटो पार्नु *v.* abbreviate

chhoto parnu छोटो पार्नु *v.* abridge

chhoto parnu छोटो पार्नु *v.* shorten

chhoto wakya छोटो वाक्य *n.* phrase

chhuchcho छुच्चो *adj.* mean

chhuchundro छुचुन्द्रो *n.* mole

chhura छुरा *n.* razor

chhura dhasnu छुरा धस्नु *v.* stab

chhuri छुरी *n.* blade

chhut छूट *n.* discount

chhut dinu छूट दिनु *v.* exempt

chhut dinu छूट दिनु *n.* exemption

chhutkara छुट्कारा *v.* acquit

chhutkara छुट्कारा *n.* discharge

chhutphut छूटफूट *n.* odds and
   ends

chhuttai छुट्टै *adj.* distinct

chhuttyaunu छुट्ट्याउनु *v.*
   distinguish

chhutyaunu छुट्याउनु *v.* sort out

chhwali छ्वाली *n.* wheat stalk

chhyap chhyap छ्यापछ्याप *n.*
   splash

chhyapi छ्यापी *n.* pearl onion

chi chya छिः छ्याः *interj.* phew

chiasmis छ्यासमिस *n.* welter

chiauko vigyan च्याउको विज्ञान *n.*
   mycology

chiaunu चियाउनु *v.* peek

chichaunu चिच्च्याउनु *v.* holler

chichindo चिचिण्डो *n.* snake-
   gourd

chichyahat चिच्याहट *n.* scream

chichyahat चिच्याहट *n.* shriek

chiddra छिद्र *n.* aperture

chidiya khana चिडियाखाना *n.* zoo

chidiya khana चिडियाखाना *n.*
   zoological garden

chidra छिद्र *n.* orifice

chihan चिहान *n.* necropolis

chihan चिहान *n.* tomb

chihan ma gadne kam चिहानमा
   गाड्ने काम *n.* burial

chiimek/aspas ko
   छिमेक/आसपासको *adj.*
   neighbo(u)ring

chij चीज *n.* stuff

chij चीज *n.* substance

chij चीज *n.* thing

chikitsa चिकित्सा *n.* therapy

chil चील *n.* eagle

chilai चिलाइ *n.* itch

chillo चिल्लो *n.* fat

chillo चिल्लो *n.* grease

chillo चिल्लो *adj.* greasy

chillo चिल्लो *adj.* oily

chilne khil चिल्ने खिल *n.* sting

chilo hunu चिल्लो हुनु *n.* glaze

chim चिम *n.* bulb

chimniko dhakni चिम्नीको ढकनी
   n. cowl

chimta चिम्टा *n.* nippers

chimta चिम्टा *n.* pineers

chimta चिम्टा *n.* tongs

chimti चिम्टी *n.* pinch

chimtra चिम्टा *n.* pincers

chin chin garnu चीँचीँ गर्नु *v.*
   squeak

china parchi na bhaeko चिनापर्ची नभएको *adj.* unacquainted

chine janeko चिनेजानेको *adj.* familiar

chingarhi चिंगड़ी *n.* prawn

chingari चिँगड़ी *n.* lobster

chinha चिन्ह *n.* symbol

chinha patra चिन्हपत्र *n.* label

chini चिनी *n.* sugar

chini mata ka wastu चिनीमाटाका वस्तु *n.* porcelain

chiniyan mtoka bhanda चिनियाँ माटोका भाडा *n.* china

chinjan चिनजान *n.* acquaintance

chinjan चिनजान *n.* introduction

chinjan/parichaya garaunu चिनजान/परिचय गराउनु *v.* introduce

chinnu चिन्नु *v.* know

chinnu चिन्नु *v.* recognize

chino चिनो *n.* emblem

chino चिनो *n.* mark

chinta चिन्ता *n.* anxiety

chinta चिन्ता *n.* worried

chinta garnu चिन्ता गर्नु *v.* worry

chintan चिन्तन *n.* reverie

chintit चिन्तित *adj.* anxious

chinu छिनु *n.* chisel

chinu चिनु *n.* keepsake

chinu चिर्नु *n.* souvenir

chiplanu चिप्लनु *v.* glide

chiplanu चिप्लनु *v.* slide

chiple kiro चिप्लेकीरो *n.* slug

chiplekira चिप्लेकीरा *n.* whelp

chiplo चिप्लो *adj.* slippery

chiplo mato चिप्लो माटो *n.* clay

chiplo r hile mato चिप्लो र हिले माटो *n.* slime

chir phar चिर फार *n.* operation

chir phar garne daktar चिरफार गर्ने डाक्टर *n.* surgeon

chir sammanit चिरसम्मानित *adj.* time-hono(u)red

chira चिरा *n.* cranny

chira चिरा *n.* interstice

chira चिरा *n.* slit

chira चिरा *n.* slot

chirchire चिरचिरे *adj.* temperamental

chirharitalta चिरहरितलता *n.* ivy

chirhaunu चिढ्याउनु *v.* rile

chirnu चिर्नु *v.* slash

chirphar चिरफार *adj.* inoperable

chirphar विरफार *n.* surgery

chirphar garn hune चिरफार गर्न हुने *adj.* operable

chiso चिसो *adj.* cold

chiso चिसो *adj.* cool

chiso चिसो *adj.* nippy

chisoparne mesin चिसो पार्ने मेसिन *n.* refrigerator

chita चिता *n.* pyre

chitaeko kura pugne kam चिताएको कुरा पुग्ने काम *n.* fruition

chitaunu चिताउनु *v.* intend

chithi चिठी *n.* epistle

chithi चिठी *n.* letter

chitra चित्र *n.* image

chitra चित्र *n.* portrait

chitra चित्र *n.* tableau

chitra adaune kathko dhancha चित्र अङ्ग्याउने काठको ढाँचा *n.* easel

chitra banaunu चित्र बनाउनु *v.* portray

chitrakar चित्रकार *n.* painter

chitrakari चित्रकारी *n.* painting

chitta dukhaune चित्त दुखाउने *adj.* heartbreaking

chittha चिट्ठा *n.* lottery

chittha चिट्ठा *n.* raffle

chituwa चितुवा *n.* leopard

chituwa चितुवा *n.* panther

chiundo चिउँडो *n.* chin

chiya चिया *n.* tea

chiya bagan चियाबगान *n.* tea estate

chiya khane chhutti चिया खाने छुट्टी *n.* tea break

chiyadan चियादान *n.* teapot

chlorine क्लोरीन *n.* chlorine

chodnu छोड्नु *v.* emit

chodnu छोड्नु *v.* let go

chodnu छोड्नु *v.* release

chodnu छोड्नु *v.* resign

choito चोइटो *n.* splint

chok चोक *n.* courtyard

chok चोक *n.* piazza

chok चोक *n.* plaza

chok bajar चोकबजार *n.* marketplace

chokar चोकर *n.* bran

chokar चोकर *n.* husk

chokho nabhayko चोखो नभएको *adj.* unchaste

cholo चोलो *n.* blouse

cholo चोलो *n.* bodice

chon छोड्नु *v.* leave off

chon छोड्नु *v.* omit

chon छोड्नु *v.* launch

choop चूप mum

chop चोप *n.* sap

chor aunla चोरआँला *n.* forefinger

chor aunla चोरआँला *n.* index finger

chorera laijanu चोरेर लैजानु *v.* walk off with

chori चोरी *n.* larceny

chori चोरी *n.* rip-off

chori चौरी *n.* theft

chori चौरी *n.* thief

chori garna lalayit hune rog चोरी गर्न लालायित हुने रोग *n.* kleptomania

choriko maal चोरीको माल *n.* swag

chornu चोर्नु *v.* rob

chornu चोर्नु *v.* steal

chot lagaunu चोट लगाउनु *v.* injure

chot lagaunu चोट लगाउनु *n.* injury

chot lagaunu va lagnu चोट लगाउनु वा लाग्नु *n.* bruise

chot lagnu चोट लाग्नु *v.* hurt

chot puryaune चोट पुन्याउने *adj.* shocking

choto r moto छोटो र मोटो *adj.* podgy

choto r rukho छोटो र रूखो *v.* curtail

chrachurangiko vigyan चराचुरूङ्गीको विज्ञान *n.* ornithology

chrachurungi rakhne thaun चराचुरूंगी राख्ने ठाउँ *n.* aviary

christmas क्रिस्मस *n.* noel

chritsmasko pachiko din क्रिस्मसको पछिको दिन *n.* boxing day

chuchcho चुच्चो *n.* beak

chuchcho चुच्चो *n.* jut

chuchcho चुच्चो *n.* point

chuchuro चुचुरो *n.* peak

chudkila घ्चुड्किला *n.* wisecrack

chuhawat चुहावट *n.* leakage

chuhine चुहिने *adj.* leaky

chuhnu चुहनु *v.* ooze

chuhyawat चुहावट *n.* leak

chukandar चुकन्दर *n.* beet

chukandar चुकन्दर *n.* sugar beet

chukaunu चुकाउनु *v.* repay

chukul चुकुल *n.* hinge

chukul चुकुल *n.* latch

chuli चुली *n.* summit

chulo चूलो *n.* oven

chumbak चुम्बक *n.* magnet

chumban चुम्बन *n.* kiss

chumban चुम्बन *n.* seal of love

chun चून *n.* lime

chun dhunga चूनदुङ्ग *n.* limestone

chun ko potai चुनको पोताइ *n.* whitewash

chun sakine छुन सकिने *adj.* tangible

chunau चुनाउ *n.* election

chunau khestra चुनाउ क्षेत्र *n.* constitutency

chunauti चुनौती *n.* challenge

chundalnu चुँडाल्नु *v.* pull off

chungi चुँगी *n.* octroi

chunnu चुन्नु *v.* elect

chunu चुन्नु *v.* opt

chup lageko चुप लागेको *adj.* silent

chup lagera चुप लागेर *adv.* silently

chupchap चुपचाप *n.* silence

chuplag चुप लाग *v.* shut up

chupriko thupro चुपरीको थुप्रो *n.* sod

chura चुरा *n.* bangle

chura चुरा *n.* bangle

chura udhayune chhala छूरा उद् याउने छाला *n.* strop

churn banaunu चूर्ण बनाउनु *v.* pulverize

churot चुरोट *n.* cigarette

churot/tamakhu khane चुरोट/तमाखु खाने *n.* smoker

churote चुरोट cheroot

chusne mithai चुस्ने मिठाई *n.* lozenge

chusnu चुस्नु *v.* suck

chut छूट *n.* omission

chutkara छुटकारा *n.* quietus

chutkilo चुट्किलो *n.* witticism

chutney चटनी *n.* chutney

chyapne purja च्याप्ने पुर्जा *n.* clamp

chyat chut parnu च्यातचुत पार्नु *v.* tear up

chyatanu च्यात्लु *v.* rend

chyau च्याउ *n.* mushroom

chyaune pwal च्याउने प्वाल *n.* peephole

chyaunu च्याउनु *v.* peep

cigar सिगार *n.* cigar

cinema सिनेमा *n.* projector

cjajami चाहनु *v.* want

cobalt कोबाल्ट *n.* cobalt

cococo beej va rukh कोकोको बीज वा रूख *n.* cacao

coughnasak कफनासक *v.* expectorant

coughnikalnu कफ निकाल्नु *v.* expectorate

crome क्रोम *n.* chrome

crore करोड़ *n.* crore

cup कप *n.* pannikin

cutlet कटलेट *n.* cutlet

D

daag दाग *n.* blemish

daag दाग *n.* smudge

daag, dhabha दाग, धब्बा *n.* fleck

daanbir दानबीर *adj.* profuse

daanshil दानशील *adj.* bountiful

daantnu डाँट्नु *v.* upbraid

daap wa myanbaat jhiknu दाप वा म्यानबाट झिक्नु *v.* unsheathe

daazu दाजु *n.* brethren

dabab दबाब *n.* pressure

dabab mahar mannu दबाबमा हार मान्नु *v.* give way

dabab samuh दबाव समूह *n.* pressure group

dabaunu दबाउनु *v.* dominate

dabaunu दबाउनु *v.* put down

dabaunu दबाउनु *v.* quell

dabaunu दबाउनु *v.* repress

dabeko haanso दबेको हाँसो *v.* chuckle

dabeko haanso दबेको हाँसो *n.* snigger

dabha दाबा *n.* claim

dad दाद *n.* eczema

dadhelo डढेलो *n.* wildfire

dadu डाडु *n.* ladle

dadura दादुरा *n.* measles

dadura दादुरा *n.* measles

dag दाग *n.* spot

dag दाग *n.* stain

dagurnu दगुर्नु *v.* run

dah sanskar दाहसंस्कार *n.* cremation

daha डाहा *n.* envy

daha डाहा *n.* malice

dahi दही *n.* curd

dahi दही *n.* yogurt, yoghurt

dahiko misthanan दही को मिष्टान्न *n.* junket

daijo दाइजो *n.* dowry

dailo दैलो *n.* door

dainik wiwaran दैनिक विवरण *n.* diary

daitya दैत्य *n.* demon

dajnu दाँज्नु *v.* collate

daju दाजु *n.* brother

dak ticket sangrah डाक टिकट संग्रह *n.* philately

dakaiti डकैती *n.* robbery

dakarmi डकर्मी *n.* mason

dakarnu डकार्नु *v.* belch

dakdak gareko awaaz ढकढक गरेको आवाज *n.* rat-tat

dakkhini दक्षिणी *adj.* southern

daknu डाक्नु *v.* summon

daksh दक्ष *adj.* adroit

daksh दक्ष *adj.* deft

daksh दक्ष *adj.* efficient

daksha दक्ष *adj.* ingenious

daksha दक्ष *adj.* talented

dakshata दक्षता *n.* efficiency

dakshin दक्षिण *n.* south

dakshin dhruv pradesh दक्षिण ध्रुव प्रदेश *adj.* antarctic

dakshini दक्षिणी *adj.* southward

dakshta दक्षता *n.* dexterity

daktar डाक्टर *n.* doctor

daktar डाक्टर *n.* physician

daktar ko shalaka डाक्टरको शलाका *n.* probe

daktari डाक्टरी *adj.* medical

daku डाकु *n.* robber

dal दल *n.* gang

dal दाल *n.* lentil

dal दाल *n.* pulse

dal chhodaha दल छोडाहा *n.* turncoat

dal dal दलदल *n.* bog

dal dal दलदल *n.* swamp

dalal दलाल *n.* broker

dalal दलाल *n.* pimp

dalbal दलबल *n.* entourage

dalchini दालचिनी *n.* cinnamon

dalera sapha garnu दलेर सफा गर्नु *n.* scrub

dalin दलिन *n.* joist

dallo डल्लो *n.* sphere

dam ka rog दमको रोग *n.* asthma

dam lagaunu दाम लगाउनु *v.* bid

daman दमन *n.* repression

daman garnu दमन गर्नु *v.* suppress

dameko chinha डामेको चिन्ह *n.* brand

dami pathar दामी पत्थर *n.* garnet

dami pathar दामी पत्थर *n.* onyx

damkal दमकल *n.* fire brigade

damkarl दमकल *n.* fire engine

damlo दाम्लो *n.* leash

dampatya दाम्पत्य *n.* marital

dan दान *n.* charity

dan/chanda dinu दान/चन्दा दिनु v. donate

dana pani दानापानी n. provisions

danadar दानादार adj. granular

danak दनक n. knock

danaw दानव n. giant

danaw दाना n. granule

dance डाँस n. gadfly

dand दण्ड n. penalty

dand/sajaya dinu दण्ड/सजाय दिनु v. punish

danda डण्डा n. bar

danda डाँडा n. ridge

dandalno डँडाल्लो n. spine

dandh दण्ड n. retribution

dandi phor डन्डीफोर n. pimple

danga दंगा n. rout

danga phasad दङ्गाफसाद n. outbreak

danjnu दाँज्नु v. compare

dank डाँक n. mail

danku डाँकु n. bandit

danku डाँकू n. dacoit

danphe डाँफे n. pheasant impeyan

dant dukhai दाँत दुखाइ n. toothache

dant ko daktar दाँतको डाक्टर n. dentist

dant ko tyaune sinko दोत कोट्याउने सिन्को toothpick

dant sambandhi दाँत सम्बन्धी adj. dental

danth डाँठ n. stalk

danth डाँठ n. stem

dantharu दाँतहरू n. teeth

dantharu दाँत n. tooth

dantpisnu दाँतपिस्नु v. gnash

dantya/pauranik katha दन्त्य/पौराणिक कथा n. legend

dap दाप n. scabbard

dar डर n. dread

dar डर n. horror

dar डर n. terror

dar lagdo डरलाग्दो adj. fearful

dar lagdo डरलाग्दो adj. ferocious

dar lagdo डरलाग्दो adj. fierce

dar lagdo डरलाग्दो adj. terrible

dar lagdo sapana डरलाग्दो सपना n. nightmare

dar le kammu डरले काम्नु v. shudder

dar r nirashako bhawna डर र निराशाको भावना n. dismay

daraeko डराएको adj. afraid

daraj दराज n. cabinet

daraj दराज n. closet

daraj दराज n. cupboard

daraj दराज n. wardrobe

darar दरार n. rift

darbaria दरबारिया n. courtier

Darha दाह्रा n. fang

Darha डर n. fear

darhi दाही n. beard

daridar दरिद्र adj. necessitous

darja दर्जा n. class

darja दर्जा *n.* degree

darja दर्जा *n.* grade

darja दर्जा *n.* rank

darja दर *n.* rate

darja दर्जामान *n.* title

darjan दर्जन *n.* dozen

darji दर्जी *n.* seamster

darji दर्जी *n.* tailor

darjini दर्जिनी *n.* seamstress

darlagdo डरलाग्दो *adj.* grisly

darlagdo डरलाग्दो *adj.* scary

darle luruk parnu डरले लुरूक्क पर्नु *v.* cower

daro दरो *adj.* stark

daro दरो *adj.* stiff

darshak दर्शक *n.* spectator

darshanik दार्शनिक *n.* philosopher

darshanshastra दर्शनशास्त्र *n.* philosophy

darta दर्ता *n.* registration

darta gareko दर्ता गरेको *adj.* registered

darta garnu दर्ता गर्नु *v.* register

das दास *n.* serf

das दास *n.* slave

das दस *n.* ten

das banaunu दास बनाउनु *v.* enslave

das lakh दस लाख *n.* million

das warsh ko samaya दस वर्षको समय *n.* decade

dasamalab दसमलब *n.* decimal

dash kharab दश खरब *n.* billion

dashko not दशको नोट *n.* tenner

dasna डसना *n.* mattress

dasna डसना *n.* mattress

dasta दासता *n.* slavery

data दाता *n.* donor

datta chitta hunu दत्तचित्त हुनु *v.* devote

dauda daud दौडादौड *n.* razor blade

daudane manchhe दौडने मान्छे *n.* runner

dauntari दाँतरी *n.* playmate

daupech दाउपेच *n.* tactics

daura दाउरा *n.* firewood

daurako bita दाउराको बिटा *n.* faggot

daure दाउरे *n.* woodcutter

daya दया *n.* compassion

daya दया *n.* kindness

daya maya lagdo दया मायालाग्दो *adj.* pathetic

daya maya lagdo दया मया लाग्दो *n.* pity

daya/kripapurwak दया/कृपापूर्वक *adv.* kindly

dayalu दयालु *adj.* benevolent

dayalu दयालु *adj.* gracious

dayalu दयालु *adj.* humane

dayalu दयालु *adj.* kind

dayalu दयालु *adj.* merciful

dayalu दयालु *adj.* warm-hearted

dayan दायाँ *adj.* right

dayitwa दायित्व *n.* liability

debre देब्रे *adj.* left

debre hat chalne देब्रे हात चल्ने *adj.* lefty

dedho डेढो *adj.* squint

dehati देहाती *n.* villager

dehati niwas देहाती निवास *n.* villa

dekha parnu देखा पर्नु *v.* appear

dekha siki garnu देखासिकी गर्नु *v.* imitate

dekhaunu देखाउनु *v.* evince

dekhaunu देखाउनु *v.* exude

dekhaunu देखाउनु *v.* flaunt

dekhaunu देखाउनु *v.* indicate

dekhawati देखावटी *adj.* showy

dekhda देख्दा *adv.* seemingly

dekhine देखिने *adj.* visible

dekhiunu देखिनु *v.* seem

dekhna na saknu देख्न नसक्नु *v.* overlook

dekhnu देख्नु *v.* descry

dekhnu देख्नु *v.* set eyes on

delhi दिली *adj.* heartfelt

desh देश *n.* country

desh bhakta देशभक्त *n.* patriot

desh drohi देशद्रोही *n.* traitor

desh nikala garnu देशनिकाला *n.* deporatation

desh nikala garnu देश निकाला गर्नु *v.* deport

deshantar देशान्तर *n.* longitude

deshbat niklanu देशभाट निकाल्नु *v.* banish

desk छेस्क *n.* desk

devdar देवदार *v.* cedar

devdoot देवदूत *n.* seraph

dewdut देवदुत *n.* angel

dewi देवी *n.* deity

dewi देवी *n.* goddess

dhaba धाबा *n.* inroad

dhabba धब्बा *n.* splotch

dhabba धब्बा *n.* tarnish

dhad ढाड *n.* backbone

dhadaka धड़ाका *n.* crash

dhadkanu धड्कनु *v.* palpitate

dhago धागो *n.* thread

dhago wa philim berne ril धागो वा फिलिम बेर्ने रिल *n.* spool

dhai धाई *n.* nurse

dhai धाई *n.* wet nurse

dhairya धैर्य *n.* fortitude

dhairya धैर्य *n.* patience

dhairyawan धैर्यवान *adj.* self-possessed

dhak ढक *n.* weight

dhak launu धाक लाउनु *v.* boast

dhakelnu धकेल्नु *v.* propel

dhakka धक्का *n.* brunt

dhakka धक्का *n.* hitch

dhakka धक्का *n.* jolt

dhakka धक्का *n.* push

dhakka धक्का *n.* shock

dhakka धक्का *n.* collision

dhakka thamne wastu ने वस्तु *n.* buffer

dhakne choli ढाक्ने चोली *n.* bra

dhaknu ढाक्नु *v.* overwhelm

dhakre ढाके *adj.* jobless

dhal ढल *n.* sewer

dhal ढाल *n.* shield

dhalnu ढल्नु *v.* collapse

dhalnu ढाल्नु *v.* mould

dhami धामी *n.* witch doctor

dhamilo धमिलो *adj.* dim

dhamilo धमिलो *adj.* nebulous

dhamilo धमिलो *adj.* turbid

dhamilo ankha bhaeko धमिलो आँखा भएको *adj.* bleary

dhamilo parnu धमिलो पर्नु *adj.* obscure

dhamiro धमिरो *n.* termite

dhamki धम्की *n.* duress

dhamki धमकी *n.* menace

dhamki धम्की *n.* threat

dhamkyaunu धम्क्याउनु *v.* intimidate

dhamkyaunu धम्क्याउनु *v.* threaten

dhamni धमनी *n.* artery

dhan धान *n.* paddy

dhan धन *n.* riches

dhan धन *n.* treasure

dhan धन *n.* wealth

dhan ko khani धनको खानी *n.* bonanza

dhan sampatti धन-सम्पत्ति *n.* possessions

dhan sampatti धन-सम्पत्ति *n.* property

dhan5 धन *n.* mammon

dhancha ढाँचा *n.* attitude

dhancha ढाँचा *n.* position

dhanchawal ढाँचावाल *adj.* stylish

dhandhali धाँधली *n.* rigging

dhani धनी *adj.* affluent

dhani धनी *adj.* rich

dhani धनी *adj.* wealthy

dhani धनी *adj.* well off

dhaniya धनिया *n.* coriander

dhanja धाँजा *n.* cleft

dhanko lobh धनको लोभ *n.* cupidity

dhanu rashi धनुराशि *n.* sagittarius

dhanush धनुष *n.* bow

dhanushtankar घनुष्टङ्कार *n.* tetanus

dhanya wad dinu धन्यवाद दिनु *v.* thank

dhanyawad धन्यवाद *inter.* thanks

dhanyawad धन्यवाद *inter.* thankyou

dhanyawad gyapan धन्यवाद-ज्ञापन *n.* vote of thanks

dhap धाप *n.* fen

dhap धाप *n.* marsh

dhap धाप *n.* pat

dhap धाप *n.* quagmire

dhar na bhaeko नभएको *adj.* blunt

dhara धारा *n.* tap

dharamistri धारामिस्त्री *n.* plumber

dharam-nishta धर्म-निष्ठ *n.* piety

dharawahik धारावाहिक *n./adj.* serial

dharka धर्का *n.* stripe

dharkanu धड़कनु *v.* pulsate

dharke धर्के *adj.* striped

dharke suti luga धर्के सूती लुगा *n.* gingham

dharm धर्म *n.* religion

dharm badalne wyakti दल्ने व्यक्ति *n.* convert

dharm nirapeksha धर्मनिरपेक्ष *n.* secular

dharm pracharak धर्मप्रचारक *n.* preacher

dharmandh धर्मान्ध *n./adj.* fanatic

dharmatma धर्मात्मा *adj.* pious

dharmgranth धर्मग्रन्थ *n.* scripture

dharmik धार्मिक *adj.* devout

dharmik धार्मिक *adj.* religious

dharmik riti धार्मिक रीति *n.* rite

dharna धारणा *n.* perception

dharnesh chara चरा *n.* hornbill

dharo धारो *n.* spout

dhatu धातु *n.* metal

dhatu pagale bharo धातु पगाल्ले भाँड़ो *n.* crucible

dhatuko maila धातु को मैला *n.* dross

dhatuko maila धातुको मैला *n.* slag

dhatuko sikka धातु को सिक्का *n.* specie

dhatuko thaal wa tray धातुको थाल वा ट्रे *n.* salver

dhaturekha धातु रेखा *n.* lode

dhaturo धतरो *n.* belladonna

dhau धाउ *n.* ore

dhawa धावा *n.* incursion

dhawa धावा *n.* raid

dhawan marg धावन मार्ग *n.* runway

dhawanse घ्वाँसे *adj.* smoky

dhayan deir padhnu ध्यान दिएर पढ़नु *v.* peruse

dheelo ढीलो *adj.* tardy

dheer धीर *adj.* sedate

dheeth ढीठ *adj.* brash

dheknu देख्नु *v.* espy

dherae धेरै *adj.* umpteen

dherai धेरै *adj.* lot(s) of

dherai धेरै *adj.* luxuriant

dherai धेरै *adj.* many

dherai धेरै *adj.* much

dherai धेरै *adj.* numerous

dherai धेरै *adj.* several

dherai धेरै *adv.* very

dherai aghi धेरै अघि *adv.* longago

dherai bahir धेरै बाहिर *adv.* way out

dherai duri ko धेरै दूरीको *adj.* long range

dherai hawa ko mar pareko धेरै हावाको मार परेको *adj.* windswept

dherai jaso धेरैजसो *adv.* mostly

dherai khane धेरै खाने *n.* glutton

dherai matle prajit garnu धेरै मतले पराजित गर्नु *v.* outvote

dherai matra धेरै मात्रा *n.* plethora

dherai nabolne धेरै नबोल्ने *adj.* reticent

dherai raksi khane रक्सी खाने *n.* drunkard

dherai raun bhaeko धेरै रौं भएको *adj.* hairy

dherai sano धेरै सानो *adj.* tiny

dherai shabd prayag garne धेरै शब्द प्रयाग गर्ने *v.* diffuse

dherai tadha najanu धेरै टाढा नजानु *v.* hangaround

dherai tala bhaeko धेरै तला भएको *adj.* high-rise

dherai tala bhaeko धेरै तला भएको *n.* multi-storey

dherai ubjani hune धेरै उब्जनी हुने *adj.* fecund

dherainiket धेरै निकट *n.* hair'sbreadth

dhika ढिका *n.* lump

dhiki chyaunkhel ढिकिच्याउँ खेल *n.* seesaw

dhiksko ढिस्को *n.* mound

dhilai ढिलाई *n.* delay

dhilo ढीलो *adj.* slow

dhilo wa chando ढिलो वा चाँडो *adv.* sooner or later

dhilogari ढीलोगरी *adv.* slowloy

dhipdhip garnu धिपधिप गर्नु *vg.* flicker

dhisko ढिस्को *n.* hummock

dhisko ढिस्को *n.* knoll

dhobi धोबी *n.* washerman

dhobi ko ghar को घर *n.* laundry

dhoka धोका *n.* fraud

dhoka adami thokeko awaaz ढोका आदिमा ठोकेको आवाज *m.* rat-a-tat-tat

dhoka dinu धोखा दिनु *v.* dupe

dhoka dinu धोखा दिनु *v.* let down

dhoke ढोका *n.* gate

dhoke ढोके *n.* gatekeeper

dhokha धोखा *n.* treachery

dhokha dinu धोखा दिनु *v.* betray

dhokha dinu धोका दिनु *v.* sell out

dhokre धोक्रे *adj.* baggy

dhokro धोक्रो *adj.* hoarse

dhol ढोल *n.* drum

dhoopghari धूप-घड़ी *n.* sundial

dhrawiya ध्रुवीय *adj.* polar

dhrisht धृष्ट *adj.* pert

dhrishtata धृष्टता *n.* effrontery

dhruvtara ध्रुवतारा *n.* lodestar

dhruwa tara ध्रुव तारा *n.* north star

dhruwa tara ध्रुवतारा *n.* pole star

dhua laer kitanuharu marnu धुँवा लाएर कीटाणुहरू मार्नु *n.* fume

dhuk dhuk ढुकढुक *n.* palpitation

dhukdhuki ढुकढुकी *n.* beat

dhukh denu दुख दिनु *v.* groan

dhuknu ढुक्नु *v.* waylay

dhukur ढुकुर *n.* dove

dhulo धूलो *n.* dust

dhulo pitho parnu धूलो पिठो पर्नु *n.* pound

dhuloko kan धूलोको कण *n.* mote

dhumdham धूमधाम *n.* fanfare

dhumketu धूमकेतु *n.* comet

dhumra pan na gaarne धूम्रपान नगर्ने *n.* non-smoker

dhun धुन *n.* craze

dhun धुन *n.* fad

dhuna hune धुन हुनु *adj.* washable

dhunga ढुङ्गा *n.* stone

dhunga chhapnu ढुङ्गा छाप्नु *v.* pave

dhunga khani ढुङ्गाखानी *n.* quarry

dhungako smarak ढुंगा को स्मारक *n.* cairn

dhunu धुनु *v.* wash

dhuri धुरी *n.* axis

dhurmrapan धूम्रपान *n.* smoking

dhurt धूर्त *n./adv.* knave

dhurt धूर्त *adj.* sly

dhusi ढुसी *n.* mildew

dhuwan धुँवा *n.* smoke

dhuwan na bhaeko धुवा नभएको *adj.* smokeless

dhuwankas चिउडो *n.* chimney

dhwaja pataka ध्वजपताका *n.* banner

dhwajawahak ध्वजावाहक *n.* standard-bearer

dhwani va shravan sambandhi ध्वनि वा श्रवण सम्बन्धी *adj.* acoustic

dhwanso ध्वाँसो *n.* soot

dhyan ध्यान *n.* meditation

dhyan ध्यान *n.* attention

dhyan dinu ध्यान दिनु *v.* heed

dhyan rakhnu ध्यान राख्नु *v.* see to

dhyan sanga hernu ध्यानसँग हेर्नु *v.* scan

dhyan sanga janchnu ध्यानसँग जाँच्नु *v.* scrutinize

dhyan/chintan garnu ध्यान/चिन्तन गर्नु *v.* meditate

dibba डिब्बा *n.* canister

dibbama band garnu डिब्बामा बन्द गर्नु *v.* encase

didi दिदी *n.* sister

diieko matra दिइएको मात्रा *n.* quantum

dijel डिजेल *n.* diesel

dikka launu दिक्क लाउनु *v.* annoy

dillagi दिल्लगी *n.* raillery

dimag दिमाग *n.* brain

din bhari दिनभरि *n.* daylong

din dinai दिनदिनै *adv.* daily

din dinai दिनदिनै *n.* day

din ko ujyalo दिनको उज्यालो *n.* daylight

din r rat saman hune samay दिन र रात समान हुने समय *n.* equinox

dinko दिनको *adj.* diurnal

dinu दिनु *v.* bestow

dinu दिनु *v.* deal

dinu दिनु *v.* endow

dinu दिनु *v.* give

dinu दिनु *v.* give away

dirghayu दीर्घायु *n.* longevity

disa दिसा *n.* f(a)eces

disa-pisab rokan naskane दिसा-पिसाब रोक्न नसक्ने *adj.* incontinent

disha दिशा *n.* direction

disha दिसा *n.* excrement

diunso दिउँसो *n.* daytime

diuso ko khana दिउसोको खना *n.* lunch

diwa bhoj दिवाभोज *n.* luncheon

diwaliya banaunu दिवालिया बनाउनु *adj.* bankrupt

diwaswapna दिवास्वप्न *n.* daydream

do bhashe दोभाषे *n.* interpreter

dobar garnu wa hunu दोबर गर्नु वा हुनु *v.* redouble

dobbar दोब्बर *adj.* double

dobhan दोभान *n.* confluence

dobhase दोभाषे *n.* bilingual

dobryaeko doro/rekha दोब्ग्राएको *n.* crease

dodhar दोधार *n.* dilemma

dodhar दोधार *n.* fix

doharine kam दोहरिने काम *n.* recurrence

dohoro दोहोरो *adj.* duplicate

dohoro दोहोरो *adj.* two-way

dohoro pushti garnu दोहोरो पुष्टि गर्नु *v.* reconfirm

dohoryaune kam दोहोन्याउने काम *n.* repetition

dohoryaunu दोहोन्यानु *v.* repeat

dohoryaunu दोहोन्याउनु *v.* revise

doman garnu दोमन गर्नु *v.* vacillate

doos डूस *n.* enema

dori डोरी *n.* cable

dori डोरी *n.* guy

dori डोरी *n.* rope

dori डोरी *n.* string

dori tanne khel डोरी तान्ने खेल *n.* tug of war

dorie डोरी *n.* cord

dosh दोष *v.* accusation

dosh दोष *n.* blame

dosh दोष *n.* drawback

dosh दोष *n.* guilt

dosh bhaeko दोष भएको *n.* defective

dosh lagannu दोष लगाउनु *v.* accuse

doshi दोषी *adj.* guilty

doshi thaharyaunu दोषी ठहन्याउनु *v.* condemn

doshi thehrin yogya दोषी ठहरिन योग्य *adj.* culpable

dosro manchhe दोस्रो मान्दे *n.* second

dosro sarwottam दोस्रो सर्वोत्तम *adj.* second best

dosrosthan दोस्रो सीन *n.* second fiddle

dridh दृढ़ *adj.* dogged

dridh दृढ *adj.* pertinacious

dridh दृढ *adj.* tenacious

dridh nishchayi दृढनिश्चयी *adj.* strong-minded

dridhta दृढता *n.* determination

drishti दृष्टि *n.* eyesight

drishti दृष्टि *n.* sight

drishti kam hune rog दृष्टि कम हुने रोग *n.* glaucoma

drishti kon दृष्टिकोण *n.* outlook

drishti sambandhi दृष्टिसम्बन्धी *n.* visual

drishtikon दृष्टिकोण *n.* standpoint

drishtikon दृष्टिकोण *n.* viewpoint

drishtikon दृष्टिकोण *n.* vision

drishtipatal दृष्टिपटल *n.* retina

drishya दृश्य *n.* scene

drishya दृश्य *n.* vista

dubaunu डुबाउनु *v.* dip

dubli ra akarshak keti दुब्ली र आकर्षक केटी *n.* gamine

dublo दुब्लो *adj.* lean

dublo bhaeko दुब्लो भएको *adj.* emaciated

dublo-patlo दुब्लो-पातलो *adj.* gaunt

dublo-patlo दुब्लो-पातलो *adj.* scrawny

dublo-patlo दुब्लो-पातलो *adj.* skinny

dubnu डुब्नु *v.* drown

dubnu डुब्नु *v.* immerse

dubnu डुब्नु *v.* plunge

dubnu डुब्नु sink

dudh दूध *n.* milk

dudh jasto दूध जस्तो *adj.* milky

dudh khwaunu दूध ख्वाउनु *v.* suckle

dudh ko दूध को *adj.* lactic

dudh ko munto दूधको मुण्टो *n.* teat

dudh paine Thaun दूघ पाइने ठाउँ *n.* dairy

dudhe balak दूधे बालक *n.* nursling

duhkh दुःख *n.* grief

duhkh दुःख *n.* trouble

duhkh ka din दुःख का दिन *n.* rainy days

duhkh/yatna/dinu दुःख/यातना दिनु *v.* torment

duhkha दुःख *n.* sorrow

duhkha दुःख *n.* woe

duhkhad ghatna दुःखद घटना *n.* tragedy

duhkhad ghatna दुःखद *adj.* tragic

duhkhi दुःखी *adj.* miserable

duhkhi दुःख *n.* misery

duhkhi दुःखी *adj.* wretched

duhurt धूर्त *n.* cunning

dui दुई *n.* twain

dui chakke ghora gadi दुई चक्के घोड़ा गाड़ी *n.* hansom

dui jana ko bhidant दुई जनाको भिडन्त *n.* duel

dui vibhajan दुई विभाजन *n.* dichotomy

dui vivah garne vyakti दुई विवाह गर्ने व्यक्ति *n.* bigamy

duijanako दुईजनाको *adj.* dual

duipalta दुईपल्ट *adv.* twice

duipalta दुईपल्ट *n.* two

dukh दुख *n.* pain

dukh दुःख *n.* tribulation

dukh dinu दुःख दिनु *v.* grieve

dukhi दुःखी *adj.* disconsolate

dukhi दुःखी *adj.* lugubrious

dukhi दुःखी *adj.* sad

dukhi दुखी *adj.* sorrowful

dukhi दुखी *adj.* stunned

dukhnu दुख्नु *n.* ache

dukkha le chhat pataunu दुःखले छटपटाउनु *v.* writhe

dul dhare दुईधारे *adj.* two-edged

dul khutte दुईखुट्टे *n.* biped

dulayamko दुई आयामको *adj.* two-dimensional

dulne डुल्ने *n.* walker

dulnu डुल्नु *v.* ramble

dulnu डुल्नु *v.* stroll

dulo दुलो *n.* hole

duluwa डुलुवा *n.* wanderer

dumsi दुम्सी *n.* porcupine

dunga डुंगा *n.* boat

dunga डुंगा *n.* ferry

dunga डुङ्गा *n.* trimaran

durachar दुराचार *n.* despite

durachar दुराचार *n.* misconduct

durachar दुराचार *n.* wrong doing

durasth दूरस्थ *adj.* outlying

durbal दुर्बल *adj.* effete

durbal banaunu दुर्बल बनाउनु *v.* enervate

durbhagya दुर्भाग्य *n.* adversity

durbhagya दुर्भाग्य *n.* misadventrue

durbhagya दुर्भाग्य *n.* mischance

durbin दुर्बिन *n.* binoculars

durbin दूरबीन *n.* telescope

durgam दुर्गम *adj.* inaccessible

durgandhi दुर्गन्थी *adj.* foul

durgandhpurn दुर्गन्धपूर्ण *adj.* malodorous

durgha Tana दुर्घटना *n* accident

durghatna दुर्घटना *n.* mishap

duri दूरी *n.* distance

durjay दुर्जेय *adj.* impregnable

durlabh दुर्लभ *adj.* rare

durooh दुरूह *adj.* recondite

durupyog दुरुपयोग *n.* misuse

durwyawahar दुर्व्यवहार *n.* ill-treatment

durwyawahar दुर्व्यवहार *n.* malpractice

durwyawahar दुर्व्यवहार *n.* maltreatment

dusaahas दुःसाहस *n.* temerity

dushan दूषण *n.* contamination

dushkaram दुष्कर्म *n.* misdeed

dusht दृष्ट *adj.* naughty

dusht दुष्ट *adj.* vicious

dusht दुष्ट *adj.* wicked

dushta दुष्ट *adj.* miscreant

dushtata दुष्टता *n.* evil

dushtta दुष्टता *n.* turpitude

dut दूत *n.* herald

dutawas दूतावास *n.* embassy

dutawas दूतावास *n.* emissary

duvidha दुविधा *n.* quandary

duwai दुवै *adj.* both

duwidha दुविधा *n.* suspense

dwandatamak द्वन्द्वात्मक *adj.* dialectic

dweepsmuh द्वीपसमूह *n.* archipelago

dyaluta दयालुता *n.* lenity

dyaudhi ड्यौढी *n.* porch

E

eghara एघार *n.* eleven

ek एक *n.* one

ek chiine एक छिन *adv.* awhile

ek chinko nidra एक छिनको निद्रा *n.* nap

ek choti एक चोटि *adv.* once

ek dam एकदम *adv.* thoroughtly

ek ek garera एकएक गरेर *adv.* one by one

ek garaunu एक गराउनु *v.* unify

ek jaatko harin एक जातको हरिण *n.* elk

ek jaatko machha एक जातको माछा *n.* trout

ek jantu एक जन्तु *n.* mink

ek jatko kukhura एक जातको कुखुरा *n.* leghorn

ek kada bastu एक कडा बस्तु *adj.* adamant

ek kisimko bandkopi एक किसिमको बन्दकोपी *n.* kale

ek kisimko ghasrne jantu एक किसिमको घस्रने जन्तु *n.* dinosaur

ek kisimko kodhalo एक किसमको कोढालो *n.* spud

ek kisimko sano baaj एक किसिमको सानो बाज *n.* kestrel

ek koshiya एक कोषीय *adj.* unicellular

ek koshiya prani एक कोषीय प्राणी *n.* amoeba

ek kuna ma एक कुना मा *n.* nook

ek mat एकमत *adj.* unanimous

ek nambar ko आफू *adj.* number one

ek nash hunu उकनाश हुनु *v.* resemble

ek nishth एकनिष्ठ *adj.* single-minded

ek prakar ko podha एक प्रकारको पौधा *n.* chicory

ek rangko एक रंगको *adj.* unicolour

ek rupta एकरूपता *n.* uniformity

ek sadaniya एक सदनीय *adj.* unicameral

ek tak ko herai एकटकको हेराइ *n.* gaze

ek tarphi एकतर्फी *adj.* one-sided

eka samayma एक समयमा *adv.* once upon a time

ekadhikar एकाधिकार *n.* monopoly

ekagrata एकाग्रता *n.* concentration

ekai एकाइ *n.* unit

ekai nas ko एकैनासको *adj.* alike

ekai nase एकैनासे *adj.* stereotyped

ekai thaun ma udi rahanu एकै ठाउँमा उडिरहनु *v.* hover

ekaichoti एकैचोटि *adv.* simultaneously

ekal pariwar एकल परिवार *n.* nuclear family

ekalei basne vyakti एक्लै बस्ने व्यक्ति *n.* recluse

ekant एकान्त *adj.* lonely

ekant bas एकान्तबासव *n.* seclusion

ekapatti एकापट्टि *adv.* aside

ekata एकता *n.* union

ekata एकता *n.* unity

ekatamak एकात्मक *adj.* unitary

ekatra hunu एकत्र हुनु *v.* turn up

eke ek garera एक-एक गरेर *adv.* piecemeal

ekh lakh एक लाख *n.* hundred thousand

ekikaran एकीकरण *n.* unification

ekka एक्का *n.* ace

ekkassi modhinu एक्कासि मोड़िनु *v.* swerve

ekkhuttama uphranu एक खुट्टामा उफ्रनु *v.* hop

ekktar garnu एकत्र गर्नु *v.* garner

eklai le एक्लै ले *adj./adv.* single-handed

eklo एक्लो *adj.* alone

eklo एक्लो *adj.* lone

eklo एक्लो *adj.* single

eklo pan एक्लोपन *n.* lonelinees

eksre एक्सरे *n.* x-ray

ektar garnu एकत्र गर्नु *v.* muster

embulens एम्बुलेन्स *n.* ambulance

ena jasto dekhine plastic padarth ऐना जस्तो देखिने प्लास्टिक पदार्थ *n.* perspex

enamel एनामेल *n.* enamel

engine ko ghumai इंजनको घुमाइ *v.* rev

engineko ghumne bhaag इंजनको घुम्ने भाग *n.* rotor

enzyme इन्जाइम *n.* enzyme

eskimo dunga एस्किमो डुङ्गा *n.* kayak

esthan ko mukh स्तनको मुख *n.* nipple

eutai एउटै *adj.* singleton

eya ऐय्या *n.* ouch

eyalkhanko rakshak इयालखानको रक्षक *n.* warder

F

fahrenheit फारेनहाइट *adj.* fahrenheit

fapar jatko saag फापर जातको साग *n.* rhubarb

fariya फरिया *n.* petiticoat

fatar-fatar bolnu फतर-फतर बोल्नु *v.* prattle

fazool kura फजुल कुरा *n.* bunkum

feerj फ़ीज *n.* froth

focusko फोक्सोको *adj.* pulmonary

fohare फोहारे *adj.* frowzy

fohor फोहोर *adj.* bawdy

fohor फोहोर *adj.* sleazy

fohori फोहोरी *adj.* blowzy

fohorko thupro फोहोरको थुप्रो *n.* midden

frakilo baato फराकिलो बाटो *n.* boulevard

french brandi फ्रेन्च ब्रान्डी *n.* cognac

french madera फ्रेन्च मदिरा *n.* champagne

furniture nabhayko फर्निचर नभएको unfurnished

G

gaali गाली *n.* reproof

gaali denu गाली दिनु *n.* abuse

gabhnu गाभ्नु *v.* include

gabhnu गाभ्नु *v.* merge

gad gadahat गडगडाहट *n.* peal

gadda गद्दा *n.* cushion

gadda गद्दा *n.* pad

gaddhi गद्दी *n.* pouffe

gadeunlo गडेएँलो *n.* worm

gadh गढ *n.* stronghold

gadha गधा *n.* ass

gadha गधा *n.* donkey

gadha kalo गाडा कालो *adj.* jet-black

gadha rato rang गाडा रातो रङ्ग *adj.* scarlet

gadnu गाड्नु *v.* bury

gadya गद्य *n.* prose

gagan chumbi bhawan गगनचुम्बी भवन *n.* skyscraper

gagro गाग्रो *n.* pitcher

gahak गाहक *n.* customer

gahana गहना *n.* jewellery

gahana गहना *n.* ornament

gahana guriya गहनगुरिया *n.* trinket

gahior sambandh गहिरो सम्बनध *n.* affinity

gahirai गहिराइ *n.* depth

gahiro गहिरो *adj.* deep

gahiro गहिरो *adj.* profound

gahiro ghau गहिरो घाउ *n.* gash

gahiro hilo गहिरो हिलो *n.* slough

gahiro nindra गहिरो निन्द्रा *n.* coma

gahiro pwal गहिरा प्वाल *n.* pothhole

gahkilo गहकिलो *adj.* momentous

gahraun गह्रौं *adj.* heavy

gahun गहुँगो *n.* wheat

gahyo गाह्रयो *adj.* difficult

gai गाई *n.* cow

gai goth गाईगोठ *n.* cowshed

gai karaunu गाई कराउनु *v.* moo

gai wastu गाईवस्तु *n.* livestock

gaiko masu गाईको मासु *n.* beef

gainda गैंडा *n.* rhinoceros

gaine गाइने *n.* minstrel

gainti गैंती *n.* mattock

gair kanuni गैरकानूनी *adj.* illegal

gair kanuni गैरकानूनी *adj.* illicit

gaivastu गाईवस्तु *n.* cattle

gaivastuko dana गाईवस्तुको दाना *n.* fodder

gajal गाजल *n.* collyrium

gajar गाजर *n.* carrot

gal bandi गलबन्दी *n.* muffler

gala गाला *n.* cheek

gala ko niman bhag गाला को निम्न भाग *n.* jowl

galafko khel गल्फको खेल *n.* golf

galaincha गलैंचा *n.* carpet

galat गलत *adj.* wrong

galat andaj garnu गलत अन्दाज गर्नु *v.* miscalculate

galat arth lagaunu गलत अर्थ लगाउनु *v.* misinterpret

galat arth laune गलत अर्थ लाउने *v.* miscontrue

galat chapnu गलत छाप्नु *v.* misprint

galat dharna गलत धारणा *n.* misconception

galat phahami गलतफहमी *n.* misunderstanding

galat samjhanu गलत सम्झनु *v.* misunderstand

galat suchana dinu गलत सूचना दिनु *v.* misinform

galat udwaran dinu गलत उद्धरण दिनु *v.* misquote

galbadi गलबन्दी *n.* scarf

galicha गलीचा *n.* rug

galli गल्ली *n.* alley

galli गल्ली *n.* lane

galti गल्ली *n.* error

galti गलती *n.* fault

galti गलती *n.* faux pas

galti garn sakne गलती गर्न सक्ने *adj.* fallible

galti garnu गल्ती गर्नु *v.* err

gam paene rukh गम पाइने रूख *n.* acacia

gambhir गंभीर *adj.* earnest

gambhir गम्भीर *adj.* grave

gambhir गम्भीर *adj.* serious

gambhir गम्भीर *adj.* solemn

gambhir गंभीर *adj.* staid

gambhir banaunu गंभीर बनाउनु *v.* aggravate

gambhir mudra गम्भीर मुद्रा *adj.*
straight face

gamla गमला *n.* flowerpot

gan tantra गणतंत्र *n.* republic

ganana गणना *n.* reckoning

ganaunu गनाउनु *v.* stench

ganaunu गनाउनु *v.* stink

gand गाँड *n.* goitre

gandabasti गन्दा बस्ती *n.* slum

gandh गन्ध *n.* odour

gandhak गन्धक *n.* brimstone

gandhak गन्धक *n.* sulphur/sulfur

gangato गँगटो *n.* crab

gangi गन्जी *n.* jarsey

ganit गणित *n.* mathematical

ganit गणित *n.* mathematics

ganji गन्जी *n.* singlet

ganji गन्जी *n.* vest

gans गाँस *n.* guip

gans गाँस *n.* morsel

gansnu गाँस्नु *v.* attach

gantavya sthan गन्तव्य स्थान *n.*
destination

gantho गाँठो *n.* knot

gantho गाँठो *n.* tumo(u)r

ganti गन्ती *n.* count

ganti गन्ती *n.* number

ganti garn sakine गन्ती गर्न सकिने
adj. numerable

ganwar गँवार *n.* lout

ganwar गँवार *adj.* uncouth

gaphi गफी *n.* gasbag

gaphi गफ *n.* gossip

gaphi गफी *adj.* talkative

gara गरा *n.* terrace

garam गर्भ *n.* womb

garam bahas गरम बहस *n.*
wrangle

garam mijas ko गरम मिजासको
adj. hot-headed

**garam thaunma hune chalako
rog** गरम ठाँउमा हुने छालाको रोग *n.*
yaws

garbh dharan गर्भधारण *n.*
gestation

garbh nirodhak गर्भनिरोधक *n.*
condom

garbhapath hunu गर्भपात हुनु *v.*
abort

garbhdharan garaunu गर्भधारण
गराउनु *n.* impregnate

garbhnirodhak गर्भनिरोध *n.*
contraception

garbhwati गर्भवती *adj.* pregnant

gardan गर्दन *n.* neck

garha rato rang गाढ़ा रातो रंग *n.*
crimson

garho गाह्रो *adj.* truing

garib गरीब *adj.* indigent

garib गरीब *adj.* poor

garib गरीब *adj.* poverty-striken

garib basti गरिब बस्ती *n.* ghetto

garibi गरीबी *n.* poverty

garjan गर्जन *n.* roar

garjane गर्जने *adj.* thunderous

garjanu गर्जनु *v.* howl

garjanu गर्जनु *n.* thunder

garmi गर्मी *n.* heat

garmi गर्मी *adj.* sultry

garmi sambandhi गर्मीसम्बन्धी *adj.* tropical

garna dinu गर्न दिनु *v.* let

garnai parne गर्नै पर्ने *adj.* compulsory

garnu गर्नु *v.* do

garnu गर्नु *v.* execute

garrha ratto rang गाढ़ा रातो रंग *n.* carmine

garwa गर्व *n.* pride

gas burner ग्यास बर्नर *n.* bunsen burner

gathiawat गठियावात *n.* arthritis

gathilo गठिलो *adj.* knotty

gathilo गठिलो *adj.* sinewy

gati गति *n.* momentum

gati गति *n.* speed

gati गति *n.* velocity

gati rodh गतिरोध *n.* impasse

gati rodhak गतिरोधक *n.* brake

gati sima गति सीमा *n.* speed limit

gati va chal badhanu गति वा चाल बढ़ाउनु *v.* accelerate

gatta गत्त *n.* cardboard

gatta गट्टा *n.* knob

gauaunu गाउनु *v.* chant

gauinu गाउनु *v.* sing

gaun गाउँ *n.* village

gaun ghar गाउँघर *n.* countryside

gaun khane katha गाउँखाने कथा *n.* riddle

gaunle गाउँले *adj.* rural

gaunle गाउँले *n.* yokel

gaunle yuvak गाउँले युवक *n.* swain

gaunthali गाँथली *n.* swallow

gawahi गवाही *n.* testimony

gayak गायक *n.* singer

gayak गायक *n.* vocalist

gayak dalko गायक-दलको *adj.* choral

gayak haru ko dal गायकहरूको दल *n.* choir

gayak haru ko dal गायकहरूको दल *n.* chorus

geda gudi गेडागुडी *n.* legume

geda phal गेडा फल *n.* berry

gene जीन *n.* gene

geru rang गेरु रङ्ग *n.* raddle

ghaantiko rog घाँटीको रोग *n.* diptheria

ghaat घाट *n.* quay

ghach ghachy aunu घचघच्याउनु *v.* jog

ghachetnu घचेट्नु *v.* shove

ghadi घडी *n.* clock

ghadi घडी *n.* timepiece

ghadi घडी *n.* watch

ghadisaj घडीसाज *n.* watchmaker

gham घाम *n.* sunshine

gham chasma घाम चस्मा *n.* sunglasses

gham chhata घाम छाता *n.* parasol

gham lageko घाम लागेको *adj.* sunny

gham ma laune kalo chasma घाममा लाउने कालो चस्मा *n.* goggles

gham pani khaeko घाम पानी खाएको *adj.* weather-beaten

ghamand घमण्ड *n.* conceit

ghamand घमण्ड *n.* vanity

ghamandi घमण्डी *adj.* haughty

ghamandi घमण्डी *adj.* haughty

ghamandi घमण्डी *adj.* hoity-toity

ghamandi घमण्डी *adj.* proud

ghamandi manchhe घमण्डी मान्छे *n.* snob

ghamaura घमौरा *n.* heat rash

ghan घन *n.* cube

ghan धन *n.* hammer

ghana घना *adj.* dense

ghana awadi bhaeko घना आवादी भएको *adj.* populous

ghanisht saathi घनिष्ठ साथी *n.* chum

ghanishth घनिष्ठ *adj.* intimate

ghankanu घन्कनु *v.* reverberate

ghanm le dadheko घामले डढेको *adj.* sunburnt

ghans khane jantu घाँस खाने जन्तु *adj.* graminivorous

ghans khane jantu घाँस *n.* grass

ghanse chaur घाँस चौर *n.* turf

ghanta घण्टा *n.* hour

ghantakar pushp घण्टाकार पुष्प *n.* tulip

ghanti घण्टी *n.* bell

ghanti घण्टी *n.* gong

ghanti घाँटी *n.* throat

ghanti sunine rog घाँटी सुनिने रोग *n.* quinsy

ghanti thunnu घाँटी थुन्नु *v.* strangle

ghar घर *n.* home

ghar घर *n.* house

ghar bhitra घरभित्र *adv.* indoors

ghar jagga घरजग्गा *n.* real estate

ghar jagga घर *n.* residence

ghar jalouney dosh घर जलाउने दोष *n.* arson

ghar ki malikni घरकी मालिक्नी *n.* matron

ghar na bhaeko घर नभएको *adj.* homeless

ghar pariwar घरपरिवार *n.* household

ghar patini घरपटिनी *n.* landlady

ghar patini घरपटी *n.* landlord

ghar samjhi rahane घर सम्झिरहने *adj.* homesich

ghar wa sathivihin vyakti घर वा साथीविहीन व्यक्ति *n.* outcaste

gharelu घरेलु उद्योग *n.* cottage industry

gharelu घरेलु *adj.* domestic

gharha घड़ा *n.* ewer

gharha khairo गाढ़ा खैरो *n. adj.* sepia

gharighari घरीघरी *adv.* frequently

gharko chal bastu घरको चल वस्तु *n.* chattle

gharma chalaune phalam ka saman घरमा चलाउने फलाम का सामान *n.* hardware

gharra घर्रा *n.* drawer

gharwihin vyakti घरबिहीन व्यक्ति *n.* waif

ghasko maidan घाँसको मैदान *n.* ley

ghasko maidan घाँसको मैदान *n.* meadow

ghasnu घस्नु *v.* smear

ghasrane jantu घस्रने जन्तु *n.* reptile

ghasranu घस्रनु *v.* crawl

ghat ko malik घट्टको मालिक miller

ghata घाटा *adj.* deficit

ghata घाटा *n.* shortfall

ghatak घातक *adj.* fatal

ghatak घातक *adj.* lethal

ghatana घटना *n.* incident

ghatau घटाउ *n.* minus

ghataunu घटाउनु *v.* diminish

ghataunu घटाउनु *v.* subtract

ghataunu घटाउ *n.* subtraction

ghatit hunu घटित हुनु *v.* take place

ghatiya घटिया *adj.* shoddy

ghatiya घटिया *adj.* third-rate

ghatna घटना *n.* event

ghatnaharu ko kramik vitran घटनाहरूको क्रमिक विवरण *n.* chronicle

ghatnapurjha bhraman घटनापूर्झा भ्रमण *n.* odyssey

ghatnasthal घटनास्थल *n.* locale

ghatnu घट्नु *v.* befall

ghatnu घट्नु *v.* subside

ghatnu घट्नु *v.* wane

ghau घाउ *n.* lesion

ghau घाउ *n.* sore

ghau घाउ *n.* ulcer

ghau घाउ *n.* wound

ghau ko papra घाउको पाप्रा *n.* scab

ghera घेरा *n.* band

ghera घेरा *n.* enclosure

ghera घेरा *n.* frame

ghernu घेर्नु *v.* enclose

ghernu घेर्नु *v.* envelop

ghernu घेर्नु *v.* surround

ghin lagdo घिनलाग्दो *adj.* hideous

ghin lagdo घिनलाग्दो *adj.* repulsive

ghine घिन *n.* dislike

ghirni घिर्नी *n.* pulley

ghirsanu घिसार्नु *v.* lug

ghisarnu घिसार्नु *v.* tow

ghoch pech घोचपोच *n.* pinprick

ghochako bar घोचाको बार *n.* paling

ghochnu घोच्नु jab

ghochnu घोच्नु *v.* poke

ghochpech घोचपेच *n.* sarcasm

ghod chadhi घोड्चढी *n.* equestrian

ghod daud kosabar घोडदौड को सबार *n.* jockey

ghoda घोडा *n.* horse

ghoda chadhnu घोडा चढ्नु *v.* mount

ghoda ko bachcha घोडा को बच्चा *n.* colt

ghoda ko jagar घोडाको जगर *n.* mane

ghodabaat ladaunu घोडाबाट लड़ाउनु *v.* unhorse

ghodi घोडी *n.* mare

ghop tinu घोप्टिनु *v.* turn turtle

ghopto घोप्टो *adj.* prone

ghor घोर *adj.* heinous

ghor घोर *adj.* tremendous

ghor apradhi घोर अपराधी *n.* felon

ghora hinhinaunu घोड़ा हिनहिनाउनु *v.* neigh

ghorako tapma nal thokne manis घोड़ा को टापमा नाल ठोक्ने मानिस *n.* farrier

ghoshana घोषणा *n.* proclamation

ghoshana garnu घोषणा गर्नु *v.* announce

ghoshana garnu घोषण गर्नु *v.* proclaim

ghoshit garnu घोषित गर्नु *v.* declare

ghoshna patra घोषणा-पत्र *n.* manifesto

ghoshnana घोषणा *n.* announcement

ghrina घृणा *n.* contempt

ghrina घृणा *n.* hate

ghrina घृणा *n.* hatred

ghrina garnu घृणा गर्नु *v.* abhor

ghrina garnu घृणा गर्नु *n.* animosity

ghrina garnu घृणा गर्नु *v.* detest

ghrinit घृणित *adj.* obnoxious

ghrinit घृणित *n.* scurvy

ghuincho घुइँचो *n.* multitude

ghuincho घुइँचो *n.* rush

ghulnu झुल्नु *n.* tilt

ghum phir garnu घुमफिर गर्नु *v.* rove

ghumakkad घुमक्कड *n.* rover

ghumante घुमन्ते *n.* tramp

ghumau घुमाउ *n.* turn

ghumhindne bekar vyakti घुमिहिँड्ने बेकार व्यक्ति *n.* hobo

ghumne iccha घुम्ने इच्छा *n.* wanderlust

ghumne yantra घुम्नु यंत्र *n.* rotary

ghumnu घुम्नु *v.* revolve

ghumnu घुम्नु *v.* wander

ghumto घुम्टो *n.* veil

ghun phir garnu घुमफिर गर्नु *v.* roam

ghunda घुँडा *n.* knee

ghunda ko chakka घुँडाको चक्का *n.* kneecap

ghunda samma ko gahiro घुँडासम्मको गहिरो *adj.* knee-deep

ghunda teknu घुँडा टेक्नु *v.* kneel

ghungro banaunu घुँगुरो बनाउनु *v.* crimp

ghurnu घुर्नु *v.* snore

ghus घूस *n.* bribe

ghus घूस *n.* graft

ghus घूस *n.* pay-off

ghus paith घुसपैठ *n.* infiltration

ghusarnu घुसार्नु *v.* push through

gija गिजा *n.* gum

gijyaunu गिज्याउनपु *v.* jeer

gilas गिलास *n.* mug

gilla garnu गिल्ला गर्नु *v.* sneer

ginni गिन्नी *n.* guinea

giraffe जिराफ *n.* giraffe

giraphtar garnu गिरफ्तार गर्नु *v.* arrest

girja गिर्जा *n.* kirk

girja ghar गिर्जाघर *n.* church

girjaghar ko khand गिर्जाघरको खण्ड *n.* aisle

girjagharka padariharu गिर्जाघरका पादरीहरू *n.* clergy

girjagharko bench wa asan गिर्जाघरको बेन्च वा आसन *n.* pew

girjagharko gajur गिर्जाघरको गजुर *n.* steeple

girjama bible rakhne desk गिर्जामा बाइबल राख्ने डेस्क *n.* lectern

girjamuniko kotha गिर्जामुनिको कोठा *n.* crypt

girkha तिर्खा *n.* gland

git गीत *n.* lyric

git गीत *n.* song

gitar गितार *n.* guitar

giti-natay गीति-नाट्य *n.* opera

glycerine ग्लिसरीन *n.* glycerine

go dhuli गोधूलि *n.* twilight

gobre kira गोब्रे कीरा *n.* beetle

goda गोडा *n.* leg

godam गोदाम *n.* godown

godam गोदाम *n.* warehouse

godawari phul गोदावरी फूल *n.* chrysanthemum

godh chadhi घोड्चढ़ी *n.* cavalier

godhuli गोधूलि *n.* dusk

godna गोदना *n.* tattoo

gohi गोही *n.* crocodile

gol गोल *adj.* round

gol bhenda गोलभेँडा *n.* tomato

gola गोला *n.* orb

golabari गोलाबारी *n.* fusillade

gola-barood गोला बारूद *n.* ammunition

golardh गोलार्ध *n.* hemisphere

goli गोली *n.* bullet

goli गोली *n.* tablet

goli handa ubhine dhang गोली हान्दा उभिने ढंग *n.* stance

golkrimi गोलकृमि *n.* roundworm

golmal गोलमाल *n.* confusion

golmal गोलमाल *n.* hubbub

gol-mal गोलमाल *n.* hanky-panky

golmej sammelan गोलमेज सम्मेलन *n.* round-table conference

golo गोलो *adj.* circular

golo गोलो *adj.* rotund

golo गोलो *adj.* spherical

golo sanu dhunga गोलो सानु ढुङ्ग *n.* pebble

golo vastu गोलो वस्तु *n.* disc, disk

goman गोमन *n.* cobra

gopniyata गोपनीयता *n.* secrecy

gopya/kura kholnu गोप्य∕कुरा खोल्नु *v.* let on

goreto गोरेटो *n.* by-road

goru गोरू *n.* bullock

goru गोरु *n.* ox

goru jasto गोरू जस्तो *adj.* bovine

goru wa bhedako charbi गोरु वा भेड़ाको चर्बी *n.* suet

goshthi गोष्ठी *n.* seminar

goswara hulak गोस्वारा हुलाक *n.* general post office

gota गोता *n.* dive

goth गोठ *n.* cote

gothalo गोठालो *n.* herdsman

graha ग्रह *n.* planet

grahak ग्राहक *n.* subscriber

grahan ग्रहण *n.* eclipse

gramophone ग्रामोफोन *n.* gramophone

gramophoneko sui ग्रामोफोनको सुई *n.* stylus

granite ग्रेनाइट *n.* granite

grantha ग्रन्थ *n.* tome

gras garnu ग्रास गर्नु *v.* engulf

grih karya गृह कार्य *n.* homework

grih prawesh samaroh गृहप्रवेश समारोह *n.* house-warming

grihini गृहिणी *n.* housewife

guchchha गुच्छा *n.* tuft

guddi hanknu गुड्डी हाँक्नु *v.* talk tall

gudi गुदी *n.* kernel

gufawasi गुफाबासी *n.* troglodyte

gujreko गुज्रेको *adj.* out of date

gula गुला *n.* testicle

gulaph गुलाफ *n.* rose

gulaph jal गुलाफजल *n.* rose water

gulaphi गुलाफी *adj.* pink

gulaphi गुलाफी *adj.* rosy

guleli गुलेली *n.* slingshot

guliyo गुलियो *adj.* sweet

gumaunu गुमाउनु *v.* forfeit

gumbaj गुम्बज *n.* cupola

gumbaj गुम्बज *n.* dome

gumbaj dar chhana गुम्बजदार छाना *n.* vault

gumnaam गुमनाम *adj.* anonymous

gun गुण *n.* merit

gun गुण *n.* quality

gun gunaunu गुनगुनाउनु *v.* hum

gun gunaunu गुनगुनाउनु *v.* murmur

gun mannu गुन मान्नु *v.* appreciate

guna गुणा *n.* multiplication

gund गुँद *n.* glue

gund गुँड *n.* nest

gunda गुंडा *n.* hoodlum

gunda गुण्डा *adj.* rovwdy

gunda गुण्डा *n.* scamp

gundri गुन्द्री *n.* pallet

gungaan गुणगान *n.* panegyric

gungan garnu गुणगान गर्नु *v.* glorify

gungunaunu गुनगुनाउनु *n.* croon

gunjan गुँजन *n.* reverberation

gunjine गुंजिने *adj.* resonant

gunnu गुन्नु *v.* multiply

gunta kasne byag गुन्टा कस्ने ब्याग *n.* holdall

gupha गुफा *n.* cave

gupha गुफा *n.* den

gupt गुप्त *adj.* covert

gupt गुप्त *adj.* occult

gupt ang गुप्त अङ्ग *n.* private parts

gupt prem garnu गुप्त प्रेम गर्नु *n.* intrigue

gupt pulis गुप्त पुलिस *n.* secret police

gupt rup ma गुप्त रूपमा *adv.* privately

gupt sabha गुप्त सभा *n.* conclave

gupt, vyaktigat गुप्त, व्यक्तिगत *adj.* privy

guptchar गुप्तचर *n.* scount

guptchar गुप्तचर *adj.* sneaking

gupti गुप्ति *n.* privacy

guptikura गुप्ति कुरा *n.* secret

guptmatdan गुप्तमतदान *n.* ballot

gurans गुराँस *n.* rhododendron

guru गुरु *n.* instructor

guru गुरु *n.* tutor

guru yojana गुरुयोजना *n.* master plan

gurutwakarshan गुरुत्वाकर्षण *n.* gravity

gurutwakarshan गुरु *n.* guru

gusseko vatavaran गुम्सेको वातावरण *n.* fug

gut गुट *n.* faction

gute गुट *n.* clique

gwala ग्वाला *n.* milkman

gyalan ग्यालन *n.* gallon

gyan ज्ञान *n.* cognition

gyan ज्ञान *n.* enlightenment

gyan ज्ञान *n.* knowledge

gyan ज्ञान *n.* wisdom

gyan ज्ञान *n.* wistful

gyane गाइने *n.* bard

gyane गाइने *n.* troubadour

gyani ज्ञानी *adj.* sapient

gyanko seema ज्ञानको सीमा *n.* ken

gyaranti ग्यारण्टी *n.* guarantee

H

haanu हान्नु *v.* smite

haar हार *adj.* resurgent

haatko isharale bolaunu हात इशाराले बोलाउनु *v.* beekon

haatmukh dhune हातमुख धुने *n.* toilet

habshi हब्शी *n.* jim crow

habsi हब्सी *n.* negro

hadbadaeko हडबडाएको *adj.* flustered

hadbadaunu हडबडाउनु *v.* bewilder

hadbadma हडबडमा *adv.* helter-skelter

haddi हड्डी *n.* bone

haddi va danthko kshay हड्डी वा दाँतको क्षय *n.* caries

hadh हद *n.* barrier

hadnata karani हाडनाता करणी *n.* incest

hadtaal हड़ताल *v.* strike

hagnu हग्नु *n.* defecate

haija हैजा *n.* cholera

haisiyat हैसियत *n.* capacity

hajam हजाम *n.* barber

hajar हजार *n.* thousand

hajar gram हजार ग्राम *n.* kologram(m)e

hajar warsh ko awadhi हजार वर्षको अवधि *n.* millennium

hajaraun हजारौँ *n.* thousands

hajir हाजिरी *adj.* present

hajir हाजिर *n.* roll-call

hajir hunu हाजिर हुनु *v.* attend

hajiri हाजिरी *n.* attendance

hajiri हाजिरी *n.* presence

hak dar हकदार *adj.* rightful

hakdar हकदार *n.* heir

hakim हाकिम *n.* boss

hal garnu हल गर्नु *v.* unriddle

hal garnu हाई गर्नु *n.* yaw

hal/samadhan garnu हल/समाधान गर्नु *v.* solve

halai हालै *adv.* lately

halat हालत *n.* condition

halat हालत *n.* plight

halbihe bhaeko हाल बिहे भएको *n./adj.* newly-wed

halchal हलचल *n.* bustle

halchal हलचल *n.* sensation

halchal हलचल *n.* shake-out

halchal हलचल *n.* shake-up

halchal garna sakne हलचल गर्न सक्ने *adj.* mobile

haledo हलेदो *n.* turmeric

halinu हल्लिनु *v.* wiggle

halka हल्का *adj.* slight

halka bear हल्का बियर *n.* lager

halka challe hanu wa chunu हल्का चालले हान्नु वा छुनु *v.* flick

halko हालको *adj.* newly

halla हल्ला *n.* din

halla हल्ला *n.* hubbub

halla हल्ला *n.* rumo(u)r

halla r vinod garne हल्ला र विनोद गर्ने *adj.* rumbustious

hallanu हल्लनु *v.* sway

hallanu हल्लनु *v.* wobble

hallaunu हल्लाउनु *v.* brandish

hallaunu हल्लाउनु *v.* shake

hallaunu हल्लाउनु *v.* wag

hallaunu हल्लाउनु *v.* waggle

halo हलो *n.* plough

halsal ko taja हालसालको ताजा *adj.* recent

halsalko हालसालको *n.* current

haluka dhangle हलुका ढंगले *adv.* gently

haluka ghussa hannu हलुका घुस्सा हान्नु *n.* rap

haluka peya हलुका पेय *n.* soft drink

haluwabed हलुवाबेद *n.* persimmon

hamesha ko lagi हमेशाको लागि *adv.* forever

hami हामी *pron.* we

hami lai हामीलाई *pron.* us

hamla हमला *n.* blitz

hamla हमला *n.* foray

hamla हमला *n.* onset

hamla garnu हमला गर्नु *v.* attack

hamla garnu हमला गर्नु *v.* zap

hamla/akraman garnu हमला/आक्रमण गर्नु *v.* invade

hamla/akraman garnu हमला/आक्रमण गर्नु *n.* invasion

hamro हाम्रो *pron.* our

hande rog हाँडे रोग *n.* mumps

hanga हाँगा *n.* branch

hanga हाँगा *n.* offshoot

hangan हाँगा *n.* bough

hangeriko raksi हंगेरीको रक्सी *n.* tokay

hani हानि *n.* damage

hani हानि *n.* detriment

hani हानि *n.* disadvantage

hani हानि *n.* harm

hani हानि *n.* harm

hani karak हानिकारक *adj.* injurious

hani karak हानिकारक *adj.* malignant

hani karak bastu हानी कारक बस्तु *n.* nuisance

hani rahit हानिरहित *adj.* harmless

hanikar हानिकर *adj.* noisome

hanikarak हानिकारक *adj.* harmful

hankai हँकाइ *n.* drive

hannu हुनु *v.* happen

hanphnu हाँप्नु *v.* gasp

hans हाँस *n.* duck

hans ko boli हाँसको बोली *n.* quack

hans kukhura adi हाँस, कुखुरा आदि *n.* poultry

hansaune gyans हँसाउने ग्याँस *n.* laughing gas

hansda galama parne khadal हाँस्दा गालामा पर्ने खाडल *n.* dimple

hansi हँसी *n.* ridicule

hansilo हँसिलो *adj.* smiling

hansiya हँसिया *n.* scythe

hansiya हँसिया *n.* sickle

hansiya हाँसिया *n.* sickle

hansnu हाँस्नु *n.* laugh

hanso हाँसो *v.* laughter

hanso हाँसो *adj.* ridiculous

hapkaunu हप्काउनु *v.* chide

hapkaunu हप्काउनु *v.* reprove

hapkaunu हप्काउनु *v.* scold

hapki हप्की *n.* rebuke

hapta ko akhiri din हप्ताको आखिरी दिन *n.* weekend

har हार *n.* necklace

har chij हर चीज *n.* everything

har mannu हार मान्नु *v.* knuckle under

har wyakti हर व्यक्ति *n.* everybody

haraeko हराएको *adj.* lost

haran garna nam milne हरण गर्न नमिल्ने *adj.* inalienable

haran garnu हरण गर्नु *v.* expropriate

haraunu हराउनु *v.* vanquish

harchur हरचुर *n.* mistletoe

hardik हार्दिक *adj.* cordial

hardik हार्दिक *adj.* hearty

harek हरेक *adj.* each

harek हरेक *adj.* every

harek tabar le हरेक तबरले *adv.* out-and-out

hareko हारेको *v.* defeated

harin हरिण *n.* antelope

hariyo हरियो *adj.* green

hariyo pariyo हरियोपरियो *n.* greenery

harkela हरकेला *n.* palm

harnu हार्नु *v.* lose

harsa हर्सा *n.* haemorrhoids

harsh हर्ष *n.* merry

harsh हर्ष *n.* rapture

harsh ashchurch adi jaher garne shabd हर्ष आश्चर्च आदि जाहेर गर्ने शब्द *int.* ha

haruwa हरूवा *n.* loser

haruwa हरुवा *n.* underdog

haryali हरियाली *n.* verdure

hasil garnu हासिल गर्नु *v.* procure

haso-khushi हाँसो-खुशी *n.* mirth

hast kala हस्तकला *n.* handicraft

hast maithun हस्तमैथुन *n.* masturbation

hast maithun हस्तमैथुन *n.* self-abuse

hastakshar हस्ताक्षर *adj.* autograph

hastakshar हस्ताक्षर *n.* handwriting

hastakshep हस्तक्षेव *n.* interference

hastmaithun garnu हस्तमैथुन गर्नु *v.* masturbate

hasurnu हसुर्नु *v.* devour

hasya abhineta हास्य-अभिनेता *n.* comedian

hasyaprad हास्यपद *adj.* ludicrous

hat हातगोला *n.* hand

hat halnu हात हाल्नु *v.* manhandle

hat le banaeko chitra हातले बनाएको वित्र *n.* sketch

hat milaunu हात मिलाउनु *v.* shake hands

hata हाता *n.* premises

hatahat हताहत *n.* casualty

hatar हतार *n.* haste

hatar हतार *n.* hurry

hatar garer हतार गरेर *adv.* pell-mell

hatar garnu हतार गर्नु *v.* hasten

hataun naskine हटाउन नसकिने *adj.* irremovable

hatauna layak ko हटाउन लायकको *adj.* removable

hataunu हटाउनु *v.* dislodge

hataunu हटाउनु *v.* displace

hataunu हटाउनु *v.* obviate

hataunu हटाउनु *v.* purge

hataunu हटाउनु *v.* remove

hataunu हटाउनु *v.* rid

hataunu हटाउनु *v.* rule out

hate byag हाते ब्याग *n.* handbag

hatemalo हातेमालो *adv.* hand in hand

hatgola हातगोला *n.* grenade

hathatiyar हातहतियार *n.* arms

hathatiyar हातहतियार *n.* munitions

hathi हठी *adj.* headstrong

hathi हठी *adj.* obdurate

hathi हठी *adj.* stubborn

hathi हठी *adj.* wayward

hathi हठी *adj.* wrong-headed

hathi r risaha हठी र रिसाहा *adj.* stroppy

hathihad हस्तिहाड *n.* ivory

hatiyar हतियार *n.* weapon

hatkadi हतकडी *n.* handcuffs

hatkadi हतकड़ी *n.* manacle

hatko nam हातको नाम *n.* cubit

hatle hirkaunu हातले हिर्काउनु *v.* pommel

hatnu हट्नु *v.* get out of

hatnu हट्नु *v.* pull out

hatnu हट्नु *v.* stand off

hatoutsaw हतोत्साह *adj.* dispirited

hatpat हातपात *n.* rough and tumble

hatpate हतपते *adj.* hasty

hatpherne हात फेर्ने *adj.* light-fingered

hattakatta हट्टा कट्टा *adj.* burly

hattakatta हट्टाकट्टा *adj.* stalwart

hattar हतार *v.* buzz

hatti हात्ती *n.* elephant

hatti ko darho हात्ती को दाह्रो *n.* tusk

hatya हत्या *n.* assassination

hatya हत्या *n.* murder

hatyara हत्यारा *n.* assassin

hatyara हत्यारा *n.* cut-throat

hatyara हत्यारा *n.* killer

hatyara हत्यारा *n.* murderer

hau bhau हाउभाउ *n.* posture

haubhau हाउभाउ *n.* pose

hausala हौसला *n.* encouragement

hausala हौसला *n.* morale

hawa हावा *n.* air

hawa हावा *n.* wind

hawa ghatt हावाघट्ट *n.* windmill

hawa ko jhokka हावा को झोक्का *n.* gust

hawa wa hawako jhoka हावा वा हावाको झोक्का *n.* flurry

hawai jahaj हवाईजहाज *n.* plane

hawai jahaj ko pankha हवाईजहाजको पङ्खा *n.* propeller

hawaiaddha हवाईअड्डा *n.* aerodrome

hawaijahaj unneko chakka हवाईजहाजको उत्रने चक्का *n.* undercarriage

hawapani हावापानी *n.* climate

hawbhaw garnu *v.* gesticulate

hayakulo हयाकुलो *n.* brisket

helicopter हेलिकाप्टर *n.* helicopter

helium हिलियम *n.* helium

helo हेलो *n./excl.* hello

hepnu हेप्नु *v.* scorn

her chah हेरचाह *v.* maintain

herai हेराइ *n.* look

herai हेराइ *n.* sight

herchah हेरचाह *n.* care

here her garnu हेराहर गर्नु *v.* stare at one another

herna layak ko हेर्न लायक को *adj.* spectacular

hernia हर्निया *n.* hernia

hernu हेर्नु *v.* behold

hernu हेर्नु despatch

hernu हेर्नु *v.* look up

hernu हेर्नु *n.* saw

hernu हेर्नु *v.* see

herwichar garnu हेरविचार गर्नु *v.* tend

herwichar/syahar garnu हेरविचार/स्याहार गर्नु *v.* look after

hichkichahat हिचकिचाहट *n.* hesitation

hichkichaune हिचकिचाउने *adj.* hesitant

hichkichaunu हिचकिचाउनु *v.* hesitate

hichkichaunu हिचकिचाउनु *v.* waver

high garnu हाई गर्नु *v.* yawn

hijje हिज्जे *n.* orthography

hijje garnu हिज्जे गर्नु *v.* spell

hilo हिलो *n.* mire

hilo हिलो *n.* mud

hilsa हिलसा *n.* herring

him manaw हिममानव *n.* snowman

him nadi हिमनदी *n.* glacier

him rekha हिमरेखा *n.* snowline

him-darar हिम-दरार *n.* crevasse

himjowar हिमज्वर *n.* malaria

himmat badhaunu हिम्मत बढ़ाउनु *v.* embolden

himmat na harne हिम्मत नहार्ने *adj.* indomitable

himmat todhnu हिम्मत तोड्नु *v.* unman

himnirodhi हिमनिरोधी *n.* antifreeze

himpat हिमपात *n.* snowfall

hindnu हिंड्नु *v.* tread

hindnu हिंड्नु *v.* walk

hinhinaunu हिनहिनाउनु *v.* whinny

hinsa हिंसा *n.* violence

hinsatmak हिंसात्मक *adj.* violent

hinsatmak wyawahar हिंसात्मक व्यवहार *n.* rampage

hinta हीनता *n.* inferiority

hira हीरा *n.* diamond

hirasat हिरासत *n.* custody

hisab garnu हिसाब गर्नु *n.* calculate

hisab garnu हिसाब गर्नु *v.* workout

hisab rakhne हिसाब राख्ने *n.* scorer

hisabkitab हिसाब-किताब *n.* account

hitaishi हितैषी *n.* well-wisher

hiun हिउँ हिउँ पर्नु *n.* snow

hiun chituwa हिउँ चितुवा *n.* snow leopard

hiun ko dallo हिउँको डल्लो *n.* snowball

hiun le dhakeko हिउँले ढाकेको *adj.* snow-capped

hiun le khaeko ghau हिउँले खाएको घाउ *n.* frostbite

hiund हिउँद *n.* winter

hiunko aandhi हिउँको आँधी *n.* blizzard

hiunko pahiro हिउँको पहिरो *n.* avalanche

ho हो *int.* o, oh

ho हो *adv.* yea

ho हो *n.* yes

ho halla होहल्ला *n.* uproar

ho halla gari ramailo garnu होहल्ला गरी रमाइलो गर्नु *v.* revel

hocho होचो *adj.* low

hochyunu हाच्याउनु *v.* degrade

hodh garne होड़ गर्ने *adj.* vying

hohalla होहल्ला *n.* commotion

hohalla होहल्ला *n.* disorder

ho-jasto garnu हो-जस्तो गर्नु *v.* simulate

hola होला *adv.* probably

hoseyar होशियार *adj.* alert

hoshiyar होशियार *adj.* careful

hoshiyar होशियार *adj.* caution

hosma bnhaeko होसमा भएको *adj.* conscious

hotel होटेल *n.* hotel

hotel ko mukhiya vansay होटलको मुख्य भान्से *n.* chef

hridaya ghat हृदयघात *n.* heart attack

hridaya widarak हृदयविदारक *adj.* heart-rending

hukka हुक्का *n.* hookah

hukka हुक्का *n.* hubble-bubble

hukum हुकुम *n.* order

hukum chalaune हुकुम चलाउने *adj.* imperious

hukum chalaunu हुकुम चलाउने *adj.* peremptory

hul हूल *n.* mob

hulak adda हुलाकअड्डा *n.* post office

hulak mahsul हुलाकमहसुल *n.* postage

hulak tikat हुलाकटिकट *n.* postage stamp

hulakadda ko hakim हुलाकअड्डाको हाकिम *n.* postmaster

hulaki हुलाकी *n.* mailman

hulaki हुलाकी *n.* postman

huldanga हूलदङ्गा *n.* riot

hullarhbaaj हुल्लड़बाज *adj.* rowdy

hulyaha हुल्याहा *n.* rioter

hulyaha हल्याहो *n.* roughneck

huna anteko हुन अँटेको *adj.* imminent

huna sakchha हुन सक्छ *adv.* possibly

huna sakhha हुनसक्छ *adv.* maybe

huna sakne हुन सक्ने *adj.* probable

hunewala हुनेवाला *adj.* would-be

hunu हुनु *v.* be

hunu हुनु *v.* become

hunu हुनु *v.* occur

hunu हुल्लु *v.* push in

huri हुरी *n.* genie

huri हुरी *n.* gnu

hurkaunu हुर्काउनु *v.* bring up

huttinu हुत्तिनु *v.* dash

hutyaunu हुत्याउनु *v.* hurl

hwel machha ह्वेल माछा *n.* whale

hydrogen bum हाइड्रोजन बम *n.* h-bomb

I

ialama sheesha halne vyakti इयालमा शीशा हाल्ने व्यक्ति *n.* glazier

iash rakhne bakas लाश राख्ने वाकस *n.* coffin

iccha gari va nagrikan इच्छा गरी वा नगरीकन *adv.* willy-nilly

ichchha इच्छा *n.* desire

ichchha इच्छा *n.* intention

ichchha dhin इच्छाधीन *adj.* optional

ichchha shakti इच्छाशक्ति *n.* will power

ichchha/kamna garnu इच्छा⁄कामना गर्नु *v.* wish

ichchhuk इच्छुक *adj.* wishful

ijjat इज्जत *n.* credit

ijjat इज्जत *n.* kudos

ijjat इज्जत *n.* prestige

ijjat इज्जत *n.* reputation

ijjat bachananu ईज्जत बचाउनु *v.* save one's face

ikh ईख *n.* grudge

ikhalu इखालु *adj.* spiteful

ikhalu इखालु *adj* jealous

imaandari ईमानदारी *n.* probity

imali इमली *n.* tamarind

imandar इमानदार *adj.* faithful

imandar इमानदार *adj.* honest

inam इनाम *n.* prize

inam इनाम *n.* reward

inchi इन्ची *n.* inch

indhan इन्धन *n.* fuel

indreni इन्द्रेणी *n.* rainbow

injiniyar इन्जिनियर *n.* engineer

inkar garnu इन्कार गर्नु *v.* deny

inkar garnu इन्कार गर्नु *n.* rejection

inkar/aswikar garnu इन्कार⁄अस्वीकार गर्नु *v.* reject

insaph इन्साफ *n.* judg(e)ment

insulin इन्सुलिन *n.* insulin

inta ईंटा *n.* brick

irshya garn yogya ईर्ष्या गर्न योग्य *adj.* enviable

irshya garnu ईर्ष्या गर्नु *v.* begrudge

isai इसाई *n.* christian

ishara इशारा *n.* gesture

Ishwar ईश्वर *n.* god

ishwar ईश्वर *n.* providence

ishwariya dan ईश्वरीय दान *n.* charisma

isotope आइसोटोप *n.* isotope

ispat इस्पात *n.* steel

isterpachiko saathon ravibar इस्टरपछिको सातौं रविबार *n.* whitsum

istkot इस्टकोट *n.* waistcoat

italyko mudra इटालीको मुद्रा *n.* lira

itihas kar इतिहासकार *n.* historian

ityadi इत्यादि *pron.* so on

J

jaali जाली *n.* grating

jaatiya जातीय *adj.* racial

jaba ki जबकि *con.* while

jaba samma जबसम्म *prep.* till

jaba samma hundaina जबसम्म....
..हुँदैन *conj.* until

jabarjasti prawesh जबर्जस्ती प्रवेश *n.* intrusion

jadibuti जडीबुटी *n.* herb

jadnu जड्नू *v.* embed

jadu जादु *n.* magic

jadugar जादुगर *n.* juggler

jadugar जादुगर *n.* magician

jag जग *n.* foundation

jag जग *n.* jug

jagaaunu जगाउनु *adj.* awake

jagaunu जगाउनु *v.* rouse

jagaunu जगाउनु *v.* wake up

jageda जगेडा *n.* spare

jageda purja haru जगेडा पुर्जाहरू *n.* spare parts

jagga जग्गा *n.* plot

jagga dhani जग्गाधनी *n.* landholder

jagga dhani जग्गाधनी *n.* landowner

jagir chodnu जागिर छोड्नु *v.* resign

jagnu जाग्नु *v.* wake

jahaj जहाज *n.* ketch

jahaj जहाज *n.* ship

jahaj chadhnu जहाज चढ्नु *v.* embark

jahaj chalaune yogya जहाज चलाउने योग्य *adj.* navigable

jahaj ko dhoka जहाज को ढोका *n.* hatch

jahaj ko pal जहाज हिँड्नु *n.* sail

jahaj ma chalan garieko mal जहाजमा चलान गरिएको माल *n.* shipment

jahaj va railma जहाज वा रेलमा *adv.prep.* aboard

jahaj wa nauko bahir rakhiyeko जहाज वा नाउको बाहिर राखिएको *adj.* outboard

jahaj/gadima lagine mal matta जहा/गाडीमा लगिने मलमत्ता *n.* cargo

jahaji जहाजी *n.* sailor

jahan जहान *n.* spouse

jahan ko tyhin rahanu जहाँको त्यहीँ रहनु *v.* stay put

jahan sukai जहाँसुकै *adv.* everywhere

jahan sukai जहाँसुकै *adv.* wherever

jai dhanya जई धान्य *n.* oats

jai-jai जय-जय *int.* hey

jaijaikar garnu जयजयकार गर्नु *v.* acclaim

jail जेल *n.* gaol

jaiphal जाइफल *n.* nutmeg

jaitun जैतून *n.* olive

jal जाली *n.* net

jal stambha जलस्तम्भ *n.* waterspout

jal widyut जल विद्युत *n.* hydroelectricity

jal yatra जलयात्रा *n.* rafting

jaladhar जलाधार *n.* watershed

jalashaya जलाशय *n.* reservoir

jalbiruwa जलबिरूवा *n.* papyrus

jaldae gareko जल्दे गरेको *adj.* aflame

jaldae gareko जल्दे गरेको *adj.* alight

jaldevi जलदेवी *n.* naiad

jali जाली *n.* web

jalo जालो *n.* network

jalpan जलपान *n.* refreshment

jamani जमांनी *n.* bail

jamghat जमघट *n.* gathering

jamghat जमघट *n.* meet

jamin जमीन *n.* land

jamin ko tukra जमीनको टुक्रा *n.* patch

jamindar जमीनदार *n.* laird

jamma जम्मा *n.* sum

jamma garnu जम्मा गर्नु *v.* collect

jamma garnu जम्मा गर्नु *v.* gather

jamma hisab जम्मा हिसाब *n.* total

jamma hunu जम्मा हुनु *v.* assemble

jammai जम्मै *adv.* altogether

jammai जम्मै *adv.* totally

jamnu जम्नु *v.* congeal

jamnu जम्नु *v.* freeze

jan abhiruchi जन अभिरुचि *n.* human interest

jan andolan जनआन्दोलन *n.* mass movement

jan ganan जनगणना *n.* census

jan jati जनजाति *n.* tribe

jan mat sangraha जनमत संग्रह *n.* referendum

jan mat sangraha जनमत-संग्रह *n.* referendum

jan sampark जन सम्पर्क *n.* public relation

jan samuh जन समूह *n.* party

jan sankhya जनसंख्या *n.* population

jan shruti जनश्रुति *n.* folklore

jana jani जानाजानी *adj.* intentional

janajani जानाजानी *adv.* purposely

janamaghi जन्मअघि *adj.* prenatal

janamkaidi जन्मकैदी *n.* lifer

janamko जन्मको *adj.* natal

janamko जन्मको *n.* nativity

janampachhi hune जन्मपछि हुने *adj.* post-natal

janana ghar जनानाघर *n.* harem

janau जनाउ *n.* intimation

janaunu जनाउनु *v.* signify

janawarko laash जनावर को लाश *n.* carcass

janch जाच *n.* censor

janch जाँच *n.* examination

janch जाँच *n.* test

janchnu जाँच्नु *v.* examine

janchnu जाँच *n.* inspection

janchpadtal जाँचपडताल *n.* investigation

janchpadtal garnu जाँचपड़ताल गर्नु *v.* investigate

jane thaun जाने ठाउँ *n.* destination

janera garieko जानेर गरिएको *adv.* deliberate

jangali जङ्गली *adj.* savage

jangalipan जङ्गलीनन *n.* savagery

jangarilo जाँगरिली *adj.* active

jangi ain जङ्गी ऐन *n.* martial law

jangi jahaj जंगी जहाज *n.* armour

jangyaha जँङ्ग्याहा *n.* sot

janijani जानीजानी *adv.* knowingly

janiph kar जानिफकार *adj.* well informed

janjir जंजीर *n.* chain

jankari जानकारी *n.* know-how

janma जन्म *n.* birth

janma patrika जन्मपत्रिका *n.* horoscope

janmada mareko *adj.* stillborn

janmadin जन्मदिन *n.* birthday

janmedekhiko janamgat जन्मैदेखिको जन्मगत *adj.* congenital

janmeko जन्मेको *adj.* born

janneke kura जानेकै कुरा *n.* truism

jansadharan जनसाधारण *n.* hoi polloi

jansankhya ghataunu जनसंख्या घटाउनु *v.* depopulate

janshunya garnu जनशून्य गर्नु *v.* unpeople

janta जनता *n.* people

janter जन्तर *v.* amulet

janto जाँतो *n.* millstone

janu जानु *v.* go

janu जानु *v.* push off

janwer जानावर *n.* animal

jao जौ *n.* oat

japani kusti जापानी कुस्ती *n.* judo

japani kusti जापानी कुश्ती *n.* karate

japhat जफत *v.* confiscate

japmala जपमाला *n.* rosary

japmala जपमाला *n.* rosary

jar जार *n.* paramour

jara जरा *n.* root

jaraekoseengh जरायोकोसीङ *n.* antler

jarajirn budhiya जराजीर्ण बुढ़िया *n.* crone

jarimana garnu जरिमाना गर्नु *v.* mulct

jarnel जर्नेल *n.* general

jaro जरो *n.* fever

jaro aaune saruwa rog जरो आउने सरूवा रोग *n.* typhus

jarooratbandh jyada khanu जरूरतभन्दा ज्यादा खानु *v.* overeat

jarurat जरुरत *n.* necessity

jaruri जरूरी *adj.* essential

jaruri जरूरी *adj.* necessary

jaruri जरूरी *adj.* urgent

jasari pani जसरी पनि *adv.* anyhow

jasoosi जासूसी *n.* expionage

jasta जस्ता *n.* zinc

jasto जस्तो *adv.* as

jasto कम महत्त्वको *adj.* like

jasto dekhinu जस्तो देखिनु *v.* look like

jasto ki जस्तो कि *adj.* such as

jasus जासूस *n.* sleuth

jasus जासूस *n.* spy

jasusi जासूसी *n.* espionage

jasusi kam जासूसी काम *n.* secret service

jate जात *n.* caste

jatha bhabi जथाभाबी *adj.* haphazar

jati bhed जाति भेद *n.* racism

jati wadi जातिवादी *n.* racist

jatil जटिल *adj.* intricate

jatir awastha जटिल अवस्था *n.* imbroglio

jatisanhar जातिसंहार *n.* genocide

jatiya जातीय *adj.* tribal

jatiya gun जातीय गुण *n.* ethos

jau जौ *n.* barley

jawaph जवाफ *n.* answer

jawaph deh जवाफदेह *adj.* liable

jawaph dinu जवाफ दिनु *v.* reply

jawaph dinu जवाफ दिनु *n.* response

jayanti जयन्ती *n.* jubilee

je hos जे होस् *adv.* anyway

je sukai जेसुकै *pron.* whatever

je sukai जेसुकै *pron.* whatsoever

jebra ghoda जेब्रा घोडा *n.* zebra

jeera जीरा *n.* caraway

jeernovastha जीर्णोवस्था disrepair

jeev जीव *n.* organism

jeevanu जीवाणु *n.* bacteria

jeevanu marne aushadhi जीवाणु मार्ने औषधि *n. adj.* antibiotic

jeevdrawya जीवद्रव्य *n.* protoplasm

jelar जेलर *n.* turnkey

jelhalnu जेल हाल्नु *v.* imprison

jelinu जेलिनु *v.* ravel

jet wiman जेटविमान *n.* jet plane

jetha जेठा *n.* status symbol

jethaju जेठाजु *n.* brother-in-law

jethimadhu जेठीमधु *n.* liquorice

jetho जेठो *adj.* elder

jetho जेठो *adj.* senior

jhaddi झाड़ी *n.* underbrush

jhadi झाड़ी *n.* bush

jhadkelo babu झड्केलो बाबु *n.* stepfather

jhagada झगडा *n.* dispute

jhagada झगडां *n.* feud

jhagada झगडा *n.* quarrel

jhagada झगडा *n.* rough house

jhagada झतडा *n.* scuffle

jhagada झगडा *n.* strife

jhagada झगडा *n.* tussle

jhagada garnu झगडा गर्नु *v.* haggle

jhagadalu झगडालु *adj.* quarrelsome

jhagadiya झगडिया *n.* suitor

jhagdalu aeimai झगड़ालु आइमाई *n.* termagant

jhagralu झगड़ालु *adj.* pugnacious

jhagrha garnu झगड़ा गर्नु *n.* brawl

jhakki झक्की *n.* eccentric

jhalak झलक *n.* glance

jhalak झलक *n.* glimpse

jhalak झलक *n.* glow

jhalkan झल्कने *adj.* lustrous

jhamaunu झम्अनु *v.* swoop

jhamtanu झम्अनु *v.* spring on

jhan झाङ *n.* thicket

jhanda झण्डा *n.* ensign

jhanda झंडा *n.* flag

jhandai jhandai झण्डैझण्डै *adj.* virtual

jhare ko phal झरेको फल *n.* windfall

jhari झाड़ी *n.* gorse

jharkanu झर्कनु *v.* growl

jharna झरना *n.* falls

jharna झर्ना *n.* fountain

jharna झरना *n.* waterfall

jharna झारण *n.* weed

jharnu झार्नु *v.* bring down

jharnu झार्नु *v.* shake down

jhaskinu झस्किनु *v.* startle

jhatka झट्का *n.* jerk

jhatkeli chhori झट्केली छोरी *n.* stepdaughter

jhatkelo chhora झट्केलो छोरा *n.* stepson

jhatoro झटारो *n.* sling

jheel झील *n.* loch

jheer झीर *n.* skewer

jhiknu झिक्नु *v.* extract

jhiknu झिक्नु *v.* take out

jhilimili parnu झिलिमिली पार्न *v.* illuminate

jhilko झिल्को *n.* flash

jhilko झिल्को *n.* spark

jhilli झिल्ली *n.* membrane

jhilmil झिलमिल *n.* shutter

jhinga झिंगा *n.* fly

jhinge machha झिंगे माछा *n.* shrimp

jhinjha झिंझा *n.* twig

jhino झिनो *adj.* slender

jhismise bihana झिसमिसे बिहान *n.* daybreak

jhok झोक *n.* rage

jhoki झोकी *adj.* edgy

jhokraeko झोक्राएको *adj.* downcast

jhokrieko झोक्रिएको *adj.* depressed

jhola झोला *n.* bag

jholunge झोलुङ्गे *n.* suspension

jholunge pul झोलुङ्गे पुल *n.* suspension bridge

jholungo झोलुङ्गो *n.* hammock

jhonki झोंकी *adj.* tetchy

jhopari झोपड़ी *n.* hovel

jhukau झुकाउ *n.* proclivity

jhukau झुकाउ *n.* tendency

jhukaw झुकाव *n.* inclination

jhukeko झुकेको *adj.* inclined

jhul झूल *n.* mosquito net

jhulana झुलना *v.* swing

jhulnu झुल्लु *v.* sag

jhundyaunu झुण्ड्याउनु *v.* hang

jhupadi झुपडी *n.* hut

jhuppa झुप्पा *n.* bunch

jhurine झुरिने *adj.* friable

jhurrinu झुर्रिनु *v.* scorch

jhutho झठो *adj.* bogus

jhuto झूटो *adj.* mendacious

jhuto bolne झूटो बोल्ने *n.* liar

jhuto kura झूटो कुरा *n.* lie

jhuto prachar झूटो प्रचार *n.* propaganda

jhuto prem झूटो प्रेम *n.* affectation

jhutro झुत्रो *n.* rag

jhutro झुत्रो *adj.* worn out

jhyal झयाल *n.* window

jhyal khana ko hakim घ्यालखानाको हाकिम *n.* jailor

jhyali झयाली *n.* cymbals

jhyalkhan झयालखान *n.* prison

jhyang pwale झयाङ्प्वाले *adj.* threadbare

jhyau झयाउ *n.* lichen

ji hajuriya जीहजुरिया *n.* yesman

jibro जिब्रो *n.* tongue

jiddi जिद्दी *adj.* pig-headed

jiddi जिद्दी *adj.* wayside

jiddi जिद्दी *adj.* wilful

jiddiwal जिद्दीबाल *adj.* obstinate

jiju bajai *n.* great grandmother

jiju baje *n.* great grandfather

jill pareko जिल्ल परेको *adj.* flabbergasted

jilla जिल्ला *n.* district

jimewari जिम्मेवारी *n.* responsibility

jimidari जिमीदारी *n.* manor

jimma जिम्मा *n.* charge

jin kapada जीन कपडा *n.* jean

jiper जिपर *n.* zipper

jipsum जिप्सम *n.* gypsum

jiri ko sag जिरीको साग *n.* lettuce

jiskyaunu जिस्क्याउनु *v.* tease

jit जीत *n.* win

jitnu जिलु *v.* conquer

jitnu जिलु *v.* excel

jitnu जिलु *v.* overpower

jitnu जिलु *v.* subdue

jitnu जिलु *v.* subjugate

jitnu जिलु *v.* surpass

jitnu जीत *n.* victory

jituwa जितुवा *n.* winner

jiundo जिउँदो *adj.* alive

jiundo जिउँदो *adj.* live

jiunu, bachnu जीउनु, बाँच्नु *v.* live

jiwan जीवन *n.* life

jiwan bima जीवनबीमा *n.* life insurance

jiwan chakra जीवनचक्र *n.* life cycle

jiwan charya जीवनचर्या *n.* career

jiwan charya जीवनचर्या *n.* way of life

jiwan dhanne wastu जीवन धान्ने वस्तु *n.* lifeblood

jiwan shakti जीवनशक्ति *n.* vitality

jiwan star जीवन स्तर *n.* standard of living

jiwanu जीवाणु *n.* microbe

jiwika जीविका *n.* livelihood

jiwika जीविका *adj.* living

jiwkosth जीवकोष्ठ *n.* cell

job sanga जोडसँग *adv.* vigorously

jod जोड *n.* link

jod dar जोडदार *adj.* vigorous

jod garnu जोड गर्नु *v.* persist

jod le kura garnu जोडले कुरा गर्नु *v.* sound off

jod le tannu जोडले तान्नु *v.* tug

joda जोडा *n.* couple

joddinu जोड दिनु *v.* insist

jodh जोड *n.* addition

jodi जोडी *n.* pair

jodinu जोडिनु *v.* ally

jodinu जोडिनु *v.* interlace

jodiyeko bhaag जोड़िएको भाग *n.* extension

jodnu जोड्नु *v.* add

jodnu जोड्नु *v.* connect

jodnu जोड्नु *v.* interlink

jodnu जोड्नु *v.* sum up

jodnu जोड्नु *v.* unite

jogini जोगिनी *n.* nun

jokhim जोखिम *n.* risk

jokhimpurn जोखिमपूर्ण *adj.* risky

jokhimpurn जोखिमपूर्ण *adj.* touch-and-go

jokhimpurn kam जोखिमपूर्ण काम *n.* escapade

jokhnu जोख्नु *v.* weep

jor जोर *n.* emphasis

jor/takita garnu जोर/ताकिता गर्नु *v.* urge

jordinu जोर दिनु *v.* accentuate

jorko awaaz जोरको आवाज *n.* bang

jorle hansnu जोरले हाँस्नु *n.* cackle

jorni जोर्नी *n.* junction

jornu जोर्नु *v.* combine

jornu जोर्नु *v.* join

josh जोश *n.* enthusiasm

josh जोश *n.* fervo(u)r

jotaha जोताहा *n.* tiller

joteko jameen जोतेको जमीन *n.*
tilth

juhari जुहारी *n.* jeweller

juka जुका *n.* leech

jukao bhaeko झुकाउ भएको *adj.*
apt

jukti जुक्ति *n.* design

jukti जुक्ति *n.* means

julab जुलाब *n.* purgative

julaf जुलाफ *n.* laxative

julum जुलुम *n.* persecution

julus जुलुस *n.* parad

julus जुलुस *n.* procession

jumlyaha जुम्ल्याहा *n.* twin

jumra haru जुम्राहरू *n.* lice

jumro जुम्रो *n.* louse

jun जून *n.* moonlight

junga जुँगा *n.* whisker

jungha जुँघा *n.* moustache

junglee haas जंगली हाँस *n.*
mallard

junglee janwarko gufa जंगली
जनावर को गुफा *n.* lair

juni जुनी *n.* lifetime

junkiri जूनकीरी *n.* firefly

junkiri जूनकीरी *n.* glow-worm

jureli जुरेली *n.* nightingale

juro जुरो *n.* crest

jutaunu जुटाउनु *v.* provide

jutho जुठो *v.* defiled

jutho pura जुठो पुरा *n.* scraps

jutta जूता *n.* boot

jutta जुत्ता *n.* footwear

jutta जुत्ता *n.* shoe

jutta ko phitta जुत्ता को फित्ता *n.*
shoelace

jutta ko phitta जुत्ता को फित्ता *n.*
shoestring

juwa जूवा *n.* gambling

juwa ghar जूवा घर *n.* casino

juwa khelnu जूवा खेल्नु *v.* gamble

juwadi जुवाडी *n.* gambler

jwala ज्वाला *n.* blaze

jwala ज्वाला *n.* flare

jwalabina jalnu ज्वालाबिना जल्नु *v.*
smoulder

jwalamukhi ज्वालामुखी *n.* volcano

jwar bhata ज्वारभाटा *n.* tide

jwar grast ज्वरग्रस्त *adj.* feverish

jwarbhatako ज्वारभाटाको *adj.* tidal

jyada ज्यादा *n.* excess

jyadae bhavuk ज्यादै भावुक *adj.*
maudlin

jyadai badhi ज्यादै बढी *adj.*
exobitant

jyadai chhoto samaya ज्यादै छोटो
समय *n.* split second

jyadai dublo ज्यादै दुब्लो *adj.* raw-
boned

jyadai harshit ज्यादै हर्षित *adj.*
overjoyed

jyadai risaunu ज्यादै रिसाउनु *v.* see
red

jyadai thulo ज्यादै ठूलो *adj.*
gigantic

jyadai thulo ज्यादै ठूलो *adj.*
immense

jyaket ज्याकोट *n.* jacket

jyalkhana झ्यालखाना *n.* jail

jyami ज्यामी *n.* labo(u)rer

jyanjane ज्यान जाने *adj.* fatal

jyasal ज्यासल *n.* foundry

jyotish shastra ज्योतिष शास्त्र *n.* astrology

jyotishi जयोतिषी *n.* astrologer

jyotishi ज्योतिषी *n.* fortune teller

jyotishi ज्योतिषी *n.* soothsayer

jyotishi ज्योतिषी *n.* stargazer

K

kaag kholnu काग खोल्नु *v.* uncork

kaarhadaar jhari कांढादार झाडी *n.* bramble

kaatar कातर *adj.* timorous

kaatnu काट्नु *v.* whittle

kabja haran garnu कब्जा हरण गर्नु *v.* dispossess

kabjiyat कब्जियत *n.* constipation

kabristan कब्रिस्तान *n.* cemetery

kabul garnu कबुल गर्नु *v.* undertake

kachaura कचौरा *n.* cup

kachchamal कच्चा माल *n.* raw material

kachha kaam garer bigarnu कच्चा काम गरेर बिगार्नु *v.* botch

kachhad कछाड *n.* loincloth

kachhuwa कछुवा *n.* tortoise

kada कड़ा *n.* acrid

kada कडा *adj.* harsh

kada कडा *adj.* severe

kada koila कड़ा कोइला *n.* anthracite

kada prayog ko lagi banaieko कडा प्रयोगको लागि बनाइएको *adj.* heavy-duty

kada ra sakht कडा र सख्त *adj.* hard and fast

kadam कदम *n.* footstep

kadam कदम *n.* pace

kadam कदम *n.* stride

kadam कदम *n.* stride

kadha parikshan कड़ा निरीक्षण *n.* surveillance

kag काग *n.* crow

kag काग *n.* rook

kagaj कागज *n.* paper

kagaj ko jilla bhaeko kitab कागजको जिल्ला भएको किताब *n.* paperback

kagaj ko panch saya tau कागज को 500 ताउ *n.* ream

kagaj patra कागजपत्र *n.* document

kagati कागती *n.* lemon

kahan काँहँ *int. pron.* where

kahan कहाँ *adv.* whither

kahile कहिले *int. pron.* when

kahile kahin कहिलेकाहीँ हुने *adv.* occasionally

kahile kahin matai कहिलेकाहीँ मात्रै *adv.* seldom

kahile kahin matai कहिलेकाहीँ *adv.* sometimes

kahile pani hoina कहिले पनि होइन *adv.* never

kahin कहीँ *adv.* somewhere

kahin katai pani hoina कहीँ कतै पनि होइन *adv.* nowhere

kahin pani कही पनि *adv.* anywere

kaida काइदा *n.* etiquette

kaida काइदा *n.* manner

kaida काइदा *n.* mode

kaida काई *n.* moss

kaida sita काइदासित *n.* orderly

kaidi कैदी *n.* prisoner

kailo-pahelo rangko कैलो-पहेंलो रंगको *adj.* tawny

kainchi कैंची *n.* scissors

kajol काजल *n.* snuff

kaju काजु *n.* cashew nut

kakh काख *n.* lap

kaki काकी *n.* aunt

kal कल *n.* engine

kal कल *n.* machine

kal chaundo कल्चौंडो *n.* udder

kala कला *n.* art

kala nirmith bastu कला निर्मित बस्तु *n.* artifact

kalakar कलाकार *n.* artist

kalam कलम *n.* pen

kalamko tuppo *n.* nib

kalank कलंक *v.* slur

kalegeo ko rog कलेजोको रोग *n.* cirrhosis

kalejo कलेजो *n.* liver

kalejo कलेजो *n.* liver

kalejoko rog कलेजोको रोग *n.* hepatitis

kali gadhi कालिगढी *n.* workmanship

kalij कालिज *n.* pheasant

kalilo कलिलो *adj.* tender

kalkothari कालकोठरी *n.* dungeon

kalo कालो *adj.* black

kalo kapal bhaeki aimai कालो कपाल भएकी आइमाई *n.* brunette

kalo rangko chattan कालो रंग का चट्टान *n.* basalt

kaloranko कालो रंगको *adj.* dusky

kalpana कल्पना *n.* imagination

kalpanik काल्पनिक *adj.* ideal

kalpanik काल्पनिक *adj* non-existent

kalpanik काल्पनिक *adj.* romantic

kalpanik काल्पनिक *adj.* fictitious

kalpanik bayan काल्पलिक बयान *n.* fiction

kalpurja sambandhi कलपुर्जासम्बन्धी *adj.* mechanical

kalushit parnu कलुषित पार्नु *v.* sully

kalyan कल्याण *n.* weakness

kalyan कल्याण *n.* weal

kalyan कल्याण *n.* welfare

kalyan कल्याण *n.* well-being

kalyankari rajya कल्याणकारी राज्य *n.* welfare state

kam काम *n.* deed

kam काम *n.* duty

kam काम *n.* employment

kam काम *n.* function

kam कम *adj.* insufficent

kam काम *n.* labo(u)r

kam कमी *adj.* less

kam काम *n.* proceeding

kam काम *n.* task

kam काम *n.* work

kam काम *n.* engagement

kam antilo कम आँटिलो *adj.* half-hearted

kam bolne कम बोल्ने *adj.* taciturn

kam chalau कामचलाउ *adj.* workable

kam chalau gyan कामचलाउ ज्ञान *n.* working knowledge

kam dinu काम दिनु *v.* employ

kam gahiro कम गहिरो *adj.* shallow

kam garai काम गराइ *n.* performance

kam gari dinu कम गरी दिनु *v.* water down

kam garne darko yunit काम गर्नू दरको युनिट *n.* horsepower

kam garnu कम गर्नु *v.* abate

kam garnu कम गर्नु *v.* alleviate

kam garnu काम गर्नु *v.* perform

kam garnu कम गर्नु *v.* reduce

kam garnu wa khali garnu कम गर्नु वा खाली गर्नु *v.* deplete

kam garnu wa khali garnu कम गर्नु वा खाली गर्नु *v.* detract

kam garnue काम गर्ने *n.* employee

kam jor hunu कमजोर हुनु *v.* run down

kam jor tuly aunu कमजोर तुल्याउनु *v.* weaken

kam kharch garne कम खर्च गर्ने *adj.* thrifty

kam kharch kiphayat garnu कम खर्च/किफायत गर्नु *v.* economize

kam kharchilo कम खर्चिलो *adj.* economical

kam ko bhar कामको भार *n.* workload

kam ma lageko/wyasta काममा लागेको/व्यस्त *adj.* engaged

kam ma lagnu काममा लाग्नु *v.* engage

kam mahattwa dinu कम महलत्त्व दिनु *v.* underrate

kam mahattwa dinu काम *n.* undertaking

kam nalagne cheej काम नलाग्ने चीज *n.* dud

kam sambhawan कम सम्भावना *n.* off chance

kam samjhanu कम सम्झनु *v.* underestimate

kam sikne vyakti काम सिक्ने व्यक्ति *n.* apprentice

kam uttejit hunu कम उत्तेजित हुनु *v.* simmer down

kam/shithil hunu कम/शिथिल हुनु *v.* let up

kamai कमाइ *n.* earning

kamal कमाल *n.* stunt

kamal ko phul कमलको फूल *n.* lotus

kamalo कमलो *adj.* soft

kamalo कमलो *adj.* soft-hearted

kamaunu कमाउनु *v.* earn

kambal कम्बल *n.* blanket

kamdar कामदार *n.* workaday

kamdarharuko thulo jamat कामदरहरूको ठूलो जमात *n.* manpower

kamdev कामदेव *n.* cupid

kami कामी *n.* blacksmith

kami कमी *n.* decrease

kami कमी *adj.* deficiency

kami कामी *n.* ironmonger

kami कमी *n.* lack

kami कमी *n.* reduction

kami कमी *n.* scarcity

kami hunu कमी हुनु *v.* run short

kami/abhaw bhaeko कमी/अभाव भएको *n.* deficient

kamij कमिज *n.* shirt

kamila कमिला *n.* ant

kamisan कमिसन *n.* commision

kamisan कमिसन *n.* kickback

kamjor कमजोर *adj.* feeble

kamjor कमजोर *adj.* unmanly

kamjor कमजोर *adj.* weak

kamjor banaunu कमजोर बनाउनु *v.* debilitate

kamjor banaunu कमजोर बनाउनु *adj.* dicky

kamlo hune कमलो हुने *adj.* pliable

kamma lyaunu काममा ल्याउनु *v.* exert

kammar कम्मर *n.* loin

kammar कम्मर *n.* loin

kammarko कम्मरको *adj.* lumbar

kammarko peerha कम्मरको पीड़ा *n.* lumbago

kamna lagne wastu काम नलाग्ने वस्तु *n.* hogwash

kamnu काम्नु *v.* dodder

kamottejak कामोत्तेजक *adj.* sexy

kampan कम्पन *n.* quake

kampan कम्पन *n.* shiver

kampan कम्पन *n.* vibration

kampani कम्पनी *n.* firms

kampas कम्पास *n.* compass

kampit swar कम्पित स्वर *n.* trill

kampyutar karya kram कम्प्युटर कार्यक्रम *n.* software

kamsal कमसल *adj.* mager/ meager

kamuk कामुक *adj.* erotic

kamuk कामुक *adj.* lewd

kamuk कामुक *adj.* randy

kamuttejanako charambindu कामोत्तेजनाको चरमबिन्दु *n.* orgasm

kan कान *n.* ear

kan कण *n.* grain

kan कण *n.* particle

kanch काँच *n.* crystal

kanch काँच *n.* glass

kanchho कान्छो *adj.* younger

kanchil garne कचिङ्गल गर्ने *adj.* fractious

kancho काँचो *adj.* immature

kancho काँचो *adj.* raw

kancho काँचो *adj.* uncooked

kancho काँचो *adj.* unripe

kand कन्द *n.* tuber

kanda काँडा *n.* prick

kanda काँडा *n.* thorn

kande काँडे *adj.* thorny

kandh काँध *n.* shoulder

kandh khum chyaunu काँध खुम्च्याउनु *v.* shrug

kangal कङ्गाल *n.* pauper

kangiyo काहीनउंदगियो *n.* comb

kanika कणिका *n.* corpuscle

kanjoos कंजूस *n.* skinflint

kanjus कंजूस *adj.* niggrdly

kanjus कन्जुस *adj.* stingy

kanjus कन्जूस *adj.* tight-fisted

kankal कङ्काल *n.* skeleton

kanko loti कानको लोती *n.* lobe

kankro काँक्रो *n.* cucumber

kano कानो *adj.* one-eyed

kanpnu काँप्नु *v.* quaver

kans काँस *n.* bronze

kanta काँटा *n.* fork

kantako bunai काँटाको बुनाइ *n.* crochet

kanth कण्ठ *n.* larynx

kantimai कान्तिमय *adj.* lambent

kanun कानून *n.* law

kanuni कानूनी *adj.* lawful

kanuni कानूनी *adj.* legal

kanya keti कन्याकेटी *n.* virgin

kanyariashi कन्या राशि *n.* virgo

kapaat कपाट *n.* valve

kapada कपडा *n.* cloth

kapada कपड़ा *n.* fabric

kapada कपडा *n.* textile

kapada ko jorni कपडाको जोर्नी *n.* seam

kapal dhukne rog कपाल दुख्ने रोग *n.* migraine

kapal ko kanta कपालको काँटा *n.* hairpin

kapal latai कपाल कटाइ *n.* haircut

kapas कपास *n.* cotton

kapati कपटी *n.* deceitful

kapati कपटी *adj.* two-faced

kaphi कफी *n.* coffee

kaphi काफी *adj.* sufficient

kaptan कप्तान *n.* captain

kapur कपूर *n.* camphor

kar laagne कर लाग्ने *adj.* ratable, rateable

kar lagaunu कर लगाउनु *v.* enforce

kar launu कर लाउनु *v.* compel

kar launu कर लाउनु *n.* compulsion

kar/badhya garaune कर/बाध्य गराउने *adj.* obligatory

kara twacha ko bahiri the कड़ा त्वचा को बाहिरी तह *n.* cuticle

karadi katai diyeko talab कर आदि कटाई दिएको तलब *n.* take-home pay

karadi katai diyeko talab कर आदि कटाई दिएको तलब *n.* tax

karalo pareko thaun करालो परेको ठाउँ *n.* escarpment

karan कारण *n.* cause

karan करङ *n.* rib

karan कर्ण *n.* rudder

karan कारण *n.* sake

karani कारण *n.* reason

karaunu कराउनु *v.* exclaim

karaunu कराउनु *v.* shout

karaunu कराउनु *v.* whoop

karbai कारबाई *n.* action

karchop कार्चोप *n.* embroidery

kardha क्रड़ा *adj.* dour

kardha कड़ा *n.* influenza

karesa bari करेसाबारी *n.* kitchen garden

karha kalo kath कड़ा कालो काठ *n.* ebony

karikadau nagarne कड़िकड़ाउ नगर्ने *adj.* lenient

karkash कर्कश *adj.* raucous

karkat rog कर्कट रोग *n.* cancer

karkhana कारखाना *n.* factory

karkhana कारखाना *n.* mill

karkhanama talabandhi कारखानामा तालाबन्दी *n.* lockout

karm chari कर्मचारी *n.* staff

karm chari/kamdar haru कर्मचारी/कामदारहरू *n.* personnel

karmchari tantra कर्मचारी तन्त्र *n.* bureaucracy

karni कर्नी *n.* trowel

karnis कार्निस *n.* cornice

karphyu कर्फ्यू *n.* curfew

karta कर्त्ता *n.* agent

karta कर्त्ता *n.* doer

kartakarak कर्त्ता कारक *n.* nominative

kartawya कर्त्तव्य *n.* obligation

karunajanak करूणाजनक *adj.* pathetic

karunras करूणरस *n.* pathos

karya कार्य *n.* affair

karya karini कार्यकारिणी *n./adj.* executive

karya kram कार्यक्रम *n.* program(m)e

karya widhi कार्यविधि *n.* procedure

karyakshetra कार्यक्षेत्र *n.* scope

karyalaya कार्यालय *n.* office

karyama parinat garnu कार्यमा परिणत गर्नु *v.* implement

karyashala कार्यशाला *n.* workshop

kasai ko kura कसैको कुरा *v.* quote

kasai to hunu कसैको हुनु *v.* belong

kasar कसर *n.* sediment

kasari कसरी *adv.* how

kasht कष्ट *n.* distress

kasht कष्ट *n.* hardship

kasht कष्ट *n.* suffering

kasht dinu कष्ट दिनु *v.* afflict

kasht dinu कष्ट दिनु *v.* bother

kasht dinu कष्ट दिनु *v.* inflict

kasieko कसिउको *adj.* tight

kasilo suruwal कसिलो सुरूवाल *n.* trews

kasingar कसिङ्गर *n.* rubbish

kasko कस्को *int.pron.* whose

kaslai कसलाई *int. pron.* whom

kasne cheej कस्ने चीज *n.* brace

kasrat कसरत *n.* gymnastics

kasrat कसरत *n.* physical exercise

kasrat dekhaune vyakti कसरत देखाउने व्यक्ति *n.* acrobat

kasturi कस्तूरी *n.* musk

kasturi mriga कस्तूरी मृग *n.* musk deer

kasur कसुर *n.* offence

katan कटान *n.* cut

katan कटान *n.* erosion

katari कटारी *n.* dagger

kath काठ *n.* wood

kath chiirne kar khana काठ चिर्ने कारखाना *n.* sawmill

kath ko mudha काठको मुढा *n.* log

kath ma naksha khanu काटमा नाक्शा खन्नु *v.* carve

katha कथा *n.* fable

katha कथा *n.* story

katha कथा *n.* tale

kathalo कठालो *n.* collar

kathalo कठालो *n.* lapel

kathar कातर *adj.* coward

kathar काथर *adj.* timid

kathawachak कथावाचक *n.* raconteur

kathchirne manchhe काठ चिर्ने मान्दे *n.* sawyer

kathe nyauri muso काठे न्याउरीमूसो *n.* weasel

kathin कठिन *adj.* arduous

kathin कठिन *n.* complex

kathin kaam कठिन काम *n.* feat

kathin pariksha कठिन परीक्षा *n.* ordeal

kathinai jhelnu कठिनाइ झेल्नु *v.* run up against

kathko काठको *adj.* wooden

kathko dhulo काठको धुलो *n.* sawdust

kathko ghar काठको घर chalet

kathko lamo patlo tukra काठको लामो पातलो टुक्रा *n.* lath

kathko mudho काठको मुढो *n.* block

kathko tero काठकोटेरो *n.* woodpecker

kathor कठोर *adj.* drastic

kathor कठोर *adj.* scathing

kathorta कठोरता *n.* rigo(u)r

kathpat काठपात *n.* timber

kathputali कठपुतली *n.* marionette

kathputali कठपुतली *n.* puppet

katla कत्ला *n.* scale

katla bhaeko कत्ला भएको *adj.* scaly

katmar काटमार *n.* massacre

katnu काट्नु *v.* amputate

katnu काट्नु *v.* deduct

katnu काट्नु *v.* slaughter

katnu काट्नु *v.* strike off

katro कात्रो *n.* shroud

kattar कातर *adj.* craven

kattar कटार *n.* dagger

kattar कातर *adj.* dastardly

kattar कट्टर *n.* hardliner

kattar कट्टर *adj.* orthodox

kattar samarthak कट्टर समर्थक *n.* zealot

kattarpanthi कट्टरपन्थी *n.* zeal

kattu कटु *adj.* caustic

kattu कट्टु *n.* shorts

kattu कटु *adj.* trenchant

katu कटु *adj.* mordant

katus कटुस *n.* acorn

katus कटुस *n.* chestnut

katusko rukh कटुसको रूख *n.* oak

kaukuti काउकुती *v.* tickle

kawach कवच *n.* panoply

kawi कवि *n.* poet

kawita कविता *n.* poem

kawita कविता *n.* poetry

kawita कविता *n.* verse

kayalnama कायलनामा *n.* confession

kayam rakhnu कायम राख्नु *v.* retain

ke के *int. pron.* what

ke ko lagi के को लागि *int. pron.* what for

kehi केही *adj.* some

kehi chhaina केही छेन *v.* never mind

kehi hoin केही होइन *n.* naught

kehi hoina केही होइन *adj.* nothing

kehi na bolne केही नबोल्ने *adj.* tight-lipped

kehi wastu केही वस्तु *pron.* something

kek केक *n.* cake

kendra केन्द्र *n.* centre (ter)

kendra केन्द्र *n.* nucleus

kendriya केन्द्रीय *adj.* central

kepasi केपासी *n.* maple

kera केरा *n.* banana

kera केरा *n.* plantain

kerau ko phul केराउको फुल *n.* sweetpea

kesh bandhne fitta केश बाँधने फिता *n.* snood

kesh sajja कश सज्जा *n.* hairdo

keshar केशर *n.* saffron

keta केटा *n.* boy

keta keti केटाकेटी *n.* kid

keti केटी *n.* girl

kettle drum केंटल ड्रम *n.* timpani

kewal केवल *adj.* only

khabar खबर *n.* news

khachakhach bhariyeko खचाखच भरिए को *adj.* overcrowded

khachchar खच्चर *n.* mule

khada खडा *adj.* upright

khadal खाडल *n.* pit

khadnu खाँदनु *v.* compress

khadyasamagri bharnu
खाद्यसामग्रीले भर्नु *v.* victual

khagol vigyansambandhi खगोल
विज्ञान सम्बन्धी *n.* astronomy

khaijandhi खैंजड़ी *n.* tambourine

khaila baila खैलाबैला *n.* tumult

khairo खैरो *adj.* brown

khairo rang खैरो रंग *n.* tan

khairo rato rang खैरो रातो रंग *n.*
maroon

khaja खाजा *n.* snack

khaja खाजा *n.* tiffin

khajanchi खजान्ची *n.* cahier

khajanchi खजांची *n.* treasurer

khajmajaunu खजमजाउनु *n.* muss

khajmajh parnu खजमज पार्नु *v.*
tousle

khajuro खजूरो *n.* millepede

khakar खकार *n.* phlegm

khaksi खक्सी *n.* sandpaper

khalbal खलबल *n.* fuss

khalbal खलबल *n.* to-do

khaldo खाल्डो *n.* ditch

khaldo खाल्डो *n.* groove

khali खालि *adv.* simply

khali खालि *adv.* solely

khali खाली *adj.* vacant

khali garnu खाली गर्नु *v.* evacuate

khallo खल्लो *adj.* insipid

khalnayak खलनायक *n.* villain

khalti खल्ती *n.* pocket

khalti ma rakhne sanu kitab'
खल्तीमा राख्ने सानु किताब *n.*
pocketbook

kham खाम *n.* envelope

kham खाम *n.* envelope

khamba खम्बा *n.* column

khamba खम्बा *n.* pillar

khamba खम्बा *n.* pole

khamba खम्बा *n.* post

khameer खमीर *n.* yeast

khamir खमीर *n.* leaven

khan nahune खान नहुने *adj.*
inedible

khana खाना *n.* meal

khana खाना *n.* repast

khana hune खान हुने *adj.* edible

khanapachhi khane mishthan
खानापाछि खाने मिष्टान्न *n.* pudding

khancho खाँचो *n.* need

khancho parda garine sewa
खाँचो पर्दा गरिने सेवा *n.* yeoman
service

khand खण्ड *n.* segment

khandan खण्डन *n.* denial

khandan garnu खण्डन गर्नु *v.*
confute

khandan garnu खण्डन गर्नु *v.*
contradict

khandilo खँदिलो *adj.* stocky

khane kura खानूकुरा *n.* eatables

khane kura खानेकुरा *n.* food

khane kura ko suchi खानेकुराको
सूची *n.* menu

khaner nikalnu खनेर निकाल्नु *v.*
unearth

khanera nikalnu खनेर निकाल्नु *v.*
excavate

khani khanne kam खानी खन्ने काम
n. mining

khanij खनिज *n.* petroleum

khanij padarh खनिज पदार्थ *n.*
mineral

khanjot खनजोत *n.* tillage

khannu खन्नु *v.* dig

khan-panma sanyami खान-पानमा
संयमी *adj.* abstemious

khanti खन्ती pickaxe

khanu खानु *v.* eat

khanyaunu खन्याउनु *v.* pour

khap tinu खप्टिनु *v.* overlap

khapada खपडा *n.* tile

khapakhap khanu खपाखप खानु *v.*
gobble

khapat/upbhog garnu
खपत/उपभोग गर्नु *v.* consume

kharab खराब *adj.* bad

kharab खराब *adj.* baleful

kharab खराब *adj.* inclement

kharab awastha खराब अवस्था *n.*
predicament

kharab bandobast garnu खराब
बन्दोबस्त गर्नु *v.* mismanage

kharab hunu खराब हुनु *v.* worsen

kharab intjam खराब इन्तजाम *n.*
mismanagement

kharab kam खराब काम *n.*
misdeed

kharab lakal खराब लकल *n.*
parody

kharani खरानी *n.* ashes

kharani ranga ko खरानी रंगको
adj. grey

kharayao खरायो *n.* rabbit

kharayo खरायो *n.* hare

kharayo rakhne khor खरायो राख्ने
खोर *n.* hutch

kharbuja खर्बुजा *n.* melong

kharch खर्च *n.* expenditure

kharch खर्च *n.* outlay

kharch garnu खर्च गर्नु *n.* spend

Kharcha garna saknu खर्च गर्न
सक्नु *v.* afford

kharchilo खर्चिलो *adj.* extravagant

kharchilo खर्चिलो *adj.*
uneconomical

kharchilo hathi खर्चिलो हात्ति *n.*
white elephant

khari खरी *n.* chalk

kharid खरीद *n.* purchase

khark खर्क *n.* pasture

kharo खरो *adj.* straightforward

khas खास *adj.* typical

khas kam ko lago kosh
chhuttyaunu खास कामको लागि
कोष छुट्टयाउनु *v.* earmark

khasi खसी *n.* mutton

khasi pareko bheda खसी पारेको
भेड़ा wether

khasi pareko ghora खसी पारेको
घोड़ा *n.* gelding

khasi pareko vyakti खसी परेको
व्यक्ति *n.* eunuch

khasnu खस्नु *v.* fall

khasre bhyaguto खस्रे भ्यागुतो *n.* toad

khasro खस्रो *adj.* coarse

khasro खस्रो *adj.* rough

khat खाट *n.* scaffolding

khat खत *n.* scar

khataeko kam खटाएको काम *n.* mission

khatam garnu खतम गर्नु *v.* exterminate

khatara ko batti खतरा को बत्ती *n.* red light

khatarako sanket खतराको संकेत *n.* alarm

khatarnak खतरनाक *adj.* dangerous

khatarnak खतरनाक *n.* hazardous

khataune/sumpane kam खटाउने/सुम्पने काम *n.* delegation

khatra खतरा *n.* danger

khatra खतरा *n.* danger

khatrama halnu खतरामा हाल्नु *v.* endanger

khaurai खौराइ *n.* shave

khediyeko gaivastuko hool खेदिएको गाई-वस्तुको हूल *n.* drove

khedo खोदो *n.* pursuit

khel खेल *n.* game

khel खेल *n.* play

khel adi shuru खेल आदि शुरू *n.* kick-off

khel bigarne manchhe खेल बिगार्ने मान्छे *n.* spoilspert

khel maidan खेल मैदान *n.* playground

khel pratiyogita खेल प्रतियोगिता *n.* tournament

kheladi खेलाडी *n.* player

kheladi खेलाडी *n.* sportsperson

khelauna खेलौना *n.* toy

khelkud खेलकूद *n.* sport(s)

khera खेर *n.* wastage

khera gaeko खेर गएको *adj.* wasted

khet खेत *n.* farm

khet खेत *n.* field

kheti खेती *n.* husbandry

kheti garnu खेती गर्नु *n.* cultivation

khichatani खिचातानी *n.* draw

khichnu खिँचिनु *v.* gravitate

khiinu खिइनु *v.* wear away

khip launu खीप लाउनु *n.* buckle

khisi, uphas खिसी, उपहास *n.* jibe

khiya खिया *n.* rust

khiya lageko खिया लागेको *adj.* rusty

khiya na lagne ispat खिया नलाग्ने इस्पात *n.* stainless steel

khoj खोज *n.* quest

khoj खोज *n.* trace

khoj talas/chhan bin garnu खोजतलास/छानबिन गर्नु *v.* look into

khoj/anweshan garnu खोज/अन्वेषण गर्नु *v.* explore

khojidal खोजी दल *n.* search party

khojnu खोज्नु *v.* look for

khojnu खोज्नु *v.* seek

khojtalash खोजतलाश *n.* search

khoknu खोक्नु *v.* cough

khokro खोक्रो *adj.* hollow

khol खोल *n.* sheath

khola खोला *n.* stream

khola ra bela खोला र बेला *n.* time and tide

kholai खोला *n.* rivulet

kholawa dhara ko pani खोला वा धाराको पानी *n.* running water

khole खोले *n.* gruel

kholinu खोलिनु *v.* unfurl

kholnu खोल्नु *v.* reveal

kholnu खोल्नु *v.* turn on

kholnu खोल्नु *v.* unbolt

kholnu खोल्नु *v.* unclench

kholnu खोल्नु *v.* unfasten

kholnu खोल्नु *v.* unfold

kholnu खोल्नु *v.* unlash

kholnu खोल्नु *v.* unleash

kholnu खोल्नु *v.* unpack

kholsa खोल्सा *n.* ravine

khonch खोंच *n.* gorge

khop खोप *n.* inoculation

khopadi खोपडी *n.* skull

khopari खोपड़ी *n.* cranium

khopaunu खोपाउनु *v.* vaccinate

khopaunu खोप *n.* vaccination

khopaunu खोप *n.* vaccine

khopilto खोपिल्टो *n.* dent

khopnu खोप्नु *v.* engrave

khor खोर *n.* coop

khor खोर *n.* fold

khorsani खोर्सानी *n.* chilli/chili

khosnu खोस्नु *v.* dismiss

khosnu खोस्नु *v.* grab

khosnu खोस्नु *v.* snatch

khot खोट *n.* flaw

khrimchinu खृम्चिनु *v.* crumple

khub khojnu खूब खोज्नु *v.* ransack

khudkila खुड्किला *n.* step

khudra खुद्रा *n.* small change

khudra bikri खुद्रा बिक्री *n.* retail

khudra pasale खुद्रा पसले *n.* retialer

khuilanu खुइलनु *v.* fade

khukulo खुकुलो *adj.* unattached

khukulo, phitlo खुकुलो, फितलो *adj.* lax

khula खुला *adj.* open

khula खुला *adj.* open-air

khula daraj खुला दराज *n.* rach

khula drishya खुला दृश्य *n.* panorama

khula motorcar खुला मोटरकार *n.* roadster

khulamanko खुला मनको *adj.* open-minded

khulast खुलस्त *adj.* heart-to-heart

khulast खुलस्त *adv.* openly

khulast खुलस्त *adj.* overt

khulast kura garne खुलस्त कुरा गर्ने *adj.* outspoken

khulast sanga खुलस्तसँग *adj.* frankly

khumchinu खुम्चिनु *v.* shrink

khup mileko खुप मिलेको *adj.* tailor-made

khur खुर *n.* hoof

khur murinu खुरमुरिनु *v.* tumble

khurpani phal खुर्पानी फल *n.* apricot

khus खुस *adj.* elated

khush खुश *adj.* happy

khush खुश *adj.* jolly

khush खुश *adj.* pleased

khush garnu खुश गर्नु *adj.* glad

khush hunu खुश हुनु *v.* rejoice

khushhal खुसहाल *adj.* well-to-do

khushi खुशी *n.* happiness

khushi खुशी *n.* joy

khushi खुशी *n.* rejoicing

khushi ko smarniya din खुशी को स्मरणीय दिन *n.* red-letter day

khushile खुशीले *adv.* happily

khusi खुसी *n.* delight

khusi खुसी *adj.* delighted

khusi parnu खुसी पार्नु *v.* gratify

khusiyali खसीयाली *n.* merriment

khuta dhakne patti खुट्टा ढाक्ने पट्टी *n.* gaiter

khuta ghisarer hindnu खुट्टा घिसारेर हिंड्नु *v.* scuff

khutta bajarer hindanu खुट्टा बजारेर हिंड्नु *v.* stomp

khutta chopne awaran खुट्टा छोप्ने आवरण *n.* leggings

khutta ghisarera hindnu खुट्टा घिसारेर हिंड्नु *v.* shuffle

khutta ko nan खुट्टाको नङ *n.* toenail

khutta na kamaune खुट्टा नकमाउने *adj.* sure-footed

khuttako chikitsa खुट्टाको चिकित्सा *n.* pedicure

khuwa खुवा *n.* cheese

khwaunu ख्वाउनु *v.* feed

khyaunu ख्याउनु *v.* erode

ki कि *conj.* whether

kichnu किच्नु *v.* crush

kihaki kapada खाकी कपडा *n.* khaki

kila किला *n.* nail

kila किला *n.* peg

kilip किलिप *n.* clip

kilkile किलकिले *n.* uvula

killa किल्ला *n.* fort

killa किल्ला *n.* fortress

kimbu किम्बु *n.* mulberry

kimti कीमती *adj.* precious

kina किन *int. pron.* why

kina bhane किनभने *adv.* inasmuch

kinaki किनकि *conj.* because

kinar किनार *n.* side

kinara किनारा *n.* brink

kinara किनारा *n.* coast

kinara nabhayeko topi किनारा नभएको टोपी *n.* tarboosh

kinarar किनारा *n.* beach

kinarma किनारमा *adv.* ashore

kinaro किनारो *n.* tatting

kinbhane किनभने *adv.* inasmuch as

kinmel किनमेल *n.* shopping

kinnu किन्नु *n.* buy

kiphayati किफायती *adj.* frugal

kira कीरा *n.* insects

kiran किरण *n.* beam

kiran किरण *n.* ray

kiraya किराया *n.* hire

kiriya किरिया *n.* oath

kiriyakhanu किरिया खानु *v.* swear

kirti कीर्ति *n.* fame

kisan किसान *n.* farmer

kisan किसान *n.* peasant

kisan warg किसानवर्ग *n.* peasantry

kishoravastha किशोरावस्था *n.* adolescence

kishorawastha किशोरावस्था *n.* salad days

kishorawastha किशोराअवस्था *n.* teens

kisim किसिम *n.* sort

kisim किसिम *n.* type

kismat किस्मत *n.* kismet

kismis किसमिस *n.* raisin

kista किस्ता *n.* instal(l)ment

kisti किस्ती *n.* tray

kitab किताब *n.* book

kitanu कीटाणु *n.* germ

kitli किट्ली *n.* kettle

kitnashak कीटनाशक *n.* insecticide

kitnu किट्नु *v.* pinpoint

ko को *prep.* of

ko chhoto roop को छोटो रूप *n.* varsity

ko choto roop को छोटो रूप gym, gymnasium

ko hunu को हुनु *v.* pertain

ko pakshma को पक्षमा *n.* behalf

ko samyama को समयमा *prep.* during

kocharnu कोचार्नु *v.* tamp

kodalo कोदालो *n.* hoe

kodalo कोदालो *n.* spade

kodhiko maal कौड़ीको माला *n.* wampum

kodo कोदो *n.* millet

kohi कोही *pron.* somebody

kohi कोही *pron.* someone

kohi hoina कोही होइन *n.* nobody

kohi pani hoina पासो *pron./adv.* no one

kohi pani hoina कोही पनि होइन *adv.* none

koila कोइला *n.* coal

kok कोक *n.* coke

kokh कोख *n.* womantizer

kolahal कोलाहल *n.* din

komal कोमल *adj.* delicate

komal कोमल *n.* pitful

komal कोमल *n.* supper

kon कोण *n.* angle

kon napne yantra कोण नाप्ने यंत्र *n.* theodolite

kopara कोपरा *n.* washabasin

kopila कोपिला *n.* bud

kopila halnu कोपिला हाल्नु *v.* burgeon

kora कोर्रा *n.* knout

korali gai कोरली गाई *n.* heifer

koram कोरम *n.* quorum

korara launu कोर्रा लाउनु *v.* flagellate

kori कोरी *n.* leper

korra कोर्रा *n.* whip

korra कोर्रा *int. pron.* who

korra hannu कोर्रा हान्नु *v.* flog

korra thoknu कोर्रा ठोक्नु *n.* lash

kosa कोसा *n.* pod

kose dhunga कोसेढुङ्गा *n.* milestone

koseli कोसेली *n.* gift

kosh कोष *n.* fund

koshish garnu कोशिश गर्नु *v.* try

koshma laune lep कोशमा लाउने लेप *n.* pomade

kosis garnu कोसिस गर्नु *v.* strive

kotha कोठा *n.* apartment

kotha कोठा *n.* chamber

kotha कोट *n.* coat

kotha कोठा *n.* room

kotha ko bhuin कोठाको *n.* floor

kothako chutiyeko bhag कोठाको छुट्टिएको भाग *n.* alcove

kothako sajawat कोठा को सजावट *n.* decor

kothama hawako jhokka कोठामा हावाको झोंक्का *n.* draught

kotyaunu कोट्याउनु *v.* pick

koya कोया *n.* bobbin

koyali कोयली *n.* cuckoo

koyha कोठा *n.* cabin

kram क्रम *n.* continuation

kram क्रम *n.* sequence

kramai le क्रमैले *adv.* respectively

krantikari क्रान्तिकारी *n.* revolutionary

kriket क्रिकेट *n.* cricket

kripa कृपा *n.* favo(u)r

kripa कृपा *n.* grace

krishi कृषि *n.* agriculture

krishi yogya कृषि-योग्य *adj.* arable

krismas क्रिसमस *n.* xmas

krismas chad क्रिस्मस चाड *n.* christmas

kritghanta कृतघनता *n.* ingfratitude

kritrim कृत्रिम *adj.* factitious

kritsankalp कृतसंकल्प *adj.* resolute

kriyapad क्रियापद *n.* verb

kriyarup banananu क्रियारूप बनाउनु *v.* conjugate

kriyasheel banaunu क्रियाशील बनाउनु *v.* activate

kriyavisheshan क्रियाविशेषण *n.* adverb

krodh क्रोध *n.* indignation

krodh क्रोध *n.* wrath

krubharuko tehkhana क्रबहरूको तहखाना *n.* catacombs

krudh parnu क्रुद्ध पार्नु *v.* enrage

kschamta क्षमता *n.* aptitude

ksham yachna क्षमायाचना *n.* apology

kshama क्षमा *n.* excuse

kshama क्षमा *n.* pardon

kshama क्षमा *n.* remission

kshan क्षण *n.* jiffy

kshariya क्षारीय *n.* alkali

kshati pura garnu क्षति पूरा गर्नु *v.* indemnify

kshati purti ko rup ma diieko wastu क्षतिपूर्तिको रूपमा दिइएको वस्तु *n.* quid pro quo

kshatipura garnu क्षति पूरा गर्नु *v.* offset

kshaya क्षय *n.* decay

kshaya rog क्षयरोग *n.* consumptive

kshaya rog क्षयरोग *n.* tuberculossis

kshepyastra क्षेप्यास्त्र *n.* missile

kshetra क्षेत्र *n.* range

kshetra क्षेत्र *n.* region

kshetra क्षेत्र *n.* sector

kshetra क्षेत्र *n.* territory

kshetra phal क्षेत्रफल *n.* area

kshetrako nap क्षेत्र को नाप *n.* hectare

kshetriya क्षेत्रीय *adj.* regional

kshetriya क्षेत्रीय *adj.* territorial

kshitij क्षितिज *n.* horizon

kshitij खितिज *n.* skyline

kubato laijanu कुबाटो लैजानु *v.* mislead

kucho कुचो *n.* broom

kucho कुचो *n.* brush

kucho launemanchhe कुचो लाउने मान्छे *n.* sweeper

kucho launu कुचो लाउनु *v.* sweep

kuddai कुद्दै *v.* romp

kuhina कुहिना *n.* elbow

kuhinu कुहिनु *v.* rot

kuhiro कुहिरो *n.* mist

kuhiro lageko कुहिरो लागेको *adj.* foggy

kuiro कुइरो *n.* fog

kukam मुकाम *n.* standstill

kukavita कुकविता *n.* doggerel

kukhura कुखुरा *n.* chicken

kukhura कुखुरा *n.* fowl

kukhuri कुखुरी *n.* hen

kukhuri कुखुरी *n.* hen

kukur कुकुर *n.* dog

kukur कुकुर *n.* doggy

kukur khor कुकुर खोर *n.* kennel

kukur ko chhauro कुकुरको छाउरो *n.* pup

kukur ko chhauro कुकुरको छाउरो *n.* puppy

kukurni कुकुर्नी *n.* bitch

kul कुल *n.* lineage

kul bansh कुल वंश *n.* clan

kulchinu कुल्चिनु *v.* trample

kuleen कुलीन *adj.* patrician

kulla garnu कुल्ला गर्नु *v.* gargle

kulli कुल्ली *n.* carrier

kulo कुलो *n.* gutter

kulpati कुलपति *n.* chancellor

kulyog कुलयोग *n.* aggregate

kumari कुमारी *n.* living goddess

kumari कुमारी *n.* mademoiselle

kumari keti कुमारी केटी *n.* maiden

kumari keti कुमारी *n.* miss

kumari meri कुमारी मेरी *n.* madonna

kumbhrashi कुम्भराशि *n.* aquarius

kumhale कुम्हाले *n.* potter

kumnai kisimle कुनै किसिमले *adv.* somehow

kun कुन *int.pron.* which

kunai कुनै *adj.* any

kunai kurama thapthaap कुनै कुरामा थपथाप eke out

kunai wyakti कुनै व्यक्ति *pron.* anyone

kunain कुनैन *n.* quinine

kunder belbutta bharnu कुँदेर बेलबुट्टा भर्नु *v.* emboss

kunjo कूँजो *n.* hunchback

kupan कुपन *n.* coupon

kuposhan कुपोषण *n.* malnutrition

kura कुरा *n.* fact

kura kholnu कुरा खोल्नु *v.* spill the beans

kura sake teliphon rakun कुरा सकेपछि टेलिफोन राख्नु *v.* hang up

kura tarnu कुरा तर्नु *v.* avert

kurakani कुराकानी *n.* chitchat

kurakani कुराकानी *n.* conversation

kurakani कुराकानी *n.* dialogue

kurakani कुराकानी *n.* talk

kurchana कुरचना *n.* malformation

kurkuchcha कुर्कुच्चा *n.* heel

kursi कुर्सी *n.* chair

kurup कुरूप *adj.* ill-favoured

kushagra कुशाग्र *adj.* subtle

kushal कुशल *adj.* safe

kushasan कुशासन *n.* misrule

kushth rog कुष्ठ रोग *n.* leprosy

kusti कुस्ती *n.* wrestling

kusti khelnu कुस्ती खेल्नु *v.* wrestie

kuti कुटी *n.* cottage

kutnaitik कूटनैतिक *adj.* diplomatic

kutnaitik shishtachar कूटनैतिक शिष्टाचार *n.* protocol

kutniti कूटनीति *n.* diplomacy

kutpit कुटपिट *n.* assault

kuwa कूवा *n.* tank

kwatar क्वाटर *n.* quarters

kyamera क्यामेरा *n.* camera

kyamp क्याम्प *n.* camp

kyampas क्याम्पस *n.* campus

kyampas क्याम्पस *n.* college

kyaset क्यासेट *n.* cassette

L

label taslu लेबल टाँस्लु *n.* labelled

labh dayak लाभदायक *adj.* beneficial

labh dayak लाभदायक *adj.* lucrative

lachakdar gadda लचकदार गद्दा *n.* trampoline

lachilo लचिलो *adj.* lithe

lachkine लक्किने *adj.* flexible

ladai लड़ाई *n.* combat

ladai लडाइँ *n.* war

ladain लडाइँ *n.* fighting

ladain ko nara लडाइँको नारा *n.* war cry

ladant लडन्त *n.* fight

ladin लडाइँ *n.* battle

ladnu लड्नू *v.* encounter

ladnu लाद्नु *v.* impose

lagaeko लगाएको *adj.* clad

lagaera hernu लगाएर हेर्नु *v.* try on

lagam लगाम *n.* bridle

lagam लगाम *n.* rein

lagan लगन *n.* perseverance

lagani garnu लगानी गर्नु *v.* invest

lagat लागत *adv.* estimate

lagatar लगातार *adj.* ceaseless

lagatar लगातार *adv.* continuously

lagatar hannu लगातार हान्नु *v.* batter

lagatar pitnu लगातार पिट्नु *v.* drub

lagatarko लगातारको *adj.* incessant

lagaunu लगाउनु *v.* put on

lagaw लगाव *n.* attachment

lagayat लगायत *prep.* including

lagbhag लगभग *prep.* about

lagbhag लगभग *adv.* nearly

laghu brahmand लघु ब्रह्माण्ड *n.* microcosm

laghu chitra लघुचित्र *n.* thumbnail sketch

laghu jawarbhata लघु ज्वारभाटा *n.* neap

laghuganak लघुगुणक *n.* logarithm

lagi rahanu लागिरहनु *v.* continue

lagnu लाग्नु *v.* turn to

lagu garne kam लागू गर्ने काम *n.* enforcement

lagu padarth लागू पदार्थ *n.* heroin

laha लाहा *n.* sealing wax

laha लाहा *mod.* shall

lahad लहड *n.* freak

lahad लहड *n.* whim

lahadi लहडी *adj.* humorous

lahadi लहडी *adj.* whimsical

lahar लहर *n.* row

lahar लहर *n.* wave

lahara लहरा *n.* vine

lahardar लहरदार *adj.* wavy

lahare khoki लहरे खोकी *n.* whooping cough

lahure phul लाहुरे फूल *n.* dahlia

lai लाई *prep.* for

lai लय *n.* lilt

lai लाई *prep.* to

lain लाइन *n.* queue

laj लज *n.* lodge

laj lageko लाज लागेको *adj.* ashamed

lajja लज्जा *n.* shame

lajjajanak लज्जाजनक *adj.* inglorious

lajjalu लज्जालु *adj.* shamefaced

lajjalu लज्जालु *adj.* sheepish

lajjalu लज्जालु *adj.* shy

lajjit लज्जित *adj.* abashed

lakhatnu लखाट्नु *v.* repulse

lakhetai लखेटाइ *n.* chase

lakhpati लखपति *n.* millionaire

laksha लक्ष्य *n.* aim

laksha लक्ष *n.* objective

lakshan लक्षण *n.* symptom

lakshyaheen लक्ष्यहीन *adj.* unaimed

lalach लालच *n.* temptation

lali लाली *n.* lipstick

lali लाली *n.* rouge

laltin लाल्टिन *n.* lantern

lalupate लालुपाते *n.* poinsettia

lam khutte लाम्खुट्टे *n.* mosquito

lama लामा *n.* lama

lama-lama khutta hune लामा-लामा खुट्टा हुने *adj.* leggy

lamb लम्ब *n.* perpendicular

lambai लम्बाइ *n.* length

lamcho लाम्चो *adj.* oblong

lami लमी *n.* matchmaker

lamo लामो *adj.* long

lamo ayu लामो आयु *n.* long life

lamo bhashan लामो भाषण *n.* disquisition

lamo chhutti लामो छुट्टी *n.* vacation

lamo duri ko लामो दुरीको *adj.* long distance

lamo duri ko uphrai लामो दूरीको उफ्राइ *n.* long jump

lamo moja लामो मोजा *n.* stocking

lamo parnu लामो पार्नु *n.* elongate

lamo poshak लामो पोशाक *n.* cassock

lamo saas phernu लामो सास फेर्नु *v.* sign

lamo sas lenu लामो साँस लिनु *n.* sigh

lamo thulo swarle karaunu लामो ठूलो स्वरले कराउनु *v.* yowl

langado लङ्गडो *n.* cripple

langado लङ्गडो *adj.* lame

langar khasalnu लंगर खसाल्नु *n.* anchor

langoor लंगूर *n.* baboon

lanu लानु *v.* take away

laparbah लापर्बाह *adj.* madcap

laparbah लापर्बाह *adj.* reckless

laparbah लापर्बाह *adj.* regardless

laparbahi लापर्वाही *n.* indifference

laparbahi लापर्बाही *n.* negligence

laparwah लापरवाह *adj.* feckless

lapetanu लपेट्नु *v.* enfold

lapetko vastu kholnu लपेटको वस्तु खोल्नु unroll

larkharaunu लर्खराउनु *v.* stagger

lash लाश *n.* cadaver

lash rakhne ghar लाश राख्ने घर *n.* mortuary

lasun लसुन *n.* garlic

lat लात *n.* kick

lat lagnu लत लाग्नु *v.* addict
lathi लाठी *n.* lathi
lathi bajra लठीबज्र *n.* mess
lathibajra लठिबज *n.* hotchpotch/ hodgepodge
lathuwa लठुवा *n.* cretain
lathuwa लठुवा *n.* dullard
lathuwa लठुवा *adj.* silly
latieko लाटिएको *adj.* numb
latkeko लट्केको *adj.* pendent
latkinu लटकिनु *v.* dangle
lato लाटो *adj.* mute
lato लाटो *adj.* speechless
lato kosero लाटोकोसेरो *n.* owl
latranu लत्रनु *v.* droop
latthaparnu लट्ठ पार्नु *v.* intoxicate
latthi लट्ठी *n.* stick
lattu लट्टु *n.* spinning top
lauka लौका *n.* gourd
launu लाउनु *v.* don
launu लाउनु *v.* wear
lawa लावा *n.* lava
laya लय *n.* tune
layak लायक *adj.* competent
layak लायक *adj.* fit
layak लायक *adj.* worsted
lebul लेबुल *n.* tag
ledo लेदो *n.* gravy
legro लेग्रो *v.* drawl
lehardar लहरदार *v.* corrugated
lehare khoki लहरे खोकी *n.* hooping cough

lekh लेख *n.* article
lekh लेख *n.* inscription
lekh padh garna janne लेखपढ गर्न जान्ने *adj.* literate
lekha janchnu लेखा जाँच्नु *v.* audit
lekha padhi लेखापढी *n.* correspondence
lekha pal लेखापाल *n.* accountant
lekha parikshak लेखा परीक्षक *n.* auditor
lekhai लेखाइ *n.* writing
lekhak लेखक *n.* author
lekhak लेखक *n.* writer
lekheko लेखेको *adj.* written
lekhera swikar/darpith garnu लेखेर स्वीकार/दरपीठ गर्नु *v.* endorse
lekhnu लेख्नु *v.* write
lekhot लेखोट *n.* memo(randum)
len den लेनदेन *n.* tally
len den garnu लेनदेन गर्नु *v.* reciprocate
lens लेन्स *n.* lens
lep लेप *n.* ointment
leshkar लेषकार punster
liera aunu लिएर आउनु *v.* fetch
likha लिखा *n.* nit
likhat लिखत *n.* record
likhit vivran लिखित विवरण *n.* record
lilam लिलाम *n.* auction
ling लिंग *n.* gender
ling लिंग *n.* penis

ling लिङ्ग *n.* sex

lipht लिफ्ट *n.* elevator

lipht लिफ्ट *n.* lift

lipi लिपि *n.* script

litre लीटर *n.* litre

lobh लोभ *n.* greed

lobh lagdo लोभलाग्दो *adj.* tempting

lobhi लोभी *adj.* greedy

lobhi लोभी *adj.* rapacious

lobhyaunu लोभ्याउनु *v.* lure

lodar लोदर *n.* hoodoo

logne लोग्ने *n.* hubby

logne लोग्ने *n.* husband

logne manchhe haru लोग्नेमान्छेहरू *n.* men

logne manchhe haru ko parti लोग्नेमान्छेहरूको पार्टी *n.* stag party

logne manis haru लोग्ने-मानिसहरू *n.* menfolk

lohar लोहार *n.* smith

lok priyata लोकप्रियता *n.* popularity

lok sangit लोकसंगीत *n.* folk music

lokgit लोकगीत *n.* folk song

lokharke लोखर्के *n.* squirrel

lokheken लोखर्कें *v.* squirrel

lokhit लोकहित *n.* philanthropy

lop garaunu लोप गराउनु *v.* eliminate

lori लोरी *n.* lullaby

lovi manis लोभी मानिस *n.* caterpillar

lu लू *n.* sunstroke

luchhnu लुछ्नु *v.* tear to pieces

luga लुगा *n.* dress

luga लुगा *n.* garb

luga लुगा *n.* garment

luga लुगा *n.* tunic

luga adi jhundyaune hyanger लुगा आदि झुण्ड्याउने हयाङ्गर *n.* hanger

luga bunne tan लुगा बुन्ने तान *n.* loom

luga ko bhitri लुगाको भित्री *n.* lining

luga lagaunu लुगा लगाउनु *vc.* attire

luga na laeko लुगा नलाएको *adj.* undressed

luga phato लुगाफाटो *n.* clothes

luga rakhne bakas लुगा राख्ने बाकस *n.* suitcase

lugaphukalnu फुकाल्नु *v.* strip

lukamari लुकामारी *n.* hide and seek

lukaunu लुकाउनु *v.* conceal

lukeko shatru लुकेको शत्रु *n.* snake in the grass

lukera garine kan लुकेर गरिने काम *n.* wirepulling

lukne thaun लुक्ने ठाउँ *n.* hideout

luknu लुक्नु *v.* hide

lulo लुलो *adj.* limp

lulo लुलो *adj.* loose

lungi लुङ्गी *n.* sarong

lut लूट *n.* hold-up

lut ko mal लूटको माल *n.* plunder
luteko mal लुटेको माल *n.* loot
lutera लुटेरा *n.* plunderer
lutko mal लूटको माल *n.* booty
lutlat लूटलाट *n.* looting
lutnu लुट्नु *v.* despoil
luto लुतो *n.* herpes
luto लुतो *n.* scabies
lwan ल्वांग *n.* clove
lyapche ल्याप्चे *n.* fingerprint
lyaunu ल्याउनु *v.* bring

M

ma मात्रा *prep.* during
ma मोटोपन *prep.* on
ma मा *prep.* upon
ma aphain म आफैँ *pron.* myself
maadh माड़ *n.* starch
maaf garnu माफ गर्नु *v.* condone
maai माई *n.* smallpox
maalyodha मल्लयोद्धा *n.* athlete
maan मान *n.* dignity
maanchirawali मानचित्रवली *n.* atlas
maanilinu मानिलिनु *v.* postulate
maathi माथि *adv* above
machan मचान *n.* sacaffold
machchaunu मच्चाउनु *v.* wield
machha vishesh माछा विशेष *n.* carp

machhako pakheta माछाको पखेटा *n.* fin
machhako pakheta माछा *n.* fish
madak/lagu padarth वर्णन गर्नु *n.* narcotic
madani मदानी *n.* churn
madat मदत *n.* help
madat/paisa dinu मदत/पैसा दिनु *v.* contribute
madhumeh मधुमेह *n.* diabetes
madhur git/sangit मधुर गीत/संगीत *n.* melody
madhur subashna मधुर सुबासमा *n.* perfume
madhya yugi मध्ययुगी *adj.* medi(a)eval
madhyagrishm मध्यग्रीष्म *n.* midsummer
madhyam मध्यम *n.* medium
madhyam warg मध्यम वर्ग *n.* middle class
madhyamarg मध्यमार्ग via-media
madhyamvargko मध्यम वर्गको *adj.* bourgeosis
madhyana मध्यान्ह *n.* noon
madhyanha मध्यान्ह *n.* midday
madhyantar मध्यान्तर *n.* half-time
madhyantar मध्यान्तर *n.* intermission
madhyantar मध्यान्तर *n.* interval
madhyasth hunu मध्यस्थ हुनु *v.* mediate
madhyauko मध्ययुको *adj.* medieval

319

madhyayugko rasayanik shashtra मध्ययुगको रासायनिक शास्त्र *n.* alchemy

madira ko bepari मदिराको बेपारी *n.* vintner

mag माग *n.* demand

magajako मगजको *adj.* cerebral

maghko dhag माँझको भाग *n.* shaft

magne माग्ने *n.* beggar

magnu माग्नु *v.* ask for

magnu माग्नु *v.* beg

maha मह *n.* honey

maha kawya महाकाव्य *n.* epic

maha mahim महामहिम *n.* excellency

maha mari महामारी *n.* scourge

maha nagar महानगर *n.* metropolis

maha wanijyadut महावाणिज्यदूत *n.* consul

mahadwip महाद्वीप *n.* continent

mahal महल *n.* castle

mahal महल *n.* chateau

mahamari महामारी *n.* epidemic

mahamari महामारी *n.* pestilence

mahamurkh vyakti महामूर्ख व्यक्ति tomfool

mahangai महँगाइ *n.* dearness

mahango महँगो *adj.* costly

mahango महँगो *adj.* expensive

mahanta महानता *n.* greatness

mahasagar महासागर *n.* ocean

mahashaya महाशय *n.* mister/Mr.

mahasul महसूल *n.* assessment

mahatthwa kam garnu महत्त्व कम गर्नु *v.* play down

mahattwa महत्त्व *n.* significance

mahattwa purn महत्वपूर्ण *adj.* important

mahattwahin महत्त्वहीन *adj.* inconsequential

mahattwahin महत्त्वहीन *adj.* unimportant

mahattwahin महत्त्वहीन *n.* urgency

mahattwapurn महत्त्वपूर्ण *adj.* significant

mahila महिला *n.* lady

mahila महिला *n.* woman

mahila haru महिलाहरू *n.* women

mahila majman महिला मेजमान *n.* hostess

mahilakawi महिला कवि *n.* poetess

mahina महिना *n.* month

mahodaya महोदया *n.* madam

mahsus garnu महसुस गर्नु *v.* feel

mahsus garnu महसुस गर्नु *v.* realize

mahuri माहुरी *n.* bee

mahuri ko chaka माहुरीको चाका *n.* beehive

maik माइक *n.* microphone

mail माइल *n.* mile

mailla parnu मैला पार्नु *v.* besmirch

main मैन *n.* wax

main batti मैनबत्ती *n.* candle

maitripurn sambandhko punh sthapan मैत्रीपूर्ण सम्बन्ध को पुन: स्थापन *n.* rapprochement

maja मजा *n.* enjoyment

majak wa thatta ko patra मजाक व ठट्टाको पात्र *n.* laughing stock

majdur sangh मजदुर संघ *n.* trade union

majetro मजेत्रो *n.* kerchief

majh माझ *adj.* middle

majhnu माझ्नु *v.* wash up

makai मकै *n.* maize

makar मकर *n.* capricorn

makarnu मर्कनु *v.* sprain

makgajarmathiko officer मकगजरमाथिको अफिसर *n.* colonel

makhan, nauni मक्खन, नौनी *n.* butter

makhmal मखमल *n.* velvet

makhmal jasto vastra मखमल जस्तो वस्त्र *n.* velour

makkiaer dhulo hunu मक्किएर धूलो हुनु *v.* moulder

makundo मकुण्डा *n.* mask

makura माकुरा *n.* arachind

makura माकुरा *n.* spider

makura ko jali माकुराको जालो *n.* cobweb

makura ko jalo माकुरा को जालो *n.* spider's web

makurako jalo माकुराको जालो *n.* gossamer

makuro माकुरो *n.* spider

mal मल *n.* fertilizer

mal माल *n.* goods

mal माल *n.* luggage

mal मल *n.* manure

mal माल *n.* material

mal ko sangalo माल को सँगालो *n.* stockpile

mal matta मालमत्ता *n.* baggage

mal utarnu माल उतार्नु *v.* unload

mala माला *n.* garland

mala माला *n.* wreath

malai मलाई *pron.* me

malai मलाई *pron.* me

malam मलम *n.* balm

malam मलम *n.* cream

malam मलम *n.* salve

malami मलामी *n.* funeral

malashaya मलाश्य *n.* rectum

maldhuwani bhada मालढुबानी भाडा *n.* freight

maldwar मलद्वार *n.* anus

malgadi मालगाडी *n.* freight train

mali माली *n.* florist

mali माली *n.* gardener

malik मालिक *n.* lord

malik मालिक *n.* master

malik मालिक *n.* owner

malik मालिक *n.* proprietor

malik मालिक *n.* proprietor

malikni मालिक्नी *n.* mistress

malin मलिन *adj.* gloomy

malis मालिस *n.* liniment**

malis मालिस *n.* massage

malis garne peshawar sthri मालिस गर्ने पेशावर स्त्री *n.* masseus

malis garnu मालिस गर्नु *v.* rub in

mallah मल्लाह *n.* fisherman

malmal मलमल *n.* muslin

malnu मल्नु *v.* rub

malpuwa मालपुवा *n.* pancake

mama मामा *n.* maternal uncle

man मन *n.* mind

man bahalaunu मन बहलाउनु *v.* entertain

man chhune मन छुने *adj.* touching

man chune मन छुने *adj.* moving

man diyera kam ma lagnu मन दिएर काममा लाग्नु *v.* knuckle down

man garnu मान गर्नु *v.* revere

man hani मानहानि *n.* loss of face

man ko awastha मन को अवस्था *n.* mood

man lagaunu मन लगाउनु *n.* pore

man pari garne मनपरी गर्ने *adj.* lawless

man pari motar hankne मनपरी मोटर हाँक्ने *n.* road hog

man phukaera kharch garnu मन फुकाएर खर्च गर्नु *adj.* lavish

man tato मनतातो *adj.* lukewarm

manahi garieko मनाही गरिएको *adj.* forbidden

manahi garnu मनाही गर्नु , prohibition

manasib मनासिब *adj.* reasonable

manasib मनासिब *adj.* valid

manasthiti मनस्थिति *n.* state of mind

manauinu मनाउनु *v.* persuade

manav vigyan मानव विज्ञान *n.* anthropology

manaw adhikar मानव अधिकार *n.* human rights

manaw swabhaw मानव स्वभाव *n.* human nature

manawiya मानवीय *adj.* human

manawiya मानवीय *n.* human (being)

manawta मानवता *n.* humanity

manch मंच *n.* dais

manch मंच *n.* forum

manch मंच *n.* platform

manch मंच *n.* rostrum

manche khane rakshas मान्छे खाने राक्षस *n.* ogre

manchhe मान्छे *n.* bloke

manchhe मान्छे *n.* man

manchinte मनचिन्ते *adj.* imaginary

mand मन्द *adj.* dull

mandal मण्डल *n.* shire

mandali मण्डली *n.* coterie

mandand मानदंड *n.* norm

mandir मन्दिर *n.* temple

mane माने *n.* meaning

mane माने *n.* prayer wheel

mangal bar मंगलबार *n.* Tuesday

322

mangal graha मंगल ग्रह *n.* mars

manik माणिक *n.* ruby

manilinu मालिलिनु *n.* assume

manjan मंजन *n.* toothpaste

manjur garnu मन्जुर गर्नु *v.* ratify

manjuri मन्जुरी *n.* approval

manjuri मन्जुरी *v.* approve

manjuri मंजुरी *n.* sanction

manjuri nama मन्जूरी नामा *n.* agreement

manko sthirta मनको स्थिरता *n.* equanimity

manlai peer parne मनलाई पीर पार्ने *adj.* poignant

manma bharnu मनमा भर्नु *v.* imbue

manniya माननीय *adj.* hono(u)rable

mannu मान्नु *v.* consent

manohar मनोहर *adj.* melodious

manonit garnu मनोनीत गर्नु *v.* nominate

manonit vyakti मनोनीत व्यक्ति *n.* nominee

manoranajan मनोरंजन *n.* recreation

manoranjan मनोरंजन *n.* amusement

manoranjan मनोरंजन *n.* entertainment

manoranjan मनोरंजन *n.* pastime

manowigyan मनोविज्ञान *n.* psychology

manpraunu मनपराउनु *v.* relish

mansahari मांसाहारी *adj.* carnivorous

mansik मानसिक *adj.* mental

mantra मन्त्र *n.* incantation

mantralaya मन्त्रालय *n.* ministry

mantri मंत्री *n.* minister

mantri ko wibhag मन्त्रीको विभाग *n.* portfolio

manu मौन *n.* hush

manushya jati मनुष्यजाति *n.* mankind

manyata मान्यता *n.* validity

map garnu माफ गर्नु *v.* write off

maph/kshama garnu माफ/क्षमा गर्नु *v.* forgive

marammat garna na sakine मरम्मत गर्न नसकिने *adj.* irreparable

marammat garnu मरम्मत गर्नु *v.* repair

maran shil मरणशील *adj.* mortal

march मार्च *n.* yearning

march mahina मार्च महीना *n.* march

mareko मरेको *adj.* dead

marg मार्ग *n.* avenue

marg chitra मार्गचित्र *n.* road map

marg darshak मार्ग दर्शक *n.* guide

marg wichalan मार्ग विचलन *adj.* deflection

markanu मर्कनु *n.* sprain

markeko मर्केको *adj.* sprained

markswad माक्र्सवाद *n.* marxism

marm prahar garnu मर्म पहार गर्नु *v.* strike home

marmarmat मरमर्मत *n.* serviciang

marmat garnu मर्मत गर्नु *v.* mend

marnottar मरणोत्तर *n.* post-mortem

marnu मर्नु *v.* die

marnu मर्नु *v.* expire

marnu मार्नु *v.* kill

marnu मार्नु *v.* liquidate

marnu मर्नु *v.* pass away

marnu मार्नु *v.* slay

marphat मार्फत *prep.* through

maru bhumi मरुभूमि *n.* desert

maryadaheen मर्यादाहीन *adj.* undignified

masakbaja मसक बाजा *n.* bagpipes

masala मसाला *n.* plaster

masaladar sasej मसालादार ससेज *n.* salami

masale dar मसालेदार *adj.* spicy

masi मसी *n.* ink

masi dani मसीदानी *n.* ink-pot

masik मासिक *adj.* monthly

masjid मस्जिद *n.* mosque

maskhara मसखरा *n.* zany

masla मसला *n.* spice(s)

mast nidaeko मस्त निदाएको *adv.* sound asleep

mast nidra मस्तनिद्रा *n.* sound sleep

mastir jaane मास्तिर जाने *adj.* upward

mastishka jwar मस्तिष्क ज्वर *n.* encephalitis

mastul मस्तूल *n.* mast

masu मासु *n.* flesh

masu मासु *n.* meat

masu khane chara मासु खाने चरा *n.* buzzard

masuma karha rubber jasto vastu मासुमा कड़ा रबर जस्तो वस्तु *n.* gristle

mat मत *n.* credo

mat मत *n.* creed

mat मत *n.* vote

mat data मतदाता *n.* voter

mat lagne मात लाग्ने *adj.* heady

mataka bhanda kunda माटाका भाँडाकुँडा *n.* pottery

mataka bhanda wa tyasko khapta माटाका भाँड़ा वा त्यसको खपटा *n.* crockery

matan मटान *n.* corridor

matar मटर *n.* pea

matdan मतदानस्थल *n.* polling booth

matdan sthal मतदान सील *n.* booth

mateko मातेको *adj.* drunk

mateko मातेको *adj.* inebriated

math मठ *n.* cloister

math मठ *n.* monastery

mathi माथि *prep.* at

mathi माथि *prep.* over

mathi माथि *prep/* up

mathi tira माथितिर *adv.* upwards

mathillo माथिल्लो *adj.* upper

mathillo hat माथिल्लो हात *n.* upperhand

mathillo tala माथिल्लो तला *n.* upstairs

matlab bujhaunu मतलब बुझाउनु *v.* imply

mato माटो *n.* soil

mato ko mathilo patra माटोको माथिल्लो पत्र *n.* topsoil

matra मात्रा *n.* dose

matra मात्रा *n.* magnitude

matra मात्रा *n.* measure

matra मात्रा *adv.* merely

matri hatya मातृहत्या *n.* matricide

matribhasha मातृभाषा *n.* mother tongue

matrihatya मातृहत्या *n.* matricide

matsyakanya मत्स्यकन्या *n.* mermaid

mattitel मट्टीतेल *n.* kerosene

mauka मौका *n.* chance

maukhik मौखिक *adj.* verbal

maukhik मौखिक *n.* word of mouth

maulaunu मौलाउनु *v.* flourish

mausam मौसम *n.* weather

mausam bhawishya wani मौसम भविष्यवाणी *n.* weather forecast

mausami मौसमी *adj.* seasonal

mausuli माउसुली *n.* gecko

mausuli माउसुली *n.* salamander

maya माया *n.* affection

maya garne माया गर्ने *adj.* fond

maya garne माया गर्ने *adj.* loving

mayagarnu माया गर्नु *v.* caress

mayalu मायालु *adj.* affestionate

mayalu मायालु *n.* heart-throb

mayapriti मायाप्रीती *n.* love affair

mayur मयूर *n.* peacock

meetha kurale fuslayanu मीठा कुराले फुस्ल्याउनु *v.* cajole

meetho मीठो *adj.* dulcet

meetho cake va roti मीठो केक वा रोटी *n.* bun

mehendi मेंहदी *n.* henna

mehko raksi महको रक्सी *n.* mead

mehnat chahine मेहनत चाहिने *adj.* onerous

mel मेल *n.* harmony

mel milap मेल मिलाप *n.* conciliation

mel milap मेलमिलाप *n.* reconcillation

mela मेला *adj.* dingy

mela मेला *n.* fair

melmilap garnu मेलमिलाप गर्नु *v.* reconcile

mero मेरो *pron.* mine

mero मेरो *pron.* my

merudandko मेरुदण्डको *adj.* spinal

mesh rashi मेष राशि *n.* aries

metaunu naskine मेटाउन नसकिने *adj.* indelible

methi मेथी *n.* fenugreek

metne rabar मेट्ने रबर *n.* eraser

metnu मेट्नु *v.* delete

metnu मेट्नु *v.* erase

metnu मेट्नु *v.* obliterate

metnu मेट्नु *v.* rub out

metnu मेट्नु *v.* wipe out

mewa मेवा *n.* papaya

mihin suto luga मिहीन सुती लुगा *n.* nainsook

mihin vastra मिहिन वस्त्र *n.* voile

mihinet मिहिनेत *n.* effort

mijas मिजास *n.* temper

mijasilo मिजासिलो *adj.* soft(ly) spoken

mila patra jhanda मिलापत्र झंडा *n.* white flag

milansaar मिलनसार *adj.* affable

milansaar मिलनसार *adj.* amiable

milansaari मिलनसारी *n.* bon-homie

milansar मिलनसार *adj.* convivial

milansar मिलनसार *adj.* debonair

milansar मिलनसार *adj.* friendly

milap garaune मिलाप गराउने *n.* mediator

milaunu मिलाउनु *v.* accommodate

milaunu मिलाउनु *v.* adjust

milaunu मिलाउनु *v.* patch up

milaunu मिलाउनु *v.* put together

milavat garnu मिलावट गर्नु *v.* adulterate

mildo मिल्दो *adj.* harmonious

milera garine kam मिलेर गरिने काम *n.* teamwork

millaunu मिलाउनु *v.* associate

milne yog मिलने योग्य *adj.* obtainable

milne/bhetne kam मिल्ने/भेट्ने काम *n.* dating

milnu मिल्नु *n.* terms

miltho bolne मीठो बौल्ने *adj.* smooth-tongued

min rashi मीन राशि *n.* pisces

minar मिनार *n.* spire

mirgalo sunine rog मिर्गौला सुनिने रोग *n.* nephritis

mirgaula मिर्गौला *n.* kidney

mirgaulako मिर्गौलाको *adj.* renal

misaha kukur मिसाहा कुकुर *n.* mongrel

misaunu मिसाउनु *v.* mix

mishra dhatu मिश्र धातु *n.* alloy

mishran मिश्रण *n.* amalgam

mishran मिश्रण *n.* compound

mishran मिश्रण *n.* mixture

mishrit मिश्रित *adj.* assorted

mishrit bhasha मिश्रित भाषा *n.* pidgin

misine kam मिसिने काम *n.* merger

misnu मिसिनु *v.* mingle

misnu मिसिनु *v.* mingle

misri मिस्री *n.* candy

mistri मिस्त्री *n.* mechanic

mitar मिटर *n.* metre/meter

mithai मिठाई *n.* confectionery

mithai मिठाई *n.* lollipop

mitho मीठो *adj.* delicious

mitho मीठो *adj.* luscious

mitho boli wa chal garer phuslaunu मीठो बोली वा चाल गरेर फुस्लाउनु *v.* inveigle

mithun rashi मिथुन राशि *n.* gemini

mithya मिथ्या *adj.* pseudo

miti मिति *n.* date

mitra मित्र *n.* colleague

mitrabhav मित्रभाव *n.* goodwill

mitrata मित्रता *n.* friendship

mitvyaye मितव्ययी *adj.* sparing

mod मोड *n.* bend

mod मोड *n.* turning

mod मोड *n.* turning point

modh मोड़ *n.* diversion

moh मोह *n.* enchantment

mohak मोहक *adj.* charming

mohit मोहित *adj.* infatuated

mohit garnu मोहित गर्नु *n.* captivate

mohit garnu मोहित गर्नु *v.* enchant

mohit garnu मोहित गर्नु *v.* enthral

mohit pamu मोहित पार्नु *v.* captivate

mohit/akarshit garnu 13 *v.* fascinate

moja मोजा *n.* sock

mokhik pariksha मौखिक परीक्षा *n.* vivavoce

mol molai मोलमोलाइ *n.* bargain

mool मूल *adj.* seminal

moorkh मूर्ख *adj.* unintelligent

motai मोटाइ *n.* thickness

motar मोटर *n.* motor

motar chadhnu मोटर चढ्नु *v.* ride

motar gadi मोटर गाड़ी *n.* car

motar karkhana मोटर कारखाना *n.* garage

motar saikal मोटरसाइकल *n.* motorcycle

motarchalak मोटरचालक *n.* chauffeur

motargadi मोटरगाड़ी *n.* automobile

motargadi haru ko lam मोटर. गाडीहरूको लाम *n.* motorcade

motarkar मोटरकार *n.* motor car

moter uhcalne aujar मोटर उचाल्ने औजार *n.* jack

moti मोती *n.* pearl

moto मोटो *adj.* corpulent

moto मोटो *adj.* thick

moto मोटो *adj.* voluminous

moto kapada मोटो कपडा *n.* canvas

moto suti luga मोटो सूती लुगा *n.* corduroy

motopan मोटोपन *n.* obesity

motorgadi मोटरगाड़ी *n.* limousine

mrigi मृगी *n.* doe

mrigko chhal मृग को छाला *n.* bickskin

mrigko masu मृगको मासु *n.* venison

mrigtrishna मृगतृष्णा *n.* mirage

mrit मृत *adj.* deceased

mrit मृत *n.* requiem

mrityu मृत्यु *n.* death

mrityu मृत्यु *n.* demise

mrityu dand मृत्युदण्ड *n.* death penality

mudda मुद्दा *n.* case

mudda मुद्दा *n.* lawsuit

mudda chalaunu मुद्दा चलाउनु *v.* prosecute

mudha haru ko beda मुढाहरूको बेडा *n.* raft

mudra मुद्रा *n.* currency

mudra sphiti मुद्रास्फीति *n.* inflation

muhan मुहान *n.* firth

muja मुजा *n.* pleat

muja मुजा *n.* ruck

muja parnu wa paarnu मुजा पर्नु वा पार्नु *v.* crinkle

mukabhinay मूकाभिनय *n.* pantomime

mukam मुकाम *n.* station

mukh मुख *n.* face

mukh मुख *n.* mouth

mukh baer hernu मुख बाएर हेर्नु *v.* gape

mukh baja मुख-बाजा *n.* harmonica

mukh chit मुख चित्त *n.* obverse

mukh ko मुखको *adj.* oral

mukh ko lali मुख को लाली *n.* flush

mukh prishth मुखपृष्ठ *n.* title page

mukh vikrati मुख-विकृति *n.* grimace

mukhbhari मुखभरि *n.* mouthful

mukhle bajaune baaja मुखले बजाउने बाजा *n.* bassoon

mukhya मुख्य *n.* arch

mukhya मुख्य *adj.* dominant

mukhya मुख्य *adj.* main

mukhya मुख्य *adj.* prime

mukhya मुख्य *adj.* salient

mukhya girijaghar मुख्य गिरजाघर *n.* cathedral

mukhya karyalaya मुख्य कार्यालय *n.* headquarters

mukhya sahara मुख्य सहारा *n.* mainstay

mukhya sahayak मुख्य सहायक *n.* right-hand man

mukhya vishya मुख्य विषय *n.* gist

mukkabaaj मुक्काबाज *n.* pugilist

mukkale pitnu मुक्काले पिट्नु *v.* pummel

mukke baj मुक्केबाज *n.* boxer

mukt garnu मुक्त गर्नु *v.* emancipate

mukt garnu मुक्त गर्नु *v.* extricate

mukta garnu मुक्त गर्नु *v.* liberate

mukta garnu मुक्त गर्नु *v.* redeem

mukthastale diaeko dan मुक्तहस्तले दिएको दान *n.* largesse

mukti मुक्ति *n.* emancipation

mukti मुक्ति *n.* liberation

mukti मुक्ति *n.* salvation

muktidata मुक्तिदाता *n.* savio(u)r

mukut kirit मुकुट किरीट *n.* diadem

mul मूल *n.* source

mul bati मूल बाटो *n.* thoroughfare

mul prawah मूलप्रवाह *n.*
mainstream

mula मूला *n.* radish

muljiu मूलजीउ *n.* trunk

mulpath मूलपाठ *n.* text

mulya मूल्य *n.* cost

mulya मूल्य *n.* price

mulya मूल्य *n.* value

mulya मूल्य *n.* worth

mulya nirdharan मूल्यनिर्धारण *n.*
valuation

mulya suchi मूल्य सूचि *n.* price list

mulya wan मूल्यवान *adj.* valuable

mulyankan मूल्यांकन *v.* evaluate

mulyankan garnu मूल्याकन गर्नु *v.*
assess

mulyawarg मूल्यवर्ग *n.*
denomination

muma bada maharani मुमा
बडामहारानी *n.* queen mother

mundri मुन्द्री *n.* ring

munga मूंगा *n.* coral

mungro मुङ्ग्रो *n.* mallet

mungro मुङ्ग्रो *n.* mallet

muni मुनि *prep.* under

muntira मुन्तिर *adv.* below

muntira मुन्तिर *adv.* underneath

murchha मूर्छा *n.* swoon

murchha मूर्छा *n.* syncope

murchhit मूर्छित *adj.* faint

murda मुर्दा *n.* corpse

murda khane pishach मुर्दा खाने
पिशाच *n.* ghoul

murda lejane gadi मुर्दा लैजाने गाड़ी
n. hearse

murkh मूर्ख *adj.* daft

murkh मूर्ख *n./adj.* fool

murkh मूर्ख *adj.* imbecile

murkh मूर्ख *n.* nincompoop

murkh मूर्ख *adj.* senseless

murkh मूर्ख *n.* simpleton

murkh मूर्ख *adj.* stupid

murkh vyakti मूर्ख व्यक्ति *n.*
dunderhead

murkh vyakti मूर्ख व्यक्ति *n.* nitwit

murkhta मूर्खता *n.* idiocy

murliwadan मुरलीवादन *n.* piping

murti मूर्ति *n.* icon

murti मूर्ति *n.* idol

murtikala मूर्तिकला *n.* sculpture

murtikar मूर्तिकार *n.* sculptor

musa haru मूसाहरू *n.* mice

musa haru मूसाहरू *n.* mouse

musa jasto jant मूसा जस्तो जन्त *n.*
vole

musal मुसल *n.* flail

musal मुसल *n.* pestle

musal dhare मुसलधारे *adj.*
torrential

musaldhar pani मुसलधार पानी *n.*
downpour

muskan मुस्कान *n.* smile

muskil le मुस्किलले *adv.* barely

muskil le मुस्किलले *adv.* scarcely

muskil le uklanu मुस्किले उक्लनु *v.* scramble

muslim मुस्लिम *n.* muslim

muslimharuko dharamgranth मुस्लिमहरूको धर्मग्रन्थ *n.* koran

muslimharuko dharmik yudh मुस्लिमहरूको धार्मिक युद्ध *n.* jihad

muslimko dharamguru मुस्लिमको धर्मगुरू *n.* imam

muslo मुस्लो *n.* torrent

muso मूसो *n.* rat

muso chhuchundro adi मूसो, छुचुन्द्रो आदि *n.* rodent

mutha मुठा *n.* roll

muthi मुट्ठी *n.* fist

muthi मुठी *n.* grasp

muthibhar ko pariman मुट्ठीभर को परिमाण *n.* handful

mutnu मुल्नु *v.* piss

mutrako मूत्रको *adj.* uric

mutrashaya मूत्राशय *n.* bladder

mutu मुटु *n.* heart

mutu मुटु *n.* hearts

mutu wa raktnali-ma khoon jamne kriya मुटु वा रक्तनली-मा खून जम्ने क्रिया *n.* thrombosis

mutuko dhukdhuki मुटुको ढुकढुकी *n.* heartbeat

myad nagheko म्याद नाघेको *adj.* overdue

myau myau म्याउम्याउ *n.* mew

myujiyam म्युजियम *n.* museum

N

na bhai na hune नभै नहुने *adj.* indispensable

na chahindo नचाहिंदो *adj.* unnecessary

na chhekieko नछेकिएको *adj.* unobstructed

na dekheko नदेखेको *adj.* unnoticed

na dekhieko नदेखिएको *adj.* unseen

na galne नगल्ने *adj.* rigid

na ramailo नरमाइलो *adj.* unpleasant

na ramro नराम्रो *adj.* ugly

na ramro sallah paeko नराम्रो सल्लाह पाएको *adj.* ill-advised

na rokine न रोकिने *adj.* non-stop

na sakne नसक्ने *adj.* unable

na ternu नटेर्नु *v.* disobey

na tirieko नतिरिएको *adj.* unpaid

naach नाच *n.* can-can

naadi नाड़ी *n.* wrist

naak नाक *n.* nose

naango नाङ्गो *adj.* unclas

nabalig apradh नाबालिग अपराध *n.* juvenile delinquency

nabbe नब्बे *n.* ninety

nabhniyeko नभनिएको *adj.* tacit

nabichari swikriti dinu नबिचारी स्वीकृति दिनु *v.* rubber-stamp

nabik officer नाविक आफिसर *n.* commodore

nabolaiko नबोलाएको *adj.* uncalled for

nabujhine नबुझिने *adj.* incomprehensible

nachoyeko नछोएको *adj.* untouched

nadi नदी *n.* river

nadi नाडी *n.* wrinkle

nadi bagne ghatti नदी बग्ने घाटी *n.* canyon

nadi helera tarnu नदी हेलेर तर्नु *v.* wade

nadiko bandh नदीको बाँध *n.* weir

nadimukh नदीमुख *n.* estuary

nagad नगद *n.* cash

nagad नगद *n.* hard cash

nagad नगद *n.* ready money

nagar नगर *n.* town

nagar palika नगरपालिका *n.* municipality

nagar pramukh नगरप्रमुख *n.* mayor

nagar yojana नगर योजना *n.* town planning

nagarpal, nagarpati नगरपाल, नगरपति *n.* mayor

nagarpalika नगरपालिका *adj.* municipal

naghateko नघटेको *adj.* unabated

nagrik नागरिक *n.* citizen

nagrikta dinu नागरिकता दिनु *v.* naturalize

nahar नहर *n.* canal

nailan नाइलन *n.* nylon

nain नाइँ *adv.* not

naitik नैतिक *n.* ethical

naitik bal नैतिक बल *n.* moral force

naitik dhang le नैतिक ढङ्गले *adv.* morally

naitik sahas नैतिक साहस *n.* moral courage

naitikta नैतिकता *n.* morality

naito नाइटो *n.* navel

naivaidhya नैवेद्य *n.* oblation

najar bandi नजरबन्दी *n.* house arrest

najeek नजीक *adv.* nigh

najeek aaunu नजीक आउनु *v.* approach

najeekma raheko नजीकमा रहेको adjacent

najekhaiko jasto garnu नदेखेको जस्तो गर्नु *v.* connive

najik नजिक *adv.* near

najik janu नजिक जानु *v.* pull in

najikai ko नजिकैको *adj.* nearby

najikari rahanu नजिकै रहनु *v.* stick aroujnd

najuk नाजुक *adj.* brittle

najuk नाजुक *adj.* critical

nak ko pwal नाकको प्वाल *n.* nostril

nakali dant नकली दाँत *n.* denture

nakali kapaal नकली कपाल *n.* toupee

nakali, jaali नकली, जाली *adj.* counterfeit

nakam नाकाम *adj.* invalid

nake नाके *adj.* nasal

nakkabandi garnu नाकाबन्दी गर्नु *v.* blockade

nakkal नक्कल *n.* mock

nakkal नक्कल प्रतिकृति *n.* replica

nakkal नक्कल *n.* imitation

nakkali नक्कली *adj.* phony

nakkali kapal नक्कली कपाल *n.* wig

nakkali wastu नक्कली वस्तु *n.* fake

nakko twaghako kathira नाकको स्वचाको खटिरो *n.* acne

nakle chunu wa dalnu नाकले छुनु वा दल्नु *v.* nuzzle

nakoreko नकोरेको *adj.* dishevelled

naksa नक्सा *n.* chart

naksa नक्सा *n.* map

nal नाल *n.* drain

nal नाल *n.* horseshoe

nala नाला *n.* runnel

nali नली *n.* duct

nali नली *n.* pipe

nali नली *n.* tube

nalihad नलिहाड *n.* shin

nalini नलिनी *n.* lily

nam नाम *n.* name

nam ko pahilo akshar नामको पहिलो अक्षर *n.* initial

namanjur/aswikar garnu नामुजूर/अस्वीकार गर्नु *v.* disagree

namannu नमान्नु *v.* disapprove

namanun नमान्नु *v.* decline

namard नामर्द *adj.* impotent

namaste नमस्ते *n.* goodbye

namaste नमस्ते *n./excl.* hi

namawali नामावली *n.* nomenclature

namawali नामावली *n.* roster

nambari sun chandi नम्बरी सुन चाँदी *n.* hallmark

nami नामी *adj.* eminent

nammatra ko नाम मात्र को *adj.* nominal

namna bhaeko नाम नभएको *adj.* nameless

namra नम्र *adj.* humble

namra नम्र *adj.* lowly

namra नम्र *adj.* meek

namra dayalu नम्र र दयालु *v.* benign

namra hunu नम्र हुनु *v.* tone down

namrata नम्रता *n.* modesty

namuna नमूना *n.* model

namuna नमूना *n.* sample

namuna नमूना *n.* specimen

nan chhuri नङछुरी *n.* whitlow

nango नांगो *adj.* bare

nango नाङ्गो *adj.* naked

nango नाङ्गो *adj.* nude

nangra नङ्ग्रा *n.* talon

nani नानी *n.* babe

naniko thana नानीको थाङ्ना *n.* nappy

nantma अन्तमा *adv.* finally

nantma नङ *n.* fingernail

nap नाप *n.* measure

nap नाप *n.* measurement

nap नाप *n.* size

napha नाफा *n.* proceeds

napha dine नाफा दिने *adj.* profitable

napkin नेपकिन *n.* serviette

napne dandi नाप्ने डन्डी *n.* ga(u)ge

napnu नाप्नु *v.* gauge

napug दपुग *adj.* inadequate

napunsak नपुंसक *adj.* neuter

nar hatya नरहत्या *n.* homicide

nara नारा *n.* slogan

naraji नाराजी *n.* displeasure

narak नरक *n.* hell

narakko नरकको *adj.* infernal

naram नरम *adj.* mild

naram नरम *adj.* silky

naram chhala नरम छाला *n.* suede

naram hunu नरम हुनु *v.* relent

naram koila नरम कोइला *n.* lignite

naran नम्र *adj.* polite

narhatya नरहत्या *n.* manslaughter

nariko cheu नाड़ीको छेउ *n.* cuff

nariwal नरिवल *n.* coconut

nariwal ko jata नरिवल को जटा *n.* coir

narkat नरकट *n.* bulrush

narsin hom नसिङ होम *n.* nursing home

nas chchhedan नसच्छेदन *n.* vasectomy

nasa नसा *n.* sinew

nasa नसा *n.* vein

nash नाश *n.* destruction

nash नाश *n.* pillage

nash garnu नाश गर्नु *v.* lay waste

nash garnu नाश गर्नु *v.* wreck

nash huna na sakne नाश हुन नसक्ने *adj.* indestructible

nash nahune नाश नहुने *adj.* imperishable

nash/nasht garnu नाश/नष्ट गर्नु *v.* destroy

nashiat नसिहत *n.* reprimand

nashkari wyakti नाशकारी व्यक्ति *n.* pest

nasht garnu नष्ट गर्नु *v.* destroy

nasht garnu नष्ट गर्नु *v.* fritter

nasingariyeko नसिँगारिएको *adj.* unadorned

nasinu नासिनु *v.* perish

naskane banaunu नसक्ने बनाउनु *v.* disable

nasochi bhannu नसोची भन्नु *v.* blurt

naspati नास्पाती *n.* pear

nasta नास्ता *n.* breakfast

nastik नास्तिक *n.* atheist

nastik नास्तिक *n.* infidel

nata नाता *n.* relation

nata dar नातादार *n.* kin

nata gota नातागोता *n.* relative

natak नाटक *n.* drama

natak नाटक *n.* re-run

natak kar नाटककार *n.* playwright

natak wa abhinaysambandhi नाटक वा अभिनयसम्बन्धी *adj.* histroinic

natawad नातावाद *n.* nepotism

nathakeekan kaam garirehne नथाकीकन काम गरिरहने *adj.* untiring

nathi नाठी *n.* flirt

natija नतिजा *n.* outcome

natikuti garne नाटीकुटी गर्ने *adj.* fussy

natini नातिनी *n.* granddaughter

natini नातिनी *n.* grandson

natirne kam नतिर्ने काम *n.* non-payment

natkiya नाटकीय *adj.* dramatic

natra नत्र *conj.* otherwise

nattune नट्टुने *adj.* indissoluble

nau नौ *n.* nine

nau khiyaune dandi नाउ ख्याउने डाँड़ी *n.* scull

nauka-daur नौका-दोड़ *n.* regatta

naulo नौलो *adj.* exotic

naulo/parai manchhe नौलो∕पराइ मान्दे *n.* stranger

nauni नौनी *n.* butter

nautal नौतल *n.* keel

nav prastar नव प्रस्तर *adj.* neolithic

nawagantuk नवागन्तुक *n.* newcomer

nawaun नवौँ *n.* ninth

nawin prawartan नवीन प्रवर्तन *n.* innovation

nawodit नवोदित *adj.* emergent

naya basne thaun dinu नयाँ बस्ने ठाउँ दिनु *v.* rehouse

naya dhangle नया ढँगले *adv.* afresh

naya jalbayuma bani parnu नयाँ जलवायुमा बानी पार्नु *v.* acclimatize

nayab नायब *n* deputy

nayab नायब *n.* junior

nayan नयाँ *pref.* neo

nayan नयाँ *adj.* new

nayan banaune kam नयाँ बनाउने काम *n.* renewal

nayan banaunu नयाँ बनाउनु *v.* renovate

nayan dishama ghumnu नयाँ दिशामा घुम्नु *v.* slew

nayan kura liaunu नयाँ कुरा ल्याउनु *v.* innovate

nayan parnu नयाँ पार्नु *v.* renew

nayan prakashan नयाँ प्रकाशन *n.* reprint

nayan shabd नयाँ शब्द *n.* neologism

nayan sipahi नयाँ सिपाही *n.* recruit

nayan suruat नयाँ सुरुआत *n.* resumption

nayan tulwa halnu नयाँ तलुवा हाल्नु *v.* resole

nayan wichar नयाँ विचार *n.* second thought

nayan/nawa warsh नयाँ∕नव वर्ष *n.* new year

nayanbasti ma basne नयाँ बस्तीमा बस्ने *n.* settler

nayaysangat न्यायसंगत *adj.* euquitable

neech नीच *adj.* ignoble

neech नीच *adj.* mingy

neeras नीरस *adj.* drab

neeras नीरस *adj.* dreary

neeras नीरस *adj.* humdrum

neeras नीरस *n.* prosy

nektai नेकटाइ *n.* necktie

nepali shaili ko mandir नेपाली शैलीको मन्दिर *n.* pagoda

neta नेता *n.* leader

neta नेता *n.* ringleader

netritava नेतृत्व *n.* hegemony

nibandh निबन्ध *n.* essay

nibhauanu निभाउनु *v.* put out

nibhaunu निभाउनु *v.* extinguish

nibhaunu निभाउनु *v.* switch off

nich नीच *adj.* vile

nicharnu निचर्नु *v.* squeeze

nichod निचोड़ *n.* conclusion

nidaeko निदाएको *v.* asleep

nidar निडर *adj.* fearless

nidar निडर *adj.* intrepid

nidar निडर *adj.* unafraid

nidhar निधार *n.* forehead

nidra निद्रा *n.* slumber

nidra lageko निद्रा लागेको *adj.* sleepy

nidra lagne chakki निद्रा लाग्ने चक्की *n.* sleeping pill

nidralu निद्रालु *adj.* somnolent

nigalo निगालो *n.* reed

nigam निगम *n.* corporation

niharika नीहारिका *n.* nebula

nihattha निहत्था *adj.* unarmed

nihuranu निहुरनु *v.* stoop

nijamati निजामती *adj.* civil

niji निजी *adj.* personal

niji निजी *adj.* private

niji gupt char निजी गुप्तचार *n.* private eye

niji udyam निजी उद्यम *n.* private enterprise

nikal निकल *n.* nickel

nikala निकाला *n.* rxpulsion

nikali dinu निकालिदिनु *n.* kick out

nikalnu निकाल्नु *v.* bring out

nikalnu निकाल्नु *v.* eject

nikalnu निकाल्नु *v.* elicit

nikalnu निकाल्नु *v.* evict

nikalnu निकाल्नु *v.* expel

nikalnu निकाल्नु *v.* oust

nikalnu निकाल्नु *v.* rusticate

nikalnu निकाल्नु *v.* throw out

nikalnu निकाल्नु *v.* turn out

nikamma निकम्मा *adj.* useless

nikamma निकम्मा *adj.* worthless

nikamma vyakti निकम्मा व्यक्ति *n.* duffer

nikas निकास *n.* outlet

nikas निकास *n.* vent

nikat निकट *adv.* up against

nikat darshi निकटदर्शी *adj.* near-skghted

nikatata निकटता *n.* proximity

nikatdarshi निकटदर्शी *adj.* short-sighted

nikkama निकम्मा *n.* rotter

niklanu निक्लनु *v.* emerge

niko निको *adj.* well

niko huna sakne निको हुनसक्ने *adj.* curable

niko hunu निको हुनु *n.* heal

niko na hune निको नहुने *adj.* incurable

niko tulyaunu निको तुल्याउनु *v.* cure

niko/aram hunu निको/आराम हुनु *v.* recover

nilamban garnu निलम्बन गर्नु *v.* suspend

nilmani नील्मणि *n.* sapphire

nilo नीलो *adj.* blue

niman madhya wargko vyakti निम्न मध्य वर्गको व्यक्ति *n.* petitbourgeois

nimanbhumi निम्नभूमि *n.* lowland

nimbuko sharbat निम्बूको शरबत *n.* lemonade

nimothnu निमोठ्नु *n.* tweak

nimtabinako pahuna निम्ताबिनाको पाहुना *n.* gatecrasher

nimto निम्तो *n.* invitation

nimto dinu निम्तो दिनु *v.* invite

ninda निन्दा *n.* calumny

ninda garnu निन्दा गर्नु *v.* dafame

ninda garnu निन्दा गर्नु *v.* denounce

ninda garnu निन्दा गर्नु *v.* tqraduce

nindra lagune aushdhi निद्रा लगाउने औषधि *n.* opiate

niphannu निफन्नु *v.* winnow

nipun निपुण *adj.* proficient

nipun निपुण *adj.* tactful

niradhar निराधार *adj.* groundless

niradhar निराधार *adj.* unsubstantial

nirakshar निरक्षर *adj.* illiterate

nirankush निरङ्कुश *adj.* tyrannical

nirantar निरन्तर *adv.* year in and year out

nirarthak निरर्थक *adj.* inane

nirarthak निरर्थक *adj.* insignificant

nirarthak निरर्थक *adj.* unmeaning

nirash निराश *adj.* hopeless

nirash garnu निराश गर्नु *v.* disappoint

nirash/hatotsah garaunu निराश/हतोत्साह गराउनु *v.* frustrate

nirasha निराश *adj.* crestfallesn

nirasha निराशा *n.* despair

nirasha निराशा *adj.* desperate

nirasha निराशा *n.* setback

nirashajanak निराशाजनक *adj.* desperate

nirashawad निराशावाद *n.* pessimism

nirbhar hunu निर्भर हुनु *v.* depend

nirday निर्दय *adj.* callous

nirday निर्दय *adj.* cruel

nirday निर्दय *adj.* unkind

nirdayi निर्दयी *adj.* brutal

nirdayi निर्दयी *adj.* cruel

nirdayi निर्दयी *adj.* inhuman

nirdayi निर्दयी *adj.* pitiless

nirdayi निर्दयी *adj.* relentless

nirdayi निर्दयी *adj.* remorseless

nirdesh dinu निर्देश दिनु *v.* direct

nirdeshak निर्देशक *n.* director

nirdeshika निर्देशिका *n.* handbook

nirdharit garnu निर्धारित गर्नु *v.* allocate

nirdishta garnu निर्दिष्ट गर्नु *v.* assign

nirdosh निर्दोष *adj.* flawless

nirdosh निर्दोष *adj.* innocent

nirdosh ghoshit garnu निर्दोष घोषित गर्नु *v.* acquit

nirdosh jhut निदोष झूट *n.* white lie

nirikshak निरीक्षक *n.* inspector

nirjal garnu निर्जल गर्नु *v.* dehydrate

nirjan निर्जन *adj.* solitary

nirjeev निर्जीव *adj.* inanimate

nirjiw wastu ko chitra निर्जीव वस्तुको चित्र *n.* still life

nirlajj निर्लज्ज *adj.* immodest

nirlajja निर्लज्ज *adj.* shameless

nirmal sthal निर्माणस्थल *n.* site

nirman निर्माण *n.* construction

nirman garnu निर्माण गर्नु *n.* build

nirmul/unmulan garnu

निर्मूल/उन्मूलन गर्नु *v.* eradicate

nirnayak निर्णायक *n.* umpire

nirutsahit garnu निरुत्साहित गर्नु *v.* discourage

nirutsashit garnu निरुत्साहित गर्नु *v.* demoralize

nirvivad निर्विवाद *adj.* indisputable

nirwan निर्वाण *n.* nirvana

nirwasit निर्वासित *n.* outlaw

niryat nikasi garnu निर्यात निकसी गर्नु *n.* export

nisasine parnu निसासिने पार्नु *v.* asphyxiate

nisasino निसासिनु *v.* stifle

nisassinu निसासिसिनु *v.* suffocate

nischit akaar निश्चित आकार *adj.* unformed

nischith निश्चित *adj.* certain

nish kapat saudebaji निष्कपट सौदेबाजी *n.* square deal

nishana निशाना *n.* target

nishchaya sanga bhannu निश्चयसँग भन्नु *v.* affirm

nishchint निश्चिन्त *adj.* uncaring

nishchit awadhi निश्चित अवधि *n.* time limit

nishedh निषेध *n.* ban

nishedh निषेध *n.* veto

nishkalank निष्कलंक *adj.* unspotted

nishkarsh nikalnu निष्कर्ष निकाल्नु *v.* conclude

nishkasan निष्कासन *n.* exile

nishkriya निष्क्रिय *adj.* passive

nishnabaz निशानाबाज *n.* marksman

nishpakshata निष्पक्षता *n.* imparitiality

nishphal निष्फल *adj.* ineffectual

nishphal hunu निष्फल हुनु *v.* fail

nishphal/parajit hunu निष्फल/पराजित हुनु *v.* go under

nishta निष्ठा *n.* allegiance

nishthur निष्ठुर *adj.* merciless

nishthur निष्ठुर *adj.* unfeeling

niskane bato निस्कने बाटो *n.* exit

nissandeh निस्सन्देह *adj.* doubtless

nissandeh निस्सन्देह *n.* no doubt

nissandeh निस्सन्देह *adv.* undoubtedly

nisswarth निस्स्वार्थ *adj.* selfless

nistej निस्तेज *adj.* lacklustre

nistej निस्तेज *adj.* muzzy

nithur निठुर *adj.* ruthless

niti नीति *n.* policy

niti shastra नीतिशास्त्र *n.* ethics

niti siksha नीतिशिक्षा *n.* moral

nitrogen नाइट्रोजन *n.* nitrogen

niwaran garnu निवारण गर्नु *v.* preclude

niwas निवास *n.* dwelling

niwasi निवासी *n.* resident

niwas-sthan निवास-सीन *n.* domicole

niyam नियम *n.* rule

niyam anusar नियमानुसार *adj.* formal

niyam bahira ko kura नियमबाहिरको कुरा *n.* exception

niyam bhang garne upaya नियम भङ्ग गर्ने *n.* loophole

niyam kanun नियम कानून *n.* rules and regulations

niyam widhi नियम विधि *n.* regulation

niyamat नियमित *adj.* regular

niyamit नियमित *v.* regulate

niyamit karya नियमित कार्य *n.* routine

niyamit rup ma नियमित रूपमा *adv.* regularly

niyantran नियन्त्रण *n.* control

niyukta garnu नियुक्त गर्नु *v.* appoint

niyukti नियुक्ति *n.* nomination

nokar नोकर *n.* lackey

nokar नोकर *n.* servant

nokarni नोकर्नी *n.* housemaid

nokarni नोकिर्नी *n.* maid

nokarni नोकर्नी *n.* maidservant

nokrani नोकर्नी *n.* handmaid

nokri नौकरी *n.* job

noksan नोक्सान *n.* loss

not ganne janchne नोट गन्ने जाँच्ने *n.* teller

nritya नृत्य *n.* ballet

nritya नृत्य *n.* dance

nsodhi lejanu नसोधी लैजानु *v.* snaffle

nuayadhish न्यायाधीश *n.* judge

nun नुन *n.* salt

nunilo नुनिलो *adj.* saline

nunilo नुनिलो *adj.* salted

nyakka toknu न्याक्क टोक्नु *v.* snap

nyano न्यानो *adj.* warlike

nyar nyur garnu ङ्यारङुर गर्नु *v.* snarl

nyarui muso न्याउरी मूसो *n.* mongoose

nyasro न्यास्रो *adj.* monotonous

nyayapalika न्यायपालिका *n.* judiciary

nyayapalika न्याय *n.* justice

nyayi न्यायी *adj.* just

nyayi न्यायी *adj.* righteous

O

obhar kot ओभरकोट *n.* topcoat

odhne ओढ्ने *n.* shawl

oilaunu ओङ्लाउनु *v.* wilt

oilaunu ओइलाउनु *v.* withdrawal

oilaunu ओइलाउनु *v.* wither

okhar ओखर *n.* wallop

okhar ओखर *n.* walnut

okhati ओखती *n.* medicine

olaama laune khol औंलामा लाउने खोल *n.* thimble

oon ऊन *pron.* he

oon katranu ऊन कत्रनु *n.* fleece

oon, dhago adiko lacha wa gucha ऊन, धागो आदिको लच्छा वा गुच्छा hank

oorja ऊर्जा *n.* energy

orali ओरालो *n.* downhill

orlanu ओर्लनु *v.* descend

orlanu ओर्लनु *v.* go down

os ओस *n.* dew

os ओस *n.* moisture

osieko ओसिएको *adj.* humid

oth ओठ *n.* lip

otharo basnu ओथारो बस्नु *v.* incubate

overcoat ओभरकोट *n.* overcoat

oxygen अक्सिजन *n.* oxygen

P

paakhura पाखुरा *n.* arm

paani jane nal पानी जाने नल *n.* conduit

paani va madirako bottle पानी वा मदिराको बोतल *n.* carafe

paatlo naram kaagat पातलो नरम कागत *n.* tissue

pacchi hatne kam पछि हट्ने काम *n.* retreat

pacchil tira पछिल्तिर *adv.* backwards

pachan kriya पाचनक्रिया *n.* digestion

pachaun kathin पचाउन कठिन *adj.* stodge

pachauni पछाउनी *n.* pancreas

pachhadi पछाडि *adv.* behind

pachhadi ko bhag पछाडिको भाग *adj.* rear

pachhariko dhoka पछाड़िको ढोका *n.* postern

pachharnu पछार्नु *v.* knock down

pachhattar keji samma ko taul केजीसम्मको तौल *n.* middleweight

pachhi पछि *prep.* after

pachhi पछि *adj.* later

pachhi bata पछि वाट *adv.* afterwards

pachhi hataunu पछि हटाउनु *v.* repel

pachhi hatnu पछि हटनु *v.* withdraw

pachhi lagnu पछिलाग्नु *v.* follow

pachhi lagnu पछि लाग्नु *v.* pursue

pachhi parnu पछि पर्नु *v.* lag

pachhi parnu पछि पर्नु *v.* tail away

pachhi sarnu पछि सार्नु *v.* postpone

pachhil tira dhakka hannu पछिल्तिर धक्का हान्नु *v.* recoil

pachhilitir jaanu पछिल्तिर जानु *v.* retrogress

pachhillo पछिल्लो *adj.* latter

pachhillo patak पछिल्लो पटक *n.* last time

pachhillo rat पछिल्लो रात *n.* last night

pachhote thaun पछौटे ठाउँ *n.* backwoods

pachhutaunu पछुताउनु *v.* repent

pachhuto पछुतो *n.* remorse

pachhuto पछुतो *n.* repentance

pachi aaune पछि आउने *adj.* subsequent

pachi hatnu पछि हटनु *v.* flinch

pachi sahara lenu पछि सहारा लिनु *v.* recline

packka पच्का *n.* syringe

pad awanati पद अवनति *n.* demotion

pad yatra पदयात्रा *n.* trekking

pad yatri पदयात्री *n.* trekker

padak पदक *n.* medal

paddonti garnu पदोन्नति गर्नु *v.* upgrade

padhai पढाइ *n.* study

padhari पादरी *n.* clerk

padhaunu पढाउनु *v.* teach

padhe lekheko पढेलेखेको *adj.* learned

padhna layak ko पढ्न लायकको *adj.* readable

padhna na sakine पढ्न नसकिने *adj.* illegible

padhna sakine पढ्न सकिने *adj.* legible

padhnu पढ्नु *v.* read

padh-parichay dinu पद-परिचय दिनु *v.* parse

padkad पकड *n.* grip

padkanu पड्कनु *v.* explode

padkanu पड्कनु *v.* go off

padkka पक्का *adj.* sure-fire

padnu पादनु *v.* fart

padri पादरी *n.* eccelesiastic

padswar पादस्वर *n.* crotchet

pagaalnu पगाल्नु *v.* smelt

pagakhana पागलखाला *n.* bedlam

pagal पागल *adj.* loony

pagal पागल *n.* lunatic

pagal kura garnu पागल कुरा गर्नु *v.* rave

pagal wa krudh banaunu पागल वा क्रुद्ध बनाउनु *n.* madden

pagalkhana पागलखाना *n.* asylum

paglanu पग्लनु *v.* melt

paglanu पग्लनु *v.* thaw

pagleko पग्लेको *adj.* molten

pagur पागुर *n.* cud

pahad पहाड *n.* hill

pahad पहाड *n.* mountain

pahad, parwat पहाड़, पर्वत *n.* hill

pahadi पहाडी *adj.* hilly

pahadi पहाडी *adj.* mountainous

pahalman पहलमान *n.* wrestler

paharedar पहरेदार *n.* guard

paharo पहरो *n.* precipice

paheli पहेली *v.* enigma

pahenlo पहेँलो *adj.* yellow

pahichan पहिचान *n.* identification

pahichan पहिचान *n.* recognition

pahile kor पहिलेको *adj.* prior

pahile na bhaeko पहिले नभएको *adj.* unprecedented

pahile nai पहिले नै *adv.* beforehand

pahile ne chetauni dinu पहिले नै चेतावनी दिनु *v.* forewarn

pahile ne dhanu पहिले नै धन्नु *v.* foretell

pahileko awasthama jaanu पहिलेको अवस्थामा जानु *v.* relapse

pahileko pad पहिलेको पद *n.* rehabilitate

pahilo पहिलो *adj.* first

pahilo bhashan पहिलो भाषण *n.* maiden speech

pahilo darja ko पहिलो दर्जाको *adj.* top-notch

pahiro पहिरो *n.* landslide

pahuna पाहुना *n.* guest

pahunch पहुँच *n.* access

paida garaunu/hunu पैदा गराउनु/हुनु *v.* originate

paidal पैदल *adv.* afoot

paidal yatra garnu पैदल यात्रा गर्नु *n.* hike

paidal yatra garnu पैदल यात्रा गर्नु *v.* trek

paidalsena पैदल सेना *n.* infantry

paidawar पैदावार *n.* yield

paikhana पाइखाना *n.* loo

paila पाइला *n.* footprint

paisa पेशा *n.* money

paisa phirta dinu पैसा फिर्ता दिनु *v.* refund

paisa tirera rakhine bhari पैसा तिरेर राखिने भारी *n.* payload

paisaadi पैसा आदि *n.* wherewithal

paisavihin पैसाविहीन *adj.* penniless

paitala पैताला *n.* sole

paitrik sampati पैतृक सम्पत्ति *n.* patrimony

paiyan पैयाँ *n.* gallop

paji पाजी *n.* rascal

pakad पकड *n.* hold

pakad पकड *n.* seizure

pakaune tarika पकाउने तरीका *n.* cuisine

pakeko पाकेको *adj.* ripe

paket rumal पकेट रुमाल *n.* hanky

pakhala पखाला *n.* diarrh(o)ea

pakhalnu पखाल्नु *v.* rinse

pakhand पाखण्ड *n.* hypocrisy

pakhe पाखे *n.* clown

pakhe पाखे *adj.* rude

pakheta पखेटा *n.* wing

pakhura पाखुरा *n.* forearm

pakka पक्का *adj.* consummate

pakka पक्का *adj.* sure

pakka पक्का *adj.* thorough

pakka garnu पक्का गर्नु *v.* insure

paknu पाक्नु *v.* fester

paknu पाक्नु *v.* maturate

paknu पाक्नु *v.* ripen

pako पाको *adj.* mature

pakranu पक्रनु *v.* take

pakrau पक्राउ *n.* capture

paksh pati पक्षपाती *adj.* unfair

paksha pat पक्षपात *n.* bias

pakshaghat पक्षाघात *n.* palsy

pakshaghat पक्षाघात *n.* paralysis

pakshpat पक्षपात *n.* partiality

pakshya tyagi पक्षत्यागी *n.* renegade

palai palo पालैपालो *adj.* alternate

palai palo sanga पालैपालोसँग *adv.* alternately

palan पालन *n.* compliance

pale पाले *n.* doorkeeper

pale पाले *n.* sentinel

pale पाले *n.* watchman

palis पालिस *n.* polish

palis garne dhatu पालिस गर्ने धातु *n.* emery

palnu पाल्नु *v.* breed

palnu पाल्नु *v.* foster

palnu पाल्नु *v.* nurture

palo dine पालो दिनु *adj.* relievign

paltan पलटन *n.* regiment

paltaunu पल्टाउनु *v.* overturn

paltindai janu पल्टिँदै जानु *v.* roll away

paltu पालतु *adj.* tame

palungo पालुङ्गो *n.* spinach

palwala dunga पालवाला डुङ्गा *n.* yacht

pan पान *n.* betel

pana पाना *n.* page

panatini पनातिनी *n.* great granddaughter

panatini पनाति *n.* great grandson

panchaun पाँचौ *adj.* fifth

panchaun पाँच *n.* five

panchbhuj पंचभुज *n.* pentagon

panchcharan पंचचरण *n.* pentameter

pandhra पन्ध्र *n.* fifteen

pandu rog पाण्डु रोग *n.* jaundice

pandulipi पाण्डुलिपि *n.* manuscript

pandulipi पाण्डुलिपि *n.* manuscript

pangremech पांग्रे मेच *n.* wheelchair

pani पनि *adv.* also

pani पनि *adv.* even

pani पनि *adj./adv./conj.* neither

pani पानी *n.* water

pani dekhi Dar पानीदेखि डर *n.* hydrophobia

pani ghatta पानीघट्ट *n.* watermill

pani khanyanu पानी खन्याउनु douse

pani ko kami पानीको कमी *n.* dehydration

pani ko paip पानीको पाइप *n.* waterpipe

pani le dhaknu/dubaunu पानीले ढाक्नु/डुबाउनु *v.* submerge

pani le na bigarne पानीले नबिगार्ने *adj.* waterproof

pani ma utrane wastu पानीमा उत्रने वस्तु *n.* float

pani ma utreko, bagi raheko पानीमा उत्रेको, बगी रहेको *adj.* afloat

paniko gahiraiko nap पानीको गहिराइको नाप *n.* fathom

panil phoka पानी फोका *n.* bubble

panile kateko kulo पानीले काटेको कुलो *n.* gully

paniun पनिउँ *n.* scoop

panja पंजा *n.* glove

panja पंजा *n.* paw

panjikadhikari पंजिकाधिकारी *n.* registrar

pank phoka पानी फोका *n.* blister

pankha पंखा *n.* fan

pankti पंक्ति *n.* line-up

panna पन्ना *n.* emerald

pannako arkopatti पन्नाको अर्कोपट्टि *adv.* overleaf

panyalo पन्यालो *adj.* watery

pap पाप *n.* sin

pap पाप *n.* vice

papi पानी *adj.* immoral

papi पापी *adj.* sinful

papra jasto पाप्रा जस्तो *adj.* crusty

par darshak पारदर्शक *adj.* see-through

para पर *adv.* beyond

para पर *adv.* further

paraalko topi परालको टोपी *n.* boater

parai परालु *n.* hay

parakasta पराकाष्ठा *n.* climax

paral पराल *n.* straw

paral ko kunyu परालको कुन्यू *n.* haystack

param परम *adj.* utmost

paramarsh garnu परामर्श गर्नु *v.* confer

paramparagat परम्परागत *adj.* traditional

parashna garnu प्रश्न गर्नु *n.* question

parasparik kriya पारस्परिक क्रिया *n.* interplay

paratan प्रर्यटन *n.* tourism

parcha पर्चा *n.* handbill

parcha पर्चा *n.* leaflet

parcha पर्चा *n.* pamphlet

parcha पर्चा *n.* poster

parchha पर्छ *mod.* must

parchha पर्छ *v./mod.* should

parda पर्दा *n.* curtain

parda पर्दा *n.* screen

pardarshi पारदर्शी *adj.* transparent

pardesh परदेश *adv.* abroad

pardeshi परदेशी *n.* aline

parela परेला *n.* eyelash

parewa परेवा *n.* pigeon

pargaman परगमन *n.* adultery

pari परी *n.* fairy

paribhasha परिभाषा *n.* definition

parichalan garnu परिचालन गर्नु *v.* steer

parichaya garaunu परिचय गराउनु *v.* acquaint

parichaya patra परिचयपत्र *n.* identity (ID) card

parichit परिचित *adj.* conversant

paridhi परिधि *n.* circumference

paridhi परिधि *n.* perimeter

pariksha linu परीक्षा लिनु *v.* try out

parinaam परिणाम *n.* sequel

parinam dine परिणाम दिने *adj.* resultant

parinam nikalnu परिणाम निकाल्नु *v.* deduce

paripakwata परिपक्वता *n.* maturity

paripreksha परिप्रेक्ष *n.* perspective

parishad परिषद् *n.* council

parishrami परिश्रमी *adj.* assiduous

parishrami परिश्रमी *adj.* industrious

parishrami परिश्रमी *adj.* laborious

parishramik नारिश्रमिक *n.* remuneration

paristhiti परिस्थिति *n.* state of affairs

parityag garnu परित्याग गर्नु *v.* renounce

parivartan nachahane परिवर्तन नचाहने *adj.* conservative

pariwar परिवार *n.* family

pariwar wa kulki mukeni परिवार वा कुलकी मुखेनी *n.* matdriarch

pariwartan परिवर्तन *n.* variation

pariwesh परिवेश *n.* ambience

parkhanu पर्खनु *v.* wait

parmaan bataunu परिमाण बताउनु *v.* quantify

parmadesh परमादेश *n.* writ

parmanu परमाणु *n.* atom

parninam परिणाम *n.* result

paro पारो *n.* merciry

paro पारो *n.* quicksilver

paroksha परोक्ष *adj.* indirect

parpachuke पारपाचुके *n.* divorce

parshram परिश्रम *n.* labour

parsi पर्सि *n.* day after tomorrow

parti dinu पार्टी दिनु *v.* throw a party

parwahan पारवाहन *n.* transit

parwatarohi पर्वतारोही *n.* mountaineer

paryapt पर्याप्त, योग्य *adj.* adequate

paryatak प्र्यटक *n.* sightseer

paryawaran पर्यावरण *n.* ecology

paryog ma lyaunu प्रयोगमा ल्याउनु *v.* apply

pasa पासा *n.* dice

pasal पसल *n.* shop

pasale पसले *n.* shopkeeper

pasarunu पसार्नु *v.* stretch out

pasaunu पसाउनु *v.* penetrate

paschim ko desha पश्चिम को दिशा *n.* occident

paschimi vayu पश्चिमी वायु *n.* zephyr

pashchim पश्चिम *n.* west

pashchim tira पश्चिमतिर *adv.* westward

pashchimi पश्चिमी *adj.* western

pashchimi ranga ma ranginu पश्चिमी रंगमा रंगिनु *v.* westernise

pashu rakhne ghera पशु राख्ने घेरा *n.* corral

pashu wigyan पशुविज्ञान *n.* zoology

pashuko chak पशुको चाक *n.* rump

pashutulya पशुतुल्य *n.* brute

pasina पसिना *n.* perspiration

pasina पसिना *n.* sweat

paskanu पस्कनु *v.* serve

pasnu पस्नु *v.* enter

pasnu पस्नु *v.* infiltrate

paso सामान्य *n.* noose

paso पासो *n.* snare

paso पासो *n.* trap

pasrinu पसिन्नु *v.* lie flat

patal पाताल *n.* underworld

patalo पातलो *adj.* thin

patalo resami kapada पातलो रेसमी कपडा *n.* georgette

patan पतन *n.* debacle

patan पतन *n.* downfall

pataunu पटाउनु *v.* irrigate

pathak पाठक *n.* reader

pathan pathan पठनपाठन *n.* reading

pathansilta पतनशीलता *adj.* deciduous

pathar पठार *n.* plateau

patharu पातहरू *n.* foliage

patharu पातहरू *n.* frond

pathaunu पठाउनु *v.* send

patheghar पाठेघर *n.* uterus

patho पाठो *n.* lamb

patho पात *n.* leaf

patho पाठो *n.* lesson

pathshala पाठशाला *n.* byre

pathshala पाठशाला *n.* school

pathya kram पाठ्यक्रम *n.* course

pathyakram पाठ्यक्रम *n.* syllabus

pathyapustak पाठ्यपुस्तक *n.* textbook

pati पाटी *n.* board

pati पाटी *n.* inn

patlieko पातलिएको *adj.* sparse

patloon पतलून *n.* pantaloons

patmurkh पटमूर्ख *n.* idiot

patra karita पत्रकारिता *n.* jornalism

patra manjusha पत्रमंजूषा *n.* letter box

patra manjusha पत्रमंजूषा *n.* mailbox

patra mitra पत्रमित्र *n.* pen pal

patra mitra पत्रमित्र *n.* penfriend

patra mitra पत्र *n.* ply

patrakar पत्रकार *n.* journalist

patrakar sammelan पत्रकार सम्मेलन *n.* press conference

patrika पत्रिका *n.* magazine

patro पात्रे *n.* almanac

patro पात्रो *n.* calendar

patta launu पत्ता लाउनु *v.* ascertain

patta launu पत्ता लाउनु *v.* detect

patta launu पत्ता लाउनु *v.* detect

patta launu पत्ता लाउनु *v.* discover

pattadata पट्टादाता *n.* lessor

pattadhari पट्टाधारी *n.* lessee

pattai पट्टाई *n.* boredom

patthar yug पत्थरयुग *n.* stone age

patti पटटी *n.* bandage

patua पटुवा *n.* hemp

patuka पटुका *n.* belt

patyarilo पत्यारिलो *adj.* credible

pau पाउ *n.* foot

pau/khutta haru पाउ खटाहरू *n.* feet

paudar पाउडर *n.* powder

paudi पौडी *n.* swimming

paudi baj पौडीबाज *n.* swimmer

paudi khelda laune poshak पौडी खेल्दा लाउने पोशाक *n.* swimming costume

paudi khelnu पौडी खेल्नु *v.* swim

paudi pokhari पौडी पोखरी *n.* swimming pool

paujeb पाउजेब *n.* anklet

paune wyaki पाउने व्यक्ति *n.* recipient

paunu पाउनु *v.* get

paunu पाउनु *v.* obtain

paunu पाउनु *v.* receive

paunu पाउनु *v.* receive

pauranik katha पौराणिक कथा *n.* myth

pauranik kathamala पौराणिक कथामाला *n.* mythology

pauroti पाउरोटी *n.* bread

pauroti पाउरोटी *n.* loaf

pauroti banaune pasal पाउरोटी बनाउने पसल *n.* bakery

paushtik पौष्टिक *adj.* nutritious

346

paushtik पौष्टिक *adj.* wholesome

pavitar parnu पवित्र पार्नु hallow

pavitra parnu पवित्र पार्नु *v.* consecrate

pavitra sthal पवित्र स्थल *n.* shrine

pawitra पवित्र *adj.* holy

pawitrata पवित्रता *n.* sanctity

pawitrata पवित्रता *n.* scredness

payak पायक *adj.* convenient

payo पायो *v.* found

pechkas पेचकस *n.* screwdriver

pechkasnu पेच कस्नु *n.* screw

peep पिप *n.* abscess

peepa पीपा *n.* keg

peer parnu पीर पार्नु *v.* disquiet

peerha पीड़ा *n.* agony

peerhanashak पीड़ानाशक *n.* aspirin

penchish पेन्चिस *n.* pliers

pensan पेन्सन *n.* pension

pensilin पेन्सिलिन *n.* penicillin

pesewar पेसेवर *adj.* professional

pesha पेशा *n.* occupation

pesha पेशा *n.* profession

pesha पेशा *n.* vocation

peski पेस्की *n.* advance

pesta पेस्ता *n.* pisctachio

pesta पेस्ता *n.* pistachio

pet पेट *n.* belly

pet पेट *n.* tummy

pet bhar bhojan पेटभर भोजन *n.* square meal

pet ko peerha पेटको पीड़ा *n.* gripses

petbokeko awastha पेट बोके को अवस्था *n.* pregnancy

peth पेट *n.* maw

pethko bachha पेटको बच्चा *n.* foetus

peti पेटी *n.* footpath

peti पेटी *n.* girdle

peti पेटी *n.* sidewalk

petko पेटको *adj.* gastric

petrol पेट्रोल *n.* gasoline

petrol पेट्रोल *n.* petrol

petrolko gun bujhaune vastu पेट्रोलको गुण बुझाउने बस्तु *n.* octane

pett पेट *n.* abdomen

petu पेटु *adj.* voracious

peya पेय *n.* drink

phachchhe फच्छे *n.* quits

phadphadahat फडफडाहट *n.* flap

phaida फाइदा *n.* advantage

phaida फाइदा *n.* gain

phaida फाइदा *n.* profit

phaida uthaunu फाइदा उठाउनु *v.* trade on

phailanu फेलनु *v.* spread

phailaunu फेलाउनु *v.* extend

phaisala फेसला *v.* decide

phaisala फैसला *n.* decision

phaisla फैसला *n.* verdict

phajul kharch garnu फजुल खर्च गर्नु *v.* squander

phajul kharchi फजुलखर्ची *n./adj.* spendthrift

phakaunu फकाउनु *v.* entice

phakaunu फकाउनु *v.* induce

phal फल *n.* consequence

phal फल *n.* fruit

phal फल *n.* product

phal vishesh फल विशेष *n.* gooseberry

phala पहल *n.* initiative

phalam फलाम *n.* iron

phalam katne aari फलाम काट्ने आरी *n.* hacksaw

phalame bar फलामे बार *n.* rail

phalame top फलामे टोप *n.* helmet

phalano फलानो *pron.* such-and-such

phalanu फलानु *pron.* so-and-so

phalatin फलाटिन *n.* flannel

phalatin फलाटिन *n.* flannel

phalayk फल्याक *n.* plank

phaldayak फलदायक *adj.* fruitful

phan phani ghumnu फनफनी घुम्नु *v.* spin

phanka khwaunu फनका ख्वाउनु *v.* whirl

phansi dine manch फाँसी दिने मंच *n.* scaffold

phansiko takhta फाँसीको तखता *n.* gallows

phansiko takhta फाँसीको तखता *n.* gibbet

phant फाँट *n.* department

phapar फापर *n.* buckwheat

pharak फरक *adj.* different

pharak फरक *n.* odds

pharakilo फराकिलो *adj.* commodious

pharakilo फराकिलो *adj.* roomy

pharakilo फराकिलो *adj.* spacious

pharasilo फरासिलो *adj.* frank

phariya फरिया *n.* gown

pharo garer chalaunu फारो गरेर चलाउनु *v.* scrimp

pharra bolne फर्र बोल्ने *adj.* fluent

pharsi फर्सी *n.* pumpkin

phasaune manis फसाउने मानिस *n.* stool pigeon

phasaunu फसाउनु *v.* enmesh

phasaunu फसाउनु *v.* entrap

phasaunu फसाउनु *v.* tempt

phasnu फसनु *v.* entangle

phat phataunu फतफताउनु *v.* mutter

phatengro फटेङ्ग्रो *n.* grasshopper

phatik फटिक *n.* quartz

phatnu फाट्नु *v.* wear out

phayankanu फ्याँक्नु *v.* dump

pheknu फेंक्नु *adj.* abject

phela parnu फेला पार्नु *v.* find

phelaiko फेलाएको *adj.* outstreched

phelaunu फेलाउनु *v.* propagate

phenyl फिनेल *n.* phenol

pheri फेरि *adv.* again

pheri bahal garnu फेरि बहाल गर्नु *v.* reappoint

pheri banaunu फेरि बनाउनु *v.* rebuild

pheri banaunu फेरि बनाउनु *v.* remake

pheri bharnu फेरि भर्नु *v.* refill

pheri bhela hunu फेरि भेला हुनु *v.* reassemble

pheri chhannu/chunnu फेरि छान्नु/चुन्नु *v.* re-elect

pheri dekha parnu फेरि देखा पर्नु *v.* reappear

pheri hunu फेरि हुनु *v.* recur

pheri lekhnu फेरि लेख्नु *v.* rewrite

pheri milaunu फेरि मिलाउनु *v.* rearrange

pheri mulya lagaunu फेरि मूल्य लगाउनु *v.* revalue

pheri paida garnu फेरि पैदा गर्नु *v.* reproduce

pheri pakranu फेरि पक्रनु *v.* recapture

pheri pasnu फेरि पस्नु *v.* re-enter

pheri sangathit hunu फेरि सङ्गठित हुनु *v.* reunite

pheri sankriya banaunu फेरि सक्रिय बनाउनु *v.* reactivate

pheri sochnu फेरि सोच्नु *v.* rethink

pheri sthapit garnu फेरि स्थापित गर्नु *v.* reassure

pheri wala फेरीवाला *n.* hawker

pheriwal फेरीवाल *n.* huckster

pheta फेटा *n.* turban

phijaiko फिँजाएको *adj.* outspread

phika baijani rang फीका बैजनी रङ्ग *n.* mauve

phikkapahenlo फिक्का पहेलो *adj.* pale

phikkapan फीकापन *n.* pallor

philtar फिल्टर *n.* filter

phinj फींज *n.* foam

phiranta फिरन्ता *n.* vagabond

phiranta jatiko sadasya फिरन्ता जातिको सदस्य *n.* gipsy

phiranta jatiko sadasya फिरन्ता जातिको सदस्य gypsy

phirauti rakam फिरौती रकम *n.* ransom

phiroj dhunga फिरोज ढुङ्गा *n.* turquoise

phirta bolaunu फिर्ता बोलाउनु *v.* recall

phirta garnu फिर्ता गर्नु *v.* restore

phirti tikat फिर्ती टिकट *n.* return ticket

phitalo फितलो *adj.* slack

phitkiri फिटकिरि *n.* alum

phitta फित्ता *n.* lace

phitta फित्ता *n.* strap

phitta फित्ता *n.* tape

phitte juka फित्तेजुका *n.* tapeworm

phiyo फियो *n.* spleen

phodnu फोड्नु *v.* smash

phohar maila फोहरमैला *n.* garbage

phohar maila फोहरमैला *n.* litter

phohor फोहोर *adj.* nasty

phohor maila फोहोर-मैला *adj.* grotty

phohor/dushit parnu फोहोर/दूषित पार्नु *v.* contaminate

phohori फोहोरी *adj.* dirty

phohori फोहोरी *adj.* filthy

phohori फोहोरी *adj.* slipshod

phohori फोहोरी *adj.* squalid

phoka फोका *n.* boil

phokso फोक्सो *n.* lung

phokso ko suj फोक्सोको सुज *n.* pneumonia

phool bechne vyakti फूल बेच्ने व्यक्ति *n.* florist

phoolko krishi फूलको कृषि *n.* floriculture

phoot फूट discord

photo फोटो *n.* photo

photocopy फोटोकापी *n.* xerox

photokapi फोटोकापी *n.* photocopy

photokapi फोटोकापी *n.* xenophobia

phukalnu फुकाल्नु *v.* put off

phukalnu फुकाल्नु *v.* take off

phukaunu फुकाउनु *v.* loosen

phukaunu फुकाउनु *v.* undo

phukaunu फुकाउनु *v.* untie

phul फूल *n.* daisy

phul फुल *n.* egg

phul फूल *n.* flower

phul ko pat फूलको पात *n.* petal

phulaunu फुलाउनु *v.* puff up

phulaunu phulnu फुलाउनु फुल्नु *v.* distend

phuldan फुलदान *n.* vase

phulko gucha फूलको गुच्छा *n.* nosegay

phulko guchchha फूलको गुच्छा *n.* bouquet

phulko seto bhag फूलको सेतो भाग *n.* albumen

phulkobhi फुलकोभी *n.* cauliflower

phulnu फुल्नु *v.* bloom

phulnu फुल्नु *n.* bulge

phulo फुलो *n.* trachoma

phurka फुर्का *n.* tassel

phursad ko samaya फुर्सद को समय *n.* spare time

phursat फुर्सत *n.* leisure

phursatma फुर्सतमा *adv.* leisurely

phurti फुर्ति *n.* elan

phurti sanga फुर्तिसँग *adv.* smartly

phurtilo फुर्तिलो *adj.* agile

phurtilo फुर्तिलो *adj.* brisk

phurtilo फुर्तिलो *adj.* dashing

phurtilo फुर्तिलो *adj.* lively

phus ko chhana फुसको छाना *n.* thatch

phuslayunu फुस्ल्याउनु *v.* wheedle

phuss niskeko hawa फुस्स निस्केको हावा *n.* whiff

phut bal फुटबल *n.* soccer

phutaunu फुटाउनु *v.* shatter

phutkanu फुक्नु *v.* escape

phutnu फुट्नु *n.* burst

phutnu फुट्नु *n.* chap

phyanknu फ्याँक्नु *v.* throw

phyauro फ्याउरो *n.* fox

phyuj फ्युज *n.* fuse

piano jasto baja पियानो जस्तो बाजा *n.* harpsichord

piaro banaunu प्यारो बनाउनु *v.* endear

piaro garer angalnu प्यारो गरेर अँगाल्नु *v.* cuddle

pichkari पिचकारी *n.* spray

pida dayi पीडादायी *adj.* painful

pida rahit पीडारहित *adj.* painless

piknik पिकनिकब *n.* picnic

pinas पिनास *n.* sinus infection

pind chhutaunu पिण्ड छुटाउनु *v.* shake off

pindalu पिँडालु *n.* taro

pindh पीण्ड *n.* base

pindh पींध *n.* bottom

pindhnu पिँध्नु *v.* grind

pinhyun ma prahar पिठ्यूँमा प्रहार *n.* stab in the back

pinjada पिँजड़ा *n.* cage

pip पीप *n.* pus

piralnu पिरल्नु *v.* fret

piramid पिरामिड *n.* pyramid

piro पिरो *adj.* pungent

pisab पिसाब *n.* urine

pishab garnu पिशाब गर्नु *v.* piddle

pishab garnu पिशाब गर्नु *v.* urnate

pishach पिशाच *n.* goblin

pisne anna पिस्ने अन्न *n.* grist

pistaul पिस्तौल *n.* revolver

pistol पिस्तोल *n.* pistol

pistol wa revolverko khol पिस्तोल वा रिभल्भरको खोल *n.* holster

pit jwar पीतज्वर *n.* yellow fever

pit patra karita पीत पत्रकारिता *n.* yellow press

pitai पिटाइ *n.* hiding

pith ma bokne jhola पीठमा बोक्ने झोला *n.* rucksack

pitho पीठो *n.* flour

pitho/matho muchhnu पिठो/माटो मुछ्नु *v.* knead

pithuma bokne jhola पिठ्यूँमा बोक्ने झोला *n.* haversack

pithuyuko पिठ्यूँको *adj.* dorsal

pithyuma पिठ्यूँमा *adv.* pickaback

pitta पित्त *n.* bile

pitta पित्त *n.* gall

pittal पित्तल *n.* brass

piun पिउन *n.* peon

piuna hune पिउन हुने *adj.* potable

piune bharho पिउने भाँड़ो *n.* goblet

piune wastu पिउने वस्तु *n.* beverage

piunu पिउनु *v.* swig

plaiud प्लाइउड *n.* plywood

plastic प्लास्टिक *n.* polythene

plastik प्लास्टिक *n.* plastic

plawika प्लाविका *n.* plasma

ple kard प्लेकार्ड *n.* placard

pohor (sal) पोहोर (साल) *n.* last year

pokhari पोखरी *n.* mere

pokhari पोखरी *n.* pond

pokhari पोखरी *n.* pool

pokhinu पोखिनु *v.* run over

pokhiyeko kura पोखिएको कुरा *n.* overspill

pokhnu पोख्नु *v.* spill

poko पोको *n.* bundle

poko पोको *n.* pack

poko पोको *n.* package

poko पोको *n.* parcel

pol na kholna diine ghus पाले नखोल्न दिइने घूस *n.* hush money

police पुलीस *v.* cop

police ko sipahi पुलीस को सिपाही *n.* bobby

polnu पोल्नु *n.* burn

polnu पोल्नु *v.* singe

poorkha पूर्खा *n.* forbear

popko dut पोपको दूत *n.* legate

poshak पोशाक *n.* costume

poshak पोशाक *n.* robe

poshan पोषण *n.* nourishment

poshan पोषण *n.* nutrition

posnu पोस्नु *v.* nourish

postbaks पोस्टबक्स *n.* postbox

poster पोस्टर *n.* poster

postkard पोस्टकार्ड *n.* postcard

pote ko geda पोतेको गेडा *n.* bead

pothi mujur पोथी मुजुर *n.* peahen

pothre dumsi पोथ्रे दुम्सी *n.* hedgehog

prabal प्रबल *adj.* ardent

prabandhak प्रबन्धक *n.* steward

prabas प्रवास *n.* domicile

prabhav parne gari bolnu प्रभाव पार्ने गरी बोल्नु *v.* declaim

prabhavmandal प्रभावमंडल *n.* nimbus

prabhaw प्रभाव *n.* impact

prabhaw प्रभाव *n.* influence

prabhaw kshetra प्रभाव क्षेत्र *n.* sphere of influence

prabhaw parnu प्रभाव पार्नु *v.* affect

prabhaw parnu प्रभाव पार्नु *v.* impress

prabhaw shali प्रभावशाली *adj.* impressive

prabhaw shali प्रभावशाली *adj.* majestic

prabhawshali प्रभावशाली *adj.* influential

prabhu satta प्रभुसत्ता *n.* sovereignty

prabhutwa प्रभुत्व *n.* domination

prachand प्रचण्ड *adj.* vehement

prachand toofan प्रचण्ड तूफान *n.* typhoon

prachar प्रचार *n.* circulation

prachar प्रचार *n.* publicity

prachar garnu प्रचार गर्नु *v.* disseminate

prachin प्राचीन *adj.* ancient

prachin प्राचीन *adj.* primitive

prachin roman phhojko company प्राचीन रोमन फौजको कम्पनी cohort

prachin samaya प्राचीन समय *n.* yore

prachlit प्रचलित *adj.* popular

prachur प्रचुर *adj.* ample

prachur प्रचुर *adj.* copious

prachur प्रचुर *adj.* galore

prachurta प्रचुरता *n.* abundance

pradan garnu प्रदान गर्नु *v.* impart

pradarshan garnu प्रदर्शन गर्नु *v.* demonstrate

pradarshan garnu प्रदर्शन *n.* display

pradarshani प्रदर्शनी *n.* exhibition

pradhan प्रधान *n.* chief

pradhan प्रधान *adj.* principal

pradhan adhyapak प्रधानाध्यापक *adv.* headmaster

pradhan mantri प्रधानमंत्री *n.* prime minister

pradhyapak प्राध्यापक *n.* professor

pradushan प्रदूषण *n.* pollution

pragati प्रगति *n.* headway

pragati प्रगति *n.* progress

pragati gardai प्रगति गर्दै *adj.* up and coming

pragatishil प्रगतिशील *adj.* progressive

prahar प्रहार *n.* stroke

praheiika प्रहेलिका *n.* charade

praidweep प्रायद्वीप *n.* peninsula

praishchit प्रायश्चित *n.* penance

prajapidak shasak प्रजापीडक शासक *n.* despot

prajatantra प्रजातन्त्र *n.* democracy

prajeet garnu पराजित गर्नु *v.* overcome

prakash प्रकाश *n.* light

prakash par'nu प्रकाश पार्नु *v.* enlighten

prakash yukta प्रकाशयुक्त *adj.* luminous

prakashak प्रकाशक *n.* publisher

prakashan प्रकाशन *n.* publication

prakashit garnu प्रकाशित गर्नु *v.* publish

prakat garnu प्रकट गर्नु *v.* disclose

prakat nabhaeko प्रकट नभएको *adj.* latent

prakhai प्रखाल *n.* parapet

prakhat ऱख्यात *adj.* fabulous

prakhyat प्रख्यात *adj.* noted

prakmukh पुमुख *adj.* leading

prakritik प्राकृतिक *adj.* natural

prakritik प्रकृति *n.* nature

prakritik drishya प्राकृतिक दृश्य *n.* scenery

prakritiwad प्रकृतिवाद *n.* naturalism

prakriya प्रकृया *n.* process

pralap garnu प्रलाप गर्नु *v.* rant

praman प्रमाण *n.* proof

praman patra प्रमाणपत्र *n.* ceritifcate

praman patra प्रमाण पत्र *n.* testimonial

pramanikaran प्रमाणीकरण *n.* verification

pramanit garnu प्रमाणित गर्नु *v.* prove

pramanit granu प्रमाणित गुर्न *n.* certify

pramanit/sabit garnu प्रमाणित/साबित गर्नु *v.* substantiate

pramarshdata परामर्शदाता *n.* mentor

pramukh प्रमुख *adj.* sailent

pramukh bhumika प्रमुख भूमिका *n.* title role

pramukh wichar प्रमुख विचार *n.* keynote

pran halnu प्राण हाल्नु *v.* animate

pranam प्रणाम *n.* obeisance

pranay-yachna प्रणय-याचना *n.* courtship

prani प्राणी *n.* creature

prani haru प्राणीहरू *n.* fauna

prani shastri प्राणीशास्त्री *n.* zoologist

prant प्रान्त *n.* county

prant प्रान्त *n.* province

prapat garnu प्राप्त गर्नु *v.* acquire

prapat garnu प्राप्त गर्नु *v.* attain

prapt garne प्राप्त गर्ने *n.* receiver

prapt garnu प्राप्त गर्नु *v.* achieve

prapt majdur sankhya प्राप्त मजदूर संख्या *n.* workforce

prapti प्राप्ति *n.* acqwuisition

prarambh प्रारम्भ *n.* inception

prarthana garnu प्रार्थना गर्नु *v.* implore

prarthana/binti garnu प्रार्थना/बिन्ती गर्नु *v.* pray

prarthanako pustak प्रार्थनाको पुस्तक *n.* breviary

prarthna patra प्रार्थना पत्र *n.* application

prarthnagaan प्रार्थनागान *n.* anthem

prasanchit प्रसन्नचित *adj.* lightsome

prasang प्रसंग *n.* episode

prasann प्रसन्न *adj.* blithe

prasanna प्रसन्न *adj.* cheerful

prasav peerha प्रसव पीड़ा travail

prashamsa प्रशंसा *n.* praise

prashansa प्रशंसा *n.* accolade

prashansagarnu प्रशंसा गर्नु *v.* admire

prashansniya प्रशंसनीय *adj.* creditable

prashasak प्रशासक *n.* administrator

prashast hava lagne प्रशस्त हावा लाग्ने *adj.* airy

prashasta प्रशस्त *adj.* abundant

prashasta hunu प्रशस्त हुनु *v.* abound

prashat प्रशस्त *n.* plenty

prashikshak प्रशिक्षक *nb.* coach

prashna प्रश्न *n.* query

prashna प्रसन्न *adj.* jubilant

prashna chinha प्रश्नचिन्ह *n.* question mark

prashna garnu प्रश्न गर्नु *v.* interrogate

prashna garnu प्रश्न गर्नु *n.* interrogation

prashnawali *n.* questionnaire

prasiddha प्रसिद्ध *adj.* famous

prasiddha प्रसिद्ध *adj.* renowned

prasiddha प्रसिद्ध *adj.* reputed

prasiddha प्रसिद्ध *adj.* well known

prasidh प्रसिद्ध *adj.* illustrious

prastavana प्रस्तावना *n.* preamble

prastaw प्रस्ताव *n.* offer

prastaw प्रस्ताव *n.* proposal

prastaw प्रस्ताव *n.* resolution

prastaw rakhnu प्रस्ताव राख्नु *v.* propose

prastawak प्रस्तावक *n.* proponent

prasthan प्रस्थान गर्नु *v.* depart

prasthan प्रस्थान *n.* exodus

prasthan rekha प्रस्थान रेखा *n.* scratch

prasuti griah प्रसूतिगृह *n.* maternity hospital

prateeksha garnu प्रतीक्षा गर्नु *v.* await

pratham प्रथम *adj.* prima

prathmikta प्राथमिकता *n.* priority

prathymik प्राथमिक *adj.* primary

prati dwandwi प्रतिद्वन्द्वी *n.* rival

prati kriya janaunu प्रतिक्रिया जनाउनु *v.* react

prati kul प्रतिकूल *adj.* unfavo(u)rable

prati kul प्रतिकूल *adj.* unfavourable

prati nidhi प्रतिनिधि *n.* proxy

prati nidhitwa प्रतिनिधित्व *n.* representation

prati nidhitwa प्रतिनिधित्व *n.* representative

prati nidhitwa garnu प्रतिनिधित्व गर्नु *v.* stand for

prati warsh प्रतिवर्ष *adj.* per annu,

prati wimba प्रतिबिम्ब *n.* reflection

prati wimbit garnu प्रतिविम्बित गर्नु *v.* reflect

prati wyakti प्रतिव्यक्ति *adj.* per capita

pratibandh garnu प्रतिबन्ध गर्नु *n.* curb

pratibhashali wyakti प्रतिभाशाली व्यक्ति *n.* genius

pratidhwani प्रतिध्वनि *n.* echo

pratigya प्रतिज्ञा *n.* promise

pratigya प्रतिज्ञा *n.* vow

pratikool प्रतिकूल *adj.* adverse

pratikriya प्रतिक्रिया जनाउनु *n.* reaction

pratikriyawadi प्रतिक्रियावादी *n.* reactionary

pratiksha suchi प्रतीक्षा सूचि *n.* waiting list

pratikshalaya प्रतीक्षालय *n.* waiting room

pratikulta प्रतिकूलता *n.* contrariety

pratilipi प्रतिलिपि *n.* copy

pratinidhi प्रतिनिधि *n.* delegate

pratinidhi mandal प्रतिनिधि-मण्डल *n.* deputation

pratinidhi niyukat garnu प्रतिनिधि नियुक्त गर्नु *v.* depute

pratirodh kayam garnu प्रतिरोध कायम गर्नु *v.* hold out

pratirup प्रतिरूप *n.* counterpart

pratisath प्रतिशत *n.* cent

pratispardha प्रतिस्पर्धा *n.* competition

pratispardha garnu प्रतिस्पर्धा गर्नु *v.* vie

pratisthapan प्रतिस्थापन *n.* replacement

pratiyogita garnu प्रतियोगिता गर्नु *v.* compete

pratyaksha प्रत्यक्ष *adj.* evident

pratyakshadarshi प्रत्यक्षदर्शी *n.* eyewitness

praudh प्रौढ *adj.* elderly

prawah प्रवाह *n.* flow

prawah प्रवाह *n.* onrush

prawah band garidinu प्रवाह बन्द गरिदिनु *v.* shut off

prawah wiparit प्रवाहविपरीत *adv.* upstream

prawakta प्रवक्ता *n.* spokesperson

prawal dweep प्रवाल द्वीप *n.* atoll

prawasi प्रवासी *n.* emigrant

prawasi प्रवासी *n.* émigré

prawasi प्रवासी *n.* migrant

praweenta प्रवीणता *n.* proficiency

prawesh प्रवेश *n.* admission

prawesh प्रवेश *n.* entrance

prawesh प्रवेश *n.* entry

prawesh garna dinu प्रवेश गर्नु दिनु *v.* let in

prawidhi प्रविधि *n.* technique

prawidhi प्रविधि *n.* technology

prawidhigya प्राविधिज्ञ *n.* technician

prawidhik प्राविधिक *adj.* technical

prawritti प्रवृत्ति *n.* trend

prayah प्रायः *adv.* almost

prayah प्रायः *adv.* mainly

prayashchit garnu प्रायश्चित गर्नु *v.* expiate

prayatna प्रयत्न *n.* endeavo(u)r

prayatna garnu प्रयत्न गर्नु *v.* attampt

prayayewachi kosh पर्यायवाची कोश *n.* thesaurus

prayog प्रयोग *n.* experiment

prayog प्रयोग *n.* trial

prayog प्रयोग *n.* usage

prayog प्रयोग *v.* use

prayog shala प्रयोगशाला *n.* laboratory

prayogshala प्रयोगशाला *n.* Lab

prayojak प्रायोजक *n.* sponsor

praytak पर्यटक *n.* tripper

prem प्रेम *n.* love

prem garihaalne प्रेम गरिहाल्ने *adj.* amorous

prem wiwah प्रेम विवाह *n.* love marriage

premalap प्रेमालाप *n.* romance

premgarnu प्रेम गर्नु *v.* woo

premi प्रेमी *n.* lover

premi प्रेमी *n.* sweetheart

premika प्रेमिका *n.* girlfriend

premika प्रेमिका *n.* sweetheart

prerana प्रेरणा *n.* impetus

prerana प्रेरणा *n.* inspiration

prerit garnu प्रेरित गर्नु *n.* goad

prerit garnu प्रेरित गर्नु *v.* inspire

pres samwaddata प्रेस संवाददाता *n.* press agent

pret प्रेत *n.* hobgoblin

prithwi पृथ्वी *n.* earth

prithwi पृथ्वी *n.* globe

priye प्रिये *n./adj.* darling

protin प्रोटीन *n.* protein

proton प्रोटोन *n.* proton

protsahan प्रोत्साहन *n.* incentive

pucchar nabhayko bandar पुच्छर नभएको बाँदर *n.* ape

puchchhar पुच्छर *n.* tail

puchhne wastu पुछ्ने वस्तु *n.* wiper

puchhnu पुछ्नु *v.* mop

puchhnu पुछ्नु *v.* winter sports

puchhnu पुछ्नु wipe

pugna sakine पुग्न सकिने *adj.* accessible

pugnu पुग्नु *v.* reach

puja garnu पूजा गर्नु *v.* adore

puja garnu पूजा गर्नु *n.* worship

pujari पुजारी *n.* priest

pujniya पूजनीय *adj.* adorable

pul पुल *n.* bridge

pul pulyaunu पुलपुल्याउनु *v.* pamper

pulao पुलाउ *n.* risotto

puling पुलिङ्ग *n.* masculine

pulis पुलिस *n.* police

pulis पुलिस *n.* policeman

pulpulaunu पुल्पुल्याउनु *v.* dote

punar ganana पुनर्गणना *v.* recount

punar janma पुनर्जन्म *n.* rebirth

punar janma पुनर्जन्म *n.* regeneration

punar jiwit garnu पुर्नजीवित गर्नु *v.* revive

punar milan पुनर्मिलन *n.* reunion

punarsthapna पुनस्थार्पना *n.* restoration

punarutpadan पुनरुत्पादन *n.* reproduction

punarwas पुनर्वास *n.* rehabilitation

punjiwad पूंजीवाद *n.* capitalism

punkeshwar पुंकेशर *n.* stamen

punkur moto पुङ्कोर मोटो *adj.* dumpy

pura पूरा *adj.* complete

pura baji marnu पूरा बाजी मार्न *v.* sweep the board

pura byunjheko पूरा ब्यूँझेको *adj.* wide awake

pura garnu पूरा गर्नु *v.* accomplish

pura garnu पूरा गर्नु *v.* fulfil

pura tawar le पूरातवरले *adv.* perfectly

purano पुरानो *adj.* old

purano पुरानो *adj.* outworn

purano पुरानो *adj.* ramshackle

purano पुरानो *adj.* second-hand

purano पुरानो *adj.* used

purano dhancha ko पुरानो ढाँचाको *adj.* old-fashioned

purano dharra ko पुरानो ढर्राको *adj.* old hat

purano dharra ko mani पुरानो ढर्राको मानिस *n.* stick-in-the-mud

purano khalko पुरानो खालको *adj.* quaint

purano thotro gadi पुरानो थोत्रो गाड़ी *n.* jalopy

puraskar पुरस्कार *n.* award

puratattva पुरातत्व *n.* archaeology

purji पूर्जी *n.* prescription

purkha पुर्खा *n.* ancestor

purkha पुर्खा *n.* forefather

purkha adi bata paunu पुर्खा आदिबाट पाउनु *v.* inherit

purn पूर्ण *adj.* absolute

purn पूर्ण *adj.* intact

purn kad पूर्णकद *adj.* life-size(d)

purn parvartan पूर्ण परिवर्तन *n.* volte-face

purn ruple पूर्ण रूपले *adv.* entirely

purna gathan garnu पुर्न गठन गर्नु *n.* reshuffle

purnta पूर्णता *n.* integrity

purntaya पूर्णतया *adv./prep.* throughout

purohit पुरोहित *n.* curate

purohitwargko shasan पुरोहितवर्गको शासन *n.* theocracy

purse परस *n.* wallet

purush natadar पुरुष नातादार *n.* kinsfolk

purushma hune पुरूषमा हुने *n.* falsetto

purushtav पुरुषत्व *n.* manhood

purvanubhav पूर्वानुभव *n.* foretaste

purv-drishya पूर्व-दृश्य *n.* flashback

purvsuchna dinu पूर्वसूचना दिनु *v.* portend

purvsuchna dinu पूर्वसूचना दिनु *v.* presage

purv-vichar पूर्वविचार *n.* forethought

purwa पूर्व *n.* east

purwabhyas पूर्वाभ्यास *n.* rehearsal

purwadhar पूर्वाधार *n.* infrastructure

purwagraha पूर्वग्रह *n.* prejudice

purwaj पूर्वज *n.* predecessor

purwaj पूर्वज *n.* progenitor

purwaka पूर्वका *n.* orient

purwi पूर्वी *adj.* eastern

purwiya पूर्वीय *adj.* oriental

puryauna janu पुन्याउन जानु *v.* see off

pushpa raj पुष्पराज *n.* topaz

pusht पुष्ट *adj.* muscular

pushti garnu पुष्टि गर्नु *v.* confirm

pushti garnu पुष्टि गर्नु *v.* corroborate

pusta पुस्ता *n.* generation

pustak adhyaksha पुस्तकाध्यक्ष *n.* librarian

pustakalaya पुस्तकालय *n.* library

pustakko akaar पुस्तकको आकार *n.* format

pustika पुस्तिका *n.* booklet

putala पुतला *n.* effigy

putali पुतली *n.* butterfly

putali पुतली *n.* doll

putli पुतली *n.* dolly

puttha पुट्ठा *n.* haunch

puttha पुट्ठा *n.* hip

putti पुति *n.* gagina

pwal parne yantra प्वाल पार्ने यंत्र *n.* punch

pwal parne yantra प्वाल पार्ने यंत्र *n.* puncture

pwankh प्वाँख *n.* feather

pwankh प्वाँख *n.* plume

pwankh प्वाँख *n.* quill

pwankh milaunu प्वाँख मिलाउनु *v.* preen

pwankhe sarpa प्वाँखे सर्प *n.* dragon

pyaj प्याज *n.* onion

pyaj jasto sabzi प्याज जस्तो सब्जी *n.* leek

pyaji प्याजी *adj.* purple

pyano प्यानो *n.* piano

pyant प्याण्ट *n.* trousers

pyarasut प्यारासुट *n.* parachute

pyaro प्यारो *adj.* dear

pyaro प्यारो *n.* favo(u)rite

pyaro wastu प्यारो बस्तु *n.* pet

pyjama पायजामा *n.* pyjamas

pyorrhoea पाइरिया *n.* pyorrhoea

R

ra र *conj.* and

raal chuhaunu राल चुहाउनु *v.* slaver

raang राङ *n.* solder

raasan रासन *n.* ration

rabad ko chhap रबडको छाप *n.* rubber stamp

rabaph रबाफ *n.* pomp

rabaph dekhaunu रबाफ देखाउनु *v.* show off

rabar रबर *n.* rubber

rabar रबर *n.* rubber

rachayita रचयिता *n.* composer

rachna रचना *n.* composition

rachnu रच्नु *v.* compose

radda/badar garnu रद्द/बदर गर्नु *v.* cancel

radda/kharej garnu रद्द/खारेज गर्नु *v.* revoke

raddhi kura रद्दी कुरा *n.* tommyrot

raddi kagaj रद्दी कागज *n.* waste paper

raddi ko tokari रद्दी को टोकरी *n.* waste(paper) basket

radh garnu रद्द गर्नु *v.* annul

radh garnu रद्द गर्नु *v.* rescind

radio रेडियो *n.* aerial

radio adiko ariel रेडियो आदि को एरियल *n.* antenna

radium रेडियम *n.* radium

ragad रगड *n.* friction

ragat रगत *n.* blood

ragat bagnu रगत बग्नु *v.* bleed

ragharne vastu रगड्ने वस्तु *n.* abrasive

rah dani राहदानी *n.* passport

rahalpahal रहलपहल *n.* oddment

rahanu रहनु *v.* stay

rahar garnu रहर गर्नु *v.* yearn

rahar/chakh lagdo रहर∕चाखलाग्दो *adj.* interesting

rahasya रहस्य *n.* mystery

rahasya रहस्य *n.* puzzle

rahasya maya रहस्यमय *adj.* mysterious

rahasyatamkata रहस्यात्मकता *n.* mystique

raheko रहेको *adj.* contained

rail ko dabba रेलको डब्बा *n.* compartment

raio रायो *n.* mustard

raj dhani राजधानी *n.* capital

raj droh राजद्रोह *n.* sedition

raj garnu राज गर्नु *n.* reign

raj hans haru राजहाँसहरू *n.* geese

raj kosh राजकोष *n.* treasury

raj kumari राजकुमारी *n.* princess

raj marg राजमार्ग *n.* highway

raj nitigya राजनैतिक *n.* political

raj nitigya राजनीतिज्ञ *n.* politics

raj patru राजपत्र *n.* gazette

raj pratinidhi ko pad राज प्रतिनिधि को पद *n.* regency

raj tantra राजतंत्र *n.* monarchy

raja राजा *n.* king

raja राजा *n.* monarch

raja राजा *n.* sovereign

raja राजा *n.* suzerain

raja ko pad राजाको पद *n.* kingship

rajako hatya राजाको हत्या *n.* regicide

rajaswala रजस्वला *n.* menstruation

rajdand राजदंड *n.* sceptre

rajdroh राजद्रोह *n.* treason

rajdut राजदूत *n.* ambassador

rajdutawas ko karyalaya राजदूतावासको कार्यालय *n.* chancery

rajgaddi राजगद्दी *n.* throne

rajgaddima rakhnu राजगद्दीमा राख्नु *v.* enthrone

rajhans राजहाँस *n.* goose

rajhans राजहाँस *n.* swan

raji राजी *adj.* willing

raji nama dinu राजीनामा दिनु *v.* step down

rajinama राजीनामा दिनु *n.* resignation

rajkiya राजकीय *adj.* royal

rajkosh राजकोष *n.* exchequer

rajpratinedhi राजप्रतिनिधि *n.* regent

rajya राज्य *n.* realm

rajyabhishek राज्याभिषेक *n.* coronation

rajyaharu sangh राज्यहरूको संघ *n.* confederacy

rajyapal राज्यपाल *n.* governor

rakam रकम *n.* amount

raket रकेट *n.* rocket

rakhbari garne thaun/manis रखबारी गर्ने ठाउे/मानिस *n.* look out

rakhne kaam राख्ने काम *n.* retention

rakhnu राख्नु *v.* keep

rakhnu राख्नु *v.* possess

rakhnu राख्नु *v.* put

raksh atmak रक्षा आत्मक *n.* defensive

raksha रक्षा *v.* defence/defense

raksha रक्षा *n.* rescue

raksha रक्षा *n.* safeguard

raksha garne रक्षा गर्ने *adj.* protective

rakshas राक्षस *n.* monster

raksi रक्सी *n.* alcohol

raksi रक्सी *n.* grog

raksi रक्सी *n.* liquor

raksi रक्सी *n.* wine

raksi r gulio tato paani रक्सी र गुलियो तातो पानी *n.* toddy

rakta pat रक्तचाप *n.* bloodshed

raktpaatpurn रक्तपातपूर्ण *adj.* sanguinary

raktranjit रक्तरंजित *adj.* gory

raktshintale pidhit रक्तक्षीनताले पीड़ित *n.* anaemia

ral राल *n.* saliva

ral chuhaunu राल चुहाउनु *v.* drool

ram रम *n.* rum

ram toriyan रामतोरियाँ *n.* lady's finger

ram toriyan रामतोरियाँ *n.* okra

ramailo रमाइलो *adj.* festive

ramailo रमाइलो *adj.* funny

ramailo रमाइलो *adj.* gay

ramailo रमाइलो *adj.* hilarious

ramailo रमाइलो *adj.* pleasant

ramana hunu रमाना *n.* departure

ramaunu रमाउनु *n.* amuse

ramaunu रमाउनु *v.* enjoy

ramniya रमणीय *adj.* scenic

ramrai chhanieko राम्ररी छानिएको *adj.* hand-picked

ramrai garieko राम्ररी गरिएको *adj.* well judged

ramrari koshish gareko राम्ररी कोशिश गरेको *adj.* well tried

ramristri राम्री स्त्री *n.* rosebud

ramro राम्रो *adj.* graceful

ramro राम्रो *adj.* handsome

ramro राम्रो *adj.* nice

ramro राम्रो *adj.* pretty

ramro राम्रो *adj.* winnowing tray

ramro bhojan tyar garne kala राम्रो भोजन तयार गर्ने कला *n.* gastronomy

ramro bolne राम्रो बोल्ने *adj.* elopquent

ramro jaankari nabhayko राम्रो जानकारी नभएको *adj.* unenlightened

ramro natija राम्रो नतिजा ल्याउनु *v.* pay off

ramro niyat ko राम्रो नियतको *adj.* well intentioned

ramroasar parne राम्रो असर पार्ने *adj.* effective

randi ghar रन्डीघर *n.* brothel

rang रंग *n.* colo(u)r

rang रङ्ग *n.* paint

rang रङ्ग *n.* tint

rang aunu रंगाउनु *n.* dye

rang manch रङ्गमंच *n.* stage

rang manch रङ्गमंच *n.* theatre/theater

ranga ko masu राँगाको मासु *n.* buff

ranga ma bhang garne रंगमा भंग गर्ने *n.* wet blanket

rangbhoomi रंगभूमि *n.* arena

rangheen gyas रंगहीन ग्यास *n.* neon

rangin pencil रंगीन पेन्सिल *n.* crayon

rangshala रङ्गशाला *n.* stadium

rani रानी *n.* queen

rankebhut राँकेभूत *n.* will-o-the-wisp

ranniti रणनीति *n.* strategy

ranthninu रन्थनिनु *v.* daze

raphphu bharnu रफ्फू भर्नु *v.* darn

raphtar रफ्तार *n.* tempo

ras रस *n.* juice

ras रस *n.* lotion

ras रस *n.* soup

rasaunu रसाउनु *v.* seep

rasayanik रासायनिक *adj.* chemical

rasdar wyanjan रसदार व्यंजन *n.* sauce

rashi राशि *n.* mass

rashi chakra राशिचक्र *n.* zodiac

rashtra राष्ट्र *n.* nation

rashtrapati राष्ट्रपति *n.* president

rashtrawad राष्ट्रवाद *n.* nationalism

rashtriya राष्ट्रीय *adj.* national

rashtriyata राष्ट्रीय *n.* nationality

rasid रसीद *n.* counterfoil

rasid रसिद *n.* receipt

rasilo रसिलो *adj.* juicy

rasksha रक्षा *n.* protection

rat रात *n.* night

rat bhari रातभरि *adv.* overnight

rat ko disa pisab रातको दिसापिसाब *n.* nightsoil

rat ko khana रातको खाना *n.* dinner

rat ko manoranjan रातको मनोरंजन *n.* nightlife

ratan रतन *n.* jewel

rath रथ *n.* chariot

ratna रत्न *n.* gem

rato रातो *adj.* red

rato french madira रातो फ्रेन्च मदिरा *n.* claret

raun कपाल *n.* hair

raunak रौनक *n.* grandeur

rawaphilo karmchari रवाफिलो कर्मचारी *n.* jack in office

redar रेडार *n.* radar

362

rediyo रेडियो *n.* radio

rediyo dharmi रेडियोधर्मी *adj.* radioactive

redkras रेडक्रस *n.* red cross

rees uthaunu रीस उठाउनु *v.* exasperate

reesko jhonk रीसको झोंक *n.* tantrum

reharlagdi रहरलाग्दी *n.* nymphet

rekard garne kam रेकर्ड गर्ने काम *n.* recording

rekard garne yantra रकेर्ड गर्ने यन्त्र *n.* recorder

rekh dekh garnu रेखदेख गर्नु *v.* supervise

rekha रेखा *n.* line

rekha chitra रेखा चित्र *n.* diagram

rekha chitra रेखाचित्र *n.* drawing

rekha ganit रेखागणित *n.* geometry

rekhale ghernu रेखाले घेर्नु *v.* curcumscribe

rel रेल *n.* train

rel gadi रेलगाडी *n.* railway train

rel ko dibba रेलको डिब्बा *n.* railway carriage

rel ko injin रेलको इन्जिन *n.* railway engine

rel marg रेलमार्ग *n.* railroad

rel marg रेलमार्ग *n.* railway

renchu रेन्चु *n.* wreckage

rephri रेफ्री *n.* referee

resham रेशम *n.* silk

resham kira रेशमकीरा *n.* silkworm

resham ko koya रेशमको कोया *n.* cocoon

reti रेती *n.* file

riban रिबन *n.* ribbon

riha garnu रिहा गर्नु *v.* let loose

rijhaunu रिझाउनु *v.* please

rikabi रिकाबी *n.* saucer

riksa रिक्सा *n.* rickshaw

rikshaw रिक्सा *n.* chaise

rikt sthan रिक्त स्थान *n.* lacuna

riktata रिक्तता *n.* blank

rile daud रिले दोड *n.* relay race

rin ऋण *n.* debt

rin ऋण *n.* dues

rin ऋण *n.* loan

rin dine sahu रिन दिने साहु *n.* moneylender

rin tirn sakne ऋण तिर्न सक्ने *adj.* solvent

rin, sapat ऋण, सापट *n.* loan

ringata रिंगटा *n.* giddiness

ringata lageko रिंगटा *adj.* dizzy

ringta रिंगटा *n.* vertigo

rini ऋणी *adj.* indebted

rini hunu ऋणी हुनु *v.* owe

rinpatra ऋणपत्र *n.* debenture

riport रिपोर्ट *n.* report

ris रिस *n.* irritation

ris रिस *n.* resentment

ris रिस *n.* wrap

ris रिसले चूर *n.* fury

ris le chur रिसले चूर *adj.* furious

ris uthaunu रिस उठाउनु *v.* irritate

ris uthaunu रिस उठाउनु *v.*
  provoke

risaeko रिसाएको *adj.* angry

risaeko रिसाएको *adj.* indignant

risaha रिसाहा *adj.* ill-temerped

risaha रिसाहा *adj.* passionate

risaha रिसाहा *adj.* rabid

risaha रिसाहा *adj.* tempered

risaunu रिसाउनु *v.* resent

rishi ऋषि *n.* sage

rit रिट *n.* wristwatch

riti thiti रीतिथिति *n.* tradition

riti/niyam purwak रीति/नियमपूर्वक
  adj. systematic

ritithiti रीतिथिति *n.* custom

riti-thiti रीति-थिति *n.* mores

ritto रित्तो *adj.* empty

ritu ऋतु *n.* season

ritu ऋतु *n.* season

robot रोबोट *n.* robot

rochak रोचक *adj.* pleasing

roda रोडा *adj.* concrete

rog रोग *n.* disease

rog khuttaunu रोग खुट्टयाउनु *v.*
  disagnose

rog nash garne रोग नाश गर्ने *adj.*
  curative

rog patta launu रोग पत्ता लाउनु *v.*
  diagnose

rog pratirodh kshamata रोग
  प्रतिरोध क्षमता *n.* immunity

rog rokne tattva रोग रोक्ने तत्व *n*
  antibody

rogi रोगी *adj.* mawkish

rogko purwanumaan रोगको
  पूर्वानुमान *n.* prognosis

rogruko vigyan रोगरूको विज्ञान *n.*
  pathology

roji रोजी *n.* option

rok रोक *n.* check

rok tham रोकथाम *n.* prevention

rokide hune रोकिँदे हुने *adj.*
  intermittent

rokka रोक्का *n.* embargo

rokka रोक्का *n.* restriction

rokne kura रोक्ने कुरा *n.* deterrent

roknu रोक्नु *v.* debar

roknu रोक्नु *v.* detain

roknu रोक्नु *n.* detention

roknu रोक्नु *v.* deter

roknu रोक्नु *v.* discontinue

roknu रोक्नु *v.* forbid

roknu रोक्नु *v.* prevent

roknu रोक्नु *v.* refrain

roknu रोक्नु *v.* restrain

roknu रोक्नु *v.* restrict

roknu रोक्नु *v.* stanch, staunch

roknu रोक्नु *v.* stop

roknu रोक्नु *v.* withhold

roknu bachanu रोक्नुबचाउनु *v.*
  ward off

roktok hataunu रोकटोक हटाउनु *v.*
  unfreeze

rom ko sena रोमको सेना *n.* legion

romanch kari रोमांचकारी *adj.*
  thrilling

roop bigarnu रूप बिगार्नु *v.* disfigure

roop-parivartan रूप-परिवर्तन *n.* metamorphosis

rooprekha रूपरेखा *n.* blueprint

rooprekha रूपरेखा *n.* contour

roosi raksi रूसी रक्सी *n.* vodka

ropnu रोप्नु *v.* impale

rorha रोड़ा *n.* ballast

rorha रोड़ा *n.* gravel

rubber adiko dudhilo ras रबर आदि को दुधिलो रस *n.* latex

ruchi रुचि *n.* liking

rugha, khoki, jwaro adi रूघा, खोकी, ज्वरो आदि *n.* flu

ruju/pramanit garnu रुजू/प्रमाणित गर्नु *v.* verify

rukawat रुकावट *n.* jam

rukh रूख *n.* tree

rukh chadne jnawar रूख चढ्ने जनावर *n.* koala

rukh haru bhaeko रूखहरू भएको *adj.* wooded

rukh kathar रूख कटहर *n.* jackfruit

rukh katnu रूख काट्नु *v.* fell

rukh ko bokra रूखको बोक्रा *n.* bark

rukh vishesh रूख विशेष *n.* elm

rukho रूखो *adj.* rugged

rumal रुमाल *n.* handkerchief

runu रुनु *v.* cry

rup रूप *n.* aspect

rup badalnu रूप बदल्नु *v.* transform

rup rekha रूपरेखा *n.* outline

rupaiyan रुपैयाँ *n.* rupee

rupwati रूपवती *adj.* shapely

rusi kisan रूसी किसान *n.* moujik

rusko mudra रुसको मुद्रा *n.* rouble

ruwai रुवाइ *n.* sob

S

saancho साँचो *adj.* veritable

saancho jasto dekine gun साँचो जस्तो देखिने गुण *n.* verisimilitude

saandhya goshti सान्ध्य गोष्ठी *n.* soiree

saano jhagda सानो झगड़ा *n.* tiff

saas chodnu सास छोड्नु *v.* exhale

saas phernu सास फेर्नु *v.* respire

saathi साथी *n.* buddy

saatnu साट्नु *v.* swop, swap

sab bhanda asal सवभन्दा असल *adj.* best

sab bhanda jetho सबभन्दा जेठो *adj.* oldest

sab bhanda kam सबभन्दा कम *n.* minimum

sab bhanda kam सबभन्दा *adj./adv.* most

sab bhanda kanchho सबभन्दा कान्छो *adj.* youngest

sab bhanda kharab सबभन्दा खराब *adj.* worst

sab bhanda mathilo सबभन्दा माथिल्लो *adj.* uppermost

sab bhanda phailo सबभन्दा पहिलो *adj.* foremost

sabai सबै *adj.* all

sabai सबै *n.* gamut

sabai bhanda thorai सबैभन्दा थोरै *adj.* least

sabai washaya ali ali janne सबै विषय अलि अलि जान्ने *n.* jack of all trades

sabbhanda ramro vyakti wa vastu सबभन्दा राम्रो व्यक्ति वा वस्तु *n.* tops

sabddhan सावधान *adj.* circumspect

saberai सबेरै *adj.* early

sabha सभा *n.* assembly

sabha सभा *n.* conference

sabha सभा *n.* congress

sabha baithak सभा बैठक *n.* meeting

sabha griha सभागृह *n.* town hall

sabha kakasha सभाकक्षा *n.* auditorium

sabhako karyasuchi सभाको कार्यसूची *n.* agenda

sabhapatitwa garnu सभापतित्व गर्नु *v.* preside

sabhel साभेल *n.* shovel

sabhyata सभ्यता *n.* civilization

sabudana साबुदानाप *n.* sago

sabun साबुन *n.* soap

sabun ko phinj साबुनको फीँज *n.* lather

sachcha सच्चा *adj.* wholehearted

sachiwalaya सचिवालय secretariat

sachyaunu सच्याउनु *v.* proofread

sachyaunu सच्याउनु *v.* rectify

sadabahar सदाबहार *adj.* evergreen

sadachari सदाचारी *adj.* virtuous

sadak सडक *n.* road

sadak सडक *n.* street

sadak ko peti सडकको पेटी *n.* pavement

sadar सादर *adj.* respectfully

sadasya सदस्य *n.* member

sade galeko सडेगलेको *adj.* rotten

sadeko masu सड़ेको मासु *n.* carrion

sadgun सद्गुण *n.* virtue

sadhain सधैँ *adv.* always

sadhain सधैँ *adv.* ever

sadhain rahane सधैँ रहने *adj.* everlasting

sadharan साधारण *adj.* mediocre

sadharan साधारण *adj.* ordinary

sadharan साधारण *adj.* run-of-the-mill

sadharan साधारण *adj.* usual

sadharan geet साधारण गीत *n.* ditty

sadharan sipahi साधारण सिपाही *n.* rank and file

sadhe साढे *n.* half-past

sadhisang judhne vaykati सँढ़िसँग जुध्ने व्यक्ति *n.* toreador

sadhu साधु *n.* hermit

sadhuharuko ashram साधुहरूको आश्रम *n.* abbey

sadi साडी *n.* sari

saghan सघन *adj.* compact

sagriye सागरीय *adj.* naval

sagwan kath सागवान काठ *n.* teak

sah bhagi सहभागी *n.* participant

saha astitwa सहअस्तित्व *n.* co-existence

saha bhagita सहभागिता *n.* complicity

saha shiksha सहशिक्षा *n.* co-education

sahabhagita सहभागिता *n.* communion

sahai naramro साहै नराम्रो *adj.* abominable

sahaj सहज *adj.* facile

sahaliya सहलिया *adj.* trite

sahan shilta सहनशीलता *n.* endurance

sahan shilta सहनशीलता *n.* tolerance

sahana na sakine सहन नसकिने *adj.* intolerable

sahanu सहनु *n.* brook

sahanu सहनु *v.* endure

sahanu सहनु *v.* put up with

sahanu सहनु *v.* suffer

sahanu सहनु *v.* tolerate

sahanu bhuti सहानुभूति *n.* sympathy

sahara सहारा *n.* standby

sahas साहस *adj.* audacious

sahas साहस *n.* courage

sahas dekhune kaam साहस देखाउने काम *n.* bravado

sahas ko kam साहसको काम *n.* venture

sahas/himmat garnu साहसे/हिम्मत गर्नु *v.* dare

sahasi साहसी *adj.* courageous

sahasi साहसी *adj.* manful

sahasi साहसी *adj.* valiant

sahasi wyakti साहसी व्यक्ति *n.* go-getter

sahasik kam साहसिक काम *n.* adventure

sahasilo साहसिलो *adj.* adventurous

sahayak सहायक *n.* assisant

sahayak nadi सहायक नदी *n.* tributary

sahayata garnu सहायता गर्नु *v.* assist

sahayata/maddat garnu सहायता/मद्दत गर्नु *n.* aid

sahayta garn inkar garnu सहायता गर्न इन्कार गर्नु disoblige

sahe moto साहै मोटो *adj.* obese

sahe sano साहै सानो *adj.* teeny

saheb साहेब *n.* sir

sahi सही *n.* signature

sahili aunla साहिली आँला *n.* ring

finger

sahitya साहित्य *n.* literature

sahityasambandhi साहित्यसम्बन्धी *adj.* literary

sahmat hunu सहमत हुनु *v,* assent

sahnu सहनु *v.* abide

sahnu सहनु *v.* endure

sahodar bhai wa bahini सहोदर भाइ वा बहिनी *n.* sibling

sahti साथी *n.* mate

sahya सहय *adj.* tolerable

sahyog garnu सहयोग गर्नु *v.* cooperate

saikal साइकल *n.* bicycle

saikal साइकल *n.* bike

sainik officer सैनिक अफिसर *n.* subaltern

sainik sarwekshan सैनिक सर्वेक्षण *n.* reconnaissance

sainik widroh सैनिक विद्रोह *n.* mutiny

saino साइनो *n.* relative

sair सैर *n.* jaunt

sair सैर *n.* trip

sais सईस *n.* ostler

saitan सैतान *n.* devil

sajaunu सजाउनु *v.* equip

sajawat सजावट *n.* layout

sajawat सजावट *n.* outfit

sajaya सजाय *n.* punishment

sajbaj साजबाज *n.* musical instrument

sajellai jalnai सजिलै जल्ने *adj.* combustible

sajha साझा *adj.* common

sajhedar साझेदार *n.* shareholder

sajilai hune kam सजिलै हुने काम *n.* pushover

sajilo सजिलो *adj.* handy

sajilo सजिलो *adj.* simple

sajilo ra saphal banaunu सजिलो र सफल बनाउनु *v.* streamline

sajilo sanga सजिलोसँग *adv.* easily

sajilo sanga सजिलोसँग *adj.* easy

sajilo sanga laij ana sakine सजिलोसँग लैजान सकिने *adj.* portable

sajilo upaya सजिलो उपाय *n.* royal road

sajilojit सजिलो जीत *n.* walkover

sajiw सजीव *adj.* vivacious

sajja सज्जा *n.* gear

sakaratmak सकारात्मक *adj.* positive

sakharkhand सखरखण्ड *n.* sweet potato

sakht सक्त *adj.* strict

sakkali सक्कली *adj.* genuine

sakkali सक्कली *adj.* original

saknu सक्नु *n.* can

saksharta साक्षरता *n.* literacy

sakshi साक्षी *n.* evidence

sakshi साक्षी *n.* witless

sakshi baknu साक्षी बक्नु *v.* testify

sakun सक्नु *mod.* may

sakundhari शंकुधारी *n.* conifer

salad *n.* salad

salah सलह *n.* locust

salah सलह *n.* locust

salai सलाई *n.* match

salai ko batta सलाईको बट्टा *n.* matchbox

salai ko kanti सलाईको काँटी *n.* matchstick

salami सलामी *n.* salute

salana battha सालाना भत्ता *n.* annuity

salesh श्लेश *n.* irony

salgam सलगम *n.* turnip

salik सालिक *n.* statue

salla, devdaru सल्ला, देवदारू *n.* fir

sallah सल्लाह *n.* advice

sallah सल्लाह *n.* counsel

sallah kar सल्लाहकार *n.* advisor

sallah linu सल्लाह लिनु *v.* conuslt

sallahkar सल्लाहकार *n.* counsellor

sallo सल्लो *n.* pine

salnal सालनाल *n.* placenta

sam lingi समलिंगी *adj.* homosexual

samachar समाचार *n.* tidings

samachar samiti समाचार समिति *n.* press agency

samachar yogya समाचारयोग्य *adj.* newsworthy

samadhan समाधान *n.* solution

samadhi समाधि *n.* masuoleum

samaj sewi समाजसेवी *n.* social worker

samajh dari समझदारी *n.* understanding

samajhdar समझदार *adj.* sensible

samajik सामाजिक *adj.* social

samajik jamghat सामाजिक जमघट *n.* get-together

samajik sewa सामाजिक सेवा *n.* social services

samajik suraksha सामाजिक सुरक्षा *n.* social security

samajik wigyan सामाजिक विज्ञान *n.* social science

samaj-vigyan समाज-विज्ञान *n.* sociology

samajvirodhi समाजविरोधी *adj.* antisocial

samajwad समाजवाद *n.* socialism

saman सामान *n.* kit

saman सामान *n.* stock

samanjasya सामंजस्य *n.* concordance

samanta समानता *n.* likeness

samanti prathako das सामन्ती प्रथाको दास *n.* villein

samanubhuti समानुभूति *n.* empathy

samanwaya garnu समन्वय गर्नु *v.* coordinate

samanya सामान्यतवरले *adj.* normal

samanya सामान्य *adj.* petty

samanya akar wa napbhanda thulo सामान्य आकार वा नापभन्दा ठूलो *adj.* outsize

samanya gyan सामान्य ज्ञान *n.* common sense

samanya gyan सामान्य ज्ञान *n.* general knowledge

samanya gyan ko prashna सामान्य ज्ञानको प्रश्न *n.* quiz

samanya tawarle सामान्यतवरले *adv.* normally

samanya ukti सामान्य उक्ति *n.* platitude

samapati समाप्ति *n.* cessation

samapt garnu समाप्त गर्नु *v.* terminate

samapt garnu समाप्त गर्नु *v.* wind up

samapt hune समाप्त हुनु *v.* run out

samapti समाप्ति *n.* termination

samaroh समाासेह *n.* ceremony

samarpit garnu समर्पित गर्नु *v.* dedicate

samarthak समर्थक *n.* follower

samarthak समर्थक *n.* supporter

samarthan garnu समर्थन गर्नु *v.* stand by

samarthan garnu समर्थन गर्नु *v.* uphold

samarupta समरूपता *n.* resemblance

samast समस्त *adj.* overall

samasya समस्या *n.* snag

samata wadi समतावादी *n.* egalitarian

samathnu समाल्नु *n.* catch

samatnu समाल्नु *v.* nab

samatnu समाल्नु *v.* round up

samatnu समाल्नु *v.* seize

samatnu समाल्नु *v.* take hold

samaya समय *n.* time

samaya bitaunu समय बिताउनु *v.* put in

samaya ko antar समयको अन्तर *n.* time lag

samaya ko palna garne समय को पालना गर्ने *adj.* punctual

samaya samaya ma hune समय समयमा हुने *adj.* periodical

samaya sima समयसीमा *n.* deadline

samaya talika समयतालिका *n.* timetable

samayatalika समयतालिका *n.* schedule

samayik सामयिक *adj.* timely

sambaddhta सम्बद्धता *n.* linkage

sambandh सम्बन्ध *n.* rapport

sambandh सम्बन्ध *n.* relationship

sambandhit समम्बन्धित *adj.* related

sambhaw सम्भव *adj.* feasible

sambhaw सम्भव *adj.* possible

sambhawana सम्भावना *n.* possibility

sambhog garnu संभोग गर्नु *v.* fuck

sambhog/maithun garnu सम्भोग/मैथुन गर्नु *v.* copulate

samhalnu सम्हाल्नु *v.* take over

samiksha समीक्षा *n.* review

samiti समिति *n.* committee

samjhana सम्झना *n.* remembrance

samjhana garanunu सम्झना गराउनु *v.* remind

samjhana layak ko समझन लायकको *adj.* memorable

samjhana layak ko समझना *n.* memory

samjhana layak ko समझन लायकको *adj.* notable

samjhanu समझनु *v.* recollect

samjhanu सम्झनु *v.* remember

samjhauta समझौता *n.* compromise

samjhauta sari sat pher garnu सम्झौतासरी साटफेर गर्नु *v.* trade off

samjhauto सम्झौटो *n.* reminder

samjhoto सम्झौटो *n.* memento

samkaleen समकालीन *adj.* contemporary

samlagna garaunu संलग्न गराउनु *v.* let in for

samlagnata संलग्नता *n.* involvement

samlingi stri समलिङ्गी स्त्री *n.* lesbian

samma सम्म *adj.* flat

samma सम्म *prep.* upto

samman dinu सम्मान दिनु *v.* dignify

samman janak सम्मानजनक *adj.* respectful

sammanit सम्मानित *adj.* reputable

sammelan सम्मेलन *n.* pow-wow

sammukh parnu सम्मुख पर्नु *v.* confront

samna garnu सामना गर्नु *v.* cope

samna garnu सामना गर्नु *n.* outface

samp gorkagjar सानो गिर्जाघर *n.* chapel

sampadan garnu सम्पादन गर्नु *v.* edit

sampanna सम्पन्न *n.* completion

sampanna सम्पन्न *adj.* prosperous

sampark सम्पर्क *n.* contact

sampark सम्पर्क *n.* intercourse

sampark सम्पर्क *n.* liaison

sampark adhikrit सम्पर्क अधिकृत *n.* liaison officer

sampati सम्पत्ति *n.* asset

sampha sanga सफासँग *adv.* neatly

samprachna संरचना *n.* structure

sampradya सम्प्रदाय *n.* sect

sampurn सम्पूर्ण *adj./adv.* whole

sampurn bhrahmand सम्पूर्ण ब्रह्मण्ड *n.* cosmos

samragi सम्राज्ञी *n.* empress

samraija wad साम्राज्यवाद *n.* imperialism

samrajya साम्राज्य *n.* empire

samrajyawadi साम्राज्यवादी *n.* imperialist

samrakshak संरक्षक *n.* patron

samrakshan संरक्षण *n.* conservation

samrakshan संरक्षण दिनु *n.* preservation

samrakshan dinu संरक्षण दिनु *v.* patronize

samrat सम्राट *n.* emperor

samrath va yogya banaunu समर्थ वा योग्य बनाउनु *v.* enable

samrathan समर्थन *v.* endorse

samsarga nishedh संसर्ग निषेध *n.* quarantine

samstha संस्था *n.* company

samsya समस्या *n.* problem

samtal maidan समतल मैदान *n.* plain

samudari chara समुद्री चरा *n.* gannet

samudari daaku समुद्री डाकू *n.* buccaneer

samudari daku समुद्री डाँकू *n.* pirate

samudari jantu समुद्री जन्तु *n.* dolphin

samudari machhako prakar समुद्री माछाको प्रकार *n.* mullet

samudaya समुदाय *n.* community

samudra par समुद्रपार *adj.* overseas

samudri bimari समुद्री बिमारी *n.* seasickness

samudri charako suli समुद्री चराको सुली *n.* guano

samudri chattan समुद्री चट्टान *n.* reef

samudri ghat समुद्री घाट *n.* seaport

samudri jhar समुद्री झार *n.* seaweed

samudri khana समुद्री खाना *n.* seafood

samudri kinar समुद्री किनार *n.* seashore

samudri sataha समुद्री सतह *n.* sea level

samudri yatri समुद्री यात्री *n.* seafarer

samudrik सामुद्रिक *adj.* marine

samudrik charo सामुद्रिक चरो *n.* albatross

samudritat समुद्रीतट *n.* sea beach

samuh समूह *n.* group

samuhik ruple सामूहिक रूपले *adv.* en masse

samundari maccha समुद्री माछा *n.* cod

samundra समुद्र *n.* sea

samwaddata संवाददाता *n.* reporter

samwedanshil संवेदनशील *adj.* sensitive

samwedik संवेदिक *adj.* sensory

samweg संवेग *n.* impulse

samwidhan संविधान *n.* constituion

samyawad साम्यवाद *n.* communism

samyawadi साम्यवादी *n.* communist

samyogant natak संयोगान्त नाटक *n.* comedy

samyukta संयुक्त *adj.* joint

samyukta संयुक्त *adj.* united

san सन *n.* jute

san laune patthar सान लाउने पत्थर *n.* whetstone

sana ghantuko tan tan awaj साना धंटी को टनटन आवाज *n.* jingal

sana hatiyar साना हतियार *n.* small arms

sana tina kura सानातिना कुरा *n.* small talk

sana-kal साना-कल *n.* gadget

sanakhat सनक *n.* ideosyncrasy

sanan स्नान *n.* ablutions

sanatak upadhi prapt nagreko vyakti स्नातक उपाधि प्राप्त नगरेको व्यक्ति *n.* undergraduate

sanchalak संचालक *n.* operator

sanchalak संचालक *n.* superintendent

sanchalak samiti संचालक समिति *n.* steering committee

sanchalan garnu संचालन गर्नु *v.* manage

sanchar संचार *n.* communication

sanchchai साँच्चै *adv.* really

sancho साँचो *n.* key

sancho साँचो *adj.* real

sancho साँचो *adj.* sincere

sancho साँचो *adj.* truthful

sancho chhiraune pwal साँचो छिराउने प्वाल *n.* keyhole

sancho haru halne rin साँचोहरु हाल्ने रिङ *n.* keyring

sandarbh संदर्भ *n.* context

sandarbh सन्दर्भ *v.* refer

sandarbh dekhaunu सन्दर्भ देखाउनु *n.* reference

sandarbh pustakalya सन्दर्भ पुस्तकालय *n.* reference library

sandeh सन्देह *n.* suspicioun

sandeh prakat garnu सन्देह प्रकट गर्नु *v.* impugn

sandesh सन्देश *n.* dispatch

sandesh सन्देश *n.* message

sandesh dinu सन्देश दिनु *v.* communicate

sandesh puraune सन्देश पुन्याउने *n.* messaenger

sandesh pury aunu/sunaidinu सन्देश पुन्याउनु/सुनाइदिनु *v.* convey

sandesh puryaunu सन्देश पुन्याउनु *v.* relay

sandhe साँढे *n.* bull

sandhi सन्धि *n.* alliance

sandhi सन्धि *n.* entente

sandhi सन्धि *n.* entente

sandhi सन्धि *n.* pact

sandhi सन्धि *n.* treaty

sandhunga सानढुङ्गा *n.* hone

sandigdhta सन्दिग्धता *n.* dubiety

sang sangai सँगसँगै *adv.* side by side

sanga सँग *prep.* by

sanga hunu सँग हुनु *v./aux.* have

sangai सँगै *adv.* together

sangai jane jahaji beda सँगै जाने जहाजी बेडा *n.* convoy

sangai rahanu सँगै रहनु *v.* co-exist

sangam संगम *n.* confluence

sangat संगत *adj.* congruous

sangathan संगठन *n.* assocation

sangeen संगीन *n.* bayonet

sangeetagya संगीतज्ञ *n.* maestro

sange-sange सँगै-सँगै *adv.prep.* abreast

sange-sange rakhnu सँगै-सँगै राख्नु *n.* juxtapose

sanghar संघार *n.* threshold

sangharsh संघर्ष *n.* struggle

sangit kar संगीकार *n.* musician

sangit rachna संगीत रचना *n.* opus

sangit sambandhi संगीत सम्बन्धी *n.* music

sanglo साहीनउंदग्ला *n.* cockroach

sangraha संग्रह *n.* storage

sangyog संयोग *n.* occurrence

sanjog parnu सन्जोग पर्नु *v.* coincide

sanjogota संयोजकता *n.* valence

sankalan सङ्कलन *n.* collection

sankat संकट *n.* crisis

sankat संकट *n.* emergency

sankat संकट *n.* hazard

sankat ko sthiti सङ्कट को स्थिति *n.* juncture

sankatma shant rehne shakti संकटमा शान्त रहने शक्ति *n.* sang-froid

sankaya सङ्काय *n.* faculty

sanket संकेत *n.* hint

sanket संकेत *n.* indication

sanket संकेत *n.* inkling

sanket सङ्केत *n.* signal

sanket chinha संकेत चिन्ह *n.* notation

sanket garnu संकेत गर्नु *v.* allude

sanket lekhak संकेत लेखक *n.* stenographer

sanket shabd संकेत शब्द *n.* watchword

sankh शंख *n.* conch

sankhya badhi hunu सङ्ख्या बढी हुनु *v.* outnumber

sanki vyakti सनकी व्यक्ति *n.* crackpot

sanki vyakti सनकी व्यक्ति *n.* crank

sankirn सङ्कीर्ण *adj.* narrow-minded

sankoch संकोच *adj.* diffident

sankochi सङ्कोषी *adj.* self-conscious

sankriyta संक्रियता *n.* activity

sanmadhan garnu समाधान गर्नु *v.* resolve

sano सानो *adj.* small

sano adhar सानो आधार *n.* toehold

sano baccha सानो बच्चा *n.* chit

sano bancharo सानो बन्चरो *n.* hatchet

sano cake सानो केक *n.* waffle

sano chamcha सानो चम्चा *n.* teaspoon

sano chutai kotha सानो छुट्टै कोठा *n.* cubicide

sano dunga सानो डुङ्गा *n.* dinghy

sano gantho सानो गाँठो *n.* nub

sano gaun सानो गाउँ *n.* hamlet

sano ghar सानो घर *n.* maisonette

sano gupha सानो गुफा *n.* grotto

sano haanga सानो हाँगा *n.* sprig

sano hunu सानो हुनु *v.* shrink

sano katai सानो कटाइ *n.* nick

sano khaat सानो खाट *n.* cot

sano khari सानो खाड़ी *n.* cove

sano khet सानो खेत *n.* croft

sano khopilti सानो खोपिल्टी *n.* dint

sano lahar सानो लहर *n.* ripple

sano nadi सानो नदी *n.* rill

sano nau सानो नाउ *n.* skiff

sano paarwartiya taal सानो पार्वतीय ताल *n.* tarn

sano r dublo सानो र दुब्लो *adj.* puny

sano rato phal सानो रातो फल *n.* cherry

sano sundar harin सानो सुन्दर हरिण *n.* gazelle

sano tarwar सानो तरवार *n.* cutlass

sano thal सानो थाल *n.* roundel

sano ulka सानो उल्का *n.* shooting star

sanokan सानो कण *n.* speck

sanomootha सानो मूठा *n.* wisp

sanrakshan संरक्षण *v.* conserve

sanrakshan संरक्षण *n.* tutelage

sansad संसद *n.* parliament

sansani सनसनी *n.* thrill

sansanipurn सनसनीपूर्ण *adj.* sensational

sansar संसार *n.* world

sansarik सांसारिक *adj.* mundane

sansarik सांसारिक *adj.* worldly

sanshodhan संशोधन *n.* revision

sanskar widhi widhan संस्कार विधि विधान *n.* ritual

sanskritik सांस्कृतिक *adj.* cultural

sanstha संस्था *n.* organization

sansthan संस्थान *n.* institute

sansthapak संस्थापक *n.* founder

sant सन्त *n.* saint

santan सन्तान *n.* issue

santan सन्तान *n.* offspring

santan सन्तान *n.* progeny

santhganth साठगाँठ *n.* collusion

santosh सन्तोष *n.* satisfaction

santosh janak सन्तोषजनक *adj.* satisfactory

santulan सन्तुलन *n.* euquilibrium

santulit सन्तुलित *adj.* well balanced

santush garnu सन्तुष्ट गर्नु *v.* appeased

santusht सन्तुष्ट *adj.* satisfied

santusht parn naskine सन्तुष्ट पार्न नसकिने *adj.* implacable

santusht parnu सन्तुष्ट पार्नु *v.* satisfy

santwana सान्त्वना *n.* solace

sanu सानु *adj.* little

sanu akar ko wastu सानु आकार को वस्तु *n.* miniature

sanu chakku सानु चक्कु *n.* penknife

sanu kad ko सानु कदको *adj.* undersized

sanu kapi सानु कापी *n.* notebook

sanu udyog प्रसन्नचित *n.* light industry

sanubot सानुबोट *n.* sapling

sanusisi सानु सिसी *n.* phial

sanyasi सन्यांसी *n.* ascetic

sanyogko safalta संयोगको सफलता *n.* fluke

sanyogle संयोगले *adv.* perchance

sanyukt rajya america संयुक्त राज्य अमेरिका *n.* dollar

sapa सफा *adj.* tidy

sapa ko tokai सर्पको टोकाइ *n.* snakebite

sapasht garnu स्पष्ट गर्नु *v.* elucidate

sapasht roople vyakt garnu स्पष्ट रूपले व्यक्त गर्नु *v.* formulate

sapashtwadita स्पष्टवादिता *n.* candour

sapat linu सापट लिनु *v.* borrow

sapat linu सापट लिनु *n.* bum

sapat/rin dinu सापट/ऋण दिनु *v.* lend

sapero सपेरो *n.* snake charmer

sapha सफा *adj.* clean

sapha सफा *adj.* neat

sapha sugghar सफा-सुग्घर *adj.* neat and clean

saphal सफल *adj.* successful

saphalta सफलता *n.* hit

saphalta सफलता *n.* success

saphalta ka din सफलता का दिन *n.* heyday

saphalta ka sath kam garnu सफलता का साथ काम गर्नु *v.* put across

saphar सफर *n.* excursion

saphar सफर *n.* outing

sapna सपना *n.* dream

sapranu सप्रनु *v.* thrive

saprinu सप्रिनु *v.* prosper

saptahik साप्ताहिक *n.* weekly

saptbhuj सप्तभुज *n.* heptagon

sar सार *n.* essence

sar सार *n.* precis

sar saman सरसामान *n.* supplies

sar sankshep सार-सङ्क्षेप *n.* round-up

sar saphai सरसफाइ *n.* sanitation

saraansh prastut garnu सारांश प्रस्तुत गर्नु *v.* recapitulate

sarahd सरहद *n.* landmark

saral सरल *adj.* candid

saral karya सरल कार्य *n.* plain sailing

sarangi सारंगी *n.* fiddle

saransh सारांश *n.* summary

sarap सराप *n.* curse

sarap सराप *n.* imprecation

sarap सराप *n.* malediction

saras सारस *n.* crane

saras सारस *n.* stork

sarauta सरौता *n.* nutcracker

sarawoth स्रोत *n.* heritage

sares सरेस *n.* gelatine

sarg सर्ग *n.* canto

sarho साह्रो *adj.* hard

sarik garaunu सरिक गराउनु *v.* implicate

sarik/samawesh garnu सरिक/समावेश गर्नु *v.* involve

saripha सरिफा *n.* custard apple

sarkar सरकार *n.* government

sarkari wakil सरकारी वकील *n.* public prosecutor

sarkas सर्कस *n.* circus

sarki सार्की *n.* cobbler

sarki सार्की *n.* shoemaker

sarne सर्ने *adj.* contagious

sarnu सर्नु *v.* budge

sarot स्रोत *n.* fount

sarpa सर्प *n.* serpent

sarpa सर्प *n.* snake

saruwa सरुवा गर्नु *v.* transfer

saruwa rog सरुवा रोग *n.* infection

saruwa rog सरुवा रोग *adj.* infectious

sarvsammati सर्वसम्मति *n.* consensus

sarvvishay gyan सर्वविषय ज्ञान *n.* omnipresence

sarwa nam सर्वनाम *n.* pronoun

sarwa shakti man सर्वशक्तिमान् *n.* almighty

sarwaushadhi सर्वौषधि *n.* panacea

sarwochcha सर्वोच्च *adj.* paramount

sarwochcha सर्वोच्च *adj.* supreme

sas linu सास लिनु *v.* inhale

sas ra hos pharkaunu सास र होस फर्काउनु *v.* resuscitate

sas roki dinu सास रोकिदिनु *v.* smother

sasej ससेज *n.* sausage

sasko jhokka सासको झोक्का *n.* puff

sasto सस्तो *adj.* cheap

sasto सस्तो *adj.* inexpensive

sasto bhadkilo vastu सस्तो भड्किलो वस्तु *adj.* trumpery

sasu सासू *n.* mother-in-law

sasura ससुरा *n.* father-in-law

sat सात *n.* seven

sata patri phul सयपत्री फूल *n.* marigold

satabarsiya शतवर्षीय *adj.* centennial

satahi सतही *adj.* unidimensional

satark rahanu सतर्क रहनु *v.* watch out

satark rahanu साता *n.* week

satarkta सतर्कता *adj.* aware

satasat साटासाट *n.* exchange

sataun सातौँ *n./adj.* seventh

sataunu सताउनु *v.* harass

sataunu सताउनु *v.* molest

sataunu सताउनु *v.* pester

sath dinu साथ दिनु *v.* accompany

sathauanu सताउनु *v.* offend

sathi साथी *n.* companion

sathi साथी *n.* comrade

sathi साथी *n.* fellow

sathi साथी *n.* folk

sathi साथी *n.* friend

sathi साथी *n.* pal

sathi साथी *n.* partner

sathi साठी *n.* sixty

sathma साथमा *prep.* along

satkar सत्कार *n.* hospitality

satkarshil सत्कारशील *adj.* hospitable

sato साटो *n.* shift

sato साटो *n.* substitue

satpher साटफेर *n.* barter

satra सत्र *n.* seventeen

satraun सत्रौं *n./adj.* seventeenth

sattama khadahunu सट्टामा खडा हुनु *v.* represent

sattan साटन *n.* satin

sattari सत्तरी *n.* seventy

satunu सताएनु *v.* persecute

satya सत्य *n.* truth

satyata सत्यता *v.* verity

saugat सौगात *n.* offering

saundarya sambandhi सौन्दर्य सम्बन्धी *adj.* aesthetic

saunf सौंफ *n.* aniseed

saur सउर *n.* birch

saur mandal सौरमण्डल *n.* solar system

sauti garnu साउती गर्नु *v.* whisper

sautini ama सौतिनी आमा *n.* stepmother

sautini bahini/didi सौतिनी बहिनी/दिदी *n.* stepsister

sautini bhai/daju सौतिनी भाइ/दाजु *n.* stepbrother

sautinidaju सौतिनी दाजु *n.* half-brothher

sawahan संवहन *n.* convection

sawar सवार *n.* rider

sawari सवारी *n.* vehicle

sawas श्वास *n.* breath

sawdhan garnu सावधान गर्नु *v.* warmth

sawdhan garnu सावधान *adj.* watchful

sawdhan hunu सावधान हुनु *v.* beware

sawdhani सावधानी *n.* precaution

saya सय *n.* hundred

saya kolo 100 किलो *n.* quintal

saya prati shat सय प्रतिशत *n.* hundred percent

sayad सायद *adv.* perhaps

sayakada सयकडा *adj.* percent

school bhagua स्कूल भगुवा *n.* truant

sdangit karyakram संगीत कार्यक्रम *n.* concert

secretari सेक्रेटरी *n.* secretary

seesa rangko सीसा रंग को *adj.* livid

sekhi na garne सेखी नगर्ने *adj.* modest

seknu सेक्नु *v.* bake

seknu सेक्नु *v.* foment

sekuwa सेकुवा *n.* roast

semestar सेमेस्टर *n.* semester

sena सेना *n.* military

sena सेना *n.* troops

senako ek bhaag सेनाको एक भाग *n.* platoon

senako ek vibhaag सेनाको एक विभाग *n.* brigade

septi pin सेप्टिपिन *n.* safety pin

sero phero सेरोफेरो *n.* surrounding

set सेट *n.* set

setho सेतो *n.* albino

seto सेतो *adj.* white

seto सेतो *adj.* white

seto dhatu सेतो धातु *n.* aluminium

seto kamal सेतो कमल *n.* water lily

seto mato सेतो माटो *n.* kaolin

sewa सेवा *n.* service

shabd शब्द *n.* word

shabd kosh शब्द कोश *n.* dictionary

shabd paheli शब्द पहेली *n.* crossword

shabd rup शब्द रूप *n.* declension

shabd yojna शब्द-योजना *n.* diction

shabdawali शब्दावली *n.* vocabulary

shadbhuj षड्भुज *n.* hexagon

shadyantra षड्यंत्र *n.* conspiracy

shahar शहर *n.* city

shahar ko bahiri bhag शहरको बाहिरी भाग *n.* outskirts

shahari हरी *adj.* urban

shahi शाही *adj.* regal

shahid शहीद *n.* martyr

shaili शैली *n.* genre

shaili शैली *n.* style

shaishaw kal शैशव काल *n.* infancy

shaitaan शैतान *n.* devil

shakha शाखा *n.* section

shakti क्ति *n.* vigo(u)r

shaktiheen parnu शक्तिहीन पार्नु *v.* devitalize

shaktihin शक्तिहीन *adj.* powerless

shaktihin wyakti शक्तिहीन व्यक्ति *n.* lame duck

shakun शकुन *n.* omen

shakun शकुन *n.* omen

shaman garnu ।मन गर्नु *v.* soothe

shamya क्षम्य *adj.* venial

shandar ।नदार *adj.* splendid

shandar शान्दार *adj.* superb

shanigraha शनिग्रह *n.* saturn

shaniwar शनिवार *n.* Saturday

shanka शंका *n.* doubt

shanka शंका *n.* jeopardy

shanka शंका *n.* misgiving

shanka janak शंकाजनक *adj.* doubtful

shanka lageko manis शंका लागेको मानिस *v.* suspect

shanka lagne शंका लाग्ने *adj.* suspicious

shanka na garine शंका नगरिने *adj.* unsuspecting

shankaspad ांकास्पद *adj.* questionable

shankha kiro शङ्खे कीरो *n.* snail

shant शान्त *adj.* demure

shant शान्त *adj.* impassive

shant शान्त *adj.* placid

shant शान्त *adj.* quiet

shant शान्त *adj.* serene

shant शान्त *adj.* sober

shanti शान्ति *n.* calm

shanti शान्ति *n.* composure

shanti शान्ति *n.* lull

shanti शान्ति *n.* peace

shanti शान्ति *n.* quietude

shanti शन्ति *n.* tranquility

shanti ko pratik शान्तिको प्रतीक *n.* olive branch

shanti kshetra शान्तिक्षेत्र *n.* zone of peace

shanti sanga शान्तिसँग *adv.* quietly

shantipurn शान्तिपूर्ण *adj.* peaceful

shantipurn sahastitwa शान्तिपूर्ण सहअस्तित्व *n.* peaceful coexistence

shapath patra ापथ पत्र *n.* affidavit

sharad ritu ारद ऋतु *n.* autumn

sharam सरम *n.* blush

sharan शरण *n.* refuge

sharan शरण *v.* resort

sharan शरण *n.* shelter

sharat शर्त *n.* proviso

shareerik शारीरिक *adj.* corporal

sharir शरीर *n.* body

sharir ko mathillo adha bhag शरीरको माथिल्लो आधा भाग *n.* bust

sharirbaat alag bhaeko शरीरबाट अलग भएको *adj.* disembodied

sharirik म्6176शारीरिक *adj.* physical

sharir-rachnako vigyan शरीर रचना को विज्ञान *n.* anatomy

sharnarthi शरणार्थी *n.* refugee

shart शर्त *n.* stipulation

shasak शासक *n.* ruler

shasan chalaunu शासन चलाउनु *v.* govern

shasan kal शासनकाल *n.* regime

shasan wyawastha शासन व्यवस्था *n.* regimen

shashan garnu ासन गर्नु *v.* administer

shat warshiki शतवार्षिकी *n.* centenary

shatabdi शताब्दी *n.* century

shatru त्रु *n.* enemy

shatru शत्रु *n.* foe

shatruta शत्रुता *n.* enmity

shauchalaya शौचालय *n.* urinal

shayad शायद *adv.* maybe

sheersh शीर्ष *n.* vertex

sheershak ीर्षक *n.* caption

sheershakheen शीर्षकहीन *adj.* untitled

sheesa सीसा lead

sheet शीत *n.* dew

shekshik शैक्षिक *adj.* scholastic

shesh शेष *n.* residue

shikar शिकार *n.* prey

shikar शिकार *n.* victim

shikar banaunu शिकार बनाउनु *v.* victimize

shikar khelnu शिकार खेल्नु *v.* hunt

shikar ko abhiyan शिकार को अभियान *n.* safari

shikari शिकारी *n.* hunter

shikari kukkur शिकारी कुकुर *n.* beagle

shikari kurkur शिकारी कुकुर *n.* hound

shikhar शिखर *n.* apex

shikhar शिखर *n.* top

shiksha शिक्षा *n.* education

shiksha dine शिक्षा दिने *adj.* didactic

shiksha dinu शिक्षा दिनु *v.* educate

shiksha va shikshan sambandhi शिक्षा वा शिक्षण संबंधी *adj.* academic

shikshadhyaksha शिक्षाध्यक्ष *n.* rector

shikshak शिक्षक *n.* teacher

shila शिला *n.* slab

shilpi शिल्पी *n.* artisan

shir dard शिरदर्द *n.* headache

shir posh शिरपोश *n.* headdress

shirako शिराको *adj.* venous

shirshak शीर्षक *n.* headline

shishtachar शिष्टाचार *n.* decorum

shishu शिशु *n.* infant

shishu widyalaya शिशु विद्यालय *n.* kindergarten

shithil शिथिल *adj.* lackadaisical

shithil/durbal hunu शिथिल/दुर्बल हुनु *v.* languish

shitil शिथिल *adj.* languid

shochniya शोचनीय *adj.* deplorable

shochniya शोचनीय *adj.* regrettable

shodh-prabandhan शोध-प्रबन्ध *n.* treatise

shok manaunu शोक मनाउनु *v.* mourn

shok-geet शोक-गीत *n.* dirge

shraddhanjali श्रद्धांजलि *n.* condolence

shraddhanjali श्रद्धांजलि *n.* homage

shradha r dar श्रद्धा र डर *n.* awe

shreni श्रेणी *n.* category

shreni baddha श्रेणीबद्ध *v.* classify

shreshth श्रेष्ठ *adj.* superior

shreshtha श्रेष्ठ *adj.* noble

shri श्री *n.* mr

shri panch ko sarkar श्री पाँचको सरकार *n.* his Majesty's Government

shrikhand श्रीखण्ड *n.* sandalwood

shrimati श्रीमती *n.* mrs

shringar श्रृंगार *n.* make-up

shripech श्रीपेच *n.* crown

shrota gan श्रोतागण *n.* audience

shubha शुभ *adj.* auspicious

shuddha ठीक *thik* correct

shuddha शुद्ध *adj.* pure

shuddha garnu शुद्ध गर्नु *v.* refine

shuddha manle शुद्ध मनले *adv.* sincerely

shuddha seto शुद्ध सेतो *adj.* snow-white

shuddha tulyaunu शुद्ध तुल्याउनु *v.* purify

shudhipatra शुद्धिपत्र *n.* corrigendum

shudhta शुद्धता *n.* purity

shukra graha शुक्रग्रह *n.* venus

shukra tara शुक्रतारा *n.* morning star

shukra war शुक्रवार *n.* Friday

shulakar stambh शुलाकार स्तम्भ *n.* obelisk

shulk dwar शुल्कद्वार *n.* turnpike

shulka शुल्क *n.* fee

shunya ून्य *adj.* desolate

shunya शून्य *n.* nil

shunyawad शून्यवाद *n.* nihillism

shuro शूरो *adj.* bold

shuru शुरु *n.* outset

shuru शुरु *n.* rudiment

shuru शुरु *n.* start

shuru garnu शरु गर्नु *v.* set about

shuru garnu शुरु गर्नु *v.* take to

shuru ko ुरुको *adj.* perliminary

shuru ko kam शुरुको काम *n.* spadework

shuruwat शुरुवात *n.* beginning

shwas prashwas वासप्रश्वास *n.* respiration

shwet patra वेतपत्र *n.* white paper

shyna सेना *n.* army

siddhant सिद्धान्त *n.* doctrine

siddhant सिद्धान्त *n.* motto

siddhant सिद्धान्त *n.* principle

siddhant सिद्धान्त *n.* tenet

siddhant सिद्धान्त *n.* theory

siddhinu सिद्धिनु *v.* exhaust

siddhinu सिद्धिनु *v.* give out

siddhyaunu सिध्याउनु *v.* finish

siddhyaunu सिद्धयाउनु *v.* use up

sidha सीधा *adj.* straight

sidha parnu सीधा पार्नु *v.* straighten

sidha sadha सीधासाधा *adj.* unaffected

sikarmi सिकर्मी *n.* carpenter

sikayat garnu सिकायत गर्नु *v.* complain

sikka सिक्का *n.* coin

sikka huttyaunu सिक्का हुत्याउनु *v.* toss up

sikka ko huttyai सिक्का को हुत्याइ *v.* toss

sikkha सुक्खा *adj.* arid

siknu सिक्नु *v.* learn

siksha diksha शिक्षादीक्षा *n.* upbringing

silai सिलाइ *n.* needlework

silai kholnu सिलाई खोल्नु *adj.* unpick

silika सिलिका *n.* silica

silot सिलोट *n.* slate

sima सीमा *n.* limit

sima rahit सीमा रहित *adj.* limitless

simana सिमाना *n.* boundary

simana सिमाना *n.* forntier

simanti सिमण्टी *n.* cement

simha सिंह *n.* lion

simhini सिंहिनी *n.* lioness

simi सिमी *n.* bean

simit सीमित *adj.* finite

simit सीमित *adj.* limited

simit rakhnu सीमित राख्नु *v.* confine

simitta सीमितता *n.* limitation

simsim pani सिमसिम पानी *n.* drizzle

simta सिम्टा *n.* pine cone

sinchai सिँचाइ *n.* irrgation

sindur सिन्दूर *n.* vermilion

sinet सिनेट *n.* senate

sinetar सिनेटर *n.* senator

singan सिंगान *n.* mucus

singareako सिंगारिएको *adj.* bedeeked

singarnu सिंगार्नु, सज्नु *v.* adorn

singarnu सिंगार्नु *v.* decorate

singarnu सिँगार्नु *v.* garnish

singh सिङ्ग *n.* horn

sinu khane pashu/chara सिनु खाने प्शु/चरा *n.* scavenger

sinudi सिउँडी *n.* cactus

sip सीप *n.* craft

sip युक्ति *n.* knack

sip सीप *n.* skill

sip सीप *n.* tact

sipahi सिपाही *n.* soldier

sipahi सिपाही *n.* warrior

sipahiharuko dera सिपाहीहरुको डेरा *n.* billet

sipalu सिपालु *adj.* adept

sipalu सिपालु *adj.* clever

sipalu सिपालु *adj.* expert

sipharish garnu सिफारिश गर्नु *v.* recommend

sipharish garnu सिफारिश गर्नु *n.* recommendation

sipi सिपी *n.* mother-of-pearl

sipi ko tank सिपीको टाँक *n.* pearl button

sippi सिपी *n.* oyster

sippi सिपी *n.* scallop

sira ko jodle chalne injin सिर्काको जोडले चल्ने इन्जिन *n.* jet endine

sirak सिरक *n.* quilt

sirka सिरका *n.* vinegar

sirka chhodnu सिर्का छोड्नु *v.* ejaculate

sisa kalam सिसाकलम *n.* pencil

sisi सिसी *n.* bottle

sisnu सिस्नु *n.* nettle

sit bhetnu सित भेट्नु *v.* encounter

sith mail khanu सित मेल खानु *v.* accord

sittai सित्तै *adj.* free of cost

sittai dieko सित्तै *adv.* gratis

sitthi सिट्ठी *n.* whistle

siune kal सिउने कल *n.* sewing machine

siunu सिउनु *v.* sew

siwaya सिवाय *prep.* except

siwaya सिवाय *prep.* short of

siyo सियो *n.* needle

skart स्कर्ट *n.* skirt

skhalan स्खलन *n.* ejaculation

skiaunu सिकाउनु *v.* instruct

skutar स्कूटर *n.* scooter

skwas khel स्क्वास खेल *n.* squash

slipin byag सिलपिङ ब्याग *n.* sleeping bag

smapat garnu समाप्त गर्नु *adj.* abolish

smarak स्मारक *n.* memorial

smarak स्मारक *n.* monument

smaran garnu स्मरण गर्नु *v.* commemorate

smiana सिमाना *n.* border

smriti-lop स्मृति लोप *n.* amnesia

snaga सँग *prep.* with

snan स्नान *n.* bath

snatak स्नातक *n.* graduate

snayu स्नायु *n.* ligament

snayu स्नायु *n.* nerve

snayu pranali स्नायु प्रणाली *n.* nervous system

snayurog स्नायुरोग *n.* neuralgia

soanp सोंप *n.* fennel

sochnu सोच्नु *v.* ponder

soda सोडा *n.* soda

soda pani सोडा पानी *n.* soda water

sodh puchh सोधपुछ *n.* inquiry

sodh puchh garnu सोधपुछ गर्नु *v.* enquire

sodhnu सोध्नु *v.* ask

sohaag सोहाग *n.* borax

sojhai सोझै *adj.* point-blank

sojho सोझो *adj.* naive

sojho सोझो *adj.* unsophisticated

sojho rakhnu सोझो राख्नु *v.* align

sokh सोख *n.* hobby

sokh sayal garne सोख सयल गर्ने *adj.* luxurious

sokhin सोखिन *n.* amateur

sokhsuchak sabdha शोकसूचक शब्द *inter.* alas

sokpa सोक्पा *n.* yeti

soli सोली *n.* funnel

somwar सोमवार *n.* monday

soot सूत *n.* yarn

sopha सोफा *n.* sofa

sorha सोरह *n.* sixteen

sosilo सोसिलो *adj.* spongy

sosnu सोस्नु *v.* absorb

spainko jahaj स्पेनको जहाज *n.* galleon

sparsh स्पर्श *n.* touch

sparshko स्पर्शको *adj.* tactile

spasht स्पष्ट *adj.* blatant

spasht स्पष्ट *adj.* clear

spasht स्पष्ट *adj.* flagrant

spasht स्पष्ट *adj.* obvious

spasht स्पष्ट *adj./adv.* outright

spasht garnu स्पष्ट गर्नु *v.* clarify

spasht sanga स्पष्टसँग *adv.* flatly

spasht wakta स्पष्टवक्ता *adj.* plainspoken

spastha स्पष्ट *adj.* apparent

sphurti dine स्फूर्ति दिने *adj.* bracing

sponj स्पोंज *n.* sponge

srijana/rachna garnu सृजना/रचना गर्नु *v.* create

srishti karta सृष्टिकर्ता *n.* creator

srot स्रोत *n.* resource

staggit garnu स्थगित गर्नु *v.* adjourn

stanpayi jantu स्तनपायी जन्तु *n.* mammal

star स्तर *n.* standard

star स्तर *n.* strata

stensil स्टेन्सिल *n.* stencil

sterin स्टेरिङ *n.* steering wheel

sthal स्थल *n.* terra firma

sthal wahini स्थल वाहिनी *n.* battalion

sthalmargbat स्थलमार्गबाट *adv.* overland

sthaniya स्थानीय *n.* location

sthaniya boli स्थानीय बोली *n.* patios

sthapana सीपना *n.* establishment

sthapana/khada garnu सीपना/खडा गर्नु *v.* establish

sthapit garnu स्थापित गर्नु *v.* install

sthayi स्थायी *adj.* permanent

sthayi adesh स्थायी आदेश *n.* standing order

sthayi samiti स्थायी समिति *n.* standing committee

sthir स्थिर *adj.* constant

sthir स्थिर *adj.* motionless

sthir स्थिर *adj.* static

sthir स्थिर *adj.* steady

sthiti स्थिति *n.* circumstance

sthiti स्थिति *n.* situation

sthiti स्थिति *n.* state

stone सङ्गमरमर *n.* marble

stri स्त्री *n.* female

stri jasto purush स्त्री जस्तो पुरुष *n.* sissy

stri rog wisheshgya स्त्रीरोग विशेषज्ञ *n.* gyn(a)ecologist

striko bhitri luga स्त्रीको भित्री लुगा *n.* undies

striko niji kotha स्त्रीको निजी कोठा *n.* boudoir

striling स्त्रीलिंग *adj.* feminine

strirog vigyan स्त्रीरोग विज्ञान *n.* gynaecology

strirulai mohit narne purush स्त्रीहरूलाई मोहित नार्ने पुरुष *n.* ladykiller

studio स्टूडियो *n.* studio

subista sanga सुविबस्तासँग *adv.* safely

suchak-shabad सूचक-शब्द *n.* catchword

suchana सूचना *n.* information

suchana सूचना *n.* notice

suchanapati सूचनापाटी साइनबोर्ड *n.* signboard

suchi सूची *n.* index

suchi सूची *n.* list

suchipatra सूचीपत्र *n.* catalogue

suchit garnu सूचित गर्नु *v.* notify

sudharnu सुधार्नु *v.* improve

sudharnu सुधार्नु *v.* recast

sudharnu सुधारनु *n.* reform

sudur pashchim सुदूरपश्चिम *adj.* westernmost

suga सुगा *n.* parrot

sugam ritile bager janu सुगम रीतीले बगेर जानु *v.* scud

sugandh सुगन्ध *n.* smell

sugandhit सुगन्धित *n.* aroma

sugandhit सुगन्धि *adj.* fragrant

sugandhit सुगन्धित *adj.* redolent

suhaoudho सुहाउँदो *adj.* appropriate

suhaundo सुहाउँदो *adj.* becoming

suhaundo सुहाउँदो *adj.* pertinent

suhaundo सुहाउँदो *adj.* suitable

sui सुई *n.* injection

sui launu सूई लाउनु *v.* inject

suidinu सुई दिनु *v.* inoculate

suj सुज *n.* inflammation

sujak सुजाक *n.* gonorrh(o)ea

sujhau dinu सुझाउ दिनु *v.* suggest

sukaeko सुकाएको *adj.* desiccated

sukeko सुकेको *adj.* dry

sukeko सूकेको *adj.* wizened

sukh duhkh सुखदुःख *n.* weal and woe

sukh va ullas ko sthiti सुख वा उल्लास को स्थिति *n.* euphoria

sukhad सुखद *n.* idyll

sukkha सुक्खा *n.* drought

suksham parikshan सूक्ष्म परीक्षण *n.* scrutiny

sukshamdarshak सूक्ष्मदर्शक *n.* microscope

sukum basi सुकुम्बासी *n.* squatter

sukumar सुकुमार *adj.* ethereal

sul सूल *n.* colic

suli सूली *n.* cross

suli सूली stake

sum sumyaunu सुमसुम्याउनु *v.* fondle

sumdhur सुमधुर *adj.* melliflous

sumlo सुम्लो *n.* muscle

sumpanu सुम्पनु *v.* entrust

sumpanu सुम्पनु *v.* extradite

sumpanu सुम्पनु *v.* handover

sumpieko kam सुम्पिएको काम *n.* assignment

sun सुन *n.* gold

sun सन *n.* hemp

sun ko jalap सुनको जलप *n.* rolled gold

sunakhari सुनाखरी *n.* orchid

sunar सुनार *n.* goldsmith

sunaulo सुनौलो *adj.* golden

sundar सुन्दर *adj.* beautiful

sundar सुन्दर *adj.* comely

sundar सुन्दर *adj.* elegant

sundar सुन्दर *adj.* lovely

sundar vastra r gehnapat सुन्दर वस्त्र र गहनापात *n.* finery

sundari naari सुन्दरी नारी *n.* belle

sundeni सुँडेनी *n.* midwife

sune anusar सुनेअनुसार *adv.* reportedly

suneko kura सुनेको कुरा *n.* hearsay

sunenischit सुनिश्चित *adj.* cocksure

sungur सुँगुर *n.* pig

sungur सुँगुर *n.* pig

sungur सुँगुर *n.* swine

sungurko khor सुङ्गुरको खोर *n.* sty

sungurko maas सुँगुरको मासु *n.* pork

sungurle bacha janmaunu सुँगरले बच्चा जन्माउनु *v.* farrow

suninu सुनिनु *v.* swell

sunna na sakine सुन्न नसकिने *adj.* inaudible

sunna sakine सुन्न सकिने *adj.* audible

sunne wyakti सुन्ने व्यक्ति *n.* listener

sunnu सुन्नु *v.* hark

sunnu सुन्नु *n.* hear

sunnu सुन्नु *v.* listejn

suntala सुन्तला *n.* citrus

suntala सुन्तला *n.* orange

sunu सुन्नु *v.* hearken

sunwai सुनवाइ *v.* hearing

supar bhajjar सुपरभाइजर *n.* supervisor

supari सुपारी *n.* betel nut

supari सुपारी *n.* nut

supathit सुपठित *adj.* well read

supt सुप्त *adj.* dormant

supurdagi सुपुर्दगी *n.* extradition

surak launu सुराक लाउनु *v.* track down

suraksha सुरक्षा *n.* security

surakshit सुरक्षित *adj.* immune

surakshit chhura सुरक्षित छुरा *n.* safety razor

surakshit garaunu सुरक्षित गराउनु *vc.* secure

surakshit garnu सुरक्षित गर्नु *v.* reserve

surakshit garnu सुरक्षित गर्नु *adj.* reserved

surath सुरथ *n.* spades

surkeni सुर्केनी *n.* loop

surkeni gantho सुर्केनी गाँठो *n.* slip-knot

surknu सुर्कनु *v.* sniff

suro सूरो *adj.* daring

suro सुरो *n.* spike

surti सुर्ती *n.* tobacco

surun सुरुङ *n.* trench

surun सुरुङ *n.* tunnel

survishesh सुरविशेष *n.* vermouth

surya सूर्य *n.* sun

surya ghadi सुर्य घडी *v.* dial

surya grahan सुर्य ग्रहण *n.* eclipse

surya grahan सूर्यग्रहण *n.* solar eclipse

surya kant mani सूर्यकान्त मणि *n.* jasper

surya ko सूर्यको *adj.* solar

surya mukhi phul सूर्यमुखी फूल *n.* sunflower

surya snan सूर्य स्नान *n.* sunbath

suryast सूर्यास्त *n.* sundown

suryast सूर्यास्त *n.* sunset

suryodaya सूर्योदय *n.* sunrise

susapshat सुस्पष्ट *adj.* unambiguous

sushankya शुशंक्य *n.* computer

sushil सुशील *adj.* courteous

sushil सुशील *adj.* seemly

sushil सुशील *adj.* well bred

sust सुस्त *adj.* weak-minded

sut सूट *n.* suit

sut सुट *n.* yard

suti kapada सुती कपडा *n.* linen

suti luga सूती लुगा *n.* calico

suti luga सूती लुगा *n.* nankeen

sutkeri bida सुत्केरी बिदा *n.* maternity leave

sutne bela ma laune kamij सुत्ने बेलामा लाउने कमिज *n.* nightshirt

sutne thau सुत्ने ठाउँ *n.* kip

sutnu सुत्नु *v.* lie down

sutnu सुत्नु *v.* sleep

sutra सूत्र *n.* formula

sutradhar सूत्रधार *n.* compere

suttuk bhagnu सुटुक्व भाग्नु *v.* abscond

sutukka/lukera janu सुटुक्क/लुकेर जानु *v.* sneak

suwidha सुविधा *n.* amenity

suwidha सुविधा *n.* facility

suwidha सुविधा *n.* privilege

swabhavik स्वाभाविक *adj.* radical

swabhavik parinam स्वाभाविक परिणाम *n.* corollary

swabhaw स्वभाव *n.* temperament

swabhaw स्वभाव *n.* trait

swabhawai le स्वभावैले *adv.* naturally

swachand स्वच्छन्द *adj.* unfettered

swad स्वाद *n.* flavo(u)r

swad स्वाद *n.* taste

swadeshi bhasha स्वदेशी भाषा *n.* vernacular

swadhinta स्वाधीनता *n.* liberty

swadilo स्वादिलो *adj.* tasteful

swadilo स्वादिलो *adj.* tasty

swadilo khana स्वादिलो खाना *n.* delicacy

swagat स्वागत *n.* reception

swagat स्वागत *n.* welcome

swagat dwar स्वागत द्वार *n.* welcome arch

swagat garne स्वागत गर्ने *n.* receptionist

swahini संवहिनी *adj.* vascular

swamitwa स्वामित्व *n.* tenure

swan swan garnu स्वाँ स्वाँ गर्नु *v.* pant

swantantra स्वतंत्र *adj.* free

swar स्वर *n.* voice

swarg स्वर्ग *n.* heaven

swarg स्वर्ग *n.* paradise

swargiya स्वर्गीय *adj.* heavenly

swarth स्वार्थ *n.* self-interest

swarth स्वार्थ *n.* selfishness

swarthi स्वार्थी *adj.* selfish

swasni स्वास्नी *n.* wife

swasni ko wash ma rahane स्वास्नीको वशमा रहने *adj.* henpecked

swasth स्वस्थ *adj.* hale

swasth स्वस्थ *adj.* sane

swasthya labh स्वास्थ्यलाभ *n.* recovery

swasthya labh स्वास्थ्य लाभ *n.* recuperation

swasthya wigyan स्वास्थ्य विज्ञान *n.* hygiene

swasthyakar स्वास्थ्यकर *adj.* sanitary

swatantra ruple स्वतंत्र रूपले *adv.* freely

swatantrata स्वतन्त्रता *n.* independence

swawlamban स्वावलम्बन *n.* self-help

swawlambi स्वावलमी *adj.* self-reliant

swayam sewak स्वयंसेवक *n.* volunteer

swayamsiddha स्वयंसिद्ध *adj.* self-evident

sweater स्वेटर *n.* cardigan

sweater स्वेटर *n.* pullover

swechchhachari स्वेच्छाचारी *adj.* high-handed

swetar स्वेटर *n.* sweater

swich स्वीच *n.* switch

swikar garnu स्वीकार गर्नु *v.* accde

swikar garnu स्वीकार गर्नु *v.* agree

swikar garnu स्वीकार गर्नु *v.* concur

swikar garnu स्वीकार गर्नु *v.* confess

swikar na garieko wyakti स्वीकार नगरिएको व्यक्ति *n.* persona non grata

swikar/manjur garnu स्वीकार/मन्जुर गर्नु *v.* accept

swlkriti स्वीकृति *n.* acknowledgement

swikriti स्वीकृति *n.* okay(ok)

syabaas स्याबास *int.* bravo

syabash स्याबाश *adj.* well done

syal स्याल *n.* jackal

syampu स्याम्पू *n.* shampoo

syandwich स्याण्डबीच *n.* sandwich

syar syar awaj niklanu स्यारस्यार आवाज निक्लनु *n.* rustle

syau स्याउ *n.* apple

T

ta pani तापनि *conj.* though

taal badlanu ताल बदल्नु *v.* syncopate

taar तार *n.* chord

taar jasto तार जस्तो *adj.* wiry

taashko khel ताशको खेल *n.* bingo

taasne vastu टाँस्ने वस्तु *adj.* adhesive

taayar टायर *n.* tyre

tab टब *n.* tub

tabela तबेला *n.* stall

tachhnu ताछ्नु *v.* scrape

tadha टाडा *adj.* aloof

tadha टाढ़ा *adv.* away

tadha टाढा *adj.* far

tadha bata garine teli phon टाढाबाट गरिने टेलिफोन *n.* trunkcall

tadha ko टाढाको *adj.* remote

tadha rahanu टाढा रहनु *v.* shun

tagaro तगारा *n.* obstacle

tagat तागत *n.* strength

tagat ko aushadi तागतको औषधि *n.* tonic

tah तह *n.* layer

tah तह *n.* level

tahudi यहूदी *n.* jew

tail chitra तैलचित्र *n.* oil painting

tainath garnu तैनाथ गर्नु *v.* deploy

tainathi तैनाथी *n.* deployment

taip raitar टाइपराइटर *n.* typewriter

taipist टाइपिस्ट *n.* typist

taja ताजा *adj.* fresh

taja garaunu ताजा गराउनु *v.* refresh

taja parnu ताजा पार्नु *v.* recreate

takhta तखता *n.* shelf

takia adima halne simalko rui तकिया आदिमा हाल्ने सिमलको रूई *n.* kapok

takiya तकिया *n.* pillow

takkaadnu टक्क अड्नु *v.* stop dead

taksar टकसार *n.* mint

tal ताल *n.* lake

tal ताल *n.* rhythm

tal jharnu तल झर्नु *v.* condescend

tala तल *n.* down

tala तला *n.* storey

tala jharne wegwan nadi तल झने बेगवान नदी *n.* rapids

tala mathi तल माथि *n.* ups and downs

tala tira तलतिर *adv.* downstairs

talab तलब *n.* pay

talab तलव *n.* salary

talab तलब *n.* wage

talabi suchi तलबी सूची *n.* payroll

talau तलाउ *n.* tier

talcha ताल्चा *n.* lock

talcha ताल्चा *n.* padlock

taleem prapt dal तालीम प्राप्त दल *n.* cadre

taleko jasto khalti टालेको जस्तो खल्ती *n.* patch pocket

talikabadh तालिकाबद्ध *adj.* tabular

talikama तालिकामा *v.* tabulate

talim तालीम *n.* training

talim paeko तालीम पाएको *adj.* trained

talime तालिमे *n.* trainee

talkanu टलकनु *v.* glint

talkaunu टलकाउनु *v.* furbish

tallo तल्लो *adj.* inferior

tallo तल्लो *adj.* lower

tallo the तल्लो तह *n.* substratum

taltul garne kam टालटुल गर्ने काम *n.* patchwork

talu khuile तालुखुइले *adj.* bald

tam tune टाम टुमे *adj.* trim

tama तामा *n.* copper

tamasa तमासा *n.* fun

tamase तमासे *n.* onlooker

tamasha तमाशा *n.* pageant

tamasha तमाशा *n.* show

tambu तम्बू *n.* tent

tamro sanga राम्रोसँग *adv.* smoothly

tan टन *n.* ton(ne)

tana marnu ताना मार्नु *v.* taunt

tana shah तानाशाह *n.* dictator

tanai तनाइ *n.* pull

tanashahi तानाशाही *n.* autocrat

tanau तनाउ *n.* strain

tanau ko kami तनाउको कमी *n.* détente

tandra तन्द्रा *n.* stupor

tandra तन्द्रा *n.* trance

tank टाँक *n.* button

tanka टाँका *n.* stitch

tankai तन्काइ *n.* stretch

tankane तन्कने *adj.* elastic

tankeko awastha तन्केको अवस्था *n.* tension

tanki टंकी *n.* vat

tankieko तन्किएको *adj.* tense

tanma haler kapda banaune wala तानमा हालेर कपड़ा बनाउने बाना *v.* wett

tanna तन्ना *n.* sheet

tannab तनाव *v.* haul

tannu तान्नु *v.* drag

tansinu टाँसिनु *v.* adhere

tansinu टाँसियनु *v.* cling

tanti ताँती *n.* cortege

tap lahar ताप लहर *n.* heatwave

tap napne ताप नाप्ने *n.* thermometer

tapani तापनि *adv.* notwithstanding

taphi टफी *n.* toffee

tapikanu तप्किनु *v.* drip

tapkane thopa तप्कने थोपा *n.* driblet

tapke ताप्के *n.* saucepan

tapkram तापक्रम *n.* temperature

tapsil तपसिल *n.* detail

tapu टापु *n.* island

tapu टापू *n.* isle

tar तार *n.* telegram

tar jhiknu तर झिक्नु *v.* skim

tara तर *conj.* but

tara तारा *n.* star

taragan तारागण *n.* constellation

taraharu madhyako ताराहरूमध्यको *adj.* interstellar

taral तरल *n.* liquid

taral padarthko tol तरल पदार्थको तौल *n.* dram

taral vastuko naap तरल वस्तुको नाप *n.* quart

taral wastu तरल वस्तु *n.* fluid

taral wastu ko nap तरल वस्तुको नाप *n.* pint

tarayukt तारायुक्त *adj.* stellar

tarbar तरबार *n.* sword

tarbuja तरबुजा *n.* melon

tarbuja तरबुजा *n.* watermelon

tarbuja तार *n.* wire

tarch lait टर्चलाइट *n.* flashlight

tarch light टर्चलाइट *n.* torch

tarika तारिका *n.* device

tariph तारिफ/प्रशंसा गर्नु *v.* appluad

tariph तारिफ गर्नु *n.* compliment

tariph garnu तारिफ गर्नु *v.* commend

tariph yogya तारिफयोग्य *adj.* praiseworthy

tark तर्क *n.* argument

tark तर्क *n.* logic

tark hin तर्कहीन *adj.* irrational

tarkari तरकारी *n.* vegetable

tarksangat तर्कसंगत *adj.* logical

tarkshastra तर्कशास्त्र *n.* logic

tarkvirudh तर्कविरुद्ध *adj.* illogical

tarnu टार्नु *v.* avoid

tarpinko tel तारपिनको तेल *n.* turpentine

tarsaunu तर्साउनु *v.* daunt

tarsaunu तर्साउनु *v.* frighten

tarsaunu तर्साउनु *v.* scare

tarul तरुल *n.* yak

tarul तरूल *n.* yam

tarun तरुण *adj.* juvenile

tarun तरुण *adj.* young

tarun तरूण *adj.* youthful

tarya तयारी *adj.* ready

tas तास *n.* card

tas तास *n.* playing card

tasalli तसल्ली *n.* consolation

taskar wyapari तस्कर व्यापारी *n.* smuggler

taskari garnu तस्करी गर्नु *v.* smuggle

tasnu टाँस्नु *n.* paste

taswir तस्वीर *n.* photograph

taswir तस्वीर *n.* picutre

taswir तस्वीर *n.* snapshot

taswir rakhne kitab तस्वीर राख्ने किताब *n.* album

tataunu तताउनु *v.* warm up

tatera rato bhaeko तातेर रातो भएको *adj.* red-hot

tatha kathit तथाकथित *adj.* so-called

tathanyak तथ्यांक *n.* data

tathastu तथास्तु *int.* amen

tatho ठाठो *adj.* keen

tathyank तथ्याङ्क *n.* statistics

tatkalik तात्कालिक *adj.* impromptu

tatkalik kshan तात्कालिक क्षण *n.* instant

tato तातो *adj.* hot

tatopani wa baph le polnu तातो पानी वा वाफ्ले पोल्नु *v.* scald

tatparta तत्परता *v.* alacrity

tatt टाट *n.* gunny

tattair piter jodnu तताएर पिटेर जोड्नु *v.* weld

tatte-phate टाटेपाटे *adj.* mottled

tatto तातो *adj.* warm

tattu टट्टु *n.* pony

tattwa तत्त्व *n.* element

tattwa तत्त्व *n.* factor

tattwawdhan तत्त्वाधान *n.* auspices

tauko टाउको *n.* pate

tauko hallaunu टाउ को हल्लाउनु *v.* nod

tauko katnu टाउको काट्नु *v.* decapitate

tauko kotne machine टाउको कोट्ने मेशिन *n.* guillotine

tauko shir टाउको, शिर *n.* head

Tauko thokine gari टाउको ठोकिने गरी *n.* headlong

tauliya तौलिया *n.* towel

tawa तावा *n.* griddle

tawa तावा *n.* pan

tayaganu त्यागनु *v.* abdicate

tayar garnu तयार गर्नु *v.* prepare

tayar hunu तयार हुनु *v.* get ready

tayar na bhaeko तयार नभएको *adj.* unprepared

tayari तयारी *n.* preparation

tayari तयारी *n.* readiness

tayari wastu तयारी वस्तु *n.* ready-made

tayksi ट्याक्सी *n.* cab

tebbar तेब्बर *adj.* triple

tebul टेबुल *n.* table

tebul poshak टेबुलपोशाक *n.* tablecloth

tebul tenis टेबुलटेनिस *n.* pingpong

tebul, kurchi, adi टेबुल, कुर्ची आदि *n.* furniture

teekho तीखो *v.* screech

teekho awaaz तीखो आवाज *n.* bleep

teekshan तीक्ष्ण *adj.* acute

teen pakshiya तीन पक्षीय *adj.* trilateral

teen rang bhaeko jhanda तीन रंग भएको झंडा *n.* tricolour

teenguna तीनगुना *adj.* triplex

teenko samuh तीनको समूह *n.* triad

tehro तेहरो *adj.* treble

tej तेज *n.* glare

tej तेज *adj.* smart

tej chal तेज चाल *n.* race

tej le तेजले *adv.* sharply

tejab तेजाब *n.* acid

tejaswi तेजस्वी *adj.* glorious

tejilo तेजिलो *adj.* speedy

tejmandeal तेजमण्डल *n.* halo

teko dinu टेको दिनु *v.* prop

tel तेल *n.* oil

tel bastu तेल बस्तु *n.* oilcake

tel ko kuwa तेलको कूवा *n.* oil well

tel lagaunu तेल लगाउनु *v.* lubricate

tel rang तेल रङ्ग *n.* oil colo(u)r

tel sapha garne karkhana तेल सफा गर्ने कारखाना *n.* refinery

teli bhijan टेलिभिजन *n.* television

teliphon टेलिफोन *n.* phone

teliphon टेलिफोन *n.* telephone

telkhani तेल खानी *n.* oilfield

teniskhel टेनिस खेल *n.* tennis

tereleem टेरीलिन *n.* terylene

terha तेह्र *n.* thirteen

terso तेर्सो *adj.* horizontal

terso तेर्सो *adj.* oblique

terso तेर्सो *adj.* slant

tesro तेस्रो *adj.* tertiary

tesro तेस्रो *adj.* third

thado ठाडो *adj.* steep

thado ठाडो *adj.* vertical

thag ठग *n.* cheat

thagnu ठगनु *v.* deceive

thaha bhaeko थाहा भएको *adj.* known

thaha dinu थाहा दिनु *v.* inform

thaha nadikana sunnu थाहा नदिकन सुन्नु *v.* overhear

thaila थैलो *n.* purse

thailo थैलो *n.* pouch

thakai थकाइ *n.* fatigue

thakai थकाइ *n.* weariness

thakai lagnu थकाइ लाग्नु *v.* tire

thakaune थकाउने *adj.* gruelling

thakaune थकाउने *adj.* tiring

thakeko थाकेको *adj.* exhausted

thakeko थाकेको *adj.* tired

thakeko थाकेको *adj.* washed out

thakeko थाकेको *adj.* weary

thakeko ghoda थकेको घोडा *n.* jade

thakit थकित *adj.* jiggered

thakkar ठक्कर *n.* blow

thakkar khanu ठक्कर खानु *v.* bump

thakkar khanu ठक्कर खानु *v.* collide

thal थाल *n.* dish

thal थाल *n.* plate

thal kamal ko phul थलकमलको फूल *n.* magnolia

thalai ma थलैमा *adv.* red-handed

thalnu थाल्नु *v.* begin

thalnu थाल्नु *v.* commence

thana थाना *n.* police station

thankyaunu थन्क्याउनु *v.* lock up

thankyaunu थन्क्याउनु *v.* put away

thanne थाङ्ने *adj.* ragged

thannu ठान्नु *v.* reckon

thap थाप *n.* plus

thap bhada wa shulak थप भाड़ा वा शुल्क *v.* surcharge

thap sahi garnu थप सही गर्नु *v.* countersigh

thapadi थपड़ी *n.* clap

thapinu थपिनु *v.* accrue

thappad थप्पड *n.* slap

thar thar aunu थरथराउनु *v.* tremble

thar thari थरथरी *n.* tremor

tharho bheer ठाड़ो भीर *n.* bluff

tharho chattan ठाड़ो चट्टान *n.* precipice

tharkanu थर्कनु *v.* vibrate

tharkeko awaj थर्केको आवाज *n.* rattle

tharmas थर्मस *n.* thermos

tharo pahad wa chattan ठाड़ो पहाड़ वा चट्टान *n.* crag

thartharaunu थरथराउनु *n.* quiver

thata garne vyakti ठट्टा गर्ने व्यक्ति *n.* joker

thatta ठट्टा *n.* joke

thatta ठट्टा *n.* pleasantry

thatta garne ठट्टा गर्ने *n.* jester

thatta garnu ठट्टा गर्नु *phr.* poke fun at

thatyaulo ठट्यौलौ *adj.* jocular

thau jahan pani khach ठाउँ जहाँ पानी खस्छ *v.* outfall

thaun ठाउँ *n.* place

thaun ठाउँ *n.* space

thedo टेढ़ो *adj.* cock-eyed

theek ठीक *adj.* precise

theek samay bataune ghari ठीक समय बताउने घड़ी *n.* chronometer

thegana ठेगाना *n.* address

thegana ठेगाना *adv.* whereabouts

thegana badli garnu ठेगाना बदली गर्नु *v.* readdress

thegnu थेग्नु *v.* sustain

thegro थेग्रो *n.* dregs

their थए *v./aux.* were

thekedar ठेकेदार *n.* contractor

thekho soar तीखो स्वर *v.* yell

thekka ठेक्का *n.* contract

thela थुम्को *n.* spur

thela gada ठेलागाडा *n.* pushcart

thes lagnu ठेस लाग्नु *v.* stumble

theula ठेउला *n.* chicken pox

thik ठीक *adj.* accurate

thik ठीक *adj.* alright

thik ठीक *adj.* exact

thik batobat hatnu ठीक बाटोबाट हट्नु *v.* deviate

thik garnu ठीक गर्नु *v.* redress

thik hisab le ठीक हिसाबले *adv.* minutely

thik sanga ठीकसँग *v.* accurately

thik sanga ठीकसँग *adv.* exactly

thik sanga ठीकसँग *adv.* precisely

thik wichar bhaeko ठीक विचार भएको *adj.* right-minded

thikari ko ठिकैको *adj.* moderate

thikkai ठिक्कै *adj/adv.* so-so

thiksang ठीकसँग *adv.* duly

thiti ठिटी *n.* damsel

thiti ठिटी *n.* wench

thito ठिटो *n.* lad

thitti ठिटी *n.* gal

thiyo थियो *v./aux.* wart

thiyo थियो *v.* was

thok थोक *n.* bulk

thok थोक *n.* wholesale

thopa थोपा *n.* drop

thopa थोपा *n.* globule

thoplo थोप्लो *n.* dot

thorae gyan थोरै ज्ञान *n.* smattering

thorae pariman थोरै परिमाण *n.* modicum

thorai थोरै *n.* jot

thorai थोरै *adj.* scant

thorai थोरै *adj.* scanty

thorai banki rahanu थोरै बाँकी रहनु *v.* run low

thorea samay matra rahne थोरै समय मात्र रहने *adj.* transitory

thos ठोस *adj.* solid

thotraraddimal थोत्रा रद्दी माल *n.* trash

thotro थोत्रो *adj.* stale

thuk थुक *n.* spit

thuk थुक *n.* spittle

thukne bhadho थुक्ने भाँड़ो *n.* spittoon

thulabadha ठूलाबाड़ा *n.* gentry

thulo ठूलो *adj.* big

thulo ठूलो *adj.* great

thulo ठूलो *adj.* large

thulo ठूलो *adj.* massive

thulo awaj hune ठूलो आवाज हुने *adj.* noisy

thulo awaj le ठूलो आवाजले *adv.* loudly

thulo ba ठूलो बा *n.* uncle

thulo bhul garnu ठूलो भूल गर्नु *n.* blunder

thulo chakku ठूलो चक्कु *n.* jackknife

thulo chingdi machha ठूलो चिङ्गडी माछा *n.* lobster

thulo dhunga ठूलो ढुंगा *n.* boulder

thulo garnu ठूलो गर्नु *v.* enlarge

thulo ghan ठूलो घन *n.* sledgehammer

thulo kathinai ma ठूलो कठिनाइमा *adv.* up against it

thulo mahtav ko ठूलो महत्त्व को *adj.* crucial

thulo ruchi ठूलो रूचि *n.* zest

thulo safalta ठूलो सफलता *n.* wow

thulo samudari machha ठूलो समुद्री माछा *n.* tuna

thulo sankhya ठूलो संख्या *n.* myriad

thulo sipi ठूलो सीपी *n.* clam

thulo sisi ठूलो सिसी *n.* jar

thulo sutne kotha ठूलो सुल्ने कोठा *n.* dormitory

thulo swarma ठूलो स्वरमा *adv.* aloud

thun थुन *n.* dug

thuna थुना *n.* detention

thuna थुना *n.* imprisonment

thunnu ठुङ्नु *v.* peck

thupro थुप्रो *adj.* heap

thupro थुप्रो *n.* hoard

thupro थुप्रो *n.* jumble

thupro थुप्रो *n.* pile

thupro थुप्रो *n.* swarm

thurpanu थुपार्नु *v.* accumulate

thussa pareko ठुस्स परेको *adj.* sullen

thussinu टुसिसनु *v.* sulk

thuta ठुटा *n.* stump

thutuno थुतुनो *n.* snout

thutunu थुतुनु *n.* muzzle

thyroid granthi थाराइड ग्रन्थि *n.* thyroid

tibi टि.बी. *n.* T.B.

tighra तिघ्रा *n.* thigh

tighrako haddi तिघ्राको हड्डी *n.* femur

tikat टिकट *n.* ticket

tika-tippani टिका-टिप्पणी *n.* comment

tikau टिकाउ *adj.* durable

tikau टिकाउ *adj.* lasting

tikharnu तिखार्नु *v.* sharpen

tikho तीखो *adj.* pointed

tikho तीखो *adj.* sharp

tikho तीखो *adj.* shrill

tik-tik awaj टिक टिक आवाज *n.* tick

til तिल *n.* sesame

timi तिमी *pron.* you

timi aphai तिमी आफै *pron.* yourself

timro तिम्रो *adj.* thy

timro तिम्रो *pron.* your

tin तीन *n.* three

tin टिन *n.* tin

tin jagayte टिन जङ्गते *adj.* tinny

tin jana ko samuha तीनजना को समूह *n.* trio

tin pangre saikal तीनपाङ्ग्रे साइकल *n.* tricycle

tini haru तिनीहरू *pron.* they

tini/uni haru ko तिनी/उनीहरूको *pron.* their

tini/uni haru lai तिनी/उनीहरूलाई *pron.* them

tipaani टिप्पणी *n.* note

tipnu टिप्नु *v.* pick up

tipnu टिप्नु *v.* pluck

tir तीर *v.* arrow

tira तिर *prep.* towards

tirkhaeko तिर्खाएको *adj.* thirsty

tirnu parne तिर्नु पर्ने *adj.* payable

tirpaal तिरपाल *n.* tarpaulin

tirth तीर्थ *n.* shrine

tis तीस *n.* thirty

titra तित्रा *n.* partidge

titra तित्रा *n.* partridge

tivra banaunu तीव्र बनाउनु *v.* exacerbate

tiwra तीव्र *adj.* intense

tiwra parnu तीव्र पार्नु *v.* tone up

tiwrata तीव्रता *n.* intensity

tiwrata तीव्रता *n.* keenness

todnu तोड्नु *v.* prise

tokari टोकरी *n.* basket

tokieko तोकिएको *adj.* scheduled

tokieko तोकिएको *adj.* specific

tokieko तोकिए को *adj.* specified

tokieko matra तोकिए को मात्रा *n.* quota

toknu टोक्नु *n.* bite

toknu तोक्नु *v.* prescribe

toknu तोक्नु *v.* specify

toli टोली *n.* squad

toli टोली *n.* team

toli टोली *n.* troop

tolko ekank तौलको एकांक *n.* ounce

tolnu तौलनु *v.* weigh

top टोप *n.* hat

top gola तोपगोला *n.* shot

topi टोपी *n.* cap

topphod तोडफोड *n.* sabotage

tori तोरी *n.* mustard green

toss ठोस *n.* gross

trabhal ejent ट्राभल एजेण्ट *n.* travel agent

traimasik त्रैमासिक *adj.* quarterly

trak ट्रक *n.* truck

trali ट्राली *n.* trolly

traphik ट्राफिक *n.* traffic

tri bhuj त्रिभुज *n.* triangle

tri khuti त्रिखुटी *n.* tripod

tri murti त्रिमूर्ति *n.* trinity

trikonmiti त्रिकोणमिति *n.* trigonometry

trimukut त्रिमुकुट *n.* tiara

tripai त्रिपाइ *n.* stool

tripat तृप्त *adj.* sated

trishul त्रिशूल *n.* trident

tryaktar ट्र्याक्टर *n.* tractor

tuch तुच्छ *adj.* peddling

tuch samjhanu तुच्छ सम्झनु *v.* disparage

tucha तुच्छा *adj.* measly

tuhine kam तुहिने काम *n.* miscariage

tuhuro टुहुरो *n.* orphan

tukra टुक्रा *n.* bit

tukra टुक्रा *n.* chip

tukra टुक्रा *n.* fragment

tukra टुक्रा *n.* piece

tukra टुक्रा *n.* scrap

tukra parnu टुका पार्नु *n.* chop

tukrukka basnu टुक्रुक्क बस्नु *v.* squat

tula rashi तुला राशि *n.* libra

tulna garn sakne तुलना गर्न सकिने *adj.* comparable

tulna garna na sakine तुलना गर्न नसकिने *adj.* peerless

tulna nahune तुलना नहुने *adj.* incommensurate

tumtum टमटम *n.* gig

tuna/mohit garnu टुना/मोहित गर्नु *v.* enchant

tungo na lageko टुङ्गो नलागेको *adj.* pending

tungoma napungame टुङ्गोमा नपुग्ने *adj.* inconclusive

tupi टुपी *n.* pigtail

tuppo टुप्पो *n.* tip

turnta hune तुरून्त हुने *adj.* immediate

turunt तुरुन्त *adv.* instantly

turunt तुरुन्त *adv.* promptly

turunt तुन्त *adv.* readily

turunt तुरुन्त *adv.* straight away

turuntai तूरून्तै *adv.* immediately

turup तुरुप *n.* trump

tusa टुसा *n.* shoot

tusaro तुसारो *n.* frost

tutaunu टुटाउनु *v.* break

tuti टुटी *n.* faucet

tuti टुटी *n.* nozzle

tuwanlo तुवाँलो *adj.* haze

tweedko luga टुवीडको लुगा *n.* tweed

tyag त्याग *n.* renunciation

tyagnu त्याग्नु *v.* discard

tyagnu त्यागनु *v.* quit

tyahan bata त्यहाँबाट *adv.* thence

tyahan bata त्यहाँबाट *adv.* there

tyahan bata त्यहाँबाट *adv.* therein

tyahandikhi त्यहाँदिखि *adj.* thence

tyaksi ट्याक्सी *n.* taxi

tyandro त्यान्द्रो *n.* shred

tyandro त्यान्द्रो *n.* wishful thinking

tyap-tyap garer ट्याप-ट्याप गरेर *adv.* pit-a-pat

tyar garnu तयार गर्नु *v.* unlimber

tyas bela dekhi त्यस बेलादेखि *adv.* since

tyas bela ko त्यसबेलाको *adj.* then

tyas karan त्यसकारण *adv./conj.* so

tyas karan त्यसकारण *adv.* therefore

tyas pachhi तयसपछि *adv.* thereafter

tyas pachhi त्यसपछि *adv.* thereupon

tyas upranta त्यसउप्रान्त *adv.* thenceforth

tyas us le त्यस उसले *adv.* thereby

tyasai gari त्यसैगरी *adv.* likewise

tyasaigari त्यसैगरी *adv.* similarly

tyaso bhae ma त्यसो भएमा *adv.* so long as

tyaso bhae ta pani त्यसो भए तापनि *adv.* however

tyaso bhae tapani त्यसो भए तापनि *adv.* nevertheless

tyastai aru kura त्यस्तै अरू कुरा *pron.* what have you

tyehan त्यहाँ *adj.adv.* yonder

tyo त्यो *pron.* that

tyo त्यो *def. art.* the

typhoid टायफाइड *n.* typhoid

tytphut टुटफुट *n.* wear and tear

tyusan टयुसन *n.* tuition

U

u aphai ऊ आफै *pron.* himself

ubhindo उभिण्डो *adj./adv.* upside down

ubhinu उभिनु *v.* stand

ubjau उब्जाउ *adj.* fertile

ubjau उब्जाउ *adj.* productive

ubrieko उब्रिएको *adj.* leftover

ucch adalatka vakil उच्च अदालत का वकील *n.* barrister

ucch darjako उच्च दर्जाको *adj.* posh

ucch pad ki mahila उच्च पद की महिला *n.* dame

ucch padka adhikari उच्च पदका अधिकारी *n.* dignitary

uccharan उच्चारण *n.* accent

ucchkotiko उच्चकोटिको *adj.* deluxe

uchai उचाइ *n.* altitude

uchai उचाइ *n.* height

uchalnu उचाल्नु *v.* elevate

uchalnu उचाल्नु *v.* hoist

uchcha nyayalaya उच्च न्यायालय *n.* high court

uchcharan garnu उच्चारण गर्नु *v.* pronounce

uchchastariya उच्चस्तरीय *adj.* high-level

uchchat lagne उच्चाट लाग्ने *adj.* tedious

uchchat lagnu उच्चाट लाग्नु *n.* bore

uchhinnu उछिन्नु *v.* overtake

uchhinu उछिन्नु outclass

uchhit उचित *adj.* reasonable

uchit उचित *v.* decent

uchit उचित *adj.* due

uchit उचित देखाउनु *v.* justify

uchit उचित *adj.* proper

uchit उचित *adj.* seemly

uchit उचित *adj.* worthwhile

uchit tarika le उचित तरिकाले *adv.* properly

udaas उदास *adj.* dismal

udahara dekhaunu उदाहरण देखाउनु *v.* set an example

udaharan ददाहरण *n.* example

udaharan उदाहरण *n.* illustration

udaharan उदाहरण *n.* instance

udan उडान *n.* flight

udar उदार *adj.* liberal

udar उदार *adj.* open-handed

udarta उदारता *n.* generosity

udasinta उदासीनता *n.* lethargy

udasinta उदासीनता *n./adj.* melancholy

udasinta उदास *adj.* moody

udaunu उदाउनु *v.* rise

uddarta उदारता *n.* bounty

uddeshya उद्देश्य *n.* goal

uddeshya उद्देश्य *n.* purpose

uddhar kosh उद्धार कोष *n.* relief fund

uddharan wakya उद्धरण वाक्य *n.* quotation

uddhrit garna layak ko उद्धृत गर्न लायकको *adj.* quotable

udgar उद्गार *n.* outpouring

udghatan उद्घाटन *n.* opening

udghatan garnu उद्घाटन गर्नु *v.* inaugurate

udghatan garnu उद्घाटन *n.* inauguration

udghatan ko उद्घाटनको *adj.* inaugural

udhanko vigyan उड़ानको विज्ञान *n.* aeronautics

udlyaman उदीयमान *adj.* rising

udus उडुस *n.* bedbug

udus उडुस *n.* bug

udwaranchinha bandh garnu उद्धरणाचिन्ह बन्द गर्नु *v.* unquote

udyam उद्यम *n.* enterprise

udyami उद्यमी *adj.* enterprising

udyami उद्यमी *n.* entrepreneur

udyan उद्यान *n.* park

udyog उद्योग *n.* industry

udyog dhanda उद्योग-धंधा *n.* industry

udyogi उद्योगी *adj.* diligent

ugatanu ओगट्नु *v.* occupy

ugra उग्र *adj.* extreme

ugra उग्र *adj.* turbulent

uhi उही *n.* ditto

uhi उही *adj.* same

uhiarth bijhaune shabd उही अर्थ बुझाउने शब्द *n.* synonym

uhile उहिले *adv.* formerly

uhile उहिले *adv.* previously

ujjadh उजाड़ *adj.* bleak

ujjawal उज्जवल *adj.* effulgent

ujjawal उज्जवल *adj.* respledent

ujjawal neelo उज्जवल नीलो *n.adj.* ultramarine

ujur उजूर *n.* grievance

ujur/bintigarnu बिन्ती गर्नु *n.* appeal

ujyalo उज्यालो *adj.* vivid

ukalo उकालो *n.* slope

ukalo उकालो *adj.* uphill

ukati उक्ति *n.* by-word

ukhaan उखान *n.* adage

ukhalnu उखाल्नु *v.* unroot

ukhan दखान *n.* proverb

ukhan उखान *n.* saying

ukhelnu उखेल्नु *v.* pull up

ukhelnu उखेल्नु *n.* root out

ukhelnu उखेल्नु *v.* uproot

ukhu उखु *n.* sugar cane

ukkanunu उक्काउनु *v.* lever up

uklanu उक्लनु *v.* ascend

uksaunu उक्साउनु *v.* encourage

uksaunu उक्साउनु *v.* instigate

ukti उक्ति *n.* maxim

ulka उल्का *n.* meteor

ullanghan उल्लंघन *v.* contravene

ullanghan उल्लंघन *n.* violation

ullanghan garnu उल्लंघन गर्नु *v.* violate

ullasit उल्लसित *adj.* ebullient

ullekh उल्लेख *n.* mention

ultai dinu उल्टाइदिनु *v.* overthrow

ultatpher उलटफेर *n.* vicissitude

ultaunu उल्टाउनु *v.* turn over

ulti उल्टी *n.* vomit

ultinu उल्टिनु *v.* upset

ulto उल्टो *adj.* opposite

ulto artha ko shabda उल्टो अर्थको शब्द *n.* antonym

ulto palto उल्टोपल्टो *adj.* topsy-turvy

umer उमेर *n.* age

umerle seto bhaeko उमेरले सेतो भएको *adj.* hoary

ummed war उम्मेदवार *n.* candidate

umranu उम्रनु *v.* germinate

umranu उम्रनु *v.* grow

un ऊन *n.* wool

un ko उनको *pron.* her

unchai ऊँचाइ *n.* elevation

unghnu उँघ्नु *v.* doze

uni उनी *pron.* she

uni ऊनी *adj.* woollen

uni aphai उनी आफै *pron.* herself

uni haru उनीहरू *pron.* those

uni suitar ऊनी सुइटर *n.* jumper

unmulan garnu उन्मूलन गर्नु *v.* extirpate

unnais उन्नाइस *n.* nineteen

unnati उन्नति *n.* prosperity

unnati उन्नति *n.* uplift

unyu उन्यू *n.* fern

up pradhyapak उपप्राध्यावक *n.* lecturer

upadhi उपाधि *n.* diploma

upadhryaha उपद्रयाहा *adj.* mischievous

upadro उपद्रो *n.* mischief

upadryaha उपद्रयाक्ष *n.* rogue

upanyas उपन्यास *n.* novel

upanyaskar उपन्यासकार *n.* novelist

upatyaka उपत्यका *n.* dale

upatyaka उपत्यका *n.* glen

upatyaka उपत्यका *n.* valley

upaya उपाय *n.* method

upaya/jukti garnu उपाय/जुक्ति गर्नु *v.* devise

upbhasha उपभाषा *n.* dialect

upchar उपचार *n.* remedy

upchar उपचार *n.* treatment

upchar grih उपचार गृह *n.* clinic

updesh उपदेश *n.* homily

updesh dinu उपदेश दिनु *v.* exhort

upeksha garnu उपेक्षा गर्नु *v.* ignore

upekshit उपेक्षित *adj.* run-down

upgraha उपग्रह *n.* satellite

uphar उपहार *n.* tribute

uphar उपहार *n.* trophy

uphrai उफ्राइ *n.* jump

uphranu उफ्रनु *v.* bounce

uphranu उफ्रनु *n.* buck

upiyan उपियाँ *n.* flea

upkaar garne उपकार गर्ने *adj.* beneficent

upkar garnu उपकार गर्नु *v.* oblige

upkaran उपकरण *n.* equipment

upkaran उपकरण *n.* appartus

upkaran va yantra उपकरण वा यन्त्र *n.* appliance

upkari उपकारी *adj.* helpful
upkhari उपखाड़ी *n.* inlet
upkulpati उपकुलपति *n.* vice chancellor
uplabdha उपलब्ध *adj.* available
uplabdhi उपलब्धि *n.* achievement
upmahadweep उपमहाद्वीप *n.* subcontinent
upmarg linu उपमार्ग लिनु *n.* by-pass
upnaam उपनाम *n.* alias
upnam उपनाम *n.* nickname
upnam उपनाम *n.* pen-name
upnam उपनाम *n.* surname
upniwesh wad उपनिवेशवाद *n.* colonialism
upniyam उपनियम *n.* by-law
uprashtrapati उपराष्ट्रपति *n.* vice president
upruyukt उपर्युक्त *adj.* aforesaid
upsanhar उपसंहार *n.* epilogue
upsaran अपसरण *n.* removal
uptpadan उत्पादन *n.* production
upwijeta उपविजेता *n.* runner-up
upyog garnu उपयोग गर्नु *v.* utilize
upyogi उपयोगी *adj.* useful
upyogi उपयोग *n.* utilization
upyogita उपयोगिता *n.* utility
urenium यूरेनियम *n.* uranium
urenus grah यूरेनस ग्रह *n.* uranus
us ko उसको *pron.* his
usineko masu r sabji उसिनेको मासु र सब्जी *n.* goulash

uslai उसलाई *pron.* him
ussinu उसिन्नु *v.* parboil
ustai उस्तै *adj.* identical
ustai उस्तै *adj.* similar
utaarnu उतार्नु *v.* unlade
utaigik bhayara uffranu उत्तेजिक भएर उफ्रनु *v.* cavort
ute ऊँट *n.* camel
uthal puthal उथलपुथल *n.* upheaval
uthaunu उठाउनु *v.* raise
uthaunu उठाउनु *v.* raise
uthnu उठ्नु *v.* arise
uthnu उठ्नु *v.* get up
utkrisht kirti उत्कृष्ट कृति *n.* masterpiece
utpadak उत्पादक *n.* producer
utpadan उत्पादन *n.* output
utpadn garnu उत्पादन गर्नु *n.* manufacture
utpat उत्पात *n.* turmoil
utpatti उत्पत्ति *n.* origin
utranu उत्रनु *v.* disembark
utranu उत्रनु *v.* touch down
utsahi उत्साही *adj.* zealous
utsahi उत्साही *n.* zero
utsav उत्सव *n.* revelry
utsavko aghilo saanjh उत्सवको अघिल्लो साँझ *n.* eve
utsaw उत्सव *n.* gala
utsaw उत्साह *n.* verve
utsaw उत्साह *n.* vim

utsaw dekhaunu उत्साह देखाउनु *v.* enthuse

utsaw manaaunu उत्सव मनाउनु *v.* celebrate

utsuk उत्सुक *adj.* avid

utsuk उत्सुक *adj.* curious

utsuk उत्सुक *adj.* eager

uttam उत्तम *adj.* excellent

uttam उत्तम *adj.* exquisite

uttapan garnu उत्पन्न गर्नु *v.* evoke

uttar उतार *n.* descent

uttar उत्तर *n.* north

uttar dinu उत्तर दिनु *v.* respond

uttar tira उत्तर तीर *adv.* northward

uttaradhikari उक्राराधिकारी *n.* successor

uttari उत्तरी *adj.* northern

uttari dhruwa उत्तरी ध्रुव *n.* north pole

uttejan उत्तेजन *n.* stimulation

uttejana उत्तेजना *n.* excitement

uttejana उत्तेजना *n.* provocation

uttejit garaunu उत्तेजित गराउनु *v.* arouse

uttejit garnu उत्तेजित गर्नु *v.* agitate

uttejit garnu उत्तेजित गर्नु *v.* excite

uttejit garnu उत्तेजित गर्नु *v.* stimulate

uttejit garnu wa hunu उत्तेजित गर्नु वा हुनु *v.* ferment

uttolak उत्तोलक *n.* lever

uttpadak-sangh उत्पादक संघ *n.* cartel

uttpan garnu उत्पन्न गर्नु *v.* engender

V

vaas वास *n.* habitation

vaasnali वासनली *n.* trachea

vachnu भाँच्नु *adj.* broke

vadi वादी *n.* plaintiff

vahya aakriti वाह्य आकृति *n.* semblance

vaidhya वैध *adj.* licit

vaigayanik वैज्ञानिक *n.* boffin

vakeel वकील *n.* advocate

vaksh वक्ष *n.* thorax

van ko devta वन को देवता *n.* satyr

vanchit garnu वंचित गर्नु *v.* divest

vanjawanu वनज्वानु *n.* thyme

vanropan वनरोपण *n.* afforestation

vanshawali वंशावली *n.* genealogy

vapas linu वापस लिनु *v.* retract

vapas paun naskine वापस पाउन नसकिने *adj.* irretrievable

varansankar वर्णसंकर *n. adj.* hybrid

vardi laune nokar वर्दी लाउने नोकर *n.* flunkey

varisht sadasya वरिष्ठ सदस्य *n.* doyen

varnan garn naskine वर्णन गर्न नसकिने *adj.* indescribable

varnan garn naskine वर्णन गर्न नसकिने *adj.* ineffable

vasiyatnama nalekhi वसयतनामा नलेखी *adj.* intestate

vayu uttapan garne वायु उत्पन्न गर्ने *n.* flatulence

vayuchapmapak वायुचापमापक *n.* barometer

vedi वेदी *n.* altar

vedna वेदना *n.* anguish

veerangna वीरांगना *n.* heroine

veerta वीरता *n.* valour

veertapurn वीरतापूर्ण *adj.* heroic

vesh वेश *n.* guise

veshya वेश्या *n.* trollop

veshya वेश्या *n.* whore

vetanbahek dine suvidha वेतनबाहेक दिइने सुविधा *n.* perquisite

vetanbhogi वेतनभोगी *n.* worker

vetanu वेताणु *n.* leucocyte

vibhin kam garnma sipalu vyakti विभिन्न काम गर्नमा सिपालु व्यक्ति *v.* handyman

vichitar विचित्र *adj.* droll

vidhyut nikalne ek yantra विद्युत् निकाल्ने एक यंत्र *n.* dynamo

vidhyut pratirodhko ekank विद्युत प्रतिरोधको एकांक *n.* ohm

vidushak विदूषक *n.* buffoon

vighatan विघटन dissolution

vigypan tasne phalyak विज्ञापन टाँस्ने फल्याक *n.* hoarding

vikaran विकर्ण *n.adj.* diagonal

vikas विकास *n.* outgrowth

vikrit garnu va hunu विकृत गर्नु वा हुनु *v.* warp

vilamb garne विलम्ब गर्ने *adj.* dilatory

vilamb wa sthagan विलम्ब वा स्थगन *n.* respite

vilap garnu विलाप गर्नु *v.* wail

vilasmaya विलासमय *adj.* plush

vimukh garaunu विमुख गराउनु *v.* estrange

vinodpurn विनोदपूर्ण *adj.* witty

violion jasto baja भाइलिन जस्तै बाजा *n.* cello

viphal hunu विफल हुनु *v.* fizzle

virakt wa wak bhaeko विरक्त वा वाक्क भएको fed

virechan विरेचन *n.* catharsis

virodh garnu विरोध गर्नु *v.* remonstrate

visamay विस्मय *n.* consternation

vish विष *n.* cyanide

vishadgrast विषादग्रस्त *adj.* melancholic

vishakt विषाक्त *adj.* septic

vishalu makura विषालु माकुरा *n.* tarantula

vishalu sarp विषालु सर्प *n.* viper

vishalu vanaspati विषालु वनस्पति *n.* hemlock

vishav विश्व *n.* consmos

vishesh विशेष *adj.* especial

vishesh adhikar विशेष अधिकार *n.* prerograive

vishesh seep विशेष सीप *n.* expertise

visheshan विशेषण *n.* adjective

vishleshan garnu विश्लेषण गर्नु *v.* analyse

vishtha विष्ठा *n.* faeces

vishthar garnu विस्तार गर्नु *v.* amplify

visphotak विस्फोटक *n.* dynamite

vitran garnu वितरण गर्नु *v.* dole

vivah yogya विवाह-योग्य *adj.* nubile

vivahit awastha विवाहित अवस्था *n.* wedlock

vivahko विवाहको *adj.* bridal

vivah-purv विवाह-पूर्व *adj.* premarital

vivash bhaer विवश भएर *adv.* perforce

vividh विविध *adj.* diverse

vridhi वृद्धि *n.* growth

vridhi garnu वृद्धि गर्नु *v.* augment

vrihat parti बृहत्पार्टी *n.* rave-up

vush भुस *n.* chaff

vyabhichar व्यभिचार *n.* fornication

vyakat garnu व्यक्त गर्नु *v.* couch

vyakhaya garn naskine व्याख्या गर्न नसकिने *adj.* inexplicable

vyaktiko chaldhal व्यक्तिको चालढाल *n.* mien

vyaktiko hissa toknu व्यक्ति को हिस्सा तोक्नु *v.* allot

vyangyapurn व्यंग्यपूर्ण *adj.* wry

vyarthe nasht bhaeko व्यर्थै न्ष्ट भएको *adj.* misspent

vyas व्यास *n.* diameter

vyavsaye-sangh व्यवसाय-संघ *n.* syndicate

W

waak garnu वाक्क गर्नु *v.* retch

wacha वाचा *n.* pledge

wachan वाचन *n.* recital

wachan वचन *n.* word fof honour

wachan baddh hunu वचनबद्ध हुनु *v.* commit

wachik वाचिक *adj.* vocal

wadwiwad वादविवाद *n.* debate

wahan sulk वाहन शुल्क *n.* carriage

wahiyat वाहियात *adv.* absurd

waidh वैध *adj.* legitimate

waigyanik वैज्ञानिक *n.* scientist

waikalpik वैकल्पिक *adj.* alternative

waiwahik वैवाहिक *adj.* matrimonial

wakil वकील *n.* lawyer

wakil वकील *n.* pleader

wakpadyati वाक्पद्धति *n.* idiom

wakta वक्ता *n.* speaker

waktawya वक्तव्य *n.* statement

wakya वाक्य *n.* sentence

wam panthi वामपन्थी *n.* leftist

wam panthi dal वामपनी दल *n.* left wing

wamsha वंश *n.* dynasty

wan वन *n.* jungle

wanaspati वनस्पति *n.* flora

wanaspati वनस्पति *n.* vegetation

wanijya वाणिज्य *n.* commerce

wapasi वापसी *n.* return

warant वारण्ट *n.* warrant

warchaswa hunu वर्चस्व हुनु *v.* rule the roost

wardan वरदान *n.* boon

warg वर्ग *n.* genus

warg mul वर्गमूल *n.* square root

warjit kam वर्जित काम *n.* taboo

warn mala वर्णमाला *adv.* alphabet

warnan garnu वर्णन गर्नु *v.* narrate

warnan lekh वर्णन लेख *v.* write-up

warnan/bayan garnu वर्णन/बयान गर्नु *n.* description

warnan/prashamsa garnu वर्णन/प्रशंसा गर्नु *v.* write up

warnungraha वरुण ग्रह *n.* neptune

warpar वारपार *prep.* across

warsh वर्ष *n.* year

warsha वर्षा *n.* rain

warsha वर्षा *n.* rainfall

warsha वर्षा *n.* shower

warsha ritu/yam वर्षाऋतु/याम *n.* rainy season

warshik वार्षिक *adj.* annual

warshik वार्षिक *adj.* yearly

warshiki वार्षिकी *n.* anniversary

warta वार्ता *n.* negotiation

wasantko वसन्तको *adj.* vernal

wasar वासर *n.* washer

wasiyatnama garer marne वसीयतनामा गरेर मर्ने *adj.* testate

wasna वासना *n.* lust

wasta na garne वास्ता नगर्ने *adj.* thoughtless

wastaw ma वास्तवमा *adv.* indeed

wastaw ma वास्तवमा *adv.* truly

wastawik वास्तविक *adj.* actual

wastawik kuro वास्तविक कुरो *n.* matter of fact

wastawikta वास्तविकता *n.* reality

wastra वस्त्र *n.* raiment

wastra dharan garnu वस्त्र धारण गर्नु *n.* apparel

wastu वस्तु *n.* matter

wastu वस्तु *n.* object

wastukar वास्तुकार *n.* architect

watawaran वातावरण *n.* environment

watawaran वातावरण *n.* milieu

wayu वायु *n.* gas

wayu sanchalan वायु संचालन *n.* ventilation

wayumandal वायुमण्डल *n.* atmosphere

wedana वेदना *n.* pang

wedhshala वेधशाला *n.* observatory

weshhah वेश्या *n.* harlot

weshya वेश्या *n.* call girl

weshya वेश्या *n.* prostitute

weshya वेश्या *n.* streetwalker

weshya mohalla वेश्या मोहल्ला *n.*
red-light area

weshyawritti वेश्यावृत्ति *n.*
prostitution

wibhag विभाग *n.* bureau

wibhajan विभाजन *n.* partition

wibhajit विभाजित *n.* split

wibhajit wyaktitwa विभाजित
व्यक्तित्व *n.* split personality

wibhinna विभिन्न *adj.* various

wichar विचार *n.* idea

wichar विचार *n.* notion

wichar विचार *n.* opinion

wichar विचार *n.* point of view

wichar विचार *n.* thought

wichar विचार *n.* view

wichar dhara विचारधारा *n.*
ideology

wichar dhara विचारधारा *n.* trend
of thought

wichar garnu विचार *n.* concept

wichar garnu विचार गर्नु *v.*
consider

wichar garnu विचार गर्नु *v.* think

wicharak विचारक *n.* thinker

wichararth wishaya विचारार्थ विषय
n. terms of reference

wicharshail विचारशील *adj.*
mindful

wicharshil विचारशील *adj.*
thoughtful

wicitra विचित्र *adj.* marval (i)ous

widambanapurn विडम्बनापूर्ण *adj.*
ironical

widesh विदेश *n.* foreign country

wideshi विदेशी *n.* foreigner

widhan sabha विधानसभा *n.*
legislature

widharm विधर्म *n.* heresy

widhwa विधवा *n.* widow

widorh garnu विद्रोह गर्नु *n.* revolt

widroh विद्रोह *n.* coup d'etat

widroh विद्रोह *n.* insurrction

widroh विद्रोह *n.* rebellion

widrohi विद्रोही *n.* rebel

widwan विद्यान् *n.* scholar

widya विद्यान *n.* learning

widyarthi विद्यार्थी *n.* student

wigat विगत *adj.* bygone

wigyan विज्ञान *n.* science

wijaya विजय *n.* conquest

wijaya विजय *n.* triumph

wijayi विजयी *adj.* victorious

wijeta विजेता *n.* champion

wijeta विजेता *n.* victor

wikas विकास *n.* evolution

wikas विकास *n.* development

wikas garnu विकास गर्नु *v.*
develop

wikhandan विखंडन *n.*
fragmentation

wikiran विकिरण *n.* radiation

wikreta विक्रेता *n.* salesman

wikreta विक्रेता *n.* seller

wikreta विक्रेता *n.* vendor

wiksit hunu wa garnu विकसित
हुनु वा गर्नु *v.* evolve

wilakshan विलक्षण *adj.* fantastic

wilap garnu विलाप गर्नु *v.* lament

wilap garnu विलाप गर्नु *v.* moan

wilasi विलासी *adj.* self-indulgent

wiman विमान *n.* aeroplane

wiman apharan garnu विमान अपहरण गर्नु *v.* hijack

wiman apharan garnu विमान अपहरण गर्नु *v.* skyjack

wiman chalak विमानचालक *n.* pilot

wiman paricharika विमान परिचारिका *n.* airhostess

wiman sewa विमानसेवा *n.* airline

wiman sthal विमानस्थल *n.* airport

winash विनाश *n.* havoc

winash विनाश *n.* ruin

wipakshi विपक्षी *adj.* hostile

wipakshi विपक्षी *n.* opponent

wiparit विपरीत *adj.* contrary

wiparit विपरीत *n.* reverse

wiprit विपरीत *adv.* vice versa

wirahi विरही *adj.* lovelorn

wirahi premi विरही प्रेमी *n.* lovesick

wiram विराम *n.* let-up

wiram विराम *n.* pause

wirodh विरोध *n.* conflict

wirodh विरोध *n.* objection

wirodh विरोध *n.* opposition

wirodh विरोध *n.* protest

wirodh विरोध *n.* restraint

wirodh garna na sakine विरोध गर्न नसकिने *adj.* irresistible

wirodh garnu विरोध गर्नु *v.* defy

wirodh garnu विरोध गर्नु *v.* gainsay

wirodh garnu विरोध गर्नु *v.* oppose

wirodh garnu विरोध गर्नु *v.* resist

wiruddha विरुद्ध *prep.* versus

wiruddha विरुद्ध *prep.* against

wiruddha hunu विरुद्ध हुनु *v.* turn against

wirudh विरुद्ध *adj.* reluctant

wirya वीर्य *n.* semen

wish विष *n.* poison

wish विष *n.* toxin

wishal विशाल *adj.* gargantuan

wishal विशाल *adj.* huge

wishal विशाल *adj.* vast

wishal विष *n.* venom

wishal bajar विशाल बजार *n.* supermarket

wishalu विषालु *adj.* poisonous

wishalu विषालु *adj.* venomous

wishaya विषय *n.* item

wishaya विषय *n.* subject

wishaya विषय *n.* theme

wishaya विषय *n.* topic

wishayabogi विषयभागी *adj.* voluptuous

wishesh विशेष *adj.* partiuclar

wishesh विशेष *adj.* special

wishesh gari विशेषगरी *adv.* especially

wishesh gari विशेषगरी *adv.*
particularly

wishesh gari विशेष गरी *adv.*
specially

wisheshagya विशेषज्ञ *n.*
specialist

wishisht विशिष्ट *adj.*
distinguished

wishisht विशिष्ट *adj.* prominent

wishisht विशिष्ट *adj.* remarkable

wishisht gun विशिष्ट गुण *n.*
characteristc

wishishtta विशिष्टता *n.* strong
point

wishist boli विशिष्ट बोली *n.* jargon

wishphotan विष्फोटन *n.* explosion

wishwa kosh विश्वकोश *n.*
encyclop(a)edia

wishwa prasiddha विश्वप्रसिद्ध
adj. world-famous

wishwa widyalaya विश्वविद्यालय *n.*
university

wishwa wyapi विश्वव्यापी *adj.*
universal

wishwas विश्वास *n.* belief

wishwas विश्वास *n.* trust

wishwas garnu विश्वास गर्नु *v.*
believe

wishwasghat विश्वासघात *n.*
infidelity

wishwasnlya विश्वसनीय *adj.*
authentic

wistar विस्तार *n.* expansion

wistar विस्तार *n.* span

wistarai umlanu विस्तारै उम्लनु *v.*
simmer

wistrit विस्तृत *adj.* elaborate

wiswas garaunu विश्वास गराउनु *v.*
convince

wiwad विवाद *n.* contest

wiwad garnu विवाद गर्नु *v.*
contend

wiwad, kalah विवाद, कलह *n.*
contention

wiwadaspad विवादास्पद *n.*
controversy

wiwah bandhan विवाहबन्धन *n.*
wedge

wiwah na bhaeko manis विवाह
नभएको मानिस *n.* bachelor

wiwah sambandhi विवाह सम्बन्धी
n. nuptial

wiwah yogya विवाहयोग्य *adj.*
marriageable

wiwahit विवाहित *adj.* married

wiwahna bhaeko विवाह नभएको
adj. unmarried

wiwaran haru विवरणहरू *n.*
particulars

wiwaran pustika विवरणपुस्तिका *n.*
manual

wiwash garnu विवश गर्नु *v.* pin
down

wiweki विवेकी *adj.* judicious

wiweki विवेकी *adj.* prudent

wiweki विवेकी *adj.* rational

wiwidh विविध *adj.* miscellaneous

wiwidh विविध *n.* varied

wiwidh manoranjan विविध मनोरंजन *n.* variety entertainment

wiyog वियोग *n.* bereavement

wriddhi वृद्धि *n.* increment

wrihaspati graha बृहस्पति ग्रह *n.* jupiter

wrishehik rashi वृश्चिक राशि *n.* scorpio

wyagra व्यग्र *adj.* fervent

wyakaran व्याकरण *n.* grammar

wyakhya व्याख्या *n.* explanation

wyakhya garnu व्याख्या गर्नु *v.* illustrate

wyakti व्यक्ति *n.* person

wyaktitwa व्यक्तित्व *n.* individual

wyaktitwa व्यक्तित्व *n.* personality

wyanga chitra व्यंग्य चित्र *n.* cartoon

wyangyapurn व्यङ्ग्यपूर्ण *adj.* sarcastic

wyanjan व्यंजन *n.* consonant

wyapak व्यापक *adj.* widespread

wyapar ka mal saman व्यापारका मालसामान *n.* merchandise

wyapari व्यापारी *n.* businessman

wyapari व्यापारी *n.* merchant

wyapari व्यापारी *n.* trader

wyaparik व्यावारिक *adj.* commercial

wyaparik chinha व्यापारिक चिन्ह *n.* trademark

wyarth व्यर्थ *adj.* vain

wyartha व्यर्थ *adj.* futile

wyasta व्यस्त *adj.* busy

wyawahar व्यवहार *n.* dealing

wyawahar garnu व्यवहार गर्नु *v.* treat

wyawahar garunu व्यवहार गर्नु *v.* behave

wyawahar garunu व्यवहार *n.* behavio(u)r

wyawashtapan व्यवस्थापन *n.* management

wyawastha व्यवस्था *n.* provision

wyawastha व्यवस्था *n.* set-up

wyawastha व्यवस्था *n.* system

wyawasthapika व्यवस्थापिका *adj.* legislative

wyawasthit व्यवस्थित *adj.* businesslike

wyawharik व्यावहारिक *adj.* fard-headed

wyawharik व्यावहारिक *adj.* practical

wyawharik व्यावहारिक *adj.* pragmatic

wyawsthapak व्यवस्थापक *n.* manager

wyayami व्यायामी *n.* gymnast

wyayamshala व्यायामशाला *n.* gymnasiu

Y

yad garnu याद गर्नु *v.* memorize

yadi यदि *conj.* if.

yadyapi यद्यपि *conj.* although

yahan यहाँ *adv.* here

yain ऐन *n.* act

yam graha यम ग्रह *n.* pluto

yas ko यसको *pron.* its

yas le यसले *adv.* hereby

yasai bich ma यसैबीचमा *adv.* meantime

yasai bich ma यसैबीचमा *adv.* meanwhile

yasari यसरी *adv.* thus

yasto यस्तो *adj.* such

yasto awaz यस्तो आवाज *v.* fizz

yata uti यताउति *adv.* to and fro

yatayat यातायात *n.* transport

yatayat ka sadhan rell, bus यातायात का साधन रेलए बस *n.* public transport

yatha sthiti यथास्थिति *n.* status quo

yathapurv sthiti यथापूर्व स्थिति statusquo

yatharthwad यथार्थवाद *n.* realism

yathesht यथेष्ट *adv.* enough

yatna यातना *n.* torture

yatra यात्रा *n.* expedition

yatra यात्र *n.* journey

yatra यात्रा *n.* peregrination

yatra यात्रा *n.* tour

yatra talika यात्रा तालिका *n.* itinerary

yatra/saphar garnu यात्र/सफर गर्नु *v.* travel

yatri यात्री *n.* passenger

yatri यात्री *n.* travel(l)er

yatri samuh यात्री समूह *n.* caravan

yatrihare basnu thaun यात्रीहरू बस्ने ठाउँ *n.* hospice

yatru यात्रु *n.* pilgrim

yaun rog योन रोग *n.* aids

yaunakarshan यौनाकर्षण *n.* sex appeal

yauwan यौवन *n.* youth

yauwanarambh यौवनारम्भु *n.* puberty

yddha wiram युद्धविराम *n.* truce

yi यी *pron.* these

yishu ka updeshharu यिशु का उपदेशहरू *n.* gospel

yisukhisht यिसुखिष्ट *n.* messiah

yo यो *pron.* it

yo यो *pron.* this

yo aphai यो आफै *pron.* itself

yoddha योद्धा *n.* warrior

yog योग *n.* yoga

yogayta योग्यता, क्षमता *n.* competence

yogayta योग्यता *n.* flair

yogi योगी *n.* monk

yogya योग्य *adj.* able

yogya योग्य *adj.* capable

yogya योग्य *adj.* meritorious

yogya योग्य *adj.* worthy

yogya bannu योग्य बन्नु *v.* qualify

yogya/layak banaunu योग्य/लायकबनाउनपु *v.* enable

yogya/uchit hunu योग्य/उचित हुनु *v.* deserve

yogyata योग्यता *n* ability

yogyata योग्यता *n.* fitness

yogyata योग्यता *n.* qualification

yogyata योग्यता *n.* talent

yogyata योग्यता *n.* worthiness

yojak chinha योजक चिन्ह *n.* hyphen

yojana योजना *n.* plan

yojana योजना *n.* planning

yojana योजना *n.* scheme

yoni योनि *n.* vagina

yuddha युद्ध *n.* warfare

yudhabhyas युद्धाभ्यास *n.* manoeuvres

yudhsmagri युद्धसमग्री *n.* ordnance

yug युग *n.* era

yug युग *n.* times

yug sandhi युगसन्धि *n.* turn of the century

yugal gan युगलगान *n.* duet

yut युत *n.* sprite

yuva vyakti युवा व्यक्ति *n.* adult

yuwaragyi युवराज्ञी *n.* heiress

yuwaraj युवराज *n.* heir apparent

yuwaraj युवराज *n.* prince

Z

zip kholnu जिप खोल्नु *v.* unzip